A NATIVE'S GUIDE TO

CHICAGO

4th Edition

www.lakeclaremont.com
Chicago

A Native's Guide To Chicago
by Lake Claremont Press

Published October 2004, Reprinted January 2008 by:

LAKE CLAREMONT PRESS

P.O. Box 25291
Chicago, IL 60625
312/226-8400
www.lakeclaremont.com

Copyright © 2004 by Lake Claremont Press
Fourth Edition

Publisher's Cataloging-in-Publication
(Provided by Quality Books, Inc.)

A native's guide to Chicago / by Lake Claremont Press. -- Updated and rev. 4th ed.
    p. cm.
    Includes index.
    LCCN 2002112556
    ISBN 1-893121-23-2

    1. Chicago (Ill.)--Guidebooks.   I. Lake Claremont Press.

F548.18.N38 2003   917.73'110444
                    QBI03-200086

09 08   10 9 8 7 6 5 4 3 2

Contents

Columbus Park, Grant and Burnham Parks, Humboldt Park, Jackson Park, Lincoln Park, Marquette Park, River Park, and Washington Park

Finding Your Way

EVERY entry in this book is coded with a geographic abbreviation: **C** (Central), **W** (West), **N** (North), **NW** (Northwest), **FN** (Far North), **S** (South), **SW** (Southwest), **FSE** (Far Southeast), and **FSW** (Far Southwest). This scheme was designed to give you a rough idea of where a place is located and to help you find things that are convenient for you. Following are the boundaries of the different regions. Consult the map on page vii for a visual representation of these areas.

Central: Bounded by North (*1600 N*), Lake Michigan, Cermak (*2200 S*), and Ashland (*1600 W*).

West: Bounded by North (*1600 N*), Ashland (*1600 W*), Cermak (*2200 S*), and the Chicago city limits (*between 4600 W and 6000 W*).

North: Bounded by Lawrence (*4800 N*), Lake Michigan, North (*1600 N*), and Kedzie (*3200 W*).

NorthWest: Bounded by Lawrence (*4800 N*), Kedzie (*3200 W*), North (*1600 N*), and the Chicago city limits (*between 7200 and 9200 W*).

Far North: Bounded by Lawrence (*4800 N*), Lake Michigan, and the Chicago city limits on the north (*between 6400 and 7600 N*) and the west (*between 7800 and 9200 W*).

South: Bounded by Cermak (*2200 S*), Lake Michigan, Marquette/67th (*6700 S*), and Halsted (*800 W*).

SouthWest: Bounded by Cermak (*2200 S*), Halsted (*800 W*), Marquette/67th (*6700 S*), and the Chicago city limits (*between 4600 and 7200 W*).

Far SouthEast: Bounded by Marquette/67th (*6700 S*), Lake Michigan, the Chicago city limits (*between 13000 and 13800 S*), and Halsted (*800 W*).

Far SouthWest: Bounded by Marquette/67th (*6700 S*), Halsted (*800 W*), and the Chicago city limits on the south (*between 11500 and 13000 S*) and on the west (*between 2400 and 4800 W*).

At least 90% of Chicago's streets fall neatly into a "grid system" that originates at State and Madison streets downtown. Street indexes and common knowledge tag these streets by their distance either north or south of Madison, or east or west of State. Eight city blocks constitute one mile. 1/8 of a mile is "100," thus, Chicago Avenue, at one mile (8 blocks) north of Madison, is considered "800 North." Ashland, being 2 miles or 16 blocks west of State, is "1600 West." 1600 W. Chicago would be at the corner of Chicago and Ashland. Major streets come every four blocks, and unless you are so far southeast that you can see Indiana, the lake is always east.

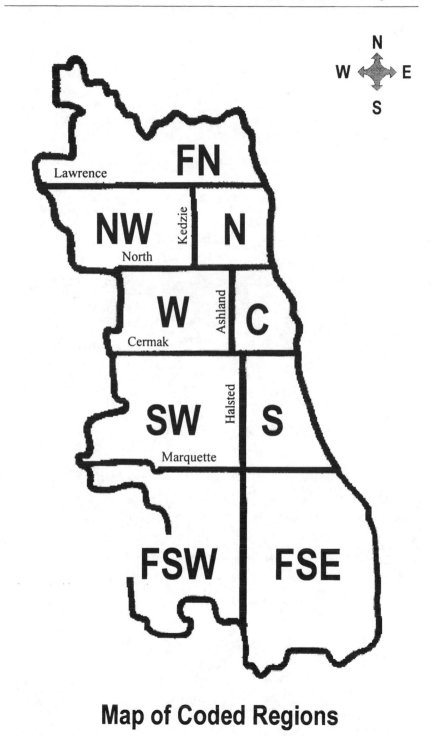

Map of Coded Regions

1

A NATIVE'S GUIDE TO CHICAGO

The CTA Green Line, a result of a 1990s project combining the city's two oldest "L" lines into one route, is one of several lines that circle the Loop.
Photo by Bill Arroyo.

A view of the Downtown riverfront (above), and a day at the New Maxwell Street Market (below). *Photos by Bill Arroyo.*

A Native's Guide to Chicago

Tenth Anniversary Edition!

FIVE years after the release of the third edition, *A Native's Guide to Chicago* is finally back—just in time to commemorate the tenth anniversary of Lake Claremont Press, a small publishing enterprise concocted to release the first edition of a quirky little budget guide in 1994. Who would have thought that one book's homage to the best, cheapest, and underappreciated of Chicago's neighborhoods would lead to an awareness of Chicago history calling to be recovered and Chicago particularities keen for attention? That ten years and 30 books of promoting, probing, and preserving all things Chicago later, Lake Claremont Press receives more great Chicago ideas and manuscripts from authors than one small press can publish? What a privilege and joy it's been to form that clamoring into books for Chicagoans and their friends, perhaps the greatest fans of any city anywhere.

What's New in Chi-Town?

ONE reason this book was so long in coming is the fact that the city has changed so much, so fast, and at a faster pace than ever in the last several years. Important forces like new immigration trends, massive gentrification and redevelopment projects, and a strong and diversified economy are altering our cityscape on a daily basis. We tried to capture much of this new energy within these pages, but all within the context of local history and culture, and never to short shrift those Chicago establishments and customs that have withstood the comings and goings of fads and the passing of time. In fact, much of this book is about paying attention to the enduring Chicago that may get overlooked with so much that is new and shiny to distract us.

What's New in This Edition?

PREVIOUS editions of *A Native's Guide to Chicago* always depended on the help of a crew of people, but this time there was also extensive help with the writing and research by fellow Chicagoists from different parts of the city—some generalists, some journalists, and some specialists. Read all about these great people on p. 477. If styles or opinions appear to vary widely, that's the cause. We may share a common spirit, but not a common mind.

We also took the "budget guide" designation out of the title and off the front cover, but we still focused on the free, the inexpensive, and the good values on every page. We hope this will bring a wider audience to the book, and everyone can still be inadvertently or less-obviously frugal.

What's the Same?

MUCH of our format is the same for this edition as past ones (though we may retire it next time for a different approach). It's thorough, it's large, but it's not everything! (I'm still working on that checking out *every single street* in the city idea.) It's a patchwork of objective facts and lots of subjective choices. 479 pages gives us a lot of room to offer a lot of advice and a lot of background on a lot of things. Sometimes we ramble, sometimes we're terse. Sometimes we're opinionated, sometimes we're straightforward. And we definitely gush. The Chicago boosterism hasn't changed.

How Do We Do It? and How Can You Do It?

THE challenges we faced in updating this guide are the same that face us as Chicago lovers: How do you keep pace with a city that's changing faster than ever? How do you maintain a fresh perspective on a place where you've lived for so long? How do you continually increase the depth and breadth of your knowledge of a place you know so well?

Below are some of the things that the contributors to this book and the Chicagoans I know do, consciously or instinctually or accidentally, that heighten their experience of the city, keep them rolling with a pulsing, international metropolis, and make them walking encyclopedias and off-kilter ambassadors of Chicago.

- **Use your out of town guests as an excuse**
  Entertaining out of town guests is a great opportunity for YOU to explore different neighborhoods and finally try out a bike path, an obscure museum, that not-so-new-anymore tapas place. Don't cringe at

another boat ride or twirl around Navy Pier, 'cause you're not going there. Instead, delight your guests *and* yourself with something unexpected.

- **Leverage other people's knowledge.**

  ✓ **Start with the people you know.** They all have hobbies, passions, and rituals that allow them to ferret out the good stuff for you. For instance, my pals Dave and Joe know sushi and golf. Matt has a sixth sense about inconspicuous bars where cool people shoot pool and drink bourbon. The Bautista family heads nearly every Sunday to Chinatown for dim sum or an Indian buffet for brunch. Their children are chickenwing and barbecue connoisseurs.

  ✓ **Ask the pros.** Concierges, tour guide professionals, the Office of Tourism's staff. They do this for a living and can handle some tough requests; they're not simply about tickets to headliner shows.

  ✓ **Ask the semi-pros.** These are the people whose jobs take them into many neighborhoods and put them into contact with people from all walks of life and/or bring them into a variety of establishments—cabbies, realtors, delivery drivers, bike messengers, cops, and city workers are all exceedingly qualified to shoot some recommendations your way. I always contend that one friend's instincts for real estate trends were honed during his days of delivering for different pizza companies.

  ✓ **Ask everyone.** The dense nature of city life brings most people into contact with new people all the time. Where does your bus driver eat lunch? Where did the gal preparing your latte go dancing last weekend? What does your Albanian hairdresser like best about her adopted city?

  ✓ **Eavesdrop.** You might as well benefit from that person yakking too loudly into their cell phone on the train or pass the time constructively while waiting in line at the bank or the DMV. People talk about Chicago and what's going here all the time.

- **Become an information junkie.**
  Read **Chapter 9: Keeping Informed** to find (and remind you of) the Chicago media best-suited to keep you abreast of the local particulars important to you. Tune in to regular shows, scan weekly papers, sign up

for e-mail newsletters. There are professionals who get paid to do this kind of scouting and reporting, and there are hobbyists who do it just for fun. Both groups need an audience to maintain their status quo. Help them out.

- **Get cultured, get active, support a nonprofit.**
  Turn to the city's cultural, social, and nonprofit groups, which are always creating new Chicago tours, lectures, and other activities with fresh twists and narrow specialties, for something bound to kickstart the Chicago enthusiasm of those who been-there-done-that-know-that. Good places to start: Chicago Neighborhood Tours (p. 78), Chicago Architecture Foundation (p. 31), Friends of the Chicago River (*www.chicagoriver.org*), the Latin School (p. 85), the Chicago Cycling Club (p. 93), and Fleet Feet Sports (p. 119). Even groups of die-hard Chicago know-it-alls, like the Chicago Windies, a group of Chicago Historical Society docents, and the Chicago Tour-Guide Professionals Association, have regular outings and customized tours to keep their chops up.

- **Volunteer.**
  Volunteering is one way many people connect with neighborhoods or fellow Chicagoans their daily lives would not otherwise put them in contact with. Some activities, like tutoring or working in community gardens, are a way of making a difference at a fundamental level. Other opportunities, like maintaining trees in city parks or leading canoe trips, can revolve around one's outdoor and environmental interests. Becoming a docent, such as in the respected Chicago Architecture Foundation Program or at the Historical Society or Field Museum, allows you to become an amateur expert while assisting these Chicago institutions. Don't forget once-a-year and special events volunteering, as for Bike the Drive or the Democratic National Convention.

- **Do everyday activities in new neighborhoods.**

  ✓ Take your laundry, post office, and banking errands to a new neighborhood, and you can cross "experience new sights and sounds" off your to-do list as well.

  ✓ Not overly adventurous? You can still move around your **dinner and a movie** night. Catching a second-run flic at the Three Penny is a chance to sample the pub grub or inexpensive ethnic eateries that serve DePaul students and the Lincoln Avenue partiers. An indie movie at the Century Landmark goes well with Lakeview classics like La Crêperie or Renaldi's. Same for an artsy Music Box offering and a Southport Avenue bistro. A blockbuster at the Burnham Plaza Theatre after dining at a new South Loop eatery is one way to keep up with the rapid changes in that area.

✓ When Jewel and Dominick's are getting humdrum and Whole Foods' "Whole Paycheck" nickname is ringing a little too true, it's time to check out the affordable and exciting options in neighborhood and ethnic groceries. Several small Albany Park grocers carry a mix of Hispanic, Middle Eastern, Eastern European, and Asian goods along with a range of fresh produce at great prices. Visits to the African-Caribbean and Vietnamese places in Uptown and Edgewater will spice up your pantry and your afternoon.

✓ Girls' Night Out? Condo board meetings? Scrabble night? Your weekend with the kids? All good times to rope others into your ventures. They're going with you to that Polish nightclub, the new gelato place, an Andersonville coffee house, or the Swap-o-Rama Flea Market.

• **Expand your notions of different activities.**
We all get into ruts, and when it's time to change them comes another opportunity for Chicagoing. In lieu of another fast food lunch downtown, there's food-court hopping to see what other buildings are like, there are brown bag lunches in different park spaces and public plazas, and there are free noontime concerts in the Cultural Center. There's another $10.95 brunch with the usual suspects, and then there's eating Sunday morning breakfast at a Maxwell Street taco stand.

• **Get creative and adventurous.**
Real people do things like this when they have more newspaper clippings to follow up on, more notes-to-self, and more Chicago to-do lists than they know what to do with.

✓ **Pick a neighborhood.**
Next time you can't decide on where to eat out, start by picking a neighborhood. Then just get yourself there and do some exploring until you happen upon the right eatery for the evening. Using this method recently brought me to one of the Italian restaurants on South Oakley, and an eavesdropping diner insisted I eat off his plate, convinced I would change my mind about not liking sword-

fish.

✓ **Pick a train stop**
Same story. It's a beautiful Sunday afternoon and you don't want to stay indoors, but you're feeling indecisive. Simply pick one unfamiliar "L" stop (or use the dart method) and spend a few hours checking out what's in its immediate vicinity.

✓ **Fish bowl**
An easy way to organize all the things you want to do in Chicago is to write them down on slips of paper, then throw them into a big container. Next time you or your pals "have no idea" what you can possibly do in Chicago, it's time to go fish.

✓ **High–low**
One interesting way to moderate an evening's costs and experience the strange juxtapositions of city life is the high–low route. Pair one high-brow activity with one low-end one: Pops for Champagne and karaoke at Carol's. Chardogs at the Wiener Circle for dinner and dessert at the top of the Hancock building.

• **Follow your bliss.**
Follow your passions and obsessions to develop your own Chicago specialties, or set a crazy goal just because. Andy Plonka became a self-made Pad Thai expert and even devoted a 'zine to the topic of Chicago's best. A group of college friends formed the "Guinness Club," which met once a month at a new pub to start off the evening with a pint. This is how we knew virtual natives Matt Wolka, Keir Graff, and John Greenfield, for instance, would make great contributors to this book. While a student at Northwestern University, Matt Wolka visited every North Side taqueria by bicycle; Keir's interest in pool halls and antiques have spiffed up those sections; and John Greenfield's made-to-order world of journalism, bike messengering, and singing/songwriting helped inform his individual perspective on Chicago.

• **Engage in some friendly competition.**
Out-Chicagoing each other affords the biggest Chi-hounds with great fun and great challenges. "I have this friend" who spent a Valentine's Day where she and he were each responsible for secretly planning alternate blocks of time throughout the evening. They forgot to allow for travel time for their farflung schemes and ended up scarfing down a Thai meal in Chinatown ten minutes before the restaurant's closing. It

wasn't romantic, but there were adventures involved. Another game "my friend" engages in is pulling four generic categories out of a hat with other friends, then challenging themselves to make an evening out of all of them. So the slips of paper once read: *Greek, ice cream, winter sports*, and *dives*. Our evening was appetizers in Greektown, ice skating at the then-new Millennium Park rink, ice cream at one of the diners with ice cream counters on Foster in North Park, and drinks and the video jukebox at the Mark II Lounge far north on Western.

Heh. Heh.

IN the first edition of *A Native's Guide to Chicago*, I said that I wrote the book I wanted to buy but couldn't find. It took only a couple more editions to recruit many talented fellow Chicago fanatics to help me write that book. Now I can benefit from much of it as an "outsider," finally having the book I wanted to help me get the utmost out of Chicago. My mental list of new things to see and do (and eat!) grew so long while editing this book, it needs its own index! I hope our fourth edition will provide you not only more information about the city's offerings, but countless real, live experiences on the streets of Chicago. Enjoy!

—Sharon Woodhouse

2

TOURING

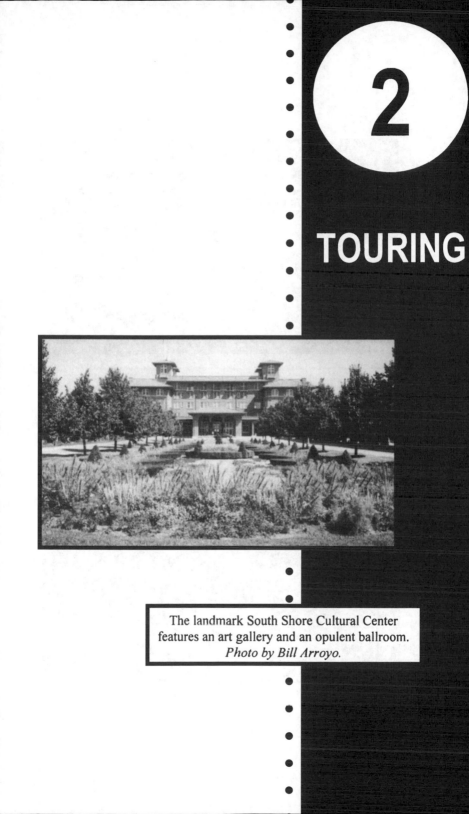

The landmark South Shore Cultural Center
features an art gallery and an opulent ballroom.
Photo by Bill Arroyo.

Touring the city: From "The Picasso" in Daley Plaza (above) to one of the many murals in the Pilsen neighborhood (below). *Photos by Bill Arroyo.*

TOURING

WHETHER YOU'RE A restless native, a frequent visitor, or a guest who wants something old and something new, this collection of places to visit should keep you occupied.

Animals

WHEN your curiosity about our fellow critters goes beyond squirrels and pigeons . . .

Animal Kingdom
2980 N. Milwaukee, 773/227-4444, *www.animalkingdominc.com*   **N**
Since the mid-1940s, **Animal Kingdom** pet store has introduced an array of unusual animals to prospective pet owners and the merely curious. Some of the animals –like the tiger my dad took us to see over two decades ago—are only for show. That long-time mascot died almost a decade ago. Among the broad assortment of animals currently in residence are a 34-year-old white-throated capuchin monkey, an African hornbill, toucans, and macaws. Open Mon.–Fri. 10 A.M.–9 P.M., Sat.–Sun. 10 A.M.–6 P.M.

Chicago is fortunate to have not one, but two free zoos . . .

Indian Boundary Park Zoo
2555 W. Estes, 312/742-7862   **FN**
Chicago's only neighborhood zoo is named for the boundary that separated the land of the Pottawatomi from that of the U.S. government back in the early 1800s. The zoo originally housed a single black bear, but today has deer, goats, llamas, pheasants, swans, and more. Add the park's active sprinklers and super playground and **Indian Boundary Park** becomes a fun summer afternoon field trip for young children. Animals are on display daily

from about 8 A.M.–4: 30 P.M.; the park is open daily from dawn until 11 P.M.

Lincoln Park Zoo
2200 N. Cannon Drive, 312/742-2000, *www.lpzoo.com*   N
One of the world's premier zoos, **Lincoln Park Zoo** is also Chicago's largest tourist attraction, the country's most visited zoo, the oldest public zoo in the United States, and one of the last free zoos in the country. Apes, endangered and big cats, flamingos, seals, elephants, and polar bears are some of the more popular attractions of the 2000 animals living here. Other highlights include the **Penguin and Seabird House** and the **Farm-in-the-Zoo**. With the **Lincoln Park Conservatory** (p. 49), **Cafe Brauer** snack shop and ice cream parlor, the lake for swimming, a pond for paddle boating, and the park for picnicking all adjacent to the zoo, this whole area is an ideal place for a family to spend the day. Be prepared for the $12 parking, or strongly consider public transit. Open daily 9 A.M.–5 P.M., until 6 P.M. during the summer, and until 7 P.M. on summer weekends.

Architecture

CHICAGO continues to be a leading architectural center, still wowing even jaded residents and well-traveled visitors with its current and emerging outcropping of buildings. Below is our partial (both in the incomplete and subjective sense) register of single buildings, and groups of buildings in a one or two block area, that are worth a visit for their architectural, historical, or social value. Following this section is the subdivision **Architecture, Religious** and further in this chapter are **Skyscrapers** (p. 75), which we thought deserved their own category. If your appetite for architecture has yet to be satisfied, our **Walking** chapter also provides information on neighborhoods loaded with structures deserving of your admiration. We've moved the **Downtown Walking Tours** of classic and contemporary downtown Chicago buildings and luxury hotel lobbies (of previous editions) to our Web site (*www.lakeclaremont.com/nativesguide*) when we ran out of space! Some of the high points of those tours have been integrated into the information below.

Central/Downtown

Government Building Tour and Things In-Between

We arranged this important string of government and commercial buildings from north to south, to make it simple to squeeze them all in to one 10-block walk. Begin at the northwest corner of Clark & Randolph:

Thompson Center
100 W. Randolph
Murphy and Jahn's squat salmon and periwinkle glass state government building (1979–1985) is often cited as Chicagoans' least favorite. In any case, there's a charm to how it matter-of-factly sits across from the classic, stone fortress of **City Hall** and kitty-cornered from the ultra-minimalist box of **Daley Center**: three government buildings from different universes just hanging out on the same corner. Its internal structure can be dizzying.

City Hall
121 N. LaSalle, *www.cityofchicago.org*
County Building
118 N. Clark, *www.co.cook.il.us*
A square block holds the square building (1911) whose western half is **City Hall** and whose eastern half is the **County Building**. The more staid exterior hides an elaborate ground floor. Wander this public-friendly building, checking out all the local governmental offices.

Richard J. Daley Center
Dearborn & Washington
The **Daley Center** (1965) appears an unremarkable, tall and narrow block of glass and steel to those unschooled in the joys of Spartanism. The plaza that contains it, however, is redeemed by **"The Picasso,"** a fountain, and the eternal flame that reside there, as well as the multitude of outdoor cultural events and activities that take place there.

Bank One Building
Dearborn & Monroe
Another Modernist skyscraper, the former First National Bank building (1969) is enhanced by its sloping design and popular plaza, which contains an enormous fountain and a Marc Chagall mosaic.

Marquette Building
140 S. Dearborn
A heavy marble staircase, bronze portrayals of Native American chiefs and European explorers, and mosaics that include glass and mother-of-pearl tiles created by Tiffany's make up some of the over $4 million in artwork ornamenting the **Marquette Building**'s (1895, renovated and restored 1980) lobby. The mosaics and bronze panels over the outside doors recount some of the adventures of French Jesuit explorer Jacques Marquette.

Chicago Federal Center
Dearborn, between Adams & Jackson
At the center of this trio of steel-and-glass block government buildings (1959–1974), one by Mies van der Rohe, stands Calder's bright orange steel sculpture, **Flamingo**, offering some color, curves, and originality.

Monadnock Building
53 W. Jackson
The tallest building with weight-bearing walls in the world (1889–1893), this is about as tall as one can build a stone building with windows (16 stories) without making the walls unreasonably wide. (They're already six feet wide at the base.) The interior has been restored to an 1890s look, which can be best appreciated by taking the elevators to the top floor and walking down the intricate staircase.

Metropolitan Correctional Center
71 W. Van Buren
Harry Weese & Associates' triangular prison and administrative center (1975) is the incarceration facility that offers every prisoner a view. A related good view is of the top floor of the adjacent parking garage, where friends and family of prisoners do all sorts of crazy things to communicate from afar with their beloved, who may be in their cell or out in the rooftop yard.

Luxury Hotel Lobbies

Tips on doing a luxury hotel lobby: Casual dress and the admiration of art, architecture, and affluence is generally acceptable, but be prepared for the occasional question or questioning looks. The size and location of a hotel, the time of day, and your demeanor and behavior all determine how easy it is to remain anonymous and free from contact with hotel personnel. "Just looking" usually suffices if someone offers to "help you with something." It's easier to wander in and out unnoticed during the day, but the view and ambiance are more spectacular at night. Once inside the lobby, feel free to explore: Climb staircases, follow hallways, and when possible, definitely peek into the ballrooms. Stay away from the floors with the guests' rooms and you should be okay. And remember, thank the doorstaff when they get the door for you.

Drake Hotel
140 E. Walton, *www.thedrakehotel.com*
White glove elegance, as they say, since 1920, the Drake Hotel sits promi-

nently at the gateway to the Magnificent Mile, visible from Lake Shore Drive as it curves near Oak Street. It has been the choice of high society, celebrity, and heads-of-state since its opening. Locals can partake via the historic **Cape Cod Room**, a fine seafood restaurant with an East Coast flair or the **Coq d'Or** piano lounge, one of the first bars to open in Chicago after Prohibition.

Hotel Burnham

1 W. Washington, 312/781-1111, *www.burnhamhotel.com*
Named for the famous city planner and original architect of the building, Daniel Burnham, the **Hotel Burnham** is a $27.5-million dollar renovation of the historic, landmark Reliance Building into a luxury boutique hotel. The steel and glass Reliance Building was one of the finest examples of a Chicago style of commercial architecture popular in the late 1800s, and considered the first structure to anticipate the modern skyscraper. The breathtaking rehab transports visitors back to early Chicago with its mosaic floor, marble ceiling and walls, filigreed metal elevator grills, mahogany doors, half-canopy beds, and antique-style staircases, archways, and elevator lobbies. Guest rooms may have the frosted windows of an early office building. If you can't bear to leave the building and can't afford to stay, coffee or a meal at the **Atwood Café** on the first floor can buy you some more time there.

Hotel Inter-Continental

505 N. Michigan, *http://chicago.intercontinental.com*
Built in 1929 as the Medinah Athletic Club, an exclusive men's club for Shriners, this landmark building reeks of musty elegance and 1920s exotica, even as it appears a sleek, modernized, deluxe hotel. A drink at the first floor piano bar is one way to literally soak more of it in. Some day, I don't know how, we all need a sneak peek of the pool room, which is purportedly gorgeous.

Palmer House Hilton

17 E. Monroe, *www.palmerhouse.hilton.com*
This is the longest continuously operating hotel in the United States, Chicago's most famous, the first entirely fireproof hotel in America, the first hotel with elevators, and the first hotel with electric lights and telephones in the rooms. It first opened in 1871 and the current building dates to 1927. However, the **Palmer House** is not about statistics but rather fabulousness. Even guests' pets receive the red carpet treatment here. For lingering amidst the grandeur, how about reading the paper in the museum-like lobby? There's also **Trader Vic's**, the dark Tiki paradise installed on their lower

level, for decades like a basement rec room, beckoning lovers and the after-work crowd with pu pus and Mai Tais.

Ritz-Carlton Hotel
160 E. Pearson, 12th Floor, *www.fourseasons.com/chicagorc*
Timeless **Ritz-Carlton** splendor in Water Tower Place since 1975! Pay a visit to the twelfth-floor lobby any time you want a shockingly peaceful and elegant alternative to Michigan Avenue crowds. Drop in for afternoon tea if you're wearied from shopping or to grab a nightcap if you're looking to prolong your evening downtown.

Sofitel Chicago
20 E. Chestnut, 312/324-4000, *www.sofitel-chicago.com*
As so many high-rise duds were going up downtown around our most recent turn-of-the-century, the French luxury hotel chain built what Chicago architects voted the best new building in Chicago in the last ten years. Each floor of this triangular, pyramidal building extends an extra foot, so the top floor juts out into the sky an additional 33 feet from the base.

Magnificent Mile

Start at the north end of the Mag Mile and head south...

860–880 Lake Shore Drive
860–880 Lake Shore Drive,
http://members.aol.com/richpat/860/860d2npm.htm
Referred to as "the glass houses" when first built between 1948 and 1951, these twin, 26-story apartment buildings were a design that architect Mies van der Rohe had had in mind since the 1920s. Not just any old high-rises, these Modernist towers became the model for future steel and glass skyscrapers, and in so doing, changed the face of urban architecture world-wide. This contribution to twentieth-century cityscapes earned **860–880 Lake Shore Drive** Chicago landmark status at the "young" age of 45 in 1996—the first Miesian building to be thus recognized.

Lake Point Tower
505 N. Lake Shore Drive, *www.lakepointtower.com/index.html*
These tripartite, glass-walled towers (1969) are based on an early-twentieth century design by Mies van der Rohe, executed much later by a couple of his students.

Water Tower and Pumping Station
806 and 811 N. Michigan
These castellated Gothic-Revival structures (1866–1869) and prominent local landmarks are most widely recognized for being the only downtown public buildings to survive the Great Chicago Fire of 1871. The **Water Tower** is on the west side of the avenue and houses the **City Gallery** (p. 54) and the **Pumping Station** on the east side contains a **Visitor Information Center** (p. 79).

Tribune Tower
435 N. Michigan
This Gothic, landmark beauty is the result of an international architecture contest calling for "the world's most beautiful office building," conducted to honor the *Tribune*'s 75th anniversary in 1922. Pieces of famous structures from all over the world (all clearly identified) are built into the lower portion of the exterior walls. Touch remnants of the Alamo, the Arc de Triomphe, the Great Pyramid, the Great Wall of China, the Taj Mahal, Westminster Abbey, and dozens more.

Wrigley Building
400 and 410 N. Michigan
Modeled after a cathedral in Seville, with a prominent clock tower, and clad in gleaming white terra-cotta tiles, this beloved architectural gem (1919–1924) is well-used as an establishing shot of Chicago in movies, TV shows, and books. Each of the 250,000 glazed, exterior tiles is classified in a computer database to track its location and maintenance! A glorious endcap to the Magnificent Mile, the building, floodlit since 1974, truly dazzles after dark.

Michigan Avenue Culture

Chicago Symphony Center/Orchestra Hall
220 S. Michigan, *www.cso.org*
A major 1997 renovation created the **Chicago Symphony Center** around **Orchestra Hall** (1905, remodeled in 1967). The updates to the building's traditional grandeur include a restaurant and expanded educational and administrative spaces.

Fine Arts Building
410 S. Michigan
Originally opened as a showroom for Studebaker vehicles (1885), Charles Curtiss turned this lovely old building into the United States' first artists'

colony about ten years later. Current tenants include voice and instrument instructors, instrument repair, violin makers, a sheet music store, rare book dealers, art studios, architects, dance groups, an interior design school, and non-profit organizations. The tenth floor walls are covered with murals from some of the colony's early occupants and its studios have skylights. There are many delightful surprises as you wander through the building, the first of which should be the fact that most of the public spaces have been untouched since an 1898 remodeling! Each floor's lobby has its own unique details. Plaques on doors commemorate famous former tenants—like Frank Lloyd Wright and Laredo Taft—and their years of occupancy. The Daughters of the American Revolution (DAR) in Room #828 has been the longest inhabitant—from 1898 to the present! Occupants open their offices and spaces to the public during monthly open houses.

Auditorium Building/Roosevelt University
430 S. Michigan, *www.auditoriumtheatre.org*
You won't be able to see this Adler & Sullivan masterpiece theater (1887–1889, restored in 1967) without a ticket for a performance, but if the box office is open, you should be able to get a quick look around the lobby. Go around the corner to Michigan, and enter **Roosevelt University**, which is in the same building. Formerly a hotel's public space, the first and second floors of the school, connected by a grand staircase, still retain much of their original splendor.

River North/North Loop

Bloomingdale's Home Store/Medinah Temple
600 N. Wabash, 312/324-7500
High-end "dome" shopping! Headquarters of the Chicago Shriners since 1912, this circus and convention center was sold in 1998 as the building crumbled. The city declared the 130,000-square-foot building, with its distinctive Moorish temple-like exterior, stained-glass windows, and Middle Eastern design flourishes, a landmark, and Bloomingdale's stepped in with their new "Home Store" concept. Re-opened in 2003 as a retail palace, the saved temple has a fixed and cleaned terra-cotta façade, restored windows and copper-clad domes, and a revitalized posh interior.

Merchandise Mart
North of the Chicago River, between Franklin & Wells
www.merchandisemart.com/mmar
Built during the roaring 1920s to centralize and consolidate Chicago's wholesale goods industry, particularly for Marshall Field, the first owner,

the Mart had a rocky start as it opened just months after the 1929 stock market crash. Field sold the 4.2-million-square-foot behemoth to the Kennedy Family in 1945, and they managed it until 1998. Spanning two blocks and rising 25 stories, the Merchandise Mart is currently the largest trade center/commercial building in the world, the largest wholesale design center, and an international business and trade show giant. It hosts over three million visitors a year, hosts 16 major trade shows, 15 co-productions, and 300 conferences and seminars. The bottom floors houses retailers, food vendors, and a CTA station. 90-minute guided tours of various showroom floors, with an introduction to the building's history, are offered to the public, Fridays at 1 P.M. Call 312/527-7762 for more information. $10 seniors, $8 students.

Marina City Towers
300 N. State, *www.marina-city.com*
Beehive? Corn cob? Once considered an innovative housing and social solution for urban singles, Bertrand Goldberg's **Marina City** (1964) was the first mixed-use apartment building in the United States. It's still considered by connoisseurs to hail from a great vision and to be an indispensable component of the city's architectural stew. It went condo in 1977. Beginning in 1994 the commercial portion of the building began to be redeveloped, eventually bringing the House of Blues, House of Blues Hotel, and other viable businesses to liven up the ground level.

333 W. Wacker
333 W. Wacker, *http://kpf.com/Projects/333wackerdrive.htm*
One of the world's most popular all-glass skyscrapers, this elegant, postmodern building (1979–1983) put the architectural firm Kohn Pedersen Fox on the map. The "famous" back side is a sheer, green surface that curves with Wacker Drive and the Chicago River, mirroring the water and reflecting the city around it. Its front is notched and faceted, a less naturalistic exterior more suited for the city it faces.

South Loop/Prairie Avenue/Chinatown

O'Leary House
137 W. DeKoven
Designed in 1901 by Zachary Davis, this is the big old home of the gambling, tavern-owning son of the woman with the notorious fire-starting cow. (It should be noted, however, that most historians have cleared the O'Leary Cow of all blame the Great Chicago Fire.) The **Chicago Fire Academy** (558 W. DeKoven) marks the spot where the fire began with or

without the help of the cow: the O'Leary barn. With its bronze flame and a shiny, fire-red, glazed brick, this very modern-looking 1960 building is where firefighters are trained. Step inside to see a horse-drawn fire engine and various displays depicting other fires and the history of firefighting in Chicago.

On Leong Chinese Merchant's Association Building
2216 S. Wentworth
Since 1928, the fabulous home of the On Leong Tong has been one of the most prominent Chinese-style buildings on the block. Previously involved in many activities of the underworld sort, they now focus on providing business and social services to the community.

Prairie Avenue Historic District
Prairie Avenue (300 E) between 16th (1600 S) and Cermak (2200 S)
This former mansion strip of Chicago's original elite includes the historically and architecturally significant **Kimball** (1801 S. Prairie—1890–1892), **Coleman** (1811 S. Prairie—1885), **Keith** (1900 S. Prairie—1870s), and **Marshall Field Jr./William H. Murray** (1919 S. Prairie—1884) houses. But the following are its two prize jewels:

- **Clarke House**, 1827 S. Indiana
  Chicago's oldest surviving building dates from its pioneer town days (1836). Instead of building a modest "balloon" house as was common at the time, the Clarkes built a sizable Greek revival home with a columned porch and broad staircase.

- **Glessner House**, 1800 S. Prairie (1885–1889)
  312/326-1480, *www.glessnerhouse.org*
  Within the bulky granite exterior lies one of the city's first modern interiors, decorated with many of the original Arts and Crafts furnishings and the Romanesque flourishes of architect Henry Hobson Richardson.

River City
800 S. Wells, *www.rivercityrentals.com*
This S-shaped building is best experienced from "River Road," which is inside the building; the view is worth the visit, even if you have to pretend you're interested in buying one of the condo units just to get inside. Originally planned as a super-dense string of towers, politics and economics forced architect Bertrand Goldberg to scale back his plans. The result, completed in 1986, is still noteworthy: a futuristic-looking complex

of residences, shops, and a marina.

Raymond M. Hilliard Center
2030 S. State
Completed in 1966 as low-cost public housing for the CHA, this innovative, undulating complex was designed to break poor inhabitants out of the boxes that characterized Chicago public housing. While other project high rises are being torn down, Hilliard is undergoing a rehabilitation that will allow mixed-income families to live side by side. Chicago architect (and native!) Bertrand Goldberg was a visionary designer whose distinctive style arose out of genuine concern for the inhabitants' well-being.

Soldier Field
Lake Shore Drive about 1400 South, 773/235-7000
www.soldierfield.net/onsiteStadiumTour.aspx
"Klingon meets Parthenon" is how *Tribune* architecture critic Blair Kamin summed up the renovation to the Chicago Bears' home stadium finished in late 2003. Indeed, most Chicagoans agree that it looks like a big, fat UFO landed atop the original's historic colonnades, and they're not too happy about it, despite new stadium amenities, a striking interior, and undoubtedly terrific sight lines. Like all once-reviled grandiosities, we suspect Chicagoans will eventually come to love and fiercely defend the new look. Other changes to the property include parkland east to the lake (with a sledding hill in winter) that connects the field to the Museum Campus just north, a memorial waterfall honoring different branches of the armed services, and a restored Doughboy statue that once stood in Garfield Park.

State Street Department Stores

Marshall Field's
111 N. State, 312/781-1000
The philosophy of "give the lady what she wants." Great clocks at State & Washington and State & Randolph immortalized by Norman Rockwell that have been meeting points over the decades for those hooking up downtown. Granite pillars (1902) at the State Street entrance second only in size to those at the Temple of Karnak in Egypt. A Tiffany ceiling (1907) of 1.6 million pieces that is the largest unbroken example of Tiffany Favrile glass in the world. Though now owned by the Target Corporation, Chicago's original, and still thriving, fashionable department store is a historic landmark not to be missed. Head to the 7th floor for the archives with photos and artifacts from the past 150 years and the Visitor Center, where you can inquire about free guided and self-guided tours.

Carson Pirie Scott & Company
1 S. State, 773/641-7000
Another Chicago landmark (1899) and a choice downtown department store for generations, **Carson**'s architectural highlight is its exterior ironwork done by architect Louis Sullivan.

West Loop/Financial District/Greektown

Chicago Board of Trade Building
141 W. Jackson, *www.cbot.com/cbot/building/home*
A remarkable building that unites a 1930 landmark with a 1980 Postmodern annex. A dramatic illustration of this union can be seen from the 12th floor's elegant 12-story atrium lobby. Dramatically floodlit at night, the **CBOT** building—perhaps Chicago's finest Art Deco work—makes the perfect anchor for the LaSalle Street financial district.

Civic Opera Building
20 N. Wacker, *www.lyricopera.org/about/house.asp*
The vision of populist billionaire industrialist, Samuel Insull, "The Prince of Electricity," the **Civic Opera Building** (1929) was conceived from the beginning to be a mixed-use, culture/commerce space. A one-block hunk of stone in the shape of a throne facing the river, this was reportedly Insull's way of "turning his back on City Hall," which he believed had "stolen" his electric utility. Designed by Graham, Anderson, Probst & White, the same firm that did the Field Museum and the Wrigley Building, it has a two-story pedestrian colonnade and a 45-story office tower; the east side's public face is in an ornate French Renaissance Revival style, while an Art Deco exterior looks out on the river. The hybrid Art Nouveau–Art Deco interior includes a famous fire curtain painted with the parade scene from *Aida* and seating for 3,563. As part of a recent $100-million rehab, every seat was refurbished and every inch completely repainted for the first time since its opening.

Jackson Boulevard Historic District
Jackson, between Ashland & Laflin
In the late 1800s, when the 30 mansions on this block were built, they stood in sharp contrast to neighborhoods—just blocks away—where immigrant populations were struggling in less than ideal conditions. Saved by early preservationists in the 1970s, until recently this strip still stood apart from the decay of surrounding streets, although those blocks have almost all been developed in the past few years.

The Rookery
209 S. LaSalle
An awe-inspiring local favorite since its 1992 restoration! The thick, ruddy exterior conceals an airy interior of spectacular lighting and lacy ironwork. Try the elevators, balcony, and spiral staircase for new sightseeing and perspectives. Designed by dynamic duo Burnham & Root (1885–1888), the original renovation was by Frank Lloyd Wright in 1907.

Skybridge
737 W. Washington, 312/787-0500, *www.skybridgechicago.com*
With so many boring residential towers thrown up into the air, mucking up our skyline and our streetscapes, architects and citizens had many reasons to laud the **Skybridge** condominiums the minute they were finished in late 2002. Sleek and narrow twin towers are strategically notched—with balconies, assorted holes that let the sky shine through, a vertical off-center gap where glass hallways on each floor link both sections of the building, and a trellis-like steel structure extending from the roof. A four-floor retail base unites the bottom portion harmoniously with the surrounding West Loop area. It also adds some excitement to the side of the Kennedy Expressway.

Union Station
210 S. Canal
Union Station's Great Hall, with its pink Tennessee marble floors, Corinthian columns, bronze torches, long, wooden benches, and 90-foot-high skylighted ceiling, will return you to a previous era. Considered one of the last of the grand train stations, the Great Hall is actually the only remaining part of the 1925 original (the rest was demolished in 1969). It was built between 1913 and 1925 from a Graham, Anderson, Probst & White design for a working "union" of four of the primary railroads of the day in a space befitting of the nation's transportation hub.

North

Edgewater

Edgewater Beach Apartments
5555 N. Sheridan
Pale pink, Art Deco, and Miami-esque, these lakefront apartment towers were created by Benjamin Marshall in 1928 as part of the now defunct, once luxurious and fashionable Edgewater Beach Hotel Complex. The lobby and ground floor shops and cafe are open to the public.

Lakeview

Alta Vista Terrace
Alta Vista Terrace, between Grace and Byron
Designed by Joseph Brompton and built by Samuel Eberly Gross between 1900 and 1904, this block of homes, characteristic of the row houses in London's Mayfair neighborhood, was the first in Chicago to be labeled a historic district in 1971. The 20 houses from Grace to Byron are replicated on the other side of the street from Byron to Grace.

Elks National Memorial Building
2750 N. Lakeview, 773/755-4876, *www.elks.org/memorial*
Finished in 1926, this extravagant, but little-visited building is dedicated to peace and freedom and memorializes the Elks that died during World War I. Adorned with sculptures, mosaics, murals, and the finest marble, the entire building is a stunner. An allegorical mural spans twelve panels in the 100-foot rotunda. Open Mon.–Fri. 9 A.M.–5 P.M. (year-round), Sat.–Sun. 10 A.M.–5 P.M. (Apr. 15–Nov. 15 only).

Uptown

Aragon Ballroom
1106 W. Lawrence, *www.aragon.com*
This 1926 former ballroom may be best-known to Chicagoans as "the Brawlroom," a rock concert venue with poor acoustics, but it's an architectural gem as well. Like the **Music Box Theater** (p. 285), the ballroom itself imitates a night sky and is a great example of 1920s "atmospheric" theaters that had exotic flourishes. Besides the fabulous interior, the Moorish architecture tells a story on the outside—if you know where to look: a bride and groom tying the knot, a two-headed eagle sharing a crown and a sword, and faces of royalty and commoners like guests at a wedding. What's it mean? The 1469 wedding of Isabella I of Castile and Ferdinand V of Aragon that unified the country we now know as Spain.

Essanay Studios
1333–45 W. Argyle
Now part of St. Augustine College, this building's most illustrious days were between 1907 and 1917 when it was used by **Essanay Studios** for the making of silent films. Prominent in both Chicago and the movie industry in general, **Essanay** worked with some of the era's biggest stars, like Charlie Chaplin and Gloria Swanson.

Hutchinson Street
Hutchinson, between Marine Drive and Hazel
This tiny landmark district contains a handsome variety of homes from the early part of the twentieth century: classic, Georgian, Prairie School, and Queen Anne. Five were designed by George Maher between 1894 and 1913: **750 W, 817 W, 826 W, 839 W,** and **840 W.**

Myron Bachman House
1244 W. Carmen
Architect Bruce Goff is known for spatially complex houses that use natural materials in a far-out way, kind of like a Frank Lloyd Wright of the twenty-first century (even though he died in the twentieth). This remodel job, with lots of corrugated metal and gobs of mortar, may be the only sample of his talents available in the city of Chicago.

Uptown Broadway Building
4707 N. Broadway
The term *horror vacui*—a fear of unadorned surface area—was applied to a brief period of the classically inspired Beaux-Arts style. This 1927 office and retail building, designed by Walter Ahlschlager, might be a perfect example of this; at any rate, it's delightfully gapeworthy. The cream and gray terra cotta cladding froths with images of cherubs, trolls, sheep, cornucopia, armor, urns, garlands and more. Persistent rumor places Al Capone as the owner—some still call it the "Al Capone Building"—but there's no evidence that this was true.

South

Beverly

Beverly Frank Lloyd Wright Houses
In the Beverly neighborhood—the country's largest urban historic district— are four Frank Lloyd Wright Prairie School houses. The two on Hoyne are prefabs from a short-term business partnership between Wright and Richard Brothers of Milwaukee.

- **9326 S. Pleasant** (1900)
- **9914 S. Longwood** (1908)
- **10410 S. Hoyne** (1917)
- **10541 S. Hoyne** (1917)

Beverly Walter Burley Griffin Prairie School Houses
104th Place in Beverly is also called Walter Burley Griffin Place after the student of Frank Lloyd Wright who designed Chicago's greatest concentration of Prairie School houses for this block.

- **The Furneaux House** (1913), 1741 W. 104th
- **The Newland House** (1913), 1737 W. 104th
- **The Salmon House** (1913), 1736 W. 104th
- **The Clarke House** (1913), 1731 W. 104th
- **The Blount House** (1911), 1724 W. 104th
- **The Jenkinson House** (1913), 1727 W. 104th
- **The Garrity House** (1909), 1712 W. 104th
- **The Van Nostrand House** (1911), 1666 W. 104th

The "Irish Castle"
10244 S. Longwood Drive, *www.buc.org*
Since the Potter Palmer Castle on Lake Shore Drive was demolished in the 1950s, this model of thirteenth and fourteenth century Irish estates apparently is the only "castle" in town. Enduring stories maintain that Robert Givens had the castle built in 1886 for his fiancée, who unfortunately died before they were wed. It is now the Beverly Unitarian Church.

Bronzeville

The Chicago Bee Building
3647–55 S. State
The facade of this former editorial office for a leading black-owned newspaper of the 1920s features terra cotta decorations. Now a branch of the Chicago Public Library, it is listed on the National Historic Register.

Chicago Daily Defender Building
2400 S. Michigan
Built in 1936 by Philip Maher for the Illinois Automobile Club, this building has housed the offices of the *Chicago Daily Defender*—a preeminent local black newspaper with a national reputation—since 1960. Since 1975, the building has been recognized as an "historical site in journalism."

Ida B. Wells/Ferdinand Lee Barnett Home
3624 S. King Drive
Wells, the noted social reformer, and Barnett, her husband and founder of

the *Conservator*, Chicago's first black-owned newspaper, lived in this three-story, rock-faced granite house from 1919 to 1930. A prime example of an urban row house of the late Victorian period, it was designated a National Historic Landmark in 1974.

Illinois Institute of Technology (IIT) Campus
3300 S. Federal, 312/567-3000, *www.iit.edu*
A conjunction of technical colleges and graduate programs, including an acclaimed College of Architecture, **IIT** has, not surprisingly, a must-visit campus of architectural and design wonders, including its first new buildings in over 25 years. Get there on the CTA's Green Line that, as it arrives at the IIT-Bronzeville-35th Street station, passes through a stainless-steel-clad tube surrounding 530 feet of "L" tracks running through the campus and over the new **McCormick Tribune Campus Center** (2003). Designed by Dutch architect Rem Koolhaas, the campus center arranges various areas around diagonal pathways, resembling interior streets that are extensions of the paths students had used to cross the campus. Also new in late 2003 was Helmut Jahn's **State Street Village** (33rd & State), a new student residence hall composed of three separate five-story buildings, joined by exterior glass sound walls that muffle noise from passing trains. Jahn studied architecture in the late 1960s at IIT under Mies van der Rohe, who designed **Crown Hall**, home of the College of Architecture and a National Historic Landmark, as well as almost a dozen other campus buildings. Free 40-minute tours of the two new buildings leave the MTCC Welcome Center Mon. 11 A.M., Wed. 11 A.M., and Thur. 3:30 P.M. Groups of eight or more must make a reservation (312/567-3077).

Jesse Binga Home
5922 S. King Drive
Binga established the first black-owned bank at 35th and State in 1908. Although the bank survived the Depression, it ultimately failed in 1930, and Binga was jailed on charges of embezzlement. His stature in the community, however, was such that a group of supporters was able to obtain his release from prison in 1938. At the height of his success, Binga lived in this house, which survived numerous fire bombings between 1918 and 1919 when hostile white residents tried to oust him from the neighborhood.

Wabash Avenue YMCA
3763 S. Wabash
It is believed that historian Carter G. Woodson founded the Association for the Study of Afro-American Life and History here in 1915. Woodson was also responsible for establishing Negro History Week, the precursor of

today's Black History Month. In the ballroom is a wall mural painted by Chicago artist William Edward Scott in 1936, depicting people of color in various professions.

Hyde Park/Kenwood

Farrakhan Home
4855 S. Woodlawn
Designed with Muslim motifs for the Nation of Islam leader, this home–fortress stands among the other mansions of Chicago's Kenwood neighborhood. It was previously the home of the Honorable Elijah Muhammad and is now the occasional residence of Minister Louis Farrakhan.

Rainbow/PUSH Building
930 E. 50th Street
Rev. Jesse Jackson's national **Rainbow/PUSH Coalition (RPC)** makes its headquarters in this 1923 Greek revival style building that was originally home to the K.A.M. Isaiah Israel Temple. RPC is committed to educational and economic equality for all people, focusing especially on the needs of African Americans, Hispanics, and people with low income.

Robie House
5757 S. Woodlawn, 708/848-1976
The internationally famous Frank Lloyd Wright masterpiece is open Mon.–Fri. for one-hour tours at 11 A.M., 1 P.M., and 3 P.M.; Sat.–Sun. 11 A.M.–3:30 P.M. every 20 minutes. Adults $9, students, seniors, and children (ages 7–18) $7.

Southwest Side

Union Stock Yards Gate
850 W. Exchange (4100 S)
This former archway to the animals' quarters serves as a solitary reminder of Chicago's stockyard past.

One of the last slaughterhouses in Chicago, **Chiappetti Lamb and Veal** (3900 S. Emerald, 773/847-1566, *www.chiappettilambandveal.com*), is also the last one that was once part of the Union Stock Yards. One of the offspring of this fourth-generation business is Chef Steven Chiappetti, the culinary mastermind behind Mango, Grapes, and Rhapsody restaurants, now with Café Le Coq in Oak Park.

West

Race Avenue and Midway Park Houses
5700–5900 West Blocks of Race and Midway Park
These grand old homes on large lots in Austin are a remnant of the area's suburban past. Seventeen of them date between 1886 and 1922. Many were designed by noted architect Frederick Schock, whose own home stands at **5804 W. Midway**. The Austin neighborhood was annexed to Chicago in 1899.

= = = = = = = = = = =

AIA's Calendar of Events
The Merchandise Mart, Suite 1049, 312/670-7770
www.aiachicago.org/events.asp **C**
Chicago's large and active chapter of the **American Institute of Architects** opens up its member lectures, tours, and other programs to the public for $15. Learn about new architectural trends and visit historic and just-built masterpieces. The Web site's also a great way to get architects' take on the buildings going up in the city.

Chicago Architecture Foundation's ArchiCenter
224 S. Michigan, 312/922-3432, *www.architecture.org* **C**
The ultimate source of building information in Chicago, **CAF** sponsors a variety of affordable opportunities to learn about local architecture. Their **ArchiCenter** in the Santa Fe Building has several components. The **Atrium Gallery** features exhibits on new design and Chicago architecture, like the current one devoted to the sustainable architecture of the future. **CitySpace** has a staffed visitor information desk, a timeline of Chicago architecture, videos of important architects speaking on Chicago, a searchable database of Chicago architecture, and rotating exhibits. The **Lecture Hall** is the sight of free Wed. lectures at 12:15 P.M on architecture and housing topics. Bring a lunch! Various walking tours of downtown, specific buildings, and city neighborhoods take place nearly every day of the year ($5–$10, many free for members), many leaving from the gift shop, which we highly endorse in our **Shopping** chapter (p. 357). **CAF** also sponsors numerous architecture tours by bus, plus a summertime river cruise that many consider the city's best overall sightseeing tour. The ArchiCenter is open Tues.–Sun. 9:30 A.M.–4 P.M.

Commission on Chicago Landmarks Tours
33 N. LaSalle, Suite 1600, 312/744-3200
www.ci.chi.il.us/Landmarks/Tours/Tours.html   **C**
The **Commission on Chicago Landmarks** Web site helps you create your
own tour with its categorization of the 202 individual landmarks and 34
districts (containing over 4,500 important structures) they've recognized to
date. Select by type of structure (say, early skyscrapers, mansions, bridges,
or innovative housing), style (perhaps Art Deco or Prairie School), theme
(music/art or labor/industry), or historical era (Civil War, pre-fire, or
post-WWII). Pick up the *Chicago Landmarks Map* from various visitor
information centers or by calling the commission.

Chicago Tribute Markers of Distinction

Since 1997, Chicago's Department of Cultural Affairs' **Chicago Tribute
Markers** (78 E. Washington, *www.chicagotribute.org*) program has installed 80 markers around the city where notable Chicagoans used to live or
work. We preserve historic buildings as landmarks; this is a way to
memorialize the people of our city's past—those whose contributions are
recognized nationally and internationally and lived or worked in Chicago
during a pivotal or formative period. A brief list of honorees reveals the
breadth of honorees: Saul Alinsky, Louis Armstrong, Mother Cabrini,
Octave Chanute, Buckminster Fuller, George Halas, Lorraine Hansberry,
Ben Hecht, Rudy Lozano, Ruth Page, Abe Saperstein, Bill Veeck, and
Harold Washington. Pick up a map at the Cultural Center.

Architecture, Religious

IN the good old days, before vandals ran rampant, one could retreat to a
house of worship any time of day or night for prayer, peace and quiet, or
aesthetic browsing. Unfortunately, most places now keep limited hours or
only open their doors for services. Call ahead to learn a good visiting hour.

Bultasa Buddhist Temple of Chicago
4358 W. Montrose, 773/286-1551, *http://bultasa.tripod.com*   **NW**
Founded in 1970, Bultasa, "gathering of the Buddhas," is the oldest and
largest worship place for Korean Buddhists in Chicago. The temple houses
an exquisite "1000 Buddha Temple Altar," not found elsewhere in the
American Midwest.

Chicago Temple
77 W. Washington, *www.chicagotemple.org*   **C**
Housing the First United Methodist Church of Chicago, this is the world's
tallest church (568 ft.) for the city's oldest congregation (1831). It's the fifth
structure the church has put on this site since 1838 (one building was wiped
out by the Great Fire). The sanctuary is open daily 7 A.M.–9 P.M., and daily
tours of its **Sky Chapel** (located in the spire) are given at 2 P.M. The chapel,
the world's highest place of worship, was created in 1952 with a donation in
honor of Charles Walgreen, founder of the local drugstore chain. Stained
glass windows on its eastern exterior wall (facing the Miro court) detail the
church's history.

Christ Universal Temple
11901 S. Ashland, 773/568-2282, *www.cu7temple.org*   **FSE**
Evoking a sports stadium, Rev. Dr. Johnnie Coleman's church is noted not
for its age or art, but merely for its capacity to accommodate thousands of
congregators at one time.

Five Holy Martyrs Church
4301 S. Richmond, 773/254-3636   **SW**
Founded in 1908 to serve the Polish families of the Brighton Park neighborhood, **Five Holy Martyrs** still offers mass in Polish several times a week.
Pope John Paul II celebrated mass here during his 1979 visit to Chicago and,
in typical Chicago fashion, a portion of 43rd Street was renamed Pope John
Paul II Drive.

Fourth Presbyterian Church
866 N. Michigan, 312/640-5376, *www.fourthchurch.org*   **C**
Their original church destroyed by the Great Chicago Fire the night of its
dedication, Fourth Church eventually rebuilt this building in 1914 on what is
now the Magnificent Mile. Include the courtyard in your appreciation of this
beautiful Gothic church; it's easy enough to peek in while walking by during
a shopping excursion.

Holy Trinity Russian Orthodox Cathedral
1121 N. Leavitt, 773 486 6064, *www.holytrinitycathedral.net*   **W**
This Louis Sullivan landmark building in Ukrainian Village is the cathedral
for the Diocese of Chicago and the Midwest of the Orthodox Church in
America. Czar Nicholas II paid for much of its construction in the late
1890s, and it was completed in 1903. The church is a remarkable combination of the Russian provincial architecture familiar to the church's original
congregation (i.e., the simple stuccoed exterior) and Sullivan's own ornate,

naturalistic detailing to create a Byzantine interior.

K.A.M. Isaiah Israel Temple
1110 E. Hyde Park, 773/924-1234, *www.kamii.org*   S
Built in 1924 by Alfred Alschuler, for the oldest Jewish congregation in the Midwest (founded 1847), this splendid old temple with Byzantine flourishes includes a 1973 addition by John Alschuler.

Midwest Buddhist Temple
435 W. Menomonee, 312/943-7801
www.midwestbuddhisttemple.com   N
The **Midwest Buddhist Temple**'s (est. 1944) "Temple of Enlightenment," designed in a traditional Japanese style, has been residing in its understated elegance on a Lincoln Park side street since 1971.

Mosque Maryam
7351 S. Stony Island, 773/324-6000, *www.noi.org*   FSE
The national center and headquarters for Minister Louis Farrakhan's Nation of Islam is a former Greek Orthodox Church, converted in 1972 and named for Mary, mother of Jesus.

Our Lady of Sorrows Basilica
3121 W. Jackson, 773/638-5820, *www.ols-chicago.org*   W
Built in the late nineteenth century and unknown to most Chicagoans, the **OLS Basilica** would be a tourist attraction if located in Florence or Rome. Its dramatic, barrel-vaulted ceiling is an immediate attention-grabber. The basilica also houses the National Shrine of St. Peregrine, patron saint of those who suffer from cancer.

Pilgrim Baptist Church
3301 S. Indiana, 312/842-5830   S
The former synagogue of Chicago's oldest Jewish congregation (K.A.M.) is an Adler and Sullivan classic (1890) that's been occupied since the 1920s by the **Pilgrim Baptist Church**. During the 1930s, this congregation, along with its longtime music director, Thomas A. Dorsey, who toured for five years with the world's greatest gospel singer ever—Mahalia Jackson—made significant contributions to the development of gospel music. Not to be confused with the **Pilgrim Baptist Church** (3235 E. 91st), where the *Blues Brothers* gospel scene was shot, famous in its own right.

Quigley Seminary and Chapel of St. James
831 N. Rush, 312/787-9343   C
With the seminary modeled after the Palais du Justisce in Rouen, France, and the chapel modeled after Paris's Sainte-Chappelle, it's not surprising that this may be Chicago's best example of French Gothic architecture. Recently added to the National Registry of Historic Places, the crowning jewels of this property are the fourteen enormous stained glass windows in the St. James Chapel. Made of antique glass, the almost 90-year-old windows are the focus of an emergency preservation campaign (*www.windows.org*) that is receiving technical assistance from the chief stained glass expert of France's Ministry of Culture. Docent tours of the chapel are given by **Friends of the Windows** (312/782-3532), Tues., Thur., Fri., Sat., noon–2 P.M. Look for special events on the grounds, including traditional choral, classical, and folk music concerts.

Quinn Chapel, African Methodist Episcopal
2401 S. Wabash, 312/791-1846   S
Chicago's oldest African-American congregation, around since 1844 and active in Chicago's abolitionist movement, had the **Quinn Chapel**, now a city landmark, built for them between 1891 and 1894.

Rockefeller Memorial Chapel
1156 E. 59th, 773/702-7059, *http://rockefeller.uchicago.edu*   S
Named for industrialist and University of Chicago founder, John D. Rockefeller, this Byzantine/Romanesque/Gothic structure is the tallest building on the U of C campus. Stop in to view the stained glass windows, ceiling tiles, and carved oak seating, and try to catch one of the scheduled concerts on the immense organ or famous carillon, an installation of large bells and the second biggest musical instrument in the world. Open daily to the public 8 A.M.–4 P.M.

St. Nicholas Ukrainian Catholic Cathedral
2238 W. Rice, 773/276-4537   W
Built in 1915, this thirteen-domed, mosaic-clad church, based on the eleventh-century cathedral of St. Sophia in Kiev, is an exquisite example of neo-Byzantine architecture. A nine-tiered chandelier hangs from the highest dome, illuminating an equally stunning interior. Take Oakley a few blocks south to the newer **St. Volodymur and Olha Ukrainian Catholic Church** (c.1975) at 739 N. Oakley for more beautiful exterior mosaic work.

St. Patrick's Roman Catholic Church
140 S. Desplaines, 312/648-1021, *www.oldstpats.org* C
Chicago's oldest public building and one of only a few to survive the Great
Fire, "Old St. Pat's" was founded by Irish immigrants and dedicated on
Christmas Day, 1856. One of the city's largest Catholic congregations, St.
Pat's manages a vibrant schedule of spiritual, social, and community-service
activities. The building itself shines from an incredible restoration in the
1990s that highlights intricate Celtic-inspired artwork from the early twenti-
eth century. Docents are available to answer questions following the 8:30
A.M. and 9:45 A.M. masses on Sunday. Tours can be scheduled by calling Jim
McLaughlin (630/852-7269).

St. Paul Roman Catholic Church
2127 W. 22nd Pl., 773/847-7622, *www.stpaulchgo.org* SW
The German immigrants who built this extravagant French Gothic masterpiece (1897), per the design of Henry Schlacks, used not a single nail (only
bricks) in its construction—a feat recognized by *Ripley's Believe It or Not.*
Its interior contains Italian mosaics and German stained glass. Later, far
beneath the church's towering 245-foot spires, St. Paul Federal Bank was
founded in the basement.

St. Thomas the Apostle
5476 S. Kimbark, 773/324-2626 S
The site of Hyde Park's Catholic parish since 1869, this majestic structure at
the corner of 55th and Kimbark was designed by Francis Barry Byrne and
built in 1923. Byrne once studied with Frank Lloyd Wright, and the church's
modernist design reflects Wright's influence and anticipates the liturgical
changes of Vatican II by four decades. Within the walls lies a tranquil
courtyard. Inside, note the bronze bas-reliefs of the Stations of the Cross
created by an Italian-born American sculptor Alfeo Faggi. The church was
added to the National Register of Historic Places in 1978.

Second Presbyterian Church
1936 S. Michigan, 312/225-4951, *www.2ndpresbyterian.org* S
Despite being a Chicago landmark and on the National Register of Historic
Places, the **Second Presbyterian Church** is one of about a dozen architecturally stunning Chicago churches in dire need of big bucks for major
repairs. Once the church of the Prairie Avenue upper class, it was designed
in 1874 by James Renwick after the 1871 Chicago fire destroyed their
previous church. Howard Van Doren Shaw remodeled it with an Arts and
Crafts interior in 1900 after another fire. Among this Gothic gem's many
dramatic features are 14 Louis Comfort Tiffany stained-glass windows.

Open Wed.–Fri. 8 A.M.–4 P.M., Sat. 8 A.M.–noon, Sun. 8 A.M.–2 P.M. (worship 11 A.M.). Tours by appointment.

Art, Indoors

Galleries

The gentrification of the River North area in the 1980s and the expanding West Side and Near South Side arts communities have helped boost Chicago's gallery scene to the scale of Manhattan or San Francisco. The sheer number of galleries, the range of art forms and styles displayed, a constantly changing lineup of exhibits, and free admission make gallery-hopping the ideal hobby for any art enthusiast. The majority of Chicago galleries are concentrated in these four areas: **River North** is the largest district, **Michigan Avenue/River East/South Loop** the ritziest, and the **West Loop/Pilsen** and the **Bucktown/Wicker Park** are the most experimental.

Chicago Gallery News
www.chicagogallerynews.com
Published three times a year (Jan., Apr., and Sept.) since 1983 and available at all listed galleries, at city visitor information centers, and major museums and hotel concierges' desks, this magazine is all you need to plan your very own art tours of Chicago and to strategically drop in at opening wine and cheese events. Better yet, visit the always-current Web site, which allows you to search the 150 participating galleries by gallery district, art specialty, and artist, as well as to see the dozens of openings and special events that take place at galleries each month.

The free weeklies, the *Chicago Reader* (Section 2) and *Newcity,* are other publications with extensive listings of gallery exhibits and goings-on.

Neighborhood Cultural Centers

Various neighborhood arts centers have free galleries.

Beacon Street Gallery and Theatre
4131 N. Broadway, 773/525-7579, *www.beaconst.org*   N
Beacon Street is one of the city's few art spaces to continually showcase both contemporary art and ethnic and folk art. As a contemporary art

---

Your Inner Poster Child
Industrious types can create another free art museum experience for themselves by hitting Chicago's vintage poster dealers:

* **Chicago Center for the Print and Poster**, 1509 W. Fullerton
  773/477-1585, *www.prints-posters.com*
* **Colletti Antique Poster Gallery**, 67 E. Oak
  312/664-6767, *www.collettigallery.com/home.html*
* **Spencer Weisz Galleries**, 215 W. Ohio
  312/527-9420, *www.spencerweisz.com*

---

gallery, Beacon Street exhibits both new and established artists of local, national, and international origin. Open Mon.–Sat. 10 A.M.–6 P.M.

Beverly Arts Center
2407 W. 111ᵗʰ, 773/445-3838, *www.beverlyartcenter.org*   **FSW**
In a 40,000-square-foot, sensational new building, the Beverly Arts Center entered the millennium better poised than ever to continue being one of the most active, multidisciplinary cultural centers in town. Open Mon.–Sat. 9 A.M.–9 P.M., Sun. noon–8 P.M. Nearby in Ridge Park, a permanent collection of works by James Whistler, Mary Cassatt, and early Chicago artist and Beverly resident John Vanderpoel are shown at the **Vanderpoel Art Association Gallery** (9625 S. Longwood, 773/779-0007), the only privately-run art gallery in the Chicago Park District system.

Boulevard Arts Center
6011 S. Justine and 1525 W. 60ᵗʰ, 773/476-4900
http://boulevardarts.ccts.cs.depaul.edu   **SW**
Opened in 1984 to provide cultural education in a neighborhood where such opportunities are scarce, the center offers arts instruction in photography, ceramics, dance, painting, drawing, music, and theater. The buildings and grounds feature colorful murals and one of the city's only neighborhood sculpture gardens. Exhibits, readings, and recitals are presented throughout the year. The gallery is on 60ᵗʰ and the artisans store on Justine. Open Mon.–Sat. 9 A.M.–9 P.M.

ETA Creative Arts Foundation
7558 S. South Chicago, 773/752-3955, *www.etacreativearts.org*   **FSE**
Created in 1971 as a showcase and training center for African-American visual and performing artists, **ETA** opens its art gallery to the public daily

from 10 A.M. to 6 P.M. Their mainstage plays have earned them a national reputation.

Near Northwest Arts Council
1741 N. Western, 773/278-7677, *www.nnwac.org*   **W**
Local artists' work rotates at this gallery supported by the **Near Northwest Arts Council**—an activist group that focuses on the power of art and creativity to build strong communities. Mon.–Fri. 10 A.M.–5 P.M., Sat. noon–5 P.M.

Hyde Park Art Center
5307 S. Hyde Park, 773/324-5520, *www.hydeparkart.org*   **S**
One of the city's oldest community art centers, the **Hyde Park Art Center** has a reputation for showing the work of emerging artists. Ed Paschke and his Hairy Who cohorts are among the artists who received early backing from the center. Open Mon.–Fri. 9 A.M.–5 P.M., Sat. noon–5 P.M.

Little Black Pearl Art & Design Center
47th & Greenwood, 773/285-1211, *www.blackpearl.org*   **S**
A non-profit organization that provides arts and cultural education (including economic self-sufficiency through the arts) for the children, teens, and adults of the struggling North Kenwood and Oakland neighborhoods, the **Little Black Pearl** exhibits local artists and hosts traveling workshops on African-American art and history. Their new building, scheduled to open in the fall of 2004, will have extra studios and workshops, a computer lab, galleries, a courtyard and other public spaces, a restaurant, and a retail store, with plans to become a tourist destination. Open Mon.–Fri. 9 A.M.–6 P.M.

North Lakeside Cultural Center
6219 N. Sheridan, 773/743-4477, *www.northlakesidecc.org*   **FN**
Housed in a renovated 1910 mansion on the lake, the **NLCC** offers a lovely and intimate parlor setting for enjoying the ten art exhibits that are featured here yearly. Author readings, performance art, concerts, recitals, drama, and dance are also held. Open Mon., Thur., Fri. 6 P.M.–9 P.M., Tues., Wed. 10 A.M.–9 P.M., Sat. 10 A.M.–3 P.M.

South Shore Cultural Center
7059 S. South Shore, 773/256-0149   **FSE**
The gallery in this grand landmark building, dating from 1906, focuses on the work of African-American artists. Except on days when special events are staged, visitors can also wander through the center's opulent ballroom. Open Mon.–Fri. 9 A.M.–6 P.M., Sat. 9 A.M.–5 P.M.

The two free public galleries of the **School of the Art Institute** are additional venues to witness the creative endeavors of both student and established artists. The **Betty Rymer Gallery** (280 S. Columbus, 312/443-3703) is open Tues.–Sat. 10 A.M.–5 P.M., and **Gallery 2** (847 W. Jackson, 312/563-5162) can be visited Tues.–Sat. 11 A.M.–6 P.M.

Art, Outdoors

CHICAGO may rank the highest among U.S. cities when it comes to quantity and quality of outdoor art. Our reputation as the nation's architectural capital goes unchallenged. Codes that favor interesting building tops keep our skyline spectacular, and ordinances promoting artistic plaza space keep the ground views fresh as well. The sculpture, murals, mosaics, fountains, and innovative landscaping that beautify downtown are just as prevalent in many neighborhoods. And, to be sure, the success of **Cows on Parade**, a public arts endeavor we borrowed from Zurich, Switzerland, a few years back, that installed hundreds of uniquely painted, life-size fiberglass cows around the city, ensures that more along the same lines are coming.

The three walking tours we published in our previous editions in the **Walking** chapter—**Public Art (Classic)**, **Public Art (Modern)**, and **Indoor Public Art**—have been moved to our Web site (*www.lakeclaremont.com/nativesguide*) in the interest of space. Even these, though, are mere introductions to the tremendous amount of public art that graces all corners of the city. A few recent books (with color photos!) do justice to this wealth in a way we cannot: *WPA-Era Murals in the Chicago Public Schools, 1904-1943* (Heather Becker and Peter J. Schulz, 2002), *A Guide to Chicago's Murals* (Mary Lackritz Gray, 2001), and *Urban Art Chicago* (Olivia Gude and Jeff Huebner, 2000).

Still, some of the public art seemed too significant to omit. Luckily, these are easily grouped in two different areas, making it convenient to see them all in one outing. The classic works are centered around the Art Institute and Grant Park; the modern pieces dominate the government and public plazas along Dearborn and Clark and can be taken in with the **Government Building Tour** outlined on p. 14.

Start the mini-tour of classic public art at Michigan Avenue and the Chicago River. A sculpted relief at each corner of the Michigan Avenue Bridge, **Defense, Regeneration, The Pioneers, and The Discoverers** (1928), recognizes the early inhabitants and history of Chicago. (Note the metal boundary lines set in the sidewalk near the bridge that mark off the site of Fort Dearborn.) Head south along Michigan about a half mile to the Art Institute. Edward Kemey's **Lions** (1894), the unforgettable bronze mascots that flank one of the world's great art museums, are an enduring symbol of Chicago. In the museum courtyard to the south of the steps is Lorado Taft's **Fountain of the Great Lakes** (1913). It's a shady, quiet, and beautiful spot to bring a summertime lunch. Further south down Michigan on either side of Congress Parkway stand **The Bowman and The Spearman** (1928), Native Americans on horseback posed as if to shoot an arrow (but with no bow) and as if to throw a spear (but with no spear). Turning and walking eastward on Congress, **Buckingham Fountain** (p. 47) will be ahead of you. Off to the left, north of the parkway, is one of Chicago's six statues of the 16th president, Augustus Saint Gaudens's **Abraham Lincoln** (1926), "The Seated Lincoln." Finally, going back north along Columbus Drive, Dankmar Adler and Louis Sullivan's **Chicago Stock Exchange Arch** (1893) sits at Monroe, saved from the 1972 wrecking ball that hit the CSE.

As with the **Government Building Tour**, we'll move north to south along this corridor to help you synch up our modern public art highlights with those sites. Starting in front of the Thompson Center at Clark and Randolph is Jean Dubuffet's **Monument with Standing Beast** (1984), a monstrous fiberglass mystery that's a suitable match for the perplexing building it guards. Crossing the intersection southeasterly brings you to Daley Plaza, home of an untitled Picasso work, we call **"The Picasso"** (1967), Chicago's original and most prominent work of modern public art. Across Washington at the south end of the Plaza, in the courtyard east of the Chicago Temple, stands another enigmatic figure by a Spanish artist, Joan Miro's **Miro's Chicago** (1981). Continue south down Dearborn to Madison. Pop into the lobby of 70 W. Madison for Henry Moore's **Large Upright Internal/ External Form** (1983), a bronze humanoid figure ("Internal Form") nestled in larger humanoid figure ("External Form"). Across the street is the Bank One plaza, home to the tallest (60 floors) building in the Loop proper and Marc Chagall's stone and glass **Four Seasons** (1974) mosaic. One more plaza south between Adams and Jackson is the Federal Plaza, where Alexander Calder's red, abstract, steel **Flamingo** (1974) provides the only spark of color around, except for the American flag. A detour a couple blocks west along Adams or Jackson will bring you to the Sears Tower, where a mobile Calder installation, **Universe** (1974), represents the cosmos through crude representations of spine, sun, flowers, pendulum, and helix.

In the city's open air galleries—neighborhood walls—are murals and mo-saics that make bold aesthetic, social, and political statements. We've also

moved these to our special Web site (*www.lakeclaremont.com/
nativesguide*), but we'd be remiss if we didn't include the Mexican neighborhood of **Pilsen** here: Named after the Czech town by its original
inhabitants, Pilsen is particularly noteworthy for its abundance of outdoor
murals. Its boundaries are roughly 16th (1600 S) on the north, Halsted (800
W) on the east, the Chicago River (about 2700 S) on the south, and Damen
(2000 W) on the west. The walls of the square at **18th & Paulina, Casa
Atzlan** community center (1831 S. Racine) and **Calles y Sueños Cultural
Center** (19th & Carpenter) make good starting points for your explorations.

Trunk Show

Fed up with his blighted neighborhood, Milton Mizenberg, Jr. took a
chainsaw to a tree stump in a vacant lot near his house about five years ago
and created an abstract work of art. Then he made another. Once he and the
city realized that the community was responding respectfully and protec-
tively of this emerging gallery, city workers came and planted 15 more oak,
ash, and poplar stumps for him to work on in that and another abandoned
lot. This striking grove of designs is now the **Oakland Museum of
Contemporary Art** (Berkeley & 41st).

Boat Rides

WITH the popularity of Navy Pier, the ongoing development of the Chicgo
River's banks, and our devotion to Lake Michigan, tour and entertainment
boats do big business in Chicago. Sightseeing and tour boat rides range from
$8 to $20. Add dinner and/or entertainment to the mix and the prices go
from $30 on up. For a quick waterways fix, try these cheaper alternatives:

Wendella RiverBus
312/337-1446, *www.wendellaboats.com*   **C**
A mere $3 (a ten-ride pass for $13 can be shared) will afford you a swift trip
down the Chicago River with commuters during morning and evening rush
hours. Board either near Union Station (Madison & Canal) or 400 N.
Michigan (at the Chicago River). Boats run Mon.–Fri. every 9–12 minutes
during rush hour and every 20–25 minutes at other times.

Shoreline Water Taxis
312/222-9328, *www.shorelinesightseeing.com*   **C**
OK, so cabs are cheaper and more flexible when it comes to routes, but these

warm weather, touristy water cabs are still fun. There are two routes: The **Harbor Taxi** shuttles between Navy Pier and the Museum Campus, the **River Taxi** between Navy Pier and the Sears Tower. Boats leave approximately every half hour between 10 A.M. and 6 P.M, Memorial Day through Labor Day. Tickets are $6 one-way and $12 for an all-day pass, $5 and $10 for seniors, $3 and $6 for children.

Cemeteries

FOR many, cemeteries are a source of fascination. They're very much alive with art, architecture, and history and make great destinations for peaceful, escapist strolls. Listed below are a few of Chicago's most noteworthy cemeteries, including the three oldest and most magnificent, along with some of their well-known inhabitants.

Bohemian National Cemetery
5255 N. Pulaski, 773/478-0373   FN
Reasons for visiting **Bohemian National Cemetery** are many. The cemetery was created to serve the needs of the Bohemian citizens of Chicago and the nation. At the time of the cemetery's founding, Chicago was the center of Czech-Bohemian nationalism. The cemetery has a unique chapel columbarium building, which includes a beautiful chapel and two side corridors which are columbaria holding the cremains and photographs of members of the Bohemian Crematory society. Bohemian National Cemetery contains a memorial to the citizens of Lidice, a town that was destroyed by Hitler in 1942. Other monuments of interest are the Hiker, which commemorates Bohemian veterans of the Spanish-American war, a Civil War memorial, and monuments to the veterans of WWI and WWII. Victims of the *Eastland* disaster in 1915 are buried at Bohemian National Cemetery. Anton Cermak, who was mistakenly assassinated instead of President Franklin Delano Roosevelt in 1933, is buried in a mausoleum here. Albin Polasek's statues, *The Grim Reaper* and *Mother*, are located in the cemetery. A map is available from the office for self-guided tours.

Graceland Cemetery (1860)
4001 N. Clark, 773/525-1105   N
Death-styles of the rich and famous! Every extravagance in funerary art and architecture has been employed for the Chicago luminaries buried here. Chicago businessmen Phillip D. Armour, Marshall Field, Cyrus McCormick, Potter Palmer, and George Pullman; architects Daniel Burnham (check that plot of shady land that juts into the lake), Ludwig Mies van der

Rohe, Louis Sullivan, and John Wellborn Root; and detective Allen Pinkerton all make **Graceland** their final resting place. Under the granite baseball lies the co-founder of the National League, William Hulbert. As you meander through the tombstones and monuments, keep an eye out for the ornate Getty family tomb (created by Louis Sullivan), Lorado Taft's chilling *Eternal Silence* monument, and for the grave markers of these people who gave their names to Chicago streets: Governor John Peter Altgeld, Ernest Robert Graham, Henry and Eliza Honore, William Kimball, John Kinzie, and Timothy Webster. The Chicago Architecture Foundation gives tours of Graceland Cemetery on Sundays in the fall for $5. You can also buy information booklets on the cemetery

Montrose Cemetery
5400 N. Pulaski, 773/478-5400   **FN**
Here the interesting monuments are to the victims of the Iroquois Theater fire and to the Japanese-Americans who were relocated during World War II. Throughout the cemetery are new markers and monuments that show the changing neighborhoods of Chicago, especially the large, unique monuments of Serbian-Americans.

Oak Woods Cemetery (1853)
1035 E. 67th, 773/288-3800   **FSE**
Within stone walls in a residential neighborhood is Chicago's oldest cemetery with four lakes, enormous mausoleums, and a large number of tall obelisk monuments. It's the final resting place for a long list of notable citizens, including Chicago's first African-American mayor, Harold Washington, civil rights leader Ida B. Wells, federal judge and first baseball commissioner Kenesaw Mountain Landis, bluesman Junior Wells, and architects Solon Beman and George Nimmons. George Fuller, builder of the Rookery and the Monadnock Building, lies in **Oak Wood**'s largest mausoleum, marked by Roman pillars and overlooking Symphony Lake. Olympic gold medalist Jesse Owens' red stone grave marker also overlooks the lake. The grave of "Cap" Anson, National League baseball player and manager of the Chicago White Stockings (precursor of the Cubs), is easily identified by two crossed baseball bats on the headstone. By contrast, physicist Enrico Fermi lies beneath a modest marker. Six thousand confederate soldiers who died while imprisoned at Camp Douglas (it once stood near 35th Street) are buried here in what is the largest northern Confederate gravesite. Their resting place is marked with the 46-foot Confederate Mound Monument. Panels list the names of 4,200 of those soldiers who were identified. A dozen Union soldiers who served as guards at the prisoner-of-war camp are also buried on the spot.

Rosehill Cemetery (1859)

5800 N. Ravenswood, 773/561-5940   FN

Rosehill's 350 acres comprised the city's first "rural park" cemetery—a Parisian concept that promoted lush, green cemeteries as tranquil, scenic escapes from the day-to-day grit of urban life. Another slate of famous folks lie here: Chicago businessmen Milton Florsheim, James Scott Kemper, Julius Rosenwald, Maurice Rothschild, Ignaz Schwinn, John G. Shedd, and A. Montgomery Ward; Coolidge's vice-president, Charles Gates Dawes; Charles Hull, who gave a house with his name to Jane Addams; and Frances E. Willard of the Women's Christian Temperance Union. Rosehill is also the final resting place of 15 Chicago mayors; 16 Civil War generals; Robert Franks, the 14-year-old victim of the 1924 Leopold/Loeb murder; and 16-year-old Lulu Fellows, who died in 1883 and is said to haunt the adjacent woods. The Chicago Architecture Foundation gives tours of Rosehill Cemetery in the spring and fall and tours of the **Rosehill Mausoleum** in the fall. Maps are available for self-guided tours of the cemetery in the Rosehill office.

St. Casimir Cemetery

111th & Pulaski   FSW

Although the word "Lithuanian" was removed from its name in the late 1990s, due to ongoing clashes between the Lithuanian community and the Archdiocese of Chicago, this is Chicago's Lithuanian Catholic cemetery. That's neither here nor there. What you need to know is that this is one unique and incredible collection of monuments, some say among the finest in the U.S. The pre-WWII headstones are traditionally and creatively decorated with intricate folk patterns, textile motifs, flowers and leafs, and religious symbols and scenes. That's impressive enough in this pleasant garden setting. The modern section, however, can be surreal. Its many abstract monuments are works of contemporary art displaying unconventional ornamentation and typefaces, and made of materials like cor-ten steel, stainless steel, fiber glass, and stained glass.

Stephen A. Douglas Tomb and Memorial

636 E 35th St.   S

How ironic that a man known as "The Little Giant" has a 96-foot monument erected for him. The Illinois politician who once vied with Abraham Lincoln for the presidency lies in Chicago at 35th Street and the lake in a landmark tomb done by Leonard Volk between 1863 and 1881.

For a more in-depth examination of Chicago cemeteries, look for Matt Hucke and Ursula Bielski's *Graveyards of Chicago* (Lake Claremont Press,

1999). Hucke's elaborate Web site, *www.graveyards.com*, provides a sneak preview and an additional 2,000 photos.

Elevator Rides

IN a city of skyscraping structures, Chicagoans are well-acquainted with elevators. Among Chicago's ear-popping rides, a few stand out as memorable:

First is the nighttime climb to the 96th floor of the **John Hancock Building** (875 N. Michigan, 312/787-9586). This is not the $9.50 trip to the 94th floor's observation deck. It's a free glide to the **Signature Lounge**, where you can opt, like so many others, to soak up breathtaking views of the glittering city below without sitting down and buying a drink—no matter how tacky or annoying to actual customers. (A drink with tax and tip from a window-side table will run in the $10 range.) Next, the old-fashioned, attendant-controlled elevators of the exquisite and musty **Fine Arts Building** (410 S. Michigan) come to mind. The operator pulls a protective iron gate across the door for the ride—just like in the old days. When you reach the top floor, wander into Curtiss Hall for a magnificent view of the lakefront. Walk your way down the ten flights of stairs stopping at any point to roam the historic hallways filled with studios, practice rooms, and music and design classes. Finally, I have a hard time forgetting the days (late 70s/early 80s) when the glass elevators of Michigan Avenue's first enclosed mall, **Water Tower Place** (845 N. Michigan), caused quite a stir. They even caught the attention of the director of the movie *Class* (1983), who used the 7-story ride as the setting for a racy love scene between Jacqueline Bisset and Andrew McCarthy.

"Factory" Tours

NEXT to gazing wide-eyed at a huge construction site, nothing feeds the inner child like a factory tour. Lookit all the cool stuff! Way up north, in North Chicago, you can actually live a childhood dream and tour a candy factory— the Jelly Belly factory, to be precise—but here in Chicago most places will tell you they can't let you in "for insurance purposes." And, since 9/11, it's no longer possible to tour the two major newspapers. Still, here's what we've got:

Eli's Cheesecake World
6701 W. Forest Preserve
773/736-3417, 773/205-3800 for groups, *www.elischeesecake.com* **NW**
Visit the 62,000-square-foot bakery and get a slice of cheesecake. "Sneak Peek" tours are available to walk-ins, Mon.–Fri. at noon. If you're with more than ten people, make a reservation for some time Mon.–Fri. 10 A.M.–3 P.M. (You can get in on the weekends, too, but the bakery is shut down.) Sneak Peek tour: Adults $3, under 12, $2. Many tour packages are available.

Federal Reserve Bank of Chicago
230 S. LaSalle, 312/322-2400, *www.chicagofed.org* **C**
Think of this as a "money factory." During the 45–60 min. tour you'll see a video, learn the Fed's main functions, and then get a look at the basement, where they process the money (no cameras, please!). You'll see a lot of cash, but this tour is 100% free. Even if you can't take a tour, the visitors' center has displays of old currency, a game, educational exhibits, and $1,000,000 in singles in a glass cube. Take home a free bag of money! (It's shredded.) Individuals and small groups can drop in for the guided tour at 1 P.M. Groups of 15 to 39 people must make an advanced reservation for a time slot between 9 A.M. and 3 P.M. Sometimes they can accommodate your group the next day; other times the next opening is several weeks ahead. Open Mon.–Fri. 9 A.M.–4:15 P.M.

United States Post Office
433 W. Harrison, 312/983-7550 **C**
It's a little-known fact that you can see where those big machines sort the mail. Tours of the two block-by-two block facility can last an hour and a half, depending on what you're interested in. Mostly you'll see the first and third floors—processing and distribution—where letters travel through some of the most modern letter-sorting machines in the world at the rate of 11–15 per second. And if that's not enough, you can buy stamps or open a P.O. box, too. Tours are given to singles or groups, but you must be 10 years or older. Call at least one week in advance for your free tour, which will be scheduled between 10 A.M. and noon, Mon.–Fri.

Fountains

Buckingham Fountain
Congress & Lake Shore Drive **C**
Buckingham Fountain—one of the world's largest, most magnificent

fountains—has remained a popular Chicago attraction since its completion in 1927. Its three-tiered, pink marble exterior; four pairs of wrought-bronze sea horses symbolizing the four states that border Lake Michigan; and a dramatic, 165-foot central geyser make it the regal centerpiece of Grant Park. The Beaux-Art-design was apparently influenced by the Fountain of Latona at Versailles. Kate Buckingham, an arts philanthropist, donated the money to build the fountain in memory of her brother Clarence. She even left an endowment, administered by the Art Institute, to maintain it. Recently, new, more intense lighting was added to help the fountain better compete with Chicago's ever brighter nighttime skyline. Water gushes daily 10 A.M.–11 P.M., Apr. 1–Nov. 1, with a spectacular colored lights display from dusk–11 P.M. Every hour on the hour after dark, there is an additional lights and music display that lasts for 20 minutes.

Nicholas J. Melas Centennial Fountain and Water Arc
McClurg Court & the Chicago River
www.mwrd.org/water/fountain.htm   **C**
Installed in 1989 to commemorate the centennial of the Metropolitan Water Reclamation District of Greater Chicago—and in a way to usher in the then-new "New East Side"—the Melas Fountain is accompanied by a stream of water that arcs across the Chicago River daily May 1–Oct. 1, for the first ten minutes of every hour, 10 A.M.–midnight, except for a 3 P.M.–4 P.M. hiatus.

Newer fountains have sprung up at **Navy Pier** and **McCormick Place** as part of the splashy and creative landscaping connected with the renovations and expansions of those sites, but the coolest new fountain in Chicago is Millennium Park's **Crown Fountain** (p. 53).

Gardens

Bergen Garden
5050 S. Lake Shore Drive, *www.regentsparkchicago.com/garden*   **S**
On top of this three-story parking garage is a one-acre paradise filled with 30,000 plants and trees, ponds and fountains. It was designed in 1982 by Phil Shipley—a California landscape architect who previously worked on the estates of such Hollywood luminaries as Clark Gable, Jean Harlow, and Walt Disney—to provide an aesthetic view for residents of the apartments above. Walkways meander through lush plantings of petunias, viburnum, daisies, English and Baltic ivy, and marigolds, shaded by Austrian pines,

flowering crab apples, and honey locust trees. A waterfall cascades into a small stream that is crossed by a footbridge. Also a designated bird sanctuary, visitors will see birds bathing in the water or eating berries from the shrubbery; a small wild duck population from the Lincoln Park Zoo spends part of the year here. Open to the public from May to October. Call to make an appointment for a free self-guided tour.

Womens Park & Gardens
Prairie Avenue, between 18th & Cullerton   C

Complementing the Prairie Avenue Historic District, these gardens join a central fountain and commemorative walkway in gracing a park specifically designed to honor the achievements of women significant in Chicago history. Open dawn–dusk. Free.

Another lesser-known garden of the same theme is the **Jane Addams Memorial Park** (on the lake, just northwest of Navy Pier), which contains the first monument in Chicago erected for a woman.

The city's two public conservatories are open daily from 9 A.M.–5 P.M. Admission is free.

Garfield Park Conservatory
300 N. Central Park, 312/746-5100, *www.garfield-conservatory.org* W

This is the largest indoor public botanical garden in the world, displaying 5,000 plant species, including one of the best cactus collections in the country. The nearby el station was recently remodeled in a Victorian style—an added incentive to take public transportation to this destination. An innovative new approach to introducing the conservatory's treasures has brought such things as the Pink Flamingo show and the use of African dinosaur skeletons and Dale Chihuly's glass art as garden sculptures among the plants. Along with the usual shows, the conservatory now offers extensive educational programs and special events like a weekly, year-round farmer's market, art shows, county fair days, heritage festivals, music performances, a garden shop, and a pedestrian mall of retail stands. Open Thurs. until 8 P.M.

Lincoln Park Conservatory
Fullerton & Stockton, 312/742-7736   N

With no need to gentrify, the smaller city conservatory in Lincoln Park holds its own slightly musty glory. Take a quick jaunt through its brief maze of rooms anytime you're passing through the park or spending a day at the zoo. Or, bring a book or your own thoughts and retreat to a bench in the fern or flower room. Annual shows include the perennial azalea, chrysanthemum, and poinsettia displays. Back in the 1960s, the chrysanthemum was designated the official flower of Chicago.

Holiday Madness

FAR from downtown's architectural majesty, Chicagoans engage in another form of arts appreciation: marveling at their neighbors' holiday displays. Please exhibit the appropriate amount of respect and restraint when it comes to private homes. While the displays are meant for public enjoyment, owners' don't expect their privacy or their lawns trampled as the price of their seasonal hobby. Their high electric bills are enough.

Christmas

"The Logan House"
2656 W. Logan   N
People from all over the North Side talk about this particular home on a large corner lot in Logan Square. Most commonly referred to as **"The Logan House,"** the more it changes from year to year, the more it stays the same. Life-size, light-studded wire figures, strands and strands of colored bulbs, shadowboxes, flags from around the world, animation, and holiday tunes playing over the speaker engorge the senses. (Note that this house is now a spectacle at Halloween time as well.)

More electric extravaganzas, including those in the decoratively-dense **Schorch Village** (bounded by Addison, Harlem, Belmont, and Narragansett) and **Sauganash** (bounded by Bryn Mawr, Cicero, Lincolnwood, and Pulaski) neighborhoods, are acknowledged in Mary Edsey's book, *The Best Christmas Decorations in Chicagoland* (Tabagio Press). Edsey offers a couple of suggestions to explain why Chicagoans seem to be even more zealous in their outdoor Christmas decorating than other Americans. First, two of the world's largest light manufacturers, Silvestri Corp. and NOMA Christmas, are located here. Secondly, from 1962 to 1966, Polk Brothers gave away 250,000 five-foot, lighted Santas with appliance and furniture purchases, surely having an impact on external holiday displays. You can still see many of these pioneering decorations on lawns, porches, and rooftops around the city. Edsey gives very merry Yuletide bus tours (773/404-9402) of mind-blowing holiday displays. She recommends **Cornelia's Restaurant** (748 W. Cornelia, 773/248-8333) for Christmas time dining because of its attractive display of antique decorations.

Apart from gaping at light displays in residential areas, Chicago has a number of Christmas-time traditions. Certain ones—like seeing *The Nutcracker Ballet* at McCormick Place's **Arie Crown Theater** or *A Christmas Carol* at the **Goodman Theater**, eating lunch under the giant Christmas tree in **Marshall Field's** 7th-floor Walnut Room, and seeing the international collection of Christmas trees at the **Museum of Science and Industry**—can be costly for the budget-minded. However, there are plenty of free and low-cost options as well. For decades, Chi-town residents have hopped on the "L" to downtown to see the super-tall city Christmas tree in **Daley Plaza** and the animated holiday window displays of the State Street department stores. (Marshall Field's decorated windows alone are a tradition that goes back over 100 years!) You can purchase a cup of hot chocolate or roasted chestnuts from street vendors. Head to the **Lincoln Park** or **Garfield Park Conservatory** (see p. 49) for the seasonal poinsettia show or to the **Adler Planetarium** (see p. 59) for their *Star of Wonder* sky show.

The City of Chicago has been enshrining new December events in our psyches, including a **Christmas Market** in Daley Plaza, and a **Santa El**. The train has Christmas decorations inside and bright neon lights on the outside. Between the middle cars of the train, a flatbed car is decorated with a sleigh upon which Santa rides. He takes breaks between stops and passes out candy canes to children riding the train. **CTA** (p. 73) employees in each car pass out transit maps and brochures. The cost of the ride is the regular fare. **Lincoln Park Zoo** (p. 14) stays open late for **ZooLights**, a spectacular display of over one million lights ($6 for adults, $4 for children).

Halloween

Outdoor decorating is not just for the yuletide anymore. Elaborate Halloween displays are appearing with greater frequency on neighborhood side streets. And, by the next edition, we can probably update you on front lawn parades of Easter décor as well.

1052 W. Wrightwood   N
Hundreds of lighted jack-o-lanterns grin and grimace from the front lawn of this Wrightwood residence.

7025 W. Berwyn   FN
A bounty of headstones, ghosts, witches, monsters, and coffin-bound mummies are barely contained by the spider web fence of this house's lawn. Visit at night to experience the full force of the light and sound effects.

Over the past 5–15 years, dozens of new Chicago Halloween traditions have emerged, many under the umbrella of the city's **"Chicagoween"** festivities, like the **Haunted Village in Daley Plaza** with spooky storytellers, pumpkin carving, and costume parades, and the **CTA's Haunted El**. For teens and adults, popular events are the **Edgar Allan Poe Readings** at **Glessner House Museum** (*www.glessnerhouse.org*), a Prairie Avenue mansion and one of the city's oldest structures, and **Redmoon Theater**'s late-night **All Hallows' Eve Ritual Celebration** (*www.redmoon.org*). Redmoon creates large, outdoor public spectacles that may combine masks, puppets, mime, performance art, juggling, fire, quirky devices, dance, physical humor, live music, and hundreds of artists and community members. Held in Logan Square from 1996–2002, refer to the Redmoon website for future locations.

Lawn Frenzy

IF you miss the seasonal shows, here is another extreme manifestation of unique exterior home decorating:

House of Crosses
1544 W. Chestnut   C
Straight from a fantastical dream (or nightmare, for some) is the eccentric **"House of Crosses"**—referred to as the "It's What I Do" House by the *American Institute of Architects Guide to Chicago*. For almost 30 years, the owners have been covering the house, lawn, and coach house with hundreds of wooden crosses, plaques, and shields. This isn't a grotesque fixation on death but an artistic tribute—primarily, *to the movies!* The names of movie stars, movie characters, and movie titles appear on these colorful structures: Ingrid Bergman, Bing Crosby, Bette Davis, Mickey Rooney, Zsa Zsa Gabor, Tarzan, Buckwheat, the Cisco Kid. Camelot, the Pope, Joan of Arc, and former mayor Jane Byrne are also among the acknowledged.

Millennium Park

MAYOR Daley had a dream. Use $160 million to transform 16 acres of old rail yards between Michigan Avenue and Grant Park for a showpiece park to mark the new millennium. Four years after its planned opening and $315 million extra dollars, eight additional acres, and much reconfiguring and political heat later, **Millennium Park** opened in July 2004. Now Mayor Daley has a legacy. An "instant" hit, most Chicagoans are delighted with it (*what botched park?*) and the international visitors and acclaim are already pouring in. (It's expected to draw two to three million visitors per year.) A true Chicago blend of accessibility and populism mixed with world-class art, architecture, and landscaping, and a smidge of edginess, commercialism, progressiveness, and wackiness, Millennium Park, now open, required zero adjustment time. It fits.

Millennium Park
Michigan, from Randolph to Monroe, *http://millenniumpark.org/*   **C**
What hasn't it got? It's our own Central Park, but conveniently condensed between downtown and the lake—and better, of course. There's a grand promenade, fountains, gardens, and interactive public art like *Cloud Gate* (already nicknamed "The Bean"), a giant silver sculpture that reflects the entire skyline, and **Crown Fountain** (p. 48), a two-towered, multi-media spectacle. It has an ice rink, gift shop, and al fresco dining. A 300-space, heated indoor bicycle parking facility offers lockers, showers, and bike repair to commuters and park visitors. The crown jewel is Frank Gehry's pavilion, an architectural and acoustic tour de force. It's the new home of the Grant Park Orchestra and countless free concerts to come. There's also a Gehry bridge (his first), a hardwood deck that snakes across Columbus Drive to Grant Park, its side clad in stainless steel. Come once, come often. Open daily 6 A.M.–11 P.M.

Museums

FOUNDATIONS, associations, philanthropists, and volunteers present us with museums of all stripes, from one-room exhibits to premier cultural treasures. Much of Chicago's thriving museum culture can be yours at no or low charge. This listing is organized for your budgeting convenience by *Always Free, Free One Day a Week, Donations Appreciated, Low Admission Charge*, and *Worth It?*

Always Free

ABA Museum of Law
321 N. Clark, 312/988-6222, *www.abanet.org/museum*   **C**
The American Bar Association pays tribute to the legal profession with their modest museum. The recent *America's Lawyer–Presidents* and *Famous Trials in American History: Cases that Shaped and Shocked the Nation* are typical of their exhibits. Open Mon.–Fri. 11 A.M.–2 P.M., Sat. 11 A.M.–5 P.M.

Chicago Cultural Center
78 E. Washington, 312/744-6630
www.cityofchicago.org\culturalcenter   C
Known as "The People's Palace" when it first opened in 1897 as the city's original public library, this national landmark still deserves every implication of that affectionate name. It remained Chicago's central library until 1977 and has been the **Cultural Center** since an extensive renovation was completed in 1991. Although Chicagoans, in true second city fashion, often brag about being number one, in the case of this cultural treasure—it really is true. As an architectural masterpiece, this beaux-art spectacle wows on every repeated visit. The Grand Staircase, Preston Bradley Hall, and G.A.R. Rotunda *are* the type of things usually associated with palaces. Try eating your lunch under the $35 million Tiffany dome (the world's largest) in Preston Bradley Hall during a **Dame Myra Hess Memorial Concert** Wednesdays at 12:15 P.M. You will feel like royalty. When it comes to the 1,000 free cultural events a year—exhibits, concerts, dance and dramatic performances, films, classes, lectures, and workshops—it is peerless. The first floor also houses a visitors information center, a photo exhibit of Chicago landmarks, several galleries, a gift shop, and cafe. Guided architectural tours begin in the Randolph Street lobby Wed., Fri., and Sat. at 1:15 P.M. Open Mon.–Thur. 10 A.M.–7 P.M., Fri. 10 A.M.–6 P.M., Sat. 10 A.M.–5 P.M., Sun. 11 A.M.–5 P.M. You'll need to pick up the monthly schedule of events to keep track of everything.

City Gallery
Historic Water Tower, 806 N. Michigan, 312/742-0808   C
Squeeze ten minutes of art into your day at the City of Chicago's free photography gallery in the historic Water Tower. About the size of a living room, there's no chance of breaking a sweat or permanently furrowing your brow—once around the tiny room and you're out. Staffed by an Office of Tourism employee and curated by the city's public art program, expect insightful takes on various slivers of Chicago: baseball photography by Sox fans vs. Cubs fans, *No Ketchup* (Chicago hot dog stands), and local fashion shots. Open Mon.–Sat. 10 A.M.–6:30 P.M., Sun. 10 A.M.–5 P.M.

D'Arcy Museum of Art
Loyola University, 6525 N. Sheridan
773/508-2679, *http://darcy.luc.edu*   FN
This intimate and elegant museum on the Loyola University campus rotates the various art works from its impressive array of Medieval, Renaissance, and Baroque art. Over 500 pieces, dating between 1150 and 1700, include sculpture, decorative arts, and paintings by Bellini, Bassano, and Tintoretto.

Open to the public when school is in session, Tues.–Sat. noon–4 P.M., Tues.–Thurs. noon–4 P.M. other times.

Harold Washington Library Center
400 S. State, 312/747-4300
www.chipublib.org/001hwlc/001hwlc.html **C**
The main branch of the Chicago Public Library offers numerous services (sign up to use pianos, computers, and AV equipment), performances, films, lectures, workshops, art exhibits, and children's programming free of charge. While touring the **HWLC**—the second largest public library in the world—don't miss the Winter Garden on the ninth floor; the Jazz, Blues, and Gospel Hall of Fame on the eighth floor; or the permanent art collection scattered throughout the building. Look for monthly schedule of events. Guided tours Mon.–Sat. at noon and 2 P.M. Open Mon.–Thur. 9 A.M.–7 P.M., Fri.–Sat. 9 A.M.–5 P.M., Sun. 1 P.M.–5 P.M.

Historic Pullman Foundation Visitor Center
11141 S. Cottage Grove, 773/785-8901 **FSW**
Turn to our **Walking** chapter (p. 305) to learn about the historic company town of Pullman. Its Visitor Center presents a continually evolving exhibition, *Pullman . . . The Man, The Car, The Company, The Model Town, The Strike, The Landmark Community in Chicago*, featuring photos, artifacts, and brief video covering the town's history up until contemporary preservation efforts. Guided walking tours of the district leave the center the first Sunday of every month at 12:30 P.M. and 1:30 P.M., May–Oct. This is a must-do! Almost 90% of the town has been preserved. Group tours are by appointment. Open Tues.–Sun. 11 A.M.–3 P.M.

Hyde Park Historical Society
5529 S. Lake Park, 773/493-1893, *www.hydeparkhistory.org* **S**
Housed in an 1893 cable station, this museum documents and displays the history of the long-flourishing Hyde Park neighborhood. Open Sat.–Sun. 2 P.M.–4 P.M.

Intuit: The Center for Intuitive and Outsider Art
1926 N. Halsted, 773/929-7122, *http://outsider.art.org* **N**
Formed in 1991 to promote the art of those who are self-taught, or rejected, ignored, marginalized, or unimpressed by the institutions of the mainstream art world, **Intuit**'s galleries are always filled with interesting and challenging works. The center also hosts dozens of lectures, discussions, film screenings, performances, tours, and parties annually, as well as runs a gift shop, *Visions*, filled with quirky products. Open Wed.–Sat. noon–5 P.M.

Louis, Louis

The Museum of Decorative Arts (4611 N. Lincoln, 773/989-4310, *www.louissullivanofchicago.com*) indeed decorates Lincoln Square with its Art Nouveau facade designed by Louis Sullivan. Built in 1922, it was Sullivan's last building commission. Inside you'll find Art Nouveau, Art Deco, and Victorian-themed coffeetable books, hats, accessories, jewelry, stationery, and gift items for sale. Their permanent collection (not for sale) includes photos of the 1893 Chicago World's Fair, photos of other Sullivan architecture, and prints of Alfonse Mucha and other famous artists of that time period. Everything in this shop is as pleasurable to explore as at any conventional museum, and, of course, since it's primarily a gift shop, it's always free to enter! Open Sat. 11 A.M.–6 P.M., Sun. noon–5 P.M.

Jane Addams' Hull House
800 S. Halsted, 312/413-5353
www.uic.edu/jaddams/hull/hull_house.html   **C**
Visit a historic building where Nobel Peace Prize winner Jane Addams and crew began their settlement house and social work projects to improve the lives of immigrants in the surrounding neighborhood. Accompanying exhibits focus on Addams, other women who lived and worked at Hull House, their social endeavors, and Chicago immigration history. Open Tues.–Fri. 10 A.M.–4 P.M., Sun. noon–4 P.M.

Mexican Fine Arts Center Museum
1852 W. 19th, 312/738-1503, *www.mfachicago.org*   **W**
The Midwest's only Mexican museum has developed an international reputation for itself and its first-rate exhibits of folk, fine, and experimental arts by local, national, and international artists. Its extensive permanent collection contains original pieces from such Mexican greats as Diego Rivera, José Orozco, and David Siquieros. The museum also sponsors performances, lectures, classes, and community events. Open Tues.–Sun. 10 A.M.–5 P.M.

Museum of Contemporary Photography
600 S. Michigan, 312/663-5554, *www.mocp.org*   **C**
On the Columbia College campus, the **MOCP** explores the roles and implications of the image in the contemporary world through exhibits employing a range of photographic styles, technologies, and interpretations. Open Mon.–Fri. 10 A.M.–5 P.M., Thur. 10 A.M.–8 P.M., Sat. noon–5 P.M.

Newberry Library
60 W. Walton, 312/943-9090, *www.newberry.org* C

Of international renown, this independent history and humanities research library boasts an astonishing collection of rare books, maps, graphics, and manuscripts—such items as a leaf from the Gutenberg Bible and original drawings for *Alice in Wonderland*. Their holdings are particularly strong in several areas, including the American West, family history and genealogy, Native American history and literature, the history of cartography, and the history of music. Free tours, Thur. 3 P.M. and Sat. 10:30 A.M. Open Tues.–Thur. 10 A.M.–6 P.M., Fri.–Sat. 9 A.M.–5 P.M.

Renaissance Society at the University of Chicago
5811 S. Ellis, 773/702-8670, *www.renaissancesociety.org* S

Established in 1915, the **Renaissance Society** has earned an international reputation as a place to discover and experience the frontiers of culture, particularly contemporary visual arts. The society was the first or one of the first institutions to recognize the talents of Picasso, Mondrian, Mies van der Rohe, Calder, Chagall, Bruce Nauman, Jenny Holzer, and Cindy Sherman, and they continue to introduce Chicago to provocative new artists. Their programming includes concerts, performance art, lectures, and film/video screenings. Open Tues.–Fri. 10 A.M.–5 P.M., Sat.–Sun. noon–5 P.M.

Rogers Park/West Ridge Historical Society
7344 N. Western, 773/764-4078, *www.rpwrhs.org* FN

The RPWR Historical Society encourages and perpetuates an interest in the history of their neighborhoods through education, preservation, and re-search. Their storefront museum displays numerous photographs and memo-rabilia depicting the rich history of these important Chicago communities. An on-site reference library includes a large collection of historical photos, maps, deeds, and other documents. Open Wed. & Fri. 10 A.M.–5 P.M., Thur. 7 A.M.–9 P.M.

Smart Museum of Art
5550 S. Greenwood, 773/702-0200
http://smartmuseum.uchicago.edu/ S

Although opened in 1974, this U of C fine art museum houses a permanent collection that began in the 1890s, the decade of the University's founding. Its 7,500-piece collection spans five millennia of Western and Eastern civilizations and includes Chinese, Neolithic, and current American art. It was named for the founders of *Esquire* magazine. Open Tues., Wed., Fri. 10 A.M.–4 P.M., Thur. 10 A.M.–8 P.M., Sat.–Sun. noon–5 P.M.

Smith Museum of Stained Glass
Navy Pier, 312/595-5024   C
Hailed as the only museum in the country dedicated to stained glass, this
section of Navy Pier's Festival Hall showcases both religious and secular
stained glass. Most of it has a Chicago neighborhood connection, having
been either in a local church or a private home. Much of the displayed work
dates between 1890 and 1920, making it a must-see for lovers of the Art
Nouveau and Art Deco styles. Famous artists such as Louis Sullivan, Frank
Lloyd Wright, and Tiffany are represented. Open daily 10 A.M.–10 P.M.

Free One Day A Week

The following museums are free to the public one day weekly. Prices listed
are admission charges for the other days of the week.

Sundays

DuSable Museum
740 E. 56th Place, 773/947-0600, *www.dusablemuseum.org*   S
Named for Chicago's first permanent settler, a Haitian man named Jean
Baptiste Pointe du Sable, this major Chicago cultural institution is devoted
to the preservation and interpretation of the history and culture of African-
Americans. Recent exhibits included a retrospective of Allen Stringfellow's
art and a look at African-American beauty industry pioneer, Annie Malone.
Mon.–Sat. 10 A.M.–5 P.M., Sun. noon–5 P.M. $3 admission, $2 students/
seniors, $1 kids (6–13).

Mondays

Chicago Historical Society
1601 N. Clark, 312/642-4600, *www.chicagohistory.org*   N
Founded in 1856, the **CHS** is Chicago's oldest cultural institution and the
country's premier urban history museum. Its wonderful exhibits chronicle
the city's history from its days as a wilderness outpost to current times, plus
throw in some regional and national history for good measure. Don't miss
the "Hands-On History Gallery," explorations of Chicago neighborhoods,
the permanent "Pioneer Life" display, and "A House Divided: America in
the Age of Lincoln." Appealing and timely programming and temporary
exhibits liven up the old stuff, as did recent coverage of Jazz Age Chicago
nightclubs, teen life in Chicago, and the city's free speech history. Open
Mon.–Sat. 9:30 A.M.–4:30 P.M., Sun. noon–5 P.M. Suggested $5 admission,
$3 students/seniors, $1 kids (6–12).

Tuesdays

Adler Planetarium
1300 S. Lake Shore Drive, 312/922-7827
www.adlerplanetarium.org   C
The country's original planetarium and the Midwest's leading museum of astronomy and space exploration features three floors of exhibits and regular sky shows in its domed theater, which is accessed by a 77-foot escalator straight from a sci-fi fantasy. These thematic sky shows combine visual effects, narration, and music to teach about comets, constellations, the solar system, or related topics. Throughout the museum, you'll encounter a remarkable assortment of antique astronomical instruments from around the world—a collection rivaled only by those in Florence and Oxford. Other favorites include the hands-on experiments with lenses and prisms and devices that tell you how much you would weigh on different planets. Open Mon.–Fri. 9:30 A.M.–4:30 P.M., Sat.–Sun. 9 A.M.–4:30 P.M. Depending on whether you're a Chicago resident and what shows you wish to see, $11–$18 admission, seniors/children (4–17) $10–$17. Sky shows on free days are an extra $5. Use the observatory's telescope to peer into outer space after the 8 P.M. sky show on Fridays.

Art Institute of Chicago
111 S. Michigan, 312/443-3600, *www.artic.edu/aic*   C
Built for the 1893 World's Fair, this internationally renowned museum boasts a consummate collection that features various genres of fine and decorative art, spanning 5,000 years and from six continents. Along with Seurat's famed *A Sunday on La Grande Jatte* and Hopper's *Nighthawks* are recognizable paintings by Caillebotte, Degas, Monet, Renoir, Picasso, O'Keefe, Toulouse-Lautrec, Van Gogh, Warhol, and Wood. Those looking for something more three-dimensional will appreciate the paperweight collection, textiles, architectural works, suits of armor, Thorne miniature rooms, and folk art and antiquities from far away lands. Open Mon.–Wed., Fri. 10:30 A.M.–4:30 P.M., Thur. 10:30 A.M.–8 P.M., Sat.–Sun. 10 A.M.–5 P.M. $12 admission, $7 students/seniors/children (6–14). This is the strongly-suggested admission price; you can technically pay what you wish as long as you pay something.

Free only Tuesday evenings, 5 P.M.–8 P.M.

Museum of Contemporary Art
220 E. Chicago, 312/280-2660, *www.mcachicago.org*   C
Enjoy the work of established and emerging contemporary artists (post-

1945) in this spectacular, new-ish building designed by German museum architect Josef Paul Kleihaus. At 151,000 square feet, the **MCA** is now the largest single building devoted to contemporary art in the country. Calder, Johns, Kline, Magritte, Nauman, Paschke, Sherman, and Warhol are among the artists featured in the museum's permanent collection, but the majority of space is left for constantly changing exhibits. Striking views of the city and lakefront, a theater for film and live performance, an education center for workshops and artist discussions, video and electronic galleries, and an outdoor sculpture garden are other notable features. Free, 45-minute tours are given daily and start in the second-floor lobby (Tues. 1 P.M. and 6 P.M., Wed.–Fri. 1 P.M., Sat.–Sun. 11 A.M, noon, 1 P.M., and 2 P.M.) Open Tues. 10 A.M.–8 P.M., Wed.–Sun. 10 A.M.–5 P.M. $10 admission, $4 students/seniors.

Cocktail Culture

As part of efforts to hook the younger set on museum attendance and cultural patronage—and to have something new and lively and social to offer its committed supporters—some of Chicago's major institutions have devised monthly cocktail party-type gatherings aimed at savvy urbanites over 21. The **Museum of Contemporary Art**'s (220 E. Chicago, 312/280-2660) monthly "First Fridays" and the **Art Institute**'s (Michigan & Adams, 312/443-3600) Thursday evening "After Hours" (3rd Thursday of every 3rd month) offer guided tours, gallery hopping, live or DJ music, appetizers, cash bar, and stimulating conversation and mingling (hopefully). The **MCA** affair runs 6 P.M.–10 P.M. ($14 cover charge, $7 for members), the **Art Institute**'s 5:30 P.M.–8 P.M. ($15 cover charge, $10 for members.) In a similar vein, the **Shedd Aquarium** and **Chicago Historical Society** have also been hosting outdoor jazz and cocktails Thursday evenings in the summer. Might want to think about that membership.

Wednesdays

Charnley–Persky House
1365 N. Astor, 312/915-0105, *www.charnleyhouse.org*   C
The Society of Architectural Historians recently began offering tours of its national headquarters, which is located in what Frank Lloyd Wright referred to as "the first modern house in America." Wright helped Louis Sullivan design the building for lumber merchant James Charnley when Wright was a young architect in Adler and Sullivan's firm. 45-minute tours are given Wed. at noon for free and Sat. at 10 A.M. and 1 P.M. for $5 (10 A.M. only

Dec.–Mar.). The Saturday tour can be extended another 45 minutes (for $5) for a walk of historic **Astor Street** and a tour of **Madlener House**, a Prairie School residence designed by Schmidt and Garden in 1901–1902.

Clarke House Museum
1827 S. Indiana, 312/326-1480   **C**
Glessner House Museum
1800 S. Prairie, 312/326-1480, *www.glessnerhouse.org*   **C**
Prairie Avenue House Museums (1800 S. Prairie, 312/326-1480) is a sophisticated organization established to preserve and promote the history, architecture, and art of the Prairie Avenue historic district. Some of their eclectic programming includes evenings with the curator, holiday tours by candlelight, and wine and cheese receptions. Chicago's oldest residence, **Clarke House**, a Greek Revival building from 1836, is furnished with artifacts from the mid-nineteenth century to recreate life on the urban frontier. A National Historic Landmark, the 1887 **Glessner House**, a fortress-like English Arts & Crafts home, was daring when first constructed in Chicago's original mansion district. It's now furnished with nineteenth-century pieces that reflect Chicago's Gilded Age. Access to both houses is by guided tour. Clarke House tours are Wed.–Sun. noon, 1 P.M., and 2 P.M.; Glessner House tours are Wed.–Sun. 1 P.M., 2 P.M., and 3 P.M. $15 admission for both houses, $12 students/seniors, $9 children (5–12); $10 for one house, $9, and $6.

Thursdays

Chicago Children's Museum
Navy Pier at 700 E. Grand, 312/527-1000
www.chichildrensmuseum.org   **C**
Since moving from its Cultural Center origins to this Navy Pier location, the **Chicago Children's Museum** has become the second most visited children's museum in the country and one of Chicago's top cultural attractions. Its three floors of exhibits, plus steady stream of workshops, performances, and special events are designed to activate the creative and intellectual potential of children from toddlers to ten-year-olds. Inventing Lab, Waterways, Treehouse Trails, Face to Face: Dealing with Prejudice and Discrimination, Artabounds Gallery, Big Backyard, and Climbing Schooner are among the delightful, permanent hands-on exhibits. Open Tues.–Sun. 10 A.M.–5 P.M., **Thur. 5 P.M.–8 P.M. is the free family night.** Open Mon. Memorial Day–Labor Day. $7 per person for an all-day pass, children less than a year old are free.

Peggy Notebaert Nature Museum
2340 N. Cannon, 773/755-5100, *www.chias.org*   **N**
This is the perfect place to take children to learn more about the environment, and to get some resource-saving tips for yourself. Located in Lincoln Park, the museum's exhibits demonstrate the relationship between nature and our modern urban surroundings. The Water Lab explains the amount of water we use in our daily lives and how clean it is. The City Science exhibit lets you tour a life-size Chicago home to see all the bacteria that reside there and all the energy that gets used. A Wilderness Walk introduces the plants and animals that ruled Chicago before we did. The highlight is the Butterfly Haven, a 2,700-square-foot glass-enclosed room with over 50 species of butterflies flitting around you. Outdoors, explore the flower garden, pond, and wildlife garden. The Butterfly Cafe serves soup, sandwiches, and salads if you need to refuel. Open Mon.–Fri. 9 A.M.–4:30 P.M., Sat.–Sun. 10 A.M.–5 P.M. $7, $5 seniors/students (13–22), $4 children. ($1 discount for Chicagoans.)

Fridays

Spertus Museum of Judaica
618 S. Michigan, 312/322-1747. *www.spertus.edu/museum.html*   **C**
Discover Jewish history and culture through an extensive collection of art and artifacts. Adults will appreciate the temporary exhibits on relevant subjects, and kids will enjoy the Artifact Center that allows them to play archaeologist in the ancient Middle East. Open Sun.–Wed. 10 A.M.–5 P.M., Thur. 10 A.M.–7 P.M., Fri. 10 A.M.–3 P.M. The Artifact Center is open Sun.–Thur. 1 P.M.–4:30 P.M., Fri. 1 P.M.–3 P.M. $5 admission, $3 students/seniors/children, $10 family maximum.

Donations Appreciated

Blues Heaven Foundation
2120 S. Michigan, 312/808-1286   **C**
The nonprofit foundation of legendary bluesman Willie Dixon (1915–1992) recently relocated to Chicago to make a home in the historic headquarters and studios of Chess Records. A multi-talented musician and perhaps the greatest blues songwriter ever—and key to the blues label's success—Dixon wrote over 500 songs for Chess. A leading force in the evolution of the blues over a career spanning five decades, Dixon also supported blues education, aspiring blues musicians, and needy blues musicians. 30–40-minute tours of the building are given Mon.–Fri. noon–3 P.M., Sat. noon–2 p.m., $10.

Hellenic Museum and Cultural Center
801 W. Adams, 4th floor, 312/655-1234, *www.hellenicmuseum.org* **C**
Once a one-room museum in the National Bank of Greece building, this museum has become an important anchor in the recent Greektown redevelopment project when it moved the corner of Halsted & Adams. The new location and the expanded hours make it easy to drop in while lunching in the area or before grabbing dinner at one of the street's classic tavernas. Exhibits focus on Greek culture, art, and history, particularly immigrant history in the U.S. Open Mon.–Fri. 10 A.M.–4 P.M., Sun. noon–5 P.M. $5 suggested donation.

Oriental Institute
1155 E. 58th, 773/702-9514, *http://oi.uchicago.edul* **S**
Since the early part of the twentieth century, the University of Chicago has been collecting and displaying artifacts from the ancient Near East and teaching Chicagoans about the history, art, archeology, and anthropology of that region's civilizations. They have recently finished a major renovation and extension project. Open Tues.–Sat. 10 A.M.–4 P.M., Wed. 10 A.M.–8:30 P.M., Sun. noon–4 P.M. Free, but suggested donation is $5, $2 children.

Peace Museum
100 N. Central Park, 773/638-6450, *www.peacemuseum.org* **W**
Relocated from its one-room River North location to the Gold Dome in Garfield Park, this little museum is just a block from the **Garfield Park Conservatory** (p. 49). Combine the two in one trip to this undervisited part of the city, each a block away from the renovated Conservatory/Central Park Green Line el station. Founded in 1981 and the first and only of its kind in the country, the **Peace Museum**'s exhibits on the peace movement, conflict resolution, and the impact of war explore these and related topics through various artistic mediums. Open Thur.–Sat. 11 A.M.–4 P.M.

Polish Museum of America
984 N. Milwaukee, 773/384-3352, *http://pma.prcua.org* **C**
Founded in 1935 and housed in a former ballroom, this is one of the largest and oldest ethnic museums in the U.S.! Among the abundant and varied Polish cultural, religious, and historical artifacts, you'll find a Picasso and a Chagall donated by prominent Polish Chicagoans. Included in the collection is an eighteenth-century Royal Sleigh, carved from a single log as a gift to Princess Maria—daughter of the Polish king, Stanislaw Leszaynski—and pre-historic objects found in Poland. They also have a 60,000-volume lending library and a full calendar of events. Open daily 11 A.M.–4 P.M.; closed Thur. $3 requested admission, $2 students, $1 children under 12.

Ukrainian Institute of Modern Art
2320 W. Chicago, 773/227-5522, *www.uima-art.org*   W
Since 1971, this sophisticated little Ukrainian Village museum built from
connected storefronts has been featuring the contemporary artwork of
Ukrainians, Chicagoans, and those of Ukrainian descent. Their main gallery
sees 5–6 major exhibits annually, while smaller side galleries house their
permanent collection. Open Wed.–Thur. and Sat.–Sun. noon–4 P.M. Donations requested.

Ukrainian National Museum
721 N. Oakley, 312/421-8020, *www.ukrntlmuseum.org*   W
Also located in the Ukrainian Village neighborhood, this museum has a
large stash of cultural and historical artifacts, including a collection of the
famous Ukrainian Easter eggs, beaded jewelry, musical instruments, and
folk costumes from 26 different regions of the Ukraine. Open Thur.–Sun. 11
A.M.–4 P.M. $2 suggested donation.

Low Entrance Fees

A. Philip Randolph Pullman Porter Museum
10406 S. Maryland, 773/928-3935
www.aphiliprandolphmuseum.com   FSE
Located in Chicago's Pullman Historic District, this relatively new museum
fills in a pivotal piece of Pullman history. The only museum in Chicago
devoted to an aspect of labor history, the museum focuses on A. Philip
Randolph, chief organizer of the Brotherhood of the Sleeping Car Porters
(the first African-American labor union in the U.S.), members of the BSCP,
African-American railroad attendants in general, and George Pullman,
owner of the Pullman Rail Car Company and founder of the planned town of
Pullman. Phillip Randolph and the Pullman Porters' struggle for equality
within the Pullman Rail Car Company led the way for future advancements
in labor history and civil rights. The story is told through the permanent
collection of historical photos and well-preserved memorabilia. Open Thur.,
Fri., Sat. 11 A.M.–4 P.M. $5 admission.

Balzekas Museum of Lithuanian Culture
6500 S. Pulaski, 773/582-6500, *www.lithaz.org/museums/balzekas*   SW
Founded in 1968 by Southwest Side car dealer Stanley Balzekas Jr., the
Balzekas Museum of Lithuanian Culture is housed in a former animal
hospital. In the various rooms, one can view traditional Lithuanian wood-
carvings—many crafted by war refugees held in displaced person camps; a
rare book collection that includes the first book printed in Lithuanian—a

1547 catechism; woven tapestries; and an extensive collection of amber, the translucent fossil resin that is found in abundance in Lithuania. The children's section is fun, even without high-tech gadgets. It includes a miniature farmhouse with accompanying animals and people, traditional Lithuanian costumes for dress-up, an enormous jigsaw puzzle depicting a suit of armor, and blocks for building replicas of the medieval castles of Lithuania. Open daily 10 A.M.–4 P.M. $4, students/seniors $3, $1 children

Museum of Holography
1134 W. Washington, 312/226-1007, *http://holographiccenter.com* **C**
This small tribute to the holographic image distinguishes itself as the nation's only all holography museum. And with a range of images so vast as to include a whirling Michael Jordan and a bladder/prostate combo, there's sure to be something to capture everyone's imagination. Open Wed.–Sun. 12:30 P.M.–4:30 P.M. $4, $3 children (6–12).

International Museum of Surgical Science
1524 N. Lake Shore Drive, 312/642-6502, *www.imss.org* **C**
Twenty-two exhibit galleries on four floors showcase the gory and glorious history of surgery and related sciences. Permanent exhibits include a nineteenth-century apothecary shop, a working iron lung, and a Civil War amputation kit, while a new exhibit looks at spinal surgery. Perhaps the most overlooked museum treasure in the city, the **IMSS** sits in one of the last remaining lakefront mansions of Chicago and the only one open to the public. Listed on the National Register of Historic Places and a city landmark, the exterior is based on a French chateau at Versailles, and the inside wows with Italian marble, decorative plastic work, antique hardware, eight exquisite fireplaces, and a gilded grand staircase. Open Tues.–Sun. 10 A.M.–4 P.M.; closed Sun. Oct.–Apr. $6 admission, $3 students/seniors.

National Vietnam Veterans Art Museum
1801 S. Indiana, 312/326-0270, *www.nvvam.org* **C**
Housed in a renovated old warehouse donated by the City of Chicago, this three-story museum is unique in its specialization in art produced by Vietnam War veterans. Artists from the U.S., Southeast Asia, and a smattering of other places have contributed over 1,000 powerful and, sometimes, disturbing paintings, drawings, sculptures, and photographic pieces to a collection that also contains North Vietnamese and Viet Cong artifacts. The museum includes a theater, library, and archives. Tues.–Fri. 11 A.M.–6 P.M., Sat. 10 A.M.–5 P.M., Sun. noon–5 P.M. $6, $5 students/seniors.

Swedish American Museum Center
5211 N. Clark, 773/728-8111, *www.samac.org*   FN
Stop in this storefront museum after breakfast at one of the Swedish
restaurants on the block. Besides regular exhibits on Swedish culture,
history, and immigration experiences, the center offers a diverse line-up of
cultural events. Their capacious auditorium comes in handy when neighbor
Women & Children First bookstore brings in big-name authors whose
crowds their little shop can't accommodate. Open Tues.–Fri. 10 A.M.–4 P.M.,
Sat.–Sun. 11 A.M.–4 P.M. $4, $3 students/seniors/children, $10 family max.

Coming Soon

Scheduled to open spring 2005 in Chinatown's old Quong Yick Company
building, the **Chinese-American Museum of Chicago** (238 W. 23rd,
312/949-1000, *www.ccamuseum.org*) will be the first of its kind in the
Midwest. Another distinctive museum is planned for a 2005 opening:
Friends of the Chicago River's **Michigan Avenue Bridgehouse Museum**
(312/939-0490, *www.chicagoriver.org*). Located on all five floors of one of
the historic bridgehouses of the Michigan Avenue bridge (the southwest
tower at Wacker), the highly-visible museum will be devoted to educating
people about the past, present, and future of the Chicago River. 2006 will
bring in the northeast tower, a public information gallery of current events
and FOCR's new offices.

Worth It?

That is, these are world-class, top-of-the-line institutions. Set aside the
collections for a moment—the buildings themselves are worth paying to
view. Because they are in a constant state of bigger-better-besting others in
their league, as well as maintaining the magnificent historic structures that
house them, they probably do need to charge their exorbitant admission fees,
which seem to have doubled out of nowhere recently. It's up to you to
decide if these fees are "worth it." For those who need to work around these
fees, there are at least four easy, reasonable options:

- Neighborhood libraries have a limited number of free passes to
  many of Chicago's museums and other cultural institutions that can
  be checked out like books. If you don't already have one, get a
  library card today!
- Although these museums have eliminated their predicable once-a-

week free days, they still each offer about 52 free or reduced-price days a year. Check their Web sites to find out when they are.

- Become a member of your favorite museum(s). If you go more than a couple times, have a family, or want to enjoy special exhibits and perks, membership will more than pay for itself.
- Become a docent or museum volunteer.

Field Museum of Natural History

Roosevelt Rd. & Lake Shore Drive, 312/922-9410

www.fieldmuseum.org **C**

Opened as the depository for the 1893 Columbian Exposition's natural history artifacts, this grand old museum now has a collection of 20 million pieces, nine acres of exhibits, and few peers on the world's museum circuit. The looming dinosaur skeletons in the lobby say it all: the classic 75-ft. mounted Brachiosaurus that greeted visitors for years as they entered the museum is now joined by *Sue*, the world's largest, most complete *Tyrannosaurus Rex*, acquired in 1997. They're finding that perfect blend of spiffed up historic offerings (the reconstructed Pawnee earth lodge, the Ancient Egypt exhibit built up around the mummy collection), temporary exhibits covering everything from shoes in culture to contemporary African life, and touring exhibits like the treasures of China's Forbidden City or the Russian Empire. Open daily 9 A.M.–5 P.M. $15–$20 admission for various packages, $11–$17 students/seniors, $7–$10 kids (3–11). Note that Chicago residents with IDs get a couple bucks discount. In lieu of their former once-a-week free day, there are now sporadic Discount Days that knock off a few more dollars (*www.fieldmuseum.org/plan_visit/discount_days.htm*).

Museum of Science and Industry

57th St. and Lake Shore Drive, 773/684-1414

www.msichicago.org **S**

Science for Dummies! Anyone can learn about science at the **MSI**, and they're bound to have a grand time of it too. Housed in the Fine Arts Building from the 1893 Columbian Exhibition, the **MSI**'s 14 acres hold countless offerings, including over 800 interactive exhibits. Attractions focus on space, manufacturing, the human body, communications, transportation, current science topics, and more, and are not at all boring like this list might imply. Although nearly half of the museum's exhibits have been newly created or refurbished over the past several years, the classics will never disappear. The coal mine, the captured German WWII submarine, a 16-foot walk-through heart, actress Colleen Moore's miniature Fairy Castle, and the annual Christmas Around the World tree display are but a few of the historical favorites. It's hard to believe that until a few years ago, this museum was always free of charge. Alas, as the busiest tourist attraction in the Midwest, the museum needed to begin charging admission fees to ensure its continued greatness. Open Mon.–Fri. 9:30 A.M.–4 P.M. (5:30 P.M. in summer), Sat.–Sun. 9:30 A.M.–5:30 P.M. $8–$22 depending on the Omnimax movies and special exhibits you want to partake in, $6.75–$18.75 seniors, $4.25–$15.50 kids (3–11). There's a $1 savings for Chicago residents with proof. They have retained some free days (including Thanksgiving and Christmas Eve), but they're not as predictable. Check the Web for dates.

Six Museums, Nine Days

For tourists who are ambitious enough to squeeze in six major attractions in under nine days and for locals who want to go on a museum-refresher blitz, there's the **City Pass** (*www.citypass.com/city/chicago.html*), which allows you to save almost 50% on admission to committing to visits to The Hancock Observatory, the Art Institute, the Field Museum, the Shedd Aquarium, the Adler Planetarium, and the Museum of Science and Industry. Pick one up at any of the six places on your first stop. $49 each, $39 children.

Shedd Aquarium
1200 S. Lake Shore Drive, 312/939-2438, *www.shedd.org*   **C**
Among the more than 8,000 aquatic animals—representing over 700 species from all parts of the world—at this, the world's largest indoor aquarium, you'll discover flashlight fish, bobbing iguanas, electric eels, venomous anemones, and hungry piranhas. Don't miss feeding time at the humongous, 90,000-gallon Caribbean coral reef tank in the museum's center. Divers hand-feed sharks, sea turtles, moray eels, and many others daily at 9:30 A.M., 11 A.M., 12:30 P.M., 1: 30 P.M., 3 P.M., and 3:30 P.M. The Oceanarium, added in 1991—with winding nature trails—houses beluga whales, dolphins, sea otters, and harbor seals in a recreation of a rugged Pacific Northwest coastline. A separate area reproduces a Falkland Islands environment for a colony of penguins. Open Mon.–Fri. 9 A.M.–5 P.M., Sat.–Sun. 9 A.M.–6 P.M. Labor Day–Mem. Day.; daily 9 A.M.–6 P.M. during the summer. This museum offers the biggest relative savings for Chicago residents: $17 for an all-access pass/$23 for others, $12 for resident seniors and kids (ages 3–11)/$16 for others. Discount Days Mon.–Tues, Oct.–Feb., are free for the main building, or $9 and $13 for all-access (Oceanarium and Wild Reef).

Natural Spaces

FROM a swampy land filled with wild smelly onions grew Chicago, whose motto since its 1833 inception has been *Urbs in Horto* (City in a Garden). Daniel Burnham's legendary, large-scale 1909 "Chicago Plan" has left us a liberal inheritance of green spaces: a lakefront preserved for culture and recreation and "The Emerald Necklace"—an extensive boulevard system that joins some of our biggest and oldest city parks. This precedent for making greenery a priority has helped put Chicago at the forefront of the current urban greening trend. The present Mayor Daley started as a well-known tree fanatic (being born on Arbor Day and all) who boosted the withering forestry department and instituted *Green Streets* programs, designed to maintain the 500,000 city-owned trees, while planting thousands of new ones annually. His offices are now leading Chicago in becoming the "greenest city in America" and doing so by exploring some of the bolder and more progressive ideas out there. City Hall has a rooftop garden designed to control energy costs. The mayor has announced that all new public buildings will be LEED (a standard for leadership in energy and environmental design) certified. Its **Center for Green Technology** may be the only platinum-certified municipal building in the country and the new Museum of Broadcast Communications building will be the first LEED gold-certified museum in the country. Stay tuned.

For the record, Chicago has 26 miles of lakefront, with 25 beaches, close to 600 parks, covering over 7,000 acres, and is surrounded by 67,000 acres of Cook County Forest Preserve. It's not quite a jungle out there but a sizable, flourishing, and expanding garden. See also **Gardens** (p. 48) in this chapter, **Birding** (p. 96) in the **Recreation** chapter, and **Parks** (p. 335) in the **Walking** chapter.

North Park Village Nature Center
5801 N. Pulaski, 312/744-5472   FN
Formerly the city's tuberculosis sanitarium (1915–1974), today **NPVNC** is the city's only nature center. (Its management was just turned over to the Chicago Park District.) Walk in woods. See animals. Be one with the environment. Annual attendance increased from 6,500 in the early 1990s to something over 100,000 currently, through a hearty commitment to education, conservation, restoration, and dynamic programming. On its 61-acre parcel is a 46-acre preserve with four distinct ecosystems teeming with native plants and wildlife: wetlands, woodlands, oak savanna, and prairie. Call/write to be put on the mailing list for a quarterly schedule of events for

From Industry to Ecology

Keep an eye on the greater **Lake Calumet Region**, an area that encompasses the Chicago neighborhoods of East Side, South Deering, Hegewisch, South Chicago, Calumet Heights, Burnside, and Pullman, as well as some of the south suburbs and parts of Northwest Indiana. Since most of the steel mills and rail operations in this area closed, leaving the area economically stagnant and environmentally emaciated for too long, many have investigated the possibilities of reviving the ecological wonderland that existed here before the region took on decades of the "dirty" work that helped make Chicago what it is. An amazing biological diversity remains in small pockets of wetlands, woodlands, and prairies. Even several threatened and rare species of birds and plants have carved out niches for themselves amidst the gross levels of pollution and decay. A montage of initiatives have arisen in response to the imposing challenges and possibilities the approximately 20-square-mile region poses. Government, community, environmental, and industrial groups continue working together to figure out how to improve the region's livability—in increased recreational opportunities, increased economic opportunities, and enhanced environmental quality. Many are looking at the thousands of acres of abandoned and unused industrial land, transit corridors, and government property available for open, public lands and ecological restoration. One fixed plan is the opening of the Ford Calumet Environmental Center in late 2006 on the Hegewisch Marsh at approximately 130th & Torrence. Note to self: Visit **Dead Stick Pond** before it's teeming with life again.

children, families, and adults. Bird watching, nature walks, star-gazing sessions, and an array of classes are all popular activities, as are the annual festivals. The Maple Sugar Festival is in March, the City Wilds Festival in June, the Harvest Festival in October, and the Winter Solstice Celebration in December. Open daily from 10 A.M.–4 P.M. Closed Thanksgiving, Christmas, and New Years Day. Free.

North Pond Wildlife Preserve
In Lincoln Park, between Fullerton and Diversey
www.friendslp.org/northpond.html   **N**
The ten-acre North Pond and surrounding region are undergoing an ecological restoration to improve water quality and preserve the area's biological diversity. Currently a refuge for fish, small mammals, and over 40 types of migratory and nesting birds, restoration efforts hope to increase the amount of wildlife by bringing more native plant species back to the water's shore.

Wolf Lake/William Powers Conservation Area
Approx. 118th to 134th Streets, Avenue "0" to Calumet   FSE
When 419 out of 580 acres of a conservation area are water, it hopefully
means there is an excellent stock of fish. Luckily fishing is permitted
year-round. **Wolf Lake**, the only state park within the city limits, belongs to
Illinois and our Hoosier neighbors, but neither state knows for sure how the
lake acquired its big, bad name. Charlevoix, an explorer in the early
eighteenth century wrote that the Native Americans called the surrounding
prairie Wolf Prairie for the abundance of wolves. Today, you'll find an
abundance of native grasses, wildflowers, and plenty of wildlife, with
accompanying picnic tables, jogging paths, and bike trails to enjoy the
surrounding nature. As a main feeder to the Mississippi flyway, Wolf Lake
is heavily traveled by migratory waterfowl. A colony of swans and the
descendants of several Monk parrots—which escaped from an experimental
project at the University of Chicago in the 1950s   have taken up permanent
residence in the area. Plaques at the bases of the trees on the drive into the
park commemorate each of Chicago's veteran organizations.

Wooded Island and Lagoon/Osaka Japanese Garden/
Paul H. Douglas Nature Sanctuary
In Jackson Park, just east of Cornell, about 5900–6200 South   S
Wooded Island, a 16-acre nature refuge protecting native Midwestern
plants, was the site of the Japanese pavilions of the 1893 Columbian
Exposition. Various Japanese gardens have come and gone since then. The
current Osaka Garden is named for Chicago's Japanese sister city, which
donated a traditional cedar entrance gate and money for restoration and
landscaping in 1995. In 2001, 6,000 additional shrubs and hundreds of trees
were planted, enhancing the already ideal, tranquil escape, with a garden ath
that winds meditatively past changing mini-environments.

Chicago Roots

There are three places in Chicago where mature stands of trees grow that
are direct descendants of the naturally-selected trees that populated this
region for the last 10,000 years. Some have a life span of about 300 years.
Jackson Park's Wooded Island (p. 337) is home to some very old oaks;
West Pullman Park (401 W. 123rd) has ancient oaks, hickories, and
cherries; and the aging burr, red, and white oaks in **Hurley Playlot Park**
(19901 W. 100th) maintain one more stately environment in Beverly.

Navy Pier

CONSTANTLY bustling with activity and attractions, it's hard to be a Chicagoan—or even a Chicago visitor—and escape acquaintance with **Navy Pier.**

Navy Pier
600 E. Grand, 312/595-PIER, 800/595-PIER (outside Chicago)
www.navypier.com   **C**
"Municipal Pier #2," constructed in 1916, has functioned as a freight center, navy training base, University of Illinois branch, and entertainment grounds (a use which continues to this day). Since its latest renovation was completed in 1995, the pier's indoor portion houses an Imax Theatre (using the latest in 3D technology), the **Chicago Children's Museum** (see p. 61), shops, restaurants, a six-story glass enclosed botanical garden, WBEZ radio station, convention facilities, and an historic ballroom with an 80-foot domed ceiling. Outside, there are picnicking areas, a beer garden, dinner and tour boats, a summertime sculpture walk (*www.pierwalk.com/about.html*), an open-air stage, a carousel, and a giant Ferris wheel (150 ft.). All in all—50 acres of fun. The Ferris wheel—which is open year-round, weather permitting—offers a spectacular view of the city, especially at nightfall. Open daily from 6 A.M.–11 P.M., the exterior region of Navy Pier is a great spot for strolling, picnicking, and skyline gazing. The building is open Sun.–Thur. 10 A.M.–10 P.M., Fri.–Sat. 10 A.M.–midnight. The restaurants and bars stay open longer. Be sure to pick up a brochure that details the many year-round events that happen here.

Politics

City Council Sessions
City Hall, 121 N. LaSalle, 312/744-5000, *www.cityofchicago.org*   **C**
Watch the mayor and council members in action from the council chambers' public viewing area on the 2nd floor; they usually convene around 9:30 or 10 A.M. Check the Web schedule (*www.chicityclerk.com/citycouncil/calendar.html*) to see what's on the agenda and when the council or any of its various committees will be in session. City Hall is very accessible, though there are a few more security guards around these days. Walk right in and wander around, popping into those offices that interest you. You might even catch the City that Works working.

Chicago Board of Elections
69 W. Washington, 312/269-7984, *www.chicagoelections.com* **C**
Serving as an election judge is the best, easiest way to glimpse the Chicago political network in action (and you get paid about $100 to do it). From 5 A.M.–9 P.M., you'll be overseeing the voting process—a role that will privy you to a non-stop barrage of gossip, opinions, insights, and instructions from voters, precinct captains, police officers, poll watchers, state's attorneys, and sometimes even candidates.

Public Transportation Touring

STILL serving its historic role as a transportation hub for the nation, Chicago is also well-connected internally when it comes to transit. There's no reason for most Chicagoans and visitors not to make most or all of their trips on our public transportation system. Getting used to a maximum number of transit routes not only helps with day-to-day practicalities, but it's also a great way to know firsthand new areas of the city and the people and places that comprise them. Hop aboard a CTA "L" (or bus) or Metra train for an inexpensive ride through the city's neighborhoods . . .

Chicago Transit Authority (CTA)

The Basics

- Call 312/836-7000 or 1-888-YourCTA, daily 4:45 A.M.–1 A.M. for questions on fares, routes, and directions to anywhere in the city.
- Visit *www.transitchicago.com* on the Internet for anything you could possibly want to know about the CTA and to download maps and schedules.
- Pick up a **CTA System Map** at any train station, at airport information booths, and at the Visitor Information Centers, or download it from their Web site.

The CTA has switched to magnetic fare cards that must be purchased from automated machines in the stations. One ride costs $1.75 and transfers (good for two transfers over a two-hour period) are $.25. Reduced fares for seniors/students/children (check specifics) are $.85 and $.15. One-day passes are $5, a 2-day pass is $9, a 3-day $12, and a 5-day $18. Not just for tourists, you Chicagoans should keep these cards in mind especially for packing in lots of errands and activities on the weekends. All local transit users should seriously consider the **Chicago Card Plus** (*www.chicago-*

card.com), a permanent and individual card that grants access to all buses and trains through a touchpad system. Your credit card is automatically charged in $10, $20, or $40 increments as necessary and each recharging comes with a 10% bonus in fare credit. There are even "passback" privileges so you can let up to six others use your card, too.

L

In Chicago, the proper spelling of the el (our elevated trains) is "L." For that matter, we generally call our subway trains the "L" too. For more information on all things "L," there's **Chicago-L.org** (*www.chicago-l.org*), the largest online resource for information on Chicago's rapid transit system—train memories, train history, future transit plans, public hearings, articles, photos, signs, arts on the trains, the "L" in movies, chronologies, facts and figures, clubs and interest groups.

Touring Tips

Riders can transfer downtown (and at certain other large stations) from one line to another without a transfer. If you have lots of time and want to see the most city with the least energy and money expenditure, you might like to try riding every line to its end and back on a single fare (perfectly legal). Nearly every station permits changing directions without paying again. See **Holiday Madness** (p. 50) for special CTA holiday "L" rides.

Routes

The CTA trains have long-been color-coded, but not so long that some of us still refer to the lines with the geographical references previously used.

- **Blue (O'Hare–Congress/Douglas) Line**
  Runs northwest from downtown to O'Hare Airport and west from downtown to DesPlaines Avenue in Forest Park and 54th/Cermak in Cicero.

- **Brown (Ravenswood) Line**
  Runs north/northwest from downtown to Kimball/Lawrence

- **Green (Lake–Jackson Park/Englewood) Line**
  Runs west from downtown to Harlem in Oak Park and south from

downtown to University/63rd and Ashland/63rd.

* **Orange (Midway) Line**
Runs southwest from downtown to Midway Airport at 55th and Cicero.

* **Red (Howard–Dan Ryan) Line**
Runs north/south between Howard Street Station (about 1600W) and
State & 95th.

Metra

The Basics

* Call 312/322-6777, weekdays 8 A.M.–5 P.M., for information on
fares, schedules, routes, etc.
* Call 312/836-7000, all other times.
* Visit *www.metrarail.com* to download maps and schedules and to
learn of new promotions.

Metra bills itself as the finest commuter rail system in the country. Its
multitude of trains and tracks connect those in certain neighborhoods,
suburbanites, and those even farther out with the city. Their bi-level,
comfortable, and large-windowed trains are perfect for sitting and sightseeing. While their weekday rates aren't the cheapest for train-hopping, a $5
weekend pass will give you unlimited rides all day Saturday and Sunday
(except, unfortunately, on the South Shore train going to Indiana Dunes
State Park). The Metra stations at Union Station (Jackson & Canal) and at
Randolph & Michigan can provide maps and information about their lines
and city and suburban destinations.

Skyscrapers

CHICAGO skyscrapers do indeed deserve their own category. Our tallest
buildings in order are: **Sears Tower** (110 stories), **Aon Center** (12th tallest
in the world), **John Hancock Center** (13th tallest in the world), **AT&T
Corporate Center, Two Prudential Plaza, 311 S. Wacker Dr., 900 N.
Michigan Ave.** (Bloomingdale's building), **Water Tower Place, Bank
One,** and **Park Tower.** When the **Trump International Hotel & Tower** is
complete in 2007, on the site of the current Chicago Sun-Times building, it
will come in fourth. By the way, national skyscraper criteria allow a
structure to lean up to one foot! This built-in "sway" helps buildings

withstand fierce winds, earthquakes, and other intemperances. The **Sears Tower**'s tilt can be 6–7 inches and the **John Hancock**'s tilt about 5-8 inches.

Aon Center
200 E. Randolph   **C**

Often overlooked, though the city's second tallest building, the former Standard Oil Building ("Big Stan") was the tallest for a couple years (1973–1974) before the Sears Tower was built. It remains the tallest building in the world without any antennae, spires, or finials at the top, and the tallest box-shaped structure too. When Amoco purchased the building, they spiffed up the plain rectangular prism with a multi-level plaza and bedecked with fountains, flora, flags, and sculpture. The six-ton layer of Italian marble that coated the building was discovered early on to be too flimsy for Midwestern winters, and in the early 1990s it was all removed and replaced with brawny granite. Now, marble from this project (that emptied the quarry that once supplied Michelangelo) can be bought in the gift shop in the form of trinkets and expensive decor. Some of the marble was crushed into decorative stone that now surrounds the Amoco refinery in Whiting, Indiana. Those who work in the Aon Center and surrounding buildings claim their food court as the best in the city.

John Hancock Building Observatory
875 N. Michigan, 888/875-VIEW, *www.hancock-observatory.com*   **C**

Apparently, looking out over our great Midwestern metropolis from 94 floors above the street in the city's third tallest building just wasn't enough for the tourists anymore. The **Hancock Observatory** finished a $2.5-million rehab project in 1997 that turned this classic attraction into a tall-building theme park experience. The price tag of that renovation is 2-1/2 times what it cost to *build* the entire structure between 1965 and 1970! The interactive, multi-media adventure begins in the ground-floor ticketing area that's designed to look like the original "Big John" construction site. Once the "world's fastest" elevators have whisked you to the observation area in 39 seconds, you can now step outdoors onto the Skywalk and experience the *windy city* first hand, where on a clear day you can see up to 80 miles and four states. Windows on Chicago virtual reality "kiosks" allow guests to navigate the cityscape and hone in on 80 major attractions for close-up virtual tours. 3-D Soundscope telescopes speak in four languages and provide sound effects to enhance the view: cheering baseball fans at Comiskey Park, crashing waves at Navy Pier. The more somber 60-foot History Wall details the city's past. Open daily 9 A.M.–11 P.M. $9.50, $7.50 seniors, $6.50 children (ages 5–12), free for children under 5. Check out their Web site for coupons, special promotions, and special events for holidays, fireworks viewings, and more. See **Elevator Rides** (p. 46) for information on drinks with a view in the Hancock's **Signature Lounge**.

Sears Tower Skydeck
233 S. Wacker, 312/875-9696 (Enter on Jackson)
www.the-skydeck.com   C
In 1996, the **Sears Tower** was pricked by a 111-foot decorative spire from Malaysia and stripped of its "tallest building in the world" title by the World Council of Tall Buildings and Urban Habitat. Upon completion of the Petronas Towers (and their spires) in Kuala Lumpur, Malaysia, the WCT-BUH declared that even though the Sears Tower had 12 more and higher occupied floors, the spires on Petronas tipped the height scale. The Sears Tower was given two consolation titles: highest occupied floor in the world, and highest roof in the world. Enter Canada. The CN Tower at over 1,800 ft. in Toronto is unarguably taller than both the Sears and Petronas Towers. However, CN Tower is not considered a building by the WCTBUH, since the majority is not functional for habitation. Nor is a spire, which renders the "spires argument" for Petronas hypocritical, but to all it should make the entire debate down right ridiculous. If you measure the Sears Tower's antennae to Petronas spires the Sears Tower is taller by 35 ft. If you put the two buildings side-by-side, and looked out from the 103rd floor of the Sears Tower Skydeck you would be looking down at Petrona's 86th floor—it's highest occupied level. So, which is the tallest building in the world? You be the judge. Oh, and they also have all the new, nifty interactive stuff like the Hancock building. Open daily Mar.–Sept. 9 A.M.–11 P.M., Oct.–Feb. 9 A.M.–10 P.M. $9.95, $7.95 seniors, $6.95 children (3–11), free for those 3 and younger. Prices don't include city admission tax.

Talk Shows

YOU may have to call several weeks in advance to book your free seat as an audience member, but that should give you plenty of time to practice your applause and heckling and develop a self-righteous opinion.

Jenny Jones
NBC Tower, 454 N. Columbus Drive, 312/836-9485   C

Jerry Springer
NBC Tower, 454 N. Columbus Drive, 312/321-5365   C

Oprah Winfrey
Harpo Studios, 1058 W. Washington, 312/591-9222   C

Tours Nouveau

NEW, more creative, less stodgy types of touring are springing up in Chicago, some straight from city offices themselves:

Chicago Greeter Program
Chicago Cultural Center, Randolph & Michigan
312/744-8000, *www.chicagogreeter.com*   C
Based on a program that began first in New York City, the Office of Tourism's **Chicago Greeter Program** is a way to give visitors a friendly, personalized introduction to a big city from the perspective of a local. Volunteer greeters, Chicagoans who love their city, are available to give small groups of guests (1–6 people) free, guided, and somewhat customized 2–4-hour experiences of Chicago, particularly of the neighborhoods and other things tourists usually don't see and do. The CTA even provides free transit for volunteers and tourists. Register online at least seven days in advance. This is meant only for visitors, not for residents, but residents can still take advantage of it by arranging one of the special, "expert" tours for their out-of-town guests.

A new **InstaGreeter** component is an on-the-spot welcoming service. Walk-in parties (with fewer than six people) to the Visitor Information Center in the **Chicago Cultural Center** can hook up with a volunteer greeter for a one-hour walking tour of downtown and North Michigan Avenue, Fri.–Sat. 10 A.M.–4 P.M., Sun. 11 A.M.–4 P.M. It's the perfect opportunity to get an initial sense of Chicago and pester your greeter for local advice and dining, shopping, and touring recommendations.

Chicago Neighborhood Tours
Chicago Cultural Center, 77 E. Randolph
312/742-1190, *www.chicagoneighborhoodtours.com*   C
The City of Chicago and Illinois tourism departments combined with the city's Neighborhood's Alive program ushered in a new breed of tour a few years back, popular with both locals and guests. Each month 2–7 from a rotating and evolving collection of about 25 tours are offered. They leave the Cultural Centers Saturdays at 10 A.M. Of the 17 **Neighborhood Tours** ($25, $20 seniors/students), some focus on history (*Soul of the South Side*), ethnic roots (*Little Italy*), arts and shopping (*Wicker Park/Bucktown*), or

architecture (*Humboldt Park*). **Special Interest Tours** ($50/$45 seniors/ students) are longer and include lunch: *Threads of Ireland* (pre-St. Patrick's Day), *WPA Murals in Chicago Public Schools*, *Literary Chicago*, and *Ethnic Food Sampling* are recent examples. **Cultural Historian's Choice Tours** ($35) are usually one-time, theme tours with surprise stops. There's been a *Historic Hotels* tour and a *Get Wet!* tour (a bathing suit was required for the mystery pools that were to be visited). Advance reservations highly recommended.

City Lit

For tourist information, visit either of the city's two Visitors Information Centers. The one at the **Chicago Cultural Center** (SW corner of Randolph & Michigan) is open Mon.–Fri. 10 A.M.–6 P.M., Sat. 10 A.M.–5 P.M., and Sun. 11 A.M.–5 P.M. The other, in the historic **Chicago Water Works** building (SE corner of Pearson & Michigan), is open daily 7:30 A.M.–7 P.M. It's not a bad idea for residents to stop in these places once in a while and raid the literature racks for information on new city programs, temporary museum exhibits, current theater and gallery offerings, and the discounts routinely offered to tourists, like the annual "Guidebook of Special Values" filled with coupons for restaurants, theater, museums, and other attractions.

Trades and Exchanges

TRADING floor after trading floor, notice how Chicago smoothly moves from its solid, earthbound reputation to the nebulous world of stocks, bonds, commodities, and futures.

Chicago Board of Trade
141 W. Jackson, 312/435-3590, *www.cbot.com*   **C**
Because of national security concerns, **CBOT**'s Visitor Center is now only open for pre-arranged groups of those ages 16 and older (free of charge). They do plan on reopening it eventually, so call or check their Web site for updates. The **Chicago Board Options Exchange** (*www.cboe.com*) and the **Chicago Stock Exchange** (*www.chx.com*) have also, hopefully temporarily, closed their visitors galleries to the public since 9/11.

Chicago Mercantile Exchange
30 S. Wacker, 312/930-8249, *www.cme.com*   **C**
Watch the swapping at the world's largest (in square footage) financial

futures exchange on its two trading floors from the fourth and eighth floor galleries. Videos and other educational displays in the fourth floor gallery provide a clue to what's happening. Schedule a group visit in advance by calling 312/930-2390. Open Mon.–Fri. 8 A.M.–4:30 P.M. Free.

Waterfalls

CHICAGO may have become great by its connection to the Great Lakes System and the Mississippi River, but cascading water is no part of that windfall. By most stretches of the imagination, waterfalls do not exist within the city limits. For purposes of touring and trivia, however, we include these:

Columbus Park Waterfalls
In Columbus Park, Adams &Central   **W**
Not large, but trickling since the 1920s when architect Jens Jensen created a small-scale replica of the Illinois river bluffs for Columbus Park.

Chicago River/River Park Waterfall
In River Park, near Argyle & Whipple   **FN**
Once accessible only to trespassers, all park visitors can now get up close and personal with the little "fall" created where the north branch of the Chicago River splits from the main branch. Walk 1/2 block north into River Park from Argyle Street, just east of Whipple and west of the river. Though you once had to listen for the tumbling current and climb through a small hole in the fence to find this waterway treasure, the city has since removed the fence and obstructive trees, and installed pavement and landscaping, making all sorts of riverbank recreation possible.

Osaka Japanese Garden Rock Waterfall
In Jackson Park, just east of Cornell, about 5900–6200 S   **S**
A rock waterfall was added during a 1981 restoration of the historic Japanese Gardens that have appeared, declined, and reappeared in various guises since the Columbian Exposition of 1893. See **Natural Spaces** (p. 69) above for more details about the garden.

3

RECREATION

Kayaking on the Chicago River makes for
a rustic adventure within the City limits.
Photo by Bill Arroyo.

Chicago has recently built new facilities to accommodate the skateboarding population, like this one at
the Wilson Avenue lakefront. *Photo by Bill Arroyo.*

The popularity of soccer is apparent when passing by
parks all around the city. *Photo by Bill Arroyo.*

RECREATION

SURROUNDED BY A bustling city and still wondering what to do? Whether you recreate passively or actively, physically or mentally, something on this list will get you going. Not only will kicking the couch potato habit reactivate your muscles and introduce you to new facets of city life, most of the time it will cost you next to nothing to do so.

Thanks to millions of taxpayers pooling their money, the visions of past and present leaders, vast land resources, including an exceptional shoreline (with 18 miles of bike paths and 15 miles of beaches), Chicagoans and their guests can enjoy the dynamic programming and impressive resources of a thriving park system. Recent surveys show that however much we Chicagoans love our parks, we still greatly underuse everything they have to offer! Many of the entries in this chapter refer to this park district bounty. For the sake of brevity, addresses and phone numbers were omitted from activities featured at a large number of parks. This information can be found at the end of the chapter in a comprehensive Chicago Park District listing.

Adaptive Sports

Rehabilitation Institute of Chicago
Virginia Wadsworth Wirtz Sports Program
710 N. Lake Shore Drive, 312/908-4292, *www.richealthfit.org*   **C**
The **Rehabilitation Institute of Chicago (RIC)** offers an incredible array of sports activities at the Helen Galvin Center for Health and Fitness on their third floor. Both recreational and competitive disabled athletes can enjoy wheelchair basketball, wheelchair softball, quad rugby, sled hockey, swim-

ming, tennis, aerobics, strength training and conditioning, sitting volleyball, fencing, golf, or just about any other sport you can think of. The sled hockey team from **RIC** won the first US gold medal in that sport in the 2002 Paralympic Games and their wheelchair softball team is one of the best in the nation. Another bonus: After a one-time initiation fee of $10–$25, the programs are free of charge.

Judd Goldman Adaptive Sailing Program
1362 S. Linn White Drive, 312/747-7684   **S**
Founded in 1990, the **Judd Goldman Adaptive Sailing Program** owns a fleet of ten specially equipped boats and runs an active program of training, racing, and recreational events. Open from Memorial Day through Labor Day.

The Chicago Park District in cooperation with the **Mayor's Office for People with Disabilities** has made ten beaches in Chicago accessible to wheelchairs through the use of special mats. For more information, call the **MOPD** (312/744-6673); they can also direct you to bowling, dancing, and other adaptive recreation options in the city. **Recreation Access Illinois** (800/900-8086, *www.recreationaccessillinois.org*) is devoted to increasing the recreational and physical activities for people with a range of disabilities and making everyone aware of the opportunities that already exist. They maintain an online searchable database of accessible programs and facilities.

Adult Education

Chicago Mercantile Exchange
www.cme.com/education/index.cfm   **C**
The **Chicago Mercantile Exchange**'s Education Department offers classroom and online courses in finance and options starting with introductory courses all the way to advanced market analysis. By completing a specific set of five courses in three years, and by passing an exam (there's always a catch), students can receive a certificate of completion from DePaul University. Courses are $150–$250. Their Web site has a series of free "instant lessons" on such topics as futures, supply and demand, risk management, and the trading pit.

Chicago Wine School
1942 S. Halsted, 312/491-0284, *www.wineschool.com/courses.html*   **C**
CWS offers five-week courses for those with a newfound interest in wine, or

those who need a refresher. Students pay about $160 and meet once a week for classes that last 90 minutes. What you'll learn in the Basic course includes the art of wine tasting and the major types of red, white, and rosé wines; ports and sherries; medium, dry, and sweet; and champagnes. Other courses delve into varietals, the wines of California and the Northwest, and the Rhone and Mediterranean regions. Seminars start at $50 and cover things like the basics, Tuscan wines, Australian wines, and French wines.

Discovery Center
2940 N. Lincoln, 773/348-8120, *www.discoverycenter.cc*   N
When life gets dull, it's time to learn proper yoga positions, computer basics, new languages, Feng Shui, fencing, investing, piano playing, kick boxing, the art of stained glass, how to uncover past lives, and how to start a business at the **Discovery Center**. They also host special events and parties—mainly for singles—such as speed flirting, coffeemating (circulate while you percolate), limo scavenger hunts, wine tastings, and the flirting safari party (how to flirt and not look like you're in heat). A new course catalog comes out every two months and can be viewed online, picked up at the office, or mailed to you. Learn something and meet somebody—Fun! Fun! Fun! Classes are held all over the city.

Impact Chicago
4770 N. Lincoln, #6, 773/338-4545, *www.impactchicago.org*   N
Impact Chicago offers a four course self-defense program that teaches students how to size up an attacker, act confident, use the voice to ward off a confrontation, and take 'em down when attacked. Classes are around $100 or $395 for the entire core program.

The Latin School of Chicago's "Live and Learn" Classes
59 W. North Avenue, 312/573-4698
www.latinschool.org/liveandlearn   C
The prestigious **Latin School** offers an exciting list of adult education courses on a quarterly basis. Many of these introduce attendees to new hobbies and recreational pursuits, as well as specific how-tos: things like crisis preparedness, buying a diamond, self-defense, cooking with top chefs, digital photography, knitting, pool, languages, computer classes, and saving for your newborn's college education. They also offer behind-the-scenes tours of little corners of Chicago: the pedway, the art collection of Playboy's corporate office, the bowels of the United Center, A Day in the Life of an Alderman, and such. A favorite is the $5 **Joke Exchange**, a two-hour, once-a-month gathering where participants bring one joke to share and leave with a treasury of fresh humor and a side split from laughter.

Lill Street Art Center
4401 N. Ravenswood, 773/769-4226, *www.lillstreet.com*   N
Lill Street outgrew its original home and recently relocated to a former industrial building in Ravenswood. Adults can sign up for courses in ceramics, drawing, painting, and metalsmithing, all taught by professionals in the field who exhibit their work locally and nationally. Classes last ten weeks and include wheel throwing, handbuilding and sculpting, and creating dinnerware and ceramic tiles. An alternative to the $200+, ten-week courses are the one-project weekend workshops where you can create, for example, a teapot, a claymation sequence, pet bowls, or a self-portrait tile. Day workshops run from $30–$80. The center also has artists' studios, galleries, a gift shop, and coffee shop/snack bar.

Old Town School of Folk Music
4544 N. Lincoln, 773/525-7793, *www.oldtownschool.org*   N
As part of their mission to advance and share the folk music of all cultures, the **OTS** teaches over 100 different classes quarterly that explore the range of international music, both vocal and instrumental, as well as dance. Some recent offerings: banjo, blues, Aztec ceremonial dance, ballet, breakdancing, fiddle, harmonica, jazz, mandolin, and songwriting. Still, as evidenced by all the young people with acoustic guitars slung across their backs, roaming down Lincoln Avenue, some of the most popular classes remain the guitar and singer/songwriter classes they've been offering Chicagoans for decades. Most classes are $140, $95 for a second class signed up for at the same time.

Oriental Institute
1155 E. 58th, 773/702-9514, *www-oi.uchicago.edu/OI*   S
Are you interested in Middle Eastern history and archaeology? If so, you'll be interested in **OI**'s many free one-day slide lectures, seminars, and films. Other fee-based courses include learning cuneiform script (one of the oldest writing systems in the world), archaeology and the Bible, family courses, literature of Ancient Egypt, and more. For more information, see the Public Programs link on the Web site.

These other cultural institutions also offer educational events, including lectures, workshops, and courses:
- **Art Institute of Chicago**, *www.artic.edu/aic/programs/aplus.html*
- **Chicago Historical Soc.**, *www.chicagohistory.org/programs_events.html*
- **Chicago Public Library**, *www.chipublib.org/003cpl/events_prog.html*
- **Field Museum**, *www.fieldmuseum.org/education/default.htm*
- **Museum of Contemporary Art**, *www.mcachicago.org*
- **Newberry Library**, *www.newberry.org/nl/programs/programshome.html*

Second City
1608 N. Wells, 312/664-3959, *www.secondcity.com*   **N**
The **Second City** comedy theater has had a second gig throughout its
history: using improvisation as a training device for performance (funny and
dramatic) and improved communication skills. Their training and education
wing offers classes that its students tend to rave about, even calling them
"life-changing"! Courses may be half a day or extend over several months.
While some are oriented for entertainment and some for business situations,
all the courses help develop students' creative, presentation, team-building,
communication, and audience-understanding skills. There are also programs
for comedy writers. Now when people say you are so funny, they'll actually
mean it.

The Palette & Chisel Academy of Fine Arts
1012 N. Dearborn, 312/642-4400, *www.paletteandchisel.org*   **C**
The **Palette & Chisel** was founded in 1895 by night students at the Art
Institute who wanted to paint during daylight hours on Sunday when the
institute was closed. Today, they offer 9- and 12-week courses from the
turn-of-the-century mansion they've occupied since 1921 in areas including
drawing human anatomy, Chinese brush painting, oil painting, watercolor
painting, and sculpture. Classes range from $150 to $250, less for members.

Arcades

City Pool Hall
640 W. Hubbard, 312/491-9690   **C**
Whatever your coin-op passion—pool, darts, foos-ball, pinball, or arcade
games, **City Pool** has them all in the classic arcade room set-up. Open daily
11 A.M.–2 A.M.

Dennis' Place for Games
957 W. Belmont, 773/528-8616   **N**
6701 N. Clark, 773/743-5207   **FN**
Dennis' has classic arcade games such as Centipede and Ms. Pac-man, as
well as newer toys. It's an all-around game place. Open Sun.–Thur. noon–2
A.M., Fri. noon–3 A.M., and Sat. noon–4 A.M.

Diversions Game Room
6259 N. McCormick, 773/588-0226   **FN**
A testing place for Midway games. Generation Xers will take comfort

recalling those days when Ma and Pa dropped them off at the arcade with a pocket full of change. **Diversions** is hailed as one totally awesome 80s arcade. Open Mon.–Thur. 11:30 A.M.–11 P.M., Fri. and Sat. 11 A.M.–12:30 A.M., and Sun. 11 A.M.–11 P.M.

Fun Zone
3641 N. Western, 773/528-3032   N
A somewhat shabby, but clean, well-lit, and safe game room that caters to the electronic gaming tastes of various generations with its nearly 50 games. Hockey, basketball, pinball, and a wide range of early video games including Galaga, Tron, Centipede, and various Pac-Man incarnations cost only one token. The latest sporting, driving, fighting, and shooting video games go for 2–4 tokens. Tokens are 5 for $1, 30 for $5. Unlimited games Sun. 10 A.M.–12:30 P.M., $4.

For pinball games found at venues around Chicagoland, pinball wizards may consult **Chicago Pinball** (*www.agvp.net/pin_locations_chicago.htm*).

Badminton

McKinley Park Badminton Club
McKinley Park, 2210 W. Pershing Road, 312/747-6527   **SW**
The only non-suburban, non-university affiliated badminton club in Chicago meets at the McKinley Park fieldhouse. Players of all ages and skill levels can drop in Tues. and Fri. 6 P.M.–9 P.M., and Sun. 11 A.M.–3 P.M. The annual fee is $35, and $5 for guests.

Baseball

THE Chicago Park District has over 200 parks with baseball facilities, with two-thirds of these parks also equipped for softball. For more information about park district facilities or to learn about joining a league, check out the park district's Web site at *www.chicagoparkdistrict.com*, or call 312/742-PLAY.

Batting Cages

Among the newer additions to the Chicago Park District holdings are batting cages. **West Lawn Park** (4233 W. 65th, 773/284-2803) has a bank of seven cages open Mon.–Fri. 11 A.M.–9 P.M. and Sat.–Sun. 10 A.M.–4:30 P.M. There are six cages at **Warren Park** (6601 N. Western, 773/262-6314) that train future sluggers on slow, medium, or fast softball or baseball pitches (15 for $1). **Palmer Park** (11100 S. Indiana, 312/747-6576) is scheduled to receive some next.

Whether you want some serious practice or a ten-minute diversion amidst other Wrigleyville sporting, **Sluggers World Class Sports Bar & Indoor Sports Facility** (3540 N. Clark, 773/472-9696) can accommodate you. When the Cubbies are out of town, you can indulge in quite a lot of hitting Mon. and Thur. 5 P.M.–10 P.M. and Sun. 6 P.M.–10 P.M. for only $5. Other times, it's 12 pitches for $1.

Basketball

IN the city where the greatest basketball player ever is simply known as "Michael," there are courts in nearly every city park. To sign up for teams, leagues, and classes or find open gym times at the park nearest you, call your regional park district office (p. 135).

Baths and Steam Rooms

Division Street Russian and Turkish Baths
1914 W. Division, 773/384-9671   **W**
Men who want a glimpse of—or indoctrination into—old, ethnic, connected Chicago and manly male camaraderie need an outing to the **Division Street Bathhouse**, the last traditional bathhouse in Chicago and one of only two in the country that are this old (est. 1906). There guys from the old country, blue collar workers, politicians, professionals, athletes, celebrities passing through, and perhaps an underworld type or two will be naked and shooting the breeze as they pass from shower room to hot room to cold bath to hot bath relaxing, soaking, rubbing themselves and each other down with oak leaves, and pouring buckets of cold water on themselves. Afterwards, they might opt for a massage, a meal in the restaurant, and a drink and a cigar in the lounge, which has a full bar. A separate facility for women with a European spa feel was added in the 1960s and was just as charming, but not as colorful; it was less communal, more private pampering. At the time of this book's printing, it was closed for remodeling. Open Mon.–Fri. 8 A.M.–10 P.M., Sat. 7 A.M.–10 P.M., Sun. 6 A.M.–10 P.M. $20 for basic, unlimited use of baths; massages, meals, etc. are extra.

Paradise Sauna
2912 W. Montrose, 773/588-3304   **N**
For an urban neighborhood adventure that's a true escape because it's both relaxing and interesting, head to the **Paradise Sauna**. (It's really a complex that includes a Japanese restaurant with sushi bar and a beauty parlor.) The crowd is predominantly Korean, but everyone is welcome. Women and men have different facilities. The $18 entrance fee buys unlimited use of the sauna, whirlpool, steam bath, hot dry bath, and hot and cold tubs. Schedule a massage for an extra charge. Open daily 7 A.M.–10 P.M.

Thousand Waves Spa for Women
1212 W. Belmont, 773/549-0700, *http://thousandwavesspa.com*   **N**
Thousands Waves feels part Zen, part grrl power. It's usually pretty tranquil with everyone keeping to themselves, but there are times—like when everyone in the Jacuzzi but me discovered they were in local bands and needed to meet each other—when animated conversation erupts. (The management takes the side of serenity.) The standard visit for the spa baths includes the three-hour use of the Redwood Sauna, Eucalyptus Steam bath, Jacuzzi Hot Tub, powerful "rain" shower, and relaxation room (free herbal tea) for $20. Towels, kimono robes, soap, shampoo, lotion, hair dryers, and lockers are provided. "Bathing Suits Optional" means just about everyone's naked, but if you're on the modest side, feel free to wear one. No appointment necessary. Two more things of note: Their $125 spa baths, herbal wrap, and one-hour massage package may be one of the city's best half-day spa deals. They also have a remarkable free stress management program for women with cancer that includes five free spa visits and five free one-hour massages. Open Tues.–Fri. noon–9 P.M., Sat. –Sun. 10 A.M.–7 P.M.

Bicycling

COMMUNITY groups and the mayor's office have taken active steps over the last several years to make Chicago a bike friendly city. One major component of the mayor's **Bike 2000 Plan** to encourage bicycle use is the establishment of a 300-mile network of bikeways in the city. Other elements include adding more bike racks and improving the Lakefront Path. Something brand new in this campaign is the 300-space, heated indoor bicycle parking facility in Millennium Park at Randolph and Columbus. The parking is free and use of lockers and showers is but a buck a day, purchased in packs of ten. (Think that's fancy? Chicago also now has free valet bike parking at the big city fests in Grant Park and free bike check-in at Wrigley Field on game days.)

The *Chicago Bicycling Map* is available free from the Chicago Department of Transportation (312/742-BIKE). A more detailed *Chicagoland Bicycle Map* which covers Chicago and the surrounding seven counties can be purchased for $6.95 from the **Chicagoland Bicycle Federation** (free with membership, see below). For any of the eight free **Cook County Forest Preserve** trail maps, call 773/261-8400 or download them from the Web (*www.fpdcc.com*). There are 100 miles of biking to be had on the Forest Preserve District's six paved trails and 200 miles of biking on mult-use trails.

Much of this progress is due to the work of the **Chicagoland Bicycle Federation** (312/42-PEDAL, *http://chibikefed.org*). In addition to advocating on behalf of cyclists, **CBF** sponsors recreational activities and dispenses useful bicycle information on local trails, urban bike safety, how to be a successful bike commuter, and more. A $25 yearly membership entitles you to a monthly newsletter, periodic ride calendars, and discounts at bike shops.

Whether it's dawn, day, dusk, or evening; winter, spring, summer, or fall; quiet or crowded; in any and all conditions, it's always an appropriate time to experience the 18½ miles of Chicago's lakefront from Kathy Osterman Beach (5800 N) to the South Shore Cultural Center (7100 S) on bicycle. Besides winding through Lincoln, Grant, Burnham, and Jackson Parks, the path will take you past sculptures, gardens, golf courses, museums, cultural institutions, the "Totem Pole," the Chess Pavilion, Soldier Field, and McCormick Place. Any of the beaches or outdoor cafés make great resting spots. The free park district *Lakefront Trail Map* outlines these and other shoreline delights. Pick up a copy at Tourist Information Centers or by calling 773/256-0949.

Other scenic off-street pedaling can be found on the dedicated bike trails of these city parks. **Legion** and **River Parks** are long parks that follow the river and are great for crossing the North Side, Peterson to Lawrence.

Bessemer Park	**Legion Park**	**Portage Park**
Calumet Park	**Marquette Park**	**Riis Park**
Douglas Park	**McKinley Park**	**River Park**
Garfield Park	**Oriole Park**	**Sherman Park**
Humboldt Park	**Oz Park**	**Warren Park**

Bike Rentals

We've all seen their gleaming rows of bikes along the lakefront and probably assumed they were just for tourists. Perhaps. But if you don't happen to have a tandem, quadcycle, or bike with baby seat in your possession, then at some time or another they may just be for you resident Chicagoans, too.

Bike Chicago/Bike and Roll
Navy Pier, 312/595-9600, *www.bikechicago.com*   C
North Avenue Beach, 773/327-2706, *www.bikerental.com*   C
This company, known as **Bike Chicago** at Navy Pier and **Bike and Roll** at North Avenue Beach, rents out a multitude of bicycle variations (with gear) and inline skates along the lake, including at their outposts at Wilson Beach, Foster Beach, and 63rd Street Beach from Memorial Day to Labor Day. Choose from over 200 mountain bikes, road bikes, comfort bikes, hybrid bikes, cruisers, tandems, quadcycles, baby seats, tag-alongs, and wagons. Maps, helmets, and locks are available free upon request. They buy new bikes from top manufacturers at the beginning of each season, so all are in excellent shape (past-season bikes may be for sale). Not all bikes are available at all locations, but Navy Pier has the largest selection. Open daily 9 A.M.–7 P.M. Apr., May, Sept., and Oct., and 8 A.M.–10 P.M. June–Aug. Rentals are $8.75 hour or $25/day on the weekends, $10/day weekdays. Higher fees for premium equipment. Discounts available for groups, longer rental periods, and for reserving online.

Bike Tours

Bike Chicago/Bike and Roll
Navy Pier, 312/595-9600, *www.bikechicago.com*   C
North Avenue Beach, 773/327-2706, *www.bikerental.com*   C
These bike rental outfits offer free guided bike tours, whether or not you rent a bike from them, to the first 15 individuals who sign up for them. Various tours leave daily, May–Sept., from Navy Pier (10:30 A.M. and 1:30 P.M.) and North Avenue Beach (11 A.M. and 2 P.M.). Rides include an easy 3-mile/60-minute ride to Grant Park or 5-mile/90-minute tour of Lincoln Park. There's a mid-range trip to Chinatown, and the longer, more challenging rides cover 11 miles of the Lakefront Trail or head to Hyde Park and the Osaka Japanese Garden. Call for more information or reserve a spot online. Groups must call for separate arrangements.

Chicago by Bike Summer Rides
312/251-9445, *www.bikeonechicago.com/summerrides.asp*
Bank One sponsors five to six free bike rides of different Chicago neighborhoods each Saturday morning from early June to late August. Led by experienced cyclists and Chicago lovers, tours take small groups (15 or fewer) to Lincoln Park, Old Town, the Gold Coast, Little Italy, Pilsen, Near West Side, Wicker Park, Chinatown, Logan Square, Andersonville, Ravenswood, Hyde Park, Bronzeville, South Loop, or Beverly and talk about local landmarks, historic sites, and other points of interest along the way and in the destination neighborhood(s). Rides start at 9 A.M., at either the downtown Bank One (Dearborn & Monroe) or the posted local branch, and last two hours. Open to riders aged 12 and older. Helmets required.

Chicago Cycling Club
773/509-8093, *www.chicagocyclingclub.org*
The **Chicago Cycling Club** takes a 15–100 mile ride most Saturday and Sunday mornings and assorted weekday evenings in summer. They typically meet at Waveland and the clock tower in Lincoln Park, and head for city, suburban, or outlying destinations, often along simple or elaborate theme routes that members take turns organizing. The Sunday and fourth Wednesday evening of the month are more leisurely, social rides. Saturday mornings are the longer, mid-range tours. And the "roadie" rides are for the serious, long-distance cyclists. Food is often involved—as a theme, say several bagel or Italian ice stops, or as a destination: *Let's ride to Superdawg (p. 180), Krispy Kreme, or Hackney's!* Other rides have focused on lesser-known areas of the city (The West Side Ride), urban elements (interesting sets of stairs to carry bikes up and down), and what appears to be everyone's favorite residential side streets in the city strung together (the annual Ultimate Neighborhood Ride). Ride with them once for free, afterwards pay an $18 annual membership fee/$23 for families. Call the ride line for upcoming events and more information.

Currently the best list of local biking events on the Web is **CBF's calendar** (*http://chibikefed.org/calendar*), which also has links to the rides listings of other clubs and organizations. Mountain bikers can also turn to the **Chicago Area Mountain Bikers (CAMB)** (*http://members.core.com/~edd/default.htm*) and tandem riders to the **Chicago Area Tandem Society (CATS)** (*http://pages.prodigy.net/waterstreet/CATS/index.htm*).

Critical Mass Bike Rides / Events

Chicago is America's best big city for biking, according to a recent *Bicycling* magazine article, but it can still be an intimidating place to ride if you're not used to heavy traffic. Whether you want to feel more comfortable on two wheels, discover new places to ride, meet fellow cyclists, or just blow off some steam at the end of the work week, you're invited to the **Critical Mass** ride, a great introduction to Chicago's cycling community.

Critical Mass is a monthly bicycle happening which originated in San Francisco in 1992 and quickly spread to cities all over the world. It promotes cycling as a cheap, efficient, healthy, and friendly form of transportation. Here in Chicago, the ride takes place on the last Friday of every month, assembling between 5:30 and 6 P.M. under the Picasso sculpture in Daley Plaza, at the intersection of Washington and Dearborn. Hundreds of people show up for the free bike party–parade and vote for one of any number of photocopied route maps, an election process known as the *Xerocracy*. The crowd of Massers then takes off for a leisurely ramble around town that usually lasts about two hours, waving to bystanders, shouting pro-bike slogans, and passing out literature. Although this un-permitted procession of bicycles delays car commuters for a few minutes as it passes by, the vibe is generally quite positive and Chicago police seem to have adopted a policy of salutary neglect towards the ride.

Folks of all ages and many walks of life participate on all kinds of bikes, ranging from thrift-store cruisers to fancy 10-speeds, from recumbents and tandems to old-fashioned high-wheelers and customized chopper bikes. Costumes, banners, boom-boxes, and the occasional two-man band towed on a bike trailer, make for a very colorful event.

The Mass usually ends as a social hour at a different bar, beach, barbecue, or arts event each month, regardless of the season. In fact, Critical Mass-associated activities heat up as the weather gets colder, when CM riders put on a wealth of activities to promote year-round cycling under the aegis of the **Bike Winter** (*www.bikewinter.org*) organization. Bike Winter events include seminars on cold-weather biking tips, the **Santa Cycle Rampage** (a costumed cruise for the benefit of holiday shoppers), the **Tiki Ride** (to a suburban Polynesian bar), a protest of the Chicago Auto Show at McCormick Place, and the annual **Critical Mass Art Show**. In 2002, the City of Chicago sponsored the first **"Bike the Drive"** event, shutting down the busy highway for bikers during the early morning hours.

Bingo

THE various games at this major bingo center benefit different community organizations. Spend a few bucks on some cards and you could walk away with tens or even hundreds of dollars. N-43, forty-three under the N . . .

Golden Tiara
3231 N. Cicero, 773/736-5350   **NW**
This former movie palace-turned-banquet hall is now the city's primary bingo parlor with a rolling Wednesday evening jackpot that can get up to $15,000 and beyond! Open daily two to three hours before games begin. Games are Mon.–Sat. 11 A.M. and 7 P.M., Sat. eve./Sun. morning at midnight, and Sun. noon and 7 P.M. There are extensive concession options, wheelchair access, and a non-smoking section.

The legendary bingo–Catholic Church connection is alive and well in Chicago. As the nation's largest Roman Catholic Archdiocese, Chicago is teeming with neighborhood churches and schools that have a weekly bingo fundraiser. Compare this with the eight fraternal lodges, six community centers, and five churches of other denominations that hold weekly games. Phone local parishes for information and pack your chips, markers, and good luck charms. Many of these can be found at **Online Bingo Halls** (*www.onlinebingohalls.com/chicago_bingo_halls.html*). If your favorite bingo-playing senior doesn't have Internet access, do them a favor and print out this list for them. And, if you'd like to volunteer to play bingo with seniors, check out **Chicago Cares** (*www.chicagocares.org*).

If you're on the younger side, are ready to bingo, and it's Monday night and there's nothing else to do, you might try . . .

Drag Queen Bingo in Rehab
Circuit, 3651 N. Halsted, 773/325-2233, *www.circuitclub.com*   **N**
Hosted by Paula Sinclaire and Miss Fozzie to the thumping disco soundtrack supplied by DJ/VJ Martin, Monday night bingo (10 P.M.–midnight) at this large gay dance club starts attracting 100+ crowds beginning at 9 P.M. No cover, no bingo fee, but queen-size cocktails are $10. Prizes on the order of squirting sunglasses. Adults over 21 welcome.

Gingerman Tavern
3740 N. Clark, 773/549-2050   **N**
Free Monday night bingo begins at this Wrigleyville tavern around 10 P.M.

and goes until the crowd loses interest, perhaps until the 2 A.M. closing on a good night. The caller makes it fun ("you know, he's kind of insulting") and distributes random, wacky prizes. Occasionally the prizes might be good—then they charge a buck.

The California Clipper
1002 N. California, 773/384-2547, *www.californiaclipper.com*   **W**
A swanky, but approachable, restored 1940s cocktail lounge, the **Clipper** also has a bingo night—the last Monday of the month, 9 P.M.–midnight. There's no cover and it comes with free pizza, free prizes, and undoubtedly a drink special. Sign up and you can call one of the games.

Birding

CHICAGO's not just a city with a diverse human population, we also have an underrecognized diversity of feathered friends flying overhead. Over 300 species of birds, some permanent, some temporary, and some passing through from the Arctic to the Amazon share the Chicago air space.

The Chicago Park District has just published a deceptively-simple brochure, **The Chicago Lakefront Birding Trail**, that is a must-have for all birding enthusiasts. In just a few pages, you'll get a brief overview of the best seasons, days, times, and places to see different types of birds, some background on the most likely birds you'll see, descriptions of some special Chicago birds, a listing of local birding organizations, and a lakefront map, coding 25 sites from Montrose Point to Calumet Park. There's also an outline of some of Chicago's bird friendly practices, including the new Lakefront Bird Habitat Guidelines that will help protect and promote bird habitats along the lakefront from future construction projects.

Some of the more prominent lakefront birding points include:

- **The "Magic Hedge" at Montrose Harbor**   **N**
Just southwest of the fishing pier, in the grouping of trees and shrubs nicknamed the **Magic Hedge**, is one of the best bird watching opportunities in the Midwest. Early morning, when things are still relatively quiet, is your best chance at spotting a rare warbler or falcon.

- **Bill Jarvis Migratory Bird Sanctuary**   **N**
A sanctuary since 1923, the woodsy area behind the Totem pole (Addison & Lake Shore Drive), was renamed in 2003 in honor of birder

Bill Jarvis, who led volunteers in maintaining the area from the 1970s through the 1990s after it had fallen into disrepair. A new group of concerned environmentalists and neighbors have recently picked up where he left off.

- **Jackson Park Bob-o-link Meadow and Wooded Island**   S
A marsh once filled for the 1893 Columbian Exposition, this land was later used for athletic fields and then an Army missile base, before it was left to the weeds. It's been a nature sanctuary since 1982, a joined effort of the Jackson Park Advisory Council and the Chicago Park District, re-seeded with native grasses and wildflowers to make a habitat more conducive for native wildlife. The **Wooded Island** is south of the Museum of Science and Industry in Jackson Park and the meadow is east of the island.

Downtown Birding on the River
In the age of fast-paced, speed everything, you can now crunch bird watching into your schedule by doing it before you go to work, or on your lunch hour, provided you work near the Chicago River. Take time to stop and check the trees and shrubs for the numerous varieties of birds that use the Chicago River as a migratory guide. A particularly fertile spot is **Wolf Point** (named for an early settlement at the fork of the river) on the south side of the Apparel Center, just west of the north end of the Orleans Street bridge.

Chicago Audubon Society's Bird Walks
Jackson Park, 6401 S. Stony Island, *www.chicagoaudubon.org*   S
Doug Anderson leads two free bird walks weekly (as he has for almost 30 years) through Jackson Park. The park was designed by Frederick Olmstead who also designed New York's Central Park. Today it is one of the best places to see birds in Northern Illinois, if not the nation! Meet at the Clarence Darrow Bridge (the lawyer's ashes were scattered in the lagoon here) behind the Museum of Science and Industry. Walks take place Wed. 7 A.M.–8:30 A.M. and Sat. 8 A.M.–10 A.M., beginning March 27 with the last tour given on New Year's Day. According to Doug Anderson, 80% of all species of birds have been sighted on the 16-acre Wooded Island giving people reason to flock from hundreds of miles away to bird watch in Chicago. Rare warblers, including the Townsend, Worm-Eating, and Frigates (only seen three times in Illinois), are a few of the rare birds you might see. According to Doug, bad weather and hurricanes in other states equal great opportunities at Wooded Island for birders as such conditions throw off the migration patterns of birds by hundreds or thousands of miles.

Beginners are encouraged to attend. Bring your binoculars. Prior registration is not required. Free.

The Chicago Ornithological Society
773/935-8439, *http://chicagobirder.org/*   N
COS, a Chicago-area birding club established in 1912, organizes year-round field trips and a monthly program at the **Margate Park Field House** (4921 N. Marine Drive) on a birding topic. They also sponsor Geoff Williamson's popular walks around North Pond in Lincoln Park, Wednesday mornings at 7 A.M. from mid-March to mid-June. Call or visit the Web site for exact dates of walks held in January and February. Meet at the north end of the North Pond at the North Pond Café.

Board Games

FOR a friendly neighborhood game of Chess, Scrabble, or Trivial Pursuit, look no father than your local independent coffeeshops, including **The Perfect Cup** (4700 N. Damen, 773/989-4177) in Lincoln Square, Café Boost (5400 N. Clark, 773/907-8674) in Andersonville, and the new hipster gourmet coffeeshop in Ukrainian Village, the **Grasshopper** (935 N. Damen, 773/394-8285). The latter is open till 2 A.M. daily. Also try the **3rd Coast** (1260 N. Dearborn, 312/649-0730, and 29 E. Delaware, 312/664-7225). And this is only the tip of the iceberg. Most small neighborhood cafés cater to regulars who enjoy cards, board games, or even those complex (and sorry, geeky) role-playing games. For bars with closets full of board games, see *Chapter 5: Entertainment* (p. 239).

Bocce Ball

FOR those with their own set of bocce balls, refine your game on courts located at one of these parks. If you're without equipment, phone the park office to learn how you can team up with local players.

Calumet Park	**Lincoln Park**	**Veteran's Mem. Plg.**
Hiawatha Park	**McGuane Park**	**Wolfe Playground**
Jackson Park	**Smith Park**	

Cody's Public House
1658 W. Barry, 773/528-4050   N
This quintessential neighborhood bar tucked on a residential corner serves its gentrified neighbors and anyone looking for an unpretentious escape with

a good beer selection, antique and dated fixtures, outdoor grill (bring and grill your own food), and regulation-size bocce ball court in the beer garden.

World Bocce Association
630/834-8349, *www.worldbocce.org*
As the **WBA** is headquartered in suburban Elmhurst, die-hard players and fans are likely to find many organized bocce events close to home.

Bowling

HERE are ten of the most, uh . . . striking neighborhood bowling alleys.

College Campus Bowling

U of I at Chicago Lanes
750 S. Halsted, 312/413-5170, *http://ccc.ops.uic.edu/rec/bbctr.html*   **C**
Guests can bowl alongside UIC students for $2 per game, $1.25 for shoe rental. Open seven days a week after 2 P.M. for non-students and open as late as 2 A.M. on weekends. Throw in their seventeen regulation pool tables ($7/hour), forty video games, and dinner at the cafeteria or in nearby Greektown, and you've got an affordable night on the town.

Glow In the Dark Bowling

Turner Bowl
6625 W. Belmont, 773/637-6654   **NW**
Fridays after 11 P.M., Saturdays after 8:30 P.M., and Sundays after 7 P.M., the house lights go off, the black lights go on, and the bowling alley is aglow. Add some music and disco lights and it's party time. Lanes rent for $25/hour for up to five people, shoe rental $2.75. Reservations necessary.

Hand-Set Pin Bowling

Southport Lanes & Billiards
3325 N. Southport, 773/472-6600, *www.southportlanes.com*   **N**
Built in 1922 by the Schlitz Brewing Company, 3325 N. Southport served, among other things, as a speakeasy and brothel before becoming a neighbor-hood bar/bowling alley. **Southport Lanes & Billiards** is one of only a handful of bowling alleys left in the United States where the pins are still set by hand and the rest of the refurbished tavern retains much of this vintage

charm. And, since it's just been redone again, it's an especially slick vintage charm. Call ahead to reserve one of the four hand-set bowling lanes. Bowling runs $20/hour per lane (pro-rated every five minutes) and pool, $12/hour per table. Shoe rental is $2.

Lawn Bowling

The Chicago Park District has bowling greens at these two locations:

Columbus Park   **Jackson Park**

Neo-Art Deco Lounge Bowling

Lucky Strike
2747 N. Lincoln, 773/549-2695
www.theluckystrike.com/lincolnpark/index.htm   **N**
1044 E. 55th, 773/347-BOWL
www.theluckystrike.com/hydepark/index.htm   **S**
Bowling, billiards, and the "Art Deco Fantasy" atmosphere serve as one more cool backdrop for adults just hanging out. The swank may be fake but much of the décor is authentic, from the vintage posters and Art Deco artifacts to some antique bowling benches, tables, and lanes. The Lincoln location is more 1920s, whereas the Hyde Park one, amidst the U of C campus, is more 40s. Food and, of course, martinis are available. Bowling costs $20/hour per lane (good for about 4–6 players), billiards, $12/hour per table. Shoe rental is $2.

Rock 'n' Roll Bowling

Diversey-River Bowl
2211 W. Diversey, 773/227-5800, *www.drbowl.com*   **N**
Established in 1958, **Diversey-River Bowl** has the feel of an old-time bowling alley, souped up with enough lights and gizmos to attract the kids. Once the leagues are finished for the night, "Rock 'n' Bowl" begins with sound-activated lights, strobes, fog machines, and thumping rock music to accompany your play. That's Wed.–Thur. starting at 11 P.M., Friday after 8:30 P.M., and Saturday at 9 P.M. Lanes run $19/hour Mon.–Thur., $26/hour Sun., and $32/hour Fri.–Sat., with up to five people allowed per lane. Shoe rental is $3. Open Sun.–Fri. noon–2 A.M., Sat. noon–3 A.M.

Second-Floor Neighborhood Bowling

Lincoln Square Lanes
4874 N. Lincoln, 773/561-8191   FN
Want to disappear for a night? Climb the worn staircase to their home above
a hardware store. $3 games, $2 shoes. Occasional live music on weekends.

24-Hour Bowling

With Marigold Bowl closing May, 2004, and Marzano's 80-lane facility
closing August, 2004, Waveland is the last 24/7/365 bowling alley in the
city. Waveland, in fact, has been open at least 380,000 consecutive hours!

Waveland Bowl
3700 N. Western, 773/472-5900, *www.wavelandbowl.com*   N
Established in 1959 and recently repackaged as a cleaner, more wholesome
family fun center, folks of all ages pack **Waveland**'s 40 lanes, snack shop,
bar, pool tables, and video games at all hours. Alley Dogs, the concession
stands, even has a few vegetarian items and ice cream shake concoctions.
Depending on the day and the hours, games are $1, $2, $3, $4, or $6/hour.
Shoe rental is $4 and includes a pair of socks for you to keep. Cozmic
Bowling creates a nightclubby vibe all ages can enjoy: the house lights go
down, the black lights come on, there's a non-stop psychedelic light show,
there's fog, and, of course, the music's pumped up. Cozmic Bowling takes
place Mondays after 7 P.M., Tues. & Thur. after 10 P.M., Fri. 3 P.M.–5 P.M.,
Sat. 1 P.M.–3 P.M. and 4 P.M.–9 P.M., and Sun. 1 P.M.–3 P.M. and after 8 P.M.

Boxing

SELF-DEFENSE. Aerobic exercise. Stress reduction. Legal aggression. Boxing
offers something for everyone and the park district teaches it to them—male
or female, young or old. Besides holding classes, these boxing rings are the
sights of numerous local shows and tournaments.

Bessemer Park	**Garfield Park**	**Loyola Park**
Calumet Park	**Hamlin Park**	**Scottsdale Plg.**
Clarendon Cmty. Ctr.	**Harrison Park**	**Stateway Park**
Fuller Park	**Humboldt Park**	

If you prefer to watch others slug it out, try the historic **St. Andrew's Gym**
(1658 W. Addison)—the center for an intensive lineup of amateur and local

boxing matches and tournaments, including all **Chicago Golden Gloves** bouts. Three good Web sites provide all the details:
* **Chicago Boxing,** *www.chicagoboxing.com*
* **Chicago Youth Boxing,** *www.chicagoyouthboxing.com*
* **Chicago Golden Gloves,** *www.chicagogoldengloves.com*

Bridge

American Bridge and Social Club
6002 N. Keating, 773/777-0700   **FN**
The **American Bridge and Social Club** (formerly in the Lincoln Village Shopping Center) focuses on bridge six days of the week. Munchies are provided and pop (a supermarket assortment) is 50 cents; no alcoholic beverages allowed. There's no need to call ahead or bring a partner—just show up. Games start promptly: Mon., Tues., Thur., and Fri. 7 P.M., Sat. 10:30 A.M., and Sun. 5:30 P.M. Members pay $8/session; non-members, $9.

Ann Sather's Restaurant
929 W. Belmont, 847/774-2247 (Gerry)   **N**
The **Lawson Bridge Club** meets in an upstairs room of Ann Sather's Restaurant, Monday nights at 6:30. The restaurant is closed then, but your $5 entrance fee includes cookies and coffee. This is a friendly group always looking for new players. Drop on by!

The Bridge Center on Sheridan
5341 N. Sheridan, 773/271-2520, *www.bridgeonsheridan.com*   **FN**
The **Bridge Center** demonstrates that this card games is alive and well and well-organized in Chicago. This fully equipped and furnished space (20 tables with supplies, kitchen, storage, computer, Internet access) allows clubs and teachers to rent affordable space without worries of overhead and maintenance. Many members of the **Chicago Contract Bridge Association** (*www.bridgeinchicago.com*) play here. Both the center's and CCBA's Web sites can easily lead you to the tournaments, classes, clubs, and dozens of organized games that happen in Chicago on a weekly basis.

Chicago Cultural Center
78 E. Washington, 312/744-4554   **C**
Renaissance Court is a subsection of the Cultural Center run by the city's Department of Aging and offers special programs for those 55+. The duplicate bridge games, Mon. 1 P.M., can draw as many as 60 people. $3 fee.

Canoeing and Kayaking

WITH a canoe or kayak and some minimal skills, you'll have access to whole new perspectives on Chicago, particularly along the 156 miles of the Chicago River system. From the river, you can newly enjoy the forest preserves and parks. There are 18 parks on the river, including **Gompers Park** up north, with its active wetlands restoration project, **Ping Tom Park** in Chinatown, with its traditional architectural flourishes, and the **Canal Origins Park** in Bridgeport, marking the origins of the now-defunct I & M Canal, the waterway that helped link Chicago to the Mississippi River and make us a great city. Along the river, paddlers also see wildlife, established residential neighborhoods, new condominium construction, light and heavy industry (barges, too!), and 45 movable bridges of various styles, a collection unrivaled in the world. It's hard to overstate the awe-inspiring experience of self-propelling a small boat through downtown's marvel of towering architectural gems. Finally, you can't miss **Bubbly Creek**. A tributary of the South Branch of the Chicago River, it is mucky and lifeless, except for the bubbles from the still-decaying carcasses tossed to the bottom of the river decades ago when the Union Stockyards dumped there.

Chicago River Canoe and Kayak

3400 N. Rockwell, 773/325-2925, *www.chicagoriverpaddle.com*   **N**
The **CRCK** base in Clark Park makes a great starting point for exploring the northern reaches of the Chicago River or for heading downstream to Goose Island and downtown. Open Sat.–Sun. 9 A.M.–sunset, Apr.–Oct., and also Wed.–Fri. noon–sunset, June–Aug. Weekdays, all boats are $10/hour. Weekends, canoes and single kayaks are $14/hour; two-person kayaks are $18/hour. The day rate is equal to a four-hour rental (they stop charging after the fourth hour). Join their special two–four-hour group outings ($25–$35) in your choice of boat, including guided tours of less-traveled stretches of the river, **Moonlight Paddles** that come with a gourmet riverside dinner, and a **Pub Yaw** that involves paddling into downtown as night falls (stunning!) and docking at Dick's Last Resort (they'll bring the boats home for you).

Chicagoland Canoe Base

4019 N. Narragansett, 773/777-1489
www.chicagolandcanoebase.com   **NW**
When you rent a canoe or kayak from the **Chicagoland Canoe Base**, you're entering the remarkable world of owner Ralph Frese. You could say he's a canoe buff, environmental activist, and local waterway expert and historian,

but that doesn't quite plumb the life of a man who's a fourth-generation blacksmith, canoe builder (including fiberglass replicas of birchbark canoes), antique watercraft collector, and the first recipient of the American Canoe Association's Legends of Paddling award. Many consider this the most unusual canoe shop in the country. It's still a great place to get a canoe with your story! Canoes or kayaks go for $40 for the first day, $20 per day up to seven days, and $15 per additional day. A special $60 weekend rate lets you pick up a canoe/kayak Friday after 3 P.M. and return it Monday before noon. Since the place is landlocked, you will need a vehicle to transport any rentals. Their New Year's Day paddle down the North Branch of the Chicago River can draw over 100 people in all weather conditions.

Lincoln Park Boat Club
www.lpbc.net   **N**
The city's oldest boat club still uses the facility that four smaller clubs joined forces to build in 1910. It sits east of Lincoln Park Zoo on the banks of the Lincoln Park Lagoon. Those interested in canoeing, kayaking, rowing, and sculling for serious fitness and competition may want to consider membership. Besides having access to their training room, instructors, and equipment for lagoon and lake, the equipment may be used off-site with permission. Memberships with all fees are close to $300, with half-year memberships available.

UIC Open Pool
UIC's Flames Athletic Center
South side of Roosevelt, ½ block west of Halsted
http://pages.ripco.net/~jwn/openpool   **C**
When it's too cold to be on Chicago's waterways, paddlers can still keep their chops wet one day each week from mid-November to late April (Wed. 7 P.M.–9:30 P.M.) at the University of Illinois's larger-than-Olympic size pool. Bring your own *clean* canoe or kayak to practice old and new skills and meet like-minded boaters with warm, still waters beneath you. A limited number of boats are available for a $10 rental fee. There's also a $10 fee per session, $5 for students and children.

For all about paddling—instruction, routes, clubs, maps, regulations—check out the **Chicago Area Paddling/Fishing Guide** (*http://pages.ripco.net/ ~jwn/*) and the **Illinois Paddling Council** (*www.illinoispaddling.org*). Besides the basics, these sites will lead to information on such events as **Caroling in Canoes and Kayaks**, when paddlers on the Chicago River sing to holiday shoppers on Michigan Avenue, celebrating afterwards at a local restaurant or bar, or Friends of the Chicago River's **Flatwater Classic**, an annual boat race (or friendly float) with a course that passes from northside residential neighborhoods through an industrial corridor to the downtown canyon of architectural giants to the working river of the near South Side.

Have canoe, need water? Most folks canoe in the Chicago River, but canoeing is also allowed in certain Chicago harbors including **Belmont Harbor, Calumet Harbor, Diversey Harbor, Jackson Park Harbor**, and **Montrose Harbor**. There's also the **Lincoln Park Lagoon**, the only park district lagoon open for non-motorized boating.

Chess

Chess Pavilion at North Avenue Beach
North Avenue and Lake Michigan   C
In this open shelter on the lake, gamesters have been dueling since the 1960s over the chess/checker boards built into cement benches. With the spectacular skyline view, lake breeze, new friends, assorted characters, and intellectual challenge found here, you have the perfect excuse to play hooky from work, or at least to hop over for a quick game during your lunch break.

Lakeview Cuyler Chess Club
Cuyler Covenant Church, Fellowship Hall, 3901 N. Marshfield
312/494-1300, x. 12 (Drew), *http://lakeviewcuylerchess.tripod.com*   N
The **Lakeview Cuyler Chess Club** welcomes all ages and all skill levels to drop in for open chess every Wednesday, 7 P.M.–10 P.M. The fee is $1 per hour of game play and includes use of tournament-standard game boards and refreshments. The club also offers lessons and holds USCF-rated events.

Wicker Park Chess Club
Myopic Books, 1468 N. Milwaukee, 773/862-4882
www.myopicbookstore.com/chess.html   C
One of Chicago's largest and most dynamic used bookstores, Myopic Books is home to the **Wicker Park Chess Club**, hosted by Patrick Jones, every Wednesday from 7 P.M. to 1 A.M. No need to call ahead—just show up. Some boards are provided; bring your own as a back-up.

For updates on Chicago-area tournaments, players can also check with the **Illinois Chess Association** (*www.illinoischess.org*).

Climbing

WHEN the day to day grind drives you up a wall . . .

Fitplex Extreme Fitness Club
1235 N. LaSalle, 312/640-1235
www.multiplexclubs.com/programs/rockclimbing.php   **C**
After becoming certified on the initial visit ($30), non-members are welcome to use this private club's climbing wall and locker room. Day passes are $12 ($80 for a 10-pass used in two months, $120 for a 20-pass used in three months), but it's $9 on Wednesdays and for students. Check Web site for staffed and unstaffed open climbing wall hours.

Hidden Peak Climbing Gym
937 W. Chestnut, 312/563-9400
www.lakeshoreacademy.com/hiddenpeak.html   **C**
After taking a class called Top Roping I ($35), enjoy the challenges of climbing over your lunch break (Mon.–Fri. noon–2 P.M.) or after work (Mon.–Fri. 5 P.M.–8:45 P.M.). Saturday and Sunday climbing is also available for the whole family, ages 5 and up. An annual pass is $375, but a day pass is only $10 ($80 for a 10-punch pass), a lunch time visit only $7. Rent all the necessary equipment for $6/visit ($40 for a 10-punch pass).

Croquet

Chicago Croquet Club
1020 S. Wabash Unit 7A, 312/692-1980
www.chicagocroquetclub.org   **S**
If you can't explain how Golf Croquet differs from Six Wicket Croquet (American or Association regulations), talk with Doug Johnson of the **Chicago Croquet Club**. A member of the 3000-member U.S. Croquet Association, the Chicago Croquet Club shares two lawns with the lawn bowlers in Jackson Park, just south of the Museum of Science and Industry. The club hosts free events, Wednesdays 6 P.M.–10 P.M., in the summer months to introduce people to the joys of whacking balls through wickets (instruction and equipment provided). A $70/season pass admits you to the lawns whenever you want (except when the lawn bowlers are there), but you need to make sure a full member is there. A full membership costs $180/season and allows access to all the equipment. Schedule lawn time with Jason Benson (312/208-1692).

Warren Park
6601 N. Western, 773/742-7888   **FN**
Warren Park also offers croquet as part of its recreational opportunities.

Darts

Windy City Darters
4340 W. Montrose, 773/286-3848, *www.windycitydarters.org*   **NW**
This clearinghouse for dart activities administers league play at over 120 neighborhood bars around the city and hosts tournaments and special events at banquet halls and convention facilities for players of all skill levels. For a ten-week season your team (4–8 players) pays $50. Additionally, individuals pay $21 annual dues and a $15 seasonal fee.

Di's Den
5100 W. Irving Park, 773/736-7170   **NW**
Di's Den hosts one of the largest weekly blind draw tournaments on the North Side on Fridays at 9 P.M. Get there by 8:30 to register. Partners are picked from a hat and may go a few rounds together. Rounds consist of one game of 301, 501, and Cricket and are played "Chicago Format." $5 entrance fee and cash prizes. All skill levels welcome.

Dodgeball and Kickball

SURE, these well-known adult sports and social clubs still sponsor the ever-popular-in-Chicago softball and beach volleyball leagues. And you may be pleasantly surprised to learn they've long since expanded their offerings to include things like floor hockey leagues, poker tournaments, kayaking classes, and ski trips. But you probably didn't know they're also your ticket to the childhood games you thought you'd never play again, but upon 20 seconds of reflection realize that, yeah, would like to play again and, gee, maybe on a weekly basis: dodgeball and kickball. Check out their Web sites to learn more and sign up for a free membership (you pay sport by sport, event by event):

- **Chicago Sport and Social Club**, *www.chicagosportandsocialclub.com*
- **Chicago Sports Monster**, *www.sportsmonster.net/chicago/index.html*
- **Players Sports Group**, *www.playerssports.net*

Dogwalking and Beyond

As there are now whole categories of North Siders who don't go anywhere without their dog in tow and at least two entire books devoted to the subject of you and your pooch in Chicago, we thought we'd highlight just a few recreational opportunities for you and your beloved.

"Bark Park"
Just north of Belmont Harbor along Lake Michigan   N
Unleash your hound on this quarter-mile, fenced-in strip of shoreline where pet owners come year round to let their dogs romp in the surf and run free in the sand. Because this is not officially a beach, the no-dogs-off-leashes on beaches rule doesn't really apply here. Technically, the only off-leash beach in Chicago is a fenced-off area at the north end of Montrose Beach. There's word that this dog-friendly area may be in jeopardy, so stay posted through the park district, dog owners' groups, and pet publications.

Wiggly Field
2645 N. Sheffield   N
This is the only park in the city where dogs can (legally) be off their leashes anywhere, anytime. The park is rigged up with almost as many fences and gates as Statesville to ensure your dog doesn't escape until you're ready to go home. Founded in 1997 as the city's first dog park, it is still considered one of the best with it's dog-level drinking fountain, seasonal activities, and mingling opportunities for singles.

Dog Friendly Areas
The rabidly-growing interest in setting aside some green spaces for dogs to run free and play with their fellows has prompted the Chicago Park District to write a step-by-step booklet on how to create Dog Friendly Areas in under-utilized sections of parks, easements, and land adjacent to el tracks. Pick one up and be prepared! It involves grass roots organizing and major planning with your neighbors or dog group. Once past the hard work of getting your site approved, your group becomes responsible for maintaining, monitoring, cleaning, managing, and fundraising for your very own DFA. There are now DFAs at **Walsh Park** (1722 N. Ashland), **Wicker Park** (1425 N. Damen), **Hamlin Park** (3035 N. Damen), **Margate Park** (4921 N. Marine Drive), and **Coliseum Park** (14th & Wabash). As you might surmise from these addresses, there's also a decent singles scene to be found at many of these parks, too. (Hey, the dogs can't have all the fun.) Dozens more doggie set-asides appear to be in the works by various canine-loving

groups, including one at **Promontory Point** (5491–93 S. South Shore).

If your dog and you make some new friends during the day, maybe you should continue a good thing later that night at **Lemming's** (1850 N. Damen, 773/862-1688). Clean, well-behaved dogs on leashes are welcome at this Wicker Park bar (fewer grooming restrictions for their owners) when it's less crowded, typically Sun.–Thur. Sunday seems to be the busiest of those days, with some regulars referring to it as "Dog Night." Other favorites include the **Marquee Lounge** (1967 N. Halsted) and **Cody's** (1658 W. Barry, 773/528-4050). When grabbing a bite, there's **Kitsch'n on Roscoe**'s backyard patio (2005 W. Roscoe, 773/248-7372), **Cactus**'s streetside patio (1112 N. State, 312/642-5999), and **Cucina Bella** (1612 N. Sedgwick, 312/274-1119 and 642 W. Diversey, 773/868-1119), where dogs get their own bowl of pasta and other royal attentions.

Who Let the Dogs In?

Let's say your spouse or significant other tells you to take the dog for a walk, but while doing so you see some friends in a passing car who tell you to hop in because they have one extra ticket to the White Sox game. But you have the dog! What to do? Bring him/her along to the ballpark and check your pet for $3, and check on your buddy as often as you like during the game. You must call ahead and make reservations (312/674-1000, x. 5503).

Euchre

The Euchre Club of Chicago
P. O. Box 30126, Chicago 60630-0126, 312/458-9010
www.euchrechicago.org   N/FN
Founded in 1990, the gay-and-lesbian-friendly **Euchre Club of Chicago** meets at the not-exclusively-gay-and-lesbian bar **Big Chicks** (5024 N. Sheridan Rd., 773/728-5511, *www.bigchicks.com*) Wed. 7:30 P.M. and Sat. 6 P.M. They also meet at the **Holiday Club**, (4000 N. Sheridan, 773/348-9600) Sun. 6 p.m. $3 buys you two to three hours of competition. After three visits, this social club asks for an annual membership of $15.

Three similar bars in Lakeview/Lincoln Park haunted by the post-college crowd host regular euchre leagues throughout the year that run $40 for a 2-person team for a 7–8-week season. There are prizes, playoffs, and cheap beer specials, too! **Duffy's** (420 ½ W. Diversey, 773/549-9090) gets going Monday nights at 6:30 P.M. and offers 50-cent sliders on top of it all. **Sedgwick's** (1935 N. Sedgwick, 312/337-7900) euchre night begins 7:30 P.M., Tuesdays. Euchre at **McGee's** (950 W. Webster, 773/549-8200) starts at 7 P.M., Mondays, but get there at 6 to start enjoying the $6 all-you-can-eat chili or taco bar.

Fencing

Chicago Fencing Club
Diana Unger, 773/685-2677, *http://chicagofencingclub.com*   **N/FN**
Splitting its time between the **Broadway Armory** (5917 N. Broadway) and the **Discovery Center** (2940 N. Lincoln, 773/348-8120), Diana Unger's **Chicago Fencing Club** provides instruction and competition for fencers of all ages. Annual membership is $100 if you're dropping by the Discovery Center on Sundays (Beginners 10 A.M.–11 A.M., Intermediate 11 A.M.–noon); $120 to practice at the Broadway Armory on Wednesdays and Thursdays (7 P.M.–9:30 P.M.); and $180 for access to both locations. Non-members are invited to fence for $5/session at the Broadway Armory. Classes are about $60 for 6 classes.

European Fencing Club
773/774-1759 (club info.), *http://totheescrime.org/efc*   **FN**
The **European Fencing Club** caters to novice, recreational, and competitive fencers over and under age 15. They meet and train in a gym in the **Jefferson Park Field House** (4922 N. Long, 312/742-7609), Mon. 4 P.M.–6 P.M., Wed. 5:30 P.M.–9:30 P.M., Fri. 6 P.M.–9:30 P.M., and Sat. 10 A.M.–noon. Most hours are for organized activities and lessons, but Fridays 7 P.M.–9:30 P.M. is for open bouting, and Saturdays for recreational fencing.

Football

NOTHING beats a little football on a crisp autumn weekend and, since the local sports teams seem to string together losing season after losing season, why not grab the pigskin yourself and head to one of 156 public football fields maintained by the park district.

If you're on the injured list and want to enjoy a little semi-pro ball—free of agents, endorsements, and contracts—check out the **Chicagoland Football League** (*www.chicagofootball.com*). Three of the leagues seven teams are in the city: The **Chicago Thunder**, which has won six of the last seven seasons, the **Chicago Chargers**, and a new team, the **Chicago Dolphins**. The home stadium for all three teams is Steinmetz High School's **Hanson Stadium** (3030 N. Mobile). In season, watch the Thunder practice at **Amundsen Park** (6200 W. Bloomingdale), Tues. and Thur. at 7 P.M., and the Chargers at **Portage Park** (Irving Park & Central), Wed. at 6:45 P.M. and Sun. at 8:45 A.M.

Golf

YOU won't golf anywhere much cheaper than on the well-kept greens of the Chicago Park District, which maintains one 18-hole course, five 9-hole courses, three driving ranges, and two miniature golf courses. Courses are open daily from dawn to dusk, with lower prices during the off season (Nov. 1–March 31) and after 4 P.M. All golf questions can be answered by the administrators, **Kemper Golf Management** (312/755-3500), or from the **Golf Information Line** (312/245-0909). When not staffed, this phone message even gives a description of each course's distinguishing features and offers 24-hour reservations. Your best bet, though, is the **Chicago Park District Golf** site (*www.cpdgolf.com*), where you can book a tee time and get all the information you need on each course: general description, course architect, photos, prices, amenities, and dress code (shirt required!).

Great courses at great prices accessible to all citizens may be one reason *Golf Digest* named Chicago as "a likely candidate for best golf city in America." Rates for juniors (under 17), seniors (with an annual $5 senior card), and twilight hours are about half the price listed for each course. If you'll be golfing frequently, consider the city's **Advantage Card** (*www.cpdgolf.com/advantage.html*) for a $3 reduction off every game and other perks. Advantage Card holders that play through the winter can join the **Polar Bear Club**. Whoever plays the most golf November through February wins unlimited free golf for the next year.

- **Robert A. Black Course**
Pratt between Western and Ridge, 312/742-7931   FN
9 holes, par 33. $14.50 weekdays/$16 weekends. Club rental, $8. Good for all skill levels.

- **Columbus Park**
500 S. Central, 312/746-5573   W
9 holes, par 35. $13 weekdays/$14.50 weekends. Club rental, $8.

- **Jackson Park**
63rd & Lake Shore Drive, 773/667-0524   S
The CPD's only 18-hole course is considered the best golf value in the area, par 70. $21 weekdays/$24 weekends. Club rental, $14.

- **Marquette Park**
6700 S. Kedzie, 312/747-2761   FSW
9 holes, par 36. $13.75 weekdays/$15 weekends. Club rental, $8. Perhaps the system's most challenging course with water surrounding seven of the nine holes.

- **Sydney R. Marovitz Course**
3600 Recreation (Waveland & the Lake), 773/742-7930   N
Its 9 holes mimic some of the nation's most challenging holes, par 36. $18 weekdays/$21 weekends. Club rental, $8. One of the more difficult courses, but perhaps the most scenic. Try it just after sunrise and finish with breakfast at the adjacent café.

- **South Shore Cultural Center**
71st & South Shore Drive, 773/256-0986   FSE
9 holes, par 33. $13 weekdays/$14.50 weekends. Club rental, $8. Another scenic lakefront course. See p. 39 for more on the South Shore Cultural Center.

More affordable golfing can be found within the **Cook County Forest Preserve System** (*www.forestpreservegolf.com*). The city tacks on a 7% sales tax on the greens fees below. Frequent golfers, seniors, and juniors should investigate the $30 annual golf card, which comes with discounted fees and other benefits. For the typical golfer, it pays for itself in six games; for seniors and juniors, it can pay for itself in two or three games.

- **Billy Caldwell Golf Course**
6200 N. Caldwell, 773/792-1930   FN
9 holes. $15 weekdays, $12 twilight/$17 weekends, $12 twilight. For die-hards, the Caldwell course is modified so that golfers can play in the snow.

- **Edgebrook Golf Course**
5900 N. Central, 773/763-8320   FN
18 holes. $21 weekdays, $14 twilight/$25 weekends, $15 twilight.

- **Indian Boundary Golf Course**
8600 W. Forest Preserve Drive, 773/625-9630   FN
18 holes. $25 weekdays, $18 twilight/$27 weekends, $20 twilight.

Visit **Golf Chicago!** (*www.golfchicago.com*) for information on private and suburban courses, indoor facilities, instruction, and equipment dealers, new and used.

Driving Ranges

Diversey Driving Range
141 W. Diversey, 312/742-7929   N
$7 for a small bucket, $10.50 for a large bucket. Get a Super Saver debit card: $90 for 10 large buckets, $135 for 16 large buckets. This is the star range in the system. It's two-tiered, with covered and heated stalls for winter months. You can also putter around on their miniature golf course. Open daily 8 A.M.–9 P.M.

Jackson Park Driving Range
63rd & Lake Shore Drive, 312/747-2762   S
$6.50 per bucket. Open daily 7 A.M.–10 P.M.

Marquette Park Driving Range
6700 S. Kedzie, 312/747-2761   FSW
$6.50 per bucket, Open daily 10 A.M.– 7 P.M.

Miniature Golf

Diversey
141 W. Diversey, 312/742-7929   N
Not on the suburban amusement park sensation scale, the Lincoln Park location of the Diversey miniature golf course more than makes up for that (at least for most adults). Its 18 holes do have some waterfalls and foot-bridges for scenery. $5.50/kids, $6.50/adults

Douglas Park
1401 S. Sacramento, 312/747-7670   W
The 3-hole learning course with putting green and hitting nets, and the 18-hole mini-golf course are *free*. This is a great excuse to visit this historic, "boulevard" park.

The Green at Grant Park
352 E. Monroe, 312/642-7888   **C**
Another tastefully-tiered and manicured mini-course, these 18 holes can be
topped off with a meal at the adjoining restaurant (full menu, patio dining)
for a lovely outing. Open daily 10 A.M.–10 P.M., May–Oct. $8 adults, $6
children.

South Side YMCA
6330 S. Stony Island, 773/947-0700   **S**
A 20,000-square-foot, 18-hole mini-golf course with trees, flowers, and
waterfalls. $3 kids, $4 adults. Open May–Sept., Mon.–Fri. 11 A.M.–8 P.M.
and Sat.–Sun. 11:30 A.M.–4 P.M. Call ahead—squirrels keep building nests in
the holes, shutting down the course.

Hi-Ball

AN unlikely combination of basketball and trampoline jumping, Hi-Ball
attracts thrill seekers to **Sluggers World Class Sports Bar's Indoor Sports
Facility** (upstairs and separate from the bar—kids are allowed) at 3540 N.
Clark (773/472-9696). Four players try to shoot baskets with a sponge ball
while bouncing around in a cylinder divided into four quadrants by 8-foot-
high netting. Unless you are unusually fit, a ten-minute session for $3/person
will probably be enough. However, the court can be rented for $40/hour if
you have a bunch of friends. In between the aerobically-taxing sessions, you
can cool down with arcade games, video games, and batting cages.

Horseshoes

THEY built the pits, you bring the horseshoes . . .

Archer Park	Grand Crossing Park	Norwood Park
Armour Square Park	Harrison Park	O'Hallaren Park
Ashe Park	Hiawatha Park	Portage Park
Beverly Park	Hoyne Plg. Park	Riis Park
Bosley Plg. Park	Independence Park	Russell Square Park
Brooks Park	Kelvyn Park	Rutherford–Sayre
Calumet Park	Kennedy Park	Senka Park
Chopin Park	LaFollette Park	Shabbona Park
Cooper Park	Lawler Park	Smith Park
Dunbar Park	Marquette Park	Strohacker Park
Dunham Park	Mather Park	Valley Forge Park

Dvorak Park	McGuane Park	Vittum Park
Foster Park	Merrimac Park	Warren Park
Galewood Park	Munroe Park	Welles Park
Gompers Park	Nat King Cole Park	West Pullman Park
		Williams Park

There are only two **NHPA** (National Horseshoe Pitching Association)-sanctioned clubs in the city, and they both play at Welles Park. Visit *www.fourdead.com/midcitychicago.htm* for more information on the **Welles Park Horseshoe Club Thursday Night League.**

Massage

NOT for those who give massages as recreation, but for those who need massages—at a discount—after recreation . . .

Chicago School of Massage Therapy
1300 W. Belmont, 773/880-1397, *www.csmt.com*   N
Book yourself some relaxation time amidst all this activity with a student massage at the **Chicago School of Massage Therapy**. Appointments can be made Mon.–Fri. 9:30 A.M.–6:30 P.M., Sat. 9:30 A.M.–6 P.M., and Sun. 9:30 A.M.–5:30 P.M. Generally, reservations must be made two weeks in advance. No requests for particular gender or level of student masseuses can be made, although all students have successfully completed their first semester. $40 per hour-long massage, 10-session package/$360.

The New School for Massage, Bodywork & Healing
800 N. Wells, 312/888-461-0114, *www.newschoolmassage.com*   C
After an analysis of the massage industry and massage schools, Emmanuel Bistas founded this school in 2002 in an effort to to improve and update both. Through the student clinic on the fourth floor, the public can enjoy one-hour therapeutic massages for $30 by an advanced student supervised by a certified massage therapist.

Origami

CHAOS (Chicago Area Origami Society)
Garfield Park Conservatory, 300 N. Central Park Ave., 312/746-5100
http://home.earthlink.net/~robertcubie/origami/chaos.html   W
Join other paper folders the second Saturday of the month from 1 P.M.–4 P.M.

to fold, create, swap ideas, and socialize. Meetings are open to all ages and all levels, and parents are encouraged to bring their children. If you want to become a regular, membership is $10 annually.

Playgrounds

FOR tykes who have seen it all . . .

Harold's Playlot
53rd and Lake Shore Drive **S**

Designed to accommodate children with disabilities, this large playground with sandbox and sprinkler is dedicated to the late mayor, Harold Washington, a Hyde Park resident.

Indian Boundary Park
2500 W. Lunt, 312/742-7887 **FN**

Just steps away from a zoo (see p. 13), duck-filled lagoon, and a sprinkler, an award-winning playground palace sprawls, bedecked with towers, tires, bridges, slides, and more.

Oz Park
2021 N. Burling, 312/742-7898 **N**

Named for the fantasy land of Chicago writer L. Frank Baum's *The Wonderful Wizard of Oz*, "Dorothy's Playlot" here employed designs by local children to create its wooden kingdom. The park's entrance is fronted by a giant Tin Man statue and there's even an "Emerald Garden."

Pool

UNFORTUNATELY, pool halls in Chicago have been on the wane lately. Break Time burned down, Stix made way for a parking lot, and North Center Lanes—one of Chicago's oldest—was torn down for condos. The owner of the St. Paul, another old-time gem, finally sold the place after a good long run. Yet, there are still a number of places you can crack a rack in the city.

Chris's Billiards
4637 N. Milwaukee, 773/286-4714 **NW**

This place gets a lot of recognition for being in *The Color of Money*, but people sometimes forget why it was featured: because it's the real deal. Smoky; no TV; the jukebox room is cordoned off with meat-locker airlocks—and hustlers will try to take your money. You can't beat it. $5.95/hour weekdays before 6 P.M., $7.25/hour after 6 P.M., every extra person pays $1.80/hour. Individuals practicing alone pay $2.55/hour before 6 P.M., $2.95 after. 47 tables available, including one snooker and five billiard. Open daily 9:30 A.M.–2 A.M. Snack bar, but no alcohol. Tournaments Wednesdays and Sundays.

Lakeview Billiard Cafe

3449 N. Lincoln, 773/871-8400 N

A rare find—a new room in Chicago. Not bad. $5/hour weekdays, $6/hour weekends, every extra player pays $2. From 1 P.M.–7 P.M. on weekdays, $7 per player flat rate. Women play free on Mondays. Fifteen 9-foot tables, snack bar, and pro shop. Open Sun.–Thur. 1 P.M.–1 A.M., Fri.–Sat. 1 P.M.–2 A.M. 9-ball tournaments on Tuesdays.

Marie's Golden Cue

3241 W. Montrose, 773/478-2555 NW

Another room for those who like the game stripped to its essence. No TV, no juke, no nothin'—just pool. Before 6 P.M., $3.75/hour (1 player), $7/hour (2 players), and $1.25/hour for each extra player. After 6 P.M., $6.75/hour (1 player), $8/hour (2 players), and $1.50/hour each extra. Nineteen 9-foot pool tables and 1 billiard table. Open Mon.–Fri. noon–2 A.M., Sat.–Sun. 11 A.M.–2 A.M. Snack bar, cues for sale.

Uno Billiards

3112 W. Lawrence, 773/267-8166 N

This pool hall has a Spanish-sounding name, is located in a Korean neighborhood, and has pictures of Brazilian soccer players on the walls. Go figure. Still, it's an attractive new room. There are ten 4½' x 9' pool tables and two 3-cushion billiard tables—the former roll pretty nice, even though they're not brand-name. Rates are a flat $9/hour, so it's no bargain for solo players, but not bad for groups. The jukebox, a mix of Korean and Euro pop and outdated American club hits, can be grueling. No booze, no snack bar, just vending machines. Open 1 P.M.–1 A.M. Sun.–Fri., 1 P.M.–2 A.M. Sat.

See **Southport Lanes & Billiards** and **Lucky Strike** under "Bowling" (pp. 99–100) for pool in upscale, retro surroundings, and **UIC Bowling** for pool in a campus setting.

Racquetball

FOLLOW the bouncing blue ball to one of four park district racquetball facilities. At $6/hour, you almost can't afford not to play!

Pottawattomie Park
7340 N. Rogers, 773/262-5835   FN
Open weekdays noon–8:30 P.M., weekends 10 A.M.–3 P.M.

Warren Park
6621 N. Western, 312/742-7888   FN
Open weekdays 3 P.M.–8 P.M., weekends 10 A.M.–3 P.M.

Washington Park
5531 S. Martin Luther King, 312/747-6823   S
Open weekdays 9 A.M.–9 P.M., weekends 9 A.M.–3 P.M.

West Lawn Park
4232 W. 65th, 312/747-7029   FSW
Open weekdays 8 A.M.–9 P.M., weekends 10 A.M.–3 P.M.

Running

THESE 33 parks have either oval or straight away tracks for the disciplined or casual runner, so you'll want to keep them in mind if they're in your neighborhood or you want a change of scenery. But, come on, everyone knows you can't beat the miles of runway along Lake Michigan. If you need any confirmation of this, or just want to enjoy *en masse* people watching, park yourself along the lakefront path between say 6 and 10 in the morning on a weekend and watch dozens of running clubs and training sessions go by, 6 to 16 runners in a pack.

Avalon Park	Grand Crossing Pk.	Munroe Park
Bessemer Park	Hamilton Park	Nat King Cole Park
California Park	Hayes Park	Norwood Park
Calumet Park	Kilbourn Park	Ogden Park
Chase Park	LaFollette Park	Orr School Park
Douglas Park	Lake Shore Park	Riis Park
Dunbar Park	Lincoln Park	Rowan Park
Ellis Park	Loyola Park	Sherman Park
Foster Park	Mandrake Park	Trumbull Park
Fuller Park	Marquette Park	Union Park
Gage Park	McKinley Park	Wrightwood Plg.

For area race, event, training, and club information, join the **Chicago Area Runners Association** (*www.cararuns.org*). Their publication *Chicago Runner Magazine* can be found in every issue of *Chicago Athlete* (see p. 440).

Fleet Feet Sports Fun Runs
4555 N. Lincoln, 773/271-3338, *www.fleetfeetchicago.com*   **N**
210 W. North, 312/587-3338   **C**
Many sporting goods and athletic shoe stores hold public events, but **Fleet Feet**'s are among the best. Their free leisurely, monthly Chicago history fun runs wind along a 4–6-mile route, stopping frequently along the way to note historic and cultural points of interest. Past theme runs have included "The Great Fire of 1871," "A Run to Wrigley," and "A Run to Riverview." They also sponsor such events as the **Elvis is Alive 5K**, voted one of the top wackiest races in the country by *Runner's World*.

Sailing

RENT a sailboat from the **Chicago Park District** at **Montrose Beach** (601 W. Montrose, 312/742-0600) for $20–$25/hour, $40/hour for catamarans, noon–8 P.M. weekdays, 9 A.M.–8 P.M. weekends. For more park district harbor and boating activities, including well-developed sailing instruction programs for children, adults, and people with disabilities, call the CPD's **Rainbow Fleet** (312/745-1700) at **Burnham Harbor** (1500 Linn White Drive). Other public access points to Lake Michigan are at the CPD facilities at **Belmont Harbor, Calumet Harbor, Chicago Harbor, Diversey Harbor, Jackson Park Harbor**, and **59th St. Harbor**.

Sail Chicago
312/409-9600, *www.sailchicago.org*
This non-profit, volunteer-run community sailing organization has been offering Chicagoans an extensive, low-cost sailing program and a serious alternative to private boat ownership since 1959. The $75–$125 annual membership provides access to affordable lessons at all skill levels, inexpensive rental ($20–$75 for 5-hour time slots), racing events, and social activities like pleasure cruises. Their fleet of 14 boats is stored at **Belmont**, **Montrose**, and **Monroe Harbors**.

Chicago Sailing Club
Belmont Harbor, 773/871-SAIL, *www.chicagosailingclub.com*   **N**
Does sailing take you away to where you always heard it could be? Do you

enjoy Christopher Cross songs? Did you know that you could rent a sailboat ($35–$90/hour) and take it solo on Lake Michigan? First you have to be certified with a 15-hour class, but once that is done ($395 plus $85 for certificate), if the wind is right you can rent a J22 or J30 and sail away!

Windy City Sailing
Belmont Harbor, 773/868-0096, *www.windycitysailing.com*   **N**
If you and some friends just want to while away a few hours and leave the skippering to others, call **Windy City Sailing**. Six friends in a boat with nothing but food, drink, and the Chicago skyline to worry about make for an indulgent summertime escapade. Go during the day to soak up the sun or plan around the Wednesday and Saturday evening fireworks displays at Navy Pier. Three-hour minimum ($75/hour weekdays, $85/hour weekends, up to $125/hour for 4th of July fireworks and special events).

If you're in the market for a sailboat, **Darfin Yachts, Ltd.** (6003 S. Archer, 773/582-8113) and **Sailboat Sales Co.** (2500 S. Corbett, 312/225-2046) are good bets for used vessels.

Shuffleboard

WHILE shuffleboard courts are found at the following parks, park district equipment may be unreliable. Call ahead to see what the park nearest you offers.

Avalon Park	**McGuane Park**	**Sr. Citizens Park**
Columbus Park	**Orr School Park**	**Union Park**
LaFollette Park	**Piotrowski Park**	**Valley Forge Park**
Lake Meadows Park	**Rosenblum Park**	**Warren Park**
Loyola Park	**Schreiber Park**	

Skateboarding

IN the old days, like a few years ago, if you wanted to see crazy kids do extreme skateboard stunts or work up to them, you had to look no farther than your neighborhood high school or park or, really, any cool ramp, hand rail, or sets of stairs lurking around you. When they made their way downtown, they'd be at the seawalls by the Shedd Aquarium. As you can see, they're still there (and ranking and sharing info. on these local spots on Web sites like *www.chiskate.com*), but they also have some serious new facilities built by the Chicago Park District.

The two major Chicago skateparks each have 20,000 square feet of spines, pyramids, bowls, launches, quarter pipes, rails, and fun boxes for stunt skateboarders and in-line skaters of varying skills. There are no fees, no supervision, no protective gear required (parents, cling to your children), and no bikes allowed. Open until dark and weather permitting.

Burnham Skate Park
31st Street Beach, 31st & Lake Shore Drive   **S**
Been there, done that; "slow and low," is what the superstars say, but that just might make it perfect for you or your kids. Or, make it an outing—take the bike ride, have a swim, and, while watching the skateboarders, enjoy **Robinson's No. 1 Ribs**, which has a concession there.

Wilson Skate Park
Wilson & Lake Shore Drive   **N**
Newer than the 31st Street skatepark, the skaters say the designers got this one right, christening it the primo spot in the city and gracing it with their presence any time it's open, and sometimes when it's not.

But that's not all . . . the CPD has installed four skateparks about one-fourth of the size of these major ones in neighborhood parks: **Rowan Park** (11546 S. Avenue "L"), **Vittum Park** (5010 W. 50th), **West Lawn Park** (4233 W. 65th), and **Warren Park** (6601 N. Western). There may be a $2 fee.

Skating, Ice

INEXPENSIVE recreation for those who refuse to hibernate! Skating at either of these high-profile rinks rewards you with great views. Try it after work for a few magical moments at dusk or combine it with a day of downtown shopping, errands, or sightseeing.

Daley Bicentennial Plaza
337 E. Randolph, 312/742-7648   **C**
Outdoor ice skating during winter months in Grant Park, just a breeze away from the lake. Open weekdays 10 A.M.–10 P.M., weekends 10 A.M.–5 P.M. Admission is $2/adults, $1/children under 14, and rental is $2/adults, $1/children. Free admission and rental for seniors.

McCormick Tribune Ice Skating Rink at Millennium Park
55 N. Michigan, 312/742-5222   **C**
This free, outdoor seasonal skating on a 16,000-square-foot rink may only

be (and that's a big maybe) rivaled by the skating at New York's Rockefeller Center. The streetside view of Michigan Avenue and the entire skyline is breathtaking, particularly at night. Skate rental is $5 for adults, $4 for children. There's even a warming center with lockers and bathrooms and a nearby café. Open 7 days/week 10 A.M.–8 P.M. or 10 P.M.

For year-round indoor skating...

McFetridge Sports Center
3843 N. California, 773/478-2609   N
This park district facility offers a variety of day and evening open skate sessions for different ages. Call for times or pick up a current schedule. $5 admission, $4 children, $3 skate rental.

The Chicago Park District and Cook County recently joined forces to build several new neighborhood skating rinks. These new rinks host occasional lessons, clinics, and competitions. Some double as in-line skating rinks in the summer. Typical skating sessions run Mon.–Fri. 3 P.M.–5 P.M. and 5:30 P.M.–7 P.M.; Sat.–Sun. 12:30 P.M.–7:30 P.M. Skating is free Mon.–Thur., and $3 all other times. Skate rental, $3.

Caldwell Woods	**Mt. Greenwood Park**	**Warren Park**
McKinley Park	**Riis Park**	**West Lawn Park**
Midway Plaisance	**Rowan Park**	

When choosing where to go, keep in mind the fireplace in the fieldhouse and the cheap tobogganing at **Caldwell Woods** (see p. 125). The **Midway Plaisance** has a nifty bi-level warming house with its ice rink, that's an extra reason to make the trip to Hyde Park if you're not already there. This joint construction between the CPD and the U of C was designed with limestone and granite to harmonize with the rest of the campus architecture, but also has vertical metal panels on one side that resemble icicles. It includes a rooftop observation deck and a café.

Skating, In-Line

THE lakefront in-line skating faction long ago became as formidable as the running and biking contingents. To participate in their glory without your own in-line skates, visit one of these rental sites:

Windward Sports (3315 N. Clark, 773/248-4970) charges $15/day during the week and $20/day on weekends. **Bike Chicago** (800/915-BIKE) offers lakefront convenience with its three stands at North Avenue Beach, Oak Street Beach, and Navy Pier for $8.75/hour, $29/4 hours, $34/day, $44/2 days. **Londo Mondo** (1100 N. Dearborn, 312/751-2794, and 2148 N. Halsted, 773/327-2218, *www.londomondo.com*) rent their in-line skates for $7/hour and $20/day. They are Chicago's first and only remaining in-line skate pro shop, making them super-knowledgeable and also a great place to get older models at reduced prices.

Get inline...Chicagoland!
www.getinlinechicagoland.com
The definitive outpost of local in-line skating information! Visit their Web site and join their free "club" of 600+ members by submitting your e-mail to receive updates and info. The site covers fitness, recreational, and racing events, offers route and trail suggestions, and suggests skate-friendly restaurants, among other useful things. Among the favorite eateries are the beachfront places (duh!), and **Mario's Italian Lemonade** (p. 187), the **Billy Goat Tavern** (p. 202), **Star of Siam** (p. 232), the **South Loop Club** (p. 202), and **Moon Palace** (p. 159). Organized group skates include a Tuesday recreational and fitness skate that meets at North Avenue Beach at 7 P.M. and a "Road Rave" that meets the first and third Friday each month at Daley Plaza.

Skating, Roller

THOUGH slick and speedy, in-line skating will never entirely replace the four-wheeled old-timer and the charm of a wooden rink.

The Rink Fitness Factory
1122 E. 87th, 773/221-2600, *http://therinkchgo.com*   **FSE**
Adults aged 21+, adults aged 27+, families, teens, and children all have designated skating sessions throughout the week at this classic roller rink, now going on 30 years in business. The first Monday of the month is a gospel skate, Saturday night is saved for teen disco, and the Saturday midnight Ramble for those over 18 rambles until 4 o'clock Sunday morning. Prices for sessions vary from $6–$10 for 3 4 hours of skating, and sometimes include rental, which is otherwise $1. Only roller skates are rented here, but in-line skates are welcome.

Grant Park (331 E. Randolph), **Daley Bicentennial Plaza** (337 E. Randolph), and **Norwood Park** (5801 N. Natoma) have large ice rinks converted for roller and in-line skating in warmer months. Norwood Park in particular is a good spot to catch some roller hockey action.

Skiing, Cross Country

CROSS country skiing is permitted anywhere in the Cook County Forest Preserves—except its golf courses—and the city parks. Large tracts of green space on city maps are a clue to Forest Preserve boundaries: On the South Side, that's the area east of Western Avenue between about 80th and 90th. Up north, it's the area on either side of the Chicago River from about Foster Avenue to Touhy. Or, try braving the lakefront! The following city parks are best equipped for cross country skiers:

Burnham Park	Horner Park	Ogden Park
Douglas Park	Humboldt Park	O'Hallaren Park
Dyett Rec. Center	Jackson Park	Olympia Park
Eugene Field Park	Lincoln Park	Oriole Park
Gage Park	Loyola Park	Peterson Park
Garfield Park	Mann Park	River Park
Grant Park	Marquette Park	Shabbona Park
Hale Park	McKinley Park	Washington Park
Hamilton Park	Mt.Greenwood Park	Wentworth Park
Hayes Park	Norwood Park	

Skiing, Downhill

IF you think "Ski Chicago!" is some kind of Polish joke, think again. The **Chicago Metropolitan Ski Council** (*http://skicmsc.com*) represents more than 80 Midwest ski clubs, many within the city. Finding someone to ski with is easy, finding a place to ski is a lot more challenging. Though you won't find any slopes in the city limits, you can find good deals on equipment at the **Viking Ski Shop** (3422 W. Fullerton, 773/276-1222, *www.vikingski.com*). All inclusive ski rental packages run $30 for the first day, $19 for the second day, and then just $10 for each additional day; children's equipment runs $20, $34, and $46 for 1, 2, and 3-day rentals.

Sledding and Tobogganing

USUALLY, as the snow begins to fly, so do the Cook County Forest Preserve budget miscalculations. Budget deficits may threaten to close the toboggan slides from year to year, but suburban **Swallow Cliffs** and the **Jensen Slides** at **Caldwell Woods** (Devon and Milwaukee, 773/631-7657) remain open. For now, as long as there's enough snow (about a 4" base) and it's cold enough (holding steady below freezing for at least 48 hours), you can't beat tobogganing for family fun. Rent toboggans for $3/hour, or pay only $1 per day for a chute pass if you own your own. Slides are open Fri. 2 P.M.–9 P.M. and Sat.–Sun. 10 A.M.–9 P.M., and 2 P.M.–9 P.M. weekdays during the end-of-the-year school holidays. There's often a fireplace going and hot chocolate for sale in the fieldhouse, but **Superdawg** (p. 180) across the street also makes a great post-sledding treat for kids and grown-ups!

Though the slides at **Dan Ryan Woods** (87th & Western, 773/233-3766) have been closed indefinitely, there is still plenty of good sledding both there and around the **Jensen Slides**. Smaller bumps around the city such as **Cricket Hill** (Montrose and Lake Michigan), **Devil's Hill** (about 2600 North along the lake across from Diversey Harbor), the **Horner Park** hill (California between Irving and Montrose), the **Indian Boundary Park** hill (2500 W. Lunt), and the **Rainey Park** hill (4350 W. 79th) always attract an enthusiastic group of kids with sleds.

Soldier Field
1410 S. Museum Campus, 312/235-7000, *www.soldierfield.net*   **C**
For special occasion sledding with fantastic lakefront and skyline views, head to the new 17-acre grounds of the renovated Soldier Field. One of its perks is a 33-foot sledding hill with a 220-foot slope behind the stadium that's open from dawn to dusk when weather allows, though a snowmaking machine is on hand to back up Mother Nature.

Soccer

HAVING played host to World Cup games in 1994, Chicago, a softball and basketball kind of town, can now boast its soccer credentials to the world. Dave Litterer's *Chicago's Soccer History* (*http://www.sover.net/~spectrum/ chicago.html*), however, points out that Chicago's soccer roots go back to the late 1800s, making the city one of only a handful of historic soccer bastions in the country. Residents have been taking advantage of the soccer fields at 157 city parks for years. Call your regional park district office (p. 135) to join a league near you or scout local parks for pick up games.

Spectating and Fandom

IF you're a fan of one of our major sports teams, there's probably not much more we can tell you about them. Visit their Web sites and indulge your passion:

- **Chicago Bears**, *www.chicagobears.com*
- **Chicago Blackhawks**, *www.chicagoblackhawks.com*
- **Chicago Bulls**, *www.nba.com/bulls*
- **Chicago Cubs**, *www.cubs.com*
- **Chicago White Sox**, *www.whitesox.com*

What we can say is if you're restless for something new in this department, nostalgic for sports free of excess commercialism, hype, and contract negotiations, or too broke to attend a major sporting event, you may do well to check out one of these local teams:

- **Chicago Blaze** (*www.nwbl.com/blaze*)
  A member of the National Women's Basketball League (NWBL), the Blaze's home games are at the Merner Field House of North Central College in suburban Naperville.
- **Chicago Fire** (*www.chicago-fire.com*)
  A member of Major League Soccer (MLS), watch their home games at Soldier Field.
- **Chicago Gems** (*www.chicagogems.com*)
  This women's baseball club is about to join the Great Lakes Women's Baseball League as an apprentice team.

Concessions to Fans

While Cubs fans will grumble about the cost of beer, hot dogs, cotton candy, pretzels, beer, peanuts, pop corn, and beer at Wrigely Field, they'll still fork over half a paycheck during a game to keep themselves sated. Their bags are inspected at the gate to make sure they're not sneaking the illicit "outside food and drink" into the ballpark. Perhaps the White Sox owners know their fans would never tolerate that or maybe they're just more respectful of their fans' pocketbooks. In any case, anyone attending a Sox game or concert at U.S. Cellular Field is allowed to bring 1 liter of their own bottled water and a small transparent plastic bag with their own food into the park. Hey Bleacher Bums, think what you could save in one season's worth of concessions! At least consider the extra change that gives you for more beer. Time to switch teams? Or ballparks?

- **Chicago Storm** (*www.chicagostorm.net*)
A member of the Major Indoor Soccer League (MISL). The inaugural season begins Oct. 2004; home games are played at the UIC pavilion.
- **Chicago Wheelchair Bulls** (*www.wheelchairbulls.com*)
The wheelchair basketball team of the Chicago bulls plays at Centennial Park in Addison, Illinois.
- **RIC Cubs** (*www.richealthfit.org/programs/softball.htm*)
The Rehabilitation Institute of Chicago's (RIC) wheelchair softball team has one of the best such teams in the country. Their home field is the state-of-the-art, specially designed wheelchair softball diamond in California Park (California & Irving Park).
- **Chicago Wolves** (*www.chicagowolves.com*)
A professional hockey team in the American Hockey League (AHL) that plays at the Allstate Arena in suburban Rosemont.

Stargazing

FOR information on what's presently going on in the heavens and what we can see in our little corner of the night sky, call the **Adler Planetarium** information line (312/922-STAR) and select the "Summary of the Current Sky" option from its recorded message. We all know, however, that the urban atmosphere permits us access to only a small portion of our sky niche. Astronomy buffs can turn next to the **Chicago Astronomical Society**—the world's oldest amateur astronomical society, founded in 1862—whose Web site (*www.chicagoastro.org*) lists many opportunities for free telescopic stargazing at the **Adler Planetarium** (1300 S. Lake Shore Drive), **North Park Village Nature Center** (5801 N. Pulaski, 312/744-5472), and other area locations.

Swimming

WITH 15 miles of beaches lining a 26-mile stretch of Chicago's shoreline and the Park District's 49 outdoor and 42 indoor pools, every Chicagoan and visitor is just minutes away from a cool—and free—dip.

Lakefront Beaches

Lakefront beaches open officially (with lifeguards on duty) the Friday of Memorial Day weekend and close the Monday of Labor Day weekend, staying open daily, weather and bacteria-count permitting, 9 A.M.–9:30 P.M.

The **Beaches and Pool Unit** (312/742-4920) can answer further questions. Also, note: some of the smaller "beaches" are not patrolled. You might consider them sandy stretches of public shoreline.

Ashe Park	Juneway Terr. Beach	Pratt Beach & Park
Burnham Park	Lane Beach & Park	Promontory Pt. Pk.
Calumet Park	Lincoln Park	Rainbow Beach
Columbia Ave. Beach	Loyola Park	Rogers Ave. Beach
Fargo Avenue Beach	Montrose Beach	South Shore
Hartigan Bch. & Park	North Avenue Beach	31st Street Beach
Howard St. Beach	North Shore Beach	12th Street Beach
Jackson Park	Northerly Island Park	
Jarvis Ave. Bch. & Pk.	Oak Street Beach	

Calling All Polar Bears

The annual New Year's Day Polar Bear Swim takes place at noon at North Avenue Beach. All that's required to fully participate is to run with the crowd into the water, dunk yourself, and refrain from whining. Any longer lingering and frolicking is up to you! Wear a bathing suit under your clothes, 'cause there's no unlocked place to change at the beach in winter. According to organizers, wet suits don't count and "spare them the nudity."

Inland Beaches

These two large, historic parks on Sacramento Boulevard, important nodes in an early Chicago plan for a grand, interconnecting park and boulevard system have their own lakes and small beaches for swimming. The lakes are large enough to interest older kids and shallow enough for younger ones. Both parks have distinguished, old fieldhouses and other remarkable buildings on the park grounds as well as enough other activities to make a full day's excursion of it. Open Memorial Day through Labor Day, 9 A.M.–dusk. Free.

- **Douglas Park**, 1400 S. Sacramento, 312/747-0832   **W**
  They also have a new, free, miniature golf course (p. 113).

- **Humboldt Park**, 1400 N. Sacramento, 312/742-7549   **W**

Outdoor Pools

The Park District's outdoor pools begin their season in mid-June and close the Monday of Labor Day weekend.

Abbott Park	Gage Park	Piotrowski Park
Ada Park	Garfield Park	Portage Park
Altgeld Park	Gompers Park	Pulaski Park
Armour Square Park	Grand Crossing Park	Riis Park
Austin Park	Hale Park	River Park
Avalon Park	Hamlin Park	Russell Square Pk.
Avondale Park	Humboldt Park	Sherman Park
Bessemer Park	Jefferson Park	Sherwood Park
Bogan Park	Kennedy Park	Smith Park
California Park	McKinley Park	Taylor Park
Carver Park	Meyering Plg.	Trumbull Park
Chase Park	Mt. Greenwood Park	Tuley Park
Columbus Park	Norwood Park	Union Park
Curie Park	Oakdale Park	Washington Park
Douglas Park	Ogden Park	Wentworth Gardens
Dvorak Park	Palmer Park	Wrightwood Park
Franklin Park		

Portage Park's Olympic-size outdoor swimming pool
was built for the 1954 Pan-American Games.

Indoor Pools

Free swimming time is scheduled for everyone at the park district's indoor pools: children, teens, families, women and men (together and separate), and lap swimmers, though in some neighborhoods lap swimmers are now charged about $20 for a 20-swim pass. Contact your neighborhood park for a seasonal time table. Swim clubs, swim teams, swimming lessons for all ages, aquafitness classes, and water polo are also available at many of these parks for no cost or a very low fee. The pools at the public high schools are also available at certain hours for community use.

Altgeld Park	Harrison Park	Portage Park
Amundsen School	Hayes Park	Ridge Park
Austin Town Hall	Independence Park	Robeson School

Blackhawk Park	Jackson Natat. Pk.	Shabbona Park
Bowen High	Juarez School	Sheridan Park
Carver School	Kelly Park	Stanton Park
Chgo. H.S. for Agr. Sci.	Kosciuszko Park	Sullivan School
Clemente Park	LaFollette Park	Washington Park
Curie Park	Leone Park & Bch.	Welles Park
Eckhart Park	Mann Park	Wentworth Park
Englewood High	Mather Park	West Pullman
Foster Park	McGuane Park	Westinghouse Sch.
Gill Park	Orr School Park	Whitney Young
Harris Rec. Ctr.	The Park @ NTA	School

Water Slides and Parks

Two city parks have noteworthy waterslides for their pools—a perfect refreshment for Chicago's inevitable scorching summer afternoons: **Washington Park Aquatic Center** (5531 S. Russell Drive, 773/256-1897) has a 36-footer and **Norwood Park** (5801 N. Natoma, 773/631-4893) boasts one 22-feet high and 110-feet long, with 4–5 ample curves.

Whealan Aquatic Center
6200 W. Devon, 773/775-1666
Located in a scenic, woodsy alcove of a Cook County Forest Preserve, the Whealan pool and water park are easy to get to and feel like a real escape from the city. The center includes a graduated-entry pool, two types of water

Public Performance Art

Our newest city park, **Millennium Park** (Michigan & Monroe), has an avant-garde installation the city is already enjoying splashing around in. The Crown Fountain—two 50-foot high, glass block towers at opposite ends of a shallow reflecting pool come alive with alternating video images of real Chicagoans' faces (from a stored collection of 1,000). Water continually cascades from the top of each tower into the pool. Then, every thirteen minutes, the eyes will blink, the mouths will pucker up, and a gushing arc of water will pour seemingly from the image's mouth before a new Chicagoan's face appears! Apparently intended by Spanish architect Jaume Plensa as a place for quiet reflection that would lure people into the park from Michigan Avenue, this has now become the coolest water attraction kids can imagine. The attention of passerbys will in reality be captured by soaking wet children (and plenty of adults) truly enjoying Millennium Park as if it were their own front yard.

slides, a playground unit with built-in sprinklers and water jets, a baby pool, and a sandy area. Amenities like the renovated historic bathhouse, well-stocked concession stand, first-aid station, free parking, and a surrounding lawn perfect for picnicking and keeping an eye on the kids make this a comfortable place to spend the day while entertaining all members of the family. Open daily during the summer 1 P.M.–8 P.M. Admission is $5/person, $3/ages 4–12, free for those 3 and under. Free parking.

Tennis

ALMOST 150 park sites around the city have a total of some 700 free outdoor courts, many of which are lit for nighttime play. A phone call to your regional park district office (p. 135) will match you with a nearby court.

Chicago Park District Tennis Association
312/458-0618, *http://eteamz.active.com/cpdta/*
Since 1943, the **Chicago Park District Tennis Association (CPDTA)**, an independent, non-profit, volunteer organization, has been using the park courts to promote competitive tennis throughout the city. Their weekend summer league of 50 or so teams play on over 40 courts across the city. Women play on Saturday mornings, men on Sundays. Team fee is $75. Call their hotline above for more information and to put yourself on the list for next season.

The Park District's better tennis courts sit along the lakefront, are lit for night play, and cost $5–$16 hour. Reserve the day of or the day before only, or just show up. Call for off-season times.

- **Diversey**, 312/742-7821   N
  $16/hour. Open daily 7 A.M.–7 P.M.

- **Grant Park North** (near Randolph), 312/742-7650   C
  $7/hour. Open 8 A.M.–10 P.M. Mon.–Fri., 8 A.M.–5 P.M. Sat.–Sun. The courts on the south end of Grant Park near Balboa are first come, first served (so to speak) and are free of charge.

- **Waveland**, 312/742-7674   N
  $5/hour. Open daily 7 A.M.–11 P.M.

Mid-Town Tennis Club
2020 W. Fullerton, 773/235-2300, *www.midtowntennisclub.com*   N
Mid-Town opened in 1969 as the first club in any major U.S. city specifi-

cally designed for tennis, and it continues to receive industry accolades for its facility and programs. If you live and breathe tennis, see what you can do about joining. If you just want to improve your game without expensive lessons, get yourself initiated for the drop-in matinee drill and open play session for all levels, Mon.–Fri., noon–4 P.M. September through May, the activation fee is $100; it drops to $50, June through August. Thereafter, you pay $25 per visit. No reservations necessary.

Ultimate Frisbee

ULTIMATE Chicago (*www.ultimatechicago.org*) is a non-profit organization that promotes and coordinates Ultimate Frisbee games, leagues, clinics, and special events for over 1,000 players in the Chicago metro area. Through them you can find out about the long-standing **Chicago Ultimate Summer League (CUSL)**, the newer **Bring Your Own Team (BYOT)** fall league, and others. League fees run $25–$50 and cover the costs of renting the fields; games are played at **Midway Plaisance**, **Washington Park**, **Jackson Park**, **Montrose Beach**, **Foster Beach**, and **Bunker Hill** in the Caldwell Woods Forest Preserve.

This is an organized bunch that even keeps good tabs on local pick-up games for Frisbee buffs: Sundays, 2:30 P.M., year-round at **Horner Park** (California & Irving); Tuesdays in winter at 7:30 P.M. at **Clarendon Park** (Clarendon & Montrose); Tuesdays in summer at 7:30 P.M. on **Montrose Beach**, Thursdays at 5:30 P.M., May–Sept. by the Petrillo Music Shell in **Grant Park**; and Thursdays at 8 P.M., year-round at **Revere Park** (Irving Park & Campbell).

Volleyball

Beach Volleyball

Yes, it's true, Chicago is a stop on the Professional Volleyball Tour. The reason is **North Avenue Beach** (North Avenue and the lake), a kind of magnificent mile of beach volleyball. If you want to play among the swarming masses, better reserve a court well in advance. $5 gets you a couple poles and two hours of sand and sun. If you need a net and/or a ball, those are just $5 each as well. Free courts are available on a first come, first served basis, but you'll have better luck finding an open spot at **Montrose**

Beach (Montrose and the lake). Rental prices for balls and nets are the same. If you have your own net and ball, the park district sets up poles only at **Foster Beach** (Foster and the lake) and **Hollywood Beach** (Ardmore and the lake). Call 312/74-BEACH between May and September for more information. For selected updates on lakefront tournaments, clinics, and other items of interest to the outdoor volleyball community, visit **Chicago Lakefront Volleyball** (*www.chlfvball.com*).

Outdoor Park District Courts

160 Chicago Parks have either indoor or outdoor facilities for volleyball. Call your regional office (p. 135) for the location nearest you. In addition, the park district seems dedicated to adding new sand volleyball courts every year. The following parks currently offer sand volleyball:

- **Beverly Park**, 2460 W. 102nd, 312/747-6024   FSW
- **Hayes Park**, 2936 W. 85th, 312/747-6177   FSW
- **Kennedy Park**, 11320 S. Western, 312/747-6198   FSW
- **Munroe Park**, 2617 W. 105th, 312/747-6561   FSW
- **Pasteur Park**, 5825 S. Kostner, 312/747-6597   SW
- **Rainey Park**, 4350 W. 79th, 312/747-6630   FSW
- **Wildwood Park**, 6950 N. Hiawatha, 312/742-7848   FN
- **Frank J. Wilson Park**, 4630 N. Milwaukee, 312/742-7616   NW

Indoor Volleyball

Almost every city park with a gymnasium offers indoor volleyball as a part of their program. Contact your regional office for more information. **Chicago Volleyball** (*www.chicagovolleyball.info*) keeps current information on competitive and recreational leagues and the more established open gym nights for true "volleyball addicts." Though many organized sports clubs offer full volleyball opportunities, only **Spike Volleyball** (773/467-9963, *www.spikevolleyballchicago.com*) specializes in volleyball—leagues, tournaments, and fun special events.

Broadway Armory Clinic
5917 N. Broadway, *www.volleyballchicagoinc.com*   FN
Fred Vargas's longstanding Latin School clinic is likely relocating here. Then, volleyballers of all levels can resume honing their skills at his Monday-night clinics, 7 P.M.–10 P.M. The cost is $20/year or $12/visit. Surely, you can go more than once! Three levels of play (beginner, interme-

diate, and advance) learn and practice skills through extensive drilling on full-size courts. That's not just passing, setting, hitting, and serving, but 4–2, 6–2, and 5–1 offensive/defensive strategies, rules of the game, and more.

Walking

Chicago Walkers
www.chicagowalkers.com   N
Join the **Chicago Walkers**, a group devoted to racewalking for all fitness levels, Saturdays at 9 A.M., in front of the east entrance of the Lincoln Park Zoo for a three-mile walk. They meet year-round but draw the bigger crowds (35–60 people) in the summer and give free racewalking clinics April through November. All ages welcome. No fee. Check their Web site for other events and activities.

Chapter 6: Walking devotes 32 pages to suggested recreational and informative walking through the streets, neighborhoods, and parks of Chicago.

Whirlyball

Chicago Whirlyball
1800 W. Fullerton, 800/8-WHIRLY
www.whirlyball.com/chicago/chicago.htm   N
This is the crazy pastime you and your friends would have invented if you'd had free reign of the amusement park's bumper cars court. **Whirlyball** has taken this imaginary game and polished it with grown-up resources. Teammates use jai-alai-type scoops to pass a ball back and forth and make "baskets" at opposite ends of the court while driving WhirlyBugs (super-maneuverable bumper cars) in a fun, fast-paced blend of basketball, polo, hockey, and lacrosse. Recruit nine friends and make a night of it. The facility has three 4,000-square-foot courts and is also a sports bar with giant-screen TVs, darts, pool, arcade games, jukebox, bar food, and drink specials. One hour of courttime during the week runs $180, weekends $200. It's not cheap, but if you bring enough for 2 full teams, that's $18–$20 per person. Call to learn of special promotions. Open Mon.–Fri. 10 A.M.–2 A.M., Sat. noon–3 A.M., and Sun. noon–2 A.M.

Yoga

WHILE most private yoga studios charge $10–$25 for a single drop-in class, many city parks offer 12-session beginning courses for $10–$25 total!

Broadway Armory	Harrison Park	Ridge Park
Commercial Club Pk.	Indian Boundary Pk.	Scottsdale Park
Daley Bicent. Plaza	Kennedy Park	Sheil Park
Dvorak Park	Loyola Park	Skinner Park
Gill Park	Marquette Park	So. Shore Cult. Ctr.
Hamlin Park	Mt. Greenwood Park	West Lawn Park

Indian Boundary Park also offers intermediate and advanced courses for $30. More parks are adding yoga classes to their roster all the time, so ask your regional office about new additions. Aerobics, weight-training, and other fitness classes can also be found at most city parks, and some maintain fitness centers, with aerobic machines and weight-lifting equipment. Though some are free, passes for these facilities typically run $20 for 20 visits.

Chicago Park District Information

IN the 1990s, the park district divided the city into six regions: North, Near North, Central, South, Southwest, and Lakefront in order to better promote and develop neighborhood parks. Your region's office or a nearby park are the best places to pick up a seasonal schedule of regional park offerings and the slick and informative new quarterly magazine of the CPD, *@Play*. Don't overlook their extensive non-athletic programming in arts and crafts, dog training, music, dance, drama, lapidary, upholstery, woodshop, GED, ESL, and more. A general directory of the entire park system and its resources is available from the **Chicago Park District's Department of Marketing and Program Support**, (425 E. McFetridge Drive; Chicago, IL 60605, *www.chicagoparkdistrict.com*). The parks mentioned in this chapter, along with their addresses and phone numbers, are listed below alphabetically, within their new region.

North Region

Regional Office:
Warren Park, 6601 N. Western, 773/262-6314   FN

South Side Youth Programs

Bronzeville Children's Museum
Evergreen Plaza-lower level   **FSW**
9600 S. Western, 708/636-9504, *www.bronzevillechildrensmuseum.com*
Located on the lower level of the Evergreen Plaza Shopping Center, the Bronzeville Children's Museum is the only African-American museum of its kind in the country. The museum features and celebrates famous African-Americans with interactive exhibits. The 1,275-square-foot space provides a full range of kid-pleasing programs, movies, crafts, games, and toys.

Children's Health & Executive Club
10928 S. Western, 733/233-4500   **FSW**
The Children's Health & Executive Club (CHEC), opened in 1999, is a unique club concept for children combining physical fitness, nutrition, self-esteem, crafts, healthy life-style instruction, and non-competitive play. The club setting resembles that of a traditional health club with an array of weight training equipment customized for children (safe for those 7 and older). The fitness programs include the warm-up, stretching, aerobics, conditioning, cool down, and rest in a fun and lively atmospher. Everyone's favorite is the climbing rock wall! CHEC offers daily drop-off and pick-up service for select neighborhood schools as well as a full after school program. A full summer program is also available.

Chocolate Chips Theatre Company
Kennedy-King College, 6800 S. Wentworth, 773/994-7400
www.chocolatesweb.org   **FSE**
Located in Kennedy-King College and one of its resident arts programs, the Chocolate Chips Theatre Company has been bringing a range of live Afro-centric theatre to children for over 20 years. Each year, the company invites young writers to submit stories of any topic related to the African-American experience for the annual storytelling festival entitled Words of Wonder (WOW). Raconteurs of national and international acclaim partici-pate with the young storytellers.

Southside Community Arts Center
3831 S. Michigan, 773/373-1026   **S**
Dedicated in 1941 by Eleanor Roosevelt in the landmark Old Comiskey Mansion, the Southside Community Arts Center served as the incubator for talents such as Margaret Burroughs, Gwendolyn Brooks, and Elizabeth Catlett. It continues the tradition as an important Bronzeville arts institution through its classes and workshops for children in painting, drawing, photog-raphy, and graphics arts, and its gallery showcasing young and established artists.

Amundsen School, 5110 N. Damen, 773/534-2320	FN
Avondale Park, 3516 W. School, 773/478-1410	NW
Brands Park, 3259 N. Elston, 773/478-2414	N
Broadway Armory Park, 5917 N. Broadway, 312/742-7502	FN
Brooks Park, 7100 N. Harlem, 773/631-4401	FN
California Park, 3843 N. California, 312/742-7585	N
Chase Park, 4701 N. Ashland, 312/742-7518	N
Chopin Park, 3420 N. Long, 773/685-3247	NW
Dunham Park, 4638 N. Melvina, 773/685-3257	NW
Emmerson Playground, 1820 W. Granville, 773/761-0433	FN
Eugene Field Park, 5100 N. Ridgeway, 773/478-9744	FN
Gale School Park, 7631 N. Ashland, 312/742-7870	FN
Gill Park, 825 W. Sheridan, 312/742-7802	N
Gompers Park, 4222 W. Foster, 773/685-3270	FN
Gross Park, 2708 W. Lawrence, 312/742-7528	FN
Hamlin Park, 3035 N. Hoyne, 312/742-7785	N
Hiawatha Park, 8029 W. Forest Preserve, 312/746-5559	FN
Hollywood Park, 3312 W. Thorndale, 773/478-3482	FN
Horner Park, 2741 W. Montrose, 773/478-3499	N
Independence Park, 3945 N. Springfield, 773/478-3538	NW
Indian Boundary Park, 2500 W. Lunt, 773/764-0338	FN
Jefferson Park, 4822 N. Long, 773/685-3316	FN
Jensen Playground, 4600 N. Lawndale, 312/742-7580	NW
Kilbourn Park, 3501 N. Kilbourn, 773/685-3351	NW
Legion Park, Peterson–Foster @ Chicago River, 312/742-7516	FN
Mather Park, 5941 N. Richmond, 312/742-7501	FN
Mayfair Park, 4550 W. Sunnyside, 773/685-3361	NW
McFetridge Sports Center, 3843 N. California, 773/478-2609	N
Merrimac Park, 6343 W. Irving Park, 773/685-3382	NW
Norwood Park, 5801 N. Natoma, 773/631-4893	FN
Olympia Park, 6566 N. Avondale, 773/631-6861	FN
Oriole Park, 5430 N. Olcott, 773/631-6197	FN
Paschen Playground, 1932 W. Lunt, 773/262-5871	FN
Peterson Park, 5801 N. Pulaski, 312/742-7584	FN
Portage Park, 4100 N. Long, 773/685-7235	NW
Pottawattomie Park, 7340 N. Rogers, 773/262-5835	FN
Revere Park, 2509 W. Irving Park, 773/478-1220	N
River Park, 5100 N. Francisco, 312/742-7516	FN
Rogers Park, 7345 N. Washtenaw, 773/262-1482	FN
Sauganash Park, 5861 N. Kostner, 773/685-6122	FN
Schreiber Playground, 1552 W. Schreiber, 773/262-6741	FN

Shabbona Park, 6935 W. Addison, 773/685-6205	NW
Sheil Park, 3505 N. Southport, 312/742-7826	N
Sullivan School, 6631 N. Bosworth, 773/534-2000	FN
Welles Park, 2333 W. Sunnyside, 312/742-7511	N
Wildwood Park, 6950 N. Hiawatha, 312/742-7856	NW
Frank J. Wilson Park, 4630 N. Milwaukee, 773/685-6454	NW
Wrightwood Park, 2534 N. Greenview, 312/742-7816	N

Near North Region

Regional Office:

Riis Park, 6100 W. Fullerton, 312/746-5363	NW

Altgeld Park, 515 S. Washtenaw, 312/746-5001	W
Amundsen Park, 6200 W. Bloomingdale, 312/746-5003	NW
Augusta Park, 4433 W. Augusta, 312/742-7544	W
Austin Town Hall Park, 5610 W. Lake, 312/746-5006	W
Bell Park, 3020 N. Oak Park, 312/746-5008	NW
Blackhawk Park, 2318 N. Lavergne, 312/746-5014	NW
Churchill Field Park, 1825 N. Damen	N
Clark Playground, 4615 W. Jackson, 312/746-5043	W
Clemente Park, 2334 W. Division, 312/742-7538	W
Columbus Park, 500 S. Central, 312/746-5046	W
Cragin Playground, 2611 N. Lockwood, 312/746-5065	NW
Eckhart Park, 1330 W. Chicago, 312/746-5490	C
Galewood Park, 5729 W. Bloomingdale, 312/746-5089	NW
Garfield Park, 100 N. Central Park, 312/746-5092	W
Haas Playground Park, 2402 N. Washtenaw, 312/742-7552	N
Holstein Park, 2200 N. Oakley, 312/742-7554	N
Humboldt Park, 1400 N. Sacramento, 312/742-7549	W
Kelvyn Park, 4438 W. Wrightwood, 312/742-7547	NW
Kosciuszko Park, 2732 N. Avers, 312/742-7546	NW
LaFollette Park, 1333 N. Laramie, 312/746-5316	W
Mozart Park, 2036 N. Avers, 312/742-7535	NW
Orr Park, 730 N. Pulaski, 312/746-5354	W
Oz Park, 2021 N. Burling, 312/742-7898	N
Pulaski Park, 1419 W. Blackhawk, 312/742-7559	C
Rutherford-Sayre Park, 6871 W. Belden, 312/746-5368	NW
Senior Citizens Park, 2238 N. Oakley, 312/742-7554	N
Seward Park, 375 W. Elm, 312/742-7895	C
Smith Park, 2526 W. Grand, 312/742-7534	W

Stanton Park, 618 W. Scott, 312/742-7896   C
Tilton Playground Park, 305 N. Kostner, 312/746-5399   W
Union Park, 1501 W. Randolph, 312/746-5494   C
Wicker Park, 1425 N. Damen, 312/742-7553   C

Central Region

Regional Office:
Hamilton Park, 513 W. 72nd, 312/747-6174   FSE

Addams Park, 1301 W. 14th, 312/746-5487   C
Armour Square Park, 3309 S. Shields, 312/747-6012   S
Back of the Yards Park, 4922 S. Throop, 312/747-6136   SW
Barrett Park, 2022 W. Cermak, 312/747-6016   W
Bosley Playground Park, 3044 S. Bonfield, 312/747-6026   SW
Commercial Club Park, 1845 W. Rice, 312/742-7558   C
Cornell Square Park, 1809 W. 50th, 312/747-6097   SW
Davis Square Park, 4430 S. Marshfield, 312/747-6107   SW
Dearborn Park, 865 South Park Terrace, 312/742-7648   C
Donovan Playground Park, 3620 S. Lituanica, 312/747-6111   SW
Douglas Park, 1401 S. Sacramento, 312/747-7670   W
Dvorak Park, 1119 W. Cullerton, 312/746-5083   C
Franklin Park, 4320 W. 15th, 312/747-7676   W
Fuller Park, 331 W. 45th, 312/747-6144   S
Harrison Park, 1824 S. Wood, 312/746-5491   W
Hoyne Playground, 3417 S. Hamilton, 312/747-6184   SW
Juarez School, 2150 S. Laflin, 773/534-6900   C
Kelly Park, 2725 W. 41st, 312/747-6197   SW
Lindblom Park, 6054 S. Damen, 312/747-6443   SW
McGuane Park, 2901 S. Poplar, 312/747-6497   SW
McKinley Park, 2210 W. Pershing, 312/747-6527   SW
Memorial Playlot Park, 149 W. 73rd, 312/747-7640   FSE
Moran Playground, 5727 S. Racine, 312/747-6560   SW
Ogden Park, 6500 S. Racine, 312/747-6572   SW
The Park at NTA, 55 W. Cermak, 312/747-1615   C
Piotrowski Park, 4247 W. 31st, 312/747-6608   SW
Sheridan Park, 910 S. Aberdeen, 312/746-5369   C
Sherman Park, 1301 W. 52nd, 312/747-6672   SW
Sherwood Park, 5701 S. Shields, 773/256-0926   S
Skinner Park, 1331 W. Adams, 312/746-5560   S
Taylor-Lauridsen Playground, 647 W. Root, 312/747-6729   S

Wentworth Gardens, 3770 S. Wentworth, 312/747-6996	S
Westinghouse School, 3301 W. Franklin, 773/534-6417	W
Whitney Young School, 210 S. Loomis, 312/656-5655	C
Wilson Community Center, 3225 S. Racine, 312/747-7001	SW
John P. Wilson Park, 1122 W. 34th, 312/747-7002	SW
Young Park, 210 S. Loomis, 312/746-5478	C

South Region

Regional Office:

Kennicott Park, 4434 S. Lake Park, 312/747-7138	S

Abbott Park, 49 E. 95th, 312/747-6001	FSE
Anderson Playground Park, 3748 S. Prairie, 312/747-6007	S
Avalon Park, 1215 E. 83rd, 312/747-6015	FSE
Bessemer Park, 8930 S. Muskegon, 312/747-6023	FSE
Bowen High School, 2710 E. 89th, 773/535-6017	FSE
Bradley Park, 9729 S. Yates, 312/747-6022	FSE
Carver Park, 939 E. 132nd, 312/747-6047	FSE
Cooper Park, 11712 S. Ada, 312/747-6096	FSW
Dunbar Park, 300 E. 31st, 312/747-7661	S
Dyett Recreational Center, 513 E. 51st, 312/747-6118	S
Ellis Park, 707 E. 37th, 312/747-0231	S
Englewood High School, 6201 S. Stewart, 535-3600, x. 124	S
Griffith Natatorium, 346 W. 104th, 312/767-7661	FSE
Haines School Park, 247 W. 23rd, 312/747-0291	S
Harris Rec. Center, 6200 S. Drexel, 312/747-7661	S
Lake Meadows Park, 3113 S. Rhodes, 312/747-6287	S
Madden Park, 3800 S. Rhodes, 312/747-6446	S
Mandrake Park, 900 E. Pershing, 312/747-7661	S
Mann Park, 13000 S. Carondolt, 312/747-6457	FSE
Meyering Playground, 7140 S. Martin Luther King, 312/747-6545	FSE
Midway Plaisance Park, 59th & Stony Island, 312/745-2470	S
Don Nash Community Center, 1833 E. 71st, 773/256-0904	FSE
Owens Park, 2032 E. 88th, 312/747-6709	FSE
Palmer Park, 11100 S. Indiana, 312/747-6576	FSE
Pietrowski Park, 9650 S. Avenue "M", 312/747-6607	FSE
Robeson School, 6835 S. Normal, 773/535-3722	FSE
Rosenblum Park, 8050 S. Chapel, 312/747-6459	FSE
Rowan Park, 11546 S. Avenue "L", 312/747-6650	FSE
Russell Square Park, 3045 E. 83rd, 312/747-6651	FSE

Stateway Park, 3658 S. State, 312/747-6707   S
Taylor Park, 41 W. 47th, 312/747-6728   S
Trumbull Park, 2400 E. 105th, 312/747-6759   FSE
Veterans' Memorial Playground, 2820 E. 98th, 312/747-6812   FSE
Washington Park, 5531 S. Martin Luther King, 773/256-1248   S
West Pullman Park, 401 W. 123rd, 312/747-7080   FSE
Williams Park, 2710 S. Dearborn, 312/747-7107   S
Wolfe Playground, 3325 E. 108th, 312/747-7005   FSE
Woodhull Playground, 7340 S. East End, 773/256-1903   FSE

Southwest Region

Regional Office:
Foster Park, 1440 W. 84th, 312/747-6135   FSW

Ada Park, 11250 S. Ada, 312/747-6002   FSW
Archer Park, 4901 S. Kilbourn, 312/747-6009   SW
Auburn Park, 406 W. Winneconna, 312/747-6135   FSE
Beverly Park, 2460 W. 102nd, 312/747-6024   FSW
Bogan Park, 3939 W. 79th, 773/284-6456   FSW
Brainerd Park, 1246 W. 92nd, 312/747-6027   FSW
Brown Memorial Park, 634 E. 86th, 312/747-6063   FSE
Chicago H.S. for Agricultural Studies, 3857 W. 111th, 535-2500   FSW
Curie Park, 4959 S. Archer, 773/284-7124   SW
Dawes Park, 8052 S. Damen, 312/747-6108   FSW
Durkin Park, 8445 S. Kolin, 773/284-7316   FSW
Gage Park, 2411 W. 55th, 312/747-6147   SW
Grand Crossing Park, 7655 S. Ingleside, 312/747-6158   FSE
Hale Park, 6258 W. 62nd, 773/229-1032   SW
Hayes Park, 2936 W. 85th, 312/747-6177   FSW
Kennedy Park, 11320 S. Western, 312/747-6198   FSW
Lawler Park, 5210 W. 64th, 773/284-7328   SW
Marquette Park, 6734 S. Kedzie, 312/747-6469   SW
Minuteman Park, 5940 S. Central, 773/284-0214   SW
Mt. Greenwood Park, 3724 W. 111th, 312/747-6564   FSW
Munroe Park, 2617 W. 105th, 312/747-6561   FSW
Nat King Cole Park, 301 E. 85th, 312/747-6063   FSE
Normandy Playground, 6660 W. 52nd, 773/229-1421   SW
Oakdale Park, 965 W. 95th, 312/747-6569   FSW
O'Hallaren, 8335 S. Honore, 312/747-6570   FSW
Pasteur Park, 5825 S. Kostner, 773/284-0530   SW

Rainey Park, 4350 W. 79th, 773/284-0696	FSW
Ridge Park, 9625 S. Longwood, 312/747-6639	FSW
Scottsdale Playground, 4620 W. 83rd, 773/284-1826	FSW
Senka Park, 5656 S. St. Louis, 312/747-7632	SW
Strohacker Park, 4347 W. 54th, 312/747-6723	SW
Tuley Park, 501 E. 90th, 312/747-6763	FSE
Valley Forge Park, 7001-7131 W. 59th, 773/229-0812	SW
Vittum Park, 5010 W. 50th, 773/284-6022	SW
Wentworth Park, 5625 S. Mobile, 312/747-6993	SW
West Lawn Park, 4233 W. 65th, 773/284-2803	SW

Lakefront Region

Regional Office:
South Shore Cultural Center

7059 S. South Shore Drive, 773/256-0149	FSE

Ashe Beach Park, 2701 E. 74th, 312/745-1479	FSE
Berger Park, 6205 N. Sheridan, 312/742-7871	FN
Burnham Park, 425 E. McFetridge, 312/747-6187	C
Calumet Park, 9801 S. Avenue "G", 312/747-6039	FSE
Clarendon Park, 4501 N. Clarendon, 312/742-7512	N
Columbia Beach Park, 1040 W. Columbia, 312/742-7857	FN
Daley Bicentennial Plaza, 337 E. Randolph, 312/742-7648	C
Fargo Avenue Beach Park, 1300 W. Fargo, 312/742-7857	FN
Foster Avenue Beach, Foster, 5200 N) and the lake, 312/742-5121	FN
Grant Park, 331 E. Randolph, 312/742-7648	C
Hartigan Park and Beach, 1031 W. Albion, 312/742-7857	FN
Howard Beach Park, 7519 N. Eastlake, 312/742-7857	FN
Jackson Park, 6401 S. Stony Island, 773/256-0903	S
Jarvis Beach and Park, 1208 W. Jarvis, 312/742-7857	FN
Juneway Terr. Beach and Park, 7751 N. Eastlake, 312/742-7857	FN
Lake Shore Park, 808 N. Lake Shore Drive, 312/742-7891	C
Lane Beach and Park, 5915 N. Sheridan, 312/742-7857	FN
Leone Park and Beach, 1222 W. Touhy, 773/262-8605	FN
Lincoln Park, 2045 Lincoln Park West, 312/742-7726	N
Loyola Park and Beach, 1230 W. Greenleaf, 773/262-8605	FN
Margate Park, 4921 N. Marine Drive, 312/742-7522	FN
Montrose Beach, Montrose, 4400 N) and the lake, 312/742-5121	N
North Avenue Beach, 1603 N. Lakeshore, 312/742-7226	C
North Shore Beach Park, 1040 W. North Shore, 312/742-7857	FN

Northerly Island Park, 1400 S. Linn White Drive, 312/747-2471 C

Oak Street Beach, Oak, 1000 N) and the lake, 312/742-5121 C

Osterman Beach, Ardmore, 5800 N) and the lake, 312/742-5121 FN

Pratt Blvd. Beach and Park, 1050 W. Pratt, 312/742-7857 FN

Promontory Point Park, 5491 S. South Shore Drive, 312/747-6187 S

Rainbow Park and Beach, 3111 E. 77th, 312/745-1479 FSE

Rogers Ave. Beach and Park, 7800 N. Rogers, 312/742-7857 FN

4

FOOD

Argyle Street is the place to go for delicious
homestyle Vietnamese cooking.
Photo by Bill Arroyo.

(Above) The 24-hour White Palace Grill offers a wonderful view of the skyline from the south. (Below) A six-block stretch of Devon Avenue presents countless options for Indian, Pakistani, and vegetarian dining. *Photos by Bill Arroyo.*

FOOD

NOT SURPRISINGLY, THIS is the only chapter in the book where you won't find a glut of free possibilities. If you're going to spend money on anything in Chicago, however, it might as well be food.

Restaurants

PLEASE note that prices, hours, and features of restaurants are particularly subject to change compared to other businesses.

African

Bolat
3346 N. Clark, 773/665-1100   N
This Wrigleyville restaurant serves a mean jollof rice ($6), which is rice cooked in a spicy tomato sauce. And, if you're in the mood for goat, this is the place to be. Served with white rice, fried rice, coconut rice, or jollof rice, curried goat dishes go for $8–$9. The tilapia is also very good. Open Mon.–Sat. 11 A.M.–midnight, Sun. 11 A.M.–9 P.M.

Couscous
1445 W. Taylor, 312/226-2408   C
A new addition to the UIC area, **Couscous** specializes in North African, Middle Eastern, and Maghrebin cuisine (dishes from Morocco, Tunisia, and Algeria). Falafel and their signature couscous dishes come highly recommended. Appetizers under $4, sandwiches under $6, dinners under $11, and desserts under $2 are served in healthy portions. Open Mon.–Sat. 11 A.M.–10 P.M., Sun. 2 P.M.–10 P.M.

Vee-Vee's African Restaurant and Cocktails
6232 N. Broadway, 773/465-2424   **FN**
This spacious restaurant with African folk touches is where native Africans
dine for home cooking. The extensive menu is organized by Bean Plates,
Stews and Soups, Yam and Plantain Specials, and Rice Entrées. **Vee-Vee's**
special *Ofe Imo* soup contains fish, shrimp, meat, pumpkin, and red pepper
and comes with semolina on the side. Entrées $6–$14, most under $9. Sun.
buffet (noon–6 P.M.), $10. Open Mon.–Sat. noon–11 P.M., Sun. noon– 9 P.M.

Argentinean

El Nandú Restaurant
2731 W. Fullerton, 773/278-0900   **N**
Exposed brick walls provide a nice backdrop for colorful artwork and an
ongoing slide show of Argentina. Start with the menu's highlight—empanadas (turnovers filled with shrimp, corn, spinach, cheese, ground beef, or
steak) that cost about $2 each. Salads, chicken, and steak comprise the
complete menu, but many go straight for the *churrasco*, a specially prepared
char-broiled NY strip. Entrées $8–$15. Open mic on Thursdays begins a
line-up of weekend entertainment. Open Mon.–Wed. 11:30 A.M.–10:30 P.M.,
Thur.–Sat. 11:30 A.M.–11:30 P.M., Sun. 5 P.M.–10 P.M.

Tango Sur
3763 N. Southport, 773/477-5466   **N**
The dance of love at this newer Argentinean restaurant is beef coupled with
more beef. Start with, say, a fried beef empanada, *chinchulin* (fried cow's
intestine), or *matambre* (cold veal roll stuffed with vegetables and egg).
Follow with one of the *parilla* (barbecue) steaks or *milanesa a caballo* (fried
breaded steak crowned with fried eggs). For variety, the *parrillada* samplers
are the house specialty. The $15 platter feeds 1–2 and contains grilled short
ribs, chorizo, *morcilla* (blood sausage), and sweetbreads; the $25 platter
feeds 2–4 and throws in one of the *vacio* steaks besides. Entrées $8–$25,
most under $15. Outdoor seating in summer. BYOB. Open Mon.–Thur. 5
P.M.–10:30 P.M., Fri.–Sat. 5 P.M.–11:30 P.M., Sun. noon–11 P.M.

Head north from either of these places to finish your meal with some
Argentinean (gelato-like) ice cream at **The Penguin** (2723 W. Lawrence,
773/271-4924). Open Mon.–Sat. 1 P.M.–10 P.M., Sun. 1 P.M.–8 P.M.

Armenian

Sayat-Nova
157 E. Ohio, 312/644-9159   C
Raw *Kibbee*–Armenian steak tartare, and *Lamajoun*—Armenian ground
lamb "pizza," join standards like hummus, baba ghannouj, and stuffed
eggplant on the *mezza* (appetizer) list. Charbroiled kebabs, couscous plates,
and Armenian dinners (including the famous lamb chops) include red lentil
soup or salad with mint vinaigrette. Lunches about $8–$12, dinners $10–
$20. Open Mon.– Sat. 11:30 A.M.–10 P.M., Sun. 2 P.M.–9 P.M.

Asian

SEE ALSO Chinese, Do-It-Yourself Stir-fry, Indian, Japanese, Korean, Laotian, Thai, and Vietnamese.

Joy Yee's Noodle Shop
2159 S. China Place, 312/328-0001   C
Tucked away in a corner of the Chinatown Mall you'll find one of the
liveliest and most whimsical restaurants in town. The walls of **Joy Yee's** are
painted in vivid shades of red, orange, yellow, and green, echoing the colors
of fresh fruit on the shelves behind the juice bar. The produce is whipped
into nearly 100 cool concoctions, including tapioca pearl-laden "bubble tea"
in such flavors as cantaloupe, lychee/papaya, and grass jelly/coconut milk
(20-ounce glass, about $3). The menu includes an equally impressive range
of Chinese, Japanese, Thai, and Vietnamese entrées, $7–$10, many served
in large, boat-shaped platters. Mixed seafood served in a coconut shell is
one of the highlights. The place is popular with teenagers and college
students, and a majority of the servers seem to be club kids with multicol-
ored hair. Open daily 11 A.M.–10:30 P.M.

Noodles, Etc.
1460 E. 53rd, 773/947-8787   S
Modest in size but powerful in taste and large in portion are the noodle
dishes served at this Hyde Park eatery. The Tom Yum Noodle soup and the
Wasabi Shu Mai are favorites amongst the Hyde Park locals. Other entrées
include a selection of wild rice noodles, soft ramen noodles, vermicelli
noodles, crispy Cantonese noodles, and Chinese egg noodles. You get the
point! A full array of soups, salads, and appetizers are also served. Most
dishes under $7. Open Mon–Sat. 11 A.M.–10 P.M., Sun. 11:30 A.M.–9:30 P.M.

Penny's Noodle Shop
950 W. Diversey, 773/281-8448   **N**
3400 N. Sheffield, 773/281-8222   **N**
1542 N. Damen, 773/394-0100   **N**
Renowned cheap-eats cafés prepare Thai, Vietnamese, and Japanese noodle specialties not far from your table's view. Delectable spring rolls, perfectly seasoned soups, and big bowls of Pad Thai, ramen, or udon noodles will leave you blissful. Beware of big crowds at the tiny original location on Sheffield. Most dishes $4–$7. Open Sun., Tues., Wed., Thurs. 11 A.M.–10 P.M., Open Fri.–Sat. 11 A.M.–10:30 P.M.

Breakfast

Chatham Pancake House
700 E. 87th, 773/874-0010   **FSE**
This neighborhood eatery is well-known for its diverse breakfast menu and large portions in a comfortable setting with quick, helpful service. Morning specialties include three pigs in a blanket, blueberry pancakes, grits, corned beef hash, and the home-style hash browns. Food items run $1.50–$6.50. Open daily 7 A.M.–3 P.M.

Golden House
4744 N. Broadway, 773/334-0406   **N**
Old paneling, a maze of sparkly, red-vinyl booths, and Uptown's mixed bag of neighbors provide an oddly relaxing environment in which to start the day. This diner/pancake house serves quite an array of good food at unbeatable prices. Top pancakes and waffles with apple, blueberry, strawberry, peach, cherry, or pineapple compote; chocolate chips; cinnamon; and, of course, plenty of whipped cream. Match your eggs with hash, pork chops, French toast, chopped ham, and more. Most items $2–$5. Open daily 6 A.M.–6:30 P.M.

The Lincoln Restaurant
4008 N. Lincoln, 773/248-1820   **N**
Honest Abe and the Civil War are the pervasive themes at this Greek-owned, country-decorated family restaurant. Recommended omelettes and egg combos are served in pewter skillets and take the names of Civil War generals. (The General Sheridan is a three-cheese omelette.) Try the granola-laced pancakes or shun breakfast conventions altogether with a fancy ice-cream sundae (named after early American presidents). Dishes $4–$7. Take home chocolate-covered Oreos from the pastry case. Open Sun.–Thur. 5:30 A.M.–10:30 P.M., Fri.–Sat. 5:30 A.M.–11 P.M.

Lou Mitchell's Restaurant
565 W. Jackson, 312/939-3111   C
Classic coffee shop (1923) efficiently and expertly serves the food that has earned recurring endorsements. (Those waiting for tables are compensated with free Milk Duds or warm, fresh doughnut holes.) Notable omelettes, waffles, thick Greek toast (with homemade orange marmalade), and homemade baked goods (brownies, muffins, cinnamon-raisin bread) hover near the top of a list of affordable favorites ($3–$7). Open Mon.–Sat. 5:30 A.M.–3 P.M., Sun. 7 A.M.–2 P.M.

Lume's
11601 S. Western, 773/233-2323   FSW
Overflowing with ready diners, you would never know that this restaurant is relatively new to the neighborhood. Beautifully appointed and entirely inviting, **Lume's** is the place for hefty portions seasoned just right! Breakfast specialties include their very own apple and German oven-baked pancakes billed as "pancakes you won't forget." Their menu with "international flair" delivers crêpes suzettes with fresh strawberries, potato pancakes with applesauce and sour cream, a Swedish extravaganza with imported loganberries, Palestine pancakes rolled with sour cream and Cointreau Liquor, and a little bit of France with cinnamon-spiral French toast smothered with cinnamon apples, plump raisins, and pecans. Other menu specialties include the homemade soups, skillet dishes, and Dagwood-sized sandwiches. Menu items run $3 $8. Open daily 5:30 A.M.–4 P.M.

Original Pancake House
22 E. Bellevue Place, 312/642-791   C
Open Mon.–Fri. 7 A.M.–3 P.M., Sat.–Sun. 7 A.M.–5 P.M.
1517 E. Hyde Park Blvd., 773/288-2322   S
Open Mon.–Fri. 7 A.M.–3 P.M., Sat.–Sun. 7 A.M.–5 P.M.
2020 N. Lincoln Park West, 773/929-8130   N
Open Mon.–Fri. 7 A.M.–3 P.M., Sat.–Sun. 7 A.M.–4 P.M.
10437 S. Western, 773/445-6100   FSW
Open Mon.–Fri. 6:30 A.M.–3 P.M., Sat.–Sun. 6:30 A.M.–5 P.M.
Diners can find breakfast bliss in all corners of the city thanks to this chain of legendary pancake houses. The menu boasts recipes handed down through generations that are hard to ignore: The Apple Pancake is a baked feast with fresh apples and cinnamon glaze served hot and fresh from the oven. Also baked is the Dutch Baby, a German pancake served with fresh lemon and powdered sugar. On future visits, you can move on to the HUGE 4-egg omelettes, the delicate fruit crêpes, and the plate-sized Belgian waffles. Children's portions available. Breakfast items $2–$8, most $4–$7.

Sweet Maple Cafe
1339 W. Taylor, 312/243-8908   **C**
Located near UIC and the medical district, this homey breakfast and lunch spot serves up tasty breakfast standards (most $4–$7) with a touch of creativity, as seen in the Taylor Street Italian omelette and challah french toast, and a touch of the South, as seen in the fresh biscuits, grits, and slabs of bone-in ham. Since they've been discovered, don't even think of coming on the weekends after 10 A.M. unless you're planning on camping out on the sidewalk while you wait. Open for breakfast Mon.–Fri. 7 A.M.–11:30 A.M., Sat.–Sun. 7 A.M.–2 P.M.

Breakfast, All Day

Clarke's Pancake House and Restaurant
2441 N. Lincoln, 773/472-3505   **N**
Healthy and innovative pancake house fare 24 hours a day. Carrot & zucchini pancakes, German pancakes, chocolate chip pancakes, spinach burritos, and such keep Lincoln Park late-nighters humming. Meals $4–$8, most under $6.

The Original Mitchell's
1953 N. Clybourn, 773/883-1157   **N**
The Mitchells have been operating family restaurants in Chicago since the 1940s. They pride themselves on their omelettes (try them pizza-style), their fresh, natural ingredients, and a wide selection of heart-healthy and vegetarian items (including "sausage" patties). Most breakfasts $3.50–$7. Open daily 6 A.M.–11:30 P.M.

Tempo Restaurant
6 E. Chestnut, 312/943-4373   **C**
If you tend to crave breakfast at unconventional hours and your nightlife often takes you to the center of town, add **Tempo** to your little black book. The people watching is good at all hours (the outdoor cafe is open until 11 P.M., weather permitting), and the food is even better. Eggs Florentine, chicken liver and eggs ("The Continental"), an artichoke/tomato/Swiss omelette over potatoes ("The Artemis"), raspberry pancakes, and egg-white French toast are but a few of the menu's highlights. Entrées $3–$9, most $4–$7. Open daily 24 hours. Cash only.

Brunch

The Bongo Room
1470 N. Milwaukee, 773/489-0690   N
Though it's true that the weekend wait is lengthy, not much has deterred
faithful diners from this ten-year-old Wicker Park hotspot, who line the
sidewalk with steaming mugs of coffee waiting for their table. The menu
changes frequently, so favorites are often short-lived, but in the past the
menu has included items such as raspberry cheesecake pancakes, roasted red
pepper and basil omelettes, chocolate chunk brioche French toast, and
shrimp Benedict with mustard and dill hollandaise. The prices are a little
steeper than other options (around $8), but the food is consistently great, the
crowd eclectic, and the atmosphere and strong coffee guaranteed to get your
day started right. Open Mon.–Fri. 8 A.M.–2:30 P.M., Sat.–Sun. 9:30 A.M.–
2:30 P.M.

Flo
1431 W. Chicago, 312/243-0477   C
For an inventive brunch with a little Santa Fe flavor, this is the place. The
chef/owner imports his chilies straight from a family farm in New Mexico
and uses the poblanos, green chilies, cayennes, and chipotles with flair. The
huevos rancheros are easily the best in the city, with fresh blue corn tortillas
smothered in New Mexican chili sauce topped with eggs and black beans.
The gigantic breakfast burrito, filled with grilled veggies and spicy chilies,
and the green chili chicken enchilada are equally popular favorites. Most
items are around $8, and traditional dishes for the spice-scared are available.
The fresh-squeezed OJ and coffee are fantastic and the unpretentious staff
and local art-covered walls make for an inviting atmosphere that turns diners
into regulars. Breakfast is served Tues.–Fri. 8:30 A.M.–2:30 P.M., Sat.–Sun.
brunch from 9 A.M.–2:30 P.M. Also open for dinner

Orange
3231 N. Clark, 773/549-4400   N
This Lakeview brunch spot serves up playful food unlike any of its surrounding diner-style competition, starting with the order slips that let
customers build their own fruit and veggie juice combos. Great attention is
paid to the ingredients here, upping the omelette ante with rosemary-roasted
ham, aged cheddar, shallots, and Dijon. Regulars like the breakfast bruschetta (multi-grain toast topped with parmesan, applewood smoked bacon,
melon, organic greens, citrus vinaigrette, and poached eggs), the jelly
doughnut pancakes (lingonberries and citrus butter), and the duck confit
hash, but you may not be able to resist trying the "green eggs and ham" or

the special pancake "flight" of the week, which offers four stacks of mini-pancakes, each a variation on the theme food of the week (such as Madagascar vanilla or tropical fruit). Most of the items are about $7–$8, their creativity well worth the price. For a fun side, check out the "frushi," an array of fresh fruit sushi made with assorted berries and cocont-infused sticky rice ($2–$3 per person). Open daily 8 A.M.–3 P.M.

Stanley's Kitchen & Tap
1970 N. Lincoln, 312/642-0007   N
Lincoln Park bar (known for its whiskey selection) and restaurant (known for its low-priced American home cooking) has a brunch buffet that can't be beat. For $10.95, fill up on fried chicken, macaroni & cheese, potatoes & gravy, biscuits & sausage gravy, bacon, home fries, fruit, muffins, biscuits, bread, bagels, and cinnamon rolls. Oh, and don't forget trips to the omelette and Belgian waffle stations! Complete with bowling trophies, family photos, antique appliances, and a contemporary flair, **Stanley's** dimly-lit backroom re-creates a mid-century roadside kitchen. For an additional $7.95, visit the build-your-own Bloody Mary bar. They start you with three shots of vodka—you add the rest. Hint: Come on Saturday to avoid the Sunday mob. Open Sat.–Sun. 11 A.M.–4 P.M.

If Stanley's is packed, try these nearby pub classics that also have a distinctive backdrop and an appealing menu for weekend brunch: **John Barleycorn Memorial Pub** (658 W. Belden, 773/348-8899) and **Four Farthings Tavern** (2060 N. Cleveland, 773/935-2060, Sun. only).

The **Original 50 Yard Line** (69 E. 75th, 773/846-0005) is a popular Chatham sports bar, serving a hard-to-pass-up $6 brunch, Sat. 2 P.M.–7 P.M. The rotating buffet menu may include baked chicken, pepper steak, meatloaf, macaroni salad, potatoes, rice, corn, string beans, greens, salad, and corn bread.

Bulgarian

Mario's Cafe
5241 N. Harlem, 773/594-9742   FN
For the longest time the only Bulgarian restaurant in the Midwest, **Mario's Cafe** has been named on *Chicago Tribune*'s list of "Top 10 Ethnic Restaurants in Chicago." Mario's recently bought out two other storefronts to seat 150 people. Bulgarian cookery bears much resemblance to Greek cooking, as is apparent in Mario's appetizers like the yogurt dip, eggplant spread, feta

cheese, and fried cheese. It also is meat-intensive, with pork predominating. Try the meatballs, sausages, and Bulgarian salami. For dessert, there's baklava, *tolumba* (fried dough with syrup), or cheese and chocolate filled pastries. Entrées hover near $10, appetizers near $5. Open daily 10 A.M.–11 P.M.

Burgers

A hot-dog-stand-with-umbrella-tables burger . . .

Big Red's Yo-Joe's
6401 W. Addison, 773/286-0131   **NW**
Carry-out their "Tummy Buster"—a 1/2 lb. of ground beef ($3), loaded with trimmings (including sauerkraut, if you so choose)—or, in warm weather, take it to the picnic tables out back. Pair it with the unique fried cheddar cheese cubes or one of their notable hot dogs for a chaser. Open daily 10:30 A.M.–10:30 P.M.

These two dark neighborhood taverns—popular, though somewhat dated or even careworn—have something else in common: burgers that Chicagoans rave about.

Boston Blackie's
164 E. Grand, 312/938-8700   **C**
Dim, bustling, and strangely like a hotel banquet hall, this stalwart neighborhood bar and grill, just a stone's throw from the sheen of ritzy North Michigan Avenue, crams folks in at lunch, dinner, and in-between for their cherished beef patties ($6). Open Mon.–Sat. 11 A.M.–11 P.M., Sun. noon–9 P.M.

Moody's Pub
5910 N. Broadway, 773/275-2696   **FN**
The award-winning 1/2 lb. Moodyburger ($6, $6.50 w/cheese) is the center of **Moody's** limited pub menu. The dark, charming, heavy wood, and fire-lit interior is perfect for winter, while the large, atmospheric beer garden makes an ideal summer retreat. Open Mon.–Fri. 11:30 A.M.–1 A.M., Sat. 11:30 A.M.–2 A.M., Sun. noon–1 A.M.

And the "newest" competitor for favorite Chicago burger . . .

Hackney's
733 S. Dearborn, 312/461-1116   **C**
This family-owned chain of suburban restaurants—defined by its burgers and blocks of french-fried onion strings—got started in the late 1930s and finally expanded to the city in 2001. This Printers Row location has a neighborhood feeling and a full bar in front. The classic Hackneyburger (that Chicagoans still happily trek out to the suburbs for) is a juicy half-pound burger served on black rye ($7.25). Share the $5 pile of onion-strings with your fellow diners. The kitchen is open Mon. 10:30 A.M.–10 P.M., Tues.–Thurs. 10:30 A.M.–10:30 P.M., Fri. 10:30 A.M.–11 P.M., Sat.–Sun. 9 A.M.–11 P.M.

The best burger deal in town is undoubtedly the $1 half-pound burger with fries (half of a plate full of them!) available with a beverage purchase Monday nights at **O'Donovan's** (see p. 218). Another polished and packed Irish pub offers a similar deals on Monday (but fries are an extra $1): **Celtic Crown** (773/4301 N. Western, 773/588-1110).

Cafeterias

Manny's Coffee Shop and Deli
1141 S. Jefferson, 312/939-2855   **C**
Big boys, old guys, and really hungry folk, be they downtown professionals, students, delivery types, cops, fire academy cadets, local pols, or longtime residents, all show up at **Manny's** for the American deli, Eastern European, and Jewish classics served at this spacious 60-year-old Maxwell Street-area fixture. Grab a tray and stand in line. It's full service—someone even pours the pop and juice—and no money is exchanged until you've finished eating. Most dishes on the vast and changing menu are priced between $3 and $8, whether they're potato pancakes and knishes; obscene corned beef and pastrami sandwiches bulging out of their rye bread confines; or hot entrées like meatloaf and liver. Manny's has a free parking lot, although it does fill up at noon. Buy your cigars at the cashier's counter on the way out. Open Mon.–Sat. 5 A.M.–4 P.M.

Valois Cafeteria
1518 E. 53rd, 773/667-0647   **S**
The **Valois** invites diners to "see your food." Folks come from every corner of Hyde Park for chicken pot pies, cheap hot sandwiches, and a changing

line-up of hearty dinners. Everything falls under $7, most dishes between $2 and $4. This place is such a neighborhood institution that in the early 1990s, U of C student Mitchell Duneier conducted a sociological study of the black working-class men who regularly meet at the Valois, eventually publishing his dissertation as a book entitled *Slim's Table*. Valois serves breakfast until 4 P.M. Open daily 5:30 A.M.–10 P.M. Cash only, free parking.

Cajun

Heaven on Seven
111 N. Wabash, 7th Floor, 312/263-6443   C
600 N. Rush, 312/280-7774   C
3478 N. Clark, 773/477-7818   N
What began as an alternative menu at the family luncheonette on the seventh floor of the Garland Building on Wabash is now a three-location Cajun empire headed by semi-celebrity chef Jimmy Bannos. The original still packs in lunchtime office workers that line up in the hall for gumbo, jambalaya, étouffee, po-boys, crayfish, crabcakes, and the like. On the first and third Fridays of the month, the restaurant closes at 3:30 and then reopens from 5:30 P.M.–9 P.M. for dinner. Open Mon.–Fri. 8:30 A.M.–5 P.M., Sat. 10 A.M.–3 P.M. While the Wabash location evokes a bayou-town kitchen, the newer spots on Rush and Clark resemble sleek Bourbon Street tourist restaurants. Both offer longer hours (Rush: Open Sun.–Thur. 11 A.M.–10 P.M., Fri.–Sat. 11 A.M.–11 P.M.; Clark: Sun.–Thur. 11 A.M.–10 P.M., Fri. 11 A.M.–11 P.M., Sat. 9 A.M.–11 P.M., Sun. 9 A.M.–10 P.M.) and brunch Sat.–Sun. (Rush: 11 A.M.–2 P.M.; Clark: 10:30 A.M.–3 P.M.). Dinners range in price from $8–$18.

The **Blues Kitchen** at **Buddy Guy's Legends** (754 S. Wabash, 312/427-0333, see p. 242) has an extensive menu of traditional Cajun food served until 11 P.M. on weeknights and midnight Sat.–Sun. Enjoy frog legs, Southern fried okra, catfish, traditional or meatless gumbo, po-boy sandwiches, and more (sandwiches $7–$9, entrées $11–$16). For a Gulf Coast fix in Lincoln Park, there's **The Local Shack** (1056 W. Webster, 773/435-3136), the snack shop cousin of the neighborly watering hole, **The Local Option** (1102 W. Webster). Stop in before 10 P.M. for some chunky gumbo or divine bread pudding (about $4) if it's "light" sustenance you need; choose among the authentic po-boys, muffulettas, and other sandwiches ($7–$10) if you still have a full evening of DePaul-area barhopping ahead of you.

Caribbean
SEE ALSO Jamaican.

Calypso Café
5211-C S. Harper, 773/995-0229   **S**
Rated one of the "Top 24 Places to Eat Now" in *Chicago Magazine*,
Calypso Café continues to share with its customers the finest, most flavorful
tropical specialties. The décor is colorful, outdone only by the spicy favorites served the "Island Way": The Island BBQ chicken is house-smoked
and served with saffron rice, sweet plantains, and blue water slaw. The jerk
chicken, jerked the Island Way, is marinated and slow-cooked over pimento
wood in the on-site jerk pits. Other entrées include peppered, peach-glazed
pork chops; red snapper in a bag; and oxtail stew slow cooked with carrots
and lima beans, and served with peas 'n' rice. End the meal with key lime
pie, coconut banana cream pie, or pineapple jump-up cake. Food items
$2–$15. Open Sun.–Thur. 11 A.M.–10 P.M., Fri.–Sat. 11 A.M.–11 P.M.

Ezuli
1415 N. Milwaukee Ave., 773/227-8200   **C**
Naming their Jamaican/Creole restaurant for a Haitian love goddess, the
owners of Ezuli paid a lot of attention to interior design, lighting, atmosphere, music selection, and menu items (as well they should in Wicker
Park), and it all comes together to enhance the dining experience (so do the
chic cosmopolitan drinks). Menu items include the catfish fry with Tabasco
honey, monk fish Creole, Jamaican catfish, and bruschetta with peanut
butter and mango. Most items $8–$15. Open Tues.–Sun. 6:30 P.M.–2 A.M.

Chili

Chili Mac's 5-Way Chili
3152 N. Broadway, 773/404-2898   **N**
Chili Mac's lets the diner create their own bowl of chili (choice of three
varieties: Texas, turkey, or 10-veggie Cincinnati vegetarian) with five
topping options (plain, with spaghetti, with cheddar cheese, with beans or
onions, or "the works"). Add chips and a frozen margarita for a complete
and affordable feast. Open daily 11 A.M.–10 P.M.

Lindy's Chili
3685 S. Archer, 773/927-7807   **SW**
Open Mon.–Thurs. 10:30 A.M.–10 P.M., Fri. 10:30 A.M.–midnight, Sat. 11
A.M.–midnight, Sun. 11 A.M.–10 P.M.

6544 S. Archer, 773/229-1512   **SW**
Open daily 10 A.M.–11 P.M.
7600 S. Pulaski, 773/582-2510   **SW**
Open daily 10 A.M.–11 P.M.
11009 S. Kedzie, 773/779-7236   **SW**
Open Mon.–Thurs. 10:30 A.M.–10 P.M., Fri.–Sat. 10:30 A.M.–11 P.M., Sun. noon–10 P.M.

A popular stop for White Sox fans after the game, the original **Lindy's** location on Archer is now part of a small chain of combined **Gertie's Ice Cream** (see p. 181) and Lindy's Chili eateries. (These local operations have been around since 1901 and 1924 respectively, and were first combined in the mid-1970s.) Start with a bowl at the restaurant (about $3), then take some home a pint, quart, or gallon for later.

Chinese

WHEREVER you go in Chicago, you're bound to find plenty of inexpensive Chinese restaurants. Dining in Chicago's tight-knit Chinese community is quite different, however, from ordering take-out chop suey from the place on the corner. As Chinatown's main strips total only a few blocks, you might try the common approach to selecting one of its many eateries of sauntering up and down Wentworth and Cermak, and through the Chinatown Square mall on Archer until a particular restaurant intrigues you, or until you find one that meets your dress, ambiance, or pricing criteria. (There's at least one there for everyone.)

A traditional gate on Wentworth (200 W) at Cermak (2200 S) welcomes you to Chinatown. The Chinatown el stop on the Red Line leaves you one block from this point. **China Café** (2300 S. Wentworth, 312/808-0202), **Dragon Court** (2414 S. Wentworth, 312/791-1882), **Emperor's Choice** (2238 S. Wentworth, 312/225-8800), and **Moon Palace** (216 W. Cermak, 312/225-4081) have different atmospheres, but all are time-tested favorites with most entrées no more than $7–$10. For something even cheaper, try **Seven Treasures** (2312 S. Wentworth, 312/225-2668). Their colossal menu lists hundreds of items priced between $3 and $12, most under $7.

Dim sum is the custom (originally Cantonese) of snacking or dining on various types of dumplings and other small portions of delicacies. While many Chinatown restaurants offer daily dim sum from mid-morning to late afternoon, weekends, particularly early Sunday afternoon, may be the best time to go for the full effect. It seems that the majority of the Chinatown neighborhood is out then, enjoying this social meal that can linger for hours.

Favorites for dim sum (typically $2–$4 per dish) are **Furama** (2828 S. Wentworth, 312/225-6888 in Chinatown; 4936 N. Broadway, 773/271-1161 in Uptown); the attractive and exceptionally popular **Phoenix** (2131 S. Archer, 2nd Floor, 312/328-0848); and the pink and cavernous **Three Happiness** (209 W. Cermak, 312/842-1964; and 2130 S. Wentworth, 312/791-1228). During busy times, select dim sum from the loaded carts that servers wind through the maze of tables. Also try **Shui Wah** (2162 S. Archer, 312/225-8811) in Chinatown Square, for a great variety of dumplings.

For lunch bargains on the South Side:

The complete lack of décor doesn't keep the local business people from packing **Arden Chinese** (6207 S. Kedzie, 773/436-6200) at lunch time. Menu selections ($2–$11) cover the entire range of Chinese and Mandarin cuisine. The chicken dishes are especially tasty. **Wing Wah Lau**'s (4340 S. Archer, 773/847-1881) lunch specials make this Brighton Park restaurant a neighborhood favorite. It's a good place for spicy chicken and beef satay.

Far East Kitchen
1509 East 53rd, 773/955-2200   S
Far East Kitchen is certainly one of the stars of Hyde Park and the South Side. The Moy family opened the restaurant in 1934 and have been offering a full variety of authentic Cantonese, Szechwan, and Mandarin style dishes ever since. Now owned and operated by the third generation of Moys, the restaurant still serves some of its original and loyal clientele! Travelers come from across the country to enjoy a fine feast here, and the restaurant has even served as a "field trip" destination for local schools. Seafood is the specialty. Other popular dishes are the Empress Chicken and the Hong Kong Steak. The egg rolls are prepared fresh daily as Mrs. Moy "puts love into each one of them." Former Mayor, Harold Washington, had his own "special table" at Far East. Food items: $3–$14. Lunch specials served 11 A.M.–1 P.M. Tues.–Sat., for $4–$7.

Papajin
1551 W. North, 773/384-9600   N
Great for anyday take-out *and* an affordable white-tablecloth place, why can't this be my local Chinese restaurant?? Dishes are MSG free and available in three degrees: mild, medium, and hot. Ten appetizers under $7 include the peerless lightly battered calamari with sesame seeds. Dozens of noodle dishes, moo shu, beef, pork, vegetable, and poultry dinners come under $10. Among those recommended are the hot pepper beef, Mandarin

pork, eggplant garlic sauce, and crispy duck. Service is top notch. Open Mon.–Thur. 11:30 A.M.–10:15 P.M., Fri. 1:30 P.M.–11:15 P.M., Sat. 2:30 P.M.–11:15 P.M., Sun. 2 P.M.–10 P.M.

Coffeehouses

IF it's teatime, dessert time, snack time, or any time for a break, Chicago has an eclectic and thriving coffee-based culture prepared to help you slow down by pumping you with caffeine, rich desserts, and, often, stimulating entertainment. This suggestion list is hardly exhaustive—Chicago's coffee league needs its own directory—but was devised to introduce a wide range of coffeehouse styles. A snack/dessert and beverage at these places will usually fall between $4 and $6. See also **Chapter 5: Entertainment**, for cafes with live music, improv comedy, and poetry readings.

Anna Held Flower Shop and Fountain Cafe
5557 N. Sheridan, 773/561-1941   **FN**
Like the pink Edgewater Beach Apartments (site of a former luxury hotel) in which it's located, the **Anna Held Flower Shop and Fountain Cafe** can jolt you into a kinder, gentler mindset, or even another era. Let the scent of fresh flowers overwhelm you as you take a seat at the soda fountain for a coffee drink, cake, or ice cream treat. Open Mon.–Sat. 10 A.M.–6 P.M.

Ennui Cafe
6981 N. Sheridan, 773/973-2233   **FN**
There's a corner table in this storefront coffeeshop that looks like a remnant of the store's (probably retail) history; a well-dressed man intent on his laptop and ignoring his coffee looks just like a window display. Step down into this comfy, sunny room and it feels just like a coffeeshop ought to: plants, art, and an almost stereotypical coffeehouse mix of denizens. Besides coffee and tea, **Ennui** serves light breakfast, soup and sandwiches, and baked goods. Open Mon.–Thur. 6 A.M.–11 P.M., Fri. 6 A.M.–midnight, Sat. 7 A.M.–midnight, Sun. 7 A.M.–11 P.M.

Cafe Jumping Bean
1439 W. 18th, 312/455-0019   **W**
An important hangout for Pilsen's **Chicago Arts District** (p. 326), **Jumping Bean** rotates the work of local artists that it displays on its walls every six weeks. Cold sandwiches, hot focaccia sandwiches, empanadas, pizza, and desserts provide ample fare to accompany a creative caffeine break. Open Mon.–Fri. 6 A.M.–10 P.M., Sat.–Sun. 8 A.M.–8 P.M.

Corona's Coffee Shop
909 W. Irving Park, 773/529-1886   **N**
With Starbucks dotting the landscape like chicken pox, it's refreshing to find
family-run coffeeshops that still thrive. **Corona's** coconut lattés are popular,
and they also sell sandwiches, pastries, and a few pieces of coffee paraphernalia. Décor is artfully rough-hewn, and music is classy. Open Mon.–Fri. 6
A.M.–7 P.M., Sun. 7 A.M.–5 P.M. (Weekdays until 8 P.M. in summer.)

Earwax Cafe
1561 N. Milwaukee, 773/772-4019   **W**
This popular Wicker Park space consists of a first floor café and video rental
in the basement, all with a side show theme fairly fitting for its location and
clientele. The primarily vegetarian menu includes veggie Mexican and
Middle Eastern dishes and vegetarian versions of typical diner fare. Daily
specials run the ethnic gamut and the dessert line-up changes weekly.
Earwax is a casual and relaxing retreat free of the attitude that plagues
similar hip, artsy places elsewhere. If you don't care for coffee, they also
have sodas, shakes, smoothies, and juices. Entrées about $4–$7. Open daily
9 A.M.–11 P.M.

Java Express
10701 S. Hale, 773/233-8557   **FSW**
Many routes collide at **Java Express**—a very friendly, relaxed, neighborhood coffee and sandwich shop. 107th is so narrow here that most of the
patrons park with the passenger-side wheels up on the curb. Bike racks
outside make it a convenient stop during a bike tour of Beverly. Train
schedules are posted inside the shop for the nearby 107th Street station of the
Rock Island line. The sound of the train pulling into the station blends in
easily with friends, neighbors, kids, and staff members passing the time of
day on knock-off oak tables and slatted Breuer-type chairs. Sandwiches
(turkey, ham, club, tuna, pb & j, veggie) are served on thick slices of
homemade bread (about $4–$6). Two homemade soups and chili are also
served each day, along with salads and cookies. When you're not having
your java express, enjoy one of their twenty-some blends of coffee—perhaps
their signature Columbian-bean Beverly Blend—in a thick white mug.
Open Mon.–Fri. 5 A.M.–4 P.M., Sat.–Sun. 7 A.M.–4 P.M.

Java Thai
4272 W. Irving Park, 773/545-6200   **NW**
Nestled in the heart of Irving Park, this place doubles as a coffeeshop and a
Thai restaurant. They serve the standard coffee drinks and bakery goods, but
their menu also offers Thai food, brunch items on Sunday, and various cafe

snacks. The Thai fruit salad and fresh veggies with peanut sauce make great, refreshing afternoon snacks. Prices are extremely reasonable—in the $4–$7 range. Open Mon., Tues., Thur. 8 A.M.–9:30 P.M., Fri.–Sat. 8 A.M.–10:30 P.M., Sun. 9 A.M.–3 P.M.

Kopi, A Traveler's Cafe
5317 N. Clark, 773/989-KOPI (5674)   FN
Kopi (named for the Indonesian word for coffee) is loosely designed for travelers to come and swap road stories and shore up on tips for the next adventure. Slip your shoes off for cross-legged lounging at low tables surrounded by decorative cushions. Perhaps a Thai iced coffee and an order of hummus will tide you over as you plan that real or imagined trip to Nepal. Food choices include scones, muffins, desserts, breakfasts, sandwiches, and international appetizers. Travel books and global treasures are for sale. Open Mon.–Thurs. 8 A.M.–11 P.M., Fri. 8 A.M.–midnight, Sat. 9 A.M.–midnight, Sun. 10 A.M.–midnight.

Colombian

El Llano
3941 N. Lincoln, 773/868-1708   N
An assortment of Colombian artifacts, photos, and sculptures give a comfortable feel to this storefront restaurant. The lunch special typifies the overall great value—grilled steak or chicken served with hefty portions of red beans, white rice, mixed salad, and sweet plantains for only $5. For dinner, the choices all stay under $14 and run the gamut from seasoned fried whole red snapper to churrascos (big chunks of marinated grilled steak), with potatoes, yuca, and sweet plantains on the side. For an invigorating beverage, try the fresh juices ($2–$2.50) in tropical flavors such as mango, passionfruit, or the adventurous lulo, a tangy green Colombian fruit. Open daily 11 A.M.–10 P.M.

Pueblito Viejo
5429 N. Lincoln, 773/784-9135   FN
Step into **Pueblito Viejo** (Old Village) and lose yourself in a recreated Colombian mountain village. The carefully decorated interior, the traditionally clad Colombian waiters, and the live music on Saturdays set the stage for the authentic food to follow. The *Picada* (seasoned and fried chunks of meat, plantain, and yucca), *Plato Montañero (*mountain platter), and *Sancocho de Gallina* (parboiled hen) are house specialties. Don't leave without trying the arepas (corn cakes) or empanadas. This is a great place to come with a group and make an evening of it. Entrées cost about $8–$12. Open

Tues.–Fri. 4 P.M.–2 A.M., Sat. 2 P.M.–3 A.M., Sun. noon–2 A.M.

To sample authentic Colombian dishes, it's hard to beat **La Fonda**'s (4758 N. Clark, 773/271-3935) lunch buffet (Tues.–Fri., 11:30 A.M.–2:30 P.M.). The spread changes from day to day but always includes variously prepared meats and poultry, salad, soup, potatoes or cassava, rice, and sweet plantains. Order empanadas and tropical juices on the side. **Las Tablas** (2965 N. Lincoln, 773/871-2414) is a Colombian steak house that also has a signature paella, seafood, and plenty of traditional sides on the menu, not to mention a city full of ardent fans. Most entrées $10–$15.

Costa Rican

Irazu
1865 N. Milwaukee, 773/252-5687   N
Grab one of the few seats at this ramshackle little shop or take your goodies to go. Sandwiches, like steak or black beans and white cheese, are about $4. Try cheap sides like cheese empanadas, plantains or cassava with garlic, and the vegetarian taco (about $2). Dinners include choices like ceviche-style fish, fried pork chunks with cassava and cabbage salad, and versions of steak, shrimp, and pork chops ($6–$12). Wash it down with a *licuado* (shake): carrot, oatmeal, tamarind, guanábana, mamey, papaya, and lemonade join more familiar flavors. Open Mon.–Sat. 10 A.M.–9 P.M.

Croatian

Casino Restaurant
9706 S. Commercial, 773/221-5189   FSE
This South Chicago restaurant specializes in traditional Croatian dishes, including *muckalica* (dried veal with grilled onions, peppers, and tomatoes) and sausages made from lamb, beef, and pork. Most entrées are $8–$15. Open daily 7 A.M.–9 P.M.

Cuban

Ambassador Café
3605 N. Ashland, 773/404-8770   N
Well-established, luncheonette-style storefront serves Cuban sandwiches and entrées from late morning to late evening. Sandwiches including the Cuban Sandwich (ham, swiss, roast pork, mustard, and pickles on crusty bread). Island-style chicken, pork, steak, and seafood entrées come with

black bean soup, fried plantains, and rice. No rum and cokes or piña coladas here, but the Cuban coffee and tropical fruit shakes are easily potable. Most sandwiches are under $6, entrées under $10, though seafood dishes run higher. Open Tues.–Sun. 11:30 A.M.–10 P.M.

Café Bolero
2252 N. Western, 773/227-9000   N

If it's the fun and flair of Cuba you're looking for, you're guaranteed to find it here at least two nights of the week. A seasonal outdoor patio, a full bar known for strong and tasty cocktails, and a stage that showcases live music Tuesdays and Thursdays provides a great atmosphere for authentic Cuban food that's consistently good. With over 20 appetizers, it's best to opt for the combo that feeds the whole table—Cuban tamales, croquettes, potato balls, and chicken-stuffed plantains. For entrées, the standard accompaniments of rice, black beans, and plantains are in decent proportions, and the rarer items, like the goat stew, are worth the $15 price tag. For dessert, the simple and classic guava shells filled with cream cheese make a great finish to the meal. The menu is a little pricier than some of the other Cuban spots in town, but a visit to Tuesday's crazed Latin jazz night will assure you that **Bolero** is more of an outing than simply dinner. Open Sun., Mon., Wed. 11 A.M.–10 P.M., Tues., Thurs. 11 A.M.–11 P.M., Fri.–Sat. 11 A.M.–midnight.

Café 28
1800 W. Irving Park, 773/528-2883   N

What used to be a cheery Cuban restaurant with a coffeehouse feel has now blossomed into a moderately upscale dining establishment, garnering critical acclaim from foodies across the city. While they may have swapped the old pastry case for a swanky bar, the service and the food remain good and consistent, even a little more creative. Cuban dishes that borrow a little Mexican flavor include the grilled duck with pasilla sauce and grilled honey jalapeño pork chops. But for the traditional fare, the classic ropa vieja (shredded beef classic) with black beans and sweet plantains has remained an old faithful. Appetizers range from $5–$8, entrées from $10–$20. Open Sun.–Mon. 5:30 P.M.–9 P.M., Tues.–Thurs. 5:30 P.M.–10 P.M., Fri.–Sat. 5:30 P.M.–10:30 P.M. Also open Tues.–Fri. 11 A.M.–2:30 P.M. for weekday lunch and 9 A.M.–2 P.M. for weekend brunch.

Sabor a Cuba
1833 W. Wilson, 773/769-6859   N

For a small ma and pa two-room restaurant, **Sabor** turns out food that could stand up to most upscale eateries in the city. For a great sampling of Cuban appetizers, try the combo—empanada, papa rellena, and two types of croquettes for only $6. Yuca lovers will appreciate the yuca three ways here: boiled with garlic mojo, stuffed yuca relleno, or sliced and fried until crispy—all for about $3. The entrées all run around $10 for jumbo portions of classics like *ropa viejo* (tender shredded beef) or *lechón asado* (roasted pork), accompanied by white rice, black beans, and delicious *maduros* (sweet fried plantains). For a special occasion, splurge for the *paella Valenciana*, a huge piping hot skillet of saffron rice and every meat and seafood item under the sun, including fresh lobster, clams, and shrimp, for $50 (feeds 2–4 depending on appetite). Open Tues.–Thurs. 11 A.M.–10 P.M., Fri.–Sat. noon–11 P.M., Sunday 11 A.M.–10 P.M.

Dinner, Other Bargains

Bertucci's Corner
300 W. 24th, 312/225-2848   S
Incongruously situated in the heart of Chinatown, this funky Italian restaurant and bar serves delicious food at very reasonable prices. The stuffed artichoke appetizer is great; so are the half dozen veal dishes. Dinners come with soup or salad and non-pasta dinners come with a side of mostaccioli (most $10–$12). Parking is at a premium, so take the Red Line to the Chinatown stop and walk the four blocks south. Open Mon.–Thurs. 11 A.M.–9:30 P.M., Fri.–Sat. 11 A.M.–10:30 P.M., Sun. 3 P.M.–9 P.M.

Bite Café
1039 N. Western, 773/395-2483   W
Internationally-influenced diner fare comes artfully prepared at this brick and wood artist-musician-bohemian neighborhood spot next door to the **Empty Bottle** (see p.253). Special daily entrées (most under $10 and including many vegetarian items) supplement a basic menu of appetizers, soups, salads, pastas, and sandwiches ($4–$8). Grab a quick bite like a grilled cheese, veggie burrito, or falafel sandwich, or a more involved bite like grilled salmon, mushroom risotto, or marinated shark. Open Mon.–Fri. 7:30 A.M.–11:30 P.M., Sat. 8 A.M.–11:30 P.M., Sun. 8 A.M.–10:30 P.M. Open for brunch Sat.–Sun. 8 A.M.–3 P.M.

Brett's Café Americain
2011 W. Roscoe, 773/248-0999   N
Arrive before 6:30 P.M. Wednesday and Thursday and enjoy a three-course meal for $15. Probably the nicest restaurant in Roscoe Village, **Brett's** is basically American food with a French twist. Enjoy salmon with chili and garlic or sesame flank steak, but keep in mind that the menu changes every

month. The weekend brunch is also a delight to the palate with a wide array of flavors and a complimentary coffee cake and sweet bread basket. Open Wed.–Fri. 10:30 A.M.–2 P.M. and 5 P.M.–10 P.M., Sat. 8 A.M.–10 P.M., Sun. 8 A.M.–9 P.M. (weekend brunch until 4 P.M.).

Kitsch'n on Roscoe
2005 W. Roscoe, 773/248-7372   N

When Chef Jon Young set about giving Roscoe Village a fun everyday dining experience that truly lives up to its name, he filled the menu with items that make a great substitute for Mom's home cooking and filled the place with as much campy retro memorabilia the two rooms could fit. A lunch of a half sandwich, soup, chips, drink and choice of Ho-Ho or Twinkie is actually served in a 70s lunchbox (not for keeps). Appetizers run from chicken fingers and crab rangoon to baked goat cheese pesto marinara and drunken coconut shrimp. Though Mom may have never made those, the entrées are certainly comfort food and a good deal at around $10. Pot pies come hearty and with a twist; garlic seared veggies, fresh fennel and chicken, or shrimp and ginger fill puff pastry bowls alongside rosemary-garlic mashed potatoes. The popular meatloaf mixes lean beef with oatmeal, portabellos, and roasted peppers, and the spinach lasagna features three cheeses and plenty of fresh veggies. The traditional southern fried chicken dinner is loved by the regulars, and desserts like Twinkie tiramisu are a perfect ending to a kitschy meal. Also popular for weekend brunch, too popular if you're really hungry! Open Tues.–Sat. 9 A.M.–10 P.M., Sun. 9 A.M.–9 P.M., Mon. 9 A.M.–3 P.M.

Medici
1327 E. 57ᵗʰ, 773/667-7394   S

Wooden booths and brick walls, adorned with graffiti and student art, chronicle the **Medici**'s decades of existence as a University of Chicago hangout. Though providing something for every taste—from salads and chicken wings to quesadillas and lamb stew—this pub-like coffeehouse is best known for its pizza (the Garbage version includes sausage, ground beef, pepperoni, mushrooms, green peppers, tomatoes, onions and garlic) and its hamburgers (topped, among other things, with barbecue sauce, olives, bacon, chili, and cheese). They say that eggs espresso (still served for breakfast) were invented here in the 60s. Plenty of vegetarian choices. Most menu items range from $5–$8. Open Sun.–Fri. 11 A.M.–11:30 P.M., Sat. 9 A.M.–1:30 P.M.

Mellow Yellow
1508 E. 53ʳᵈ, 773/667-2000   S

Classic, nouvelle, casual, eclectic: the American/lightly French food at this energetic and attractive Hyde Park restaurant includes beloved rotisserie chicken and Taste of Chicago award-winning chili! Vegetarian chili of equal caliber is also on the menu. For a delicious meal under $8, choose one of the menu's numerous lighter options including crepes and baked potato meals. Most sandwiches are under $8, entrées with soup or salad under $10. Open Sun.–Thurs. 6 A.M.–10 P.M., Fri.–Sat. 6 A.M.–11 P.M.

Stanley's Kitchen & Tap
1970 N. Lincoln, 312/642-0007   N
How can you resist a place with a sign outside that boasts the daily availability of homemade mashed potatoes and bourbon? (Stanley's list of American whiskeys and bourbons is reputed to be Chicago's largest.) This homey tavern offers upscale home-cooking at great prices. Blackened chicken and catfish, gourmet burgers on black bread, chicken fried steak, veggie lasagna, toasted mac and cheese, meatloaf, pork chops, crabcake po-boys, and pies. Sandwiches are served with mashed potatoes, french fries, sweet potato fries or tater tots; supper items with a side dish of choice. Read about their not-to-miss brunch on p. 154. Open Mon.–Fri. 6 A.M.–2 A.M., Sat. 11 A.M.–3 A.M., Sun. 11 A.M.–2 A.M.

Do-It-Yourself Stir-fry

Flat Top Grill
3200 N. Southport, 773/665-8100   N
Open Sun.–Thurs. 11:30 A.M.–10 P.M., Fri.–Sat. 11:30 A.M.–11 P.M.
319 W. North, 312/787-7676   C
Open Sun.–Thurs. 11:30 A.M.–10 P.M., Fri.–Sat. 11:30 A.M.–10 P.M.
1000 W. Washington, 312/829-4800   C
Open Mon.–Thurs. 11 A.M.– 9:30 P.M., Fri. 11 A.M.–10:30 P.M., Sat. noon–10:30 P.M., Sun. noon–9 P.M.
Choose the ingredients for your personal stir-fry from an extensive buffet of meats (chicken, beef, pork, chicken livers, turkey, shrimp, squid), tofu, egg, vegetables, fruits, oils, sauces, vinegars, and flavored waters and deliver it to a chef at the flat top grill for cooking. A wall-sized chalkboard behind the buffet advises on time-tested combinations and proportions. You also select how to enjoy your stir-fry: over noodles (4 kinds), with rice (5 kinds), in a broth, atop lettuce as a salad, and occasionally, folded in pancake-style wrappers, like a burrito. Unlimited trips to the buffet/grill, $12; lunch $8.
For a couple bucks extra, **BD's Mongolian Barbecue** (3330 N. Clark, 773/325-2300) offers the same concept, with a larger selection of meat and

seafood, plus a soup and salad bar. "One-bowl" lunch is available at a lower price.

Doughnuts

Huck Finn Donuts and Snack Shop
3414 S. Archer, 773/247-5515   SW
6650 S. Pulaski, 773/581-4285   SW
Retirees, workers, families, and couples all come to these popular, South Side diners for the excellent homemade doughnuts available at all hours. They call their other areas of specialty "food" and "ice cream." The Donut Delight dessert combines your choice of doughnut and ice cream and tops it with whipped cream and a cherry. Open daily 24 hours.

Tommy's Rock 'n' Roll Café
2500 W. Chicago, 773/486-6768   W
Care for a Fender with your fritter? This unassuming storefront is a dough-nut shop that sells guitars (or a guitar store that sells doughnuts). Work up an appetite jamming on one of the used instruments for sale, checking out the kitschy rock memorabilia on the walls or the 80s concert videos on television. Then treat yourself to **Tommy's** excellent doughnuts, pecan rolls, and coffee, or an inexpensive sandwich. Just be sure to wipe off your fingers before you pick up that vintage Stratocaster again. Open Mon. 7:30 A.M.–3 P.M., Tues.–Fri. 7:30 A.M.–6 P.M., Sat. 7 A.M.–3:30 P.M.

Ecuadorian

La Peña Restaurante
4212 N. Milwaukee, 773/736-9498   NW
This spacious, full-bar, giant-menu Jefferson Park Ecuadorian restaurant is best considered a club to come with a number of people for sharing traditional sides and ample entrées and making an evening out of lingering, drinking, and nibbling to the live music. Their seating and waitstaff are prepared for the several large groups that show up nightly, but be prepared for the delays these parties can cause in the kitchen. Music may be folk, Latin dance, or karaoke. Open Tues.–Wed. 4 P.M.–10 P.M., Thur.–Sat. 4 P.M.–2 A.M., Sun. noon–2 A.M.

English

The Red Lion Restaurant and Pub
2446 N. Lincoln, 773/348-2695   **N**
The Red Lion is a classic English pub with good tavern fare (bangers and mash, fish and chips, shepherd's pie, Cornish pasties, seafood chowder, and more), a better beer selection, and just the right atmosphere to make it the perfect place to be stranded during a snowstorm. (That's my winter-weathered Chicago imagination in action.) Most dishes $4–$10. Look for the occasional Monday night poetry and "Twilight Tales," for readers and writers of all things spooky. Open Mon.–Thurs. noon–11 P.M., Fri.–Sat. noon–midnight, Sun. noon–10 P.M.

Ethiopian

The number of Ethiopian restaurants in town has more than doubled in recent years with the opening of several new injera eateries in Edgewater, a neighborhood that's home to many African immigrants. **Ethiopian Market and Restaurant** (5403 N. Broadway, 773/878-2353) is a small storefront with tiny carved horses, goats, birds, and elephants in the window. Breakfasts include an eggs-and-meat scramble with beef, onions, jalapeños, and fresh tomatoes. For dinner a whole fried tilapia served with salad and spicy lentils comes for $10. **Ras Dashen** (5846 N. Broadway, 773/506-9601), named after Ethiopia's tallest mountain, offers a wide array of interesting dishes. Entrées, $8.50–$12, include *komodoro ferfet*, a cold, tangy salad of injera, tomatoes, red and green onions, and green peppers; *doro alicha*, chicken and eggs in a mild sauce of onions, garlic, ginger, and green peppers; and *yebeg dereq tibs*, lamb tips fried with onions, garlic, and spices. Finish your meal with gelato, baklava, or bread pudding made with injera, raisins, nuts, and roasted flax seeds. **Ethiopian Diamond** (6120 N. Broadway, 773/338-6100), which opened in the late 90s, is a spacious, inviting room, great for celebrating with a large group of friends.

The established Wrigleyville places have had more time to work on their ambiance and still offer their great locations and prices: **Addis Abeba** (3521 N. Clark, 773/929-9383) still dominates the scene. **Ethio (Ethiopian Village) Café** (3462 N. Clark, 773/929-8300) is striking with its red walls, black and tan African tablecloths, and glass tabletops, *and* you can catch the ballgame on the tube from time to time. Check out the weekend buffet. At **Mama Desta's** (3218 N. Clark. 773/935-7561), candles and white tablecloths turn a basic storefront into an intimate dining environment.

Filipino

Pampanga's Cuisine (6407 N. Caldwell, 773/763-1781), near the city's edge, provides a friendly and tasty introduction to the Spanish-influenced Asian cooking of the Philippines. Suckling charcoal-roasted pig, cured barbecue pork, *longanisa* (spicy sausage), *lumpianitas* (spring rolls), and *pancit* (thick or thin rice noodles) will content the majority of newcomers. Most entrées are under $8. Open Wed.–Mon. 11:30 A.M.–8:30 P.M. To sample a wider variety of Philippine dishes, head to **Little Quiapo**'s (4423 N. Clark, 773/271-5441) for $9 daily buffets. Open for lunch 11 A.M.–3 P.M., for dinner 5 P.M.–9 P.M.

French

IN a major metropolis like Chicago, it takes beaucoup francs to experience the *crème de la crème* of the town's French cooking. These bistros and cafes, however, make charming and affordable alternatives.

Bistro Margot

1437–39 N. Wells, 312/587-3660   **C**

Red walls, black chairs, white linen covered tables—it's as French as the Eiffel Tower. The Sunday brunch menu includes soup, *terrine de legumes* (vegetable terrine with goat cheese, greens, and tomato vinaigrette), salads, *pain perdue* (brioche French toast with apple cinnamon butter), *saumon fume* (smoked salmon on a bagel with cream cheese, onion, tomato, and capers), *poulet roti* (roasted chicken with garlic, lemon, herbs, and *pommes frites*), and sandwiches such as the steak au poivre (sliced steak with peppercorn sauce on a baguette) for about $4–$10. The food is presented as an artform (should you eat it or frame it?). The dinner menu is out of "budget" range, but a nice ending to an evening would be French wine ($6.50/glass) and pastries including *mousse au chocolate* (chocolate mousse and raspberry sauce) or crème brulée for $6. Open Mon. 11:30 A.M.–9 P.M., Tue.–Thur. 11:30 A.M.–10 P.M., Fri. 11:30 A.M.–11 P.M., Sat. 10:30 A.M.–11 P.M., Sun. 10:30 A.M.–9 P.M. Lunch served weekdays 11:30 A.M.–4 P.M. Brunch served on weekends 10:30 A.M.–3 P.M.

Café Bernard

2100 N. Halsted, 773/871-2100   **N**

Big tip: to cat at this fine restaurant for only $5 on your birthday, go to their Web site (*www.cafebernard.com*) and click on the coupon link. Dinner entrées, with the exception of the vegetarian plate and the boneless chicken are $16 and up, but the appetizers, soups, salads, and desserts are reasonably priced. Appetizers run from $6–$12 and include shiitake mushrooms with goat cheese, *escargot sous feuillete*, lobster ravioli, and duck pate. Soups are $4, and salads are under $6 and include the apple and blue cheese salad with mustard vinaigrette. Desserts range from $5–$8, with decadent choices like white chocolate mousse cake, apple tart, crème brulée, and velvet chocolate cake. Reservations suggested. Open daily 5 P.M.–11 P.M.

La Crêperie
2845 N. Clark, 773/528-9050   **N**
This small, dark restaurant is in its 26th year of catering to Chicago's Francophiles via its *Crêpes Bretonnes*—buckwheat crêpes with fillings like *coq au vin*, broccoli & cheese, ratatouille, and seafood in cream sauce. With its candlelit outdoor garden tables (May–Sept.); the occasional live accordion music; dessert crêpes dripping with fresh fruit, chocolate, Nutella, crème caramel, and liqueurs; and some of the city's best prices for French wine, **La Crêperie** offers continental romance on a budget. Crêpes, $3.50–$9. Complete $16 dinner comes with soup or salad, one dinner crêpe, and one dessert crêpe. Open Tue.–Fri. 11:30 A.M.–3:30 P.M. (lunch) and 5 P.M.–11 P.M. (dinner), Sat. 11 A.M.–11 P.M., Sun. 11 A.M.–9:30 P.M.

Red Rooster Cafe and Wine Bar
2100 N. Halsted, 773/929-7660 (Entrance on Dickens)   **N**
Rustic and romantic, this cozy, wood-walled restaurant tucked on a Lincoln Park side street woos diners with such dishes as duck à la orange, filet mignon, mustard chicken, and grilled salmon in cabernet sauce. Entrées $10–$15, prix fixe menu available Sun.–Wed. Open Mon.–Thur. 5 P.M.–10:30 P.M., Fri.–Sat. 5 P.M.–11:30 P.M., Sun. 5 P.M.–10 P.M.

French Fries

Demon Dogs
944 W. Fullerton, 773/281-2001   **N**
$1.50 will buy you a glorious bulging brown sack of crispy, salty, greasy fries with the skins still on at this memorable hot dog stand. Owned by Peter Schivarelli, former 43rd ward sanitation superintendent and manager of the band *Chicago*, this little shop, tucked under the Fullerton el and sharing the blue demon mascot of nearby DePaul, declares that its food is a "hard habit to break." Can you name that 80s tune? The walls are covered with *Chicago* mementos, including a gold record. Most menu items are under $3. Open Mon.–Fri. 6:30 A.M.–10 P.M., Sat.–Sun. 9:30 A.M.–8 P.M.

Grant's Wonderburger
11045 S. Kedzie, 773/238-7200   **FSW**
In their "wah wah" speech, did your parents ever whine "you kids are
spoiled, they didn't have curly fries when I was a kid!" Well, I'm here to tell
you they were lying! **Grant's Wonderburger** introduced their Curly Q fries
on March 8, 1954. The Q fries (don't be shocked to get the occasional C or
O) are a heaping helping of heaven for less than $2 (add .50 for cheese on
your heaven). An added bonus of the Q fry is its ability to be just as yummy
cold, so you can let it sit around for hours and hours and then go back and
munch some more. Open Mon.–Sat. 10:30 A.M.–8 P.M.

Wiener Circle
2622 N. Clark, 773/477-7444   **N**
"Oh-my-gosh" will be your outcry after the cook hands you this mound of
melted cheese (trust me there are fries under there.) Cost, only $2.85. Open
daily 11 A.M.–4 A.M.

Game

While game is often found at pricier restaurants, these casual tavern settings
are known for their unusual meats. **Grizzly's Lodge** (3831 N. Lincoln,
773/281-5112) recreates a North Woods hideaway and boasts buffalo,
venison, elk, quail, and wild boar on its menu ($6–$27). Open Sun.–Fri. 11
A.M.–2 A.M., Sat. 11 A.M.–3 A.M. The **Lincoln Tavern & Restaurant** (1858
W. Wabansia, 773/342-7778)—also with a lodge-like interior—has a Friday
night (6 P.M.–9 P.M.) roast duck special for $12.95, including soup and salad.
Call ahead for reservations. Open Mon.– Sat. 11 A.M.–2 A.M.

German

Berghoff Cafe/Berghoff Restaurant
17 W. Adams, 312/427-3170   **C**
Serving German and American food and their own beers since 1898, this
bastion of tradition was the first tavern in Chicago to receive a post-
Prohibition liquor license. Only in the last part of the twentieth century did
they begin hiring women for their uniformed waitstaff. Although every
penny you spend in the restaurant on sauerbraten, schnitzels, and creamed
spinach will be worth it, the more affordable route is the cafe's sandwich
line and grill. This is not a modern day concession, but an important element
of the **Berghoff** tradition. The dark wood room is adorned with intricate
carvings, stained glass, murals, mirrors, and a long, antique bar complete

with brass rail where diners stand to eat. Cafe classics include the hot corned beef, roast beef, fried halibut, and bratwurst sandwiches on homemade rye (most $7–$9). Enjoy with Berghoff's own beers, bourbons, or root beer on the side. Open Mon.–Thur. 11 A.M.–9 P.M., Fri. 11 A.M.–9:30 P.M., Sat. 11:30 A.M.–10 P.M.

Chicago Brauhaus
4732 N. Lincoln, 773/784-4444   **N**
Large, atmospheric restaurant, beer hall, and night club in Lincoln Square reverberates with live music (German, international, and American) for dancing (slow, fast, polka, ballroom) Wed.–Mon. 7 P.M.–2 A.M. Schnitzels (veal or pork tenderloins), sauerbraten, roast goose, *leberkäse* (thick fried pork/veal "bologna"), and *Königsberger klopse* (meatballs with caper sauce) top the entrée list ($9–$18). Sausage plates fall under $8. Popular with groups, older couples, and dancers. Two warnings: Service can be slow (go dance in the meantime), and the stage isn't visible from most tables in the tiny non-smoking section. Lunch $7–$12. Kitchen open weekdays (closed Tues.) 11 A.M.–midnight, Fri.–Sat. 11 A.M.–2 A.M.

Meyer's Delicatessen
4750 N. Lincoln, 773/561-3377   **N**
Tucked amidst the last German businesses in Lincoln Square (a couple doors from the **Brauhaus**), **Meyer's** sells a wide array of homemade sausages and breads, along with imported chocolates, mustards, cheeses, German specialty products, beer, and more. Come at the holidays just to experience everyone packed in the tiny space buying traditional holiday goodies to haul back to the suburbs. Deutsch is spoken. Open Mon.–Sat. 9 A.M.–7 P.M., Sun. 10 A.M.–5 P.M.

Stop in the picturesque **Merz Apothecary** (4716 N. Lincoln, 773/989-0900), which has been down the block for over a century, for homeopathic remedies, fine soaps and bath products, imported shampoos and toothpastes, and Euro-style counter service. They just opened a boutique, mini-version of themselves on the first floor of Marshall Field's State Street store, a testament to their charm and timeless appeal. Open Mon.–Sat. 9 A.M.–6 P.M.

Resi's Bierstube
2034 W. Irving Park, 773/472-1749   **N**
Beer garden, beer garden, beer garden. Large portions of exceptional homemade food, a friendly all-ages crowd, over 160 imported beers, reasonable prices, and the charming, aforementioned beer garden have brought **Resi's** a high percentage of regulars over the last few decades. Many groups

seem to congregate here, from Germans, Poles, Romanians, Latvians, Greek, Irish, and Mexicans to boaters, skiers, rugby players, cops, contractors, bankers, and pub crawlers, though those groups keep getting less-defined and younger. You won't find a lineup of depressing barflies on these barstools: the multi-generational regulars are more likely be discussing politics, history, sports, travel, or sex than drowning their sorrows in good beer. After putting in three years of weekend waitressing here, I feel qualified to recommend the *jagerschnitzel* (pork schnitzel with a brown mushroom gravy), potato pancakes, goulash soup (cold weather months), kassler ribs (smoked pork chops), Russian Eggs (needs too much explanation), wurst dinners (pick 2 from 7 kinds of sausage, plus potato salad and kraut), and homemade soups. Try a weiss beer (2 on tap, over 16 in bottles)—Resi's was the first tavern in the city to import this German specialty. Dinners ($9–$16) include a bowl of homemade soup or a house salad and noodles or potatoes. Sandwiches, $6–$9; sides, $3–$4. Open daily 3 P.M.–2 A.M. (Sat. until 3 A.M.). Kitchen open 5 P.M.–10 P.M. (Closed Mon.).

Greek

THIS three-block commercial strip on Halsted is all that remains of Chicago's once, much larger Greektown. However, it has seen some recent cosmetic improvements (note the classical columns), and its many restaurants are as vibrant and crowded as ever. Here are some all-round deals for food, atmosphere, service, and price.

Artopolis
306 S. Halsted, 312/559-9000   C
Artopolis, Greek for "breadtown," is a bakery/café/social haven/restaurant all wrapped into one. You'll not only find Grecian foods here, but French and Italian as well, making it an all-around Mediterranean café. Appetizers ($3–$8) include the Mediterranean Fest (hummus, fava, baba ghanoush, tzatziki, tabouleh, and olives) and seasonal soups. Signature sandwiches ($6–$8) include the café sandwich, a special creation of the day. Pick from eight salads under $9 including Frutti Di Mare (shrimp, octopus and calamari, marinated in olive oil and lemon) and the Jardin (greens, walnuts, tomatoes, Brie, pear, and raspberry vinaigrette.) Artopolis also serves pizzas, pastas, coffees, teas, and a large dessert selection. This a great place to grab a sandwich or a snack during the day. Seating is on two levels, with views out onto Halsted. Live music is sometimes played in the evening. Open Sun.–Thur. 9 A.M.–midnight, Fri.–Sat. 9 A.M.–1 A.M.

Athena Restaurant
212 S. Halsted, 312/655-0000   C

Athena, one of the nicer restaurants in Greektown, has a stunning outdoor eating area (waterfall included). Menu items include *moussaka* (eggplant, zucchini, potatoes, ground beef and béchamel sauce), *Kotopoulo kebob* (chicken, onion, tomato, green pepper and rice pilaf), s*panakopita*, and Alexander chicken stuffed with cheeses and served with rice pilaf ($10–$12). For the newbie to Greek cuisine, consider ordering the appetizers tapas style. Athena offers a nice selection of hot and cold appetizers ($4–$12) including *saganaki*, assorted Greek cheeses and olives, *melitzanosalata* (roasted eggplant spread), *octapodi* (octopus), *tiropitakia* (small cheese pies), *loukaniko* (Greek sausage), and *ortikia* (quail.) Athena offers several Greek salads and authentic Greek dinners for under $12 including Chicken Riganati (baked chicken with lemon and oregano). Desserts include *galaktobouriko* (lemon flavored custard in honey-dipped filo dough) and *rizogalo* (rice pudding). Open daily 11 A.M.–midnight.

Greek Islands
200 S. Halsted, 312/782-9855   C

This Greektown classic may draw the biggest crowds on Halsted, with its perpetual bustle, Greek village atmosphere, and great food. Braised lamb in various forms, seafood (sea bass, red snapper, octopus, calamari, cod), moussaka, pastichio, and most other meals keep customers returning. Half portions are available. Entrées, including the daily specials $8–$18, most under $11. Open Sun.–Thur. 11 A.M.–midnight, Fri.–Sat. 11 A.M.–1 A.M.

Pan Hellenic
322 S. Halsted, 312/454-1886   C

Regular items at this 30-year family-owned and operated bakery include *amigdalta* (sweet and chewy almond cookies), *koulovria*, *kourabiedes* (Greek wedding cookies), *kataifi*, *floyeres* (also comes dipped in chocolate), *paximadio*, and Louie's cookies (a chewy double-decker chocolate cookie with brownie characteristics, and our favorite), *melomakarouka*, *saragio* (Greek Christmas cookies), baklava, custard cakes, and breads. Prices range from $7–$10/lb. Buy in bulk to go (prepackaged goodies are ready for quick sale on tables in middle of store) or relax at one of the tables and eat your pastry with a nice cup of coffee and conversation with Louie (one of the best treats in the place.) Open Mon.–Thur. 9 A.M.–8 P.M., Fri.–Sat. 9 A.M.–9 P.M., Sun. noon–6 P.M.

Parthenon
314 S. Halsted, 312/726-2407   C

The oldest restaurant in Greektown (1968) claims to have both created flaming saganaki (a melted cheese appetizer delivered with cries of

"Opaa!") and to have introduced gyros to Chicago. Its polished, contemporary dining room is the site of hearty eating, ouzo swilling, spirited gatherings, and intimate meetings. Of the dozens of entrées, narrow your selection to the lamb (roasted, barbecued, braised, chops) and seafood (red snapper, codfish, shrimp or scallops flambé) dishes. Grazing from the appetizer list makes a fine meal, too. Appetizers $3–$9. Entrées $5–$20, most under $12. Ouzo is sold by the carafe. Open Sun.–Thur. 11 A.M.–midnight, Fri.–Sat. 11 A.M.–12:30 A.M.

Pegasus
130 S. Halsted, 312/226-4666   **C**
Greektown is situated just south and west enough of the Loop to offer a wonderful view. Enjoy it even more while enjoying the Greek/Mediterranean cuisine on the rooftop at **Pegasus**. Appetizers include saganaki, *tiropitakia* (feta cheese in filo dough), and taramasalata (red Greek caviar) for about $4 to $6. Many of the dinners, including *arni kokkinisto* (lamb served with vegetables, rice, or potato), Yiayias Fry Pan (Greek-style fajitas), and *makaronada* (imported macaroni), are under $10. Open Mon.–Sat. 11 A.M.–midnight, Sun. noon–midnight.

Roditys Restaurant
222 S. Halsted, 312/454-0800   **C**
Try some of their original Greek dishes for under $10: *moussaka* (eggplant and ground beef), *dolmades* (stuffed grape leaves with ground beef, rice, and cream sauce), spanikopita (spinach and cheese pie), the Grecian-style chicken, lamb shishkabob, homemade Greek sausage, or *keftedes* (Greek meatballs). Other menu items include lamb (loin, leg, braised, shishkabob, fried liver), steer, seafood (shrimp, squid, swordfish), and broiled chicken. Let that all digest with a cup of Greek coffee. Check daily specials for good deals. Open Sun.–Thur. 11 A.M.–midnight, Fri.–Sat. 11 A.M.–1 A.M.

Guatemalan

Café Las Delicias
4911 N. Western, 773/293-0656   **FN**
This tiny Lincoln Square family-run restaurant serves up some of the best *pupusas* in town. Cornmeal patties stuffed with pork, beans, cheese, seafood, or grilled zucchini, these made-to-order classics are under $2 each and reason enough to stop by. Guatemalan style tamales, tostadas, and tacos join traditional Mexican entrées like fajitas and chili rellenos, and breakfast specials include delicious coffee and plantains. Prices here are cheap and the food is fresh and high quality, though the interior is lacking and might be

why the delivery and carry-out business does so well. Open Sun.–Thur. 10 A.M.–10 P.M., Fri.–Sat. 10 A.M.–11 P.M.

El Tinajón
2054 W. Roscoe, 773/525-8455   N
Decorated with wind chimes, clay dolls, and colorful photos and textiles of Guatemala, **El Tinajón** gives off a warm and friendly atmosphere for enjoying Guatemalan versions of tamales, tacos, and tostadas, along with more distinctive dishes like the *paches de papa* (potato tamales) or *shepes* (corn tamales filled with black beans). Entrées all run around $10 and come with plenty of sides, such as plantains, pinto beans, and homemade tortillas. For a great party with a couple of friends, try the *El Tablazo*—an assortment of pork, beef, and chicken simmered in house sauces and served with grilled shrimp, veggie shish kabobs, plenty of sides, and a bucket of beer (serves four). There's also a small but full-service bar. Open Mon.–Thur. 11 A.M.–10 P.M., Fri.–Sat. 10 A.M.–11 P.M., Sun. 9 A.M.–9 P.M.

Hot Dogs

FOR newcomers, visitors, and any residents who need reminding, a Chicago-style hot dog arrives with yellow mustard, relish, raw onions, tomatoes (no ketchup), and celery salt on a poppyseed bun. Grilled onions, a pickle spear, and hot peppers are acceptable additions. (Every contributor had their favorites, so we got a little windy here.)

Carm's Beef & Italian Ice
1057 W. Polk, 312/738-1046   C
Get a hot dog and fries for only $2, or two Vienna hot dogs with fries ($3.15). Open Mon.–Fri. 8 A.M.–7 P.M., Sat. 8 A.M.–5 P.M.

Comiskey Park/U.S. Cellular Field
333 W. 35th, 312/674-1000   S
At weekend evening games, the smell of fried onions wafting from the Kosher hot dog carts is enough to make any hot dog lover woozy with desire. The stands are only operable on weekends, however, and are located at various places on the main concourse.

Fat Tommy's
3256 W. 111th, 773/233-3287   FSW
Fat Tommy's is a little red restaurant with a big history. Named for Thomas Rakein, the 18-time hot dog eating champion, this restaurant proudly serves up the Fat Tommy Hot Dog with fries and a large drink for $3.75. Open Mon.–Fri. 11 A.M.–8:30 P.M., Fri.–Sat. 11 A.M.–8 P.M.

Fluky's
6821 N. Western, 773/274-3652   FN
Fluky's, home of the Chicago-style hot dog, started serving dogs on Maxwell and Halsted Streets in 1929 for a nickel. Having been voted Chicago's #1 hot dog in blind taste tests, this is one experience you're not going to want to miss. Choose from a pure beef, a fat-free hog dog, Polish sausage, and more. By the way, Fluky's helps celebrate Chicago's home-grown Pulaski Day holiday (1ˢᵗ Monday in March) by giving a free hot dog to anyone can prove that their first, middle, or last name ends in "ski." Open Mon.–Thur. 6 A.M.–10:30 P.M., Fri.–Sat. 6 A.M.– 11 P.M., Sun. 7 A.M.–10 P.M.

Gilhooley's Grand Saloon
3901 W. 103ʳᵈ Street, 773/233-2200   FSW
Gilhooley's is the local hangout for St. Xavier Students as the university is across the street. Check for daily specials. Open daily 11 A.M.–1 A.M.

Hot Doug's
2314 W. Roscoe, 773/348-0326   N
The Britney Spears (fire hot dog), the Psycho Ronnie Raines (corn dog), the Howard Devoto (veggie dog), the Charlie & James Sohn (bagel dogs & tater tots), and the Dog (Chicago-style hot dog) are just a few of the eats available at **Hot Doug's**. Other items include the Roseanne Tellez (bratwurst), the Luca Brasi (Italian sausage), and don't forget to check the Jackie Bange and Mash (daily special sausage with fries). Prices start at $1.50. Tempoarily closed because of a fire somewhere else on the property and looking for a new home, we still had to include them because we love this fast-food "home of encased meats."

Janson's Drive-in
9900 S. Western, 773/238-3612   SW
This low-priced drive-in has been selling hot dog favorites and carrying on the mysterious tradition of taking orders on brown paper bags since 1960. Red hots, spicy dogs, cheese dogs, chili dogs, and chili cheese dogs run under $3. Most of the items on the decently-sized menu are under $5. Among their shakes, floats, sundaes, and other ice cream offerings, the fresh strawberry and fresh banana shakes are exceptionally worthy. Monthly specials posted inside. Open Mon.–Sat. 10 A.M.–10 P.M., Sun. 11 A.M.–6 P.M.

Pop's
10337 S. Kedzie, 773/239-1243   FSW
Pop's has some of the best deals around–hot dog and fries or Swiss burgers are under $2, and the heartier appetite can feast on a half slab of ribs with

fries and cole slaw for about $8. Open Sun.–Thur. 11 A.M.–9 P.M., Fri.–Sat. 11 A.M.–10 P.M.

Superdawg
6363 N. Milwaukee, 773/763-0660   **FN**
Mr. Hot Dog with his caveman leopard skin, goofy bravado, and red blinking-light eyes poses with a coy Ms. Hot Dog, in her matching dress and bow, atop this landmark (1948) hot dog stand. The pure beef Superdawg ($3.95 with tax) comes dressed with all the trimmings (mustard, NO ketchup, piccalilli, a kosher dill, chopped onions, green tomatoes, and the optional hot peppers) on a poppyseed bun, accompanied by the highly touted crinkle-cut fries. Burgers, chicken, fish, and Polishes also come Super-style and include fries. Call your order over the intercom at your parking spot and a carhop will deliver the goods (and pick up trash later) for in-car dining. Open Sun.–Thur. 11 A.M.–1 A.M., Fri.–Sat. 11 A.M.–2 A.M.

The Wiener Circle
2622 N. Clark, 773/477-7444   **N**
The grand prize winner for many is the char-dog ($2.58) at this compact hot dog stand. It's split and darkened on the grill, then dressed appropriately for Windy City palettes. Enhance your meal by visiting after hours with other diehard fans of the charbroiled pup. Open daily 11 A.M.–4 A.M.

Hungarian

Paprikash Hungarian Restaurant
5210 W. Diversey, 773/736-4949   **NW**
Chicago's only Hungarian eatery, this large, friendly bar/restaurant would shine even if it did have competitors. The Hungarian Farmer's Plate appetizer offers tastes of homeland sausages, salamis, and cheeses; vegetarians can try the potato pancake with *lecso* (mixed steamed vegetables). Succulent entrées ($8–$14) like chicken paprikash, veal paprikash, beef goulash, and broiled pork chops will keep you smiling from start to finish. *Somloi* (yellow sponge cake with mixed fruit, custard, chocolate sauce, and whipped cream) or *parecsinpa* (crepes with strawberry, apricot, or sweet cheese filling) for dessert are additional delights. This is a great place to linger . . . pick out one of their 30 kinds of Hungarian wine to accompany your meal and follow everything with some Hungarian schnapps or brandy. Music most weekends. Open Wed.–Fri. 5 P.M.–midnight, Sat.–Sun.11 A.M.–midnight

Ice Cream

Gertie's Ice Cream

3685 S. Archer, 773/927-7807	SW
6544 S. Archer, 773/229-1512	SW
7600 S. Pulaski, 773/582-2510	SW
11009 S. Kedzie, 773/779-7236	SW

Now part of the **Gertie's Ice Cream** and **Lindy's Chili** chain (see p.158), this old-time ice cream parlor is notable not only for the great homemade ice cream but the over-sized stuffed animals peering through the store-front windows. Phosphates, sodas, shakes, sundaes, splits, and other creations of homemade ice cream, yogurt, and whipped cream run about $2 to $5. Open daily, hours vary from location to location.

Margie's Candies

1960 N. Western, 773/384-1035   N

Everything in the Poulos's old-fashioned ice cream parlor and candy shop (around since 1921) throws you back to an earlier era of ice cream eating: the uniforms, service, dishes, and décor. Ice cream creations start around $3 to $4 for most individual servings and run up to $35 for a group monstrosity. Also for sale are the hand-dipped candies, balloons, flowers, and stuffed animals. Open Sun.–Thur. 9 A.M.–midnight, Fri.–Sat. 9 A.M.–1 A.M.

Mario & Gino's

2057 W. Roscoe, 773/529-8664   N

This small Roscoe Village parlor serves Double Rainbow brand ice cream, gelato, and sorbet. Sugar-free and soy ice cream varieties are available, making **Mario's** a summer staple for those with restricted diets. Open Sun.–Thur. noon–10 P.M., Fri.–Sat. noon–11 P.M.

Original Rainbow Cone

9233 S. Western 773/238-7075   SW

In the summer, the line at this Southwest Wide institution can stretch out the door and around the corner. Family-owned since 1926, the store's namesake cone is a pile of chocolate, strawberry, Palmer House (New York vanilla with cherries and walnuts), pistachio, and orange sherbet. Other delights include sundaes, shakes, and banana splits. **Rainbow Cone** also has a stand in Union Station's underground food court and is a popular booth at the yearly **Taste of Chicago** (p. 289). Open Sun.–Thur. 1 P.M.–9 P.M., Fri.–Sat. 1 P.M.–10 P.M. Closed from Dec. 23 to Feb. 1.

Zephyr Ice Cream Restaurant
1777 W. Wilson, 773/728-6070   **N**
Much of the reputation of this ice cream asylum is due to its Art Deco décor
and theme menu. Individual ice cream concoctions run $2.50–$4.50. Try the
famous French fried ice cream or share the ten-scoop "War of the Worlds"
sundae. Open Sun.–Thur. 8 A.M.–midnight, Fri.–Sat. 8 A.M.–1 A.M.

Indian/Pakistani

THE best spot for Indian dining is Devon Avenue (from about 2200–2700
West), the lifeline of Chicago's Indian/Pakistani community. Top off your
lunch or dinner here with a stroll and a browse (see p. 315).

Four time-tested, all-round good deals:

Gandhi Indian
2601 W. Devon, 773/761-8714   **FN**
Various vegetarian, chicken, and lamb dishes round out the tandoori specialties from the clay oven ($8–$12) and biryani rice specialties ($8–$10).
All-inclusive sampler dinners are about $12. Open Sun.–Thur. 11:30 A.M.–
10 P.M., Fri.–Sat. 11:30 A.M.–11 P.M.

Hema's Kitchen
6406 N. Oakley, 773/338-1627   **FN**
Once upon a time not too long ago, **Hema's** was a no-frills, super-cheap
one-person business in a narrow, side-street storefront. Then Hema's decorated a little and continued serving her fresh, homemade, made-to-order
Indian specialties. Then WTTW's *Check, Please!* (see p. 431) profiled
Hema's Kitchen. She's now the belle of the ball, has tripled the size of her
restaurant, and we all continue to eat there happily ever after. Hema
recommends the chicken masala—boneless chicken in a rich gravy—for
meat-eaters and the spinach & cheese, eggplant & potato, or lentil dishes for
vegetarians. Most dishes $4–$8. Open Mon.–Sat. 10 A.M.–9 P.M., Sun. 11
A.M.–7 P.M.

Mysore Woodland
2548 W. Devon, 773/338-8160   **FN**
This Southern Indian restaurant features an all-vegetarian menu and is as
popular with India natives as it is with adventurous Chicagoans. A little
cheaper than its sister restaurant, **Indian Garden**, this is a great option for
vegetarians who can really fill up for about $12. The vegetable samosas are
perfectly spiced and flaky and a deal at $3. Traditional South Indian
pancakes are excellent here, available in the topped *uthappam* or filled *dosai*

styles for around $7. But it's the *pongal avial* that is the house specialty—lentil and rice mash accompanied by stewed veggies and topped with a perfectly balanced masala sauce for $8. Traditional *paratha* bread and *lassi* drinks are consistently good bets. Open Sun.–Thur. 11:30 A.M.–9:30 P.M., Fri.–Sat. 11:30 A.M.–10 P.M.

Udupi Palace
2543 W. Devon, 773/338-2152   FN
Though the décor targets the commoners, the completely vegetarian food is fit for royalty. South Indian favorites include *dosai* (filled with potato and onions) and *udhapam* ("Indian-style pizza" with various toppings). Crowded on the weekends. Entrées $4–$16, most under $9, lunch specials $8.

This strip abounds with lunch and dinner buffets of various stripes ($5–$10), which make a tasty introduction to Indian and Pakistani cuisine. For starters, try **Indian Garden** (2546 W. Devon, 773/338-2929) and **Sher-a-Punjab** (2510 W. Devon, 773/973-4000).

When it's time to go classy (white tablecloths and the like), head to **Indian Garden**, **Tiffin** (2536 W. Devon, 773/338-2143), or **Viceroy of India** (2520 W. Devon, 773/743-4100), where the prices are higher, but still inexpensive, and you can order a beer.

Besides serving tasty, inexpensive Indian and Pakistani cuisine, the centrally located **Zaiqa** (858 N. Orleans, 312/280-6807) offers other special features for its customers. Muslims will appreciate their Halal meat and five daily prayer sessions in the basement. Everyone will enjoy the charming outdoor dining. Open daily, 24 hours.

Another North Side option...

Standard India
917 W. Belmont, 773/929-1123   N
A favorite among the Lakeview locals and commonly referred to simply as "SIR," this decade-old buffet restaurant lives up to its name. Nothing fancy or out of the ordinary here, but good traditional dishes and all-you-can-eat for $9 ($8 for lunch). The buffet changes only slightly, keeping the vegetarian soup, samosas, pakoras, tandoori chicken, chick peas, saffron rice and *malak paneer* (cheese and peas in mildly spicy sauce) as its constants. The main dishes usually cover one type of curry (usually chicken) and one vindaloo (usually lamb). For vegetarians, the spicy chick peas, potatoes with mushrooms, sauteed spinach and paneer are almost always present. The

buffet also includes a sweet ending, with both rice pudding and gulab jamon (small cheese doughnuts floating in honey sauce). Open Mon.–Fri. 9 A.M.–5 P.M., Sat. 9 A.M.–midnight.

Irish

Abbey Pub and Restaurant
3420 W. Grace, 773/478-4408   **NW**
This multi-faceted Irish nightclub darling caters to many needs. They offer decent Irish and pub fare (entrées $7–$12, most under $9), live music (Irish, folk, rock, other), Irish sports TV, and neighborhood bar amenities (darts, pool, beer specials). Open Sun.–Fri. 10 A.M.–2 A.M., Sat. 10 A.M.–3 A.M.

Chief O'Neill's Pub and Restaurant
3471 N. Elston, 773/583-3066   **N**
A large, inviting pub in the Avondale neighborhood, **Chief O'Neill's** serves Irish and American pub food including a seafood stew brimming with mussels and the requisite corned beef. Live music on Sundays and Tuesdays, and an awesome fireplace. Sunday brunch 10:30 A.M.–3 P.M. $10.95 for adults, $5.95 for kids under 10. Open Mon.–Fri. 11:30 A.M.–2 A.M., Sat. 11:30 A.M.–3 A.M., Sun. 10:30 A.M.–1 A.M.

Fifth Province
4626 N. Knox, 773/282-7035   **NW**
Housed in the **Irish American Heritage Center,** the name of this pub refers to Irish President Mary Robinson's remark that the Irish in America consti-tute the country's "Fifth Province." Open on Fridays and Saturdays with traditional food, drink, and music. Open Fri.–Sat. 6 P.M.–1 A.M. (food is served until 10 P.M.).

The Irish Oak
3511 N. Clark, 773/935-6669   **N**
An Irish pub that feels like it's been there since the Potato Famine. The décor: faded damask-covered booths and an Oscar Wilde quote over the bar ("I have nothing to offer this country except my genius"). Our food recom-mendations: the excellent seafood chowder served with a thick slice of grainy soda bread, Irish chips topped with red cheddar cheese sauce, and an Irish breakfast served all day. Open Mon.–Fri. 11 A.M.–2 A.M., Sat 11 A.M.–3 A.M., Sun. 11 A.M.– 2 A.M.

Kitty O'Shea's
720 S. Michigan, 312/922-4400 x. 4455   **C**
Named for a Dublin pub, this hotel (Chicago Hilton & Towers) bar even imports some of its staff from the old sod. Irish chow and American pub food line the menu. After a meal of shepherd's pie, Scotch eggs (hard-boiled eggs rolled in a mixture of chopped sausage and bread crumbs), fish & chips, lamb stew, or corned beef and cabbage, enjoy some bread pudding for dessert, another Guinness or Harp, and the live Irish music. Entrées $8–$14. Live music Mon.–Sat. 9:30 P.M.–1 A.M.

Follow up late weekend nights at the bars with a hearty Irish breakfast in the pubs first thing Saturday or Sunday Morning. The classic Irish breakfast is a food spree bound to soak up last night's hangover: eggs, bangers (sausage), black and white puddings (sausage-like), rashers (bacon), grilled tomato, potatoes, mushrooms, and soda bread. The **Abbey Pub** (see above) offers this feast 9 A.M.–2 P.M. for $8.95, and the **Hidden Shamrock** (2723 N. Halsted, 773/883-0304) starting at 10:30 A.M. on Sat. and 11 A.M. on Sun. for $8.95. When you feel like an Irish breakfast for supper, both locations also serve this treat on weekdays after 4 P.M.

Israeli
SEE ALSO Kosher.

Hashalom Restaurant
2905 W. Devon, 773/465-5675   **FN**
The honorary street sign "Golda Meir Boulevard" at the corner of Devon and Francisco says it all. In the midst of the small concentration of Kosher bakeries and shops around this intersection, **Hashalom** serves up Israeli and Mediterranean cuisine to culinary adventurers, regular customers, and recent immigrants. A clock on the wall keeps Tel Aviv time. Substantial appetizers and salads range from $2 to $8 and entrées are generally under $10. Finish your meal with steaming hot Turkish coffee served in a glass with no handles. Open Mon.–Fri. noon–9 P.M. Closed for Jewish holidays.

Italian

Taylor Street

Caffé LaScala
626 S. Racine, 312/421-7262   **C**
All of Rico's antipasta salads (11) are under $10; choices include *vongole*

crude (fresh clams), calamari, broiled octopus, and *frisella alla napoletana* (Italian bread with tomatoes, olives, onions, garlic and cheese). Eleven of their Italian specialty dinners are under $10 and include vermicelli alla puttanesca (with olives and capers), fettuccine alfredo, spaghetti, cavatelli, and fidelini al pomodoro (homemade egg noodle angel hair pasta.) Many Italian (Sicilian, Venetian, Tuscan) wines for under $5 per glass! Besides great food, **Caffé LaScala** offers a laid back atmosphere in a location oozing with character and history. Open Mon.–Fri. 11 A.M.–2 P.M. for lunch, Mon.–Thur. 4 P.M.–9:30 P.M. for dinner, Fri.–Sat. 4 P.M.–10:30 P.M. for dinner.

Café Viaggio
1435 W. Taylor, 312/226-9009   C

We suggest you stop in for lunch, an early dinner, or drinks—chocolate martini—as one way around pastas and entrées that are $13 and up. Instead, opt for the five hearty appetizers under $10 and five salads under $10. The signature salad is baby greens with roasted red peppers, gorgonzola cheese, artichoke hearts, and red onions with house dressing $7. Open Tues.–Thur. 5 P.M.–9 P.M., Fri. 11:30 A.M.–10 P.M., Sat. 4:30 P.M.–10:30 P.M., Sun. 8 A.M.–2 P.M. for breakfast, 4 P.M.–9 P.M. for dinner.

Little Joe's
1041 W. Taylor, 312/829-5888   C

This restaurant/bar serves dinner (with soup and salad for $7 to $12) including baked eggplant, pan-fried cheese ravioli, and Sicilian sausage. Sandwiches ($4–$6) include selections like charbroiled Sicilian sausage, and an eggplant foccacia sandwich. Appetizers run $3 and up and include clams and seafood. Open Sun.–Fri. at 3 P.M., Sat. at 5 P.M., no set hours for closing.

The Rosebud
1500 W. Taylor, 312/942-1117   C

This Windy City classic—ideal for both romantic outings and lively group dinners—is the proud originator of Chicken Vesuvio. Though this famed invention is still a good bet, take heed of **The Rosebud**'s recent nomination as one of the top 15 pasta restaurants in the country. A single order of one of their signature homemade cavatelli (finger-like dumplings) dishes may be the tastiest pasta bargain in town. The $14.95 entrée portion can literally feed 2–4. Add an antipasto salad, a side of Italian sausage, and tiramisu for dessert and you have an affordable feast. Open Mon.–Thur. 11 A.M.–10:30 P.M., Fri. 11 A.M.–11:30 P.M., Sat. 5 P.M.–11:30 P.M., Sun. 11 A.M.–10:30 P.M.

To grab some good food fast on Taylor Street, stop in the **Pompei Bakery** (p. 213) for their singular pizza concoctions or **Al's #1 Italian Beef** (p. 189) for an Italian beef tradition.

A pilgrimage to be made at least once each summer . . .

Mario's Italian Lemonade
1068 W. Taylor   C
This seasonal Taylor Street stand is a Chicago landmark for Italian lemonade. A dozen slushy flavors can be enjoyed in a range of sizes, from a small cup (about a buck) to a small bucket (around $5). The watermelon and traditional lemonade flavors are hits. Open May 1–Oct. 1

South Oakley: Chicago's "Heart of Italy"

"Hidden" away just east of Western Avenue is a 3-block strip of Italian restaurants dating back to when diminutive alderman Vito Marzullo ruled a large portion of Chicago's Southwest Side. The restaurants are small and cozy, but can have a mythical feel—like you're eating in the kitchen of someone's Italian grandmother, in a faded-glory banquet hall, and on a movie set of the old neighborhood all rolled into one. **Bruna's Ristorante** (2424 S. Oakley, 773/254-5550) was opened in 1933, making it the oldest of the lot. Entrées range from $8 to $17, with most under $12. Other affordable options include **Bacchanalia Ristorante** (2413 S. Oakley, 773/254-6555), and **La Fontanella** (2414 S. Oakley, 773/927-5249).

Pasta cheap-eats in other neighborhoods:

Carm's Beef & Italian Ice
1057 W. Polk, 312/738-1046   C
1603 N. Lake Shore Drive (North Ave. Beach: Summer hours only.)   N
Carm's and **Fontano's Subs** (across the street on Polk) are family-owned operations (second and third generations) that originally started in 1929, when UIC started to build up. Carm's is no secret to those in the UIC area, particularly students. The hefty helpings and thrifty prices allow college kids to spend more money, on, um, beer . . . posters for their dorm room walls. Sub sandwiches (28 varieties) run $3–$5 (small), $4–$6 (medium), $5–$7 (large), and $18–$26 for the three-footer. Italian ice is also available starting at $1 for a number of fresh fruit flavors. Summer and winter hours differ. Open Mon.–Fri. 8 A.M.–7 P.M., Sat. 8 A.M.–5 P.M. (These are the winter hours; the summer hours vary.)

Pasta Palazzo
1966 N. Halsted, 773/248-1400   N
Cross a slick diner with bursts of color and you have the lively setting for this affordable pasta lollapalooza. Try the Classico (shells with Italian sausage and red bell peppers) or Cavatappi Polo (corkscrews with grilled chicken, mushrooms, sun-dried tomato, and cream sauce) and you're bound to come back for more. Fresh soups, grilled calamari, and polenta appetizers make it harder to finish the main dish. Dinners run $8–$15. Open Mon.–Thur. 11:30 A.M.–9:30 P.M., Fri.–Sat. 11:30 A.M.–10:30 P.M., Sun 11:30 A.M. 8:30 P.M.

Trattoria Caterina
616 S. Dearborn, 312/939-7606   C
Printer's Row trattoria offers 27 fantastic pasta dishes along with a handful of chicken entrées and hot Italian sandwiches. Linguine with mussels, ziti marinera, angel hair with sun-dried tomatoes, fettucine alfredo, or lasagna rolls: no entrée is more than $12 and most run $8–$10. BYOB. Open Mon.–Thur. 11 A.M.–9 P.M., Fri. 11A.M.–10 P.M., Sat. 5 P.M. – 9 P.M.

Trattoria E Oggi Cafe
1378 W. Grand, 312/733-0442   C
Pasta dishes include spaghetti with meatballs, manicotti, stuffed shells, and the Oggi special (angel hair pasta served with their special matarocco sauce) all for under $8. Open Mon.–Thur. 11 A.M.–10 P.M., Fri. 11 A.M.–11 P.M., Sat. 11 A.M.–10 P.M., Sun. 11 A.M.–9 P.M.

The truly patient who want a neighborhood pasta and pizza powerhouse a step up from the cheap-eats can head to **Mia Francesca** (3311 N. Clark, 773/281-3310). The nightly crowds and hour-long waits (at times, an underestimate) testify to its worthiness.

Old-world baked goods . . .

D'Amato's Bakery (1124 W. Grand, 312/733-5456) not only bakes some of the greatest Italian breads, but also sells their unique pizza in baker's sheets (party size) for $27–$29. The city's oldest (est. 1908) and largest Italian pastry shop, **Ferrara's Original Bakery** (2210 W. Taylor, 312/666-2200) transports you to a previous era the minute your foot crosses the threshold.

Italian Beefs/Italian Sausages

"BEEFS," as we say in these parts, are a Chicago original that have been around since the late 1940s. Thinly sliced beef (with all the fat trimmed) is piled into an Italian or French bread bun, topped with sweet green peppers or hot giardiniera, and given a ritual drenching in the cooking juices (unless you order it "dry.")

Al's #1 Italian Beef
1079 W. Taylor, 312/226-4017   C
Featured in Jane and Michael Stern's *Road Food*, in *Gourmet* magazine, on the *Today Show*, and on *Good Morning America*, **Al's** 65-year-old sandwich shop has caught the nation's attention as the apparent inventor and favored vendor of this Chicago culinary icon. Al's Beef was served at Hillary Clinton's 50th birthday party (even though she is now a New Yorker). Beefs with a drink run under $5. Open Mon.–Thur. 10 A.M.–11 P.M., Fri.–Sat. 10 A.M.–1 A.M.

Mr. Beef
666 N. Orleans, 312/337-8500   C
Another contender for Chicago's best, **Mr. Beef**'s has been serving beefs ($5) with their special giardiniera for 20 years. This is Jay Leno's favorite place in Chicago to snag a beef sandwich. (They all need celebrity endorsements.) Open Mon.–Fri. 9 A.M.–5 P.M., Sat. 10:30 A.M.–2 P.M.

Another uniquely Chicago snack, a spicy Italian sausage, parked in a crusty roll and blanketed with soft green peppers, shouldn't be missed by those seeking out regional delicacies.

Benedict's Delicatezzi Italiano
2501 S. Archer, 312/225-1122 (no answer or voice mail)   SW
An eye-catching little place perched on a corner near Archer and Halsted, **Benedict's** serves an outstanding Italian sausage sandwich smothered in cheese, red sauce, and peppers, and an equally yummy Italian sub sandwich loaded with capicola, salami, mortadella and provolone cheeses, and Benedict's flavored olive oil. Most sandwiches under $5. Benedict's also serves homemade cannoli and Eli's Famous Cheesecake.

Go with a friend and get one of each . . .

Boston Bar-B-Q
2932 W. Chicago, 773/486-9536 **W**
Some of the best and biggest, since 1949. Beefs and Italian sausages about
$4, an extra quarter for peppers. Open Mon.–Sat. 9 A.M.–10 P.M.

Freddie's
701 W. 31st, 312/808-0149 **S**
Scrumptious monster beefs and Italian sausages under $5, under $6 with
fries. Open daily 9:30 A.M.–midnight.

Jamaican
FOR home-cooked Jamaican carry-outs and fast food:

The **Caribbean American Baking Company** (1539 N. Howard, 773/761-
0700) prepares Jamaican baked goods, sweets, and beef patties daily. **Taste
of Jamaica**, part of Nathan's Deli, (1372 E. 53rd, 773/955-4373) makes
authentic jerk and curry dishes, escoveitch fish, and beef patties, most under
$7. For sit-down dining, you can probably escape the homey **Linette's
Jamaican Kitchen** (7366 N. Clark, 773/761-4823) with a full stomach of
Jamaican specialties (seafood, beef and vegetable patties, jerk chicken, and
pork) for under $15.

Japanese
NEARLY every close-in North Side neighborhood boasts hip new sushi
restaurants at various price points. Here's but a handful of the old-timers
with one newbie for contrast.

Matsuya Restaurant
3469 N. Clark, 773/248-2677 **N**
Beloved and mobbed: This is Chicago's best all-things-considered Japanese
dining, from the grilled squid and soft-shell crab appetizers, to the Osaka-
style sushi and the teriyaki entrées. If you're not already going with a sushi
combination, pick up a piece of salmon, red snapper, or mackerel on the
side. Appetizers and sushi $2–$7, rice/noodle dishes $6–$8, main dishes
$8–$20, many under $12. Open Mon.–Fri. 5 P.M.–11:30 P.M., Sat.–Sun.
noon–11:30 P.M.

Nohana
3136 N. Broadway, 773/528-1902 **N**
Price-dueling for years with other longstanding neighborhood sushi joints,
Nohana offers deals aplenty. Deluxe sushi dinners with miso soup, rolls, an

array of fresh fish (tuna, flounder, salmon, red snapper, mackerel, octopus), and tea go for $8 to $10, Mon.–Sat. During the "happy hours" of noon–1 P.M. and 5 P.M.–6 P.M. Mon.–Sat., they do a brisk business in $1 nigiri pieces and $2–$2.75 maki rolls. Open Mon.–Thur. 5 P.M.–9:30 P.M., Fri. 5 P.M.–10 P.M., Sat. 12 P.M.–10 P.M., Sun. 5 P.M.–9 P.M.

Sai Café (2010 N. Sheffield, 773/472-8080), a relaxed and convivial Lincoln Park favorite for affordable sushi, served nontraditional roll combinations like the salmon and cream cheese bagel maki before it was hip in a bustling, nondescript setting. **Hey Sushi** (2630 N. Clark, 773/248-3900), on the other hand, has the wide variety of maki (Octopus in a Hawaiian-style marinade, American tuna salad, sweet corn in a creamy sauce, panko encrusted pork and cucumber), along with sake-tinis, cocktails blended with energy drinks, dining from couches or the lunch-style counter, and a Tokyo club feel. Rolls and nigiri (2 pieces/order) run $2.50–$7, most under $5. Food prices are good; they get you on the drinks.

And for a complete evening of traditional Japanese dining and entertainment, head to **Midori** (3310 W. Bryn Mawr Ave., 773/267-9733). Call ahead to reserve one of their four tatami rooms for intimate feasting with friends; afterwards head next door to work off your meal with late night crooning in one of their private karaoke rooms.

Korean

Chicago Kalbi House
3752 W. Lawrence Ave., 773/604-8183   NW
In a unique twist on Chicago dining, this is a Korean restaurant with Japanese owners (in Chicago it is common for Japanese restaurants to have Korean owners). This is THE place to go if you are a Japanese visitor. It is listed in all of the Japanese guidebooks to Chicago, and tourists, along with many Japanese celebrities, flock to it (you can see their photos and autographs on one of the walls of the restaurant). Apparently, Scottie Pippin likes this place too, as there are many pictures of him looking like he just finished a plate of yummy grilled food. **CKH** gives you that unique Asian touch of seating your party in a separate "private" room, so you won't actually see the visiting celebs. Open Wed.–Mon. 5 P.M.–midnight.

Cho Sun OK
4200 N. Lincoln, 773/549-5555   N
Happy confusion reigns at **Cho Sun OK**. If you are unfamiliar with Korean

restaurants (or the Korean language), this is one of those places that will make you feel like you've just landed in Seoul, without the 14-hour flight. The customers are mostly Korean, most of the waitresses don't speak English, the menu doesn't really help you, the TV is blaring local Korean programming, and the ventilation is bad (which is a good thing, as the place smells of barbecuing meat, and so do you after you leave). You might have to randomly point at a menu item or two, or the owner might stop by to help—his English is fine, and he's super friendly. Either way, you'll probably get some of the best Korean food this side of the 38th parallel. Open Mon.–Sat. 10:30 A.M.–10 P.M., Sun. 10:30 A.M.–9:30 P.M.

Jim's Grill
1429 W. Irving Park, 773/525-4050   N
Korean-American breakfast and lunch shop with a greasy-spoon vibe caters predominantly to vegetarians. Morning meals include teriyaki and shitaki mushroom omelettes. Vegetarian lunch offerings range from huge bowls of various noodle dishes to items like vegetable pancakes and vegetable tempura. Most dishes $4–$6. Open Mon.–Sat. 9 A.M.–3:30 P.M.

For grilling Korean barbecue dishes at your own table, head further north and west. **Jang Mo Lim** (6320 N. Lincoln, 773/509-0211) and **Hai Woon Dae** (6240 N. California, 773/764-8018) are popular neighborhood places with table-top grills. Most entrées, $7–$14.

Korean, Vegan, and Buddhist

Amitabul
6207 N. Milwaukee, 773/774-0276   FN
Relocated to the Norwood Park neighborhood from its original location on Southport, **Amitabul** still specializes in delicious noodle dishes, veggie pancakes, "cure-all" noodle soups, and revitalizing fruit drinks that enlighten the mind and body. Recommended items include the Mandoo Vegan Dumplings, "Dark Side of the Moon" (an array of mushrooms in black bean miso sauce), and the Spicy Kimchi Tofu Bi Bim Bop. A fountain/garden display adds to the soothing atmosphere. Most entrées fall in the $8 range for huge portions. Prepare for culinary nirvana. Open Tues.–Sat. noon–8:30 P.M., Sun. noon–7:30 P.M.

Kosher

2700–3000 W. Devon Avenue   FN

When the signs on the shops change over from Hindi to Russian and Hebrew, you know you've reached the city's largest concentration of kosher delis, bakeries, grocers, and fish markets. If you've never had challah or gefilte fish, treat yourself with a trip to this neighborhood. Down the street is the city's only kosher **Dunkin' Donuts** (3132 W. Devon, 773/262-4560) and kosher Chinese restaurant, **Mi Tsu Yun** (3010 W. Devon, 773/262-4630). Around the corner is the only kosher pizzeria:

Tel Aviv Kosher Pizza
6349 N. California, 773/764-3776   FN
Good food must run in the family since the owners of **Tel Aviv Kosher Pizza** and **Hashalom** (p. 185) are brothers. The all-vegetarian menu is strictly Kosher, and also delicious! Open Sun.–Thurs. 11 A.M.–11 P.M., Fri. 11 A.M.–3 P.M., Sat. open one hour after sundown–1 A.M. Closed for Jewish holidays.

Other notables in the area are **North Shore Baking** (2919 W. Touhy, 773/262-0600) and their famous potato knishes, the **Romanian Kosher Sausage Shop** (7200 N. Clark, 773/761-4141), and the **Tel-Aviv Kosher Bakery** (2944 W. Devon, 773/764-8877). Far from this strip, **Ashkenaz** (12 E. Cedar, 312/944-5006) is a kosher deli in the Rush Street area that serves a good bagel and cream cheese, lox, herring, and corned beef.

Laotian

Nhu Hoa Café
1020 W. Argyle, 773/878-0618   FN
Pleasant and attractive eatery proffers 40+ Laotian dishes alongside four times as many Vietnamese ones! **Nhu Hoa Café** has been serving up specials such as garlic shrimp, sweet & sour stuffed squid, tamarind duck, and beef salads garnished to perfection with fresh Vietnamese herbs for almost 15 years. Everything here is outstanding, so pick a few things from different categories and share. Be sure to include some roll-your-own spring rolls, or something that comes with the puffy shrimp chips for scooping. BYOB. Menu items $5–$25, most under $8. Open daily 10 A.M.–10 P.M.

Late-Night Wonders

Café Ibérico
739 N. LaSalle, 312/573-1510   C
This bustling, authentic tapas (appetizers) bar has won accolades from all

major local newspapers and was elected "The Best Hispanic Restaurant in Illinois" by *Hispanic Magazine*. A large bar area, huge dining room, and a downstairs *bodega* (cellar) can barely contain the enthusiastic crowds. The cold tapas ($3–$7) list contains all the Spanish standards: olives, artichokes, toasted bread with Manchego cheese, *tortilla española* (potato omelette), cured ham, cold octopus. The hot tapas ($3–$9) selection does just as well with its special preparations of mussels, scallops, clams, chorizo, squid, and goat cheese. Desserts heavy with caramel and custard are also great for sharing. Affordable brandy, amontillado, sherry, vino tinto, and sangria await. Open Sun.–Thur. 11 A.M.–11 P.M., Fri. 11 A.M.– 1:30 A.M., Sat. noon–1:30 A.M., Sun. noon–11 P.M.

Holiday Club
4000 N. Sheridan, 773/348-9600   N
Billing itself as "the swingers mecca," this mid-size bar has a sort of Vegas-meets-Chicago feel, with tongue-in-cheek Rat Pack décor. The original Wicker Park location was up and running for ten years (it's now closed), doing so well the owner was prompted to open a second location in early 2002. The kitchen turns out pretty good food for a bar that focuses on daily half price food or drink specials. Favorites include the Holiday hamburger (a 1/4 lb. burger with choice of house potatoes, mashed & gravy or salad for $7.50), the homemade soup of the day ($3), and the house-made pizzas (pesto or bacon, spinach, tomato are good bets for $8 to $9). Monday nights are a good initiation into the crowd, who pack it in for half price imported pints and $.25 chicken wings. Open Mon.–Fri. 6 P.M. –2 A.M., Sat. 6 P.M.–3 A.M., Sun. 10 A.M.–2 A.M.

Iggy's
1840 W. North, 312/829-4449   C
This swanky restaurant and bar with a nightclub feel moved from its original Milwaukee Avenue home, but is still "devoted to the pleasures of late-night dining." Grilled asparagus salad with almonds and Dijon dressing, artichoke heart fritters, crab and ricotta stuffed mushroom caps, jambalaya risotto, and scrambled eggs with cream cheese and scallions epitomize the menu offerings. The coffee (made with espresso and cinnamon) is peerless; the desserts (like Rustica—a richer tiramisu), phenomenal; and the almost 50 signature martinis (like the "Blue Velvet"), alluring. The food is worth the bucks. Salads and appetizers $6–$11, egg dishes and entrées $10–$17. Food served Sun.–Fri. until 1:15 A.M., Sat. until 2:15 A.M. Open Mon.–Thur. 5 P.M.–2 A.M, Fri. 3 P.M.–2 A.M., Sat. 11 A.M.–3 A.M., Sun. 11 A.M.–2 A.M.

Korean Restaurant
2659 W. Lawrence, 773/878-2095   N
When the newfangled Korean coffeehouses, pool halls, karaoke bars, and other hangouts close, this 24-hour corner storefront still provides sustenance. They prepare tasty marinated and grilled meats, ribs, kim chee, vegetarian pancakes, noodles galore, and a host of exotic soups that should quell any late-night hunger pangs. Entrées $6–$16, most under $9. Open daily, 24 hours.

For lighter Asian fare, there's Old Town's **Kamehachi** (1400 N. Wells, 312/664-3663), quite affordable if you stick with the sushi and maki rolls for your after clubbing noshing. Open Mon.–Sat. until 2 A.M., Sun. until midnight.

Los Dos Laredos
3120 W. 26th St., 773/376-3218   W
Head to the Mexican Little Village neighborhood for a fun way to cure your insomnia. The late-night **Los Dos Laredos** has been serving their authentic specialties for over 30 years. Fajitas, gorditas, burritos, tacos, and more accompanied by a jumbo 36-ounce margarita are sure to make you full and sleepy. Open 24 hours on the weekends, Sun. until 2 A.M., Mon.–Thur. 8 A.M.–midnight.

Two inexpensive and informal taco restaurants sit conveniently at the corner of Western & Armitage cheerfully filling people up all day and all night for just a few bucks. **Arturo's** (2001 N. Western 773/772-4944) is open 24/7, **Lazo's Tacos** (2009 N. Western, 773/486-3303) almost just as long. Flashier, even faster, with better vegetarian options, and right on Wicker Park's main intersection is everyone's favorite **Flash Taco** (1570 N. Damen, 773/772-1997). Open Mon.–Fri. until 5 A.M., Sat. until 6 A.M., and Sun until 3 A.M., what a great place to spend your last few pesos after a neighborhood show.

Lucille's Tavern & Tapas
2470 N. Lincoln, 773/929-0660   N
A casual, sophisticated bar, specializing in wonderful tapas and fine cocktails, **Lucille's** serves food nightly until 1 A.M. Peanut-crusted catfish with a hoisin and wasabi swirl, pancetta-wrapped shrimp with Chardonnay buerre blanc, and drunken chicken and Monterey jack quesadillas typify their various tapas plates ($4–$9) which are geared for sharing. Try the daily specials. Open Sun.–Fri. 5 A.M.–2 A.M., Sat. 5 A.M.–3 A.M.

The Maxwell Street Depot
411 W. 31st, 312/326-3514   S
Known for its pork chop sandwiches and Polish sausage, this Bridgeport
eatery never closes . . . ever.

Pick Me Up Café
3408 N. Clark, 773/248-6613   N
Maybe one of the small handful of vegan-friendly restaurants in the city, this
late night spot is a favorite with that strange segment of twenty-somethings
who smoke like chimneys but wouldn't think of putting harmful meat in their
bodies. Regulars swear by the three-cheese grilled cheese with seasoned
fries, the huge burritos available veggie style, and the gigantic margarita
glass ice cream sundaes. The menu ranges from delicious artery-clogging
cheese fries and stuffed mushrooms to health-conscious hummus with fresh
veggies and pita. Both coffee drinks and dessert are available vegan-friendly
(made with soy), and a non-smoking section is available for a little more
quiet than the boisterous main room. With appetizers around $4–$8 and
entrées around $7–$11, it's a little pricier than 24-hour greasy spoons, but
it's not quite as greasy and, again, aimed at non-meat eaters. Open 24 hours
on the weekends, Sun.–Thur. until 3 A.M. Mon.–Thur. the restaurant opens at
3 P.M.

River Kwai Seafood II
1650 W. Belmont, 773/472-1013   N
Carved from the seedy streets of Bangkok and inserted in Chicago's trendy
North Side, this late-night, sub-level dive's menu is a welcome departure
from standard after-hours fare. But the tasty (and cheap!) Thai/Chinese eats
don't come easy. If you don't phone first, be prepared to wait up to an hour
for your dish—especially on weekends when the bars close. The portions are
large. The food is good. The proprietor is a hoot. But be warned! The wait
can be torturous—particularly if you've tied one on that night. And the
plastic lawn furniture, crawlspace-like dining area, and sometimes freakish
clientele can be a bad trip if you're not mentally prepared. Phone in your
order—or bring something to pass the time (e.g., deck of cards, good book,
or pen for napkin art). Most find this adventure in dining worthwhile, which
speaks volumes about the food. Recommended dishes include Spicy Noodle,
Lad Nar, Green Curry, and all soups offered. Plus, you can wash it all down
with River Kwai's version of the Big Gulp—a 32-oz. bottomless Thai iced
coffee! Located stumbling distance from the bars near Lincoln & Belmont
and a mere crawl from Gunther Murphy's. Open daily 11 P.M.–6 A.M.

Twisted Spoke
501 N. Ogden, 312/666-1500   C
Appealing to the "weekend warrior" in all of us, this biker motif restaurant/
bar is best known for three things: a human skeleton riding a motorcycle
perched atop the roof, the good 'n' greasy "Fat Boy" burgers, and the best
Bloody Mary in town. Gaining in popularity is the Saturday night "Smut 'n'

Mount Olympus, 24/7

THESE diner–fast-food eateries in Greektown are available 24/7 to help mere
mortals afflicted with stomach rumbling in the wee hours of the night.

Greektown Gyros
239 S. Halsted, 312/236-9310   C
$3 breakfast items include the Basic Breakfast (two eggs, potatoes, and
bread), Panorama (three vanilla pancakes), and French toast (Greek toast
with vanilla–cinnamon flavoring). Lunches include *Yeeros* (Gyros) sandwich with homemade tzatiziki sauce, *souvlaki* (pork kabob), and an array of
sandwiches, burgers, and salads ($3–$6.) Dinners include Greek-style
chicken, steak Mediterranean, Yerros Market, and the Souvlaki plate
($5–$7). **Greektown Gyros** is packed late-night and during lunchtime so
plan accordingly. Greek wines and beers are served daily from 11 A.M.–
4 A.M.

Mr. Greek Gyros
234 S. Halsted, 312/906-8731   C
Mr. GG is a good man because he offers some great meal deals in the $5
range like gyros, fries, and medium drink, souvlaki dinners, and spinach pie
dinners. He also has sandwiches such as rib eye steak and shishkabob, and
subs ($2–$5), and salads starting at $2. Omelettes are also available,
including the gyros omelette, hash browns, and toast for $4, and traditional
pastries under $3.

Zorba's House
301 S. Halsted, 312/454-1397   C
This late night diner offers a few Greek-themed omelette selections like the
gyros omelette or feta cheese one (both with hash browns and toast for
under $5.) For lunch try their pork chops, corned beef, Italian beef, and
sausage combo sandwiches ($3–$6). Dinners such as the Greek chicken,
veal cutlet, fried shrimp, and New York Steak include your choice of potato
and vegetable ($5–$10). Pizza, salads, and soups round out the menu. Late
nights and weekends you'll find mostly a college crowd.

Eggs," a late-night brunch served midnight–2:30 A.M. while vintage porn movies play in the background. Obviously not exactly a "family restaurant," the **Spoke** is however a great place to go for a great time, with loud music, a sarcastic staff (but actually funny), and wrecked bike remnants everywhere. The aforementioned burger and its equally greasy partners, pulled pork, cheesesteak, and BBQ chicken sandwiches, are all around $8 and come with hand-cut fries, slaw, and pickle. Food is served until 1 A.M. during the week and 2 A.M. on weekends. Open Sun.–Fri. 11 A.M.–2 A.M., Sat. 11 A.M.–3 A.M.

White Palace Grill
1159 S. Canal, 312/939-7167   C
Newly remodeled and expanded in 2002, the **White Palace** has been a South Loop institution since 1939. It serves up breakfast and diner food 24 hours a day, mostly under $6. Check out the spectacular view of the skyline as well as a mural of Chicago legends, from Al Capone to the Blues Brothers to Sammy Sosa. If it's steak and eggs, liver and onions, chili and the like you're hankering for, this is the place to be.

Lithuanian

CHICAGO boasts the nation's strongest Lithuanian community, most of which was once centered on the South and Southwest Sides, particularly in the area bounded by 69th (Lithuania Plaza Court), 71st, Western, and California. Although most of the original immigrants' descendants have moved to the suburbs, a couple Lithuanian restaurants remain in the area.

Healthy Food Lithuanian Restaurant
3226 S. Halsted, 312/326-2724   SW
Claimed to be the oldest Lithuanian restaurant in the world (est. 1938), **Healthy Food** serves traditional Lithuanian dishes, including *koldunai* (boiled meat dumplings), *kugelis* (potato pudding with bacon), and *blynai* (Lithuanian pancakes). Sauerkraut soup and chicken noodle soup are also specialties of the house. Most entrées range from $6–$9. The place feels like an old-world diner, and the service is quick and firendly. Open Mon.–Wed. 7 A.M.–4 P.M., Thur.–Sat. 7 A.M.–8 P.M., Sun. 7:30 A.M.–5 P.M.

Seklycia
2711 W. 71st, 773/476-1680   FSW
This small restaurant serves traditional Lithuanian food, such as *kugelis*, blintzes, and dumplings, as well as American standards, including grilled and broiled fish, chicken, and meatloaf. Entrées in the $8 range. Open daily 8 A.M.–7 P.M.

Lunch

SOME places with lunch we really liked that didn't fit elsewhere. . .

American/Mexican Restaurant & Mini Market
2300 Lincoln Park West, Arcade Level, 773/404-2564   **N**
Spending the day at the zoo or elsewhere in Lincoln Park and it's just too darned sunny or rainy or snowy? Impress your crowd by marching them across the park and into this residential high-rise. Downstairs on the arcade level is a cute, compact eatery serving delicious homemade American and Mexican diner fare for really low prices. Most items $3–$6. Open daily 7 A.M.–10 P.M.

Café Penelope
230 S. Ashland, 312/243-3600   **W**
Incongruent pink and quaint cafe in the land of union halls (and just three blocks from the United Center) offers hearty and healthy hot and cold sandwiches, soups, salads, and pizza. Brown bag lunches come with a sandwich (picks like roast beef, Greek feta, and curried eggplant), fresh fruit cup, and homemade cookie. Wonderful hot sandwiches with roasted potatoes include baked meatloaf, Maryland crabcake, and ham barbecue. Dine alfresco under the garden's grape vines. Soups and salads $2–$7, sandwiches $5–$9. Open Mon.–Fri. 7 A.M.–9 P.M.

Café Society
1801 S. Indiana, 312/842-4210   **C**
Located in the **National Vietnam Veterans Art Museum** (p. 65), just a block from the Prairie Avenue Historic district, **Café Society** is an appetizing beginning to an afternoon of cultural touring. This small lunch place has a larger patio for summer dining. Sandwiches range from $4 for a vegetarian to $6 for a grilled chicken. The menu also includes a multitude of salads, soups, Mexican and Italian entrées, quiches, and coffee drinks. French toast is the highlight of the weekend brunch. Open Mon.–Wed. 7 A.M.–4 P.M., Thur.–Fri. 7 A.M.–11 P.M., Sat. 8 A.M.–11 P.M., Sun. 8 A.M.–5 P.M.

La Cocina Criolla
2420 W. Fullerton, 773/235-7377   **N**
$5–$7 buys authentic Puerto Rican cooking for lunch at this neighborhood bar, grill, and banquet center. Hot sandwiches come with soup or salad and seasoned rice for $5 to $6. Other specials include the stewed chicken or pork, and jibaritos—green plantains stuffed with steak, tomatoes, and onions. Open Mon.–Sat. 11 A.M.–9:30 P.M., Sun. noon–8 P.M.

La Milanese
3156 S. May, 773/254-9543   SW
Italian/Sicilian sandwich shop on a residential corner of Bridgeport is
popular for its enormous sandwiches (Italian beefs and sausages, meat ball,
pepper and egg, etc.), including the best breaded steak sandwich in town.
Sandwiches cost $3–$7, most under $4. Open Mon.–Fri. 10 A.M.–7 P.M.

Manzo's
3210 W. Irving, 773/478-3070   NW
Long a neighborhood favorite for thick pizza, **Manzo's** has expanded into
the lunch trade with a kingly weekday buffet. For $7.60 (including tax), the
ever-changing lineup may include cheese and sausage pizza, soup, chicken,
BBQ ribs, rice, potatoes, salad, fruit, garlic bread, and more. Buffet is open
Tues.–Fri. 11 A.M.–3 P.M.

Nikki & Pete's Fabulous Deli
1520 N. Halsted, 312/943-6100   C
Sleek and spotless little breakfast and lunch deli sits inside an auto shop!
Adorned with models of classic cars, this eatery serves soups, salads,
muffins, and bagels, along with its specialty sandwiches: The '56 T-Bird is
a hot smoked ham and baby swiss, the '59 Vette contains roasted veggies,
fresh mozzarella, and special sauce, and the Lamborghini is a marinated
chicken breast piled with spinach, fresh basil, and shallots. Sandwiches
about $4 to $6. Open Mon.–Fri. 8 A.M.–4:30 P.M., Sat. 8 A.M.–4 P.M.

Rancho Luna
3357 W. Peterson, 773/509-9332   NW
Colorful, cool, and clean, the atmosphere at this small storefront soothes,
while the merengue music, wonderful food, and good lunch prices rejuvenate. Choose from sandwiches like shredded beef, roast pork, and BBQ
chicken ($4–$6), fruit shakes ($3), side dishes like yucca, congri, and
tostones ($2–$3), and special lunch plates ($6—11 A.M.–3 P.M. weekdays
only). Dinner $8–$15. Open Mon.–Thur. 11 A.M.–11 P.M., Fri. 11 A.M.–2
A.M., Sat. 11 A.M.–3 A.M., Sun. noon–11 P.M.

There's a certain type of city worker who always has a new recommendation
for a great place to eat. Their jobs take them into all neighborhoods, and
they have the discerning appetite and sense of value necessary to seek out
the best lunch joints. Dennis Foley, a former Streets & Sanitation Department electrician, is just such a person. Lucky for us, Dennis decided to share
his particular treasury of knowledge with the world in the form of *The
Streets & San Man's Guide to Chicago Eats*, reviews of 75 of the best

mom-and-pop eateries in Chicago where one can have an all-inclusive lunch for $5–$10.

Lunch in Bars

Blackie's
755 S. Clark, 312/786-1161 C

Blackie's has been the neighborhood bar of Printers Row for decades but was remodeled a number of years ago. Club sandwiches, salads, burgers, and the like make this a modest, but satisfying lunch spot. Outdoor seating on Polk Street is available, although limited, during the summer months. They also serve a great weekend brunch. Expect to pay about $8 for a lunch entrée and beverage. Open Mon.–Thur. 11 A.M.–10 P.M., Fri.–Sat. 7:30 A.M.–10 P.M., Sun. 7:30 A.M.–3:30 P.M.

Cactus
404 S. Wells, 312/922-3830 C

Cactus "makes the world safer for margaritas" and urges traders not to "drink and trade" though many drink here directly afterwards. For lunch we suggest one of the best (and largest) chicken Caesar salads in the city, even tastier when eaten in the outdoor area. The atmosphere, crowd, drink specials, pool table, darts, and music make this a popular after-work Loop hangout. Open Mon.–Fri. 11 A.M.–11 P.M.

Cavanaugh's
53 W. Jackson, 312/939-3125 C

This cozy neighborhood bar—reminiscent of *Cheers*—serves sandwiches and salads during the week. Tucked away in the Monadnock Building in the Loop, you can enter through the lobby or from the alley. Open Mon.–Fri. 11 A.M.–10 P.M. (kitchen open until 8 P.M.).

Govnor's Pub
207 N. State, 312/236-3696 C

There's sometimes a chance you'll rub elbows with local political wheelers and dealers at **Govnor's Pub** at lunchtime and always a chance you'll rub elbows with downtown office workers in training for Happy Hour. Serving hearty burgers, sandwiches, soup, salads, nachos, and chili in a bread bowl, Govnor's also dishes up high-profile outdoor seating on State Street and a thick fog of smoke inside. Open Mon.–Fri. 11 A.M.–2 P.M., Sat. 11 A.M.–midnight, Sun. 11:30 A.M.–8 P.M.

Jury's Food & Drink
4337 N. Lincoln, 773/935-2255   N
Most lunch menu items are in the $6–$8 range at this classy Lincoln Square bar and eatery (their award-winning cheeseburgers are their claim to fame). Better yet, bring a business card so you can enter a drawing for a free $12 meal. During warmer months, the secluded outdoor patio is open in back. Dinner specials may include things like "$10 night," when all bottles of wine are $10. Open Mon.–Thur. 11 A.M.–10 P.M., Fri.–Sat. 11 A.M.–11 P.M., Sun. 2 P.M.–9 P.M.

Speaking of Juries

What to do for lunch when you're on jury duty, or, uh, going to testify in the criminal courts building at 26ᵗʰ & California? Join lawyers, judges, cops, and other court personnel at **Jean's Restaurant & Bar** (2532 S. California, 773/847-3600), long a place to grab a bite and a brew (when not working, that is.)

South Loop Club
701 S. State, 312/427-2787   C
A popular hangout of students from Columbia and DePaul's Loop campus, this sports bar has two sides: Enter the bar on State Street, but order food from the grill like juicy burgers, ribs, pizza, and sandwiches on Balbo. Note the closing time: you can also eat lunch here if you work the second shift. Open daily 11 A.M.–4 A.M.

Wild Goose
4265 N. Lincoln, 773/281-7112   N
$3.99 lunches Mon.–Fri. That says it all—almost. The portions are big, sides like French fries are included, and a few non-bar food items like blackened tuna in pita and high-end tacos make the menu. Most people go for the standard burgers, reubens, and chicken sandwiches. A dozen televisions in the bar ensure that some—any—sporting event is within view. Open Sun.–Fri. 11 A.M.–2 A.M., Sat. 11 A.M.–3 A.M.

Lunch, Downtown

Billy Goat Tavern
430 N. Michigan, 312/222-1525   C
This place is certainly a Chicago institution, especially for journalists, tourists, and others looking to escape to its underground, lower Michigan

locale. **The Goat** has been around since 1934 and is known for its cheese-burgers, chips (no fries), and Cokes, as immortalized by John Belushi on *Saturday Night Live* in the 70s. Billy Sianas, the founder, was not allowed into Wrigley Field for the 1945 World Series with his pet goat. So, he placed a curse on the Cubs, who haven't won a World Series in almost 100 years. Open Mon.–Fri. 6 A.M.–2 A.M., Sat. 7 A.M.–2 A.M., Sun. 11 A.M.–2 A.M.

Boni Vino
111 W. Van Buren, 312/427-0231   C
Since 1967, downtown diners have been sitting down at this south Loop Italian restaurant for a relaxing and affordable lunch. Stick with the daily special, pasta, fish, sandwiches, or pizza and your meal will come in under $8. Open Mon.–Fri. 10 A.M.–2 A.M.

Fast Track
629 W. Lake, 312/993-9300   C
Fresh, high-quality fast food: hot dogs, polishes, corned beef, burgers, Italian beefs and sausages, salads, and ice cream shakes and sundaes. Located near the el tracks, **Fast Track** carries a train theme throughout, including a motorized miniature train and elevated track that circles the place. Dine at the outdoor picnic tables during warm weather. Sides $1–$3, salads and sandwiches $2–$6. Open Mon.–Fri. 6 A.M.–7 P.M., Sat. 9 A.M.–4 P.M. ("But if you spend a lot of money, we wait.") Closed Sun. ("We stay home with the wives.")

Food Life
Water Tower Place, 835 N. Michigan, 312/335-3663   C
Espresso/Juice Bar and Bakery: Open Sun.–Thur. 7:30 A.M.–8 P.M., Fri.–Sat. 7:30 A.M.–9 P.M.
Kiosks: Open Sun.–Thur. 11 A.M.–8 P.M., Fri.–Sat. 11 A.M.–9 P.M.
Market: Open Mon.–Sat. 10:30 A.M.–8 P.M., Sun. 11 A.M.–7 P.M.
This upscale food court is fun and inexpensive. With over a dozen places to choose from, you can enjoy Southern cooking, Asian, health food, Mexican, and gourmet pizza, among others. Eat at separate tables or at the larger community table. Most lunch items are about $6–$7.

Two other food courts downtown veterans routinely crow about are **Under 55** (55 E. Monroe) on the lower level of that building and the one in the **Aon Center** (200 E. Randolph). The various vendors at Under 55 each offer at least one freshly-made daily special with a drink and small frozen yogurt for $6–$7. The food emporium in our second-tallest building is known for having higher-end items like sushi.

Los Amigos Grill and **Café Gioia**
436 S. Wabash, 312/566-0208   C

Housed in the International Youth Hostel building/Columbia College dorm is this pair of new, cheerful eateries where you can lunch surrounded by visitors from around the world. **Café Gioia** is an Italian-style coffee shop serving baked goods, coffee drinks, panini sandwiches ($3–$5), signature sandwiches (around $6), including the Tuscan Turkey and Mediterranean Veggie, and classic sandwiches like peanut butter and jelly, and ham and cheese ($4–$5). Next door, **Los Amigos Grill** dishes out breakfasts, burritos, tacos, tostadas, quesadillas, tortas, fajitas, and more. The vegetarian versions, featuring grilled zucchini, eggplant, red onion, sweet peppers, and corn, are particularly intriguing. Inexpensive beer is also available. Open Mon.–Fri. 8 A.M.–7 P.M., Sat. 10 A.M.–4 P.M. **Los Amigos Grill** closed Sun.

Mac Kelly's Greens and Things
21 E. Adams, 312/431-1373   C
Open Mon.–Fri. 6:30 A.M.–3 P.M.
216 N. Jackson, 312/346-8072   C
Open Mon.–Fri. 6 A.M.–4 P.M.
177 N. Wells, 312/899-9022   C
Open Mon.–Fri. 6:30 A.M.–3 P.M.
225 N. Michigan, 312/540-0071   C
Open Mon.–Fri. 6:30 A.M.–3 P.M.
123 W. Madison, 312/214-6401   C
Open Mon.–Fri. 6:30 A.M.–3 P.M.

Build a lunch piece by piece at this do-it-yourself headquarters. Choose from coolers packed with waters, juices, sodas, and fruit; racks lined with bagels, muffins, cookies, and doughnuts; an 80-item salad bar; soup and chili; sandwich and pasta bar; and hot daily specials. Carry out only. Most diners can eat well for $4 to $7.

Ronny's Steakhouse
347 S. Wabash, 312/346-9487   C
Open daily 7 A.M.–midnight
110 W. Randolph, 312/939-6010   C
Open daily 7 A.M.–8 P.M.

Huge meals at really great—sometimes unbelievable—prices abound here at these warm, family-friendly cafeterias. The Wabash location is practically under the el tracks and has a lot of dining space (you can fully lose track of the city din in the downstairs eating area). Full meals or lighter lunches include steak, pizza, ribs, sandwiches, and daily specials. Feel free to enjoy long lunches here, as there's no pressure to eat and run.

Sixty-Five Seafood Restaurant
336 N. Michigan, 312/372-0306   C
225 S. Canal, 312/474-0065   C
In the mood for Chinese comfort food? Then this is the place. Hot-and-sour shrimp, beef and broccoli, and lemon chicken are just some of the cheap items on the menu. Although **Sixty-Five** does a good business, there's always an empty booth. Takeout is available and quite popular. Most prices under $7. Open Mon.–Fri. 11 A.M.–7:30 P.M., Sat.–Sun. 11 A.M.–7 P.M.

Sopraffina Marketcaffè
10 N. Dearborn, 312/984-0044   C
111 E. Wacker, 312/861-0200   C
175 W. Jackson, 312/583-1100   C
222 W. Adams, 312/726-4800   C
200 E. Randolph, 312/729-9200   C
Classy Italian cafeteria affiliated with the celebrated Trattoria No. 10 dining spot at the original location. Line up for soups, salads, pastas (lasagna toscano, stuffed shells), pizza (Margherita, homemade sausage with three cheeses), and classic Italian sandwiches (chicken Caesar salad, grilled portabello mushrooms, roast beef and avocado). The Randolph Street location has outdoor seating during the warmer months. Open Mon.–Fri. 6 A.M.–7:30 P.M. closed weekends. Lunch runs under $10, usually around $7.

Standing Room Only (SRO)
610 S. Dearborn, 312/360-1776   C
Endorsed once by Mayor Daley as the "Best Turkey Burger in Chicago" and former Governor Edgar as the "Best Turkey Burger in Illinois," **SRO**'s char-grilled, hand packed, 100% turkey burger dominates a menu loaded with plenty of sandwich and salad temptations. They nominate their char-grilled, fresh (never frozen) chicken breast sandwich and falafel in whole wheat pita as "Best in Chicago," but I'd also stand behind their Cajun style chicken and tuna steak sandwiches. Over fifty percent of the menu is heart healthy, including a half-dozen vegetarian choices. Sandwiches $4–$8, most about $6; salads $4–$9. Despite the name, there's ample seating in this slick Chicago sports-themed sandwich shop. Open Mon.–Fri. 11 A.M.–9 P.M., Sat. 11:30 A.M.–8 P.M.

Mexican

WITH the hundreds (especially if you include carts and stands) of Mexican eateries in Chicago, most affordably priced and many worth trying, the following are but a few great deals and some of the authors' and their pals' favorites:

Cesar's Restaurant
3166 N. Clark, 773/248-2835   **N**
Home of the "Killer Margarita," **Cesar's** encompasses a large eating and bar area. The flautas are excellent, as are the veggie fajitas. Most dishes are under $8. For those not into margaritas or looking for a non-alcoholic alternative, try the sangria soda. Open Mon.–Thur. 11 A.M.–11 P.M., Fri.–Sat. 11 A.M.–midnight, Sun. 1 P.M.–8 P.M.

Doña Torta
3057 N. Ashland, 773/871-8999   **N**
From the outside—and well, the inside too—**Doña Torta** appears to be just another Mexican fast food place. It's when you first glimpse the menu, take your first bite, or pay your first bill with pocket change that you realize you've found a winner. Let's start with the fourteen Super Tortas (sandwiches) à la Mexico City. None are priced over $4 and come in such combinations as grilled steak with bacon & sliced ham, and ham & cheese omelette with onions. There are also Super Burritos (around $4)—of the *grande* size we accept as normal in Chicago. The 14 options for Super Tacos—priced under $2—include pork butt and cheese, eggs with chorizo, fried fish with lemon wedge, breaded steak, and beef tongue. There's more. Seven additional burritos are low calorie, four of those are vegetarian. Along with the fresh fruit Super Shakes, la Doña serves Vitamin Shakes (nutritional powder added), Energy Shakes (carbohydrate powder added), and Protein Shakes (with egg, protein powder, and carbs added). Open daily 7 A.M.–midnight

La Fiesta Restaurant
3333 W. 111th, 773/779-4844   **FSW**
Open the large, heavy red doors to this Mexican restaurant and prepare yourself to be pleasantly surprised. Start your meal off with a large selection of appetizers from shrimp poppers (shrimp and cheese wrapped in a jalapeño pepper) to guacamole. Some of their entrées include *Bistec á la Mexicana* (steak simmered in their own pico sauce) served with rice, beans, and tortillas, fajita dinners, seafood (perch, shrimp), tacos, burritos, enchiladas, tostadas, combination specials, and more. Open Mon.–Thur. 11 A.M.–10 P.M., Fri.–Sat. 11 A.M.–11 P.M., Sun. 11 A.M.–9 P.M.

LaLo's
3515 W. 26th, 773/522-0345   **SW**
Open Mon.–Fri. 10 A.M.–10 P.M., Sat.–Sun. 9 A.M.–11 P.M.

4126 W. 26th, 773/762-1505   SW
Open Mon.–Fri. 10 A.M.–10 P.M., Sat.–Sun. 9 A.M.–11 P.M.
1960 N. Clybourn, 773/880-5256   N
Open Sun.–Thur. 11 A.M.–11 P.M., Fri.–Sat. 11 A.M.–midnight
2747 W. 63rd, 773/476-8207   SW
Open Mon.–Fri. 10 A.M.–10 P.M., Sat.–Sun. 9 A.M.–11 P.M.
500 N. LaSalle, 312/329-0030   C
Open Sun. 12 P.M.–10 P.M., Mon.–Tues. 11 A.M.–10 P.M., Wed. 11 A.M.–11
P.M. (bar until 1 A.M.), salsa lessons 9 P.M.–10 P.M. (no cover), Thur. 11
A.M.–11 P.M., Fri.–Sat. 11 a.m.–midnight (bar until 2 A.M.)
Suck down a hefty margarita and dig into the chips & salsa and marinated
veggies (carrots, cauliflower, jalapeños, mild whole garlic cloves), while
you peruse the menu at this animated and colorful Mexican neighborhood
favorite. (They started on 26th Street and spread.) Go with a standard (you'll
enjoy it) or opt for one of the house or seafood specialties: beef tongue
simmered in tomatillo sauce, butterfly-cut skirt steak with guacamole, sopa
marina five-seafood soup, shrimp fajitas. They also serve up great fruity
margaritas, including strawberry, raspberry, peach and guava. Entrées $4–
$14, most under $9.

Maravilla's Restaurant
5211-G S. Harper, 773/643-3155   S
Maravilla's Restaurant serves up authentic Mexican food to a loyal group
of customers. They're most popular with the local students but offer great
dishes for everyone. Popular food items include the freshly-made burritos,
tostadas, flautas, and enchiladas, and entrées like the *Carne a la
Tampiqueña* (marinated and grilled strip steak served with refried beans
topped with cheese and an enchilada) as well as *Bistec à la Mexicana*
(skewered tenderloin of mariachis with onions, peppers, and tomato marinated in a spicy sauce). Food items $2–$10. Open Mon.–Sat. 9 A.M.–11 P.M.,
Sun. 10 A.M.–10 P.M.

Nuevo Leon
1515 W. 18th, 312/421-1517   C
Open Mon.–Sat. 7 A.M.–midnight, Sun. 7 A.M.-11 P.M.
3657 W. 26th, 773/522-1515   SW
Open Sun.–Thur. 8 A.M.–11 P.M., Fri. 8 A.M.–midnight, Sat. 8 A.M.–1 A.M.
Modest family restaurant serves cherished stews, enchiladas, and *mole*
dishes. Other specialties include the Steak Nuevo Leon and *Machacado*
(scrambled eggs and meat). Entrées $4–$10, many $5–$6. The 26th St.
location has been going strong since 1962.

Rique's Regional Mexican Food
5004 N. Sheridan, 773/728-6200   **FN**
This new restaurant is a real find—genuinely cheap and unbelievably delicious. Chef and owner Enrique Cortés (with partner George Kozel) opened his small storefront in November 2002, with a goal of serving "very indigenous food, very basic things that have existed forever." Citing Aztec, Mayan, and colonial Spanish influences, Cortés recreates dishes he enjoyed eating while a child in northern Sonora, Mexico. Particularly perfect are dishes like the achiote-marinated grilled chicken breast in tomatillo and pumpkin seed sauce, and a Yucatan salad with orange, red bell pepper, red onions, green apples, and cilantro. They even serve breakfast—try the unique *huevos motuleños*, a drowned torta, simmered in a thick red sauce. They offer take-out, delivery (between 6 P.M.– 9P.M. and 11 P.M.–2 A.M.), and have a party room that's free to use, as long as Enrique's cooking. Most food items $6–$10. BYOB. Open Mon. 4 P.M.–10 P.M., Tues.–Fri. 11 A.M.–11 P.M., Sat.–Sun. 10 A.M.–11 P.M.

For vegetarians who want something other than refried beans . . .

Garcia's
4749 N. Western, 773/769-5600   **N**
Open Sun. 10 A.M.–midnight, Mon.–Thur. 10 A.M.–1 A.M., Fri. 10 A.M.–3 A.M., Sat. 10 A.M.–4 A.M.
1758 W. Lawrence, 773/784-1212   **N**
Open Mon.–Fri. 4 P.M.–midnight (bar until 1 A.M.), Sat.–Sun. 2 P.M.–midnight (bar until 2 A.M.)
Busy, family-owned restaurants offer a cheesy, piquant chile relleno nestled in a soft corn tortilla, making a filling and unusual taco for only $2.50. Or try the broccoli, spinach, and rice burrito with choice of cheese or sour cream for $4 (even tastier when you add avocado for another small fee).

Taco and Burrito Palace #2
2441 N. Halsted, 773/248-0740   **N**
Heavy-traffic, fast-food Mexican place/palace substitutes the typical refried beans in their vegetarian burrito with loads of grilled onions and peppers. Huge and messy. A great place to stop in on the weekends when you have those 'round-midnight munchies. Open Sun.–Tues. 9 A.M.–3 A.M., Wed.–Sat. 9 A.M.–5 A.M.

Meat-eaters who want something a little heartier in their salsa and a little more "kick" to their Mexican options can't pass up **Rocky's Tacos** (7043 N. Clark, 773/274-4634, 3054 W. Montrose, 773/604-5067): Their salsa is made with diced ham, rock en espanol blares over the speakers, and their house theme is soccer. The specialty—super tortas (sub-like sandwiches)—are named for Mexican soccer teams and players, with a few jabs thrown in. Among the over 50 variations are *La Taximaroa* with bacon, pork chop, ham, and pineapple, and *La E. Romanazo*, with steak, melted mozzarella, and cactus. Tortas about $4–$5. Open daily 9 A.M.–midnight.

Middle Eastern

Since the early 1990s, a variety of Middle Eastern restaurants, bakeries, and grocery stores have opened on 63rd Street between Kedzie and Pulaski. The first was **Steve's Shishkabab House** (3816 W. 63rd, 773/581-8920, closed Wed.). In addition to the skewered and grilled meats of its name, **Steve's** also serves other delicious chicken and lamb dishes, garlicky hummus, and warm homemade pitas. Local rumor has it that the chef at **The Jerusalem** (3534 W. 63rd, 773/776-6133) once toiled in the kitchen of the Jordanian royal palace. Try the *arrayes* appetizer—finely chopped, seasoned lamb grilled inside pita bread. **The Nile** (3259 W. 63rd, 773/434-7218) is a good place for lunch that puts together fresh and tasty sandwiches in a hurry.

Andie's Restaurant
5253 N. Clark, 773/784-8616   FN
Open daily 11 A.M.–midnight, Sun. 10 A.M.–midnight
1467 W. Montrose, 773/348-0654   N
Open Sun.–Thur. 11 A.M.–10 P.M., Fri.–Sat. 11 A.M.–11 P.M.
So popular they first expanded to a second location, then built up their original Clark Street storefront into a a palace by comparison. One of the first eateries to really popularize Middle Eastern dining on the North Side, Andie's continues to earn loyal converts to its classic Lebanese meals and their extensive vegetarian dishes (about half the menu). Entrées run $5–$15 (most under $8).

Cedar's of Lebanon
1206 E. 53rd, 773/324-6227   S
Cedar's offers an authentic taste of Lebanese cuisine at this simple and elegant restaurant. Among the large portions served at reasonable prices are the grilled vegetable platters, shish kebabs, falafel, curry chicken, and an outstanding hummus. Vegetarian meals, sandwiches, and salads from Cedar's Garden are other highlights. Food items $3–$10. Open daily 11:30 A.M.–10 P.M.

Cousin's
2833 N. Broadway, 773/880-0063   N

Mouth-watering Turkish, Mediterranean, and vegetarian dishes should please nearly every palette at **Cousin's**, where the emphasis is on healthy, fresh, and innovative cooking. Vegetarian moussaka, *imam bayildi* (stuffed baby eggplant), and *manti* (spinach, asparagus, and cheese-filled ravioli topped with fresh pesto, pine nuts, and diced tomatoes) are among the dozen vegetarian entrées that can be vegan with the omission of feta cheese. Chicken doner (a chicken "gyro"), lamb chops, saffron shrimp, and more join delectable shish kebabs for meat eaters. Turkish wines, beer, tea, coffee and imported juices complement the food, and baklava or custard make great finales if you find yourself in the unusual circumstance of still having room after dinner. Sides under $3, appetizers and sandwiches $4–$6, kebabs and entrées $8–$15, most under $9. Open Sun.–Thur. 11:30 A.M.–10:30 P.M., Fri.–Sat. 11:30 A.M.–11:30 P.M.

Cousin's
3038 W. Irving Park, 773/478-6868   N

Not to be confused with the separately owned **Cousin's** on Broadway, the original chef from the now defunct Clark St. Cousin's location recently opened this Albany Park gem. Touting their menu as "contemporary Turkish cuisine with vegetarian flair," they have ever-changing daily specials, and tango dancing on Monday evenings. They also have a small selection of Turkish wine to accompany your meal. Open Mon. 4 P.M.–midnight, Sun., Tues.–Thurs. 4 P.M.–10 P.M., Fri.–Sat. 4 P.M.–11 P.M. Call ahead for lunch hours.

Noon-O-Kabab
4661 N. Kedzie, 773/279-8899   NW

Described as "Fine Persian Food," the menu features beef, chicken, and shrimp kabab dishes, but also includes creative vegetarian offerings like Shirin Polo (sweet & sour Persian rice with nuts and berries) and a mixed vegetable plate with light cinnamon tomato sauce. The baba ganoush appetizer served with marinated diced vegetables is highly recommended. Open Mon.–Sat. 11 A.M.–10 P.M., Sun. 11 A.M.–7 P.M.

Reza's
5255 N. Clark, 773/561-1898   FN
432 W. Ontario, 312/664-4500   C

Chicago's favorite Persian restaurants, acknowledged by nearly every critic for food, service, atmosphere, and price. The voluminous menu holds a specialty for everyone: A separate vegetarian appetizer and entrée list

($4–$8 and $10–$14), 11 lamb dishes from shanks, to chops, to kabobs ($10–$16), 10 poultry dishes including turkey, Cornish hen, quail and skinless, low-fat chicken dishes ($10–$14), seafood delights like salmon kabobs and shrimp and scallop combos ($10–$16), and more. Lunch entrées $7–$10. Open daily 11 A.M.–midnight.

Moroccan

Andalous Moroccan Restaurant
3307 N. Clark, 773/281-6885   N

Quaint Moroccan décor makes for a cozy experience at **Andalous**. Owner Hadj will introduce specialty dishes to diners new to the cuisine. The lamb couscous and chicken tangine (roasted in a clay pot with herbs and olives) and other entrées average around $8–$9. Mint tea is very popular in Morocco and is served here. An outdoor patio is open during warmer months. BYOB. Open Sun.–Thurs. 2 P.M.–10 P.M., Fri.–Sat. 2 P.M.–11:30 P.M.

Peruvian

Rinconcito Sudamericano
1954 W. Armitage, 773/489-3126   N

Established Peruvian place caters more to the big appetite and the palate than aesthetic inclinations. Peru's lengthy coastline supplies plenty of seafood recipes (stuffed squid, seafood-packed rice, port-style mussels, lobster, shrimp). Most other entrées are chicken and beef based (like the *anticuchos*—grilled beef hearts), but there's lamb, tripe, and rabbit, too. Many of the dishes are cooked with wine, onions, and cilantro, and all are excellent. Entrées $8–$15, most under $10. Open Mon. 5 P.M.–10 P.M., Tues.–Sat. 1 P.M.–10 P.M., Sun. 1 P.M.–8 P.M.

Taste of Peru
6545 N. Clark, 773/381-4540   FN

Excellent food (particularly seafood) and immense portions, plus inexpensive prices make **Taste of Peru** well worth your while—and wait. While the service is friendly, it is not a fast food restaurant. BYOB. Sun.–Thur. 11:30 A.M.–10 P.M., Fri.–Sat. 11:30 A.M.–11 P.M.

Pizza

WHERE do you start listing worthy pizza in the pizza capital of Chicago?

Dishing out perhaps the best-known pizza anywhere, **Pizzeria Uno** (29 E. Ohio, 312/321-1000) birthed the deep-dish pizza that made Chicago famous, back in 1943. Soon afterwards, its sister, **Pizzeria Due** (619 N. Wabash, 312/943-2400), was opened across the street to accommodate the crowds that have persisted to this day. Be forewarned: you must order your pizza at these places before you're even seated.

Other major players on the Chicago-style deep dish and stuffed pizza scene to look for are the many **Bacino's** (heart-healthy stuffed spinach), **Connie's** (you must go to their Archer location), **Edwardo's** (all natural), **Gino's**, **Giordano's**, **Ranalli's**, and **Suparossa's** restaurants scattered across town. They don't disappoint. Once you've clogged your gills with their cheesy indulgences, check out the other pizza renditions and environments of the following places:

Chicago Pizza and Oven Grinder Company
2121 N. Clark, 773/248-2570   N

The individual pizza pot-pies are this dark, wooden, and atmospheric pizzeria's original claim to fame. Customers love just about everything else on the limited menu as well: the Mediterranean bread (a crispy, seasoned round appetizer that about covers the table), the Salad Dinners (salad concoctions that serve as a meal for 2–4 diners), and the Oven Grinders (overflowing baked sub sandwiches). Pot-pies—half-pounder $8.75, one pounder $17.50, oven grinders $9.75–$10.25, sharing-size Mediterranean bread $5.50, and must-share salad dinners $10.25–$21.75. Lincoln Parkers wait 1–2 hours to be seated on the weekends; the host's memory functions as the waiting list. No reservations accepted. Cash only. Open Mon.–Thurs. 4 P.M.–11 P.M., Fri. 4 P.M.–midnight, Sat. noon–midnight, Sun. noon–11 P.M.

Gulliver's
2727 W. Howard, 773/338-2166   FN

Perhaps the best-looking pizza parlor in the city, **Gulliver's** has an immense stained glass, lighting, and architectural artifacts collection (primarily from 1910s to 1930s) that spruces up its heavy wooden tables and booths, making it both ornate and cozy. The ceiling is covered literally "wall-to-wall" with antique lighting styles. The must-have "world famous pizza in the pan" is accompanied by a broad menu of Italian (stuffed shells, veal parmesan, fried calamari . . .), Mexican (red snapper, chimichangas, burritos . . .), and American (stuffed steakburgers, ribs, grilled tuna, BLT club . . .) dishes. Sandwiches run about $6–$9, entrées $9–$18, most in the mid-range. Open Mon.–Thurs. 11 A.M.–1 A.M., Fri.–Sat. 11 A.M.–2 A.M., Sun. noon–1 A.M.

Pizza Metro
1707 W. Division, 773/278-1753   C
For authentic Italian pizza, made by actual Italian-speaking people, check
out **Pizza Metro** (fittingly located near a scooter shop.) The tasty option at
Pizza Metro is that you can order the various pizzas whole ($7–$23) or by
the slice ($2–$4), allowing diners to try not just one, but many of their
delicious combinations. The rosemary potato pizza is highly recommended,
as are the garbage, veggie, and chicken pizzas. You can also create your own
pizza like the grilled chicken, onion, and bleu cheese combo we created.
Their gnocchi, lasagna, ravioli, and tortellini are hearty helpings of homemade pasta in their own marinara sauce and served with homemade bread
($6–$8). It is just as mouth-watering as similar dishes in Rome! The turkey
panini is huge and dripping with a special sauce (request extra napkins.)
Finish off the meal with tiramisu, apple tart, or an Italian doughnut. If you
dine in, arrive early, as Pizza Metro is as narrow as a boot. Open Mon.–
Thur. 11 A.M.–1 A.M., Fri.–Sat. 11 A.M.–4 A.M., Sun. noon–1 A.M.

Pompei Bakery
1531 W. Taylor, 312/421-5179   C
This longtime storefront pizza parlor and bakery, opened in 1909, recently
moved down the street and recreated itself in a glossier fashion.
"Emporium" comes to mind. The pizza is still outstanding and varied.
They've got original square, open-faced (look for baked clams with a lemon
wedge on Fridays during Lent), and stuffed pizza, along with their signature
"pizza strudel"—a delightful concoction that comes in flavors like "poor
boy," roast beef, turkey stuffing, and steak fajita. Hefty slices start around
$3. A smaller, second location, **Pompei's Little Italy** (2955 N. Sheffield,
773/325-1900) is in Lincoln Park. Open Mon.–Sat. 11 A.M.–10 P.M., Sun. 11
A.M.–9 P.M.

For maximum pizza possibilities, you can't beat Chicago's family-owned
chain of **Leona's** restaurants. Choose thin crust or pan; traditional, whole
wheat, or garlic parmesan crust; regular or soy cheese; Alfredo, pesto, or
tomato sauce; and toppings from a list of two dozen (ricotta cheese, Genoa
salami, turkey breast, artichokes, pineapple . . .). Complimentary cookies
arrive with the check.
1936 W. Augusta, 773/292-4300   W
This is the original location, where the restaurant was built around the
family's home. Open Mon.–Thur. 11 A.M.–11 P.M., Fri. 11 A.M.–1 A.M., Sat.
noon–1 A.M., Sun. noon–10:30 P.M.
3215 N. Sheffield, 773/327-8861   N
Open Sun.–Thur. 11 A.M.–11:30 P.M., Fri.–Sat. 11 A.M.– 1 A.M.

3877 N. Elston, 773/267-7287 **NW**
Open Mon.–Thur. 11:30 A.M.–10:30 P.M., Fri. 11:30 A.M.–11:30 P.M., Sat. noon–11:30 P.M., Sun. noon–10 P.M.

7443 W. Irving Park, 773/625-3636 **NW**
Open Mon.–Thur. 4 P.M.–9:30 P.M., Fri. 11 A.M.–11 P.M., Sat. noon–11 P.M., Sun. noon–9:30 P.M.

6935 N. Sheridan, 773/764-5757 **FN**
Open Mon.–Thur., 11:30 A.M.–11 P.M., Fri.–Sat. 11:30 A.M.–12:30 A.M., Sun. 10:30 A.M.–10:30 P.M.

1419 W. Taylor, 312/850-2222 **C**
Open Mon.–Thur. 11:30 A.M.–10:30 P.M., Fri. 11:30 A.M.–midnight, Sat. noon–midnight, Sun. noon–10:30 P.M.

53rd & Woodlawn, 773/363-2600 **S**
Open Mon.–Thur. 11:30 A.M.–11 P.M., Fri. 11:30 A.M.–12:30 A.M., Sat. noon–12:30 A.M., Sun. noon–10:30 P.M.

25th & Western, 773/523-9696 **SW**
Open Mon. –Thur. 11:30 A.M.–10 P.M., Fri. 11:30 A.M.–11 P.M., Sat. noon–11 P.M., Sun. noon–10 P.M.

111th & Western, 773/881-7700 **FSW**
Open Mon.–Thur. 11 A.M.–11 P.M., Fri. 11 A.M.–12:30 A.M., Sat. noon–12:30 A.M., Sun. noon–10:30 P.M.

645 N. Franklin, 312/867-0101 **C**
Open Mon.–Thur. 11 A.M.–11 P.M., Fri.–Sat. 11 A.M.–midnight, Sun. noon–10:30 P.M.

7601 S. Cicero, 773/838-8383 **SW**
Open Mon.–Thur. 11 A.M.–9:30 P.M., Fri. 11 A.M.–10:30 A.M., Sat. noon–10:30 P.M., Sun. noon–9:30 P.M.

Lou Malnati's Pizzeria
3859 W. Ogden, 773/762-0800 **W**
This big-name Chicago pizza chain opened a West Side location in 1996 in conjunction with the Lawndale Community Church in hopes of both revitalizing the area's long gone business district (much of it ravaged in the riots of 1967) and earning money for the church's community programs. All profits are re-invested in the community, folks needing a second chance are given jobs, and transitional housing is available upstairs for the homeless. Having become a popular community hangout and meeting place, insiders refer to the pizzeria as "Malnati's Lighthouse." They serve the same great deep dish pizza and reasonably-priced Italian specialties as the other locations. Open Mon.–Thur. 11 A.M.–9 P.M., Fri.–Sat. 11 A.M.–10 P.M., Sun. 12:30 P.M.–8 P.M. Other locations: 958 W. Wrightwood, 773/832-4030; 439 N. Wells, 312/828-9800.

Piece
1927 W. North, 773/772-4422   N
This Wicker Park hipster pizzeria was first made famous by employing cast
members of MTV's *The Real World: Chicago*, but it's the New Haven-style
thin-crust pies and house-brewed beers that have kept patrons loyal. The
huge, hand-shaped pies come in three varieties: plain (tomato sauce, garlic,
Parmesan), white (olive oil, garlic, mozzarella), and red (tomato sauce,
mozzarella) with your choice of toppings. A few appetizers like baked goat
cheese and spinach dip join the menu, along with at least seven house-
brewed beers and ten microbrews on any given day. The skylight ceiling,
sunken lounge, huge curved bar and numerous tables indicate some out of
the "pizza box" thinking occurred in design. Truly refreshing and unique to
Chicago, you definitely want a piece of this. Open Sun.–Fri. 11:30 A.M.–2
A.M., Sat. 11:30 A.M.–3 A.M.

Sean's Rhino Bar
10330 S. Western, 773/238-2060   FSW
A decent beer selection, Irish flair, and good food prices are about what you
might expect from a nice Beverly neighborhood pub named Sean's—and
you get that here. But you also get what may be the best homemade salsa in
an Irish bar, Mexican grub muy autentico, and absolutely the best paper-thin
crust pizza in the city. So crispy and perfectly flavored with fennel and other
spices—it melts in your mouth and rolls your eyes to the back of your head.
(And I'm sure that wasn't the Guinness talking.)

Lunch time bargains at some favorite pizzerias: **Home Run Inn** (4254 W.
31st, 773/247-9696) has been a South Side wonder since 1947. They pitch a
winning weekday buffet for $7.50. The feast includes seven kinds of pizza,
two soups, pasta, salad, and dessert. Open Mon.–Fri. 11 A.M.–2 P.M. On the
North Side, **Giordano's** (2124 W. Lawrence, 773/271-9696) serves a
stuffed individual pizza with your choice of three ingredients, plus beer or
pop, for just $5.18. Mon.–Fri. 11 A.M.–3 P.M. Call ahead so it's ready when
you arrive!

For the biggest pizza puff in the city . . .

Damenzo's Pizza and Restaurant
2324 W. Taylor, 312/421-1142   W
Family owned and operated joint in the old Italian neighborhood offers the
largest pizza puff/calzone in the city for $6. Other deals include the gigantic
slice of pizza with a pop for $3.80. Open Sun.–Thurs. 10 A.M.–midnight,
Fri.–Sat. 10 A.M.–1 A.M.

Mea Culpa

In ten years of releasing the *Native's Guide to Chicago*, only one restaurant came up again and again as an egregious omission: **Vito & Nick's** (8433 S. Pulaski, 773/735-2050), the South Side family pizza institution known for its ultra-thin pies and carpeted walls, which you must rub for good luck before you leave.

Polish

WITH Chicago's Polish population second only to Warsaw, it's no surprise that Milwaukee Avenue, between Diversey and Addison, is rapidly developing into a little Warsaw. In recent years, a new influx of young, professional Polish immigrants has increased the demand for modern Polish restaurants, coffeehouses, delis, and video stores.

Andrzej Grill
1022 N. Western, 773/489-3566   **W**
Don't be deterred by the shaded windows of this tiny diner. Come on in for Polish specialties such as pierogis, beef borscht, potato pancakes stuffed with pork, and stuffed cabbage. Expect huge portions for small price tags: lunches are about $5–$6, dinners $6–$8. A vegetarian menu is available. Open Mon.–Sat. 11 A.M.–7:30 P.M.

Angelica's Restaurant
3244 N. Milwaukee, 773/736-1186   **NW**
Angelica's is new to the slew of Polish restaurants on Milwaukee Avenue. If you like what you eat at Angelica's, stop next door at **Wally's International Market**, a full grocery owned by Angelica's father, Walter Mulica. If you are feeling adventurous, try the *flaczki* (tripe soup). Open daily 11 A.M.–9 P.M.

Caesar's Deli
901 N. Damen, 773/486-6190   **W**
Fans come from near and far for **Caesar's** 12 types of pierogi, including the late columnist Mike Royko who called them "the Rolls-Royce of pierogi." Fillings include sauerkraut, cheese, potato, peach, plum, and the summertime special—organically grown Michigan strawberries. Take along more goodies from the freezer or deli counter: *nalenski* (rolled crepes filled with apple, cheese, apricot or prune), *golabki* (stuffed cabbage), potato dumplings, *kolaczki,* cruellers, Polish rye, homemade soup, chop suey... Open Mon.–Wed. 8 A.M.–6 P.M., Thur.–Fri. 8 A.M.–7 P.M., Sat. 8 A.M.–5 P.M.

Szalas Restaurant
5214 S. Archer, 773/582-0300   SW
Based on the food and décor, Szalas is the kind of place you'd think had
stood the test of time and continued to lure back several generations for
well-loved favorites and great memories. A rustic and charming chalet–log
cabin interior evokes a Polish Highlander setting with its stone fireplace,
water wheel, hand-carved surfaces, and traditional clothing and artifacts on
the walls. The bilingual staff serves a bountiful menu of pierogis and
traditional items, along with various stews and fish and lamb dishes.
Soups/appetizers $3–$9, entrées $10–$25 (many under $14), weekday lunch
specials $5–$8. Open daily 11 A.M.–11 P.M., Fri.–Sun. the bar stays open
until 2 A.M.

Tatra Inn
6040 S. Pulaski, 773/582-8313   SW
If your mother ever told you to clean your plate, she might have had this
place in mind. Tatra serves up a huge buffet of all-you-can-eat goodies—
provided that you go back for refills with a clean plate. A sign even states
that you'll be charged for any wasted food. All fried food is cooked with
canola oil. Open Tues.–Thur. 11:30 A.M.–8 P.M., Fri. 11:30 A.M.–9 P.M., Sat.
noon–9 P.M., Sun. noon–8 P.M.

Other popular Polish buffets, well-tested by Chicago's hearty winter appetites, include the **Ambassador Restaurant** (7050 W. Belmont, 773/286-
9337), open for lunch and dinner, and **Czerwone Jabluszko (Red Apple)
Restaurant** (3121 N. Milwaukee, 773/588-5781), an inexpensive favorite
that serves up good, old fashioned home cooking. All meals include soup,
entrée, dessert, and non-alcoholic beverage. They can be quite crowded on
Sundays after church.

Pub Grub

Dante's
1200 W. Hubbard, 312/243-9350   C
How does **Dante's** keep the young and the restless, the bold and the
beautiful returning to its infernal and very red clubby bar? Cheap, cheap
food, of course. Mondays are ten-cent chicken wings, Tuesdays $1 burger
and fries, Wednesdays $3 pasta, Thursdays $5 pizzas, and Fridays $4
lasagna. Nightly drink specials are fairly predicatable (and decent), but the
Wednesday $7 wine flights is something extraordinary. Open Mon.–Fri. 4
P.M.–2 A.M., Sat. 9 P.M.–3 A.M.

Goose Island Brewing Company
1800 N. Clybourn, 312/915-0071   N
3535 N. Clark, 773/832-9040   N

Considered to be one of the nation's top brewpubs and known to be Chicago's oldest and largest, **Goose Island** has an impressive menu that rivals their vast lineup of award-winning beers. Favorites such as Honkers Ale battered fish 'n' chips, grilled cider-rubbed Atlantic salmon with wild rice & fruit pilaf, the Carolina pulled pork BBQ sandwich, and a pepper-crusted burger with stilton on pumpernickel roll are made with their own beers. A free basket of thick, seasoned, homemade potato chips starts all meals and compliment a pre-meal beer sampling session. Select three or more draft beers to taste and each 5-ounce glass costs only $1. $3 tours of the brewpub are given Sundays at 3 P.M. and are followed with brewer-led tastings. Entrées $10–$17, most under $12, hearty appetizers, pizzas, salads, and sandwiches $3–$9, most $5–$7. Open Sun.–Thurs. 11 A.M.–1 A.M., Fri.–Sat. 11 A.M.–2 A.M.

Hog Head McDunna's
1505 W. Fullerton, 773/929-0944   N

Hog Head McDunna's serves what is arguably Chicago's finest pub food, with specials that can't be beat. Headlining burgers and veggie burgers (macho enough for red meat eaters) with topping options like roasted garlic, black olives, portabello mushrooms, or jalapeño jack cheese lead the broad menu. Guinness Stout Steak, Teriyaki Salmon, and Hawaiian Pizza are other choices. This is hearty, homemade, and—relatively-speaking—healthy eating, with better-than-average presentation for a neighborhood saloon. With a drink purchase, customers can relish these dinner time deals: $3 BLT/Turkey Club/Turkey Reuben on Sundays, twenty-five-cent wings (Chicago's Wingfest Champions 2002!), $3 nachos, and $1.50 chili on Mondays, $5 Surf 'n' Turf Dinner on Tuesdays, $3 Italian Sausage and Italian Beef on Wednesdays, and $2 burger-n-fries on Thursdays. Mon.–Fri. 11 A.M.–4 P.M. order anything on the menu for $5, with a drink purchase. Open Sun.–Fri. 11 A.M.–2 A.M., Sat. 11 A.M.–3 A.M.

O'Donovan's
2100 W. Irving Park, 773/478-2100   N

This new Northcenter favorite replaced the longstanding Schulien's a few years back with a contemporary Irish-Chicagoan pub, popular after Cubs games, for their daily specials, and just because people like them and their year-round outdoor patio. Specials include $1 burger & fries on Mondays, twenty-cent wings on Tuesdays, $1.95 "Mama's Midway Meatloaf and

Mashed Mayhem" on Wednesdays, and $4.95 all-you-can-eat Fish 'n' Chips on Fridays. Specials are subject to change and require a drink purchase. Open Sun.–Fri. 11 A.M.–2 A.M., Sat. 11 A.M.–3 A.M.

Schaller's Pump
3714 S. Halsted, 773/376-6332   S
A firm Bridgeport address, unshakable White Sox allegiance, past and present politicos from the ward office across the street (including the former Mayor Richard J. Daley) as regulars, St. Patrick's Day revelry, a red meat menu, and the city's oldest liquor license (1881) staunchly establish **Schaller's** South Side credentials. Something "light" from the menu, perhaps corned beef, burgers, or steak sandwiches with the legendary hash browns will run $6–$8. Dinner specials (say, pork chops, stuffed cabbage, chicken, or ribs) with soup and salad are priced in the $8–$10 range. If you miss the traditional weekend accordion music, the jukebox comes well-stocked with 50s through 90s classics. Open Mon.–Fri. 11 A.M.–2 A.M., Sat. 4 P.M.–2 A.M., Sun. 3 P.M.–2 A.M. (kitchen is open nightly until 9 P.M.).

Sedgwick's Bar & Grill
1935 N. Sedgwick, 312/337-7900   N
Capacious Lincoln Park gathering place offers homemade victuals that are more than just food to drink by. Appetizing pastas, sandwiches, salads, quesadillas, and appetizers ($3–$8.50, most under $7) are served until 1 A.M. nightly. The specials change weekly and range from pasta salad or a sandwich served with salad and a side dish to beef stroganoff, jerk chicken, and Caribbean-style ribs. A Friday evening happy hour buffet (5:30 P.M.–7:30 P.M.) and a Saturday pre-closing buffet (midnight–2 A.M.) are absolutely free. Munch on tasty buffalo wings, pizza slices, pasta, egg rolls, raw veggies, and more. Pop in on Sunday for a creative brunch menu combined with pool and big-screen satellite TV (10 A.M.–2 P.M.). Open Sun.–Fri. 10 A.M.–2 A.M., Sat. 10 A.M.–3 A.M.

Puerto Rican

Borinquén Restaurant
1720 N. California, 773/227-6038   NW
Borinquén's specialty is the *jíbarito* (peasant) sandwich, made with fried plantains instead of bread, filled with meat (steak, pork roast, chicken, or ham), vegetables, cheese, lettuce, tomato, mayo, and mashed garlic! Prices are very reasonable, mostly under $7. Open Sun.–Thurs. 9 A.M.–10 P.M., Fri.–Sat. 10 A.M.–midnight.

La Bruqueña
2726 W. Division, 773/276-2915   **W**
One of the most popular Puerto Rican restaurants in the city, **La Bruqueña's** green bananas and fried pork, seafood dishes, *mofongo* (mashed green plantain), and *mondogo* (tripe soup) are house favorites. Live music on some weekends. Open daily 9 A.M.–11:30 P.M.

Latin American Restaurant and Lounge
2743 W. Division, 773/235-7290   **W**
The specialties of this small **Paseo Boricua** (Puerto Rican Division Street) restaurant include *cuchifrito* (pig ears), *tostones* (fried plantains), lobster, shrimp soup, *guineo* (boiled banana), and *morcilla* (spicy blood sausage). Most entrées cost under $8. Open Sun.–Thur. 8 A.M.–10:30 P.M., Fri.–Sat. 8 A.M.–11:30 P.M.

Ribs
SEE ALSO Soul Food and Southern Eclectic for more restaurants known for their ribs.

After debating the best pizza in town, Chicagoans can launch right into the merits of their favorite rib joints. It was for good reason that Hawkeye Pierce ordered ribs all the way from Chicago on the popular television show *M.A.S.H.* Don't miss the new annual **Ribfest** in Northcenter (Lincoln/ Damen/Irving) in mid-June. The rest of the year, chow down on some of these favorites.

These take-out places draw fans from around the city:

Lem's Bar-B-Que House
311 E. 75th, 773/994-2428   **FSE**
A South Side institution, **Lem's** has a lot to brag about, and so do its customers of 30 years. An island along the 75th Street corridor, Lem's serves tender and flavorful pit-oven smoked ribs, rib tips, and hot links. All orders served with french fries and Lem's Bar-B-Que sauce (available for purchase in individual to gallon-size servings). The side extras include potato salad and cole slaw; fried chicken and fried shrimp complete the menu. Menu items run $3–$18. Open Sun., Mon., Wed., Thur. 2 P.M.–2 A.M., Fri.–Sat. 2 P.M.–4 A.M.

Leon's Bar-B-Q
8251 S. Cottage Grove 773/488-4556 (the original location)   **FSE**

Open daily 11 A.M.–3 A.M.
1640 E. 79th, 773/731-1454   **FSE**
Open daily 11 A.M.–3 A.M.
1158 W. 59th, 773/778-7828   **SW**
Open Mon.–Thurs. 11 A.M.–3 A.M., Fri. 11 A.M.–4 A.M., Sat. 10 A.M.–4 A.M.,
Sun. 10 A.M.–3 A.M.
4550 S. Archer, 773/247-4171   **SW**
Open daily 11 A.M.–10 P.M.
When you see the big, round pig logo, you know you've found **Leon's**—
some of the best ribs around. Slices of white bread come with the order to
wipe up the extra sauce. These can be dangerous neighborhoods, however,
evidenced by the bullet-proof windows at the order counters.

Coleman's #1 Hickory Bar-B-Que (555 N. Cicero, 773/626-9299 and
5754 W. Chicago, 773/287-0363) on Cicero comes recommended by school
bus drivers from a nearby depot.

For dine-in ribs, these distinctive barbecue restaurants carry easier price tags
than many and should not be overlooked:

Twin Anchors (1655 N. Sedgwick, 312/266-1616) has occupied the same
leafy, residential corner in Old Town for nearly 75 years, maintaining its
pre-gentrification ambiance and Sinatra on the jukebox. Much of the film
Return to Me (2000) was filmed here and photos from the movie are
prominently displayed. The funky, part-diner, part-club **Smoke Daddy**
(1804 W. Division, 773/772-6656) imported a special pit-oven from down
south for its authentic, smoky ribs. Other barbecue pleasures include the
pork shoulder sandwich, vegetarian sandwich, and chicken breasts.
Live blues or jazz nightly, check the events calendar online:
www.thesmokedaddy.com. Open Mon.–Wed. 11:30 A.M.–midnight, Thur.–
Sun. 11:30 A.M.–1 A.M.

Kenny's Ribs & Chicken
1461 E. Hyde Park, 773/241-5550   **S**
Open Mon.–Thurs. 10:30 A.M.–midnight, Fri. 10:30 A.M.–2 A.M., Sat. noon–
2 A.M., Sun. noon–11 P.M.
11142 S. Halsted, 773/568-9404   **FSE**
Open Mon.–Thurs. 11 A.M.–midnight, Fri.–Sat. 11 A.M.–1 A.M., Sun. noon–
10 P.M.
8601 S. Stony Island, 773/221-6466   **FSE**
Open Mon.–Thurs. 11 A.M.–midnight, Fri.–Sat. 11 A.M.–2 A.M., Sun. 1 P.M.–
10 P.M.

Treat yourself to one of the South Side's best BBQ houses. Quick and helpful service is the rule. Chockfull of slow-cooked, wood-flavored foods with no wrong choices: Ribs, rib tips, hot links, barbecued chicken, southern fried chicken, and seafood. Meals include fries, bread, and coleslaw. There are party specials and daily lunch specials, and even student specials at select locations. Daily lunch specials are served Mon.–Fri. 11 A.M.–6 P.M. Holidays excluded. Food items about $3–$20 (for combos).

Ribs 'N' Bibs
5300 S. Dorchester, 773/493-0400   S
"Lip smackin' satisfaction" for over 35 years, **Ribs 'N' Bibs** has been serving the community and the country with its tender hickory-smoked ribs. A vintage neighborhood site, the restaurant offers tips 'n' link combos, maverick munchies (rib tips), western sandwiches and dinners, and of course, The Boss (a whole slab of ribs). "Branded . . . best food in town with gallopin' fast service." Menu choice range from $2–$16. Open Sun.–Thur. 11 A.M.–11 P.M., Fri.–Sat. 11 A.M.–midnight.

To grab a slab downtown before or after a symphonic or theatrical event, try these casual Loop favorites: The **Exchequer Restaurant and Pub** (226 S. Wabash, 312/939-5633) serves food nightly until 11 P.M. from a dining room plastered with Chicago memorabilia. The kitchen at **Miller's Pub** (134 S. Wabash, 312/263-4988) stays open until 2 A.M. (the bar until 4 A.M.).

Russian

Russian Tea Time
77 E. Adams, 312/360-0000   C
Although it's in the name, **Russian Tea Time** has not always served afternoon tea. It does now, but tea is only one option on a menu of outstanding, healthy Russian, Ukrainian, Georgian, Azerbajiani, and Uzbeki offerings. (Not to mention several vodkas, including many flavored ones.) Dough creations like Russian *piroshki*, Ukrainian potato dumplings, and Uzbeki *samsa* make great afternoon appetizers. Quail, calf's liver, and chicken croquettes appear on the hot entrée list, while vegetarians can delight in an impressive array that includes stuffed eggplant, beet caviar with walnuts and prunes, and Azerbajiani stuffed mushrooms. The sumptious surroundings are perfect for pairing with nearby Orchestra Hall or Art Institute events. Salads $5–$9, soups about $3, appetizers $3–$8, lunch $6–$11, dinner $10–$20. Open Sun.–Mon. 11 A.M.–9 P.M., Tues.–Thur. 11 A.M.–11 P.M.., Fri.–Sat. 11 A.M.–midnight.

Three Sisters Delicatessen & Gift Shop
2854 W. Devon, 773/973-1919   **FN**
Everything you need for a homemade Russian smorgasbord is here (both the ingredients for making it from scratch and already prepared items): cheese, chocolate, dumplings, stuffed cabbage, smoked meats, fresh and smoked fish (lots of herring choices), and kosher deli tems. The sisters' gift shop has *matrioshka* (stacking) dolls, ceramic figurincs, crystal goblets, Russian tea sets, and plenty of unusual items for that person who has everything. Open daily 9 A.M.–9 P.M.

Salvadoran

Izalco
1511 W. Lawrence, 773/769-1225   **N**
Closed for a while in 2001 for renovations, **Izalco** is up and running again with three rooms instead of one. This neighborhood restaurant features tamales, empanadas, pasteles, and daily specials like a ranchero steak priced under $5! Otherwise, entrées and soups are in the $5–$15 range, but most are well under $10. Mexican and Puerto Rican cuisines are also featured on the menu. Open Sun.–Wed. 11 A.M.–10 P.M., Fri.–Sat. 11 A.M.–11 P.M.

Sausage

When it comes to Old World butcher shop needs in the encased meats deparment, each side of town is lucky to have at least one stand-out sausage standby. Both have been around for decades, have over 100 specialties, and draw customers from miles around. South Siders rely on **Bobak's** (5275 S. Archer, 773/735-5334), where Polish sausage and other Polish meat preparations only head a stuffed list of choices. North Siders (including certain restaurants) go to **Paulina Meat Market** (3501 N. Lincoln, 773/248-6272) for German sausages (well beyond the standard veal brat), as well as other ethnic groups' recipes.

Scones

A Taste of Heaven
5401 N. Clark, 773/989-0151   **FN**
Truly divine scones in chocolate chip, raisin, and various fruit flavors take center stage while sinful bread pudding, eclairs, raspberry crumble bars, lemon bars, brownie bars, rugelah, monster cookies, and such tempt you from the sidelines. Open Mon.–Thurs. 6:30 A.M.–11 P.M., Fri.–Sat. 6:30

A.M.–midnight, Sun. 7 A.M.–10 P.M.

The 3ʳᵈ Coast
1260 N. Dearborn, 312/649-0730   **C**
This cozy Euro-style cafe serves up big and tasty homemade scones and
keeps late hours. At $3 each, they're a little pricey, but hey, **The 3ʳᵈ Coast**
is located in the Gold Coast. Open Mon.–Thurs. 7 A.M.–2 A.M., Fri. 7 A.M.–3
A.M., Sat. 8 A.M.–3 A.M., Sun. 8 A.M.–2 A.M.

Scottish

The Duke of Perth
2913 N. Clark, 773/477–1741   **N**
This Scottish pub/restaurant serves up shepherd's pie, steak and kidney pie,
and excellent fish and chips alongside more Americanized offerings (for
instance, the "William Wallace Cheese Burger"). The sizeable beer selection accompanies an unsurpassed 70–75 brands of single-malt Scotch.
Recommended beverages include McEwan's beers and the 16-year-old
Lagavulin Scotch. Entrées $7–$11, most under $8. All-you-can-eat fish and
chips on Wednesday and Friday for $8.95. The kitchen is open Sun.–Thur.
until 11 P.M., Fri.–Sat. until midnight.

Seafood

THIS is one of those categories where a full treatment is best left to food
critics and guides not working with our same budget orientation. Instead, we
give you a takeout joint on the river…

Lawrence Fisheries
2120 S. Canal, 312/225-2113   **C**
You wonder what wholesome motive draws someone to a deserted riverside
neighborhood in the middle of the night? 24-hour fried shrimp, fish chips,
frog legs, scallops, clam strips, catfish, smoked chubs, and seafood gumbo.
That's what. Dinners run about $3–$12, many under $6 (if you go with the
smaller version). Items are also sold by the pound or half-pound. You never
know who you might run into here.

And, takeout not on the river…

DiCola's
10754 S. Western, 773/238-7071   **FSW**
Primarily a fish market, **DiCola's** also cooks up some carry-out items.

Catfish is the main event, but shrimp, oysters, smelt, and frog legs are also popular. On the weekends and around holidays, the wait can be as long as an hour. Keep yourself entertained by people watching and gazing at the giant fish murals. Open Mon.–Thurs. 9 A.M.–9 P.M., Fri. 9 A.M.–10 P.M., Sat. 9 A.M.–9:30 P.M., Sun. 11 A.M.–7 P.M.

On the Northwest Side, stop in **Hagen's Fish Market** (5835 W. Montrose, 773/283-1944) for fresh, smoked, and fried fish, as Chicagoans have since 1946, when this family enterprise served a primarily Scandinavian clientele. The have the last hardwood smokehouse in the city, so bring your own fresh catch by for them to smoke for you.

Serbian

Simplon Orient Express
4520 N. Lincoln, 773/275-5522 **N**
Intimate and polished Serbian restaurant, which almost feels like you're sitting in a train car, proffers Serbianized specialties from every country that the regal Orient Express train passed through on its historic path from Constantinople to Paris, along with a handful of Serbian classics. Switzerland, Italy, Bulgaria, Turkey, Greece, and Romania all have their national dish. There's veal goulash from Hungary, Wiener schnitzel from Austria, and veal cordon bleu from France. European entrées $10–$18, Serbian entrées $10–$14, sides $3–$5. Open Mon.–Sat. 4 P.M.–2 A.M., Sun. noon–midnight.

Skadarlija
4024 N. Kedzie, 773/463-5600 **NW**
A cozy, windowless Serbian restaurant and nightspot, **Skadarlija** specializes in veal schnitzel, shish kebab, muckalica (pork tenderloin with peppers and tomatoes). The $32 Gypcy Plate includes traditional sausages, meat patties, and skewered chunks of pork and feeds 2–4, but most dishes run $8–$16. Music begins at 9 P.M., occasionally a cover charge for live acts. Open Wed.–Thur., Sun. 6 A.M.–2 A.M., Fri.–Sat. 6 A.M.–3 A.M.

Soul Food
SEE ALSO Southern Eclectic.

Army and Lou's Restaurant
422 E. 75th, 773/483-3100 **FSE**
Known as a South Side treasure, **Army and Lou's** has been dishing up soul

food since 1945. It is one of the oldest black-owned restaurants in the Midwest. Its sophisticated décor features walls lined with African and Haitian art. This award-winning restaurant was once a favorite dining spot for Harold Washington, Chicago's first black mayor. The restaurant has a large loyal clientele and remains a favorite among Chicago politicians and business owners. The fried chicken has been coined "arguably the best in town." The menu is filled with Southern specialties: baby back ribs, chicken livers, short ribs of beef, smothered chicken, Creole shrimp, and chitterlings. Live jazz Friday evenings 6 P.M.–10 P.M. Most dishes $3–$15. Open Wed.– Mon. 9 A.M.–10 P.M.

BJ's Market & Bakery
8374 S. Stony Island, 773/374-4700   **FSE**
9645 S. Western, 773/445-3400   **FSW**
Described as "Soul Satisfying" by *Chicago Magazine* and "A Must Visit Chicago Restaurant" by *Ebony Magazine*, **BJ's Market** serves up some of the very best soul food Chicago has to offer (and the stylish and sophisticated décor is welcoming). The mustard-fried catfish is the signature dish of the restaurant. Other noted dishes are the rotisserie smoked chicken, smothered smoked turkey wings, catfish teasers, beef short ribs, and salmon fillet. Their famous hot sides include fried green tomatoes, cornbread dressing, red beans and rice, and greens with smoked turkey. Dessert items include fresh baked peach cobbler, banana pudding, or bread pudding with rum sauce. Kids menu and senior discounts offered. Menu items range from $2 to $10. Open Mon.–Thur. 11 A.M.–9 P.M., Fri.–Sat. 11 A.M.–10 P.M., Sun. 11 A.M.–8 P.M. There's a Sunday buffet at Stony Island location.

Captain's Hard Time Dining
436–440 E. 79th, 773/487-2900   **FSE**
As you enter **Captain's Hard Time**, it is suggested on the entryway to "get ready to tantalize your taste buds and satisfy your hunger with soul delicious food." This South Side restaurant is beautifully decorated and appointed with fine artwork; table linens coordinate with the colorful décor. It's not uncommon to find local politicians, local business owners, and celebrities any time of the day or evening here. The menu is filled with southern classics: BBQ spareribs, salmon croquettes, oxtails, and short ribs of beef. Southern classic side dishes include steamed cabbage, mixed greens, pickled beets, and candied sweets. Business lunch specials offered. Breakfast, lunch, and dinner served daily. Food items $2–$14. Open Tues.–Thur. 8 A.M.–11 P.M., Fri. 8 A.M.–midnight, Sat. 11 A.M.–midnight, Sun. 11 A.M.–10 P.M.

Gladys' Luncheonette
4527 S. Indiana, 773/548-6848   **S**
The Formica counters and green booths may be what you'd imagine as "luncheonette" décor, but **Gladys'** food surpasses any "luncheonette" expectations. Since 1945, Gladys has been drawing South Siders for memorable dishes like smothered chicken, rib tips, oxtails, fried catfish, and ham hocks. Entrées come with your choice of sides (collard greens, black-eyed peas, corn muffins, biscuits, and then some). Though you won't have room, it will be hard to pass on dessert. Sweet potato pie, lemon meringue pie, bread pudding, and peach cobbler are but a few of the favorites. The menu changes daily. Most breakfasts are under $6. Lunch and dinner entrées are $6–$12, most under $7. Brunch early Sunday afternoon with a dressed-up after-church crowd. Cash only. Open Sept.–Feb., Tues.–Sun. 7 A.M.–10 P.M.

Pearl's Place
3901 S. Michigan, 773/285-1700   **S**
Touted as the restaurant that offers "Southern soul with a touch of Creole." Located in the heart of Bronzeville, **Pearl's** is a Chicago legend offering friendly service and a full array of soul food. The "Bronzeville Bits" (appetizers) include Pearl's crabcakes, Cajun BBQ shrimp, and fiery chicken wings. The "Smells Like Sunday" entrées include plantation fried chicken, salmon croquettes, liver and onions, and smothered steak. Sample side dishes include collard greens, candied yams, macaroni and cheese, and whipped potatoes. Dishes are about $5–$14. Open Mon.–Thur. 8 A.M.–8 P.M., Fri.–Sat. 8 A.M.–9 P.M., Sun. 8 A.M.–7 P.M.

Soul Queen
9031 S. Stony Island, 773/731-3366   **FSE**
Advertising "Soul Food for all Souls," this South Side institution has been around for 50 years, starting in the Bronzeville area and then moving to its current address in Pill Hill. You'll recognize it not only by the huge sign but by owner Helen Maybell's green Excalibur parked out front. Open Sun.–Thurs. 11 A.M.–11:30 P.M., Fri.–Sat. 11 A.M.–1 A.M.

For meatless, healthy versions of many of these dishes, head a block or so east to **Soul Vegetarian East** (205 E. 75th, 773/224-0104)—a warm and laid-back restaurant serving breakfast, lunch, and dinner.

Soup

Soupbox
2943 N. Broadway, 773/935-9800   N
Just six weeks before Seinfeld's infamous "Soup Nazi" episode, enterprising (and psychic?) 20-something Jamie Taerbaum converted his summertime Italian Ice shop (**Icebox**) into a literal soup kitchen for the cold months. It's all soup here, so you have only two choices: *What kind?* (12 kettles of homemade soup daily, from a rotating selection of 70) and *What size?* Tortellini with Chicken, Cream of Asparagus, Tomato Florentine, Minestrone, Chili, Pizza Lover's, Albondigas (Spanish meatballs), Split Pea with Ham, Clam Chowder....Mmmm Good. Open daily 11 A.M.–11 P.M.

Southern Eclectic

Dixie Kitchen & Bait Shop
5225 S. Harper, 773/363-4943   S
Cheerful re-creation of a bayou joint issues first-rate and plentiful Cajun and southern favorites. Start with fried green tomatoes, peach-glazed chicken wings, or crayfish and corn fritters ($4–$6). Sandwiches like the Oyster Po'boy and North Carolina Pulled Pork come with cole slaw and your choice of a side ($6–$9). Gumbo, jambalaya, and red beans & rice are served with a corn muffin, and entrées like blackened catfish and country-fried steak come with cole slaw, corn muffin and two sides (about $8–$12). Sides include black-eyed peas, mashed potatoes, greens, and corn. Please save room for dessert: bread pudding with whiskey sauce, peach cobbler, and pecan pie. Open Sun.–Thur. 11 A.M.–10 P.M., Fri.–Sat. 11 A.M.–11 P.M.

Wishbone
1001 W. Washington, 312/850-2663   C
Open Mon. 7 A.M.–3 P.M., Tues.–Fri. 7 A.M.–3 P.M. & 5 P.M.–10 P.M., Sat. 8 A.M.–3 P.M. & 5 P.M.–10 P.M., Sun. 8 A.M.–3 P.M.
3300 N. Lincoln, 773/549-2663   N
Open Mon. 7 A.M.–3 P.M., Tues.–Fri. 7 A.M.–3 P.M. & 5 P.M.–10 P.M. (with limited pub grub menu from 3 P.M.–5 P.M.), Sat.–Sun. 8 A.M.–2:30 P.M. & 5 P.M.–10 P.M.
Whimsical depictions of barnyard animals and sea life decorate the converted warehouse on Washington where the energetic crowd never lags until the last grit is served at the end of the day. The menu, inviting and lighthearted in its takes on Southern classics, wows with its choices for every meal of the day. (Weekend brunch really packs in the devoted.) The

food itself pleases any serious diner, including the health-conscious: baked bone-in-ham with honey mustard sauce, Hoppin' John, cheesy grits, bean cakes with mango salsa, Eggplant Elegant, blue claw crab cakes, stuffed acorn squash. Breakfast, lunch, and dinner entrées around $6–$12.

Subs/Deli Sandwiches

SURE there are more, like our beloved **Potbelly Sandwich Works**, which has exploded into a 16-store local chain, but these are a couple you may not know about...

Home of the Hoagy
1312 W. 111th, 773/238-7171   FSW

Venture to **Home of the Hoagy**, and be prepared to wait in line because this place is always hopping and the line is often out the door. They're known for steak sandwiches with hot peppers, regular and turkey hoagies, and "get your fingers messy" fries drenched in Ro's special secret sauce. Hot dogs and Polishes are also on the menu . . . and you can't leave without getting a cup or pint of the hand-packed ice cream. Open Mon.–Sat. 10 A.M.–11 P.M.

Morry's Deli
5500 S. Cornell, 773/363-3800   S

Touted as being "the closest to New York-style deli as you'll ever find," **Morry's** infamous Sky High triple-decker club sandwiches are served day in and day out with potato salad and pickles. Doubled-up sandwich selections include corned beef with New York pastrami, corned beef with roast beef, and breast of turkey with pastrami. The Ultimate Reuben Sandwich is offered with your choice of meat, sauerkraut, eggs, onions, Swiss cheese, and dressing served on toasted bread. Check them out for breakfast too: the Egg McMorry stacks an omelette, cheese, pastrami, and salami on a bagel. Food items $2–$8. Open Mon.–Sat. 7 A.M.–7:30 P.M., Sun. 9 A.M.–4 P.M.

Swedish

SEE the **Andersonville** entry (p. 308) in **Chapter 6: Walking** for more information on Chicago's original Swedish neighborhood and two of its long-standing delicatessens.

Ann Sather's Restaurant (and **Cafés**)
5207 N. Clark, 773/271-6677   FN
Open Mon., Wed.–Fri. 7 A.M.–2:30 P.M., Sat.–Sun. 7 A.M.–4 P.M.
929 W. Belmont, 773/348-2378   N
Open Mon.–Tues. 7 A.M.–3 P.M., Wed.–Sun. 7 A.M.–9 P.M.

3411 N. Broadway, 773/305-0024   N
Open Mon.–Fri. 7 A.M.–3 P.M., Sat.–Sun. 7 A.M.–4 P.M.
3416 N. Southport, 773/404-4475   N
Open daily 7 A.M.–2 P.M.
1448 N. Milwaukee, 773/394-1812   N
Open Mon.–Fri. 8 A.M.–2 P.M., Sat.–Sun. 8 A.M.–3 P.M.
Extraordinary cinnamon rolls, marvelous homemade food, large portions, cozy atmosphere, and great prices continually put the **Ann Sather's** restaurants at the top of Chicagoans' lists of favorite breakfast spots. [Note: The cafés have limited menus.] Swedish pancakes and meatballs, Swedish waffles with ice cream and strawberries, potato sausage, limpa rye, and lingonberry syrup join more conventional breakfast items on the menu. Special touches accent all meals: try peach, zucchini, or crab in the delectable omelettes. Choose homemade cinnamon rolls, biscuits, or muffins instead of toast, and homemade applesauce or fresh fruit instead of hash browns, as accompaniments to your egg dishes. Enjoy freshly made potato pancakes and ham with the bone left in. Take home cinnamon rolls, loaves of limpa, fruit pies, or monstrous cocoa-laden brownies from the bakery. Breakfasts $4–$9, most under $7, sides $1–$4.

Svea Restaurant
5236 N. Clark, 773/275-7738   FN
In lieu of **Ann Sather's** big city bustle, cross the street to **Svea**'s sleepy, down-to-earth charm. The Swedish pancakes, Swedish omelette, and Swedish meatballs are as Swedish as they profess. Other authentic favorites, like lox, egg & anchovies, and herring, can be found atop an open-faced sandwich. Menu items range from $3–$8, most under $5. Open Mon.–Fri. 7 A.M.–3 P.M., Sat.–Sun. 7 A.M.–4 P.M.

Swedish Bakery
5348 N. Clark, 773/561-8919   FN
A smorgasbord of low-priced and generously portioned baked goods for every occasion: breads (Stockholm limpa, sweet rye), muffins (sour cream poppyseed, cranberry), slices (custard streusel, Italian plum, pumpkin), candies (carrot cake truffles, mini cannoli), coffee cakes (apple walnut, cardamom raisin), cakes (mocha log, chocolate raspberry buttercream), cookies (Swedish butter cookies, filbert sandwich), and more. Waits can be long on weekends, giving you plenty of time to scope out the three walls of goods and make some choices. Open Mon.–Fri. 6:30 A.M.–6:30 P.M., Sat. 6:30 A.M.–5 P.M.

Tre Kronor
3258 W. Foster, 773/267-9888   FN
Picturesque Swedish and Norwegian café serves a limited but sufficient
menu of omelettes, quiches, soups, salads, and sandwiches for breakfast and
lunch ($4–$7). Try the Oslo Omelette filled with smoked salmon, dill, and
cream cheese, or the Stockholm, with caraway and cheese. Limpa bread and
potato sausages make good additions for those with Viking appetites. With
fresh flowers and candle lit tables in the evening, the dinner ambiance
becomes less quaint and more romantic. Lamb, salmon, and meatballs are
house specialties. Complete dinners are under $12. Open Mon.–Sat. 7
A.M.–10 P.M., Sun. 9 A.M.–3 P.M.

Thai

Cozy Noodles & Rice
3456 N. Sheffield, 773/327-0100   N
Cozy? Maybe they mean crazy—in the best possible sense. This new
Wrigleyville Thai shop is bright, colorful, and cheerful, and why wouldn't it
be, when most possible surfaces are covered with toys (many from **Quake
Collectibles**, p. 386). Rows of transformers, trucks, action figures, ther-
moses, and vintage radios neatly line the walls and hundreds of Pez
dispensers are tacked up in the women's restroom. Tables are made of old
sewing machine stands with mosaic tabletops. The food will bring you back,
too (you'll want to show your friends anyway). It's all delicious. Nearly
everything's under $6, plus there are combo lunch specials and delivery
coupons! Open Sun.–Thur. 11 A.M.–10 P.M., Fri.–Sat. 11 A.M.–11: 30 P.M.

Dao Thai Restaurant
230 E. Ohio, 312/337-0000   C
Fresh meat, fish, and vegetables are purchased daily, and the herbs and
spices home-grown for the memorable dishes served at this haven for "old
fashioned Thai cuisine." In the summer, savor every spicy morsel on the
lovely outdoor deck. Year round, relish the incredibly low check. Entrées
run $5–$9 and nearly all are under $7. Open Sun.–Thurs. 11 A.M.–10 P.M.,
Fri.–Sat. 11 A.M.–11 P.M.

Noodles in the Pot
2453 N. Halsted, 773/975-6177   N
This attractive little storefront stresses their noodle dishes: *Pad Thai* with
chicken, shrimp, or tofu; thick egg noodles topped with broccoli and roasted
duck; *Lard Nar* (fried rice noodles) with chicken or beef. Most entrées cost
$6–$8, lunch bargains are even less. Open Sun.–Thurs. 10 A.M.–10 P.M.,

Fri.–Sat. 10 A.M.–11 P.M.

Siam Café
4712 N. Sheridan, 773/769-6602   **N**
Around since before we became a Thai-savvy town, this modest neighborhood restaurant continues to serve inexpensive meals, including house specialties like pork satay, curries, catfish, cuttlefish, oysters, and greens fried in oyster sauce. Most entrées $5–$7. Open daily 11:30 A.M.–9 P.M.

Star of Siam
11 E. Illinois, 312/670-0100   **C**
Downtown's first Thai restaurant (1984), the **Star of Siam** claims to have helped popularize Thai food in Chicago and the country. Located in a rehabbed warehouse appointed with Thai folk art and some unique seating, this cheap eatery draws a fashionable clientele who gobble the cashew chicken, *Pad Thai*, and chicken satay. Hot fried curry chicken, spicy ginger chicken, and brandy-beef with green curry appear on the specials list. Entrées $6–$18, most under $8. Open Mon.–Thurs. 10 A.M.–9:30 P.M., Fri.–Sat. 10 A.M.–10:30 P.M., Sun. 11 A.M.–9:30 P.M.

Standing out for their fresh, healthy ingredients, fair prices, options for vegetarians, and all-round quality are **Bamee Noodle Shop** (3120–22 N. Broadway, 773/281-2641) and **Thai Wild Ginger** (2203 N. Clybourn, 773/883-0344). Most entrées at both places fall between $6 and $8. **Thai Wild Ginger** has $5–$6 weekday lunch specials (11:30 A.M.–3:30 P.M.) that come with soup, salad, and choice of entrée.

Vegetarian

A Natural Harvest
7122 S. Jeffery, 773/363-3939   **FSE**
The Taste of Chicago (p. 289) has exposed thousands (if not millions) over the years to the vegetarian tamales and corn dogs of this South Shore deli and health food store. Make a trip for other veggie substitutes. Ham, salami, chicken, burgers, steaks, tacos, and hot dogs are among the other mock meats/meat dishes prepared to go. The premises include a fresh juice bar that also supplies a range of energy drinks. Items range from $2–$6. Open Mon.–Fri. 10 A.M.–7P.M., Sat. 10 A.M.–6:30 P.M.

Chicago Diner
3411 N. Halsted, 773/935-6696   **N**

"Love animals, don't eat them," they say here at Chicago's chief, 20-something vegetarian restaurant, where typical vegetarian ingredients dominate the menu's dishes. Tofu, tempeh, sea vegetables, brown rice, legumes, kale, sprouts, soy cheese, et. al. create standards like burgers, salads, stir–fries, and noodle dishes. Breakfast favorites include biscuits & gravy and the potato hash with tempeh. At dinner, lentil loaf, seitan fajitas, and the future burger are frequent requests. Most entrées $6–$11. Don't forget to take home a tasty treat from their 100% vegan bakery (muffins, tofu "cheese" cake, and chocolate mousse cake come highly recommended). Open Mon.–Thur. 11 A.M.–10 P.M., Fri. 11 A.M.–10:30 P.M., Sat. 10 A.M.–10:30 P.M., Sun. 10 A.M.–10:00 P.M. (slightly longer hours in summer).

Heartland Cafe and Buffalo Bar
7000 N. Glenwood, 773/465-8005   FN

This peace–love complex and Rogers Park cultural nexus includes a healthy vegetarian (soy, tempeh, tofu, rice, beans) and non-vegetarian (burgers, chicken, turkey) restaurant with a spacious outdoor patio, a bar with an impressive and diverse entertainment lineup, a book store/gift shop, and a newspaper with a message. The nachos, chili with cornbread, outdoor dining, and entertainment are just a few reasons to stop by. Breakfasts run under $6; lunch and dinner, $5–$10. Open Mon.–Fri. 7 A.M.–10 P.M., Sat.–Sun. 8 A.M.–10 P.M. (longer hours in summer months).

Victory's Banner
2100 W. Roscoe, 773/665-0227   N

Just the Indian-inspired atmosphere, with the waitresses wearing saris and the spiritual music softly playing in the background, is worth the trek to this serene Roscoe Village restaurant. But the vegetarian wraps, omelettes, burgers, and salads give any veggie eater plenty of creative menu options to choose from. Many dishes include soy sausage, Fakin' Bacon, or tofu, and they offer plenty of dairy-free options. That's transcendental bliss for local vegans. Open for breakfast and lunch, most entrées range from $5–$8, and the sunny, bright room makes it a great place to meet friends. Be prepared for lines on weekends, as its fan base has outgrown the small room. Open Wed.–Mon. 8 A.M.–3 P.M.

Every two-bit diner and coffeehouse has at least one vegetarian sandwich these days, but sometimes you have to wonder if they've ever tasted their own recipes. Two coffeeshops that really know what they're doing and never fail to deliver food delicious and nutritious are **Bourgeois Pig** (738 W. Fullerton, 773/883-5282) and **Beans & Bagels** (1812 W. Montrose, 773/769-2000; 2601 W. Leland, 773/649-0015). **B&B** deserves heaps of praise too for their prices ($3–$5!), portions (sometimes enough for two servings), and variety of breads and vegetable toppings. Try one of their sandwich combos on the grilled whole wheat pita wrap or add marinated mushrooms.

Vietnamese

THE so-called "New Chinatown," along the 1000 and 1100 blocks of Argyle Street, is actually dominated by Vietnamese shops and restaurants, almost all of which are inexpensive and most of which offer at least 100 dishes. Explore this two block stretch, venturing into a restaurant that interests you, or take one of these recommendations:

New Pho Hung Cafe
1129 W. Argyle, 773/275-1112   FN
Encyclopedic menu offers 156 fascinating choices (fancy stuffed crabs with house sauce; sizzling platter of abalone, shrimp, crab, fish cakes, and vegetables; sautéed eel in curry and satay sauce) and Vietnamese classics in a no-frills storefront. Most dishes $5–$9. Lunch special includes appetizer, entrée, and soft drink for under $5. They also serve bubble tea! Open daily 10 A.M.–9 P.M.

Tien Giang Restaurant
1104–06 W. Argyle, 773/275-8691   FN
Perhaps Argyle Street's best. Outstanding food and low prices far outweigh the ho-hum décor. Clay-pot specials like shrimp soup with fresh pineapple and catfish soup with sour mustard and taro just nick the surface of the dozens of good finds you'll discover on this 187-item menu. Dishes $4–$13, most under $6. Open Mon.–Thur. 10 A.M.–10 P.M., Fri.–Sun. 9 A.M.–10 P.M.

Thai Binh
1113 W. Argyle, 773/728-0283   FN
This family-run Argyle street staple is sparsely decorated, but that won't matter to your happy taste buds. Head over in the early evening and the owners' daughter, Linda, will be happy to help you select your meal from the huge menu. Highlights include a stunning variety of shrimp dishes, clay pot meals, and tasty shakes including avocado–coconut. Sun.–Thur. 9 A.M.–10:30 P.M., Fri.–Sat. 9 A.M.–11 P.M. (But the best place on the block for an avocado shake—for there or to go—is **Pho 777** at 1065 W. Argyle. It doesn't matter how it sounds; trust us, you'll like it!)

Internet Resources

Chowhounds Chicago

www.chowhound.com/midwest/boards/chicago/chicago.html
Tastiest fish in Ravenswood? Best Black Forest cake? Where can I find Szechuan peppers? Seeking stuffed challah? If these are the types of questions you like to ask and answer, get yourself to the Chowhounds Chicago online message board.

Eatchicago.net

www.eatchicago.net
A Chicago foodie's blog filled with reviews, essays, news, and photos devoted to eating in and dining out in Chicago.

Savoring Chicago

www.savoringchicago.com
This bimonthly subscription newsletter devoted to discovering the best food stores, bakeries, pastry shops, butchers, fishmongers, ethnic grocers, gourmet specialty shops, cafés, wine stores, etc. in the city and suburbs includes ample excerpts with lots of local color on its Web site.

Slow Food

www.slowfoodchicago.org
The Chicago chapter of the international movement that promotes the pleasures of slow eating, sustainable agriculture, artisanal and authentic products, and diversity of food traditions and ingredients.

These local, online restaurant guides offer features like searchable databases (by all sorts of criteria), articles, top 10 lists, professional and amateur reviews, and more:

- **Centerstage Chicago: Restaurant Guide**, *http://centerstage.net/restaurants*
- **Chicago Reader Restaurant Finder**, *www1.chicagoreader.com/cgi-bin/rrr/form.cgi*
- **Citysearch's Restaurant Guide**, *http://chicago.citysearch.com/section/restaurants*
- **Cuisine Net Chicago**, *www.cuisinenet.com/restaurant/chicago*
- **Metromix**, *www.metromix.chicagotribune.com/dining*

Outlet Stores

WHAT'S better these days than more carbs? Day-old carbs at a discount!

The Affy Tapple
7110 N. Clark, 773/338-1100   **FN**
These folks lay claim to "The Original Caramel Apple," and after 50 years in business, who's gonna argue with them? The factory store, which deals in cash only, sells **Affy Tapples**, pretzel rods, frozen bananas, fairies ("like turtles but cute"), and caramel cups at well off retail. Affy Tapples are just fifty cents, half what you'd pay in a store. Open Mon.–Fri. 9 A.M.–5 P.M., Sat. 8 A.M.–noon.

Butternut Bread Thrift Stores
10 E. Garfield, 773/536-7700   **S**
2925 W. Montrose, 773/478-8875   **N**
Additional 10% discount Tuesdays. Open Mon.–Sat. 9 A.M.–6 P.M.

Eli's Cheesecake World
6701 W. Forest Preserve Drive, 773/736-3417   **N**
The yearly taste of **Eli's** celebration is usually in August or September. Call for this year's date. Open Mon.–Fri. 8 A.M.–6 P.M., Sat. 9 A.M.–5 P.M., Sun. 11 A.M.–5 P.M.

Entenmann's Thrift Stores
2945 W. Addison (Addison Mall), 773/463-6570   **N**
Open Mon.–Sat. 9 A.M.–6 P.M., Sun. 9 A.M.–5 P.M.

Heinemann's Bakery Plant Outlet Store
3925 W. 43rd, 773/523-5000   **SW**
Open daily 6 A.M.–6 P.M.

Hostess Cakes/Wonder Bread Outlet Stores
1301 W. Diversey, 773/281-6700   **N**
Open Mon.–Fri. 9 A.M.–7 P.M., Sat. 9 A.M.–6 P.M., Sun. 10 A.M.–5 P.M.
5702 W. 55th, 773/585-7474   **SW**
Open Mon.–Fri. 9 A.M.–7 P.M., Sat.–Sun. 9 A.M.–5 P.M.

Sara Lee Outlet Stores
4028 W. 59th, 773/581-9408   **SW**
Open Mon.–Fri. 9 A.M.–7 P.M., Sat. 9 A.M.–6 P.M., Sun. 10 A.M.–4 P.M.
6210 N. Western, 773/973-6210   **FN**

Open Mon.–Fri. 9 A.M.–7 P.M., Sat. 9 A.M.–6 P.M., Sun. 10 A.M.–4 P.M.
7650 W. Touhy, 773/763-4785 **FN**
Open Mon.–Thur., Sat. 9 A.M.–6 P.M., Fri. 9 A.M.–7 P.M., Sun. 10 A.M.–4 P.M.

Vienna Beef Factory Store & Deli
2501 N. Damen, 773/235-6652 **N**
Open Mon.–Fri. 8 A.M.–3 P.M., Sat. 10 A.M.–3 P.M.

World's Finest Chocolate Outlet Store
5007 S. Lawndale, 773/847-4600 **SW**
If you've lived in Chicago for any length of time, you're probably familiar with the chunky chocolate candy bars wrapped in silver foil and a fast-food coupon commonly sold by local children for school fundraising programs. Now, if the kids haven't come around in a while, you can take yourself over to the outlet store for some really sweet deals (they offer a larger selection, too!). Chocolate bars are almost always at least half the price of what you usually pay. The company has taken care to make this into a legitimate gift shop, though, with a selection of decorative glassware or small vases already filled with one of the company's candies and then attractively wrapped. There are special arrangements for the holiday, and usually a small selection of decorated tins or wicker baskets so you can put together your own gift packages. Open Mon.–Fri. 8 A.M.–6 P.M., Sat. 9 A.M.–4 P.M.

Farmers Markets

FOR four months of the year, from late June to late October, the city of Chicago's **Farmers Market** program offers ample opportunities to purchase fresh and inexpensive produce from regional farmers. Arrive early (7 A.M.–8 A.M.) for the best selection, but come near closing (2 P.M.–3 P.M.) for the best bargains. Complete schedules are available in season at the information desk in **City Hall** (121 N. LaSalle) or by calling the **Mayor's Office of Special Events** (312/744-3315). Visit the Special Events department on the City of Chicago site (*www.cityofchicago.org*) for a schedule and to see what's in season.

5

ENTERTAINMENT

The outdoor stage with state-of-the art sound at
Millennium Park is the city's newest spot to enjoy
free summer concerts. *Photo by Bill Arroyo.*

Two of Chicago's favorite venues for live entertainment: The historic Green Mill (above) for jazz and poetry slams, and The Old Town School of Folk Music (*below*) for folk and world music. (*Photos by Rames Shrestha.*)

5

···· # ENTERTAINMENT ····

WHEN IT'S TIME for some rest and relaxation, leaf through this section to find some of the best ways to spend an evening in Chicago. You can amuse yourself and others by volunteer ushering; attending festivals; learning about beer; dancing; or participating in improv comedy, open mic poetry, and open music jams. Or, let them entertain you with live music, movies, theater, comedy, dance, and poetry. We've got hard-to-beat blues and jazz, improvised *Sopranos*, free classical music in the afternoon, midnight movies, reggae clubs, spoken word performance forums, Euro-style dance clubs, build-your-own Bloody Mary bars, neighborhood gospel festivals . . .

Live Music

Blues

In the blues capital of the northern U.S. (we like to collect such titles here), big-name blues can be heard seven days a week all over town for very low entrance fees.

Artis' Lounge
1249 E. 87th, 773/734-0491   **FSE**
An upwardly-mobile, well-dressed crowd gathers nightly at **Artis'** to enjoy blues and R&B. Legendary DJ Herb Kent ("the Cool Gent") mans the controls on the first Tuesday of every month beginning at 8 P.M. Local bands such as Billy Branch and the Sons of the Blues appear on Sunday and Monday nights at 9 P.M. Open Sun.–Fri. 11 A.M.–2 A.M., Sat. 10 A.M.–3 A.M. No cover.

Blue Chicago
536 N. Clark, 312/661-0100 (Closed Mon.)   C
736 N. Clark, 312/642-6261 (Closed Sun.)   C
Packed with both tourists and residents, these bars remain down-to-earth and friendly in a trendy nightlife area. The clubs open at 8 P.M., the music begins at 9 P.M. and goes past midnight. $6–$7 cover allows admission to both clubs. Visit *www.bluechicago.com* for current schedules.

B.L.U.E.S. on Halsted
2519 N. Halsted, 773/528-1012, *www.chicagobluesbar.com*   N
Small club provides an intimate, quintessential blues bar experience with some Chicago greats: Big Time Sarah, Magic Slim & The Teardrops, Son Seals. Music begins nightly around 9:30 P.M. Most covers $5–$10.

Buddy Guy's Legends
754 S. Wabash, 312/427-0333, *www.buddyguys.com*   C
The Grammy winner's club presents local and national acts in a roomy storefront. Two pool tables and a full kitchen with great BBQ (serving until midnight) expand your options. On certain nights you might catch the legend himself roaming through the crowd or working the door. Nightly music, cover $10–$15.

Kingston Mines
2548 N. Halsted, 773/477-4646, *www.kingstonmines.com*   N
This 35-year-old blues club has an atmosphere that the owner Doc claims, "will return you to the birth of the blues." Seven nights a week you'll find the blues on both stages in this large two-room restaurant/bar, belting out both classics and originals amongst muraled walls and regulars who swear by the Southern style BBQ and fried catfish. Staying open every night until 4 A.M. and even 5 A.M. on Saturdays, this is the only place on the North Side to catch a late-night bite to the beat of the blues. Cover $12–$15; cheaper with a student I.D. and cheaper as the night goes on. No cover for students (with I.D.) Sun.–Wed.

Lee's Unleaded Blues
7401 S. South Chicago, 773/493-3477   FSE
The blues begin at 9 P.M. and go until 2 A.M. Fri.–Mon. at this cozy, South Side night spot. No cover, but the drinks do cost at least fifty cents more during music sessions.

Rosa's Lounge
3420 W. Armitage, 773/342-0452, *www.rosaslounge.com*   NW

"Chicago's Friendliest Blues Lounge" is owned by a transplanted Italian blues drummer and his mama, Rosa. Visit the Web site to join the mailing list to have schedules mailed to you. Music begins 9:30 P.M. Tues.–Fri., 10 P.M. Sat. Cover $5–$7, $10 for the likes of Sugar Blue and Melvin Taylor.

Smoke Daddy
1804 W. Division, 773/772-6656, *www.thesmokedaddy.com*   **W**
A sleek, diner-like BBQ restaurant and lounge with blues/jazz nightly, 9:30 P.M. Never a cover.

The **Chicago Blues Exchange** (72 E. Randolph), a gallery devoted to blues in the Chicago Tourism Center, hosts free blues Mon. and Wed. at noon, Fri. at 5:30 p.m.

Classical

There's no better place to start than **Orchestra Hall** (220 S. Michigan) for world-class classical music. The 1997 creation of **Symphony Center** came with a remodeling of Orchestra Hall that includes improved acoustics, new seating, and renovated public areas. Though generally quite pricey, it's possible to get tickets for as low as $11 here—for the **Chicago Symphony Orchestra** (312/294-3000, *www.cso.org*), as well as for other local ensembles/soloists and visiting musicians. The **Civic Orchestra of Chicago** (the "minor leagues" for the **CSO**, comprised of college and graduate musicians, is free, but tickets are required, 312/294-3420), the **Chicago Sinfonietta** (a more progressive orchestra, 312/236-3681, *chicagosinfonietta.org*), and the **Chicago Youth Symphony Orchestra** (high school-aged virtuosos, 312/939-2207, *www.cyso.org*) routinely play at Orchestra Hall (as well as occasional free concerts elsewhere) and come recommended.

In sharp contrast to the high ticket prices that even lesser-known classical groups command, some of the best classical music in Chicago can be heard for absolutely nothing. The **Chicago Cultural Center** (pp. 53, 283) and the **Harold Washington Library Center** (pp. 54, 287) are often the sites of free performances by noted regional ensembles like the **Newberry Consort** (312/255-3610), **Chicago Chamber Orchestra** (312/922-5570), and the **Classical Symphony Orchestra** (312/341-1521). Many of these shows take place on the lunch hour, evenings, and Sunday afternoons. Monthly schedules are available. Elegant neighborhood cultural centers, particularly the **North Lakeside Cultural Center** (6219 N. Sheridan, 773/743-4477), the **Three Arts Club** (1300 N. Dearborn, 312/944-6250), and the **South Shore**

Cultural Center (7059 S. South Shore Drive, 312/747-2536), likewise offer impressive classical concerts free of charge. Finally, no summer would be complete without enjoying at least one of the many free outdoor concerts performed by the **Grant Park Symphony** (312/742-7638) each season.

Schools, universities, and churches are another solid source of free and inexpensive classical music and opera. **DePaul University** (1 E. Jackson Blvd., 312/362-8000) and the **University of Chicago** (5801 S. Ellis, 773/702-1234), in particular, present both high-quality student perfor-mances and well-known guests. **Northeastern Illinois University** (5300 N. St. Louis, 773/442-4636) offers a concert series featuring a wide array of performers. **Roosevelt University** (430 S. Michigan, 312/341-3500) is dependable for free performances, and the reputable **Sherwood Conserva-tory of Music** (1312 S. Michigan, 312/427-6267) showcases their diamonds-in-the-rough at low cost. Head to Hyde Park where the stunning **Rockefeller Memorial Chapel** (5850 S. Woodlawn, 773/702-2100) spon-sors favorites like the Chapel Choir and Carillon concerts. **St. Luke's Evangelical Church** (1500 W. Belmont, 773/472-3383) has a popular cantata series.

Coffeehouses

Café Luna
1742 W. 99th, 773/239-8990   **FSW**
An elegant old-European coffeehouse/bistro, graced with classic tin ceilings, ceramic floors and sturdy oak doors, offers folk music every Saturday at 8 P.M. with no cover charge. The atmosphere is artsy and upscale. Coffees run $.92–$3.02. Sandwiches (with names like Half Moon, Harvest Moon, Tuna Moon, and New Moon) range in price from $3–$7. Luscious homemade desserts include brownies, lemon squares, pies, cakes, and ice cream; homemade breads are baked daily. There also is an enclosed garden open in the warmer months, a children's corner with books and games, and a monthly art exhibit.

Hotti Biscotti
3545 W. Fullerton, 773/772-9970, *www.hottibiscotti.com*   **NW**
A classic old-time Chicago bar transformed into a cozy Logan Square coffeeshop has become a hangout for the hip art crowd. There is a variety (folk, funk, rock) of music five or six nights a week, and they have recently begun serving alcohol in addition to coffee. Art displayed on the walls changes monthly. Open Tues.–Sun. 10 A.M.–2 A.M. Sandwiches range in

price from $3–$6, baked goods $1–$12, coffee $1.50–$3.

Mountain Moving Coffeehouse for Womyn and Children
1700 W. Farragut, 312/409-0276, *www.angelfire.com/il2/mmch/*   **N**
Open one Saturday a month from 7:30 P.M.–10 P.M., the **Mountain Moving Coffeehouse** is the oldest women-only coffeehouse in the country. No males over the age of 2 are allowed, not even male-to-female transexuals. Music, poetry, literature, and comedy, along with coffee, tea, and baked goods are what you're likely to find at this all-girl coffeehouse located inside the Summerdale Community Church/Good Shepherd Parish. A $15–$20 dollar donation is suggested but not mandatory. Call for details. No alcohol.

Uncommon Ground Café
1214 W. Grace, 773/929-3680, *www.uncommonground.com*   **N**
Established in 1990, this popular establishment was the first smoke-free neighborhood coffeehouse in Chicago. The comfortable, cozy atmosphere has become a favorite performance space for both local and national acts. There is an open mic on Mondays, and on Wednesdays you can enjoy your world jazz and wine tasting from 7–8 P.M. Folk/rock musicians also play on Tues. and Thur.–Sun., with 2–3 sets a night. All covers are a donation. Breakfast, lunch, and dinner are served; the menu is more than half vegetarian. Hours are Sun.–Thur. 9 A.M.–11 P.M., Fri.–Sat. 9 A.M.–midnight.

The comfortable **Ennui Cafe** (p. 161) has an old-hippie flavor with an eclectic mix of furniture for lounging while listening to jazz performers at 7:30 P.M. on Sundays. With its overstuffed chairs and wood-paneled walls, **Katerina's** (1920 W. Irving Park, 773/348-7592, *www.katerinas.com*) has a comfortable European flavor and is a self-described "eclectic club with its soul in the arts." Local musicians perform Tues.–Thur. at 9:00 P.M., Fri. at 6:30 P.M. and 10 P.M., Sat. at 10 P.M., and Sun. at 7 P.M. and 8:30 P.M. Music varies from soul jazz to latin percussion, and the cover is always $5.

Country

A funny thing happened in Uptown (p. 26) the last couple years as that neighborhood stands on the brink of another major transition in its colorful history: The young people moving in, and a diverse group of others who really get around, have discovered the country bars previously strictly for regulars and those seeking to not be found. At first they may have gone for their kitsch, adventure, or transgression value. Now it appears that they just plain have a good time there. Can you believe it?

Carol's Pub
4659 N. Clark, 773/334-2402   N
During the day and Monday through Wednesday evenings, this is still the
sleepy, spacious neighborhood tavern with cheap beer that could just as
easily be in any slow-going Midwestern town. But when it comes to
Thursday night karaoke (9 P.M.–1 A.M.), the live band Fri.–Sat. 9 P.M.–2 A.M.,
or the Sunday night open jam (9 P.M.–1 A.M.), be prepared for a free-
wheeling good time. The regulars and the unpredictable newcomers happily
co-exist, separate but equal, once in a while exchanging barbs and pleas-
antries. A recent karaoke night had regulars and retro-clothes gals singing
old school country, a sorority sister doing the best Aerosmith ever, a
professional opera star belting out Frank, and actors from the Cornservatory
hamming up 80s tunes, with groups of Catholic school employees and
middle-aged lesbians amongst the onlookers. The house band that's been
playing there for years delivers seven sets of old and new country, oldies,
rockabilly, R&B, and other faves for the dancing fools in the audience.
Never a cover.

Lakeview Lounge
5110 N. Broadway, 773/769-0994   FN
A small neighborhood bar that harkens back to country when country wasn't
cool. Their country and western bands play Thur.–Sat. from 10 P.M. to early
morning from a behind-the-bar perch. No cover, but the drink prices sure
have gone up lately.

Ethnic Tunes

For Eastern European music, visit **Skadarlija** (see p. 225) Serbian restaurant Wed.–Sun. 8:30 P.M., 773/463-5600, when the house ensemble per-
forms. **El Nandú** (see p. 148) Argentinean restaurant hosts a Latin singer-
guitarist Thur.–Sat. at 7 P.M., 773/278-0900. The house band at **Juliana**
(3001 W. Peterson, 773/334-0000) Arabic restaurant plays a variety of
Middle Eastern and American music Fri.–Sun. 9:30 P.M.–2 A.M. At **Plava
Laguna** (2610 W. Peterson, 773/465-1483), Bosnian folk music is featured
Fri.–Sat. at 9 P.M. The Ecuadorian restaurant, **La Peña** (4212 N. Milwaukee,
773/545-7022), features Andean music Fri.–Sat. at 7 P.M. and 10:30 P.M. and
Latin music Thur. and Mon. at 7:30 P.M. and 10:30 P.M. Turkish music
brightens up the **Arkadasha Café** (5721 N. Clark, 773/506-2233) at 8:30
P.M. Wed., and Fri.–Sun. For African pop and jazz check out the **Ethiopian
Diamond** (see p. 170) Fri. at 7 P.M.

Folk

Abbey Pub

3240 W. Grace, 773/478-4408, *www.abbeypub.com*   **NW**
Irish bar and nightclub (p. 184) regularly features folk, bluegrass, and alternative country musicians in addition to traditional Irish and rock bands. Free open acoustic stages Tues. Covers FREE–$15, sometimes more for major acts.

The Old Town School of Folk Music

4544 N. Lincoln, 773/728-6000, *www.oldtownschool.org*   **N**
Established in 1957, this venerable folk music school and performance space has become the world's largest center devoted to folk music with its move (Sept. 1998) to the renovated Art Deco building of the former Hild Regional Library. Expect a diverse lineup of folk acts, both big and small. Bluegrass, Celtic, Native American, Zydeco, Latin, blues, jazz, country, world music, and then some. Tickets $12–$25. The annual **Folk and Roots Festival** is held on a July weekend in nearby Welles Park.

Schubas

3159 N. Southport, 773/525-2508, *www.schubas.com*   **N**
Large tavern and restaurant has a comfortable room for intimate live performances. While the club has moved toward a growing roster of rock acts (p. 254), it continues to feature a fine lineup of acoustic, folk-rock, folk-country, alternative country, bluegrass, etc. Many of the acoustic shows are early (7 P.M.). Typical covers $6–$15, most $6–$10.

Irish

Abbey Pub

3240 W. Grace, 773/478-4408, *www.abbeypub.com*   **NW**
Large Irish nightclub and bar hosts a free Sunday night Irish jam session, the oldest in the city. While the club has moved to diversify its bookings, it hasn't given up on the nationally-known Irish bands, as well as local performers, who helped put the club on the map. See above for information on the Abbey's folk music schedule, p. 252 for its rock schedule, and p. 184 for a look at its menu offerings.

Celtic Crossings
751 N. Clark, 312/337-1005   C
Irish pub-club enlivened with artwork, two fireplaces, conversation (no TV), and plenty of Guinness offers traditional Irish music Sat. 9:30 P.M.–midnight., 6 P.M.–10 P.M. No cover.

Chief O'Neill's
3741 N. Elston, 773/583-3066, *www.chiefoneillspub.com*   NW
Slick pub and restaurant is named after Chief Daniel Francis O'Neill, the policeman credited with keeping Irish music alive in Chicago. In front of the fireplace on Tuesdays from 9 P.M.–11 P.M., an array of Irish musicians gather for an invigorating jam session. Bands are featured Sunday evening. No cover.

Cullen's Bar and Grill
3741 N. Southport, 773/975-0600   N
Attached to the Mercury Theater, this dark, wood-paneled bar/restaurant attracts a young, trendy crowd. Music includes an Irish jam at 9 P.M. Tues. and bands Thur.–Sun. at 9:30 P.M. Get there early, especially on Sunday which seems to be the most popular night for year-round Irish merriment. No cover.

Fifth Province Pub
Irish American Heritage Center
4626 N. Knox,773/282-7035, *www.irishamhc.com/fifthprovince.asp* NW
Tucked away in this 86,000-square-foot former public school building dedicated to everything Irish is an authentic Irish pub. Local and national bands perform at 9 P.M. Fri.–Sat. Shows are always free, and there is plenty of free parking available.

Kitty O'Shea's
720 S. Michigan, 312/922-4400   C
Named for a Dublin pub, this casual Irish bar and restaurant in the Chicago Hilton and Towers Hotel features Irish music Mon.–Sat. 9:30 P.M.–1 A.M. No cover. (See p. 185).

Martyrs'
3855 N. Lincoln, 773/404-9494, *www.martyrslive.com*   N
A long-time supporter of local Irish musicians, **Martyrs'** holds one of the city's best Irish jams at 9 P.M. Mon. (see p. 253 for rock schedule). Enjoy the free Celtic sounds along with drink specials and half-price pizzas.

McNamara's
4328 W. Irving Park, 773/725-1800   N
Neighborhood restaurant/bar in the Old Irving Park neighborhood features
an Irish jam session on Sat. at 7 P.M. No cover.

Jazz

Andy's
11 E. Hubbard, 312/642-6805   C
Jazz bar and restaurant, popular with all types, has a free noontime jazz set
Mon.–Fri., a $5 after-work set Mon.–Fri. at 5 P.M., and a later set at 9 P.M. for
$5. Live music Mon.–Thur. noon–2:30 A.M., Fri. noon–1:30 A.M., Sat. 6
P.M.–1:30 A.M., and Sun. 7 P.M.–12 A.M. Covers $5–$10, with a two-drink
minimum on Sat. The kitchen stays open until midnight.

The Cotton Club
1710 S. Michigan, 312/341-9787, *www.thecottonclub.info*   C
Evoking a feel similar to the mythical Harlem club it's named for, this sleek
and classy club (dress code enforced) features live jazz music Fri.–Sat. 10
P.M.–3 A.M. for a $10 cover. Sundays and Tuesdays are Reggae, and
Mondays and Wednesdays offer comedians and some excellent fledgling
musicians a chance to shine with a night of open mic. Complimentary buffet
after 8 P.M., Fri. and Sat. nights. Cover on weeknights varies depending on
the entertainment, so remember to phone first. Thursday nights ladies get in
free before 11 P.M.

Green Mill
4802 N. Broadway, 773/878-5552   N
Although it's been open since the early 1900s and popular in nearly every
successive decade, what remains and what's remembered of the **Green Mill**
are the speakeasy days when Al Capone frequented the place. It was also a
favorite of silent movie giants Charlie Chaplin and Gloria Swanson during
their days at Essanay Studios on nearby Argyle Street. Regular features
include a wee-hour jam session from 1:30 A.M.–4 A.M. Fri., and the long-
running, heckling poet's paradise, the Sunday-evening **Uptown Poetry
Slam** (see p. 280). The Green Mill doesn't disappoint; it's always there for
a weeknight, late-night, romantic, or glamorous escape. Black, white,
brown, tourists, locals, lovebirds, and diehards—everyone grooves here
together. Live jazz Mon.–Thur. 9 P.M.–1 A.M., Fri. 9 P.M.–4 A.M., Sat. 9
P.M.–5 A.M., Sun. 11 P.M.–1 A.M. Covers usually $5–$10.

Joel Siegel's Jazz Showcase
59 W. Grand, 312/670-2473, *www.jazzshowcase.com*   C
A roster of national acts are served up year round at this nightspot where the true jazz aficionados gather to keep up on what's happening in the genre. **The Jazz Showcase** is the second-oldest jazz club in the city, and Siegel himself has been announcing every act for the last 50 years! The popular Sunday afternoon show is geared for families and is the perfect time to introduce children to jazz. Shows are Fri.–Sat. 9 P.M. and 11 P.M., Sun. 4 P.M., 8 P.M., and 10 P.M., Tues.–Thur. 8 P.M. and 10 P.M. Covers average around $20, sometimes less, sometimes more, depending on the act.

Joe's Be-Bop Cafe & Jazz Emporium
Navy Pier, 700 E. Grand, 312/595-5299, *www.joesbebop.com*   C
A friendly cafe/club that offers performances by local artists as well as talented jazz bands from area colleges. The summer schedule presents live music at 6 P.M nightly; the rest of the year Mon.–Thur. 5 P.M.–10 P.M., Fri.–Sat. 6 P.M.–11 P.M., Sun. 4 P.M.–10 P.M. No cover.

Pops for Champagne
2934 N. Sheffield, 773/472-1000   N
Trendy but comfortable club offers a non-stop roster of jazz musicians that have made it a popular destination for cool jazz groupies. Music begins at 8:30 P.M. Mon.–Thur., 9 P.M. Fri.–Sun. No cover Sun.–Tues., $5 Wed.–Thur., $10 Fri–Sat.

Underground Wonder Bar
10 E. Walton, 312/266-7761, *www.undergroundwonderbar.com*   C
Cozy, low-key, subterranean bar features nightly jazz (classic, Latin, piano, and other styles) until 4 A.M. Cover $5–$10; free until 9 P.M. Sun.–Thur., and until 8 P.M. Fri.–Sat.

Velvet Lounge
2128-1/2 S. Indiana, 312/791-9050, *www.velvetlounge.net*   C
Chicago jazzman Fred Anderson's bare-bones place, where serious fans and players come for the Sunday night free-form jam from 6:30 P.M.–11 P.M. ($4) and jazz bands at 9:30 P.M. Wed.–Sat. Covers range from $4–$15.

Aspiring musicians can visit the **New Apartment Lounge** (504 E. 75th, 773/483-7728) for an open jazz jam every Tues. at 10 P.M.

Piano Bars

Slightly higher-priced drinks compensate for the absent cover charge at these establishments.

Coq d'Or Lounge
140 E. Walton, 312/787-2200, *www.thedrakehotel.com*   C
The Drake Hotel Lounge that's been serving since the end of Prohibition features a variety of pianists, 7 P.M.–1:30 A.M. Mon.–Sat., 8:30 P.M.–12:30 A.M. Sun. There is also a jazz brunch on Sun. from 11:30 A.M.–3:30 P.M. No cover.

Davenport's
1383 N. Milwaukee, 773/278-1830, *www.davenportspianobar.com* N
A friendly Wicker Park establishment that opened in the fall of 1998. Pianists tinkle the ivories in the piano bar and draw out the occasional guest vocalist (usually patrons and students). Bigger names perform in the comfortable cabaret room. No cover for the piano bar; $20 and under for the cabaret. Open Mon.-Thur. 7 P.M.–midnight, Fri.–Sat. until 2 A.M., and Sun. 3 P.M.–11 P.M.

The Red Head Piano Bar
16 W. Ontario, 312/640-1000   C
Polished, dress-up place attracts an older and spiffy crowd. Dress code enforced. Music Sun.–Fri. 7 P.M.–4 A.M., Sat. 7 P.M.–5 A.M. No cover.

Zebra Lounge   C
1220 N. State, 312/642-5140
In business since 1932, this dark, space-constricted lounge with a pervasive zebra motif draws a mixed, upscale crowd for its animated sing-alongs. Sun.–Fri. 9 P.M.–1:30 A.M., until 2:30 A.M. Sat. No cover.

Punk

Fireside Bowl
2646 W. Fullerton, 773/486-2700, *www.firesidebowl.com*   N
Chicago's premier venue for punk rock shows just happens to be a bowling alley! Cover is usually $6–$10 for three bands. All ages welcome; bar available for those over 21. Be warned that the restrooms may be the most disgusting you've ever experienced.

Keep an eye on these other clubs that also showcase punk bands: **Empty Bottle** (see p. 253) shows are usually Thur.–Sat. The **Metro** (see p. 255) features the big acts, and the **Hideout** (see p. 253) and **Double Door** (see p. 253) present a big show occasionally as well.

Reggae

Exedus II
3477 N. Clark, 773/348-3998   N
With the stage in the window of this small storefront club, you'll have to push your way to the back of the tight room for your allotted inches of dance floor. The live reggae bands begin after 10 P.M. Cover generally runs $5–$10, but there's no cover Sun.–Mon. or before 10:30 P.M. Wed. Closed Tues.

Wild Hare
3530 N. Clark, 773/327-4273, *www.wildharereggae.com*   N
Founded in 1979, the **Wild Hare** may be one of the nation's oldest reggae clubs; it's known as "America's Reggae Capital." The club offers a mix of reggae and world music seven nights a week. Club opens at 7 P.M., bands start at 9:30 P.M. No cover charge collected before 9 P.M.; after that it's $5 Sun., Wed.–Thur., $10 Fri., $12 Sat. Sunday is reggae jam night. Mon.–Tues. no cover, Wed. no cover for women.

Rock/Alternative

For both national and up-and-coming local alternative rock, pop rock, and alternative country, these bar-clubs are a must:

Abbey Pub
3240 W. Grace, 773/478-4408, *www.abbeypub.com*   NW
Once known only as a venue for Irish, folk, or bluegrass, the **Abbey Pub** has expanded its music schedule with a fresh lineup of local rock and alternative country bands, as well as national rock and pop acts. The smaller pub stage brings local bands for around $5–$10, while the main 550-seat music venue draws popular national acts for $10–$25.

Double Door

1572 N. Milwaukee, 773/489-3160, *www.doubledoor.com* **W**

Though some find the **Double Door** a clear indication of Wicker Park's gentrification, most find this spacious club's band bookings in line with the neighborhood's cutting-edge reputation. Live music Tues.–Sat., beginning at 9 P.M., 10 P.M. on Sat. Open until 2 A.M. Cover $5–$15, higher for big names.

Empty Bottle

1035 N. Western, 773/276-3600, *www.emptybottle.com* **W**

This off-the-beaten-path bar probably presents the most truly on-the-fringe bands, though its offerings range widely to include jazz, punk, local talent, and indie rock. Live music nightly, beginning after 9 P.M. Opens at noon on Sat.–Sun., 5 P.M. Mon.–Wed., and 3 P.M. Thur.–Fri; closes at 2 A.M., 3 A.M. on Sat. Cover charges typically run $5–$12, usually at the lower end. Join their e-mail list to receive the weekly show schedule and a free drink coupon!

The Hideout

1354 W. Wabansia, 773/227-4433, *www.hideoutchicago.com* **N**

Without losing any of its old-time flavor, this decades-old, working-man's watering hole has been transformed into a cutting edge music and performance venue that has a friendly, come-as-you-are atmosphere. Quickly becoming one of the biggest supporters of the local independent music scene in the city, it's a great place to catch Chicago bands before they garner regional and even national attention. Other events include off-beat films, theatrical events, poetry readings, and benefits. There's usually something going on every night, beginning at 9:30 P.M., 10 P.M. on the weekends. Covers are $10 or less, often for a combination of events. A two-day block party in September has become a popular end-of-the-summer destination. (You can only get there off of Elston; it *is* down that dark looking street.)

Martyrs'

3855 N. Lincoln, 773/404-9494, *www.martyrslive.com* **N**

This clean, spacious, and relaxed club has catapulted the North Center neighborhood onto the nightlife map with its attention-getting bookings. The hottest local acts, some big names on tour, and a few interesting no-names are all just as likely to appear on **Martyrs'** ample stage in a given week. Although its name refers to deceased greats from the rock world, you're going to find a lot more than classic rock 'n' roll here—anything from the local Irish band with the African-American drummer and Asian bass player to new-agey percussionists. Covers run about $5–$10, sometimes more depending on the band. Monday night features an Irish jam (p. 248).

Phyllis' Musical Inn
1800 W. Division, 773/486-9862   N
This club remains from the late 1940s when this section of Division was filled with polka clubs and referred to as "Polish Broadway." **Phyllis'** now hands the stage over to rock groups, jazz ensembles, and bands of every stripe in between looking to break into better local-act venues. Tues. is free open mic night. Covers are $3–$5 the rest of the week.

Schubas
3159 N. Southport, 773/525-2508, *www.schubas.com*   N
One of the city's best intimate venues, **Schubas** made a name with folk, bluegrass and alternative country acts (p. 247 for folk listing). Recently, it has turned over a good portion of its schedule to pop and alternative rock bands. The intense schedule features music every night, with up to three acts performing. A separate restaurant serves better-than-bar American comfort food, and features a local showcase sponsored by the tongue-in-cheek paper *The Onion* the first Wednesday of each month. Covers average $8.

Wise Fools Pub
2270 N. Lincoln, 773/929-1300, *www.wisefoolspub.com*   N
The legendary blues club was reborn in 2001 and now promises a more eclectic roster of acts. With its exposed brick and tiny wall lamps, the 250-seat listening room looks like it did in 1979. Bookings range from blues to folk to rock and even some of the old-timers show up now and then. Music starts at 8 P.M. weekdays, 10 P.M. weekends. Open Tues.–Sun. Covers around $10.

Fun and inexpensive spots to see local bands include **Beat Kitchen** (2100 W. Belmont, 773/281-4444, *www.beatkitchen.com*) with its interesting musical offerings and creative menu. In the heart of Wrigleyville, the **Cubby Bear** (1059 W. Addison, 773/327-1662, *www.cubbybear.com*) offers local bands as well as national acts. While two bar/restaurants with music, **Joe's** (940 W. Weed, 312/337-3486) and **Boulevard Café** (3137 W. Logan, 773/384-8600, *www.boulevardcafe.com*), feature a lineup of rock and pop acts, they also have become known for showcasing the growing number of national jam-band acts. The **California Clipper** (1002 N. California, 773/384-2547, *www.californiaclipper.com*), an old speakeasy, has a great atmosphere and a variety of music. **Gallery Cabaret** (2020 N. Oakley, 773/489-5471) features a packed lineup of local bands. Most cover charges at these places run from $5–$15 depending on the act.

These distinctive and, to different degrees, historical, mid-sized concert halls should be visited at least once. Wait for your favorite national acts to come to town. The **Aragon** (1106 W. Lawrence, 773/561-9500), with its dated, exotic Mediterranean decor, still stands after an earlier heyday as a 1940s big band dance hall. An old-time theater, the **Metro** (3730 N. Clark, 773/549-0203) now hosts pop, rock, alternative, and punk bands. The **Park West** (322 W. Armitage, 773/929-5959, *www.parkwestchicago.com*) went from a strip club to an eclectic entertainment center with a kind of 70s panache. Also serving many entertainment functions since it was built in 1918, the **Riviera** (4746 N. Racine, 773/275-6800) now presents a range of concerts, including major rock, alternative, rap, and jazz acts. The **Congress Theater** (2135 N. Milwaukee, 773/252-4000), which has hosted everything from films to boxing matches since its 1926 opening, now features various DJs and bands booked by independent promoters.

World Music

HotHouse
31 E. Balbo, 312/362-9707, *www.hothouse.net*   **C**
Subtitled "The Center for International Performance and Exhibition" or "Chicago's home for the Progressive Arts," the **HotHouse** is both home to a host of progressive political and artistic groups and a hip nightclub, showcasing an eclectic program of music, dance, poetry, and performance art. In a given month, the music selection can encompass mambo, flamenco, samba, fandango, jazz, big band, cabaret, performances by multimedia artists and a wide variety of internationally-known world-music artists. With hot orange-red walls, warehouse-high ceilings, colorful artwork, interesting sculptures, big-window views of the city, full bar, and a dizzying entertainment schedule, HotHouse makes for a sensational South Loop club. Open daily two hours before showtime. Covers range from about $5–$20, most $10.

Clubs

Dance Clubs

Small-to-medium-sized neighborhood dance clubs are typically free of the attitude of the nightclub scene, are generally more affordable, and can even be more interesting as well.

Exit (1315 W. North, 773/395-2700, *www.exitchicago.com*) is Chicago's punk headquarters, where dancers can listen to plenty of music from the good old days, plus current metal, ska, and anything hardcore. Open 10 P.M.–4 A.M. nightly, Sat. until 5 A.M. Call for nightly themes. Covers FREE–$5. Still another alternative old-timer, **Neo** (2350 N. Clark, 773/528-2622, *www.neochicago.com*) features techno, industrial, new wave, and other dark and alternative dance music at the DJ table. Open Wed.–Fri. from 10 P.M. to 4 A.M., Sat. to 5 A.M. Covers FREE–$5. Located underneath the **Metro**, the **Smart Bar** (3730 N. Clark, 773/549-4140) plays some jazz, but mostly house and other urban dance styles, nightly from 10 P.M.–4 A.M., Sat. until 5 A.M. Covers run from $5–$10. **The Hideout** (see p. 253) spins progressive and trance music beginning at 12:30 A.M. Sat. DJs spin hip-hop, R&B and reggae at **Zentra** (923 W. Weed, 312/787-0400, *www.zentranightclub.com*) from 10 P.M.–4 A.M. Thur., Fri., and Sun.; until 5 A.M. on Sat. **Liar's Club** (1665 W. Fullerton, 773/665-1110) spins house and hip-hop; Thur. is metal night. Opens nightly at 9 P.M.

With weekend cover charges starting around $10 and moving towards $20 at the city's biggest and best nightclubs, the bargain bet would be to test drive them first at a lower price during the week.

Outrageous, enormous, extreme, and body-pounding loud, **Crobar** (1543 N. Kingsbury, 312/266-1900, *www.crobar.com*) attracts wild crowds. Techno, disco, and anything with a low and definite beat rule the expansive floor of dance-crazed patrons. When it's busy, if you don't have "the look," you may be waiting outside all night. Thur.–Sat. covers from $10–$30. Sunday is gay and lesbian night, cover is usually $10. The Asian-themed **Dragon Room** (809 W. Evergreen, 312/751-2900, *www.w36.com/inactive/dragonroom/*) draws a moneyed, urbane crowd for sushi and all-night dancing. For a sexy, elegant evening visit **Le Passage** (1 Oak Place, 312/255-0022), a darkly lit, French colonial nightclub/restaurant where the dance music is urban contemporary and ranges from house and acid jazz to hip-hop. Wed.–Fri. 7 P.M.–4 A.M., Sat. to 5 A.M. Cover on Wed. is the cheapest at $4, with $4 drink and food specials and 80s and 90s tunes; weekends are $20.

Some of the bigger clubs with more affordable weekend fees are the **Excalibur Entertainment Complex** (632 N. Dearborn, 312/266-1944) and **Biology Bar** (1520 N. Fremont, 312/266-1234). The **Excalibur Entertainment Complex** joins a lounge area, dance club, singles bar, restaurant, arcade, pool hall, and more in 60,000 square feet under the roof of one castle-like fortress. Listening and dance music may be "Top 40," house, retro, R&B, disco, Latin, industrial, alternative, lounge, or jazz at any given moment or in any particular corner. Open 5 P.M.–4 A.M. nightly, until 5 A.M. Sat. There is typically no cover to enter, but charges for certain rooms may hover in the area of $5–$10. **Biology Bar** is, you guessed it, a laboratory-themed club featuring house-techno music. Cocktails are served in test tubes and beakers. Wed.–Fri. 9 P.M.–4 A.M., Sat. until 5 A.M. Covers $15 or less.

Depending on what you want or what you can tolerate, the Division Street singles bars clustered between Dearborn and State make for an inexpensive evening of dancing, drinking, and mingling.

Far from the moneyed or edgy crowds of the city's top nightclubs, these pubs o' fun draw just-barely-post-collegiate types, frat drinkers, out-of-towners, suburban kids, sports buffs, neighborhood party people having a big evening downtown, or any combination thereof. The young and the reckless certainly appreciate the absence of cover charges and the ridiculously cheap drink and shot specials—particularly for the womenfolk. The following bars have the most active dance floors of the pack: **Finn Mc-Cool's** (15 W. Division, 312/337-4349), **Bootleggers** (13 W. Division, 312/266-0944), and **Mother's** (26 W. Division, 312/642-7251). Located a block or so off the strip, **Hangge-Uppe's** (14 W. Elm, 312/337-0561) has probably the best dancing crowd and facilities of them all, with first floor and lower level DJs spinning different types of music for each dance floor. Open until 4 A.M. Fri., 5 A.M. Sat. Cover $2–$3.

Folk

Folk dancers should access the **Folk Dance Council of Chicago** web page at *http://members.aol.com/fdccpub/index.html*. With a few clicks, you'll be in touch with all the clubs, dances, and lessons you can hope for. Bulgarian singing and basic Balkan dance lessons, Irish set dancing, Scottish country dancing, international folk dancing for seniors, Norwegian folk dancing performances, ethnic dance parties, and Cajun/Zydeco lessons are just a few of the many options that are happening nearly every week in Chicagoland.

Gay and Lesbian

Berlin
954 W. Belmont, 773/348-4975, *www.berlinchicago.com*   **N**
This big, 20-year-old video dance club, with frequently-changing theme nights, attracts mostly gay men during the week and a mix of gays, straights, and "I'm too drunk to cares" on the weekends. Male dancers, drag contests,

disco balls, feather boas, dancing platforms, and lots of camp. Every Wednesday is Women's Obsession Night for lesbians, and the last Wednesday of the month is Disco Wednesday. Open Sun.–Mon. 8 P.M.–4 A.M., Tues.–Fri. 5 P.M.–4 A.M., until 5 A.M. Sat. Cover charge $3 weeknights, $5 weekends.

The "Boystown" neighborhood (p. 311) offers an abundance of nightlife opportunities for gay men. **Sidetrack's** (3349 N. Halsted, 773/477-9189) is a video bar with TVs at every turn to watch videos with varying nightly themes, such as show tunes, comedy, and 60s, 70s, and 80s music. **Roscoe's** (3356 N. Halsted, 773/281-3355) combines a café, neighborhood bar (TV watching, pool tables, couches), dance floor, and ever-changing entertainment gimmicks like dinner-and-a-movie nights, amatuer drag shows, and wet boxer contests. **Spin** (800 W. Belmont, 773/327-7711) is open nightly for dancing and various theme events until 2 A.M., Sat. until 3 A.M. Cover charges range from FREE–$5. For country/western dancing, including lessons Mon. at 7:30 P.M., head to **Charlie's** (3726 N. Broadway, 773/871-8887), where there are regular drink specials and free admission.

Among the good neighborhood bars are **Big Chick's** (5024 N. Sheridan, 773/728-5511), a predominantly-gay, used-to-be-lesbian neighborhood bar with great drink prices, weeknight euchre (see p. 109), and weekend dancing. Guys and gals also gather at **Scot's** (1829 W. Montrose, 773/528-3253) bar in Ravenswood. **Charmer's** (1502 W. Jarvis, 773/465-2811) Art Deco establishment in Rogers Park has been standing since 1929 and now lures mostly gay men, some women, and some neighbors for its friendly bar atmosphere. **Star Gaze** (5419 N. Clark, 773/562-7363) is a gay and lesbian neighborhood dance club, restaurant, and beer garden in Andersonville, but it's mostly about the ladies.

Other entertainment alternatives include the mostly-gay **Gentry** (440 N. State, 312/836-0933, *www.gentryofchicago.com*) cabaret/piano bar, where there's never a cover charge.

German

Chicago Brauhaus
4732 N. Lincoln, 773/784-4444, *www.chicagobrauhaus.com*   **N**
The authentically-clad house band at this large restaurant/beer hall (p. 174) plays German, American, international, polka, ballroom, and popular music for dancing from 7 P.M.–midnight Mon. & Wed., 7 P.M.–1 A.M. Fri., 1 P.M.–5

P.M. and 7 P.M.–2 A.M. Sat., and 1 P.M.–5 P.M. and 7 P.M.–midnight Sun. Closed Tues. No cover.

Latin Dance

Nacional 27
325 W. Huron, 312/664-2727   **C**
A chic club featuring salsa, merengue, cha cha and mambo dancing on Fri. and Sat. beginning at 11 P.M. Covers are $10 on Fri. (ladies free); $10 on Sat.

Polish

On the Northwest Side, a string of small-to-medium-sized dance clubs featuring both DJs and live bands, cater predominantly to Polish and Polish-American crowds with other Europeans and neighbors mixed in. Most of these places either have no cover charge or a minimal one, tend to be dressier than other neighborhood spots, and play a range of international pop/dance music.

Jedynka
5610 W. Diversey, 773/889-7171, *www.jedynka.com*   **NW**
With 10,000 square feet, three rooms, and four bars, Jedynka is probably the largest nightclub on Chicago's Northwest Side. It takes that responsibility seriously and delivers big for its patrons. Their facilities include a vodka bar, a cappuccino bar, pool tables (tournament pool on Wed.), "champion" DJs playing Europe's newest dance music, and elaborate hi-tech light shows. Brimming with a variety of contests and special events, the club has a tradition of packing the last Friday of every month with gifts and surprises for those whose birthdays occur in that month. They've also been known to give away free bottles of champagne on guests' birthdays or name days. Open Wed.–Fri. and Sun 8 P.M.–2 A.M., until 3 A.M. Sat. No cover before 10 P.M. Sunday is 70s & 80s Euro-retro night with drink specials until 10 P.M. Wed. offers free admission for ladies and $2 drinks for all.

Dance from 10 P.M.–2 A.M. every night of the week (until 3 A.M. Sat.) at the **New Polonia Club** (6101 W. Belmont, 773/237-0571), and from 8 P.M.–4 A.M. nightly at **Chicago 21 Night Club** (6020 W. Belmont, 773/777-5208). Neither charge covers.

12-Step Polka

For a modern spin on the old classics, check out Chicago's own **Polka-holics**, who mix polka tunes with rock n' roll. As their Web site (*http:// polkaholics.chicagogigs.com*), states, they're "hot as a grilled kielbasa, crunchy as a potato pancake." The site lists their upcoming local shows, and offers MP3 song samples. For more information, you can also drop them a line at P.O. Box 803664, Chicago, IL, 60680-3664. The young polka scene is thriving in Chicago, and *PolkaSceneZine* (*www.geocities.com/polka-scenezine*) gives you all the current info on gigs, hot spots, and the culture. Never forget the polka version of Carpe Diem: *In heaven there is no beer, that's why we drink it here!*

Polka

Major Hall
5600 W. Grand, 773/237-8089   NW
Don't fight it, polka is back! And every Tuesday morning from 10 A.M.–1 P.M. the Major Hall holds polka parties, showing that, at least for some people, it never went away. The "Pensionaires" play their brand of polka to an almost all-seniors crowd, though anyone with "happy feet" is welcome. Lunch is $2 and coffee costs a quarter. If anything, this is the only wholesome place in the city where you can get a mixed drink at 10 in the morning.

Polonia Banquet Hall
4604 S. Archer, 773/523-7980   SW
The site of many a Southwest-side wedding reception, Polonia holds frequent polka nights. One of the most popular celebrates Paczki Day (pronounced "poonch-key"), the Polish version of Mardi Gras, centering around the consumption of paczki, jelly-filled pastries sprinkled with powdered sugar. Cover charge is $10–$12. Call for upcoming events.

Local polka dance groups meet at varying locations—sort of a floating polka party. For a current list, contact the International Polka Association (4608 S. Archer, 773/254-7771).

Stepping

If you have to ask what this is, don't show up at one of the clubs until you've learned a few steps. But we'll give you this hint: it's a uniquely Chicago African-American dance phenomenon, often compared to gliding across the dance floor. When you're ready to join the couples on the dance floor, try one of these places:

The New Dating Game
8926 S. Stony Island, 773/374-8883   S
This ritzy night-spot guarantees a mature crowd with a 25 years and older age requirement. The **Dating Game** oozes sleek elegance and class with its mirrored walls accenting the black décor. The main bar is lowered in the middle of the room and adorned with a few televisions. There are tables and booths surrounding the bar on the main level, and another bar against the wall. If you want a challenge, try to guess the identities of those pictured in the photos displayed along the walls. There's a small dance floor for those who want to get a little closer, as the DJ spins some mellow hits from his booth seven nights a week. No cover charge. Drink tickets can be purchased for $5/drink. And if you're looking to fine-tune your moves, The Dating Game offers $10 Stepping lessons Mon., Thur. and Sat., 6 P.M.–9 P.M. Free Salsa lessons are given on Thur. around 10 P.M.

Taste Entertainment Center
6331 S. Lowe, 773/873-6700   S
"The Taste is the place to be." With 23 years of experience hosting parties, the **Taste** is one of the oldest clubs in the city, so come dressed to impress. When you walk into this club, you'll be greeted by the Big Bear Police, reminding you to behave, and the red lips adorning the walls let you know you're in for a luscious time on any given day of the week. Every 4th Sunday is all about the Steppers, which is to be expected in the stepping capital of the world. Tuesdays are gay night, complete with female impersonators. Every 1st Wednesday, the Taste hosts nearly 600 seniors for food and dancing from noon until 5. Thursdays are ladies' nights, and male dancers are on the menu as the special treat. Friday is the weekly fish fry from 5 P.M.–11 P.M. served with classic "dusties" and local radio personalities on the turntable. After that, get ready to move your body to the sounds of reggae on Friday nights. On Saturdays, popular Chicago DJs take the stage to get the party jumping; more male dancers are swinging it for the ladies. But men…don't stay at home—there is a lingerie show for you. The cover at the Taste ranges from about $10–$15.

Other neighborhood spots for stepping on the far Southeast Side: **East of the Ryan** (914 E. 79th, 773/488-1000), **Mr. G's** (1547 W. 87th, 773/445-2020), and **Original 50 Yard Line** (see p. 154).

Swing

Want to really learn the ins and outs of swing dancing? The **Chicago Swing Dance Society** (*http://swing.uchicago.edu*) offers lessons and info on dances. Based at the University of Chicago, most of their events take place at Ida Noyes Hall (1212 E. 59th).

Drink

Bars for Beer Education

The Map Room
1949 N. Hoyne, 773/252-7636, *www.maproom.com*   N
With 26 beers on tap, a first-rate imported beer and microbrew selection, and daily drink specials, **The Map Room** is the perfect classroom for learning more about beer *and* geography! Maps line the tables and walls, globes are scattered about, and a travel club convenes here. They offer monthly Saturday beer classes (about $15 to sample). Drink specials, imported coffees, and international theme nights add to the enticing brew at this comfortable bar. Look for the free buffet of ethnic foods Tues. at 7:30 P.M.

Sheffield's
3258 N. Sheffield, 773/281-4989   N
Serene and atmospheric in the winter, thanks in part to dim lighting, wooden features, and a fireplace, this well-loved bar gets crowded and crazy when the beer garden opens in the summer. Join the Joseph Sheffield Memorial Beer Society by trying every beer on the menu (free t-shirt and two **Sheffield's** pint glasses upon completion). A booklet explains each of the over five dozen kinds to help you learn the differences between ales, porters, Pilsners, bocks, ciders, rye beers, wheat beers, oatmeal stouts, cream stouts, lambics, pale ales, lagers, and any stray cousins. The bar also sponsors quarterly beer tastings and special events to further their support of the current beer renaissance. Open 2 P.M.–2 A.M. Mon.–Fri., noon–3 A.M. Sat., and noon–2 A.M. Sun.

Bars for Beer Selection

Hop Leaf
5148 N. Clark, 773/334-9851   FN
Posters on the walls; wooden tables, chairs, and stools; big booths; candles; and interesting magazines and jukebox make for a spiffy neighborhood tavern. You'll want to return repeatedly to try the 18 different beers on tap, a rotating selection of over 110 bottled beers (1/4 are Belgian), and the Swedish Glögg. Ask for recommendations. Free pretzels and chips. Open daily 3 P.M.–2 A.M., until 3 A.M. Sat.

Quenchers
2401 N. Western, 773/276-9730, *www.quenchers.com*   N
Beer lovers can always have their thirst for just about anything quenched at this large corner bar, established in 1979, before the current beer boom. With 225 different kinds of bottled beer (many unusual and most imported) and 17 more on tap (try the rogue or Belgian ales), this is most likely the largest assortment of beer assembled in Chicago. The owner's famous chili and the standard bar popcorn will intensify your need for something thirst-quenching. Have another—these prices are easily some of the best in town for this type of selection. Open daily 11 A.M.–2 A.M., Sat. until 3 A.M. They now have free live music Mon.–Sat. after 9 P.M.

Village Tap
2055 W. Roscoe 773/883-0817   N
The over 30 draft beers on hand at the **Village Tap** is not only an impressive quantity, but one of the most craftily maintained collections of microbrews around. They like to push Midwestern labels, including Bell's from Michigan and Chicago's Goose Island. The backyard beer garden is a big draw; indoor accessories include board games, a pinball machine, and an encyclopedia set. Open Mon.–Thur. 5 P.M.–2 A.M., Fri. 3 P.M.–2 A.M., Sat.–Sun. noon–2 A.M.

Bars for Games

The Blue Frog Bar and Grill
676 N. LaSalle, 312/943-8900   C
Folks head to the Blue Frog to play one of their 100+ board games, including the ever-popular Trivial Pursuit, Operation, Mousetrap, and Don't Break the Ice. A well-stocked bar and a full-service kitchen keep gamesters satisfied, whether they're waiting to "get out of jail free" or watching others

"roll again." Open Mon., Wed., 11:30 A.M.–midnight, Tues., Thur.-Fri. 11:30 A.M.–2 A.M., Sat. 6 P.M.–3 A.M. Closed Sun.

Guthrie's
1300 W. Addison, 773/477-2900   N
Large windows, high wooden stools, checkered tablecloths, old maps, and pictures of boats and harbors make this quiet and quaint neighborhood tavern (when not packed on weekends or after Cubs games) perfect for spending an evening with friends and one of the board games from the backroom cabinet. Bar prices are on the higher side of average. Open Mon.–Fri. 5 P.M.–2 A.M., Sat. 5 P.M.–3 A.M., Sun. 2 P.M.–2 A.M.

Bars, Just Some Favorites

Artful Dodger
1734 W. Wabansia, 773/227-6859   N
The funky 20-year-old Bucktown/Wicker Park neighborhood bar that once promoted its glow-in-the-dark signature drink, "The Aqua Velva," is now cashing in on the fine booze, beer, and cocktail craze and pushing their remarkable stock of aged tequilas, wines, sherries, ports, cognacs, single malt scotches, rums, bourbons, microbrews, and imported beers. Open 5 P.M. daily, Sat.–Sun. at 8 P.M. DJ spins alternative music Wed.–Sat. in its back, black-lit dance room. No cover.

Bohica
5518 S. Archer, 773/581-0397, *www.bohicabar.com*   SW
Bohica welcomes diversity. Word has gotten around that everyone who enters this Southwest Side bar is made to feel at home, which means the crowd ranges from nerdy to funky. The outdoor beer garden is popular in warm weather. Open until 2 A.M. Mon.–Fri., 3 A.M. Sat., closed Sun.

Danny's
1951 W. Dickens, 773/489-6457   N
This house-turned-bar has been spruced up with plush couches, crazy artwork, candles, low and colored lighting, unique furniture, and plenty of turns and alcoves. Grab a niche for lounging, romancing, or their reading series. Open Sun.–Fri. 7 P.M.–2 A.M., Sat. 7 P.M.–3 A.M.

Delilah's
2771 N. Lincoln, 773/472-2771   N
A host of odd and splendid bottles call to you from behind the bar— particularly the impressive assemblages of bourbon, scotch, beer, and wine.

To accompany the liquid experimenting, you couldn't ask for more eclectic background entertainment. Punk rock, ska, gothic, old metal, and more have their theme-nights at the DJ table. Similarly, the music spinners pay a musical tribute to folks like Johnny Cash, Tammy Wynette, and Johnny Thunder on their birthdays. Expect the occasional fashion show or look-alike contest. Screenings of offbeat films and cult classics every Sat. and Sun. at 6 P.M., rock 'n' roll related films every Tues. at 7 P.M. Wed. is insurgent country night. Open Sun.–Fri. 4 P.M.–2 A.M., Sat. 4 P.M.–3 A.M. Never a cover charge.

Estelle's
2013 W. North, 773/782-0450   W
Locals love to lounge at this stylish, lazy, late-night bar in the Wicker Park/Bucktown area. Some bar hoppers even call it the best late-night bar in Chicago (are they fishing for free drinks or what?). Open Mon.–Fri. and Sun. until 4 A.M., Sat. until 5 A.M.

Mark 2 Lounge
7436 N. Western, 773/465-9675   FN
Ever wonder what happened to the diverse, middle-of-the-road crowd you likely grew up with in a typical Chicago neighborhood in the 70s and 80s? I think they're here at the **Mark 2**, hiding behind the divey façade, escaping their gentrified cohorts elsewhere. This is one nice bar—and with a 4 A.M./5 A.M. license, too—offering reasonably-priced drinks, a good selection, several well-kept pool tables and dartboards, foosball, and a video jukebox room all in an inviting, cozy setting.

Old Town Ale House
219 W. North, 312/944-7020   C
Journalists, writers, actors, and late-night employees are among those who join the more down-and-out at this shoddy, shabby, and uniquely-adorned neighborhood fixture. Its bookshelf is filled with classics, its walls filled with portraits, its jukebox filled with everything (classical, jazz, opera, rock, soul, oldies), and its bar stools filled with characters. Located in one of Chicago's ritziest 'hoods, this decidedly downscale place with a 70s flair seems to make it on everyone's list of favorite Chicago bars. Open noon–4 A.M. daily, until 5 A.M. Sat.

Skylark
2149 S. Halsted, 312/948-5275   C
Once a Bohemian bar when Pilsen was Czech, the recently re-opened Skylark may be the sign of new bohemian joints to come to the east side of

Pilsen and western edge of Chinatown. It's a large and fairly empty neighborhood tavern, visited by artists, young slackers, and others who venture to dark streets where nothing else is going on (i.e. a great place to take a breather from hyped-up areas and enjoy the low-cost cheap beer). Other items of interest are its lonely black velvet paintings, the giant 1940s urinals in the men's room, and the Southern-style comfort food. Open daily 4 p.m.–2 A.M., Sat. until 3 A.M.

Coffee at Night

Café Lura
3184 N. Milwaukee, 773/736-3033   NW
Sharing a name with a pub in Lodz, Poland, **Café Lura** is quite a discovery for anyone whose beaten path doesn't include the Northwest-side Polish stronghold where it's located. The dark and heavy wood-and-brick gothic decor is unlike any American coffeehouses in these parts. The glowing, black-lit side room with mirrors, trellises, vines, and a faded velvet sofa or two (and the storefront windows darkened) is like a set for an avante-garde *Midsummer Night's Dream*. Beyond espresso, cappuccino, and other caffeinated beverages, cocktails, ice cream, dessert, and a small food menu are available to support your nighttime lounging. A cover charge of $5–$10 may apply for evenings of live jazz, blues, or Polish music, but most shows are free. Open Sun.–Fri. 5 P.M.–2 A.M., Sat. 5 P.M.–3 A.M.

Filter
1585 N. Milwaukee, 773/227-4850   N
Newer addition to the North/Milwaukee/Damen area, from the same owners as Gourmand, (see below) offers a similar menu in another cozy location. A nice place to unwind after an early show lets out in the area. Open Mon.–Fri. 7 A.M.–midnight, Sat. 8 A.M.–midnight, and Sun. 8 A.M.–11 P.M.

Gourmand
728 S. Dearborn, 312/427-2610   C
The Dearborn location of this large, comfortable coffeeshop is a beloved place of Columbia students and staff members. Open till midnight in the spring and summer months, they offer reasonable espresso prices, a huge breakfast menu, delicious cakes, scones, and lunch options that include sandwiches and homemade cous cous. With their home-brewed coffee, late hours, and salon-type atmosphere, this neighborhood favorite shines above the usual chain shops. Open Mon.–Fri. 7 A.M.–10 P.M., Sat. 8 A.M.–10 P.M., and Sun. 8 A.M.–9 P.M.

Theater

WHEN it comes to a vibrant theater scene, Chicago is second only to New York City. This section will hopefully bring theater-going into your realm of daily activity options. Relieve the theater of its special occasion status, bring it down to the routine level of movie-watching, and your life will change. While theater can at times be an expensive venture, there are several ways—half price previews, as well as half-price tickets at Hot Tix—to bring down the price at the higher end theaters. Volunteer ushering is even cheaper; do a little work and you're in free. The Friday editions of the *Chicago Sun-Times* and the *Chicago Tribune* and the weekly editions of the *Reader* (free) and *Newcity* (free) are the best places to find comprehensive listings of what's playing where, when, and for how much.

Inexpensive Theater Options

Chicago's theater scene holds something for everyone: drama and comedy; experimental, political, and classic works; student, amateur, and professional performances; works-in-progress. Many of the productions staged at the theaters below cost under $15. Scan the newspaper listings carefully—some of these theaters have "pay what you can" nights and most have a week, or at least a few nights, of half-price preview performances.

$—$10 & under
$$—$10.01–$20

A Red Orchid Theatre ($$)
1531 N. Wells, 312/943-8722, *www.a-red-orchid.com*   N

American Theater Company ($$)
1909 W. Byron, 773/929-1031, *www.atcweb.org*   N

Angel Island Theatre ($/$$)
731 W. Sheridan, 773/871-0442   N

Athenaeum Theatre ($/$$)
2936 N. Southport, 773/935-6860, *www.athenaeumtheatre.com*   N

Bailiwick Repertory ($/$$)
Bailiwick Arts Center, 1229 W. Belmont
773/883-1090, *www.bailiwick.org*   N

Beverly Arts Center ($/$$)
2153 W. 111th, 773/445-3838, *www.beverlyartcenter.org*   FSW
For more information on the Beverly Arts Center, see p.38

Black Ensemble Theatre ($$)
Uptown Center Hull House, 4520 N. Beacon, 773/769-4451   FN
Known for its musical-biographies of African-American artists such as
Muddy Waters, Jackie Wilson, etc.

Boulevard Art Center ($/$$)
6011 S. Justine
773/476-4900, *http://boulevardarts.ccts.cs.depaul.edu/*   SW

Boxer Rebellion Theater ($/$$)
1257 W. Loyola, 773/465-7325   N

Breadline Theatre ($/$$)
1802 W. Berenice, 773/327-6096   N

Cenacle Theatre ($$)
Pilsen Theatre, 556 W. 18th, 312/491-8484   C

Chicago Center for the Performing Arts ($$)
777 N. Green, 312/327-2000

Chicago Cultural Center Studio Theater and Claudia Cassidy Theater
(FREE/$)
77 E. Randolph, 312/744/6630, *www.theaterland.com*   C

Chicago Dramatists ($$)
1105 W. Chicago, 312/633-0630, *www.chicagodramatists.org*   C
In addition to a regular season, plays-in-progress by Chicago playwrights are
featured Sat. at 2 P.M. for $3.

Chicago Kids Company ($)
Richard J. Daley College
7500 S. Pulaski, 773/539-0455, *www.chicagokidscompany.com*   FSW
Wright College
4300 N. Narragansett, 773/539-0455   NW

Chicago State University Breakey Theatre ($/$$)
9501 S. Martin Luther King Jr. Drive, 773/995-4511   FSE

Chicago Theatre Company ($$)
500 E. 67th, 773/493-0901, *www.chicagotheatrecompany.com*   **S**
One of Chicago's five theaters specifically devoted to works by and about African-Americans.

Chocolate Chips Theatre Company ($/$$)
Kennedy–King College, Katherine Dunham Theatre
6800 S. Wentworth, 773/994-7400   **FSE**

Chopin Theatre ($$)
1543 W. Division, 773/278-1500, *www.chopintheatre.com*   **C**

City Lit Theater ($$)
1020 W. Bryn Mawr, 773/293-3682   **FN**

Columbia College Theater ($)
72 E. 11th, 312/344-6126   **C**

The Cornservatory ($/$$)
4210 N. Lincoln, 312/409-6435   **N**
The home of the offbeat Corn Productions.

Curious Theatre Branch ($/$$/'pay what you can')
7001 N. Glenwood
773/274-6660, *www.curioustheaterbranch.com*   **FN**
The home of the annual Rhinoceros Theatre Festival, a muti-week event featuring theater artists from Chicago's fringe.

ETA Creative Arts Foundation (FREE/$/$$)
7558 S. South Chicago, 773/752-3955   **S**
An African-American cultural center, **ETA Creative Arts Foundation** offers an ambitious schedule of original works by African and African-American playwrights. See p. 38 for a more detailed look at its comprehensive arts programming.

The Free Associates ($$)
Royal George Theatre, 1641 N. Halsted, 312/988-9000   **N**
An accomplished troupe known for its spoofs of pop-culture icons.

The Garage at Steppenwolf ($/$$)
1624 N. Halsted, 312/335-1650, *www.steppenwolf.org*   N
Showcases works by up-and-coming playwrights and directors, as well as the work of younger theater companies.

Griffin Theatre Company ($/$$)
5405 N. Clark, 773/769-2228, *www.griffintheatre.com*   FN
The company also produces children's theater.

Heartland Studio ($/$$)
7000 N. Glenwood, 773/465-8005, *www.heartlandcafe.com*   FN
This performance space is part of a healthy foods restaurant/bar/store complex (p. 233).

Lakeshore Theater ($/$$)
3175 N. Broadway, 773/472-3492, *www.lakeshoretheater.com*   N

Lifeline Theatre ($$)
6912 N. Glenwood, 773/761-4477, *www.lifelinetheatre.com*   FN
The company, dedicated to producing adaptations of literature and popular fiction, also is known for its children's theater season.

Live Bait Theater ($$)
3914 N. Clark, 773/871/1212, *www.livebaittheater.org*   N

Lookingglass Theatre ($$)
821 N. Michigan, 312/337-0665, *www.lookingglasstheatre.org*   C

Loyola University Theatre ($$)
6525 N. Sheridan, 773/508-3847
www.luc.edu/depts/theatre/season.htm   FN

Mary-Arrchie Theatre Company ($/$$)   N
Angel Island, 731 W. Sheridan, 773/871-0442, *www.maryarrchie.com*

Merle Reskin Theatre ($/$$)
60 E. Balbo, 312/922-1999, *http://theatreschool.depaul.edu*   C
Expect a diverse theater schedule, including works by the DePaul Theatre School and plays for children.

National Pastime Theater ($$)
4139 N. Broadway, 773/327-7077, *www.npt2.com*   N

Neo-Futurarium ($/$$)
5153 N. Ashland, 773/275-5255, *www.neofuturists.org*   FN
Located above a funeral parlor, the **Neo-Futurarium** has been performing "Too Much Light Makes the Baby Go Blind," their popular 30 plays in 60 minutes requiring audience participation, since 1988. Shows Fri.–Sat. 11:30 P.M., Sun. 7 P.M. Pay $5 plus the roll of a die ($6–$11). Doors open at 11 P.M. on Fri.–Sat., 6:30 P.M. Sun. No reservations are accepted, so get there early because the theater fills up quickly. Crowds are lighter on Sundays.

Northeastern Illinois University ($)
Stage Center, 5500 N. St. Louis
773/442-4274, *www.neiu.edu/~stagectr/*   FN

Paul Robeson Theater ($)
South Shore Cultural Center
7059 S. South Shore, 773/256-0149   FSE

Pegasus Players ($$)
O'Rourke Performing Arts Center, Truman College
1145 W. Wilson, 773/878-9761, *www.pegasusplayers.org*

Playground Theatre ($)
3209 N. Halsted, 773/871-3793, *www.the-playground.com*   N

Profiles Theatre ($$)
4147 N. Broadway, 773/549-1815, *www.profilestheatre.org*   N

Prop Theatre ($$)
3502–4 N. Elston, 773/539-7838, *http://propthtr.lilyput.com*   N

Puppet Parlor Theatre ($/$$)
1922 W. Montrose, 773/774-2919
www.thenationalmarionettecompanyofchicago.com   N
Included among their various marionette extravaganzas is **Les Petites Follies**, an adults-only show modeled after the Ziegfield Follies, Follies Bergeres, and Vaudeville acts.

Raven Theatre ($$)
6157 N. Clark, 773/338-2177, *www.raventheatre.com*   FN

The Shakespeare Project of Chicago (FREE)
Harold Washington Library Center, 400 S. State   **C**
Berger Park Cultural Center, 6205 N. Sheridan   **FN**
773/334-8771, *www.shakespeareprojectchicago.org*
Free staged readings of the Bard's works.

Shapeshifters Theatre ($/$$)
4626 N. Knox, 773/282-7035, *www.irishamhc.com/shapeshifters.asp* **NW**
The resident theater of the Irish American Heritage Center.

St. Sebastian Players ($/$$)
St. Bonaventure Church
1625 W. Diversey, 773/404-7922   **N**

Stage Left Theatre ($$)
3408 N. Sheffield, 773/883-8830, *www.stagelefttheatre.com*   **N**

Steppenwolf Studio Theatre ($$)
1650 N. Halsted, 312/335-1650, *www.steppenwolf.org*   **N**

Storefront Theater ($/$$)
66 E. Randolph, 312/742-8497, *www.storefronttheater.org*   **C**

Strawdog Theatre ($$)
3829 N. Broadway, 773/528-9696, *www.strawdog.org*   **N**

Theatre Building Chicago ($$)
1225 W. Belmont, 773/327-5252, *www.theatrebuildingchicago.org* **N**

Theater on the Lake ($)
Fullerton and the Lake, 312/742-7994
www.cityofchicago.org/specialevents   **N**
The Chicago Department of Cultural Affairs sponsors a full summer lineup
of popular plays staged by local theater companies.

TimeLine Theatre ($/$$)
615 W. Wellington, 773/281-8463, *www.timelinetheatre.com*   **N**

Trap Door Theatre ($$)
1655 W. Cortland, 773/384-0494, *www.trapdoortheatre.com*   **N**

University of Chicago University Theater ($)
Reynolds Club, 5706 S. University
773/702-3414, *http://ut.uchicago.edu*   S

University of Illinois at Chicago Theatre ($/$$)
1040 W. Harrison, 312/996-2939, *www.uic.edu/depts/adpa*   C

Viaduct Theater ($/$$)
3111 N. Western, 773/296-6024, *www.viaducttheater.com*   N

WNEP Theatre ($/$$)
3026 N. Hoyne, 773/755-1693, *www.wneptheater.org*   N

Itinerant Theaters

Some theater companies don't have the luxury of a permanent site in which to perform. But that small matter doesn't stop them from being some of Chicago's best and most creative troupes. Instead, these companies rent space from venues such as Victory Gardens, Angel Island, the Theatre Building, the Athenaeum Theatre, Chicago Dramatists, the Cultural Center, the Storefront Theater, Live Bait Theater, and the Viaduct.

About Face Theatre ($$)

Annoyance Productions, 773/929-6200 ($/$$)

CollaborAction Theatre, 312/409-2741 ($$)

Congo Square Theatre, 312/913-5808 ($$)
The newest of Chicago's African-American theater companies.

Defiant Theatre, 312/409-0585 ($$)

Eclipse Theatre, 312/409-1687 ($$)

Emerald City Theatre, 773/529-2690 ($)
Theater for children and families.

European Repertory Theatre, 773/248-0577 ($$)

Factory Theater, 312/409-3247 ($/$$)

Famous Door Theatre, 773/404-8283 ($$)

Frump Tucker Theatre, 312/409-2689 ($$)

The Hypocrites, 312/409-5578 ($$)

Latino Chicago Theater Company, 773/486-5120 ($$)

The Mammals Theatre, 773/293-0431 ($$)

Open Eye Productions, 773/293-1557 ($$)

Pendulum Theatre, 773/529-2692 ($$)

Plasticene Physical Theater Company, 312/409-0400 ($/$$)

Porchlight Theatre, 773/325-9884 ($$)

Redmoon Theater, 773/388-9031 (FREE/$$)
The creative company known for its annual Halloween spectacle, as well as an annual winter pageant and wonderful mainstage productions.

Rivendell Theatre, 773/472-1169 ($$)

Roadworks Productions, 312/492-7150 ($$)

Seanachai Theatre, 773/878-3727 ($$)

Shattered Globe, 773/404-1237 ($$)

ShawChicago, 312/409-5605, (FREE/$$)
Free readings of works by George Bernard Shaw, as well as mainstage productions.

Shining Through Productions, 773/743-3591 ($$)

Steep Theatre Company, 312/458-9424 ($$)

Teatro Luna, 312/683-5248 ($$)
Chicago's first all-Latina theater ensemble.

Theo Ubique Theatre, 773/338-7258 ($$)

Tin Fish Productions, 773/474-0201 ($$)

Wing & Groove Theatre, 773/782-9416 ($$)

Zeppo Theater, 312/458-9877 ($$)

Theaters That Use Ushers

Volunteer ushering is an ideal way to keep current with what's playing on the moderate to high-priced theater front. It involves little more than dressing in black and white (and sometimes a bowtie), collecting tickets, passing out programs, directing patrons to their seats, making sure no intermission refreshments leave the lobby, and picking up left-behind programs at the end. Show up an hour early for a briefing of the theater and its seating policies, perform your simple duties, and take an empty seat once the show begins.

There are three basic ways to connect with ushering opportunities: 1) Almost all of the theaters below depend solely on volunteer ushers. Find the dates and times of their current productions in a newspaper and call with the specific day and time you would like to work. If it's open, they'll pencil you in. If not, you can talk about other available shows. 2) Theaters that still need ushers for upcoming shows often put a notice in the *Reader* classifieds (section 4) under the Theater/Performing Arts or Wanted headings. 3) Some theaters have a volunteer list/organization from which they draw their ushers. Contact the theaters you're interested in and sign up.

Bailiwick Repertory
1229 W. Belmont, 773/883-1090   N

Briar Street Theatre
3133 N. Halsted, 773/348-4000   N

Chopin Theatre
1543 W. Division, 773/278-1500   C

Goodman Theatre
170 N. Dearborn, 312/443-3800   C

The Saints

If you enjoy volunteer ushering, you might want to join **The Saints** (773/559-5510, *www.saintschicago.org*), a volunteer group that supports the performing arts. In addition to ushering, Saints members are offered other ways to volunteer for theater groups in exchange for show tickets. Some of the city's best theaters like the Shubert, Oriental, Palace or Chicago Theater, as well as Chicago Shakespeare, Court Theatre, Victory Gardens, and the Athenaeum, only use Saints members for their volunteer ushers. Monthly meetings have guest speakers from Chicago's theater community and allow ushers to sign up to usher several shows at once. Annual fee: $55, $25 for students ages 16–24.

Lookingglass Theatre
Michigan and Pearson, 312/337-0665   C

Mercury Theater
3745 N. Southport, 773/325-1700   N

Royal George Theatre Center
1641 N. Halsted, 312/988-9000   N

Steppenwolf Theatre
1650 N. Halsted, 312/335-1650   N

Theatre Building
1225 W. Belmont, 773/743-4438   N

Theatre on the Lake
Fullerton and the Lake, 312/742-7994   N

Discount Theater Tickets

Finally, if you want to see the big-time stuff and don't want to pass out programs in exchange, you have the wonderful **Hot Tix** alternative.

Hot Tix Booths:
78 W. Randolph   C
Michigan & Pearson (Water Tower Visitors Center)   C
214 S. Wabash (Tower Records—cash only)   C

214 S. Wabash (Tower Records—cash only)   C
2301 N. Clark (Tower Records—cash only)   N
Buy your theater tickets the day of the performance, in person at one of the
Hot Tix booths, and get them for 1/2 price. To see what's available before
you go, check out *www.hottix.org*, which is updated Tues.–Sat. at 10 A.M.
and 2 P.M., Sun. at noon. Hours for the 78 W. Randolph location are
Tues.–Fri. 8:30 A.M.–6 P.M., Sat. 10 A.M.–6 P.M., Sun. noon–5 P.M. All other
locations are open Tues.–Sat. 10 A.M.–6 P.M., Sun. noon–5 P.M.

League of Chicago Theatres
http://chicagoplays.com
The full-service site of the **League of Chicago Theatres** shows you at a
glance what's opening soon, what's closing soon, and what's playing
tonight.

Centerstage's Chicago Theatre Directory
http://centerstage.net/chicago/theatre/theatres/directory
Phone numbers and addresses for 200 Chicago theaters.

Comedy and Improv

MOST comedy clubs have the last laugh as they tack on the two (over-
priced)-drink minimum rule to your already too-high cover charge. This list
omits those types and employs the same code used for theaters to lead you to
a performance that's kinder on your pocketbook. Again, a weekly *Newcity*
or *Reader* can give you details for current shows.

FREE—Indicates no charge, but please, if at a café or bar, have at least one
drink to support the establishment.
$—$10 and under
$$—$10.01–$15

ComedySportz Theatre ($/$$)
2851 N. Halsted, 773/549-8080   N
A mainstay on the local comedy scene, **ComedySportz** involves two teams
competing in short improv games. Thur. 8 P.M., Fri.–Sat. 8 P.M. and 10:30
P.M. The theater also presents other improv shows and comedic stage
productions.

Cornservatory ($)
4210 N. Lincoln, 773/865-7731   N

Cornball troupe has ongoing late-night show, *Chemically Imbalanced Comedy Saturday Night Showcase.* Sat. 10 P.M., $8.

Frankie J's Methadone Theater ($)
4437 N. Broadway, 2ⁿᵈ floor, 773/769-2959   N
A performance space above the restaurant/bar features various local improv groups (Sat. 10:30 P.M., $10) and a stand-up open mic (Wed. 9 P.M., $3).

ImprovOlympic Theatre ($/$$)
3541 N. Clark, 773/880-0199   N
Long-form improv shows and some sketch comedy can be seen at this informal Wrigleyville club (bar available). Tues. 8 P.M., Wed. 8 P.M. and 11 P.M., Thur.–Sat. 8 P.M. and 10:30 P.M., Sun. 8 P.M. "Improv Jams" Sat. at midnight are free for participants. Shows $5–$14, though occasionally they're free!

Lincoln Restaurant ($)
4008 N. Lincoln, 773/296-4029   N
A stand-up comedy and variety showcase in a side room at this family restaurant. (They have a full bar and ice cream sundaes). Fri. in season 8 P.M., $6.

Playground Theater ($)
3209 N. Halsted, 773/871-3793   N
The Playground is a consortium of some of the city's best new improv ensembles. Its member groups perform on a rotating basis. Thur.–Sat. 8 P.M. $5–$10 cover.

Second City ($$)
1616 N. Wells, 312/337-3992   N
The famed, original Chicago comedy company. Tues.–Thur. at 8:30 P.M., Fri.–Sat. at 8 P.M. and 11 P.M., Sun. at 8 P.M., $17–$19, some $10, no drink minimums. Come (or stay) after the last show of the evening for the free improv set (that's about two hours after it starts).

Second City's Donny's Skybox Studio ($)
1608 N. Wells, 4ᵗʰ Floor, 312/337-3992   N
More comic stage productions from the funny Second City People, particularly those in training who may not be quite as funny as the main stagers. Shows Thur.–Sun. $5–$10.

Second City E.T.C. ($$)
1608 N. Wells, 312/337-3992   **N**
Second City's second stage performs improv shows Thur. at 8:30 P.M.,
Fri.–Sat. at 8 P.M. and 11 P.M., Sun. at 8 P.M. Like Second City on Wells, they
host a free improv set after the last show of the evening.

Several new **free** open mic, stand-up comedy nights make it easy to move on
to the next one if you're laughing as much as you'd like (occasionally a poet,
rapper, musician, or great orator will take the stage). Sundays, try **Bad Dog
Tavern** (4535 N. Lincoln, 773/334-4040) at 9:45 P.M.; Mondays, **Tequila
Roadhouse** (1653 N. Wells, 312/440-0535) at 8:30 P.M. and **Xavier's** (4500
S. Western, 773/376-1992), 1st & 3rd Mondays only, 9:30 P.M. Tuesdays, try
Islands (3856 N. Ashland, 773/871-5585) first at 8:30 P.M. and **Phyllis'
Musical Inn** (1800 W. Division, 773/486-9862) after 9:30 p.m. On
Wednesdays, your options are **Big Horse** (1558 N. Milwaukee, 773/770-
2039) at 8 P.M. and **Hog Head McDunna's** (1505 W. Fullerton, 773/929-
0944) at 9 P.M.

Poetry and Spoken Word

THOUGH still the greatest strugglers in the starving artists' club, poets do have
a variety of changing and established forums in Chicago where they can
publicly express themselves. For audiences who lean toward the creative and
the literary, this means a whole new world of inexpensive entertainment.
Most poetry readings will cost you no more than the amount of coffee or
alcohol you want to drink. To keep abreast of new developments in the
poetry circuit, look to the weekly arts newspaper, *Newcity* ("Words" listing),
and the weekly alternative newspaper, the Chicago *Reader* ("Open Mikes &
Jams" section). Both of these periodicals are free and can be found in
abundance at coffee shops and various alternative venues.

Big Horse Lounge
1558 N. Milwaukee, 312/525-0917   **C**
Walk past the Mexican takeout place in front to the lounge in back! **Impact
Night** is their weekly spoken-word open mic event with DJ backup. Tues. 9
P.M., $4 cover, $3 for participants.

Funky Buddha Lounge
728 W. Grand, 312/666-1695   **C**
An open mic, with jazz accompaniment, for poets, spoken word artists, and
other vocalists is part of this funky nightclubs Supa Soul Sunday lineup.

Outspoken

The unassuming **Lincoln Restaurant** (4008 N. Lincoln), already profiled in this book for its delectable omelettes named for Civil War generals, offers a home once a week to a wacky and delightful Chicago free speech forum that's been in existence since 1951: **The College of Complexes**, a.k.a. The Playground for People Who Think. Some people in the crowd look like they're on the 50-year college plan. Each week features a guest speaker spouting off on anything under the sun from any perspective on or off the spectrum. After a question and answer period come the rebuttals and remarks (limited to five minutes) from the faculty (that's you in the audience who have a few choice words or brilliant insights to share), then a chance for the poor speaker to defend themselves in reply. The atmosphere is lively, offcenter, relatively civilized, and true to the spirit of founder Slim Brundage, Industrial Workers of the World organizer and first-rate hobo. Saturdays 8 P.M., $3 tuition, plus food or drink purchase. Get a schedule of upcoming topics: *www.collegeofcomplexes.org.*

Sun. 9 P.M.–11 P.M., $10 cover.

Gallery Cabaret
2020 N. Oakley, 773/489-5471   **N**
Low-key, arts-oriented bar hosts a performance open mic. Thur. 9 P.M., FREE.

Green Mill's Uptown Poetry Slam
4753 N. Broadway, 773/878-5552   **FN**
Hosted at the legendary **Green Mill** jazz club by founder Marc Smith since 1987, this internationally known poetry open mic/variety show includes a role for the opinionated audience. The opinions seem to carry over into the bathrooms—this is some of the best graffiti in the city. Sun. open mic 7 P.M., featured guest 8 P.M., slam 9 P.M., $6.

Heartland Cafe
7000 N. Glenwood, 773/465-8005   **FN**
The popular Rogers Park restaurant (see p. 233) features **In One Ear**, an open mic performance showcase of poetry and spoken word. Wed. 10 P.M., $2.

Myopic Bookstore
1564 N. Milwaukee, 773/862-4882   **W**
Large and literary Wicker Park bookstore hosts the **Myopic Poetry Series**, featuring poets reading and discussing their own work, Sun. 7 P.M., FREE.

New Glass House
7911 S. Halsted, 312/525-0917   **FSE**
K-SO G and DJ Pierre host another **Impact Night** spoken-word open mic at
this South Side club. Mon. 10 P.M., $5 cover, $4 for participants.

Subterranean Café & Cabaret
2011 W. North, 773/278-6600   **W**
Large, multi-purpose club turns over the stage for open mic poetry and
spoken word, Thur. 6 P.M.–1: 30 A.M., FREE.

Dance

FOLLOWING are the most likely places you can see dance performances in
Chicago for under $20; many hover around $10. To keep up with the dance
set, pick up a **Chicago Dance and Music Alliance** (312/987-9296) monthly
calendar at the tourist information booth in the **Chicago Cultural Center**
(78 E. Washington) or check out the coalition's Web site at
www.chicagoperformances.org.

The Athenaeum Theatre
2936 N. Southport, 773/ 935-6860, *www.athenaeumtheatre.com*   N

Chicago Cultural Center
78 E. Washington, 312/744-6630, *http://egov.cityofchicago.org*   C

Dance Center of Columbia College
1306 S. Michigan, 312/ 344-8300, *www.dancecenter.org*   C

Harold Washington Library Center
400 S. State, 312/747-4800, *www.chipublib.org*   C

Links Hall
3435 N. Sheffield, 773/281-0824, *www.linkshall.org*   N

Museum of Contemporary Art
220 E. Chicago, 312/397-4010, *www.mcachicago.org*   C

Northeastern Illinois University
5500 N. St. Louis, 773/442-5941, *www.neiu.edu/~music*   FN

Movies

WITH the following list in hand, you will never have to pay over $9 for a movie in Chicago again. Paying less won't interfere with seeing first-run or big-name movies. Nor does seeing such movies "second-run" make them a second-rate experience. Use moviegoing to expand your knowledge of the cityscape. With the wide range of inexpensive movie choices in Chicago, it's easy to combine the familiar escape to the silver screen with an adventure to a new neighborhood.

Matinees

Loews/Cineplex Cinemas dominate first-run moviegoing in Chicago, as does **AMC** with a fairly new 21-plex just off the Magnificent Mile, a 14-plex in the Ford City Shopping Center, and the 14-plex on N. Western— demanding $8–$10 per show. Matinees are your ticket around those prices. The 8-screen **Century Centre Cinema** shows mostly independent and art films. Each of the following theaters offers discounted prices before 5 P.M. or 6 P.M. during the week and for the first show on weekends and holidays. Bargain prices are $5–$6. Seniors and children under 12 always pay the reduced rate.

62nd & Western, 2258 W. 62nd, 773/476-4959	SW
600 N. Michigan, 600 N. Michigan, 312/255-9340	C
Burnham Plaza, 826 S. Wabash, 312/554-9100	C
Century Centre Cinema, 2828 N. Clark, 773/509-4949	N
City North 14, 2600 N. Western, 773/394-1601	N
Esquire, 58 E. Oak, 312/280-0101	C
Ford City 14, 7601 S. Cicero, 773/582-1838	FSW
Lawndale, 3330 W. Roosevelt, 773/265-1010	W
Lincoln Village, 6341 N. McCormick, 773/604-4747	FN
Pipers Alley, 1608 N. Wells, 312/642-7500	N
River East 21, 322 E. Illinois, 312/596-0333	C
Webster Place, 1471 W. Webster, 773/327-3100	N

The Cheap Movie Theaters

Chicago has lost most of the second-run "dollar shows" we used to know, love, and rely upon, but some still prevail, and we do have a few cherished and affordable independent theaters in our neighborhoods.

Brew & View at the Vic
3145 N. Sheffield, 773/929-6713   **N**
The historic **Vic Theatre** wisely added cheap movie house to its list of incarnations (both a former theater and nightclub, it still doubles as a concert hall) several years ago. Admission is always $5 for 2 to 3 movies. The first one starts around 8 P.M., the second at 10 P.M., and the third movie (Thur.–Sat.) at midnight. There's a full bar (with various drink specials nightly), full concession stand, a grand staircase to the second floor balcony, and a gutted first floor with benches and tables for more convivial viewing. This is a rowdy time—like renting videos with your closest two hundred friends. Must be 18 to enter, and 21 with ID to drink.

Finish an evening at **Brew & View** with a trip to the local **Dunkin' Donuts** (Belmont & Clark), so long a notorious hangout for rebel teens that it is sometimes referred to as the *Punkin' Donuts*.

Davis Theatre
4614 N. Lincoln, 773/784-0893   **N**
The **Davis** splits its four screens between first-run blockbusters and independent/art films. While it is no longer a "bargain" theater, it's top price is still cheaper than the other large movie houses. Pay $5 until 6 P.M., $7.50 after.

Logan Theatre
2646 N. Milwaukee, 773/252-0627   **NW**
The **Logan** is the only neighborhood theater that has matinees daily. They show 4–6 movies weekly, with some double features. Pay $3 at all times.

Three Penny Cinema
2424 N. Lincoln, 773/525–3449   **N**
The features here tend to be critically-acclaimed, art, independent, or foreign flics. Keep an eye out for midnight shows. The cheap Monday night movie ranges from $2.50–$4.50, depending on the movie. The normal price tag is $7.50, $5.00 for seniors and students. A six-movie discount pass is $27. The concession stand offers herbal iced tea, sparkling water, fancy juice combos, and popcorn refills.

The Village Theatre
1548 N. Clark, 312/642-2403   **C**
Four–six different movies are shown weekly, often including a double

feature. Prices are $4 before 6 P.M., $6 after. All movies are $4 on Tuesdays, and $4 all days/times for students and seniors. The Village has popularized midnight shows in Chicago as an alternative to the weekend bar scene.

A sister theater of **The Village** is **The Village North Theatre** (6746 N. Sheridan, 773/764-9100) which is the community theater for the Loyola/ Rogers Park area, showing 4–6 movie selections a week. Prices are $4.50 daily before 6 P.M. and $6.50 after 6 P.M. Seniors, college students with IDs, and children under 12 pay $4.50.

Alternative Movie Houses

Chicago Filmmakers
5243 N. Clark, 773/293-1447, *www.chicagofilmmakers.org*   **FN**
Chicago Filmmakers is a 28-year-old independent film house and forum/ resource center for filmmakers. They usually screen a couple of movies, mostly experimental stuff, weekly. Films are $7–$10, but members pay a reduced admission. Memberships begin at $25, or $20 for filmmakers, students, and seniors. A $50 Co-op Membership gives filmmakers access to equipment and classes. Consider volunteering and seeing movies for free.

Facets Multimedia
1517 W. Fullerton, 773/281-4114, *www.facets.org*   **N**
The **Facets** complex includes three theaters (for film, video, and live performance), classroom/conference space, and an enormous one-of-a-kind video rental library. A broad range of independent, unusual, classic, and rare movies are shown (at least one each day) for $9 a piece, $5 for members. A $50 Cinematheque Membership gets you ten free movie passes and numerous other perks, including discounted admission and video rental fees. Call for a film schedule or pick up a bimonthly calendar at various locations.

Gene Siskel Film Center
164 N. State, 312/846-2800
www.artic.edu/webspaces/siskelfilmcenter   **C**
In June, 2001, the **Film Center** set up its marquee at its great new location on State Street directly across from the **Chicago Theatre**. Renamed after the late Chicago film critic, the venue now features three comfortable theaters, a café, concessions, and film-related exhibitions. But even with its higher profile, the Film Center continues its mission as a research center and archive, as well as a non-profit theater that offers one of the nation's best programs of independent, international, and classic films. Pick up the

center's monthly *Gazette* or call the number above for information on upcoming films. Over 500 are shown annually; most cost $9. For film buffs, you can't beat gold card membership: $60/year for 1 or $85/year for 2 (the members can live at different addresses). Besides entitling you to some free passes, a subscription to the *Gazette*, free weekly lectures, and a discounted admission price of $4, gold card membership allows you to see sneak previews of major new releases (i.e., many Hollywood films) for free. For membership details, call 312/846-2600.

Music Box Theatre
3733 N. Southport, 773/871-6604   N
Although with tickets priced at $8.75 the **Music Box** is no longer an inexpensive movie option, this classic theater, renovated a few years back, is a must-see and do for its architecture and offerings. Some consider its lineup of foreign films, art movies, documentaries, animation fests, weekend midnight shows, and classics to be the country's best. Save by buying a $30 pass for 5 movies. Check out Sat. and Sun. matinee classics at 11:30 A.M. for $6.75, when a live organist regularly plays in the main theater. Quarterly schedules are available outside the theater and periodically in the *Reader*.

Other Film Venues

LaSalle Classic Film Series
4901 W. Irving Park, 312/904-9442   NW
See old movie classics on the big screen at this bank's clean and roomy theater (also used for financial seminars and community events) Sat. at 8 P.M. for $5, seniors and children under ten, $3. Popcorn $.75–$1, buttered $1–$1.25. Enter through the parking lot behind the bank. Pick up or call for a seasonal schedule.

University of Chicago Doc Films
Max Palevsky Cinema at Ida Noyes Hall
1212 E. 59th, 773/702-8574   S
University of Chicago film group shows recent, classic, and documentary movies daily during the academic year, both for the campus community and all Chicagoans. Named "Best Student Film Society" in the country by *Entertainment Weekly*, this is the country's longest continuously running student film society (since 1932). The Max Palevsky Cinema is even outfitted with the latest Dolby SR surround sound technology. Movie times are approximate: Mon.–Wed. at 7 P.M., Thur. at 7 P.M. and 9:15 P.M., Fri.–Sat. 7 P.M., 9 P.M., 11 P.M., and Sun. at 2 P.M. and 7 P.M. Admission is $4, $3 for the Sunday matinee. Call for recorded message of weekly and

upcoming offerings, 773/702-8575.

Chicago Outdoor Film Festival
Grant Park, Butler Field, Lake Shore Dr. & Monroe
773/744-3315   C
From mid-July to the end of August, spend Tuesday nights watching free
classic movies under the stars. A 23-by-46-foot movie screen sets the scene
for this urban "walk-in" with a skyline. It's never completely dark and sirens
and traffic noises blend in with the film. Bring a blanket, food, and friends.
With the demise of most revival movie houses, it's a rare chance to see
classic Hollywood films on a wide screen.

Chicago Silent Film Festival
Gateway Theatre in the Copernicus Center
5216 W. Lawrence, 773/777-9438   FN
Retaining its glorious original movie palace features, the Gateway Theatre is
the ideal venue for Chicago's Silent Film Society's increasingly popular
(like close to 1,000 in attendance for each gig) **Silent Summer** film series.
For six Fridays in late July through late August at 8 P.M., a different silent
classic is shown to organ accompaniment. At least one show in the series has
a full orchestra and a special celebrity guest.

Movies in the Parks
City parks
Another terrific (and free!) summertime movie outing for friends and
families are the classics, musicals, cartoons, blockbusters, and family-style
tearjerkers shown outdoors by the Chicago Park District. One hundred parks
each show one film for the season, and three or four possibilites are
available to you in a given week. Again, bring a chair or blanket and
munchies. Movies begin at dusk. Pick up a schedule at your local park's
fieldhouse.

To learn about movies currently being filmed in Chicago, extras casting,
procedures for filming, and things of that nature, contact the **Chicago Film
Office** (*www.cityofchicago.org/FilmOffice/about*).

Downtown and Free

FOUR grand central city institutions offer continuous and diverse complimentary programming for the public.

Chicago Cultural Center
78 E. Washington, 312/744-6630   C
A monthly schedule and the FINE-ART (312/346-3278) hotline can provide
you with specific information regarding the procession of free entertainment
offered at Chicago's public cultural headquarters. Especially popular are the
classical **Dame Myra Hess Memorial Concerts** held Wednesdays at 12:15
P.M. in the exquisite Preston Bradley Hall.

Harold Washington Library Center
400 S. State, 312/747-4800   C
The auditorium in the lower level of the main branch of Chicago's library
system is frequently open for free public music, dance, and drama performances. Pick up a monthly schedule of shows in the library's lobby or at the
Chicago Cultural Center. You can also call 312/747-4800 for dance,
312/747-4700 for drama, and 312/747-4850 for music information.

James R. Thompson Center
100 W. Randolph, 312/814-6684   C
Regular noon-time entertainment is offered in the atrium mall of this state
government building. Pick up the monthly *Center Stage* brochure at 100 W.
Randolph or call for details.

Under the Picasso
Daley Civic Center, Washington & Dearborn, 312/346-3278   C
Every weekday of the year from noon–1 P.M., near the Picasso in the Daley
Civic Center plaza, the City of Chicago's Department of Cultural Affairs
sponsors a range of cultural events: choral and instrumental music concerts,
drama, dance, lectures, ethnic celebrations, fashion shows, exhibits, farmers
markets, and much more. For the monthly schedule, stop by City Hall. For
the week's activities, call FINE-ART (312/346-3278).

Public Celebrations

SUMMER in Chicago is our reward for surviving the harsh, grueling winters.
May through September, a constant stream of music fests, food feasts, art
fairs, block parties, parades, fireworks, street fairs, historical house and
garden walks, neighborhood fests, church carnivals, ethnic festivals, and
picnics offers us abundant opportunities for eating, drinking, music listening, dancing, hanging out, spectating, browsing, marching, playing, gambling, lounging, strolling, meeting our fellow Chicagoans, and out-and-out
carousing. Consult weekend newspapers, tourist information centers, or the
events hotlines for exact times and dates. (See **Chapter 9: Keeping In-**

formed on p. 415 for more details on these resources.) To use as a rough guideline, the last line of each festival entry gives the typical time of year for the event. For a consistently updated list of summer events, check out the City of Chicago Web site at *www.cityofchicago.org/specialevents.*

The Big Grant Park/Lakefront Summer Events

Ahhh . . . There's nothing quite like partying with hundreds of thousands of your neighbors in Chicago's grassy front yard of Grant Park or on the sandy shores of Lake Michigan: World-class music and summertime food favorites abound, the music and people watching are free and sensational, there are surprisingly few problems considering the number of people hoarded together, and the amount spent on eating and drinking is up to you . . .

Chicago Gospel Festival, 312/744-3315   C
Grant Park (Jackson & Columbus)
A continuation of Chicago's historical involvement in the evolution of gospel music, the city hosts the country's largest free fest devoted to the genre for over a quarter of a million fans. Local and national acts, and soloists and choirs, perform traditional and contemporary gospel styles.
1ˢᵗ weekend in June

Chicago Blues Festival, 312/744-3315   C
Grant Park (Jackson & Columbus)
Food and art have joined this music extravaganza as the Chicago favorite (over 650,000 attend) and world's largest free blues fest continues to grow.
2ⁿᵈ weekend in June

Grant Park Music Festival, 312/742-4763   C
Millennium Park (Michigan & Ranolph)
The Chicago Department of Cultural Affairs and the Chicago Park District took over in 2001 where the Grant Park Concerts Society left off after 60 years of presenting free, evening summer concerts. Pick up a schedule in the Cultural Center. Bring dinner, beverages, and a blanket; stretch out; and enjoy a relaxing evening under the stars!
Concerts run mid-June through late August

Summer Dance, 312/742-4007   C
Grant Park, Sprit of Music Garden, 601 S. Michigan
www.cityofchicago.org/CulturalAffairs/SummerDance/
Summer Dance brings 200–500 people out onto a 3,500-square-foot,

open-air dance floor Thursdays through Sundays for 11 weeks in the summer for a *different* dance lesson and live band every night, weather permitting. Rumba, samba, chacha, salsa, merengue, foxtrot, waltz, African, Greek folk, polka, stepping, and swing...you can learn them all and more in one easy summer. There's no need to bring a partner; it's usually easy enough to find one or many in the crowd if necessary. A new **DJ Series** has been added with local and internationally-known DJs spinning various genres of electronic dance music Wed. 6:30 P.M.–9:30 P.M. (no lessons). Thur.–Sat. lesson at 6 P.M., music 7 P.M.–9:30 P.M., Sun. lesson at 4 P.M., music 5 P.M.–7 P.M. Concessions available.
Mid-June to late August

Chicago Country Music Festival, 312/744-3315   C
Grant Park (Jackson & Columbus)
Listening and dancing to regional and major country artists—again the largest free outdoor event of its kind.
Last weekend in June

Taste of Chicago, 312/744-3370   C
Streets extending from Jackson & Columbus intersection
Lavish food-sampling fest of 70+ area restaurants accompanied by loads of street musicians/performers and a packed schedule of "official" musicians and performers. Pay for the food; the music, as always, is free. With an attendance estimated at 3.5 million, this is Chicagoans' number one public extravaganza.
Usually the ten days up to and including the July 4th weekend

Fourth of July Concert and Fireworks, 312/742-7638   C
Lakefront/Grant Park/Navy Pier for viewing fireworks; begins after dark.
Hard-to-beat fireworks fete and accompanying classical music concert lures millions to the lakefront for an Independence Day celebration.
July 3, yearly

Venetian Night, 312/744-3315   C
Viewing area along lakefront between Navy Pier and the Adler Planetarium, begins after dark.
For over 40 years, this annual parade of illuminated and decorated boats coasts along Lake Michigan, with fireworks and the Grant Park Symphony in the background, for the enjoyment of over a half-million viewers.
A Saturday between late July and mid-August

Air and Water Show, 312/744-3315   C
Best lakefront viewing spot is North Ave. Beach.
Two million people have packed the lakefront for over 45 years to view stunt
pilots and power boat racers in the country's oldest such event and its largest
two-day spectator event.
Late August, though date tends to vary

Viva! Chicago Latin Music Festival, 312/744-3315   C
Grant Park (Jackson & Columbus)
Top local, national, and international performers provide a weekend of Latin
jazz, merengue, and salsa along with newer forms.
Usually a weekend in August

Chicago Celtic Music Festival, 312/744-3315   C
Grant Park (Jackson & Columbus)
Celebrates the music, dance, and Celtic traditions from Brittany, Galícia,
Ireland, Canada, the United Kingdom, and the United States. There's a harp
tent, bagpipe competition, and of course, the Trinity Irish Dancers.
Weekend in mid-September

Chicago Jazz Festival, 312/744-3315   C
Grant Park (Jackson & Columbus)
World's largest (surprise!) free outdoor jazz fest showcases the many faces
of jazz with local, national, and international acts for 350,000 Chicagoans
and visitors. This is the oldest (est. 1979) of the free lakefront music fests
Labor Day weekend

Chicago World Music Festival, 312/742-1938   C
Grant Park (Jackson & Columbus) & at a host of local venues
The newest of the city's music festivals—2004 is its sixth year—this is a
grand spectacle of music from all corners of the globe. International performers who rarely come to Chicago can be found here, as well as singers
and musicians from Chicago's own growing world music scene.
Usually runs 7–10 days at the end of September

Music Festivals

43rd Street Blues Fest, 773/924-1330   S
Mandrake Park, Oakwood and Cottage Grove
This free, one-day celebration of "gut-wrenching blues" is sponsored by the
Mid-South Planning and Development Commission not only to provide

entertainment for the community, but to educate people about the rich local talent. Past performers have included the late Junior Wells, Vance Kelly, and Otis Rush.
Wednesday before the annual city Blues Festival, the 2nd weekend in June

Belmont–Sheffield Music Festival, 773/868-3010   N
Sheffield, between Belmont and School
Arts and crafts, food, and top national music acts. Small entrance fee.
1st weekend in June

Chicago Folk & Roots Festival, 773/728-6000   N
Welles Park, 4200 N. Lincoln
The Old Town School of Folk Music's outdoor event features tons of music, from country to rock to world beat, as well as a dance tent and kids' tent. Food and crafts, too.
2nd or 3rd weekend in July

Concerts in the Parks, 312/742-7529
Citywide
The Chicago Park District sponsors over 80 summer concerts in over 60 Chicago parks. Call for a schedule.
Various dates/times throughout July and August

Jazz Heritage Fest, 773/734-2000   FSE
South Shore Cultural Center, 71st & South Shore Drive
1st weekend in August

Art Fairs

57th Street Art Fair, 773/493-3247   S
57th & Kimbark
Established in 1948, this is the oldest juried art fair in the Midwest. It attracts almost 300 serious artists from throughout North America, who exhibit their paintings, photography, sculpture, woodworking, etc. A wide variety of food and refreshments are available at the Ray School. FREE.
1st weekend in June

Hyde Park–University of Chicago Art Festival, 773/702-4195   S
Park your car for free at the University of Chicago, and hop a free trolley around Hyde Park to visit up to 30 neighborhood art institutes. The tour includes the **57th Street Art Fair** (see above) and the **Hyde Park Commu-**

nity **Art Fair** (below), which features work from local artists. Admission to most of the museums on the tour is free. Tours begin at 10 A.M.
1ˢᵗ weekend in June

Hyde Park Community Art Fair, 773/363-8282   **S**
57ᵗʰ & Dorchester
An offshoot of the **57ᵗʰ Street Art Fair**, this juried fine arts and fine crafts fair is sponsored by the Harper Court Arts Council. FREE.
1ˢᵗ weekend in June

Old Town Art Fair, 312/337-1938   **N**
1800 N. Lincoln Park West & 1800 N. Orleans
Chicago's oldest (55 years & counting) outdoor art fair is also among the most prestigious of America's top 20 art fairs, and one of the nation's oldest as well. Over 250 artists are represented. $5 donation.
2ⁿᵈ weekend in June

Wells Street Art Festival, 773/868-3010   **C**
Wells, from North to Division
30-year-old Chicago staple with 275+ artists, music, and a children's area. $5 donation.
2ⁿᵈ weekend in June

Annual Art Experiences, 312/751-2500   **C**
Various downtown locations
The American Society of Artists sponsors four to five downtown art fairs every summer. Call for the year's list of events.

Beverly Arts Fair, 773/445-3838   **FSW**
Beverly Art Center, 2407 W. 111ᵗʰ
Besides art, this family-oriented festival centers around ethnic music, dance, food, and children's events.
3ʳᵈ weekend in June

DuSable Arts & Crafts Festival, 773/947-0600   **S**
DuSable Museum, 740 E. 56ᵗʰ Place
Arts and crafts fair and family festival of the **DuSable Museum of African-American History and Culture**.
Weekend in mid-July

Gold Coast Art Fair, 847/444-9600   **C**
River North neighborhood, bounded by Ontario, Wells, Superior, and State

In its 47th year, another important Chicago fine arts fair.
1st or 2nd weekend in August

Bucktown Arts Fest, 312/409-8305   N
2300 N. Oakley
A Bohemian art, food, and entertainment event in its 18th year.
Last weekend in August

African Festival of the Arts, 773/955-2787   S
Washington Park, 55th & King
An annual festival of African culture, with live performances, fine art,
jewelry, sculpture, and clothing ,going on its 16th year. $10/day or $25/4-day
pass.
Four days over Labor Day weekend

Around the Coyote Art Exhibition, 773/342-6777   W
Milwaukee, North, and Damen
Visit the studios and galleries of Wicker Park's cutting-edge visual and performing artists. They have a winter version as well, in February.
2[nd]weekend in Sept. after Labor Day

Neighborhood Fests

St. Casimir's Day Festival, 773/778-7500   SW
Lithuanian Youth Center, 5620 S. Claremont
A free celebration of the feast day of the patron saint of Lithuania and of the
Lithuanian Boys and Girls Scouts of Chicago who sponsor this arts and
crafts festival. Visitors also enjoy ethnic food, entertainment, and games.
1st Sunday in March

Hyde Park Garden Fair, 773/947-8313
Weekend in mid-May

Printers Row Book Fair, 312/222-3986   C
Dearborn, from Congress to Polk (and spreading)
The Midwest's largest book fair, now owned by the *Chicago Tribune*, has
been drawing tens of thousands for 20 years to this former printing/publish-
ing district for buying new, used, and antiquarian books; attending author
signings, panel discussions, and workshops; and enjoying the literary ambiance. With expanding options for food and kids.
1st weekend in June

Humboldt Park Fest, 773/406-4968   FW
California & Division
Five-day Latino street fair features music, food, and art.
Late May or early June

Unity Day Picnic, 773/324-1447
Washington Park, 55th & King Drive   S
Sponsored by Jamaican-American Association of Illinois.
Weekend in June, noon

Park West Antique and Flower Fair, 773/506-4460   N
Main gate at 600 W. Fullerton
Summer streetfest focusing on buying, selling, and admiring antiques. $6
donation.
1st weekend in June

Fiesta Back of the Yards, 773/247-5100   S
47th, from Paulina to Damen
Food, music, arts and crafts in the historic Chicago neighborhood.
2nd weekend in June

Fiestas Puertoriqueñas, 773/292-1414   W
Humboldt Park, California & Division
Large Puerto Rican summer fest and independence day celebration includes
carnival rides, games, live music, traditional Puerto Rican specialties, and
other international foods.
Six days leading up to the 2nd or 3rd Sunday in June

Andersonville Midsommarfest, 773/665-4682   FN
Clark from Foster to Balmoral
Swedish mid-summer fest with food, drink, arts and crafts vendors, and local
bands.
2nd or 3rd weekend in June

Lincoln Park Fest, 773/868-3010   N
Clark & Armitage
Situated in the historic Lincoln Park neighborhood, this hip festival features
fine arts, food, and entertainment. Small entrance fee.
Weekend in mid-June

NAES Annual Pow Wow, 773/761-5000   FN
Mather Park, California & Peterson

A celebration of Native American cultures, sponsored by **Native American Educational Services (NAES)**, includes food, crafts, entertainment, and ceremony. Donation required for entrance.
3rd weekend in June

Jeff Fest, 773/868-3010   **NW**
Higgins, between Milwaukee & Gale
The Jefferson Park Community Festival offers some of the best local entertainment, as well as food, crafts, and family fun. Small admission fee.
Weekend in late June

Lakeview Arts & Music Festival, 773/472-7171   **N**
Belmont, Lincoln, and Ashland
Festival features top recording artists, as well as food, fine arts, and crafts.
Weekend in late June

Taste of Randolph Street, 312/458-9401   **C**
Randolph, between Peoria & Racine
Three-day event in the Randolph St. corridor West of the Loop features food from area restaurants, art and world market vendors, and entertainment.
Weekend in late June

Calumet/Giles/Prairie Historical Fest and House Walk
773/225-2257   **S**
3100 S. Calumet
Tours of historic homes and attendant festivities.
Saturday in late June

Bronzeville Historic House Tour, 773/924-1330   **S**
3402 S. King Dr.
The Mid-South Planning Board sponsors tours of the beautiful, restored homes in the historic African-American neighborhood.
Sunday in late June

St. Symphorosa Festival, 773/767-1523   **SW**
St. Symphorosa Church, 6200 S. Austin
This block party that has grown into a festival features food booths hosted by area restaurants, bingo, beer tent, raffle, adult and kiddie games, and entertainment.
Usually the 1st weekend after the Fourth of July

Annual "I Have a Vision" Community Gospel Festival   **FSE**
Hoard Park, 7200 S. Dobson, 312/861-8990
The **"I Have a Vision" Festival** is an all-day affair aimed at allowing the South Shore community to take back the streets and bring something positive to their neighborhood. This "Golden Gospel" festival brings well-known gospel acts to the neighborhood for free. Vendor booths, each with free giveaways, clowns, a basketball tournament, talent show and special appearances by the Chicago Police Department Canine Unit and some professional basketball players, it is known to be a fun-filled, spiritual, action-packed day.
2ⁿᵈ weekend in July, 11 A.M.

Rock Around the Block, 773/665-4682   **N**
Lincoln, between Addison and Roscoe
For a $5 donation, enjoy 30 local bands on three stages, food, and arts and crafts vendors.
2ⁿᵈ weekend in July

Taste of Logan Square, 773/868-3010   **N**
Fullerton & Kedzie
Popular neighborhood fest draws 25,000+ along the boulevards of this diverse neighborhood.
Four days in mid-July

Korean Street Festival, 773/583-1700   **FN**
3200–3400 W. Bryn Mawr
Korean crafts, food, and music.
Weekend in mid-July

Roots Festival, 773/373-3228   **S**
The **Roots Festival** is a free, one-day music and cultural extravaganza organized by 3ʳᵈ Ward Alderman Dorothy Tillman. With normally more than 200,000 people in attendance, the summertime event hosts great world and local entertainers, as well as vendors, local businesses, and food.
Weekend in mid-July

Sheffield Garden Walk, 773/929-9255   **N**
Webster & Sheffield
A tour through nearly 100 neighborhood gardens, as well as entertainment, food, and a children's corner.
Weekend in mid-July

Taste of Ireland, 773/282-7035   N
Irish American Heritage Center, 4626 N. Knox
A celebration of Irish culture, music, food, and drink.
Weekend in mid-July

Wicker Park's Summerfest, 773/665-4682   N
Division, between Damen & North
The arty neighborhood comes alive with art, music, and food.
Weekend in mid-July

Wrigleyville's Addison–Clark Street Fair, 773/880-5822   N
Clark & Addison
Wrigleyville street fair offers continuous live music, tastings from area
restaurants, and goods from local merchants.
Weekend in mid-July

Chinatown Summer Fair, 312/326-5320   S
Wentworth, from Cermak to 24th
Fireworks, sidewalk sale, traditional arts and crafts, food, children's carnival, folk dancing, and martial arts.
3rd or 4thSunday in July

Newberry Library Book Fair & Bughouse Square Debates   C
60 W. Walton, 312/255-3510
Noted humanities library combines humongous not-to-miss book fair with
its historic debate fest for well-known orators and those on a soapbox.
Last weekend in July

Taste of Lincoln Avenue, 773/348-6784   N
Lincoln, between Fullerton & Wrightwood
Taste of Lincoln Avenue draws 50,000+ people and features the food of
300 eateries, 25 bands playing on four stages, and a wide array of sidewalk
vendors.
Last weekend in July

Fiesta del Sol (Festival of the Sun), 312/666-2663   S
Cermak, from Throop to Morgan
Mexican street festival draws 1 million+ for food, entertainment, music,
dancing, arts and crafts, carnival rides, etc.
Last week in July or 1stweek in August

Dearborn Garden Walk & Heritage Festival, 312/632-1241   N
Dearborn, from Division to North
A walking tour of the fabulous gardens on Chicago's north side, along with food, entertainment and children's events. Architectural tours are also offered. Small admission fee includes a map of the garden walk.
A Sunday in July

Old Timers of Lilydale Festival, 773/568-1172   FSE
Abbott Park, 49 E. 95th
Jazz and gospel music set the stage for dancing, food, and art exhibits.
1st Saturday in August

South Chicago Festival, 773/768-1221   FSE
8700–9200 Commercial Ave.
Sponsored by South Chicago Chamber of Commerce.
1st weekend in August

Retro on Roscoe, 773/665-4682   N
Roscoe & Damen
An antique car and motorcycle show with music, food, and arts and crafts.
Weekend in early August

Taste of Midway Festival, 773/767-8183   SW
5500 S. Lorel
St. Camillus's parish five-day food fest with beer garden, music, games, rides, and children's activities.
1st or 2nd week in August

"Northalsted" Market Days, 773/868-3010   N
Halsted, between Belmont and Addison
Large (i.e. the largest 2-day street fair in the Midwest) food, art, and entertainment carnival, organized and heavily-attended by Chicago's gay community.
2nd weekend in August

Argyle Street Fair, 773/769-3776   FN
1100 block of W. Argyle
Festival features the food, crafts, and culture of the Asian and Asian-American populations centered in this area.
Weekend in mid-August

Midwest Buddhist Temple's Ginza Festival, 312/943-7801   N
435 W. Menomonee
Japanese food, dancing, drumming, crafts, and martial arts. $4 donation.
2nd or 3rd weekend in August

Belize Day in the Park Festival, 773/881-0412   S
Washington Park, 55th & King Drive
Music, food, and kid's activities to celebrate Belizean culture.
A weekend day in August

Celebrate the Spirit of South Shore, 773/324-0494   FSE
1809 E. 71st, 70th & Jeffrey Blvd., 71st & South Shore, 75th & Jeffrey Blvd.
A weekend day in August

Taste of Polonia Festival, 773/777-8898   FN
Copernicus Plaza, 5216 W. Lawrence
Polish and American music, dancing, folk dance performances, bingo, and
20+ Polish and American food vendors. Small entrance fee.
Labor Day weekend

German-American Fest, 630/653-3018   N
Lincoln & Leland
Folk dance, musical performances, and carnival games serve as the background for lots of German food and even more beer.
1st or 2nd weekend in September

57th Street Children's Book Fair, 773/619-8371   S
57th, between Kimbark and Kenwood
An annual celebration of children's literature.
Sunday in late September

Parades

FOR more parade news, check out *www.cityofchicago.org/SpecialEvents/*.

Chinese New Year Parade, 312/225-6198   S
24th Place & Wentworth to Cermak & Princeton, 1 P.M.
Usually Sunday after the Chinese New Year's Day. Generally, February.

Chinese New Year Parade on Argyle, 773/334-6537   **FN**
Argyle between Broadway & Sheridan. Call for time.
Around the same time as the Chinatown Parade in February.

South Side Irish St. Patrick's Day Parade, 773/239-7755   **FSW**
Western between 103rd and 115th, noon
Supposedly the largest Irish neighborhood parade outside of Ireland—a
raucous event that can last up to three hours (before it gets moved to
backyards and pubs).
Sunday before March 17

St. Patrick's Day Parade, 312/942-9188   **C**
Columbus Drive between Balbo & Monroe, noon
Vegetable dye turns the Chicago River bright green for the day!
Usually the Saturday before St. Patrick's Day

O'Really?

A Chicago pipefitter's union is responsible for the time-honored tradition of
dying the river green on St. Patrick's Day. They use fluorescein dye, a
chemical used scientifically for tests in moving water.

Hellenic Heritage Parade, 847/962-9678   **C**
Halsted, from Randolph to 400 South, 2:30 P.M.
Sunday in late March

St. Jude Police Memorial Parade, 312/745-6210   **C**
Michigan, between the Chicago River and Chicago Ave., 8:30 A.M.
1st Sunday in May

Polish Constitution Day Parade, 847/451-1480   **C**
Columbus Drive, between Balbo & Monroe, 11:30 A.M.
Saturday in early May

Chicago's Memorial Day Parade, 312/744-3315   **C**
State, between Lake and Van Buren, noon
Saturday of Memorial Day weekend

Puerto Rican Day Parade, 773/292-1414   **C**
Columbus Drive between Balbo & Monroe, noon
Saturday in mid-June

Juneteenth Celebration and Parade, 312/744-3315   **FSE**
79th & Stony Island to Rainbow Beach, 10 A.M.
Juneteenth is the oldest celebration of the freedom of African-Americans in the United States. Originating in Texas in 1865, the Chicago celebration kicks off with a parade of pride highlighting a different aspect each year of African-American history. A celebration follows that includes remarks from local politicians and school principals, music, school bands, and refreshments. Adding to the special day is a salute from the Tuskegee Airmen. The event is free.
3rd Saturday in June

Gay and Lesbian Pride Parade, 773/348-8243   **N**
Halsted, from Belmont to Broadway, south to Diversey, east to Sheridan, noon.
Last Sunday in June

Bud Billiken Parade and Picnic, 312/225-2400   **S**
King Drive, from 35th to 55th, 10 A.M.
Sponsored by the Chicago Defender Charities, the historic, African-American **Bud Billiken Parade** has been around for 75 years. Named after a cartoon character from the paper, a billiken is a Chinese figure that is believed to be the guardian of children. The five-hour-long back-to-school parade highlights under-privileged children, and is the country's third largest parade, after the Rose Bowl Parade in Pasadena and Macy's Thanksgiving Day Parade in Manhattan. Following the stroll of school bands, dance groups, local dignitaries and floats, is a barbecue held in Washington Park featuring entertainment from around the country.
2nd Saturday in August

Pakistan Independence Parade, 773/338-3492   **FN**
Devon, between Damen and Western, noon
2nd weekend in August

India Independence Day Parade, 312/744-3315   **FN**
Devon between Western and California, noon
3rd weekend in August

Mexican Independence Day Parade—Pilsen, 312/744-3315   **SW**
18th St., from Newberry to Wolcott, noon
Labor Day

Mexican Independence Day Parade—South Chicago
312/744-3315   C
Columbus, from Balbo to Monroe, noon
Saturday in early September

Mexican Independence Day Parade—South Chicago
312/744-3315   FSE
8700 S. Commerical to 100th, noon
Sunday in early September

Mexican Independence Day Parade—Little Village
312/744-3315   SW
26th, between Albany & Kostner, noon
Sunday in mid-September

Central American Independence Parade, 312/744-3315   C
Montrose, between Kimball and California, noon
Saturday or Sunday after Labor Day

Von Steuben German Day Parade, 312/744-3315   C
Lincoln, between Irving Park and Lawrence, 2 P.M.
Saturday in early September

Double-Ten Parade, 312/225-6198   S
Wentworth, from 24th Street to Cermak, 12:30 P.M.
Chinatown parade commemorates the 1911 overthrow of the Manchu dynasty by Sun Yat-Sen and his Nationalistic Party.
1st Sunday in October

North Halsted Halloween Parade, 773/868-3010   N
Halsted, between Belmont & Addison, 7 P.M.–10 P.M.
A costume extravaganaza in true Boystown spirit.
Halloween Day

Columbus Day Parade, 312/744-3315   C
Columbus, between Balbo & Monroe, 1 P.M.
Columbus Day

Magnificent Mile Lights Festival and Procession, 312/409-5560   C
Michigan, from Oak to Wacker, 5 P.M.
Kick-off parade for the downtown holiday shopping (and lights!) season.

As the parade goes by at dusk, the lights go on.
Saturday before Thanksgiving

State Street Thanksgiving Day Parade, 312/781-5681   **C**
State, between Congress & Randolph, 8:30 A.M.
Thanksgiving Day

63rd Street Christmas Parade, 773/436-1000   **SW**
63rd, from Tripp to Western
This is the city's largest holiday parade, averaging 75 entrants with some 20 floats, 12 performing groups, the requisite politicians, and of course, Santa Claus. Neighborhood residents line up along 63rd Street early in the day to stake out their spots with lawn chairs and to visit with each other.
Saturday before Thanksgiving

6

WALKING

The Gothic University of Chicago campus, modeled after Cambridge, is loaded with inviting and imposing buildings. *Photo by Bill Arroyo.*

Strolling along the lakefront path is a great way to get to know the city for residents and visitors alike. *Photo by Bill Arroyo.*

Cloud Gate (already nicknamed "The Bean"), is a giant silver sculpture in Millennium Park that reflects the entire skyline. *Photo by Bill Arroyo.*

········ # WALKING ··········

WALKING EARNED ITS own chapter in this book because it is the ideal way to know any place intimately. Much of the information in this book, in fact, comes from the thousands of miles we have hiked on Chicago sidewalks over our lifetimes.

Walking intimately exposes us to our surroundings. It allows us to pick up more environmental information than any other mode of transport. Walking is an active endeavor that requires attention and decision making. This close contact with the streets helps us to develop ever more intricate mental maps of Chicago, which then provide us with increasingly reliable information about the city. And, as the budget-conscious know, walking is free entertainment.

The two sections of this chapter: **Neighborhoods, Historic Districts, and Ethnic Enclaves for Roaming and Exploring** and **Good Parks for Walking** should provide a good start for your efforts to better know and appreciate the sights and sounds of the Chicago streets. Visit our Web site at *www.lakeclaremont.com/nativesguide*, where we'll continue to share and update our own neighborhood explorations.

Neighborhoods, Historic Districts, and Ethnic Enclaves for Roaming and Exploring

HERE'S a hefty introduction to "the city of neighborhoods." The approximate boundaries and brief descriptions of 45 distinct areas of the city given here, matched with your spirit of adventure and lots of free time, should be all you need to begin your exploring.

Andersonville FN
Clark (about 1500 W) from Foster (5200 N) to Bryn Mawr (5600 N)

Once a somewhat dour, working-class Swedish neighborhood, **Andersonville** has exploded into an exuberant pastiche of Swedish, Middle Eastern, and Japanese eateries, with a strong selection of nonchain stores, all shoe-horned into an eminently walkable four-block strip (although benches on side streets encourage lounging). A sure sign of cultural blend: **Andie's** Mediterranean restaurant (p. 209) sells glögg, the hot, spiced, Swedish holiday drink. Andersonville's escalating popularity may eventually price it out of the range of many Chicagoans as a place to live—and the SUV-jams are starting to increase—but it's such a terrific place to hang out that it's no wonder people want to live there. The Swedish influence is still strong, of course: visit the **Swedish American Museum Center** (p. 66) and **The Landmark** (5301 N. Clark), the latter a three-story mall of arts, crafts, and Scandinavian goods. **Erickson's Delicatessen** (5250 N. Clark) and **Wikstrom's Gourmet Foods** (5247 N. Clark), some of the country's only Swedish delis outside Minnesota, have thrived here since the early 1920s. Drop in to stock up on imported cheese, sausage, jams, syrups, chocolate, cookies, fresh and frozen lingonberries, salt cod, and herring of all persuasions. Take a number and stand in line at **The Swedish Bakery** (p. 230) to gawk at a wonderland of sugary delights under glass. And when winter comes, go to **Simon's** (5210 N. Clark)—not Andie's—for glögg, the spiced and fruity wine of the season. Traditional festivities for **St. Morten's Gos Day** (Sat. in early Nov.) and **St. Lucia Day** (Sat. in early Dec.) make Andersonville a great destination for atmospheric holiday shopping. A few non-Swedish food places you should know about include: **Taste of Lebanon** (1509 W. Foster), which offers a great, cheap lunch or dinner; **Middle Eastern Bakery and Pastry** (1512 W. Foster); and **Sunshine Cafe** (5449 N. Clark), cheap, home-style Japanese cooking for a Japanese crowd (they serve noodles, not sushi). **Pars Persian Store** (5260 N. Clark), sells Iranian food, beautiful hookahs and mild, fruit-flavored tobacco, board games, music, and books; **Sabrina Gift Shop** (5202 N. Clark) offers an interesting variety of Egyptian wares. If you prefer to give Starbuck's the cold shoulder, enjoy coffee at **Kopi, A Traveler's Cafe** (p. 163) or **Cafe Boost** (5400 N. Clark). Defiantly non-chain, **Women and Children First** (5233 N. Clark) sells feminist and children's books. Bargain-basement Beau Brummels will enjoy the $5 manicure or the $6 haircut at **Mac Daniel's Beauty School** (5228 N. Clark). For nightlife, besides Simon's, Andersonville is host to a number of friendly bars, including the **Balmoral Clark Tap** (1507 W. Balmoral). Cap a long day in Andersonville by taking in 30 plays in 60 minutes at the **Neo-Futurarium** (p. 271).

Argyle Street FN

Argyle (5000 N) between Broadway (1200 W) and Sheridan (1000 W) and Broadway between Lawrence (4800 N) and Foster (5200 N)

The pagoda stop on the Red Line marks the epicenter of a bustling "New Chinatown"—really a misnomer because the bulk of this area's Asian immigrants are Vietnamese, Thai, Laotian, and Cambodian. At a quarter of a century old, this district offers a plentiful array of Asian goods and services. You might start a day visit here with breakfast, either dim sum at **Furama** (4936 N. Broadway) or congee, a traditional Chinese rice porridge, at **Sun Wah** (1134 W. Argyle). Fortified, begin a pleasant day of browsing and shopping. **Hiep Loi** (1125 W. Argyle) sells Chinatown-type gifts that range from tacky to lovely. **New World Watch Sales and Repair** (1038 W. Argyle) has a fun, goofy selection of clocks and loads of Hello Kitty paraphernalia. **Hong Kong Fashion** (1027 W. Argyle) has colorful clothes, both modern and traditional. Jewelry stores selling beautiful gold and jade aren't hard to find. **Argyle** abounds in fascinating food, and not just restaurant dining. Carry out baked goods from **Chiu Quon Bakery** (1127 W. Argyle); many are savory, not sweet, a surprise to Western palates. On Saturdays, Argyle slows to a crawl and parking lots overflow as Asian families go shopping. Three of the best grocery stores are **Viet Hoa** (1051 W. Argyle), **Tai Nam** (4925 N. Broadway), and **Thuong Xa My A Broadway Supermarket** (4879 N. Broadway). You'll be amazed by the selection of fresh fish and vegetables, and the sheer variety of sauces, soups, noodles, grains, and the like. If nothing else, you'll take home some ramen that beats Jewel brands by a mile. Prices are often very cheap. Take a side trip to see **Essanay Studios** (p. 26) and the **Myron Bachman House** (p. 27). Check out the simple but pretty stained glass at **Agudas Achim North Shore Congregation** (5029 N. Kenmore), the last traditional cathedral-style synagogue in the greater Chicago area. If you'd like some feline companionship, whether to take home or maybe just for a visit, drop by the **Tree House Animal Foundation** (1212 W. Carmen), a no-kill shelter that has rooms and rooms of free-range kitties. Need a break from the pavement? Grab an avocado and coconut shake from **Thai Binh** (1113-5 W. Argyle) and walk down Argyle to Lincoln Park—you're just a stone's throw from the water. For dinner, you can't go wrong with **Nhu Hoa** (1020 W. Argyle, p. 193), which serves delicious Vietnamese and Laotian cuisine (try #142, the tangy shrimp soup!), and **Sun Wah** (see above) serves terrific barbecue and seafood in a traditional Chinese manner. Exhausted? Cap the evening by having a drink with the friendly folks at **Big Chicks** (5024 N. Sheridan, p. 258). Try not to think about the dozens of other places not even mentioned here.

Belmont & Clark and Diversey & Clark N

Clark Street between just north of Belmont (3200 N) & just south of Diversey (2800 N)

Considered part of "Lakeview East," these two intersections rival any in the city for quality people-watching, hip hanging out, and diverse shopping opportunities. Immediately west and south of **Boystown** (p. 311) and north of **Lincoln Park** (p. 322), Clark and the environs teem with a good urban mix of offbeat independents and national chains, established off-Loop theater, alternative clothing, shoes, and housewares, pick-of-the-litter resale shops, and affordable eateries galore. Unlike the **Clybourn Corridor** (p. 314), this is highly walkable territory. Don't miss the **Alternative Shopping Complex** (p. 377) and the **"Punkin' Donuts"** (the national donut chain frequented by those of all persuasions and hair colors) at Belmont & Clark and the **Century Shopping Centre** at Diversey & Clark. In between, there's **Binny's** (p. 370) and used bookstores (p. 390). **La Creperie** (p. 172), **Duke of Perth** (p. 224), and **Renaldi's** (2827 N. Broadway) are neighborhood classics to know, while **Orange** (p. 153) is among the winning newcomers.

Belmont Cragin NW

Bounded by Belmont (3200 N), Cicero (4800 W), Grand (slanting about 1800–2300 N), and Narragansett (6400 W)

A solid, middle-class residential neighborhood with classic Chicago housing down every side street, **Belmont Cragin's** longstanding retail center at Belmont & Central offers anything from crafts supplies to homemade sausage and imported foodstuffs. Many of its businesses cater to a strong base of both older and younger Polish immigrants. The esteemed **Gene's Sausage Shop** (5530 W. Belmont) has served a couple generations. Newer places include **Back to Nature** (5556 W. Belmont) and **Live With Nature** (5223 W. Belmont) for loose herbs, vitamins, herbal supplements, and health foods, and the **Paris Café** (5301 W. Belmont) and **Euro Cappuccino** (5759 W. Belmont) for coffee sipping and camaraderie. **Blackstone's** (5415 W. Belmont) and **Metro Sales** (5416 W. Belmont) both offer warehouse prices on party, craft, and wedding supplies.

Beverly/Morgan Park FSW

Bounded by the curving Prospect (about 1500 W), 115th (1500 S), Hoyne (2100 W), and 89th (8900 S)

Here in the middle of the Illinois flatlands are hills created some 12,000 years ago by the waters of the long-gone Lake Chicago and a continental glacier. Longwood Drive, which runs north and south through the neighborhood, rides the crest of the Blue Island Ridge. After Lake Chicago receded, marshlands and prairie grasses flourished. These eventually produced a lush, rolling terrain. Today, beyond the wide expanses of lawn and towering trees are 3,000 homes and other structures that are on the National Historic Register. **Longwood Drive** [91st to 115th] and **Walter Burley Griffin Place** [104th between Wood (1800 W) and Prospect (1600 W) and named for the architect–student of F.L. Wright] are also Chicago landmark districts. Within these streets are roughly 50 Prairie style houses as well as examples of 14 other styles including Queen Anne, Victorian, Gothic Revival, Tudor, Italianate, and English Country. Beverly's **"Irish Castle"** (p. 28), now home to a Unitarian church, is technically the only "castle" within the city's boundaries. The fate of **Beverly Hills/Morgan Park** was of great concern in the early 1970s when African-American families began moving into the area and rumors about white homeowners fleeing to the suburbs circulated. The **Beverly Area Planning Association (BAPA)** (10233 S. Wood, 773/233-3100) worked to allay these fears and to bring about a rejuvenation of the area. Today Beverly Hills/Morgan Park is reasonably well-integrated and home to many professional couples and their families. House values into the high six-figures give the name Beverly Hills a double meaning. Pick up maps for walking and biking tours at the **BAPA** office. Other organizations critical to Beverly's vitality are the **Ridge Historical Society,** headquartered in the 1922 English Manor-style **Driscoll House** (10621 S. Seeley, 773/881-1675), and the newly-enhanced **Beverly Arts Center** (p. 38).

Boystown   N

Broadway (600 W) from Grace (3800 N) to Diversey (2800 N) and Halsted (800 W) from Grace to Belmont (3200 N)
These sections of Broadway and Halsted in Lakeview are the main drags of gay Chicago. There's eclectic shopping during the day and restaurants, bars, and clubs galore at night (see Entertainment, p. 239 for specific suggestions). For three days in August a large section of Halsted is blocked off for the annual street party known as "Market Days," which attracts thousands of people to the area (p. 298). The party is a celebration of gay pride crossed with a neighborhood fest complete with music, food and drink booths, transvestite square dancers, the ROTC (Righteously Outrageous Twirling Corps), vendors, and a good dose of bare skin and outrageous outfits. Although always accepting of people of all persuasions, large clubs such as **Roscoe's, Spin** and **Circuit** are attracting a more eclectic and racially diverse crowd of gay and straight these days. The city of Chicago has recognized the area as gay and lesbian friendly with special rainbow gateways, street improvements, landscaping, and new street lights. It is the first officially designated gay district in the United States.

Bridgeport
S/SW

Bound by Wentworth (200 W), Pershing (3900 S), Ashland (1600 W), the diagonal Archer, and the Stevenson Expressway

One of Chicago's oldest and most famous neighborhoods, **Bridgeport** gets its name from the port created when a too-low bridge at Ashland Avenue and the Chicago River necessitated the unloading and reloading of barges in order to pass. Its fame stems in part from its being the center of Chicago's Democratic Party machine and as the site of **Comiskey Park**, now named **U.S. Cellular Field** (333 W. 35th), home of the Chicago White Sox. Although first populated by European immigrants, people of Mexican, Chinese, and Italian descent now comprise 50% of its population. But, thanks to politics, it is the Irish who are most associated with Bridgeport. This working-class neighborhood has produced several Chicago mayors, including the Daleys, and more than its fair share of police officers and firefighters. Much of the political power emanates from the **Hamburg Athletic Association** (3523 S. Emerald) whose members have included the first Mayor Daley, federal judge Abraham Lincoln Marovitz, and the current Mayor Daley. The original 1910 **Comiskey Park** (called White Sox Park by the locals) was razed in 1991 and replaced across the street by a modern stadium complete with skyboxes. A plaque commemorating the original park stands in the north parking lot. Bridgeport's architecture is quintessential Chicago with blocks of brick bungalows and two-flats. In recent years, however, a number of upscale town homes and condominiums have been constructed. Another neighborhood renovation project is underway at **Bubbly Creek** (p. 103), part of the South Branch of the Chicago River and long a place of legend in the neighborhood. It's only fitting to cap off a tour of Bridgeport with a beer at a classic neighborhood pub like **Schaller's** (p. 219) or **Puffer's** (3356 S. Halsted).

Bronzeville
S

Bounded by 31st, Pershing (39th), the Dan Ryan Expressway, and Cottage Grove (800 E)

In the early 1900s, thousands of African-Americans migrated from the Southern states to Chicago in search of jobs. Racially and politically motivated housing restrictions caused many of them to settle in this South Side neighborhood near the lakefront. By the 1930s, **Bronzeville**, as this area came to be known, was a mecca of African-American culture. Duke Ellington, Louis Armstrong, Scott Joplin, and Nat "King" Cole all lived here for a time in the early days of jazz and ragtime. Gwendolyn Brooks, Bessie Coleman, Sammy Davis Jr., Mahalia Jackson, BB King, Joe Louis, Muddy Waters, Ida B. Wells, and Richard Wright are a few of the other historic luminaries with strong ties to Bronzeville. Stately graystones, many of which are still standing today, occupied the residential streets. Black-owned businesses flourished, including Supreme Life, the nation's first black-owned and operated insurance company, the Binga Bank, one of the first black-owned banks, and the *Chicago Defender* newspaper (2400 S. Michigan). At the **Wabash Avenue YMCA** (38th & Wabash, p. 29), Carter G. Woodson established Negro History Week in 1926, the precursor to Black History Month. After the second world war, housing opportunities opened up and most of Bronzeville's more well-to-do residents moved elsewhere. The Chicago Stockyards closed, putting much of Bronzeville's working class out of work. Buildings fell into decay. In the late 1990s, a group of local business people began to revitalize Bronzeville. The wide boulevards have been cleaned up, homes are being restored, townhouse and condo developments have sprung up, and new businesses are opening. Nine buildings in the area were designated historic landmarks by the Chicago City Council in 1998. These include the **Eighth Regiment Armory** (3533 S. Giles), the home of African-American soldiers during World War I, which was re-opened as The Chicago Military Academy high school in 1999; and the **Supreme Life Insurance Building** (3501 S. Martin Luther King Dr.), which is slated to become an African-American tourism and visitors center. Other projects include establishing a retail and entertainment complex in the **Alco Drugs Building** (35th & King). Contact the **Mid-South Planning Commission** (773/924-1330) for information on the progress of these projects. A bronze map, designed by Gregg LeFevre, sits in the median strip at 35th and King Drive, identifying over 120 historic sites between 21st and 52nd and Wentworth Avenue and the lakefront. At 3624 S. King Drive, for example, you will find the former home of social reformer Ida B. Wells and Ferdinand Lee Barnett, founder of the *Conservator*, Chicago's first black-owned newspaper. The house was designated a National Historic Landmark in 1974. The campus of the **Illinois Institute of Technology (IIT)** (p. 29) occupies the eastern edge of Bronzeville.

Chinatown   S

Cermak (2200 S) between Princeton (300 W) & Wentworth (200 W), and Wentworth from Cermak to 24th Place (2450 S)
The original "Old Chinatown" in Chicago overlapped with the Levee vice district near Clark and Harrison in the south Loop. In 1905, however, various civic organizations and the state's attorney pushed the vice lords south to 22nd and Wabash. The Chinese, who could not afford the rents of their new, unwelcoming landlords, followed the crime bosses south, where they established themselves along Wentworth. **Chinatown** remains to this

day perhaps the most tightly preserved ethnic community in Chicago. Chinese gift shops, grocers, and restaurants line these two blocks of Wentworth and a block of Cermak Road. **Chinatown Square** (2130 S. Archer), a 1993 outdoor mall incorporating traditional design elements, contains two levels of restaurants, bookstores, gift shops, and other retailers on either side of a pedestrian thoroughfare. The discovery and revitalization of all neighborhoods near south have not missed Chinatown. The staff, décor, and menus of the newer eateries are more Pan-Asian, with a slicker, global-village feel, naturally drawing the younger crowds who are moving into the adjacent neighborhoods. There is little chance, however, that the Chinese character of this area will diminish. There is not enough housing in Chinatown, first of all, to accommodate all the Chinese immigrants who'd like to settle there. Then, new additions to the neighborhood have only solidified its Chinese character, including **Ping Tom Park** (300 W. 19th) on the river, a **Nine Dragon Wall** (2131 S. Wentworth)—a 30-foot long by 18-foot high mosaic, inexpensive **pedicab** rides through Chinatown's streets, and the coming **Chinese-American Museum of Chicago** (p. 66). See p. 159 for some restaurant recommendations.

Clybourn Corridor   N

Along Clybourn, from the Chicago River & Fullerton (2400 N) on the north to Halsted (800 W) & North (1600 N) on the south
Aggressive development has transformed this neighborhood as radically as any in Chicago. As recently as the early 1990s, creaky junk trucks crept up and down Clybourn taking their loads to the scrap yards along the Chicago River. Now, a solid belt of suburban-style mini-malls with every major mid-level chain store you can think of congests Clybourn with BMWs and SUVs. At the southern end of the corridor, retail giants such as Crate and Barrel, Smith and Hawken, Gap, Erehwon, Best Buy, Whole Foods, Cost Plus Market, Container Store, Workbench, and Pottery Barn have left just enough space to cover everything else with parking lots. Don't miss local treasures like **Sam's Wines and Spirits** (p. 369) with its incredible selection of all things alcoholic. The **Goose Island Brew Pub** (p. 218) moved into the neighborhood in 1988 and serves up an eye-opening assortment of beers brewed in Chicago as well as a full menu of well-prepared bar-style food. As you continue north on Clybourn, smaller retailers and "nicer" fast food places like **Panera Bread** and **Chipotle Grill** have carved out spots near old-timers like **Solly's Drive In** (1982 N. Clybourn, 773/248-7233). **Webster Place** shopping mall, with its movie theaters, Barnes and Noble Booksellers, Kozy's Cyclery, and Bally's Total Fitness club, marks the end of the retail strip. Make sure to stop for a slice at **Pequod's Pizzeria** (2207

N. Clybourn). This self-proclaimed home of hockey in Chicago serves New York style pizza with whatever you want on it. If you keep walking you will come to the **Salvation Army Adult Rehabilitation Center** and its well-stocked **Thrift Store** (p. 407). When you are done shopping, enjoy the nightlife at the **Weed Street Entertainment District** just south of North Avenue between Fremont (900 W) and Kingsbury (a diagonal street running parallel to Clybourn). The names of the clubs are constantly changing, but the hip, young, affluent crowd remains the same. DJs at **Crobar** (1543 N. Kingsbury) have been spinning fresh grooves since the early 90s. Clubs that are more likely to be here today and gone tomorrow include: **Zentra** (923 W. Weed), **Joe's** (940 W. Weed), and **Biology Bar** (1520 N. Fremont). Other clubs worth mentioning on Clybourn include **Glow** (1615 N. Clybourn), **Copa** (1637 N. Clybourn), **Zella's** (1938 N. Clybourn), and **Kustom** (1997 N. Clybourn).

Devon Avenue   FN
Devon (6400 N) from Leavitt (2200 W) to Kedzie (3200 W)
English immigrants renamed Church Street **"Devon"** in the 1850s after their home country, but it wasn't long before the neighborhood began its steady growth toward the "International Market Place" to which it currently likens itself. (Note to non-native Chicagoans: It's pronounced "duh-VON" not "DEH-vun.") While West Rogers Park—through which Devon runs—was once exclusively a Jewish community, the Indian presence expanded rapidly in the 1970s and 1980s. Today, Indian and Pakistani concerns (or "Indo-Pak" as they are abbreviated on signs) are the dominant presence on Devon, although the thoroughfare is an exciting cultural mélange: Devon at Leavitt begins a full strip of Indian and Pakistani restaurants, services, sari shops, jewelers, video rental stores, and general merchandisers; Washtenaw (2700 W) marks the start of a stretch of Jewish and Russian shops, kosher restaurants, delis, bakeries, grocers, and fish markets. There are also emerging Arabic and Assyrian businesses and occasional Chinese or Greek eateries. The **Croatian Cultural Center** is at 2845 W. Devon. There are too many worthwhile (and cheap!) restaurants to attempt an objective recommendation process (but see p. 182 for some time-tested deals); the best way to approach eating on Devon is just to dive in. Browse at **Russian Books** (2746 W. Devon, 773/761-3233), a truly eclectic collection of books (some in English), paintings (from terrific to terrible), jewelry, antiques and Soviet-era leftovers. Musty, and filled with voluble Russian-speakers, you half expect to step back outside into St. Petersburg. Other bookstores serve their local contingents, from **Rosen-blum's World of Judaica** (2906 W. Devon), where you can buy a

basketball-style yarmulke for a youth, to **Iqra' Book Center** (2751 W. Devon), a spacious and airy Islamic bookstore, to **India Bookhouse and Journals** (2551 W. Devon). It's interesting to note that, despite the clashes that often mark relations in the Middle East (i.e., Israel–Palestine, India–Pakistan) these groups still chose to share real estate in a foreign country. A few other shopping spots of note include: **Patel Brothers** (2610 W. Devon), one of largest and nicest groceries; **Devon Discount Distributors** (p. 365), where you can buy drugstore items and perfume at deep discounts (though not as deep as they once were); **India Handicrafts and Gifts** (2657 W. Devon), a gallery of gorgeous statuary and inlaid-wood artwork; and **A & T International Bakery** (2858 W. Devon), with a great selection of Russian and Hungarian sausages, cheese, smoked fish, imported treats, and fresh-baked bread. Incongruous in the middle of this foreign fare is the **Republic Bank**, a.k.a. "Independence Hall," at 2720 W. Devon. It's not architecturally significant, but it is worth noting for the faded but extensive display of patriotic plaques, pictures, and statuary. Dedicated to America's military efforts in the Spanish-American War and the subsequent "Philippine Insurrection," this colonial-styled ode to colonialism seems downright ironic in the midst of Indian émigrés—themselves a people who know a thing or two about the subject.

Division Street

C/W

Division Street (1200 N) between Ashland (1600 W) and Leavitt (2200 W)
This ain't Studs Terkel's **Division Street** and it ain't your grandfather's Polish Broadway. Puerto Rican Chicago is to its west and all those barely-legal/tourist/aging swingers bars are still east of Clark. This is the latest dense distillation of upscale and trendy restaurants and boutiques to materialize in almost a blink to serve the swells of young and younger professionals moving in. Post WWII, this was a "Polish Broadway" with 45 taverns lining Division between Ashland and Damen, many with music. Polka bands were king, and a Chicago Hop style of polka was born of them. (You can see actual footage of those days in Jimmy Stewart's *Call Northside 777*.) **Phyllis' Musical Inn** (1800 W. Division)—still with music!—and the **Gold Star Bar** (1755 W. Division) remain from that era. Other historic sites are the **Russian Baths** (p. 89) and **Holy Trinity Russian Orthodox Cathedral** (p. 33). **Hilary's Urban Eatery (HUE)** (1500 W. Division), **Smoke Daddy** (p. 243), and **Leo's Lunchroom** (1809 W. Division) have been around since early in the latest revival and continue offering good food and good vibes at good prices. Sushi, gelato, high-end cocktails, hookahs, swanky make-out corners, expensive shoes, independent caffeine, and sidewalk outposts keep the buzz high.

Downtown at Night C

For nighttime downtown strolling, try Michigan Avenue from Oak (100 N) to Balbo (700 S).
The areas on the east of the Michigan Avenue contain elegant hotels and homes along with office buildings, night life, and green space. Follow the Chicago River too for spectacular and romantic views.

Edgewater/Bryn Mawr Avenue FN

Bounded by Foster (5200 N), Lake Michigan, Devon (6400 N), and Ravenswood (1800 W)
Known in the mid-1800s as the celery-growing capital of the Midwest, and in the 1920s for a swanky lakeside resort, **Edgewater** continues to be a neighborhood of interesting contrasts. High-rises with private beaches barricade much of the lakefront, just blocks from pockets of urban desperation. With the listing of a four-block stretch of **Bryn Mawr** (5600 N) on The National Register of Historic Places, and the renovation of nearby buildings, some of the incongruities are becoming more acute. While a number of low-rent storefront operations remain, others lie empty, and still others are making way for upscale rustic furniture outlets, high-end restaurants, and the inevitable Starbucks. Poorer locals enjoy cheap Mexican, BBQ, Caribbean, Greek, and Chinese cuisine, while the well-heeled dress down for $20–30 entrees at places like **Pasteur** (5525 N. Broadway) and **Francesca's** (1039 W. Bryn Mawr). Make sure to gape at the gorgeously renovated **Belle Shore Apartment Hotel** (1062 W. Bryn Mawr)—its green-blue terra cotta glistening—and reflect on the fact that when **Manor House** (1021–1031 W. Bryn Mawr) was built, the palatial building consisted of only six apartment units, two with their own ballrooms. **St. Ita's Church** (1220 W. Catalpa) is worth a look for its thirteenth-century Gothic style, and the **Beaconsfield-Hollywood Apartments** (1055–1065 W. Hollywood) are worth noting for their whimsical terra cotta ornamentation. At the lake end of the street, the pink **Edgewater Beach Apartments** (5555 N. Sheridan, p. 25) is all that remains of the Edgewater Beach Hotel complex, a swanky Jazz Age resort that once boasted its own radio station. Stop in at the **Anna Held Flower and Fountain Cafe** (p. 161), located on the ground floor, for an ice cream concoction at the gorgeous old soda fountain. For nightlife, **Hollywood East** (5650 N. Broadway, 773/271-4711) offers live Reggae, stepping (see p. 260 for more about this style of dance), and Caribbean food.

Gold Coast
C

Bounded by La Salle (150 W), North (1600 N), Lake Shore Drive and Michigan on the east (about 100 E), and Chicago (800 N)

The **Gold Coast** began as the big money, big power place it is today when Bertha and Potter Palmer (of Palmer House fame) boldly packed up from their posh Prairie Avenue neighborhood in 1882 and moved north of downtown. It has the highest concentration of wealth in the Chicago area and one of the highest in the country. The historic parts on Dearborn (36 W), State (0 E/W), and Astor (50 E), between North and Division (1200 N) contain the grandest structures, including the **McCormick Mansion** (1500 N. Astor) and the **Residence of the Roman Catholic Archbishop** of Chicago (1555 N. State Parkway). The **Charnley-Persky House** (1365 N. Astor), designed by Frank Lloyd Wright when working as a draftsman for Adler and Sullivan in 1891, is open for tours (p. 60).

Greektown
C

Halsted (800 W) from Madison (0 N/S) to Van Buren (400 S)

The building of the University of Illinois and the Eisenhower Expressway in the 1960s disrupted, and ultimately destroyed, large portions of **Greektown**. Yet, its concentration of restaurants on Halsted Street has always endured as a popular destination for both out-of-towners and city dwellers in search of affordable food, fun, and drink. Along with several commendable Greek restaurants, the strip holds Greek bakeries, grocers, gifts shops, and bars. Like with Chinatown (p. 313), economic development decisions are reinforcing the area's Greekness and focusing on the spillover advantages from adjoining hotspots (UIC, West Loop, Randolph Street restaurants, East Village). New "gateway" columns anchor the street, as does the new **Hellenic Museum** (p. 63) location.

Hegewisch
FSE

Bounded by 100th (10000 S), the Calumet River (roughly 2800–3000 E), Brainerd (slanting from about 13000 to 13800 S), and the state of Indiana

One of Chicago's least-known neighborhoods, **Hegewisch** is tucked away in the far southeast corner of Cook County, a stone's throw from Indiana. It was founded in 1883 by Adolph Hegewisch, the president of U.S. Rolling Stock Company. Like his fellow railroad car manufacturing magnate George Pullman, Hegewisch wanted to create a company town. His attempt failed miserably and, in 1889, Hegewisch became part of the city of Chicago. Local rumor has it that Adolph Hegewisch took off for Mexico to escape his creditors. A predominately white, blue-collar community of modest bungalows, Hegewisch feels more like a small town than a neighborhood in a large metropolis. Most families have lived here for generations and many of the houses are known by the family name. Hegewisch has produced its share of colorful citizens including White Sox player and automobile dealer Tony Piet, lightweight boxing champion Battling Nelson, writer Eugene Izzi, and former alderman turn radio-talk show host Ed Vrdolyak, who earned the nickname Darth Vader during the infamous Council Wars waged after the election of Chicago's first African-American mayor, Harold Washington. Hegewisch boasts the only state park within city limits (**Wolf Lake/William Powers Conservation Area**, see p. 71), the only goose and duck hunting within city limits, a PGA golf course (**Harborside**), and 40-plus taverns serving its 8,000 residents. A feisty group of those residents has successfully fended off attempts to raze the neighborhood and build an airport, and is currently working to revitalize the area, particularly **Wolf Lake**. Check out **Aniol's True Value Hardware** (13416 Baltimore). It's been family-owned and operated for three generations and the current proprietor is the unofficial historian of Hegewisch. Make time to visit one or two of the local eating and drinking establishments such as **Doreen's Pizzeria** (13201 Baltimore) or **Club 81 Too** (13157 Avenue M)—a friendly tavern that serves lobster tails at its Friday night fish fry.

Hyde Park   s

Bounded by Cottage Grove (800 E), Hyde Park (5100 S), Lake Michigan, and 61st (6100 S)

Developed by attorney Paul Cornell in the mid-1880s as a strictly residential suburb, **Hyde Park's** name was chosen to evoke the gracious living associated with London's park of the same name. Thanks to Cornell's active involvement to create a park system south of Chicago, Hyde Park is bounded by Jackson Park to the south and Washington Park to the west. In spite of vehement opposition from Cornell and other residents, Hyde Park was annexed to Chicago with several other large townships in 1889 to increase the city's odds for hosting the 1893 Columbian Exposition. Cornell's dream of luring a major academic institution to Hyde Park was realized in 1890 when John D. Rockefeller and the Baptist Church founded the **University of Chicago**. The university, whose faculty collects Nobel Prizes (77!) like some people collect parking tickets, is the focal point of the community. The Gothic campus, modeled after Cambridge, is loaded with inviting and imposing buildings, but you can start with the stunning **Rockefeller Chapel** (p. 35) and grab a bite at the castle-like **Reynolds Club** (57th & University). Hyde Park has retained a somewhat independent status, a sort of idyllic island surrounded by blighted neighborhoods, though there are signs of hope in many of those communities these days. It is alternately seen as progressive, snobbish, integrated, segregated, elitist, and populist, depending on the speaker's point of view. In any event, it is a thriving, bustling community with architectural jewels, eclectic and affordable restaurants, and the wide variety of the kind of funky stores that usually inhabit a college town. **57ᵗʰ Street** has several bookstores, **53ʳᵈ Street** several restaurants. Don't miss **Jimmy's Woodlawn Tap** (1172 E. 55ᵗʰ), a kind of divish college bar found only in the University of Chicago universe. **The Hyde Park Art Center** (p. 39) hosts a multitude of art exhibits, holds classes for adults and children, and has an outreach program that reaches over 4000 people every year. Hyde Park is also home to the 57ᵗʰ Street Art Fair, which always held the first weekend in June. It is the oldest juried art fair in the Midwest.

Jefferson Park   NW/FN
Bounded by Montrose (4400 N), Narragansett (6400 W), Bryn Mawr (5600 N), and Cicero (4800 W)

If you grew up in a nice, working- or middle-class Chicago neighborhood on the North Side and are looking to recreate that childhood for your own kids—but in a place you might be able to afford—chances are you've considered a move to **Jefferson Park**. The homes and lawns are interesting and well-maintained, the streets are safe, and the CTA/Metra/Expressway nexus near Lawrence and Milwaukee can easily get you to where you need to go. The actual **Jefferson Park** (4822 N. Long) and the **Copernicus Center** (5216 W. Lawrence) are two primary recreational centers. The former Gateway Theater movie palace, the Copernicus Center is home to the Polish Cultural Center, but is also used for a host of other ethnic and non-ethnic cultural events. A prominent new use is for the increasingly popular summertime **Silent Film Series** (with live organ music), ironic considering this was the first theater in Chicago built exclusively for "talking" pictures. Jefferson Park and its surrounding areas are also home to some of the Northwest Side's most beloved 24-hour diner hangouts. The **Blue Angel** (5310 N. Milwaukee), **The Big Top** (6348 W. Higgins), and **Sally's** (5454 N. Harlem) are all reliable places for endless coffee refills and huge breakfast portions at any hour of the day. The plaza at Foster and Northwest Highway holds **American Science and Surplus** (see p. 387), where you can get bargains on school project or art supplies, as well as **Js Vitamins** (5316 N. Milwaukee), for your nutritional needs.

Kenwood Mansions   S

*Bounded by Cottage Grove (800 E), 47ᵗʰ (4700 S), Blackstone (1500 E), and
Hyde Park (5100 S)*
This square of **Kenwood** has the city's largest concentration of mansions
(many built between 1870 and 1930), earning it a Chicago landmark district
designation in 1979. Known for being a pillar of black/white racial harmony
in an infamously segregated city, Kenwood is bounded by the University of
Chicago to its south and some of Chicago's most hurting neighborhoods to
the north and west. It was founded by Chicago dentist John A. Kennicott in
1856, who named it after his mother's ancestral Scotland estate. Other
wealthy families soon built palatial homes in the area. Kennicott's house
once stood at 43ʳᵈ Street and the Central Railroad line. Among those still
standing are the **C.S. Bouton House** (4812 S. Woodlawn), an example of
the Italianate style; the **Elijah Muhammad House** (4835 S. Woodlawn),
now the home of Nation of Islam leader Louis Farrakhan; the **Julius
Rosenwald House** (4901 S. Ellis), built for the Sears executive and major
Chicago philanthropist; and two Frank Lloyd Wright-designed houses (4852
and 4858 S. Kenwood). Also keep an eye out for the **K.A.M. Isaiah Israel
Temple** (1100 E. Hyde Park), home of Chicago's oldest Jewish congregation, and Jesse Jackson's **Rainbow/PUSH headquarters** (930 E. 50ᵗʰ). The
John A. McGill House (4938 S. Drexel), a 20,000-square-foot 1890
mansion, was purchased years ago in a crumbling state for $41,000, consci-
entiously restored, and subdivided into apartments. Upgraded again recently
to the McGill Pare condominiums, the units sell for prices attractive by
North Side standards.

Lakefront   FSE/S/C/N/FN

Chicago has about 26 miles of Lake Michigan shoreline as its eastern
boundary with 25 beaches dotting that strip from **Rogers Park** (about *7700
N*) to **Calumet Beach** (about *10000 S*). Walking, running, biking, in-line
skating, wading, swimming, sunning, picnicking, romantic strolling: the
lakefront offers endless possibilities for relaxation and rejuvenation. (And,
it's hard to overdo this lakefront bonanza!) Here's an introductory checklist
of lakefront opportunities:

- Any lakefront activity in spring, summer, fall, and winter.
- Any lakefront activity in the rain and the snow (with ice on the
  water), including the New Year's Day Polar Bear Swim (p. 128).
- Any lakefront activity at sunrise and dusk.
- Any lakefront activity after dark [note: beaches technically close at
  11 P.M.] At night, the grassy, hilly stretch of land that juts into the

lake and leads to the Adler Planetarium is a popular spot for lovers to lounge and stargaze.

- Chicago skyline view from the north, as from the North Avenue Chess Pavilion (p. 105).
- Chicago skyline view from the south, as from Promontory Point at 55th and the lake.
- Lakefront people watching the first warm days of spring and the first hot days of summer.
- Being packed at the shore with tens or hundreds of thousands of others out for an event like the **Air and Water Show** or **Venetian Night** (see the **Public Celebrations** section on p. 287 in **Chapter 5: Entertainment**, for more details).
- The Fourth of July fireworks display on the 3rd of July.

Lincoln Park   N

Bounded by North (1600 N), Diversey (2800 N), the Chicago River, and Lake Michigan.

While technically **Lincoln Park** covers a much wider region (most of which is good for meandering and admiring costly homes), its accepted hub is Fullerton/Halsted/Lincoln—the "DePaul Area." Packed with chic shops, used book and music stores, caffeine outposts, restaurants, bars, and clubs, Lincoln Park surges with activity from dawn to well past midnight. The nightlife, much aimed at just post-college types, is concentrated along Lincoln from Armitage (2000 N) to Diversey (2800 N), with Halsted being home to some prominent blues clubs (see p. 242). Another strip of Lincoln Park where commerce is in full bloom is on Clark Street from Belden (2300 N) to the intersection of Clark, Broadway, and Diversey (2800 N). There's a heavy emphasis on unconventional (and pricey) clothing stores, but you'll also find low-key diners and cheap takeout from **Flash Taco** (Mexican, 2556 N. Clark, 773/248-2901) or the **Wiener Circle** (p. 180). There is a sizable market here for new-and-used record stores like **Hi-Fi** (p. 402), **Reckless Records** (p. 404), and the dance music-centered **Gramaphone** (p. 402), while the comic book contingent is represented by **Graham Crackers Comics** (2562 N. Clark). **Halsted**, between Webster and Armitage, and **Armitage**, between Halsted and Racine, offer some of the most stylish shopping outside of downtown; **Webster**, between Halsted and Southport, is a chockfull, but slower-paced business district; and the **Clybourn Corridor** (p. 314) is its own animal.

Lincoln Square

N/FN

Lincoln from Sunnyside (4500 N) to Lawrence (4800 N)

After a brief stint in the 1960s as the "New Greek Town," **Lincoln Square** began fortifying the last vestiges of Lincoln Avenue's German roots and molding a unique one-block commercial strip (between Lawrence & Leland) for itself to preserve this heritage. As a result, German delis, bars, a restaurant, gift shop, and apothecary now do an energetic business in the area. It is also the site of Chicago's annual Oktoberfest, an event which draws tens of thousands for a weekend of brats, traditional music festivities, and enough beer to fill another Great Lake. The German stuff, however, is really about history and flavor and not a reflection of the actual neighborhood (longtime Greek and Mexican restaurants are just as popular). There's also an established toy store, an upscale café, one of the best martial arts academies in the city, a new bookstore/winebar ,and turn-of-the-century ice cream parlor. All of this is tucked in an outdoor mall setting complete with a shady bench-lined courtyard, fountain, and active events lineup. Lincoln Square may have become "one of the hottest neighborhoods on the planet" as supposed by one late-90s travel magazine, but it is its own type of hot. Perhaps a friendlier, artsy-lite, wackier, more family-oriented gentrification. Perhaps. Lincoln Avenue between Leland and Sunnyside may be even more important for this new flair. Entertainment anchors like the saved-by-the-neighborhood **Davis Theater** (p. 283) and the **Old Town School of Folk Music** (p. 247) can't be underestimated forces, nor can idiosyncratic shops we've highlighted elsewhere like **Quake Collectibles** (p. 386) and **Laurie's Planet of Sound** (p. 403). That trendy restaurants of all ethnicities and persuasions fill in the remaining storefronts is a given.

Little Village/"La Villita"

SW

Bounded by Ogden, Western (2400 W), the Chicago Sanitary and Ship Canal, and the city limits at the train tracks (about 4600 W)

The bustling 26th Street commercial district between Sacramento and Kostner in South Lawndale plays a crucial role in the village-like atmosphere of this tight-knit, predominantly Mexican community. It's just that there's nothing *little* about it. The concentration of Mexican goods, food, and culture it offers draws regular visits not only from the population of 600,000 new Mexican immigrants living in the Chicagoland area, but from Mexican-Americans living in other parts of the Midwest as well. *This compact business strip pays the second-highest amount of Illinois sales tax in the city*, second only to the Magnificent Mile (p. 324)! They come here for arts and crafts, clothing, fresh tortillas, specialty ingredients, piñatas, authentic cuisine, and umpteen other things, and you can, too. It's a one-day trip to

Mexico.

Logan Square/Boulevards Historic District　N

Logan (2600N) from Western to Kedzie, Kedzie (3200 W) between Palmer (2200 N) & Logan, Humboldt (3000 W) between Milwaukee & North ending in Humboldt Park, Palmer Square at Palmer & Kedzie, and Logan Square at Milwaukee (about 3100 W) & Logan

While many feared a homogenized gentrification for **Logan Square** when its solid, reasonably-priced bungalows, two-flats, and graystones were discovered, more restrained development over the last twenty years still leaves the neighborhood socially diverse. The mansion-like graystones that line **Logan Boulevard** (2600 W to 3000 W) are the heritage of its first turn of the century residents who earned the street the early "Boulevard of Millionaires" nickname. These and other homes along Logan Square's massive boulevards, with their expansive green stretches, make up the **Boulevards Historic District** which contains the northwestern portion of Chicago's boulevard system as outlined by Daniel Burnham's visionary 1909 "Chicago Plan." Working-class families inhabited the surrounding streets at the community's origin and have continued to predominate until the present. Although the commercial areas reflect the largely Hispanic population, newer businesses are catering to a growing number of young professionals and artist-types. A slate of taco places agreeably co-exists with the **Boulevard Cafe** (3137 W. Logan) supper club, which appeals to a diverse clientele with drink specials Mon.–Thur. and live music Thur.–Sat.

"The Loop"　C

Bounded by Lake (200 N), Wabash (50 E), Van Buren (400 S), and Wells (200 W)

Chicago's downtown core gets its name **"The Loop"** from the late 1800s' streetcar tracks that encircled the central business district. Today's el tracks trace that same route. See **Architecture, Central/Downtown**, for mini-walking tours of *Government Buildings* (p. 14), *State Street Department Stores* (p. 23), and *Luxury Hotel Lobbies* (p. 16) in this area. **Art, Outdoors** (p. 40) devotes a paragraph to some of the most famous public artworks in the Loop.

Magnificent Mile　C

Michigan (100 E) from Oak (1000 N) to the Chicago River (about 400 N)

Still Chicago's closest thing to a Rodeo Drive or Champs-Elysees, Michigan Avenue's three-quarters-of-a-mile stretch of magnificently expensive shopping has more recently come to offer brand-name retailers for a range of pocketbooks alongside the exclusive stuff.

Old Edgebrook   FN
Bounded by Devon (6400 N), the diagonal Caldwell (about 5600 W), the diagonal Lehigh following the railroad tracks (about 5400 W), Central (about 5350 W), and the North Branch of the Chicago River.
Tucked in the forest preserves of northwest Chicago stands this charming mini-neighborhood developed in 1894 as a suburb for railroad executives. Recently, many young couples have migrated to the general **Edgebrook** area to raise families, and the result is an enclave of trendy Italian restaurants, coffee shops, and sports bars near the Metra railroad tracks (Devon & Caldwell). Still retaining a calm, suburban feel, the area's trendiness is steadily trickling in from other sophisticated North Side neighborhoods.

Old Town   N
Bounded by Armitage (2000 N), Lincoln Park (just west of the lake), North (1600 N), and Halsted (800 W)
Perhaps the original gentrified neighborhood, the **Old Town** section of Lincoln Park abounds with boutiques and restaurants—especially along Wells (200 W), Halsted (800 W), and Armitage (2000 N)—that cater to people who not only have a taste for the finer things in life, but also the money to pay for them. Well-kept, well-gardened old houses and tree-lined streets (some with cobblestone and old-fashioned street lamps) make aimless meandering a worthy Old Town diversion. The entertainment this neighborhood is known for, however, stems from the fabled **Second City** (p. 278) and **Steppenwolf** (p. 272) theaters. The birthplace of improvised comedy, **Second City** is where members of the original and subsequent casts of *Saturday Night Live* got their starts. Original ensemble members John Malkovich, Laurie Metcalf, and Gary Sinise, are among the many TV and film stars who have performed on the **Steppenwolf** stage. Certain immortal businesses linger from previous eras, their characters never diminishing with the polish around them—the **Old Town Ale House** (219 W. North), still retaining a nice 60s/70s-dive patina, and **Twin Anchors** (1655 N. Sedgwick), serving neighborhood ribs since 1932, are among them. Plaques along Wells provide background on significant buildings and features in the neighborhood and help keep Old Town's history hanging around.

Pill Hill   FSE
Bounded by 91st (9100 S), Euclid (1934 E), 93rd (9300 S), and East End (1700 E)
The most affluent section of Calumet Heights, this four-block square of

suburban-like residences was built in the 1960s, mainly for white doctors. Other health-care professionals soon moved in, some who worked from their homes. Thus, the name. Today the area is inhabited primarily by black professionals. The ranch and split level homes are enormous (some are luxurious, too), often dwarfing the city lots on which they sit. Note that the 60s-style landscaping has been retained in many places.

Pilsen   W

Bounded by 16th (1600 S), Halsted (800 W), the Chicago River (about 2700 S), and Damen (2000 W)

Pilsen was originally settled by Czechoslovakian immigrants who named their new home after the Czech town where the Pilsner brewing process was invented. It was the power base from which Anton Cermak rose to the mayor's office only to be killed in Miami, in 1933, in an assassination attempt on President Franklin Delano Roosevelt. Pilsen began its transformation into a heavy-on-the-arts, Mexican community in the 1950s. Many of Pilsen's structures are adorned with murals, mosaics, and other outdoor artwork. The vibrantly decorated **Casa Aztlan** (1831 S. Racine) serves as a center for dance, art, and theater instruction, and the premier **Mexican Fine Arts Center Museum** (p. 56) is not-to-be-missed. Two annual festivals bring crowds of people to Pilsen. One is the **Fiesta del Sol**, a warm weather feast of food, music, and culture traditionally held the last week of July and/or the first week of August. The other, more solemn celebration is the **Via Cruces**, or Way of the Cross, which reenacts the Christian story of the Last Supper and Jesus' journey to his crucifixion each Good Friday. The procession begins at **Providence of God Church** (built in the 1920s), at 18th & Union. Increasingly since the 1990s, as artists have moved in in search of

Pilsen East

One reason that young, non-Mexican artists have been moving to Pilsen is because there's been an almost 35-year history of artists doing so. In 1970, third-generation Pilsen native, John Podmajersky, and his wife Ann, began their first efforts of developing live/work studios for artists in a "colony" setting (*www.podmajerksy.com*). Hundreds of artists (sculptors, painters, ceramists, writers, actors, photographers, and arts educators and entrepreneurs) now live in a 12-square-block area off Halsted between 16th and Cermak, in a dense and supportive community network, with many loft spaces opening onto tranquil communal gardens and courtyards. Previously known as the **Pilsen East Artists Colony**, this expanding effort is known as the **Chicago Arts District** (*www.chicagoartsdistrict.org*).

cheap rent, Pilsen has been thought of as a Mexican neighborhood and as an emerging artists' neighborhood, with those classifications only occasionally overlapping. And, like every good artsy neighborhood, Pilsen has its requisite coffeehouse, in the form of **Cafe Jumping Bean** (p. 161), and hipster dive, the reclaimed Bohemian (literally) pub **Skylark** (p. 265).

Pullman Historic District   FSE

Bounded by 111th (11000 S), Langley (700 E), 115th (11500 S), and Cottage Grove (slanting and running parallel to the train tracks at about 500 E)
George M. Pullman built this community in the 1880s to house the employees of his Pullman Palace Car Company, which manufactured railroad sleeping cars. Designed by architect Solon S. Beman and landscape architect Nathan Barrett, the town was self-sufficient with houses, a school, a church, a shopping arcade, a theater, stables, a hotel, and a market. Note the varying sizes and styles of the houses; they correspond to the level of the workers who once lived within. You will also notice that most of the structures are red brick with green and red trim, echoing the colors of the original Pullman cars. The 1894 strike by Pullman employees, led by union organizer Eugene Debs, resulted in more control for the workers and changed the face of U.S. management-labor relations. Two years later, **Pullman** received the "World's Most Perfect Town" award. Pullman was annexed by the city of Chicago in 1889. In 1960, developers threatened to raze the neighborhood in order to build an industrial park. The Pullman Civic Organization was formed to preserve the area. It became a state landmark in 1969, a national landmark district in 1971, and a City of Chicago landmark in 1972. Today, Pullman's residents are typically teachers, retirees, police officers, and students. In addition to the civic organization, the community has several other active community groups including the Historic Pullman Foundation, the Gay and Lesbian Association, the Arcade Park Garden Club, and the Pullman Seniors Club. The shopping arcade was demolished in 1926. In its place stands a utilitarian building housing the **Historic Pullman Visitors Center** (p. 55, for walking tour information). Be sure to see the **Greenstone Church** (112th & St. Lawrence) and the lavish **Hotel Florence** (11111 S. Forrestville), the latter of which is closed for massive renovations (*http://members.aol.com/PullmanIL/florence.html*). Pullman himself stayed at the **Hotel Florence**, named for his daughter, when he was "in town," but his own home was on Prairie Avenue (p. 61). The family had that building torn down to prevent anyone else from purchasing it.

River North   C

Bounded by the Chicago River (on the southern and western edges), Oak

(1000 N), and Wabash (50 E)
Marked with non-stop growth and re-creation since its successful 80s gentrification, this former industrial zone now encompasses the largest concentration of galleries in Chicago (and one of the largest in the country). Factories and warehouses of yesteryear have been either razed or remodeled for lofts, condos, auction houses, fine antique dealers, pricey furniture retailers, elite health clubs, day spas, sleek hair salons, restaurants galore, trendy clubs, and plenty of martinis and expensive shoes. There is also a collection of oversized, overdone, theme-park-style dining experiences, starting with: **Ed Debevic's** interactive 50s diner (640 N. Wells), the **Hard Rock Cafe** (63 W. Ontario), the **Rock 'n' Roll McDonald's** (600 N. Clark), and **Portillo's Hot Dogs** (100 W. Ontario), whose two-story interior recreates a Chicago neighborhood of the 30s and 40s. As the neighborhood's ad people say, there's something for everyone from the "most wide-eyed visitor to the most jaded urbanite." Guess who goes where? Refer to *www.chicagogallerynews.com* for gallery listings and descriptions.

Rogers Park   FN

Bounded by Lake Michigan, Devon (6400 N), Ridge (running diagonally from about 1850 W to 2100 W), Howard (7600 N), Hermitage (1732 W), and Juneway (7736 N)
This most northeastern of Chicago neighborhoods is unique in that has always served both as a settling place (with its spacious single-family homes) and a transition neighborhood—especially for newly arrived immigrants (almost 80% of residents rent rather than own). Settled first by Native Americans, followed by Luxembourgers, Germans, English, and Irish, then later by Russian Jews and African Americans, and most recently by Hispanics, Asians, Caribbean Islanders, and Middle Easterners, **Rogers Park's** eclectic population includes large numbers of Loyola and Northwestern University students, young families, and retirees. Basically, the neighborhood has been home to members of every ethnic and religious group just short of Yoda's, with each group leaving their mark on the neighborhood in the form of shops, restaurants, churches, graffiti, etc. A sampling of Rogers Park congregations turns up African-American Baptists, Nigerian Christians, Mennonites, orthodox and reform Jews, Buddhists, Hindus, Muslims, Sikhs, and Hare Krishnas. Not surprisingly, a recent study of fifty cities across the U.S. ranked Rogers Park first in economic, racial, and religious diversity. Visitors enjoy its beaches, bars, coffeehouses, bookstores, and theaters. Residents benefit as well from an active neighborhood known for its schools, grass roots activism, and strong community organizations. Rogers Park doesn't have a main drag as such, but several commercial

streets are worth noting. Clark offers an array of Mexican and Belizean restaurants (like **Flower's Pot**; 7328 N. Clark), taverns, Western wear shops, and is home to the **Clark Mall** (p. 412), a terrific assortment of stalls where you can buy clothes, luggage, CDs, videos, shoes, perfume, cell phones, electronics, jewelry, manicures, haircuts, and exotic lingerie, all under one roof. Howard, at the end of the Red Line, is a minor commercial strip with a few eateries and retail shops. Try **Tickie's Belizean Cuisine** (7605 N. Paulina) or walk towards Clark for tasty hot wings at **Buffalo Joes** (1849 W. Howard); shop for antiques at **Lost Eras** (p. 394). A walk down Sheridan takes you past a number of beaches and several coffee shops— including **Cafe Ennui** (see p. 161), **Chase Cafe** (7301 N. Sheridan), and **Panini Panini** (6764 N. Sheridan)—and down to **Loyola University** (where Sheridan turns east). Stop at the **Village Theatre North** (p. 284) for a movie if you get too footsore. The last noteworthy commercial concentration in Rogers Park is anchored by the **Heartland Cafe and Buffalo Bar** (see. p. 233) around the Morse stop on the Red Line. Here you'll find a small cluster of bars, a bookstore, coffee shops, and storefront theaters.

Roscoe Village N

Bounded by Western (2400 W), Belmont (3200 N), Cornelia (3500 N), and Ravenswood (1800 W)

Roscoe Village—one of those picturesque names coined by real estate agents and developers to draw new life to an old neighborhood—refers in most minds to an eclectic, low-key business district along Roscoe between Western (2400 W) and Ravenswood (1800 W). This one-time underdog has steadily grown into a certified, happening place, adding new shops, restaurants, and of course, condos, all the time to service the rise in yuppie families and 20-something residents. Daytime strollers can browse **Sterns Psychology Book Store** (2004 W. Roscoe), **Shangrila's** (p. 395), for a great selection of vintage clothing, pulp fiction, and LPs, or the gigantic **Village Discount** resale store (p. 409), for super bargains. Stop in **Big Hair** (2012 W. Roscoe) for a cheap haircut or to witness the latest in alternative hair styles and dye jobs. Diners like the retro and cheeky **Kitsch'n** (2005 N. Roscoe) and serene and vegetarian **Victory's Banner** (p. 233) guarantee good food and friendly atmosphere for both young friends and large families. Note that two blocks south on Belmont is **Antique Row** (p. 374). Hip, neighborly nightlife can be found at **Village Tap** (p. 263), and up-and-coming rock bands play nightly at the **Beat Kitchen** (p. 254).

South Chicago FSE

Bounded by the Calumet River (about 9500 S), the slanting South Chicago

Avenue, Lake Michigan, and 79th (7900 S)

The burgeoning steel industry brought European immigrants seeking jobs at the Wisconsin Steel Company and USX Corporation South Works plants from the late 1800s to the First World War. They were then joined by Mexican workers and their families. (For 90 years Mexicans and Mexican-Americans have settled here, and **South Chicago** remains the center of Chicago's Southeast Side Mexican community.) The area thrived until a dark day in March of 1980 when the Wisconsin Steel Company closed. Although the closing of the South Works steel plant in 1992 has only added to the neighborhood's depressed state, the community somehow manages to hold together in the face of continued unemployment. On the plus side, the Southeast Chicago Development Commission is working hard to get city, state, and federal funds to rejuvenate South Chicago. (See p. 70 for ecological restoration projects in the area.) **Our Lady of Guadalupe Church** (3200 E. 91st) was founded in 1926, making it the city's oldest Mexican immigrant church. Ironically for South Chicago, the church also houses the **National Shrine of St. Jude** (3200 E. 91st), the patron saint of lost causes.

South Loop/Printers Row   C

Bounded by Clark (100 W), Congress (500 S), the lakefront, and I-55 to the South

The **South Loop** is a fashionable neighborhood on the rise (even the mayor—a lifelong Bridgeport resident—moved here some years back), prized for its convenient just-south-of-the-Loop, just-west-of-the-lakefront location. Major housing developments (quite suburban-like); art galleries; and jazz, blues, and comedy clubs now join the long-standing Lake Shore Drive museum trio (**Aquarium**, **Planetarium**, and **Natural History**) and **Grant Park**, where once there were crumbling buildings, long-gone industry, and unused railroad yards. South Loop housing developments like the ground-breaking **River City** (p. 22); **Dearborn Park** (between Polk & Roosevelt, west of State), a three-decades-long private, "urban renewal" success in the making; and **Central Station**, a complex of different housing options at the south end of Grant Park, have paved the way for new development in areas like Chinatown, Pilsen, Bronzeville, and Bridgeport, as those who can't afford to buy on the North Side are discovering these closer-in South Side neighborhoods. And, while quirky retailers like the **Laughing Iguana** (1247 S. Wabash) are moving in and adding to the neighborhood feeling, so are Target and other big box retailers, bringing the suburbs right into downtown. Home to **Columbia College** (600 S. Michigan), the South Loop maintains many coffeehouses and casual restaurants where students, faculty, and local business people relax on their off-time.

Dearborn Street between Congress and Polk is "**Printers Row**," the former printers' strip that now contains restaurants, bars, a hotel, and a bookstore. **Gourmand** (see p. 266) serves coffee and snacks in Printers Row, and **Cafe Gioia** (see p. 204) does the same for both locals and visitors staying at **Hostelling International** (24 E. Congress, see p. 351). **The South Loop Club** (1 E. Balbo, 312/427-2787) offers plenty of space, a variety of local and imported beers, and greasy grub to entertain any group of friends. **Printing House Row** is a city landmark district that developed in the late nineteenth and early twentieth centuries by printing and publishing firms who needed facilities close to the South Loop's train stations, freighthouses, and river. It was anchored by the 1885 **Dearborn Station** (Polk & Dearborn), a Romanesque building that's still standing, though it closed as one of the city's major train depots in 1971. Printing businesses began leaving the area in the 1960s and 70s, and by the 1980s, the conversions of office and loft buildings to condos and apartments began taking place, and the kinds of businesses needed to make a residential neighborhood complete popped up. Not to be missed are the annual **Printers Row Book Fair** (p. 293), the Midwest's largest bookfest, in June, and the **Historic Printers' Row Neighbors' Annual Loft Walk** in December, a self-guided walking tour in and out of the private homes in these converted printing houses.

South Shore FSE

Bounded by the lakefront, 79ʰ (7900 S), South Chicago (running diagonally from 400 E–1600 E), the IC tracks (about 200 E), and 67ʰ (6700 S)
Long the home of an upwardly mobile middle-class—first WASPs, then Irish Catholics and Jews, now African-Americans. The community's crowning jewel is the **South Shore Cultural Center** (7059 South Shore Drive), overlooking Lake Michigan. The approach to the center's front door is framed by a columned promenade. Its 65 attendant acres include a beach (known for its romantic ambiance and spectacular view of downtown Chicago), a public golf course, tennis courts, stables, and a stage. Built in 1906 as the preeminent South Shore Country Club (White Christians only, please. Blacks and Jews need not apply), the building and grounds were purchased by the Chicago Park District in 1974. In its infinite wisdom, the park district announced plans to demolish the building. Luckily the community banded together to save it. After you've visited the Cultural Center's art gallery and peered into its ballrooms, dining rooms, and solarium, hike up 71ˢᵗ Street to the **Jeffery-Cyril Historic District** [the 700 S blocks of Cyril (1934 E) and Jeffery (2000 E)] to view a patch of 1920s apartments, many of which have been rehabbed. On the other side of 71ˢᵗ, running to 67ᵗʰ, Constance (1836 E), Bennett (1900 E), and Euclid (1934 E) is **Jackson**

Park Highlands, a ridge-top neighborhood developed between 1905 and 1940 and home to a trendy, integrated middle-class. Your visit should also include Chicago's oldest cemetery, **Oak Woods** (p. 44); Chicago's premier African-American theater, the ornate, muraled, Middle Eastern-inspired **New Regal Theater** (79th & Stony Island); and the Afrocentric **ETA Creative Arts Foundation/Cultural Center** (p. 38). For dinner, try **Army & Lou's** (p. 225), a soul food staple; for music and cocktails, **The New Apartment Lounge** (p. 250).

Southport   N
Southport (1400 W) from Belmont (3200 N) and Irving Park (4000 N)
Just a hop, skip, and a drunken stumble from Wrigley Field—**Southport** is one more booming sliver of Lakeview. Once home only to a few pizza joints, several neighborhood taverns, and a multitude of closed shops, the auspicious arrival of Starbucks in the early 1990s would change this nondescript stretch for good. Over a decade later, this is a hip strip of yuppie commerce with unique ethnic eateries, upscale French and Italian dining, vintage clothiers, antique dealers, and pricey home furnishings and gift boutiques. Entertainment options include the classic **Music Box Theatre** (p. 285) for an artsy foreign flic, **Southport Lanes** (p. 99) for hand-set pin bowling, or the **Saga Launder Bar** (1334 N. Newport) for combining laundry day with a trip to the corner bar.

Streeterville   C
Bounded by Michigan (100 E), Oak (1000 N), Lake Shore Dr. (cutting diagonally from about 240 E to 500 E), and Water (about 420 N)
Named for George Wellington "Cap" Streeter, who set up house in 1889 on a sandbar that his steamboat ran into, this neighborhood east of Michigan Avenue is now one of the city's most moneyed areas. Declaring the sandbar (where the **John Hancock Building** now stands) and an increasing area of landfill, "The Independent District of Lake Michigan," Streeter and his wife were joined by a ragtag cadre of undesirables who collectively fought for their right to the land until Streeter's death in 1921. "Picture postcard" Chicago, **Streeterville** has long since been home to numerous luxury hotels and apartments, restaurants, bars, **Navy Pier** (p. 72), and plenty of up, upscale shopping.

Taylor Street/Near West Side   C
Taylor (1000 S) from Morgan (1000 W) to Ashland (1600 W)
Once the lifeline of Chicago's Near West Side Italian community, **Taylor**

Street might now be the closest thing in Chicago with the feel of a college town's main drag. There are so many inexpensive and ethnic restaurants here (it seems like there's "one of each"), you could almost eat at a different one every day for a month. Old-schoolers **Mario's Italian Lemonade** (p. 187), **Al's Beef** (p. 189), and the **Pompei Bakery** (p. 213) are still among the favorites, and lasting Italian businesses like the **Conte di Savoia** (1438 W. Taylor) deli help retain some of the hood's original character. On one block around here you'll feel the decades of the arrival of new immigrants, decay, and urban renewal, on others the dominating presence of UIC and the West Side Medical District, and on still others quaint Italian village scenes emerge Brigadoon-like side by side with rehab projects. Another major going-on in the vicinity is the developers' aggressive renaming of the area centered on Roosevelt and Halsted as **University Village**, "Chicago's new exciting neighborhood." (We bet it was pretty exciting all those decades it served as a major port-of-entry neighborhood for dozens of immigrant groups and those 120+ years when the Maxwell Street Market thrived.) Historically, the neighborhood is home to two notable sights, the **Hull House Museum** (p. 56), in honor of the huge amount of social work done in the area by Jane Adams, and the **Chicago Fire Academy** (p. 21), built on the spot where the legendary Chicago Fire allegedly started.

Tri-Taylor Historic District   C/W

Bounded by Oakley (2300 W), Polk (800 S), and Ogden (cutting diagonally from about 2300 W to 1932 W)
Triangular near south district has been on the National Register of Historic Places since 1983 for its well-preserved two- and three-story row houses from the late 1800s. See **Taylor Street** above for an idea of what's new on the commercial strip.

Villa Historic District   NW

Bounded by the diagonal Avondale which runs parallel to the Kennedy Expressway (about 3750 N), Hamlin (3800 W), Addison (3600 N), and Pulaski (4000 W)
Procured in 1907 by developers Albert Haentze and Charles M. Wheeler for the purpose of single-family bungalow building, this area still has at least 120 historically significant bungalows, many with Prairie-School touches. Mostly Chicago and California-style bungalows, they are amongst the biggest and most handsome in the city; the oldest sit on lots 50 feet wide. Part of the larger "Old Irving Park" neighborhood on the Northwest Side, the general community is comprised of quiet, tree-lined, and non-flashy residential streets. Its small business districts contain mostly unassuming,

independent retailers, bars, bakeries, and delis, some reflecting an ample Polish population.

Wicker Park/Bucktown   N/W
Bounded by Western (2400 W), Fullerton (2400 N), the Kennedy Expressway (cutting diagonally from about 2200 W to 1300 W), and Division (1200 N)

Once the stomping grounds of writer Nelson Algren, the bustling commercial intersection of Damen, Milwaukee, and North Avenue (sometimes referred to as "the crotch") joins **Wicker Park** (to the south) and **Bucktown** (to the north). These two once neglected neighborhoods were rediscovered by artists and have long since skyrocketed to heights of hipness and gentrification. After Manhattan and San Francisco, Wicker Park/Bucktown recently held the United States' highest concentration of working artists, with their talent still showcased every winter and fall in the **Around the Coyote** festival (p. 293). It has also been the breeding ground for various indie label musicians who achieved national and international fame in the 1990s. The area's galleries, artists' work spaces, coffee shops, slick eateries, poetry open mics, performance spaces, and four o'clock bars testify to this convergence of creativity and trendiness. Bucktown's wealth has increasingly overwhelmed Wicker Park's old-school artist faction (that overwhelmed the former Hispanic population that replaced the earlier Polish residents that...), but the main intersection still serves as an urban catwalk (tattoos, piercing, zines, anarchists, WiFi, and connoisseurs of all things hip). Both include side streets filling up with incredible and pricey rehab projects and commercial strips filling up with pricey clothing, shoes, eyewear, and everything boutiques. Coffeehouses like **Earwax** (p. 162) and **Filter** (p. 266) and bookstores such as **Myopic** (p. 390) and **Quimby's** (p. 383) preserve the area's alternative leanings. Check out Wicker Park's **Beer Baron Row** on Hoyne (2100 W) between Pierce (1532 N) and Schiller (1400 N), and the **Pierce Avenue Mansions** around the block. While German brewery chiefs like Schlitz were living it up in these 1880s mansions, humbler German immigrants were tending to their backyard goat "buck" farms further north in Bucktown.

Wrigleyville   N
Bounded by Byron (3900 N), Sheffield (1000 W), Newport (3434 W), and Southport (1400 W)

This section of residential Lakeview overflows with nightlife for the youngish, thanks in part to the beer and bar culture surrounding **Wrigley**

Field (Clark & Addison). The area is active all year round but really kicks into gear in spring, when baseball returns to the North Side, bringing with it cars, street vendors, and crowds of people spilling out of the bars, shouting: *Cubs win! Cubs win!* (on a good day). Despite the neighborhood's frat party image, you'll find great Mexican and Asian food, three of Chicago's oldest Ethiopian restaurants (p. 170), the city's two most popular reggae clubs (see p. 252), a handful of small theater companies and comedy clubs, used book and music stores, vintage clothing, antique dealers, and the **Metro** (p. 255)—a common venue for highly-alternative music—in the immediate vicinity of the ballpark. Clark Street, **Wrigleyville's** main artery, has remained a well-traveled path since its origins as Green Bay Road—a busy Indian trail that stretched all the way to Green Bay, Wisconsin.

Good Parks for Walking

OF Chicago's 560+ parks, these eight stand out for their size, greenery, beauty, popularity, and recreational opportunities. All provide a refreshing, scenic escape from the city din; but be careful, not all are located in the safest of neighborhoods, particularly after dark.

Columbus Park

Bounded by Austin (6000 W), Adams (200 S), Central (5600 W), and the Eisenhower Exp. (about 750 S)   **W**

Leading Prairie-school landscape architect, Jens Jensen, designed **Columbus Park** in 1920 to celebrate the area's natural topography and as a tribute to Midwestern landscapes in general. Although he worked on re-designs of other parks, Jensen built this one from scratch, and it's considered his masterpiece. A 1992 Park District renovation focused on restoring this original plan. Handsome and historic park buildings, wildflower gardens, lagoons, small waterfalls (p. 80), a great golf course for beginners (p. 111), and plenty of picnicking space all say "Sunday afternoon in the park." While you're here, visit the **Race Avenue and Midway Park Houses** (p. 31).

Grant and Burnham Parks   C/S

Bounded by Randolph (150 N), the lakefront, 56th (5600 S), and on the west, Michigan (100 E) from Randolph to 11th (1100 S) and the train tracks from 11th to 56th

Designed by architect Daniel Burnham in the mid-1890s, **Burnham Park** linked downtown with Jackson Park on the South Side. In 1933–34, it was the site of Chicago's second World's Fair. Later additions to the park included the construction of Meigs Field, Chicago's third airport, in 1946, and the McCormick Place convention center in 1960. Mayor Richard M. Daley created the Museum Campus along the lakefront at Roosevelt Road (1200 S) to unite the museums in a beautiful landscaped and pedestrian setting, and hurried along his plans to convert Meigs into more natural park space in the mid-2000s by a surprise bulldozer attack on the runways under the cover of night in March 2003. **Grant Park** is Chicago's answer to Central Park, named after our 18th President and commissioned by the city's residents in 1835 to protect the open lakefront space. In the summer, enjoy a different outdoor activity every night: symphony concerts, salsa dancing classes, movies under the stars, **Buckingham Fountain** light shows (p. 47), and one of Chicago's many summer festivals (Taste of Chicago, the Blues Fest, Jazz Fest, and Gospel Fest, to name a few). Historical note: We do all this on the same site where the disturbances of the 1968 Democratic Convention took place. See pp. 52–53 for information on **Millennium Park**, Grant's new neighbor and cultural competitor to the east.

Humboldt Park   W

Bounded roughly by North (1600 N), California (2800 W), Division (1200 N), and Kedzie (3200 W)
A recreational center for Chicago's Puerto Rican community and grounds for various annual ethnic festivities, **Humboldt Park** is one of Chicago's grand, historic parks of the West Side boulevard system. Its carefully designed grounds and "prairie river" that connects with the parks lagoons (there's also a lake, p. 128) are more Prairie-school handiwork of landscape genius Jens Jensen. With the Chicago Park District and City of Chicago's growing interest in greening activities and renewable energy, the once crumbling Humboldt Park is a perfect candidate for their experiments. It's no surprise that they're working on restoring the park's fields with native prairie grasses and wildflowers and looking into a sustainable energy system for its waterways. Landmarks on the property are the **boathouse**, designed by Frank Lloyd Wright contemporary Hugh Garden, and the **stable building**, a Germanesque stable with sloping roofs and stately turrets on a hefty stone foundation. Park employees once hitched horses.

Jackson Park   S

Bounded by 56th (5600 S), the lakefront, 67th (6700 S), and Stony Island (1600 E)
Located on the lake and behind the **Museum of Science and Industry** (p.

67), the venerable tenant of the 1893 Columbian Exposition's Fine Arts Palace building, much of this park's 1,055 acres were developed for the expo and designed by leading landscape architect Frederick Law Olmsted. Don't miss the Japanese garden on the **"Wooded Isle"** (p. 71) that has existed in various forms since that era. It's now called the **Osaka Garden** for Chicago's Japanese sister city, which donated a traditional cedar entrance gate and money for restoration and landscaping in 1995. Other park highlights include the still, reflective **Columbian Basin** (behind the museum) that leads to the lagoon system, the "Golden Lady" statue, and **Promontory Point** with its lighthouse-looking field house and great view of the cityscape. Declared "The Best City Park" by *Chicago Magazine* in 1999, **Jackson Park** boasts the home of the first golf course west of the Alleghenies, two beaches, 24 tennis courts, a yacht club and marina, soccer fields, bowling green, a baseball field, fitness center, meeting rooms and assembly halls, a walking/jogging/biking path, and a gymnasium.

Lincoln Park

FN/N/C

Bounded by Ardmore (5800 N), Lake Michigan, Grand (530 N), and on the west, roughly, Lake Shore Drive (about 1000 W–250 E)

Lincoln Park is the city's largest (1,212 acres) and perhaps best-maintained and most used park. In addition to its great amenities for lakefront recreation, Lincoln Park also contains **Lincoln Park Zoo** (p. 14), **Lincoln Park Conservatory** (p. 49), the **Peggy Notabaert Nature Museum** (p. 62), the **Chicago Historical Society** (p. 58), **Theatre on the Lake** (p. 276), an historic rookery undergoing renovation, a new wildlife preserve, lagoons, ponds, cafés, numerous monuments, and countless sports facilities. Focus on a certain area or activity, or go on bike and take a whirl past everything.

Marquette Park

FSW

Bounded by Central Park (3600 W), Marquette (6700 S), California (2800 W), and 71ˢᵗ (7100 S)

Named after the French Jesuit missionary and explorer, Father Jacques Marquette (1637–1675), **Marquette Park** has over 300 acres of land. An 18-hole golf course (p. 112) is situated on two islands, surrounded by man-made lagoons and connected by footbridges. The park also has a field house, skating area for winter outdoor skating, tennis courts, a playground, and a huge nursery of 90,000 trees and shrubs. A monument commemorating two Lithuanian-American aviators, Darius and Girenas, was designed and placed in Marquette Park in the mid-1930s. Free concerts are held in the park, as is a big carnival on Memorial Day weekend.

River Park   FN

On both sides of the Chicago River, between about 2850–2950 W.
Lawrence (4800 N) and 3200–3300 W. Devon (6400 N)
At 30 acres, this is the largest of the parks that line the north branch of the
Chicago River. A gently meandering paved walkway explores both sides of
the river and is perfect for biking, roller blading, jogging or walking. Don't
miss the beautiful 1929 field house designed by Chicago architect Clarence
Hatzfeld. Some lovely residential neighborhoods abut the entire span of this
elongated park.

Washington Park   S

Bounded by Martin Luther King Dr. (400 E), 51st (5100 S), Cottage Grove
(800 E), and 60th (6000 S)
Planned and landscaped in the 1870s, this 366 acre park just west of the
University of Chicago has a large lagoon, plenty of shade, and a new
aquatic center. Through a special program with the famed Morton Arboretum in suburban Lisle, **Washington Park** is also home to Chicago's first
"Arboretum in the Park." Sunrise to sunset, visitors can wind through a
special grouping of trees, amongst the largest and most unusual in the city,
on interconnected trails. Lindens, hickories, sycamores, bur oaks, and at
least 45 other types are outlined on a map for self-guided tours. The **Lessing
Monument** in the park's rose garden (57th & Cottage Grove) commemorates
an eighteenth-century German writer whose plays spoke for religious toler-
ance, particularly towards Jews. While wandering around, be on the lookout
for the ghost of Studs Lonigan, title character from James T. Farrell's famed
trilogy. Both author and character hung out here as boys in the 1920s. The
DuSable Museum of African-American History is on park grounds, in the
administration building originally used for the South Park Commission, and
several annual festivals aimed at the black community take place in the park
as well.

7

LODGING

The Lincoln Motel is one of the few remaining rest stops on the once thriving Lincoln Avenue motel strip. *Photo by Bill Arroyo.*

Many visitors are surprised to discover the array of affordable accommodations in the heart of downtown Chicago. *Photo by Bill Arroyo.*

LODGING

BIG-NAME HOTEL CHAINS, local bargain hotels, quaint boutique hotels, bed and breakfasts, youth hostels, university dorms, retreat centers, and outlying motels provide a wide range of lodging choices for Chicago visitors who inevitably have a wide range of preferences for where they lay their head and hat, as well as varying interpretations of affordable accommodations.

Downtown Hotels

ONE can usually find a room at the following downtown hotels in the $79–$129/night range. Rates may vary with availability, convention schedules, day of the week, and season, but most can be cut with the help of various discount travel services and simple Internet searches. If you're reserving by phone, ask for weekend rates, as many hotels empty out when business travelers and conventioneers go home.

Web tip: Click "Book a Hotel" at *www.877chicago.com* to sort hotels by weekday and weekend price (low to high) for the current and upcoming months. You *will* find the $79–$99 rooms here. The "Listing of All Hotels" on the Convention and Tourism Bureau's accommodations page, *www.choosechicago.com/accommodations.html*, marks hotels with an exclamation point that are currently offering special promotions, from lower rooms and free meals to bonus tours, shows, and seasonal treats.

Magnificent Mile

These four options are in the heart of the Magnificent Mile shopping strip in the Gold Coast neighborhood. You're blocks away from the river, lake,

Sleeping in Luxury

The Internet is your best bet to quickly find the random bargain price at better downtown hotels. Typing a phrase like *cheap Chicago hotel rooms* or *discount Chicago hotel rooms* into your favorite search engine will yield pages of room reservation services. Visit at least three or four and enter your travel dates and number of travelers. Better and more interesting downtown hotels like **House of Blues Hotel** (333 N. Dearborn), **The Seneca Hotel & Suites** (200 E. Chestnut), **Talbott Hotel** (20 E. Delaware), **The Tremont Hotel** (100 E. Chestnut), **The Raphael Hotel** (201 E. Delaware), **The Whitehall Hotel** (105 E. Delaware) routinely appear with a room in the vicinity of $100 per night. Another interesting thing we noticed was that often the lower-priced hotel chains were sold out months in advance for holiday weekends and special events (say, Blues Fest or Jazz Fest weekend), but these better hotels still had rooms available at prices identical to the economy hotels.

Navy Pier, Water Tower Place, and the John Hancock Building, surrounded by umpteen restaurants, nightlife possibilities, and other attractions.

Allerton Crowne Plaza Hotel
701 N. Michigan, 312/440-1500, *http://cpchicago.felcor.com*
Recently renovated, the Allerton Crowne Plaza is a historic landmark hotel worthy of the extra dough if you can spare it.

Best Western
162 E. Ohio, 312/787-3100

Comfort Inn & Suites
15 E. Ohio, 312/894-0900, *www.chicagocomfortinn.com*
The renovation of this 1920s hotel has kept many of the Art Deco touches in the memorable lobby and other common areas.

Red Roof Inn
162 E. Ontario, 312/787-3580
The best chain bargain to be found in downtown Chicago.

River North

The restaurant, nightlife, and art gallery district of River North offers these reliable quarters within walking distance of Michigan Avenue, the Loop,

Indy Operators in River North

Cass Hotel
640 N. Wabash, 312/787-4030, *www.casshotel.com*
When you can't find a good deal elsewhere, you can always rely on the Cass Hotel, where singles run $59 to $69 and doubles $79 to $89, depending on the season and the promotion, and often include breakfast. Rooms are small, and the place is old and quirky, but cost-conscious travelers develop a fondness for the Cass. Many say its Sea of Happiness lounge is a great place to meet foreigners and budget-minded travelers, and its café has free Wi-Fi.

Ohio House Motel
600 N. LaSalle, 312/943-6000
A contender with the Cass for best cheap sleep downtown, the Ohio House has all the feel of a careworn, roadside motel but just happens to be in the center of a major metropolis. Free parking in their lot.

Lenox Suites Hotel
616 N. Rush, 312/337-1000, *www.lenoxsuites.com*
Another Chicago original, Lenox Suites has a more conventional and upscale feel than either the Cass Hotel or Ohio House and is definitely worth the few extra bucks if those things are important to you. Various lodging/attractions packages are always available, and the ones for families seem particularly reasonable. Lenox Suites has won industry awards for its commitment to Chicago, community service, and business leadership.

and the lakefront.

Best Western
125 W. Ohio, 312/467-0800

South Loop

Those spending the night in the South Loop are but a quick walk to the Sears Tower, Grant Park, Museum Campus, lakefront, Printers Row, and Soldier Field; and McCormick Place is but a quick bus, shuttle, or cab ride away. The fabulous view from many of the rooms of the Michigan Avenue motels is an amenity not to be underestimated.

Best Western Grant Park Hotel
1100 S. Michigan, 312/922-2900

Chicago's Essex Inn
800 S. Michigan, 312/939-2800, *www.essexinn.com*
Another recently-renovated hotel, the Essex Inn is especially proud of its
intimate feel and the new fourth-floor rooftop Garden Pool and Fitness
Center, which sports a retractable glass roof and an elaborate deck overlooking Grant Park and Michigan Avenue.

Congress Plaza
520 S. Michigan, 312/427-3800, *www.congressplazahotel.com*
Designed and built to host visitors to the 1893 World's Columbian Exposition, the spacious rooms and grand lobby here are a couple of the many
reminders of the previous decades this facility has seen.

Travelodge Hotel
65 E. Harrison, 312/427-8000

West Loop

A few blocks west of the river and the Loop and in walking distance of
Greektown, UIC, the Sears Tower, Amtrak, and Greyhound, these West
Loop locations shouldn't be overlooked. However, they're right off the
expressway and light sleepers should be aware of that never-ending noise in
advance. It helps to remember that Greektown and late-night ouzo shots are
only yards away.

Quality Inn & Suites
1 S. Halsted, 312/829-5000

Rodeway Inn Mid-City Plaza
1 Mid-City Plaza, Halsted & Madison, 312/829-5000

Hotels in Other Areas

THESE strategically located hotels provide lower-priced, quality rooms in
popular areas. Expect to pay the same room rates as for the downtown hotels
above, and follow the same Web advice to secure the best prices.

Transient Hotel in Transition?

Sheffield House (3834 N. Sheffield, 773/248-3500) is a former residential hotel reconfigured and repackaged for the budget traveler, though some say it doesn't seem to have made the full transition. It's cheap ($55 for the basic double room), a stone's throw from Wrigley Field, and just fine for the right sort of traveler. You probably already know if this is or isn't you, but visit *www.sheffieldhouse.com* and you might be surprised.

Lakeview/Lincoln Park   N

Staying in these popular, dense, and active lakefront Near North Side neighborhoods sets you amidst the everyday surroundings of many Chicagoans. Because even if they don't live here, many North Siders routinely find themselves in the Lakeview and Lincoln Park neighborhoods for the shopping, dining, bars, clubs, Cubs games, and vibe.

Best Western Hawthorne
3434 N. Broadway, 773/244-3434

Inn at Lincoln Park
601 W. Diversey, 773/348-2810
Jacuzzi suites also available.

Days Inn Gold Coast
1816 N. Clark, 312/664-3040
Located across the street from Lincoln Park and Lincoln Park Zoo.

Days Inn Lincoln Park North
644 W. Diversey, 773/525-7010

Midway Airport   FSW

Four Points Sheraton Midway
7353 S. Cicero, 773/581-5300

Holiday Inn Express Hotel & Suites Chicago/Midway Airport
Midway Hotel Center, 6500 S. Cicero, 773/458-0202

FYI

Visitors to **The Budget Traveller's Guide to Sleeping in Airports** Web site (*www.sleepinginairports.com*) give O'Hare and Midway Airports mixed reviews for their overnight comfort. Recent postings note Midway Airport's pervasive Chicago theme (smiley face) and that O'Hare security does not allow you to fall asleep there (skull and cross bones).

O'Hare Airport FN

Clarion Barceló Hotel at O'Hare
5615 N. Cumberland, 773/693-5800

Holiday Inn Chicago O'Hare/Kennedy
8201 W. Higgins, 773/693-2323
Near O'Hare Airport and Rosemont theaters and convention facilities.

Hyde Park S

Ramada Inn Lake Shore
4900 S. Lake Shore Drive, 773/288-5820
Located across from Lake Michigan, near Hyde Park and the University of Chicago, on the city's South Side.

Room Link-Up Services

FOR discounted rooms at better hotels, make use of one of the link-up services below. Be sure to also consult discount travel services connected with AAA, banks, credit cards, entertainment cards, frequent flyer clubs, and professional organizations.

Hot Rooms
773/468-7666, 800/HOTEL-00, *www.hotrooms.com*
Free reservation service links you with discounted (up to 50%) rooms at 22 downtown hotels, up to four months in advance. Be warned: even after big price cuts, nightly rates generally range from $79 to $225.

Hotel Reservation Network
800/715-7666, *www.hoteldiscount.com*
"A chocolate on your pillow doesn't have to cost you a mint." Free hotel booking service reserves blocks of rooms at major economy, first class, and

deluxe hotels, and passes the savings (up to 65%) on to you. The Hotel Reservation Network guarantees their low rates.

Discount Chicago Hotels
800/311-5045, *www.discountchicagohotels.com*
Free reservation service offers discounted (up to 60%) rooms for 89 of Chicago's hotels. Visit their Web site for a full description of the hotel's services and take a sneak peak at the rooms available. Prices range from $60 to $295.

Neighborhood Inns of Chicago

NEIGHBORHOOD Inns of Chicago (*www.cityinns.com*) has renovated three old transient residences, turning them into charming, one-of-a-kind, boutique hotels. Located in the lively Lakeview East neighborhood, each hotel is just a short walk from numerous restaurants, clubs, theaters, trendy shopping, the lakefront, and Wrigley Field. Check the "Specials" tab on their Web site for occasional discounts and package deals.

City Suites Hotel
933 W. Belmont, 773/404-3400, 800/248-9108   N
With its vintage architecture and Art Deco interiors, City Suites maintains its original Prohibitian-era charm. Its 45 rooms and suites run $119–$189.

Majestic Hotel
528 W. Brompton, 773/404-3499, 800/727-5108   N
Escape to the gentility of the quaint and elegant English style at the Majestic, where coffee, tea, and afternoon cookies are available daily in the lobby. Its 52 rooms/suites run $139–$199. Suites contain butler pantries.

Willows Hotel
555 W. Surf, 773/528-8400, 800/787-3108   N
Tucked on a quiet and pleasant side street, the Willows' 55 rooms evoke the nineteenth-century French countryside and range from $89 to $199.

Bed & Breakfasts

YOU won't be staying in the typical country inn bed & breakfast in Chicago, but you probably didn't want to anyway. Instead, the companies below will connect you with charming urban alternatives, ranging from cozy coach houses to elegant town homes and stunning high-rise apartments. For helpful

Purple Roofs

Purple Roofs (*www.purpleroofs.com/usa/illinois.html*) directs travelers to gay-friendly lodging in the Chicago area, including **Wooded Isle Suites** in Hyde Park (5750 S. Stony Island, 773/288-6305). Most of the guest houses, apartments, and bed & breakfasts on their site are open to people of all persuasions. Prices range from $30 to $600 per night, most $100–$150.

room descriptions, photos, and price specifics, visit their Web sites.

At Home Inn Chicago
312/640-1050, 800/375-7084, *www.athomeinnchicago*
This reservation service will find a room for in you in one of the 29 locations they work with in the Downtown, Gold Coast, Old Town, Lincoln Park, Bucktown/Wicker Park, and Lakeview/Wrigleyville neighborhoods. Prices for six of these quarters go for $105 to $125 per night; another 13 accommodations run from $135 to $155.

Bed & Breakfast Chicago
773/248-0005, 800/375-7084, *www.chicago-bed-breakfast.com*
One of the first B & B reservation services in the country, Bed & Breakfast Chicago links travelers with about a dozen memorable residences in Chicago's Old Town, Gold Coast, Bridgeport, Wicker Park, Lakeview, Lincoln Park, and Wrigleyville neighborhoods. Rooms with breakfast have a two-night minimum and run $85–$125 per night. Self-contained apartments have a three-night minimum and cost $115–$350 a night.

= = = = = = = = = = =

For an extra touch of Chicago, the rooms at Lincoln Park's Victorian **Windy City Urban Inn** (607 W. Deming, 773/248-7091, 877/897-7091, *www.windycityinn.com*) are named for famous Chicago writers and the common areas decorated with Chicago memorabilia. Stay in the Mike Royko, Carl Sandburg, or Gwendolyn Brooks room ($115–$150/night), the Sara Paretsky, with a Jacuzzi ($165–$185), or the romantic Nelson Algren and Simone de Beauvoir Suite ($185–$225).

A great B&B bargain in Rogers Park, the **Greenview Inn B&B** (7318 N. Greenview, 773/743-1043, *www.thegreenviewinn*) is two blocks from the el and priced right at $85/night for solo travelers and $95/night double occupancy. Wicker Park's **The House of Two Urns** (1239 N. Greenview, 773/235-1408, *www.twourns.com*) is notable not only for its great location

Bronzeville Renaissance

Bronzeville's 1st Bed & Breakfast
3911 S. Martin Luther King Dr., 773/373-8081
www.bronzevillesbnb.com
Situated in the historic Goldblatt's Mansion is **Bronzeville's 1ˢᵗ Bed & Breakfast.** The fully restored mansion is a glorious blend of luxury accommodations, exquisite dining, day spa, full-service salon, and arts and entertainment center. Real estate developer and professional model of 20 years, Pamela Johnson, is the owner and visionary behind this magnificent endeavor. Opened in 1999, the B&B first collaborated with local ministries to host out-of-town guests. The word spread quickly of its well-appointed rooms, down home gourmet meals, and impeccable service—a place where "old" meets a discriminating and eclectic mix of "new." Johnson has since hosted international visitors; local and national politicians; and famous musicians, artists, performers, writers, and athletes.

Rooms run $135–$150 per night and the guest house is $375. The Honeymoon Suite, with a two-seat Jacuzzi and a rooftop deck offering views of the ballpark fireworks when the White Sox are at home, costs $230. Prices are based on double occupancy and *include 3 meals daily plus butler service.* Menu choices focus on soul food, Creole, Caribbean, African, and vegan/vegetarian cuisine and may be brought to your room upon request.

Located just three minutes from the Chicago McCormick Convention Center and ten minutes from downtown, **Bronzeville's 1st Bed & Breakfast** is part of the ongoing revival of the historic Bronzeville neighborhood, once a thriving cultural center of Chicago's African-American community. Its "wall of fame" features black and white photos of African-Americans past and present.

The mansion is available for special events, family gatherings, receptions, holiday parties, and corporate events. Check the Web site for details on spa and salon services and the entertainment calendar. They welcome walk-ins daily from noon to 6 P.M. who would like a tour of the facilities.

and Victorian and quirky charms, but for better than average prices ($69–$150/night) and its quarters for families ($125–$180).

Hostels and Dorms

NOT just for youths, hostels are the ideal choice for anyone who doesn't need big hotel amenities (like a private bathroom), for people who like to meet other travelers, or for those who would prefer spreading their money around the city rather than concentrating it in the hands of a hotelier. Likewise, unused college dorm rooms can provide basic, affordable accomodations for the flexible traveler. Reservations are strongly recommended, especially in the summer when space/rooms go fast. Prices quoted are per night.

Arlington House International Hostel
616 W. Arlington Place, 773/929-5380   **N**
At $19.50 for those with a hostel membership, $41 for a private single (no bath), $48 for private double (no bath), $55 for a private double (with bath), and $76 for a triple, anyone wanting convenient access to the lake, downtown, and Near North Side neighborhoods should keep this hostel in mind. 24-hour check-in and access.

Chicago International Hostel
6318 N. Winthrop, 773/262-1011   **FN**
Near Loyola University, Rogers Park, Evanston, and great transportation, the $15 for basic accommodations, $35 for a private double (with bath), and $48 for a private room with three beds (no bath) are true deals. Groups of 10 or more pay $13 per person. Family rooms are available. Check-in 7 A.M.–10 A.M. and 4 P.M.–midnight. There's a midnight curfew, which extends to 2 A.M. on weekends.

Holy Roofs

Spiritual seekers and those practicing particular faiths may prefer to return to the peaceful surroundings of a retreat center after long days of business meetings or sightseeing. For modest rooms in the $20 to $50 range, consider the Zen Buddhist **Urban Meditation Retreat Center** (1730 W. Cornelia, 773/528-8685), which offers morning meditation and kitchen facilities; **Quaker House** (5615 S. Woodlawn, 773/288-3066), for members of the Society of Friends and their friends; and the Catholic **St. Benedict House** (1049 W. 31st St., 773/927-7424), for a monastic experience of silence and solitude. On the same property is the **Benedictine Bed & Breakfast**, a private retreat, complete with modern amenities and a hot breakfast, on the grounds of this urban monastery ($145/night for 1–2 guests; $185/night for 3–4 guests). For other options in the Chicago suburbs, try *www.findthedivine.com* and *www.retreatfinder.com*.

Chicago International House
1414 E. 59th, 773/753-2270   S
Located on the U of C campus, guests must be at least 18 years old and a
student or friend or family member of someone affiliated with the University
of Chicago. All rooms are private and cost $45/night. Reservations are
mandatory.

Hostelling International Chicago
The Ira & Nicki Harris Family Hostel
24 E. Congress, 312/360-0330, *www.hichicago.org*   C
With its prime downtown location—within walking distance of the el,
Amtrak, Greyhound, Grant Park, the Sears Tower, the Art Institute, and the
Museum Campus—how can any budget-conscious traveler not consider
overnighting it here? This seven-story, renovated loft building, built in 1886,
operates as a year-round hostel (with 500 beds!), but half the space houses
Columbia College students during the school year. They are also serviced by
a student center, performance center, and library on the premises. There's an
information center on the first floor, free walking tours, low-cost sailboat
rides, and other discounts and perks for guests. Six to 10 people share a
room. 24-hour access. $30 members, $33 non-members.

Illinois Institute of Technology
3200 S. Wabash, 312/808-6403   S
Three miles directly south of downtown and near Sox Park (a.k.a. U.S.
Cellular Field, hiss)—just a bus or el ride away—the IIT dorm rooms have
an attractive price for summer travelers of all ages. Private rooms for one
person are $28/night with linen, $23 without linen. Double rooms are $23
per person with linen, $18 per person without linen. Community bathrooms
are located on each floor. Laundry and cafeteria available. One-time linen
set-up included. Reservations accepted one week in advance with credit card
guarantee.

No-Frills Neighborhood Motels

CHICAGO is not a Club Med sort of destination where one's lodging is an
integral part of the experience. Stay inside and you might as well have
stayed home. The hardier, more adventurous, more tolerant, more finan-
cially constrained traveler may prefer saving their dollars for seeing the
town and check into one of these no-frills neighborhood motels.

All are easily accessible by public transportation and cost somewhere between $45 and $90 a night—at least half the price of a downtown hotel. Granted, some of these establishments make more money as outposts for amorous trysts and spicy cable TV programming than on visits from thrifty tourists, and yes, more than one has served as a clandestine site for partying teens. However, even at these locations, the linen is clean and the rooms are safe.

For the budget-conscious and for the not so particular who will be out exploring Chicago all day anyway, the neighborhood motels present a viable alternative to pricier accommodations. Borrowing a Motel 6 motto, *These are rooms to stay in, not to live in.*

Far North

These motels on the far North Side are a cut above the other neighborhood motels. All but the Heart O'Chicago are within walking distance of Lake Michigan and a CTA Red Line station.

Chicago Lodge
920 W. Foster, 773/334-5600, *www.chicagolodge.com*
A room with one bed for up to two guests, $80/night; two beds for up to four guests, $87/night; three beds for up to six guests, $98/night; and Jacuzzi suites, $121/night.

Esquire Motel
6145 N. Elston, 773/774-2700
$59/single, $69/double.

Heart O' Chicago Motel
5990 N. Ridge, 773/271-9181, *www.heartochicago.com*
$58/single, $70/double, king or two double beds. AAA rated. Continental breakfast included.

Lakeside Motel
5440 N. Sheridan, 773/275-2700
$58.95/single, $69.95/double. Rates *include* the 14.9% hotel tax.

Super 8 Loyola
7300 N. Sheridan, 773/973-7440
$77/single, $89/double.
Located near Loyola University's Lake Shore Campus.

North Lincoln Avenue Strip

This rapidly disappearing collection of drive-up motels seems out of place in the middle of the city. Built during the 50s when Lincoln Avenue (Highway 41) conducted northbound travelers to the Edens Expressway at Peterson, these motels were left stranded in urbanization when the Kennedy Expressway bypassed them. It seems like no one could possibly come up with a legitimate reason why they stay in business, but I've never seen one of their parking lots empty. However, the **Riverside Motel** is now a grassy park, and the infamous **Spa Motel**, stopping point for every two-bit band hoping to be Led Zeppelin, is now the 20th District's new Police Headquarters. Others are sure to follow as developers continue to push north and west, in what's now being dubbed the "Lincoln Bend" neighborhood.

Apache Motel
5535 N. Lincoln, 773/728-9400
$50/weekdays, $58/weekends.

Diplomat Motel
5230 N. Lincoln, 773/271-5400
$62/all rooms.

Guest House Motel
2600 W. Bryn Mawr, 773/561-6811
$45/weekdays, $55/weekends.

Lincoln Inn
5952 N. Lincoln, 773/784-1118
$45/weekdays, $55/weekends.

Lincoln Motel
5900 N. Lincoln, 773/561-3170
$45/weekdays, $50–$55 weekends.

O-Mi Motel
5611 N. Lincoln, 773/561-6488
$45/weekdays, $65/weekends.

Patio Motel
6250 N. Lincoln, 773/588-8400
$51/weekdays, $71/weekends.

Stars Motel
6100 N. Lincoln, 773/478-6900
$50/weekdays, $65/weekends.

Summit Motel
5308 N. Lincoln, 773/561-3762
$50/single, $60/double.

Tip Top Motel
6060 N. Lincoln, 773/539-4800
$43/weekdays, $55/weekends.

Share the Love

Artist Michele Walker is collecting stories, artwork, and memories of the Lincoln Avenue motels for various projects. Contact her through *www.michelewalker.com* to participate.

South

The Amber Inn
3901 S. Michigan, 773/285-1000
$59–$79/all rooms.
Conveniently next to I-90, this "better" neighborhood motel also distinguishes itself with **Pearl's Place**, a southern soul food/creole restaurant on the premises.

Super Motel
6625 S. Martin Luther King Drive, 773/667-5118
$50/single, $65/deluxe rooms.

Royal Michigan Motel
3756 S. Michigan, 773/536-4100
$46/all rooms.

Southwest

Rainbow Motel and Pink Palace
7050 W. Archer, 773/229-0707

Budget-minded travelers check in at the Rainbow Motel for $65/single, $75/double, and romantically-inclined couples stay at the Pink Palace's fantasy-themed suites for $139 Sun.–Thur., $169 on weekends. If the Wine and Rose's heart-shaped bed or the Hawaiian room's artificial flowers don't do it for you, maybe the large cards on the Vegas room wall or the space-capsule bed of Space Walk will!

These three are all within 1/2 mile of Midway Airport:

Rollin' Wheels Motor Hotel
5335 S. Pulaski, 773/582-9600
$62/all rooms.

Sportsman's Inn Motel
4501 S. Cicero, 773/582-3700
$63/all rooms.

Tangiers Motel
4944 S. Archer, 773/582-0900
$74/1 bed, $92/2 beds.

Far Southeast

Barbara Ann's Motel 2
7621 S. Cottage Grove, 773/487-5800
$45/weekdays, $73/weekends.

Camelot Motel
9118 S. Cottage Grove, 773/488-3100
$30–50/all rooms.

New Riviera Motel
9132 S. Stony Island, 773/221-6600
$52/all rooms.

Seville Motel
9101 S. Stony Island, 773/731-6600
$46/all rooms.

Zanzibar Motel
8161 S. Stony Island, 773/768-1430
$50/all rooms.

Far Southwest

Aloha Motel
8515 S. Cicero, 773/767-3100
$45/weekdays, $55/weekends.

Grand Motel
10022 S. Halsted, 773/881-3500
$53/all rooms.

Hogan's Motel
8903 S. Ashland, 773/881-4200
$52/all rooms.

Regency Castle Lodge II
1140 W. 95th, 773/238-8500
$55/all rooms.

Saratoga Motor Inn
7701 S. Cicero, 773/582-8400
$70/double, $60 king. Water beds and hot tubs cost extra.

8

SHOPPING

Definitely not your suburban shopping center:
the Logan Square Megamall offers a unique
atmosphere for bargain hunting and snacking.
Photo by Rames Shrestha.

Voting With Your Wallet
by Keir Graff

IT'S A SEEMINGLY endless trend: small, unique businesses are replaced by chain stores that look the same whether they're plunked down in Manhattan, New York, or Manhattan, Kansas. In conversation, strangers locate themselves by the chain stores available to them: Do you have Steak 'n Shake? Fuddrucker's? Big Boy? Ironically, in a nation that celebrates the rugged individual, we're cocooning ourselves with safe, predictable retail environments. Yet travel loses its thrill when neighborhoods in Seattle, San Francisco, and Miami feature the same signs on the same buildings, and when you can eat at McDonald's in Paris or KFC in Beijing. Indeed, it's arguable whether you *have* traveled if you simply stay at the Marriott, eat at T.G.I. Friday's, and shop at the Gap. Everywhere is in danger of becoming nowhere. Chicago is no different, and long-time residents can tick off dozens of wonderful, individually-owned establishments that have knuckled under to either chains or "concept" establishments. When an Irish tavern closes, you can bet that a Disney-style "authentic Irish pub" is opening soon.

Too many of us pay lip service to our neighborhood shops, only to contribute to their impending demise. We browse in them, and then drive to a big chain store to actually shop. But there's something simple we can all do to help preserve the wonderful places that remain in Chicago, or anywhere: patronize them. Even if our politicians were so inclined, they haven't shown much aptitude for legislating diverse, thriving neighborhoods. But since this is a capitalist country, the dollar is stronger than a vote anyway. Every dollar you spend has importance, so give it to someone whom you want to have it. It's amazing how much better it feels to spend money at the local coffee shop than at Starbuck's.

My wife Marya and I have resolved to buy locally whenever possible. We're supporting businesses that have faces, that don't treat their employees like simple units of labor. We're supporting the idea of a bustling local retail district, and sometimes, a quirky way of doing business where the clerk is allowed to be grumpy or chatty depending on how they feel. Would *you* want to work somewhere where you had to read from a script?

It's true that there are drawbacks: We pay a little more for groceries, or luxuries like electronics, and sometimes we don't have as many choices or we have to wait for something to come into stock. There are also immediate payoffs, like not having to sit in rush-hour traffic or having someone who knows what they're talking about explain how a product works.

It's easy to make the argument that we're too poor to shop locally, that it doesn't make sense to pay extra dollars at a small shop when we can find cheap goods at megastores or on the Web. But only looking for the lowest price carries hidden costs, whether in the time and gas we expend getting to the big-box store or in the isolation we create for ourselves in front of computers. In fact, buying into this mentality is the only way we become truly poor—spiritually and culturally.

And what's more important to you: your money or your life?

SHOPPING

BECAUSE WE COULDN'T advise on all your shopping needs in one chapter, we began by focusing on those businesses and categories of stores that offered the best deals. We filled out that mixture with local classics, multi-generational, family-owned institutions, dealers in the kinds of goods one only finds in very big cities, types of retailers that any savvy urbanite needs to be familiar with, great places to browse, and places that are as much fun for people-watching as they are for shopping. We hope this approach brings some adventure to otherwise mundane shopping trips and gives you additional reasons to venture to unfamiliar areas of the city.

Outlet Stores

OUTLET stores sell new, generally brand-name merchandise at reduced prices. The items they carry may be last year's model, have slight imperfections, or merely be overstock that a manufacturer is trying to push. Included among the outlet stores in this list are some off-price shops and major discount centers, also well-loved for their great bargains.

Audio Equipment

Saturday Audio Exchange
1021 W. Belmont, 773/935-HIFI, *www.saturdayaudio.com*   **N**
Open only on Thursday evenings (5:30 P.M.–9 P.M.), Saturdays (10:30 A.M.–5:30 P.M.), and Sundays (noon–4 P.M.), the **Saturday Audio Exchange** sells, buys, and exchanges home audio and home-theater audio equipment. Although the stock is made up of samples, demos, seconds, and used items, everything comes well-guaranteed. All merchandise comes with a 90-day full exchange option. From 90 days to a year after purchase, products may

be returned for a store credit of two-thirds the price paid. Many items also come with full manufacturer's warranties.

20th Century TV & Stereo Center
1615 W. Montrose, 773/528-1728   N
In a world where electronic gadgets often become obsolete before we even learn how to use them, it's nice to know there is an alternative to buying disposable goods. Since 1970, Mitch and Ursula Lewczuk have operated on the principle that quality is what counts. Using their extensive experience, they buy, refurbish, and sell audio and TV equipment that they know is reliable—even if it's 20 or 30 years old. And if you bring your stuff in for repair, they'll give you a fair estimate and won't perform a quick fix if what you really need is an overhaul. For this, their customers come even from out of state. They do deal in CD players, but you can find or fix old speakers, reel-to-reel tape recorders, turntables with changers, and more. They stock cartridges, needles, belts, and accessories, some that aren't made anymore. Everything comes with a warranty, and they strive for quick turnaround (two weeks is usually the upper limit). The emphasis is more on audio than video, and the Lewczuks no longer service cameras and camcorders. Open Mon.– Sat. 10 A.M.–8 P.M., Sun. noon–6 P.M.

Baby Goods

Rubens Baby Factory Store
2340 N. Racine, 773/348-6200   N
No tedious browsing through rack after rack at this minimalist outlet: discounted goods are displayed in a small section of the factory's office. Crib and bassinet sheets, bibs, cotton diapers, pajamas, and the ever-favorite $1.99 assortment of undershirts comprise the majority of available products. Open Mon.–Fri. 9 A.M.–3:30 P.M.

Cameras, Film, and Film Processing

Central Camera Company
230 S. Wabash, 312/427-5580, *www.central-camera.com*   C
In business since 1899, **Central Camera** still offers old-fashioned style counter service and the area's largest selection of discounted new and used photo equipment (includes binoculars, books, camera bags, and dark room supplies) from its cramped quarters. With its convenient downtown location, their color film developing service is a blessing for tourists. Bring film in by 10 A.M. and pick it up the next day with a free second set of prints. Central

Camera has now expanded its business to include digital printing services, as well as digital camera equipment and accessories. Go online to see *everything*, especially used cameras, closeouts, and the gear impossible to find elsewhere. Open Mon.–Fri. 8:30 A.M.–5:30 P.M., Sat. 8:30 A.M.–5 P.M.

Triangle Camera
3445 N. Broadway, 773/472-1015, *www.trianglecamera.com*   N
This family-owned camera shop has been in business for almost 50 years, offering a wide range of processing services and new and used equipment at a great price. They also offer rentable darkrooms and studios for the aspiring photographer, as well as a full spectrum of photography classes at prices that beat the pants off of local colleges. The well-stocked supply of professional films and papers is available at discount for those taking classes. Open Mon.–Fri. 9:30 A.M.–6 P.M., Sat. 10 A.M.–5 P.M., Sun. noon–4 P.M.

Clothing

Burlington Coat Factory
4520 S. Damen, 773/254-0054   SW
7340 W. Foster, 773/763-6006   FN
www.coat.com
While off-price coats—for every season and occasion, from all possible materials—are the emphasis here, some women's sportswear and designer clothing, men's suits and ties, and children's togs are also sold. Everything is 10–70% below department store prices. Open Mon.–Sat. 10 A.M.–9 P.M., Sun. 11 A.M.–6 P.M.

Filene's Basement
1 N. State, 312/553-1055   C
Open Mon.–Sat. 9 A.M.–8 P.M., Sun. 11 A.M.–6 P.M.
830 N. Michigan, 312/482-8918   C
Open Mon.–Fri. 9 A.M.–9 P.M., Sat. 9 A.M.–8 P.M., Sun. 10 A.M.–7 P.M.
Founded in Boston in 1908, **Filene's Basement** is the country's oldest off-price store. They're known for their downtown locations that attract the downtown work force on their lunch hour and after work to shop for brand name, designer, and occasionally couture fashion for women and men, particularly careerwear. They also carry some home furnishings and gift items.

Fox's
2150 N. Halsted, 773/281-0700   **N**
Women's off-price designer clothing store features sportswear, suits, dresses, and coats at 40–70% off retail prices. This is the only big-city store of the 13 in the Fox family of stores, which means it doesn't have to share any inventory suitable for urban audiences with other locations...it all comes here. Mon.–Wed. 11 A.M.–7 P.M., Thur.–Fri. 11 A.M.–8 P.M., Sat. 10 A.M.–6 P.M., Sun. noon–5 P.M.

The Gap Factory Outlet
2778 N. Milwaukee, 773/252-0594   **NW**
Irregular and discontinued Gap clothing and accessories for men, women, children, and babies. Heavy on the jeans, trousers, and cotton shirts. Mon.–Sat 10 A.M.–8 P.M., Sun. 11 A.M.–6 P.M.

Gingiss Formalwear Outlet
542 W. Roosevelt, 312/347-9911   **C**
Know one of those nice guys that will end up going to half a dozen proms? Send them here to buy used (previously rented) tuxes, formalwear, and accessories. Buying one of these tuxes is cheaper than renting one twice— coat, pants, shirt, cummerbund, and bow tie packages start at just over $100. Open Mon.–Fri. 10 A.M.–6 P.M., Sat. 9 A.M.–5 P.M., Sun. 11 A.M.–4 P.M.

Mark Shale Outlet
2593 N. Elston, 773/772-9600   **N**
Spiffy work and play clothes for the urban professional from local clothier Mark Shale (est. 1929) and others at 40–60% discounts. Translation: You can find a $375 suit for a low $149. Open Mon.–Fri. 10 A.M.–8 P.M., Sat. 10 A.M.–6 P.M., Sun. Noon–5 P.M.

Marshall's
600 N. Michigan, 312/280-7506   **C**
Open Mon.–Sat. 9 A.M.–9 P.M., Sun. 10 A.M.–6 P.M.
1834 W. Fullerton, 773/296-4494   **N**
Open Mon.–Sat. 9:30 A.M.–9:30 P.M., Sun. 10 A.M.–7 P.M.
3131 N. Clark, 773/327-2711   **N**
Open Mon.–Sat. 9:30 A.M.–9:30 P.M., Sun. 11 A.M.–7 P.M.
4937 W. North, 773/342-8637   **W**
Open Mon.–Sat. 9:30 A.M.–9:30 P.M., Sun. 11 A.M.–6 P.M.
4612 W. Irving Park, 773/282-0078   **NW**
Open Mon.–Sat. 9:30 A.M.–9:30 P.M., Sun. 11 A.M.–6 P.M.
One of the country's largest off-price clothing retailers for men, women, and

Haberdashery on Roosevelt Road

A small stretch of Roosevelt Road, just south of downtown and not far from the old Maxwell Street Market, has long been noted for its reputable haberdashers. In fact, the notorious zoot suit was invented along this strip by Harold Fox of **Fox Brothers Tailors** (556 W. Roosevelt, 312/922-5865) back in the early 1940s. Today this area is still a men's wear center where one can find today's zoot suit progeny like dapper pink and orange silk suits. It's also particularly known for high-quality, off-price clothing. **555 W. Roosevelt Road** is home to three such clothiers: **Eisenstein Clothing** (312/738-0028) carries brand name irregulars, returns, and closeouts (mostly suits) for 50% to 75% off. Any flaws are pointed out to the customer. **Meyerson Associated Clothing** (312/421-5580) specializes in large sizes at a 20–30% discount. The only place in the United States to buy certain current-season European designer clothes at a discount is in the chockfull, second-floor store of **Morris & Sons** (312/243-5635). Expect 30–50% markdowns—more in the clearance section. On the same street, you can buy a tux for a bargain at **Gingiss Formalwear Outlet** (p. 362) or stock up on low-cost necessities at **Chicago Hosiery and Underwear Company** (601 W. Roosevelt, 312/226-0055).

children, Marshall's promises "brand names for less, every day." Their selection of brand name and designer apparel and accessories is priced at least 20–60% off the deparment store or specialty catalog tags. Smaller sections of their store are devoted to discounted home furnishings and gourmet food gifts.

Motherhood Maternity Outlet
1730 W. Fullerton, 773/529-0564   N

This outlet store combines the discounted wares from **Motherhood Maternity**, **Mimi Maternity**, and **A Pea in the Pod**, taking care of all the clothing needs of fashion-conscious mothers-to-be with their ample selection of casual clothes, careerwear, lingerie, nursing garb, swimwear, special occasion outfits, and more. Open Mon.–Fri. 10 A.M.–9 P.M., Sat. 10 A.M.–6 P.M., Sun. noon–4 P.M.

The Sock Shoppe
4012 W. 63rd St., 773/582-4787   SW

Stock up on clothing essentials at this cozy little business. Prices vary depending upon the brand name and size, but six pairs of white athletic socks usually cost you about $5. Athletic socks are the big sellers, but you'll often find ladies' trouser socks or men's dress socks at bargain prices. Depending upon size, sweat shirts or sweat pants are usually in the $5–$10 price range. T-shirts, pajamas, and even sunglasses can also be had for bargain prices, though some merchandise has minor imperfections. Open Mon., Wed., Fri. 8:30 A.M.–8 P.M., Tues. & Thur. 8:30 A.M.–7 P.M., Sat. 8 A.M.–7 P.M., Sun. 10 A.M.–6 P.M.

T.J. Maxx
11 N. State, 312/553-0515   C
Open Mon.–Sat. 9 A.M.–8 P.M., Sun. 11 A.M.–6 P.M.
1745 W. Fullerton, 773/327-1124   N
Open Mon.–Sat. 9:30 A.M.–9:30 P.M., Sun. 11 A.M.–7 P.M.
2840 N. Broadway, 773/975-2347   N
Open Mon.–Sat. 9:30 A.M.–9:30 P.M., Sun. 11 A.M.–6 P.M.
6456 W. Irving Park, 773/725-9400   NW
Open Mon.–Sat. 9:30 A.M.–9:30 P.M., Sun. 11 A.M.–6 P.M.
The largest off-price apparel retailer in the U.S., **T.J. Maxx**'s discounts on brand-name clothing, shoes, accessories, and jewelry range from about 20% to 60% the list price.

Computers and Supplies

Chicago Computer Supply
27 N. Wacker, 312/202-0237, *www.chicagocomputersupply.com*   C
Always priced below retail, **Chicago Computer Supply** prices their brand-name hardware, software, and accessories competitively and helps you select what you need with superior customer service. Also save big with "new open box" and "refurbished" items. Open Mon.–Fri. 9 A.M.–6 P.M.

Computer Discount Warehouse
315 W. Grand, 312/527-2700, *www.cdw.com*   C
When it comes to the 30,000 products (major computer brands, peripherals, and accessories) they sell, not only does **CDW** pass on the "right price" to its customers, but they pride themselves on passing on the "right advice" as well. Readers of *Computer Shopper* agree: they recently awarded them six first-place titles—best place to buy notebook PCs, printers, scanners, monitors, and software, and best vendor Web site. Open Mon.–Fri. 8 A.M.–6 P.M.

Cosmetics

Devon Discount Distributors
2454–59 W. Devon, 773/743-1058   **FN**
Largest independent fragrance distributor in Chicago sells name-brand and
designer (Armani, Versace, Gaultier, and pals) fragrances and related products at discounts up to 85%. Drastic discounts also apply to their cosmetics,
health and beauty supplies, film, and batteries. Open Mon. & Thur. 10
A.M.–8 P.M., Tues., Wed., Fri. 10 A.M.–6 P.M., Sun. 11 A.M.–5 P.M.

Crafts

Gone to Pot
1432 W. Irving Park, 773/472-2274   **N**
For one-of-a-kind items for gift giving or home use, make a trip to this
"seconds" outlet to find irregular and discontinued handmade crafts from
artisans around the country. Pottery, blown glass, sculpture, wood, jewelry,
frames, clocks, lanterns, switchplates, quilts, and more carry price tags
30–60% less than retail. Open Tues.–Fri. noon–6 P.M., Sat 11 A.M.–5 P.M.,
Sun. noon–5 P.M.

Fabric

Hallmark Textiles, Inc.
2820 N. Elston, 773/489-7707   **N**
In business since 1958, this wholesaler recently opened its doors to the
public. Hallmark buys discontinued fabrics and sells them at deep discounts.
Great bargains on upholstery, drapes, vinyl, and outdoor and marine fabrics.
Open Mon.–Fri. 8 A.M.–4 P.M.

Textile Discount Outlet
2121 W. 21st Place, 773/847-0572   **W**
Four rooms on each of three floors take up thousands of square feet to
display thousands of fabrics, trimmings, and sewing doodads. Whether it's
for outfitting the bride, re-upholstering a chair, or any project in between,
you will—if you spend enough time—find what you're looking for. If you
don't, it's because you discovered something better and at a better price.
Open Mon. & Thur. 9:30 A.M.–7 P.M., Tues. & Wed. 9:30 A.M.–5 P.M., Fri.
9:30 A.M.–4:30 P.M., Sun. 10 A.M.–4 P.M.

Vogue Fabrics
623–27 W. Roosevelt Rd., 312/829-2505, *www.voguefabrics.com*   C
Known for low prices, frequent sales, exhaustive inventory, and sections devoted to designer materials and draperies, this family business has become one of the country's largest and most beloved fabric dealers. Before heading to the store, check out online the bargain fabrics, designer fabrics, equipment, and notions currently on sale. Open Mon.–Sat. 9 A.M.–6 P.M., Thur. 9:30 A.M.–6 P.M., Sun. noon–5 P.M.

Furniture
THE typical finds at these furniture outlets and liquidators are listed below:

Affordable Portables
2608 N. Clark, 773/935-6160, *www.affordableportables.net*   N
Over 2,500 types of futons, futon frames, futon covers, bedroom furniture, desks, book shelves, entertainment centers, sofas, and cocktail/coffee tables. They're at 25 years of supplying "trendy furniture for frugal people" from their overcrowded store. Open Mon.–Fri. 10:30 A.M.–7 P.M., Sat. 10:30 A.M.–6 P.M., Sun. noon–5 P.M.

American Furniture Liquidators
4343 S. Ashland, 773/579-0200   SW
1441 E 75th, 773/643-0002   FSE
Living and dining room pieces, carpeting, headboards, mattresses, bunk beds, stereos, TVs, and VCRs. Open Mon.–Fri. 10 A.M.–7 P.M., Sat. 10 A.M.–6 P.M., Sun. 11 A.M.–5 P.M.

Chicago Furniture Liquidation Company
5923 N. Clark, 773/275-0200   FN
Living room and dining room furniture, futons, mattresses, rugs, bunk beds, and daybeds. Open Mon.–Fri. 10 A.M.–8 P.M., Sat. 10 A.M.–6 P.M., Sun. 11 A.M.–5 P.M.

Furniture Factory Outlet
2700 N. Elston, 773/276-3000   N
Bedroom, dining room, living room, and kitchen sets. No desks/entertainment centers. Layaway and delivery available. Open 10 A.M.–7:30 P.M., Sat. 10 A.M.–6 P.M., Sun. 10 A.M.–5 P.M.

Marjen of Chicago
1536 W. Devon, 773/338-6636, *www.marjenofchicago.com*   **FN**
Full sets for the bedroom, dining room, living room, kitchen, and computer room, plus all the rest: canopy and brass beds, armoires, breakfast bars, bookcases, entertainment centers, telephone stands, room dividers, coat racks, mirrors, and more. Open Mon. & Thur. 10:30 A.M.–8 P.M., Tues., Wed., Fri. 10:30 A.M.–7 P.M., Sat. 10 A.M.–6 P.M., Sun. 11 A.M.–5 P.M.

Golf & Tennis Equipment

Chicago Tennis & Golf Company
3365 N. Drake, 773/489-2999, *www.chicagotennisgolf.com*   **N**
For $55/year, serious golfers and tennis players stand to save a bundle by joining the **Chicago Tennis & Golf**'s buyer's club. Membership entitles them to a price much lower than the discounts already found at this independent, family-owned store. For example, a golf bag marked down to $160 recently went for $119 for club participants. Top equipment and apparel brands include Callaway, Titleist, Cobra, Prince, Foot-Joy, Wilson, Head, Nike, and more. Indoor golf and tennis demo lanes available to test the products. Trade in used golf equipment for store credit. Open Mon.–Thur. 10 A.M–7 P.M., Fri.–Sat. 10 A.M.–6 P.M., Sun. 11 A.M.–5 P.M.

Nevada Bob's Discount Golf
60 E. Lake, 312/726-4653, *www.nevadabobs.com*   **C**
Especially proud of their deals on premium golf club brands, **Nevada Bob**'s guarantees the lowest prices on clubs, clothing, shoes, and other tee-time accessories. Open Mon.–Fri. 9 A.M.–7 P.M., Sat. 9 A.M.–6 P.M., Sun. 11 A.M.–5 P.M.

2nd Swing
1730 W. Fullerton, 773/244-0011, *www.2ndswing.com*   **N**
"Pre-swung" golf equipment is the specialty of this Twin Cities-based retailer. They buy used equipment from individuals, both outright and as trade-ins, and from pro shops and country clubs nationwide. They've identified over 50,000 different codes for types and condition of equipment to offer sellers a maximum, pre-determined price. Their store has separate women's and juniors' sections. Open Mon.–Fri. 10 A.M.–7 P.M., Sat. 10 A.M.–6 P.M., Sun. noon–6 P.M.

House and Garden

1730 Outlet Company
1730 W. Wrightwood, 773/871-4331   N
1730 is the home accessories clearance center of the Trade Associate Group, an import-export home furnishings company. They deliver savings of 50–70% on miscellaneous high-quality housewares for indoors (dishes, baskets, cloth napkins, placemats, dish towels, candles, candleholders, area rugs, and frames) and out (lanterns, citronella and other garden torches, wooden window boxes, and flower baskets). Open Mon.–Sat 10 A.M.–4 P.M.

Crate & Barrel Outlet
1864 N. Clybourn, 312/787-4775   N
The **C&B Outlet** moved from its longtime North & Halsted location to a couple blocks north underneath the new Trader Joe's. You can expect their signature tableware, kitchen gadgets, glassware, home accessories, gift items, and furniture at a decent discount. Open Mon.–Fri. 10 A.M.–8 P.M., Sat. 10 A.M.–7 P.M., Sun. 11 A.M.–6 P.M.

Northwestern Cutlery and Supply
810 W. Lake, 312/421-3666   C
Most come here for deals of up to 35% off on kitchen knives, particularly the Henckels and Wusthof brands. Knife-sharpening services and bargains on cutlery sets and Swiss army knives are another draw. Open Mon. 9 A.M.–5 P.M., Tues., Thur., Fri. 7 A.M.–5 P.M., Wed. 7 A.M.–7 P.M., Sat. 8 A.M.–5 P.M.

Smith & Hawken Outlet
1780 N. Marcey, 312/266-1948   N
Leftovers from the upscale **Smith & Hawken** catalog—which sells everything remotely related to gardening—can be found here across the patio from the Smith & Hawken retail store at healthy discounts. Some standard buys are plants, tools, bulk seeds, statuary, fencing, topiaries and topiary supplies, and metal and rattan outdoor furniture. Open Mon.–Wed. 10 A.M.–7 P.M., Thur. 10 A.M.–8 P.M., Fri. 10 A.M.–7 P.M., Sat. 10 A.M.–6 P.M., Sun. 11 A.M.–5 P.M.

Yardifacts
1864 N. Damen Ave., 773/342-9273   N
Stephanie Fenza, who started **Yardifacts** in 1999, deals with salvagers and has a regular inventory of architectural embellishments, chandeliers, and old mantels. The inventory consists of new and old from wrought iron planters

to statues, fountains, hand blown hummingbird feeders, hand-designed mobiles/windchimes, and handmade jewelry. The store has a relaxed, charming country feel, so take your time to enjoy everything. Items are ideal for balconies, small and large yards, even interior design. Also take advantage of the sales in fall and spring and save around 50%! Open Tues.–Sat. 11 A.M.–6 P.M., Sun. 1 P.M.–5 P.M.

Liquor

Cardinal Liquors
3501 N. Central, 773/725-0900   NW
Open Mon.–Sat. 9 A.M.–9 P.M., Sun. 11 A.M.–7 P.M.
4905 N. Lincoln, 773/561-0270   FN
Open Mon.–Sat. 9 A.M.–Midnight, Sun. 11 A.M.–8 P.M.
With their great selection, low prices, and even better sales, it's no wonder that these full-service neighborhood liquor stores have been in business for 60 years. Some of their can't-find-anywhere-else stock includes specialty Polish, Hungarian, and Russian products.

Sam's Wines & Spirits
1720 N. Marcey, 312/664-4394, *www.sams-wine.com*   N
Over close to six decades, this family warehouse business has grown to become a Chicago institution with a legendary collection of alcohol, particularly wine. With one visit to their 33,000-square-foot store, stocked with over 20,000 wines, spirits, beers, gourmet food items, cigars, and accessories at some of the lowest prices available, you'll be inclined to agree that they are the "single leading beverage retailer in the world." Weekend shopping in this area can be a traffic nightmare, but do come once in a while for one of the frequent wine tastings. And, if you can bear the crowds, do come at the holidays, too, to watch entertainers from around the city pile their carts with hundreds and thousands of dollars worth of booze. Open Mon.–Sat. 8 A.M.–9 P.M., Sun. 11 A.M.–6 P.M.

Wine Discount Center
1826 1/2 N. Elston, 773/489-3454, *www.winediscountcenter.com*   N
An impressive wine selection, which ranges from low-end, unusual, and obscure brands to fine labels—all at hard-to-beat prices—is what has allowed the **Wine Discount Center** to operate successfully for 20 years just a stone's throw from the mega stores. If you're the kind of wine shopper that chooses by price, grape type, and bottle aesthetics, you can't go wrong here—they don't carry products that don't earn their "above averarage," "exceptional," or "extraordinary" rating. They have in-store wine tastings

every Saturday from noon to 4 p.m., monthly sales, and special events like wine dinners and classes. Open Mon.–Fri. 10 A.M.–7 P.M., Sat. 9 A.M.–8 P.M., Sun. noon–5 P.M.

Binny's Beverage Depot
213 W. Grand, 312/332-0012   C
Open Mon.–Thur. 8 A.M.–8 P.M., Fri. 8 A.M.–9 P.M., Sat. 9 A.M.–9 P.M., Sun. 11 A.M.–6 P.M.
1531 E. 53rd, 773/324-5000   S
Open Mon.–Fri. 10 A.M.–7 P.M., Sat. 9 A.M.–7 P.M., Sun. 11 A.M.–6 P.M.
3000 N. Clark, 773/935-9400   N
Open Mon.–Sat. 9 A.M.–9 P.M., Sun. 11 A.M.–6 P.M.
www.binnys.com
They may have no rum from the Ukraine, no Aquavit from Guatemala, and no brandy from Holland, but these three Chicago links in the beloved 15-superstore Chicagoland chain may carry everything else you're looking for at the prices you're hoping for. Go to their Web site to do searches of their inventory (like above) by country and spirit type. While you're there, you can also sign up by e-mail for the free **Frugal Wine Lover's Club**. Their downtown store, which took over the 70-year-old Zimmerman's Discount Liquors, also has a wine cellar, gourmet foods, and a walk-in humidor. The Hyde Park location is a more compact, "express" set-up, though they too sell cigars. The Lakeview store, maintaining the castle-like exterior of decades of previous tenants, has a "catacombs tasting room," wine cellar, wine storage, walk-in humidor, and a gourmet grocery section, and is the most memborable.

Luggage

Irv's Luggage Warehouse
820 W. North, 312/787-4787, *www.irvs.com*   N
Pay a visit to Irv's before your next trip for the best name brands in luggage at factory direct prices. Whether you need a garment bag, duffel bag, passport pouch, or full set of luggage, you'll appreciate the 20–70% cut in prices—not to mention additional savings from the regular coupon offers in local papers and their "lowest price guaranteed" policy. Find current styles, discontinued models, closeouts, and irregulars from makers like Hartmann, Samsonite, TravelPro, Swiss Army, Pathfinder, North Face, High Sierra, Brent Haven, and Jack Georges, to name a few. Also save money with their luggage repair service. Open Mon.–Fri. 10 A.M.–7 P.M., Sat. 10 A.M.–6 P.M., Sun. noon–5 P.M.

Mattresses

Wholesale Mattress Factory Outlet
4227 W. 43rd, 773/254-0700, *www.mattfac.com*   **SW**
The Heller family business—for three generations and more than 80 years—sells a range of bedding sizes and styles for about 50% of what you'd pay elsewhere. They even welcome you to tour their facility (directly attached to their showroom) and see the manufacturing in process. If you also want customized bedding for children, non-standard sizes, institutional settings, or to meet hypoallergenic and orthopedic needs, they can accommodate you. They've even helped out Oprah and movie props people. Open Mon., Tues., Thur., Fri. 8 A.M.–5 P.M., Wed. 8 A.M.–8 P.M., Sat. 10 A.M.–4 P.M., Sun. 8 A.M.–noon.

Mattress King
1444 W. Belmont, 773/472-5120, *www.mattresskingchicago.com*   **N**
For 20 years Mattress King has been selling all of their mattresses, box springs, futons, and frames to the public at wholesale prices. At these rates, you can afford that customized mattress you've needed but put off—for boats, RVs, rollaway beds, bunk beds, hospital beds, and more. If you refer a friend within three months of your purchase, both you and they receive $15 rebates. Senior citizens get special prices on Wednesdays. Open Mon.–Fri. 11 A.M.–6 p.m., Thur. 11 A.M.–7 P.M., Sun. 11 A.M.–4 P.M.

Marjen of Chicago Discount Furniture & Bedding
1536 W. Devon, 773/338-6636, *www.marjenofchicago.com*   **FN**
With 35 years under its belt, Marjen bills itself as Chicago's oldest and largest furniture discounter, which makes it a great place to get an off-price bedroom set to go around your new, affordable mattress or futon. In addition to their wholesale prices, they have immediate delivery and home set-up. Open Mon. & Thur. 10:30 A.M.–8 P.M., Tues., Wed., Fri. 10:30 A.M.–7 P.M., Sat. 10 A.M.–6 P.M., Sun. 11 A.M.–5 P.M.

Office Supplies

Xpedx Paper Store
3555 N. Kimball, 773/463-0822, *www.xpedx.com*   **NW**
This warehouse, formerly Arvey Paper, stocks more paper and envelope styles than you can imagine, plus all the other office and shipping supplies your home, business, or graphic design project could need. Although the everyday low prices, monthly sales, and volume discounts are outstanding,

even more remarkable is the friendly, helpful staff, most of whom seem to be high school- and college-aged students. Open Mon.–Fri. 7:30 A.M.–6:30 P.M., Sat. 8 A.M.–5:30 P.M., Sun. noon–5 P.M.

Party Supplies and Greeting Cards

Card & Party Giant
1880 W. Fullerton, 773/342-1500   **N**
6253 N. McCormick, 773/478-6200   **FN**
www.cardandpartygiant.com
Helping outfit parties for over a decade, **Card & Party Giant** bills itself as the "largest party store in Chicago" at over 15,000 square feet at each location. They specialize in printed party goods for holidays and theme parties that sell for at least half off the manufacturer's suggested retail price. In addition to costumes, catering supplies, greeting cards, and gift wrap, check out the more than 100 mylar balloon types available. Open Mon.–Fri. 9 A.M.–9 P.M., Sat. 9 A.M.–7 P.M., Sun. 9 A.M.–6 P.M.

Doolin's
511–513 N. Halsted, 312/666-8070, *www.doolins.com*   **C**
When outfitting and accessorizing any event, season, fundraiser, or special occasion, simplify the task by starting at **Doolin's**. In one fell swoop, you can pick up all manner of holiday decorations, coordinated table- and partyware, gaming and big-event supplies, glow products, decorative lighting, balloons and helium tanks, and more. With fifty years in the business, they have found the right way to blend the benefits of big and small businesses for the benefit of their customers. Open Mon.–Fri. 9 A.M.–4:30 P.M., Sat. 9 A.M.–3 P.M.

Factory Card Outlet
6520 W. Fullerton, 773/637-4874   **NW**
Open Mon.–Sat. 9 A.M.–9 P.M., Sun. 10 A.M.–6 P.M.
8045 S. Cicero, 773/582-7787   **FSW**
Open Mon.–Fri. 9:30 A.M.–9 P.M., Sat. 9 A.M.–8 P.M., Sun. 10:30 A.M.–6 P.M.
www.factorycard.com
One of the oldest and largest discount superstores for party supplies, greeting cards, and special occasion merchandise, **Factory Card Outlet** offers 20–60% off coordinated party supplies, and over 4,000 top quality greeting cards at a fraction of what you'd pay elsewhere. They also carry party favors and novelties, serving ware, costumes, seasonal decorations, gift wrap, piñatas, banners, and more.

Restaurant Supplies For the Home

Edward Don Co. Outlet
2525 N. Elston, 773/489-7739 N
While you can find an astounding range of glassware, dinnerware, flatware, commercial cookware, utensils, and cleaning supplies at **Edward Don**, the epicenter here is their kitchen gadgetry. Five hundred kitchen gadgets—most specialized and many imported from Switzerland, Hungary, and Poland—draw those who want just the right flour sifter or cheese grater. Open Mon.–Fri. 10 A.M.–6 P.M., Sat. 9 A.M.–5 P.M., Sun. 11 A.M.–4 P.M.

Krasny & Company
2829 N. Clybourn, 773/477-5504, *www.krasnyco.com* N
Founded in 1918, this is Chicago's original restaurant supply house. From the ketchup and syrup dispensers, bread baskets, and ashtrays used at corner diners to the over 600 kinds of specialty glassware found behind hotel bars. **Krasny** has the kind of items you've long admired at eating and drinking establishments of every caliber and have always wanted to take home. Other perks of shopping at this accessible wholesaler include the industrial cookware and bulk herbs and spices. Open Mon.–Fri. 9 A.M.–6 P.M.

Shoes

Adams Factory Shoe Outlet
3655 W. Irving Park, 773/539-4120 NW
If sturdiness means more to you than fashion, then read on. Since 1945, this family shoe store has dealt in irregulars, closeouts, and overstocks of American made shoes, becoming known for their wide range of sizes—women's 1–14, men's 5–18, and wide-widths. Their "full-service" includes a cup of good coffee! There's a small parking lot behind the store. Open Mon.–Sat. 9 A.M.–6 P.M., Sun 10 A.M.–4:30 P.M.

DSW Shoe Warehouse
3131 N. Clark, 773/975-7182; *www.dswshoes.com* C
Located in The Pointe shopping center at Clark and Broadway, **DSW** sells an expansive variety of men's and women's shoes at 25–50% discounts (30–80% when these go on clearance). Women may love Chicago's growing collection of cute shoe boutiques, but this is where they're shopping for day-to-day purchases. They also carry socks, belts, and handbags. Free parking is available in the shopping center garage. Open Mon.–Fri. 10 A.M.–9 P.M., Sat. 10 A.M.–8 P.M., Sun. 11 A.M.–6 P.M.

Nine West Outlet
2739 N. Clark, 773/281-9132   **N**
2058 N. Halsted, 773/871-4154   **N**
These two **Nine West** outlets carry shoes manufactured solely for outlet sales, though the Clark location also sells some of last year's models at clearance prices. Look for frequent two-for-one sales. Open Mon.–Fri. 10 A.M.–8 P.M. (Clark St. until 9 P.M.), Sat. 10 A.M.–7 P.M., Sun. 11 A.M.–6 P.M.

Antiques

THOUGH Chicago has antique stores of one kind or another tucked into just about every neighborhood, there are two main areas where you'll find a concentration of shops that are easy to walk to. The first, **Antique Row**, is an eight-block stretch of Belmont, from Ashland to Western (although it more properly starts around Ravenswood). Although it is Chicago's oldest antique district (around since the 1970s), an incursion of pricey new condos has driven up property values and is beginning to change the flavor of the neighborhood. The antique malls—Phil's and the two Belmont malls—are gone, as well as several other stalwart shops, and remaining dealers note that foot traffic has diminished somewhat. But don't be misled; there are still a lot of great antique shops in the area, and there are signs that a whole new crop of dealers may be moving in.

The second noteworthy concentration of antique dealers is nearby, on a short stretch of Lincoln just below Belmont. A couple of big antique malls—mixed with several very different solo dealers—make for a great afternoon's browsing. Plan a weekend if you want to really give both districts their due.

Antique Mall on Clark
6122 N. Clark, 773/465-1200   **FN**
Formerly the International Antique Center, this place has Antiques with a capital "A"—not kitschy collectibles—and offers excellent browsing if you're interested in seeing how the other half used to live. Open daily 11:30 A.M.–5:30 P.M.

Broadway Antique Mall
6130 W. Broadway, 773/743-5444   **FN**
Uprooted from its Wrigleyville digs (and renamed in the process), this incredible emporium now has twice the room (20,000 square feet) to showcase its phenomenal collection of goods, mostly representing "mid-century modern" (1930s through 1960s). They also feature arts & crafts,

pottery, and a second floor that's all furniture, all the time. Not cheap, but the quality is top-notch and it's worth it just as a field trip. Open Mon.–Sat. 11 A.M.–7 P.M., Sun. 11 A.M.–6 P.M.

Chicago Antique Centre
3045 N. Lincoln, 773/929-0200 **N**
For the non-tycoon looking for everything from kitsch to treasures, this modest-sized mall of 30 dealers offers the best browsing in the Lincoln–Belmont area. With about 30 dealers in 12,000 square feet on two floors, they offer "Mission to Modern," mostly twentieth-century wares. They sell some furniture, but more small items: art, barware, clothing, magazines, vintage cheesecake, and much, much more. Open daily 11 A.M.–6 P.M.

Design in Mind
1901 W. Belmont, 773/975-7460 **N**
This small store feels like the backstage area at a Vaudeville show or maybe an old warehouse for an advertising firm. Goods are big, bold, and prop-like: an oversized wooden straight razor, a barber pole, a mannequin torso with organs showing, a bunch of fake hands for modeling gloves. There's also a great selection of truly unusual old movie posters and displays. It's not surprising to learn the owner has also decorated a Leona's and a Fuddrucker's. Open Mon.–Sat. 11 A.M.–6 P.M., Sun. noon–5 P.M.

Father Time Antiques
2108 W. Belmont, 773/880-5599, *www.fathertimeantiques.com* **N**
The expensive clocks, furniture, and jewelry are *not* for bargain hunters, but the store is worth a visit as a timepiece museum. Gorgeous, fascinating clocks and watches will make you long for the predigital era—and perhaps consider a home equity loan so you can take one home. Open Wed.–Sun. noon–5 P.M.

Gold Coast Gallery
3020 N. Lincoln, 773/327-7600, *www.goldcoastantiquesofil.com* **N**
In business since 1968, this enormous store (25,500 square feet) deals mostly in furniture, from antique to new, from domestic to imported, from the exquisite to the exquisitely tacky. The long, narrow aisles can be a bit maze-like—take a wrong turn and you dead-end—but there's a lot to see. Open Mon.–Sat. 10 A.M.–6 P.M., Sun. noon–6 P.M.

Lincoln Antique Mall
3141 N. Lincoln, 773/244-1440 **N**
With 20 dealers and 11,000 square feet, the Lincoln Antique Mall tries to

live up to its motto, "If you didn't get it in the will you can get it here." Over the years, this place has grown a little more chi-chi; they're heavy on furniture, chandeliers, oil paintings, and the like. *Objets* range from French and traditional mahogany to Deco and mid-century modern. A city lot provides parking right behind the store. Open daily 11 A.M.–7 P.M.

Park West Antiques Fair
600 W. Fullerton, 773/935-3751   N
Generally the first Saturday and Sunday in June, this annual summerfest provides a background of music and food for a weekend of serious antique shopping.

Red Eye Antiques
3050 N. Lincoln, 773/975-2020   N
Owner Bob Lutz takes pride in his broad buying and selling criteria: If it's from the 1500s to the 1970s, if it's of high quality and very unusual, you might find it in his store. **Red Eye** was featured in a *Chicago* magazine's "Secret City" issue, though it's not much of a secret any more. Lots of paintings and a nice selection of not-too-naughty girlie mags, among many other things. Open Wed., Fri., Sat. 11 A.M.–6 P.M., Thur., Sun. noon–6 P.M.

Toy Town Museum and Gifts
1903 W. Belmont, 773/975-7460   N
The appellation "museum" may be a bit coy—this here's a store—but **Toy Town** has a pretty amazing collection of (mostly) very old toys. Not much bubble-wrap crap here. Open Mon.–Sat. 11 A.M.–6 P.M., Sun. noon–5 P.M.

Vintage Deluxe
2127 W. Belmont, 773/529-7008   N
This small store is packed with great stuff from the 1930s through the 1960s: eyeglasses, Tiki and bamboo kitsch, barware, lighting, posters, and prints. They also do prop rentals, notably for the recently filmed *Road to Perdition*. Open daily 11 A.M.–6 P.M.

Antique Starr

Pick up the *Guide to Antiques on Lincoln Avenue*—a free brochure outlining 33 sources for antiques on Lincoln Avenue between Fullerton and Lawrence from the **Steve Starr Studios** (2779 N. Lincoln, 773/525-6530). Steve Starr, an antique frames specialist, compiles and regularly updates the guide, which contains addresses, phone numbers, hours, and merchandise descriptions.

Unique Browsing

THINGS you would find only in a big city. Things that are great to look at, but you don't need, don't want, or can't afford. Things that make distinctive, memorable gifts. Things that make you go hmm . . .

Alternative Stuff

Alternative Shopping Complex
Clark & Belmont, 773/883-1800, *www.altshopcomplex.com*   **N**
Six stores under one roof sell "alternative" products for the urban hip: **The Alley** (Clark entrance, x.219) deals in motorcycle gear, leather jackets, boots, clothing, jewelry, and alternative lifestyle paraphernalia. At the **Architectural Revolution** (Clark entrance, x.232), find columns, statues, gargoyles, and other decorative plaster items to spruce up the house and garden. **Blue Havana** (Belmont entrance, x.224) is a premium cigar shop, with a decent selection of ashtrays and humidors. **Jive Monkey** (Belmont entrance, x.229) sells new and used clothing and accessories. **The Silver District** (Clark entrance, x.215) carries silver jewelry and accessories to suit urbanites of all stripes. And, for those of age, **Taboo-Tabou** (Belmont, x.223) carries lingerie, condoms, and adult toys. Hours vary. The stores open at 11 A.M. or noon and stay open until at least 8 P.M. (Tabou Tabou and the Alley until 10 P.M.), and most until midnight Fri.–Sat.

99th Floor
3406 N. Halsted, 773/348-7781   **N**
Welcome to a world of leather, latex, hardware, hair dye, and Zippo lighters. The 99th Floor traffics in "eclectic and extreme" shoes, boots, clothing, jewelry, and accessories for an underground and alternative clientele, including punks, Goths, ravers, metalheads, and fetishists. Open Mon., Thurs., and Fri. 3 P.M.–10 P.M., Sat. noon–10 P.M., and Sun. noon–7 P.M.; Closed Tues.–Wed. They are planning to extend hours in the near future.

Architecture and Design Stuff

Chicago Architecture Foundation Gift Shop
224 S. Michigan, 312/922-3432   **C**
875 N. Michigan, 312/751-1380   **C**
www.shopcaf.org
Architecture books, Tiffany-style lamps, decorative gargoyles, jewelry, and

assorted home accessories—many with Frank Lloyd Wright motifs—are among the carefully chosen items for sale. Distinctive and educational children's toys like Archiblocks, Geomobiles, and origami and rubber stamp kits are also architecturally inspired. Check out the rest of the stunning Santa Fe building and ArchiCenter while you're here. Open Mon.–Sat. 9 A.M.–6:30 P.M., Sun. 9 A.M.–6 P.M.

City of Chicago Store
163 E. Pearson, 312/742-8811   **C**
Primarily souvenir purveyors, the **City of Chicago Store** also carries salvaged goodies from city departments for Chicagoans who want to accent their lives with that municipal touch: traffic lights, retired transit route and park district signs, street signs, sewer covers, parking meters, jewelry and doodads made of old CTA tokens, and more. Open Mon.–Sat. 9 A.M.–6 P.M., Sun. 10 A.M.–5 P.M.

The Stadium Seat Store
810 W. Irving Park, 773/404-7975, *www.stadiumseats.com*   **N**
If you can't always attend services at the Church of Baseball—Wrigley Field—maybe you'd like to make a shrine at home. Proprietor Peter Gottstein sells seats, and sometimes bricks or other architectural bric-a-brac, from the home of the Cubs. "The chairs are meant to be used," he says. "They're in working order and they'll last forever. The only thing I recommend you do with 'em is have a couple of Buds on 'em, or Old Styles." They ain't cheap, but there is a limited supply of this stuff. Bring cash and make an offer—this is Chicago. Irregular hours; call for an appointment.

Salvage One
1840 W. Hubbard, 312/733-0098, *www.salvageone.com*   **W**
Though not inexpensive, **Salvage One** boasts the largest collection of "used" building materials in Chicago. Much of the material has been salvaged from structures slated for demolition. Huge piles of doors, bins of doorknobs, and racks of switchplates whet your appetite for the main course: handrails, gates, chandeliers, mirrors, benches, bars, urns, statuary, and mantels. Throw in some stained and leaded glass, finials, columns, marble, ironwork, woodwork, paneling, and terra cotta for dessert and your home remodeling project will be done. Open Mon.–Sat. 11 A.M.–5 P.M., Sun. noon–4 P.M.

On a smaller (and dog-friendly!) scale, **Architectural Artifacts, Inc.** (4325 N. Ravenswood, 773/348-0622, *www.archartifacts.com*) sells stained glass windows, chandeliers and other period lighting, mirrors, fireplace mantels, garden furnishings, religious articles, tiles, cast and wrought iron, terra cotta, carved stone, other salvaged building materials, and a catch-all category they describe as "funkadelics" all cleaned up and ready to use. Open daily 10 A.M.–5 P.M.

Venture Statuary
5040 N. Clark, 773/334-3656   **FN**
Need a mini replica of the Statue of Liberty? The motto of this family-owned lawn statuary store is, "For the person who has everything, say it with concrete" (although they do also sell some plaster products). The jumbled showroom offers great browsing, with a fantasia of statues, birdbaths, and planters (although sometimes we worry about the proprietors, amidst the strong paint fumes). Word to the wise: Call ahead, as their hours are not etched in stone, though they're technically open daily 10:30 A.M.–5 P.M.

Art by Locals

Gallery 37 Store
66 E. Randolph, 312/744-7274, *http://gallery37.org/store/*   **C**
Chicago's extensive Gallery 37 programs apprentice young people ages 14–21 with established artists in a range of genres. Their works are then sold here to help support the program. Find paintings, sculptures, textiles, clothing, jewelry, wood carvings, ceramics, painted furniture, CDs, poetry books, and more—perfect for irreplaceable gifts. Open Mon.–Fri. 10 A.M.–6 P.M., Sat. 11 A.M.–4 P.M.

Illinois Artisans Shop
100 W. Randolph, 312/814-5321   **C**
Located in the James R. Thompson Center, this gift boutique markets arts and crafts from Illinois artisans. Woodworkers, feltmakers, quilters, beaders, photographers, painters, potters, and 60 different jewelry artisans are among the dozens of artists displaying their handiwork here. From fine art to county fair crafts, from the practical to the purely decorative, the **Illinois Artisans Shop** is impressive in its range of merchandise and its reasonable price tags. Open Mon.–Fri. 9 A.M.–5 P.M.

Bikes

A stone's throw from the Cabrini Green housing projects, in a former storefront church, is **Yojimbo's Garage** (1310 N. Clybourn, 312/587-0878). Although bike messengers make up the bulk of the clientele and the stock consists mostly of ultra-light road and track (single-gear, no hand breaks) bikes, all cyclists who visit will appreciate the welcoming atmosphere and detail-oriented wrenching at this small shop. Yojimbo's also sponsors the **Tour da Chicago**, an early-morning, messenger-style racing series which brings out dozens of riders of all abilities every other weekend during the dead of winter.

Urban Bikes (4653 N. Broadway, 773/728-5212) on the North Side and **The Blackstone Bicycle Works** (6100 S. Blackstone, 773/425-2011, *www.blackstonebike.com*) on the South Side are community-oriented shops that recycle old bikes and provide skills training for neighborhood children. Both offer programs where kids can learn about bikes while earning their own bicycles by putting in time fixing flats, repairing bikes for resale, and cleaning up the space. In 2001 the building that housed the Blackstone Bike Works was gutted by a fire, and the following year the program was moved to a temporary location at 61st and Kenwood. A new facility, **Experimental Station**, is being built at the old site to house Bike Works as well as artists and other environmental projects. It's scheduled to open Spring 2005.

Comic Books

Larry's Comic Book Store
1219 W. Devon, 773/274-1832, *www.scifispy.com*   FN
Most comic book stores these days feature "graphic novels," adult-oriented fare that's just as likely to have a nerd as the protagonist as it is a superhero. Larry's harks back to an earlier time, featuring flimsy-paged sagas of superheroes, spies, swordsmen, soldiers, and cowboys. In business since 1972, Owner Larry Charet estimates that he's got 20,000–30,000 comics and magazines for sale. Although he's got "a little bit of everything" (including some Japanese manga), he has especially good collections of Dr. Who and James Bond, and Sci Fi and movie magazines. The shop is dim, with peeling blue paint, but it only adds to the feeling that you might find some hidden treasure here. Open Mon.–Sat. noon–6 P.M., Sun. 1 P.M.–5 P.M.

Costumes

Beverly Costumes Inc.
11628 S. Western Ave., 773/779-0068   FSW
Have you ever wanted to be a banana? A Peanut? A Candy Bar? Or even a tooth? To make sure that your next Pirate attack isn't tacky or your next Roman Banquet is chic, give **Beverly Costumes** a call! No occasion is too

small or production too large for this neighborhood masterpiece. They have in stock a large selection of Santas, witches, angels, elves, farm animals, zoo animals, cops & crooks, sultans & slaves, and French maids & butlers to name a few. Outfit your harem, wagon train, or revolutionary war. The majority of costumes are for adults, but they do have a children's selection as well. Open Mon. 11 A.M.–4 P.M., Tue., Wed., Fri. 11 A.M.–5 P.M., Thur. 11 A.M.–7 P.M., Sat. 10 A.M.–2 P.M.

Fantasy Headquarters
4065 N. Milwaukee, 773/777-0222, *www.fantasycostumes.com*   **NW**
A block-long mega store equipped for every disguise and party need: 5,000 masks, 10,000 costumes for sale or rent, makeup and accessories (stage blood, fake noses, glow-in-the-dark facial decorations), 1,000 wigs on display (30,000 in stock), adult novelties and gag gifts, and party goods (luau decorations, streamers, helium tanks). Medieval garb, gangster attire, and Blues Brothers costumes are perennial favorites, and characters from the latest blockbuster or political campaign have a high turnover, too. Come too close to Halloween and even this superstore can't hold you—*you'll be waiting in line around the block*! Open Mon.–Fri. 9:30 A.M.–8 P.M., Sat. 9:30 A.M.–6 P.M., Sun. 11 A.M.–5 P.M.

Hats

Hats Plus
4706 W. Irving Park, 773/286-5577, *www.hats-plus.com*   **NW**
Revamp your image again and again from the 10,000 hats and 10,000 caps in over 500 styles at **Hats Plus**. The management lists the Panama and straw hats; fedoras; 30s and 40s style hats; golf, fishing, and baseball caps; and Greek fisherman's caps as their most popular styles. But if you prefer, you can always walk away topped with a propeller beanie, ear-flap hat, lambskin beret, Stetson, or furry Siberian number. Open Mon.–Wed. & Fri.–Sat. 10 A.M.–6 P.M., Thur. 10 A.M.–8 P.M., Sun. 11 A.M.–5 P.M.

Magazines and Newspapers

City Newsstand
4018 N. Cicero, 773/545-7377, *www.citynewsstand.com*   **NW**
This small and friendly neighborhood store has a periodical lineup that can't be beat in Chicago—or maybe anywhere else for that matter. You'll find Sunday papers from Maui and Prague, old monster magazines, France's *Purple Fashion*, *Armchair General*, *Mahogany Brides*, obscure literary

journals, and at least 6,000 other newspapers, magazines, and publications, including their own monthly newsletter, *The Mag Bag*, which has such priceless features as "Top 10 Tabloid Headlines" and "Things We Learned Reading Magazines." Open daily 7 A.M.–11 P.M.

Just getting started and taking a while to fill up their racks, **Wrigleyville News** (3420 N. Sheffield, 773/935-0058, *www.wrigleyvillenews.com*) also aspires to be the city's largest periodical dealer. What they lack in quantity, they're beginning to make up for in quality. Open daily 10 A.M.–9 P.M.

Quimby's Bookstore
1854 W. North, 773/342-0910, *www.quimbys.com*   **W**
Not surprisingly, the literate, eclectic, and supremely alternative **Quimby's Bookstore** says it better than anyone: they're "specialists in the importation, distribution, and sale of unusual publications, aberrant periodicals, saucy comic booklets and assorted fancies as well as a comprehensive miscellany of the latest independent 'zines' that all the kids have been talking about." That's all the books, graphic novels, comics, 'zines, chapbooks, vintage erotica, revolution, conspiracy, alchemy, mayhem, lowbrow art, and highbrow criticism you can handle. Open Mon.–Fri. noon–10 P.M., Sat. 11 A.M.–10 P.M., Sun. noon–6 P.M.

Magic

Izzy Rizzy's House of Tricks
6034 S. Pulaski Rd., 773/735-7370, *www.izzyrizzy.com*   **SW**
From the outside of this converted South Side house, you would never guess the amount of magic supplies, costumes, clown accessories, books, videos, pranks, novelties, bachelor(ette) party supplies, and odds and ends that are tucked away in this 35-year-old fun house. What used to be a popular ventriloquist school is now the only magic shop on the South Side and still prides itself on the personal instruction offered to those looking to enter the world of magic. Open Mon.–Fri. 10 A.M.–8 P.M., Sat. 10 A.M.–7 P.M.

Ash's Magic Shop (4955 N. Western, 773/271-4030, *www.ashs-magic.com*) is a small but overflowing magic shop, run by Ash (a veteran magician with 30 years under his belt) and his wife, that has been plugging along for over two decades. The friendly couple is quick to offer a cup of coffee and truthful advice to any aspiring magician browsing through the selection of tricks, gags, and instructional material. Just a couple blocks away is the granddaddy of Chicago magic shops: **Magic Inc.** (5082 N.

Lincoln, 73/334-2855, *www.magicinc.com*). According to owner Jay Marshall, "every magician who's anybody" has walked through the doors of this 80-year-old company's doors. As the dean of The Society of American Magicians, he should know. The family-run business caters to not only the amateur magician looking for supplies or instruction (they publish their own magic manuals to sell along with other tried-and-true books), but assist the professional magician with building props and stage illusions. **Magic Masters** (Navy Pier, 312/321-1100, *www.magicmasters.com*), the product of a 30-year-old company that targets touristy areas across America, is still pretty neat (and popular with the kids) despite being part of a chain. Intended for beginner magicians, this recreation of Houdini's library features a bookcase that spins the trick-buyer around into a secret room where the in-house magicians teach the "magic."

Models

Chicagoland Hobby
6017 N. Northwest Hwy., 773/775-4848, *www.chicagoland-hobby.com* **FN**
This 30-year-old hobby shop is predominantly a train fanatics dream, but also carries a few model cars and boats. Not only are they a "Kline Superstore," they have one of the largest selections of popular-again vintage models, sell new and used trains, do custom work and extensive repairs, and carry books and videos on model-making and railroad history. Open Mon.–Thur. 11 A.M.–7 P.M., Fri. 11 A.M.–8:30 P.M., Sat. 10 A.M.–5 P.M., Sun. noon–4:30 P.M. Closed Sun. May–Sept.

Musical Instruments

Snukst Music
6611 S. Pulaski Rd., 773/585-7923   **SW**
Somewhere between a museum and a shopping experience, **Snukst**'s has developed a loyal following among accomplished musicians and youngsters in school band programs. Wind your way through narrow aisles bumping into racks crowded with some of the most beautiful instruments imaginable, whether its guitars like the ones the Beatles played, handcrafted rhythm instruments, reed instruments for orchestras, or a handbook on how to play the penny whistle. Open Mon.–Sat. 10:30 A.M–8 P.M., Sun. 10:30 A.M.–5 P.M.

Chicago Music Exchange (3270 N. Clark, 773/477-0830, *www.chicagomusicexchange.com*) consists of two storefronts with four rooms of vintage instruments to explore, including many odd birds. The collection of old acoustic guitars in the back room is especially impressive, with many beautiful old models, some costing thousands of dollars. Open Mon.–Fri. 11 A.M.–7 P.M., Sat. 11 A.M.–6 P.M., Sun. noon–5 p.m. **The Different Strummer** at the Old Town School of Folk Music (4544 N. Lincoln, 773/751-3398, *www.oldtownschool.org/Strummer*), with it's knowledgeable, attitude-free staff, is a great place to buy your first acoustic guitar (or bass, banjo, mandolin, or dulcimer). The collection of international percussion instruments is also impressive. Look for their annual garage sale one weekend each August. Open Mon.–Thur. 10 A.M.–5:30 P.M., Fri.–Sat. 10 A.M.–5 P.M. **Midwest Music Exchange** (6019 W. Irving Park, 773/545-2020) is a small, disorganized shop where Chicago's rock musicians go to unearth strange old electric guitars and amplifiers. Drop by every month or so to see what new treasures have washed up. It's also a good place to sell or trade your old gear. Open Mon.–Tues. 10 A.M.–6 P.M., Wed. noon–6 P.M., Thur.–Fri. noon–7 P.M., Sat. 10 A.M.–5 P.M.

Occult/Metaphysical

Alchemy Arts Metaphysical Books and Supplies
1203 W. Bryn Mawr, 773/769-4970, 800/348-6766
www.alchemy-arts.com   FN
This spacious Edgewater store may be clean, tidy, and well-lit, but, they assure us, they are "not New Age." Focusing on "older-style occult and metaphysical," they offer books, incense, herbs, candles, oils, magazines, figurines, amulets, jewelry, and curios (like the skull replica toilet brush holder). **Alchemy Arts** has been around in various incarnations (once it was strictly mail order) and at various locations for 20 years, and now offers rare arcana to a clientele both local and global. Open Sun.–Tue. noon–6 P.M., Wed.–Sat. 11 A.M.–7 P.M.

Augustine's Spiritual Goods
3114 S. Halsted, 312/326-5467, *www.augustinespiritualgoods.com*   SW
The owners of this Bridgeport shop, PaPa Doc and Miss Alice, native Chicagoans themselves, take their voodoo and spirituality seriously. Jokesters and unattended children will be asked, politely but firmly, to leave. The shop's wide-ranging inventory includes potions, amulets, talismans, house blessings, tarot cards, candles, books on Wicca and witchcraft, and Christian religious statues. Augustine's also provides astrological services such as natal and relationship reports. Open Mon.–Thur. 11 A.M.–7 P.M., Fri.–Sat. 11 A.M.–6 P.M.

Occult Bookstore
1579 N. Milwaukee, Ste. 321, 773/292-0995
http://users.rcn.com/occult/occulus   **W**
In business for almost 90 years in various locations, the **Occult Bookstore** moved from a Milwaukee Avenue storefront to a third-floor space in the Flat Iron Building some years back, but all else remains the same. The stacks of new and used books cover magick, metaphysics, Wicca, UFOs, tarot, astrology, alternative healing, Kabbalah, freemasonry, Theosophy, Eastern religions, esoteric Christianity, Santeria, and more. There's also a large selection of candles, herbs, incense, and similar supplies. Open Mon.–Thur. noon–7 P.M., Fri.–Sat. noon–8 P.M., Sun. noon–6 P.M.

Paper

Alphabétique
701 W. Armitage, 312/751-2920, *www.alphabetiquechicago.com*   **N**
A common bond over paper led sisters Kristyn and Karyn to open this high-end paper boutique that carries virtually every type of paper from Japanese Yuzen to Thai Marbled, from those with simple patterns to the most ornate. For the correspondence devotees, the handsewn envelopes with matching paper, the scented Italian ink, and the colorful wax seals transform everyday letters into a beautiful experience. And for special occasions, either one of the owners or staff will sit down for a private consultation to help you choose custom letterpress invitations, cards, and extras in any style that you can dream up. A little pricey but comparable for the quality. Open Mon.–Fri. 11 A.M.–7 P.M., Sat. 10 A.M.–6 P.M., Sun. noon–5 P.M.

Paper Boy
1351 W. Belmont, 773/388-8811
www.unclefunchicago.com/pboy.html   **N**
This full-service stationer features handmade papers from as far away as India and Japan and as nearby as Chicago. Paper and envelopes are sold by the piece or in sets for a pretty fair price. Custom thermography and letterpress are available, and local work includes Snow & Graham letterpress and the popular "Unique Artistry" from Andrea Ummel. Open Mon.–Fri. noon–7 P.M., Sat. 11 A.M.–7 P.M., Sun. 11 A.M.–5 P.M. The sister store, **Fly Paper** (3402 N. Southport, 773/296-4339, *www.unclefunchicago.com/fly.html*), is a tiny storefront that acts more as a neighborhood card store with an array of cute cards, wrapping paper, and gifts. Both are owned by the popular old toy store, **Uncle Fun** (p. 386). Open Tues.–Fri. noon–7 P.M., Sat. 11 A.M.–7 P.M., Sun. 11 A.M.–5 P.M.

The Paper Source
232 W. Chicago, 312/337-0798   C
919 W. Armitage, 773/525-7300   N
www.paper-source.com
Chicago's original fancy paper store, **The Paper Source**'s extravagant array of homemade papers, paper and wood gifts, classy stationery items, extensive rubber stamp and ink pad collection, and supplies for book binding, calligraphy, and collage-making retain customer loyalty even as competitors keep popping up. Open Mon.–Fri. 10 A.M.–7 P.M., Sat. 10 A.M.–6 P.M., Sun. noon–5 P.M.

Pop Culture Stuff

Quake Collectibles
4628 N. Lincoln, 773/878-4288   N
This 15-year-old shop of collectible toys and pop culture artifacts transfixes people of all ages and all walks of life—some so much so that they linger for hours or volunteer to organize the GI Joe section so they can continue hanging out. Besides the fact that it's never the same store twice, the beauty is you can find a mountain of things in the $1–$10 bracket or stumble on that rare find for $400. Looking for Stars Wars everything, vintage lunch boxes, Pez dispensers, old board games, action figures, transformers, concert T-shirts, or all manner of mugs, banks, alarm clocks—anything—emblazoned with folks like Snoopy, Daisy Duke, Mr. Spock, the Incredible Hulk, and Ronald McDonald? Owner David Gutterman's your man. If it's not in the store, it may be in the basement or in the collection of someone he knows. He'll locate the object of your desire and probably memorize your collection preferences for next time. Open Mon. & Wed.–Fri. 1 P.M.–6 P.M., Fri. noon–6 P.M., Sat. noon–5 P.M.

Uncle Fun
1388 W. Belmont, 773/477-8223, *www.unclefunchicago.com*   N
This Belmont Avenue essential proclaims itself to be "a toy store and so much more," and it must be experienced first hand to fully understand the truth to this statement. It's really *is* like visiting a fun uncle, one that happens to have an eye for merchandising. Quirky pop culture collectibles mingle with novelties, gags, fun gifts, and unusual toys from around the world. The prices are so low you'll never leave empty handed. Open Tues.–Fri. noon–7 P.M., Sat. 11 A.M.–7 P.M., Sun. 11 A.M.–5 P.M.

Yesterday
1143 W. Addison, 773/248-8087   **N**
You've seen it . . . the odd, little misfit building everyone passes on the south
side of Addision on the long walk from their car to Wrigley Field. Now
you'll know what's inside: If it's old, made of paper, and referring to bygone
days of movies, television, sports, celebrities, and historic events, it's
probably somewhere in **Yesterday**'s collection of newspapers, magazines,
comics, posters, cardboard cut-outs, baseball cards, and photographs.
There's currently lots of 70s stuff. Open Mon.–Sat. 1 P.M.–7 P.M., Sun. 2
P.M.–6 P.M.

Posters

Poster Plus
200 S. Michigan, 312/461-9277, *www.posterplus.com*   **C**
Idle away a couple of hours in their three-floor shop across from the Art
Institute poring over the thousands of vintage and contemporary posters on
display. Once inspired, you may want some of their fine art for everyday
life: O'Keefe mousepads, Degas serving trays, Kandinsky mugs, Magritte
puzzles, etc. Founded in 1969, this is Chicago's oldest poster store and
remains the most comprehensive. Open Mon.–Fri. 10 A.M.–6 P.M. (Tues. 'til
8 P.M.), Sat. 9:30 A.M.–6 P.M., Sun. 11 A.M.–6 P.M.

Surplus Stuff

American Science and Surplus
5316 N. Milwaukee, 773/763-0313, *www.sciplus.com*   **FN**
Being useful since about 1937! Countless aisles and bins overflow with an
extraordinary array of other companies' unrelated baubles, leftovers, mis-
takes, and pieces–parts, etc. Find what you need for that science, art, or
home improvement project super cheap: tubes, cords, magnets, wires,
motors, lenses, compasses, doll heads, plastic body parts, rubber animals,
light blue masking tape, vinyl bank bags, and thousands of additional items.
Open Mon.–Fri. 10 A.M.–8 P.M. (Thur. 'til 9 P.M.), Sat. 9 A.M.–5 P.M., Sun. 11
A.M.–5 P.M.

Creative Reuse Warehouse
222 E.135th Pl., 312/421-3640
www.resourcecenterchicago.org/crw.html   **C**
Reduce, reuse, recycle is the idea behind this non-profit distributor of
business scraps and surplus. **Creative Reuse Warehouse** makes items

otherwise headed for a landfill available at low cost to teachers, artists, non-profit groups, and the public. Select items have price tags, but the general fee is a few bucks per bag. Most of these goodies are "raw" (fabrics, leather, yarns, plastics, wood pieces, metals, and plenty of whatchimacallits) and require *imaginative* re-use. Open Mon.–Fri. 10 A.M.–3 P.M., Sat. 10 A.M.–6 P.M.

Wine

Kafka Wine Co.
3325 N. Halsted, 773/975-9463, *www.kafkawine.com*   **N**
Kafka refers to owner Joe Kafka, but this is a wine store metamorphosis nonetheless. The shop is oriented entirely for the typical wine drinker and not anyone who might be snooty enough to call themselves an *oenophile* (or even know what one is). That is, it's non-intimidating, user-friendly, afford-able, and commonsense. Nearly every bottle is under $15, and the wines are organized by flavor traits, not grapes: earthy, toasty, fruity, spicy, floral, herbal, etc. Throw in the care of the staff in choosing the wines to begin with, add their expertise in directing you to what you'll like, and you'll walk away with a winner every time. Open Mon.–Sat. noon–10 P.M., Sun. noon–7 P.M.

Resale Shopping

EXTENSIVE coverage of Chicago's resale options is provided below for various reasons. First and foremost, this is where you'll spend the least amount of money for the most stuff. Secondly, as most of these places are operated by individuals or non-profit organizations, they are unique to Chicago. K-Mart, Sears, and Marshall Field's can be patronized in any old city. These stores and markets can lure you into new neighborhoods to explore. Then, as any experienced resale shopper can tell you, it's not just about acquiring things—it's a hobby, an adventure. You'll often have to search for what you want, but those we know who work this circuit often can find almost *anything* they want in a week or less, and usually by visiting just a handful of stores in one afternoon. What about the societal gains? This is recycling far beyond the realm of bottles and cans. Local charitable organi-zations benefit when you buy from them. Finally, second-hand merchandise is the perfect affordable option for those who don't want to wear or own the same things as everyone else.

Specialty Resale Stores

You won't be rummaging through a haystack of junk to find the needle you want at these places. This listing contains specialized resale shops, most dealing with high-quality merchandise. They sell the sorts of things you may not mind buying used: appliances, books, building parts, children's clothing and goods, furniture for home and office (including hotel/motel furniture), men's suits, music, sporting goods, vintage clothing, and women's designer and consignment clothing.

Appliances

Before shelling out for big-ticket appliances like stoves, refrigerators, washers, and dryers, you may want to check out the second hand items available at **McCoy New & Used Furniture & Appliance** (7259 S. Halsted, 773/994-9000), **M&G Appliances** (3248 W. North Ave., 773/862-4688), and **BUA Used Appliances** (4226 S. Ashland, 773/927-1665). For these appliances plus temperature control appliances (heating units, water heaters, air conditioners, etc.), there's **Vargus Used Appliances** (3248 W. 25th, 773/762-2340).

Books

After-Words
23 E. Illinois, 312/464-1110   C
The only used bookstore on the north side of downtown sells new books on its ground level and 30,000 used books in its basement. In a renovated old warehouse on a relatively quiet stretch, just a stone's throw from Michigan Avenue, **After-Words** makes a great escape. Their titles span from the popular to the unusual to the obscure and are fairly priced. Coffee and internet access available. Open Mon.–Thur. 10:30 A.M.–10 P.M., Fri.–Sat. 10:30 A.M.–11 P.M., Sun. noon–7 P.M.

The Armadillo's Pillow
6753 N. Sheridan, 773/761-2558   FN
Small, general used bookstore draws Loyola University students and neighbors for the carefully culled offerings sold at reasonable prices. Natural history, fiction, and children's book offerings are particularly noteworthy. The jewelry, gifts, incense, and rustic Bohemian charm make it a bona fide Rogers Park establishment. Open daily noon–8 P.M.

Bookleggers Used Books
2904 N. Broadway, 773/404-8780   N
Packed shelves, narrow aisles, decent organization, and a varied, quality collection of respectable art, photography, architecture, fiction, literature, literary criticism, philosophy, religion, Chicago history, and audio/video sections give bibliophiles all they need to be loyal patrons. Open daily noon–9 P.M.

The Bookworks
3444 N. Clark, 773/871-5318   N
Bookworks' rare and general used book collection includes art, photography, history, psychology, literature, contemporary fiction, CDs, vinyl, and enough sports in the window to nab the eye of Cubs' fans on the way to or from Wrigley. Open Mon.–Thur. noon–10 P.M., Fri.–Sat. noon–11 P.M., Sun. noon–6 P.M.

The Gallery Bookstore Ltd.
923 W. Belmont, 773/975-8200   N
Established in 1927, the Gallery Bookstore is a general used bookstore, though its **Florence Hanley Memorial Wing**, devoted to vintage, collectible, and quality mystery, science fiction, and horror is in itself the city's oldest and last "genre shop." Some of its holdings date back to the early twentieth century and occasionally some predate that. Open Mon.–Fri. 1 P.M.–8 P.M., Sat. noon–8 P.M., Sun. noon–7 P.M.

Myopic Books
1564 N. Milwaukee, 773/862-4882, *www.myopicbookstore.com*   W
Open until 1 A.M. six nights a week, **Myopic** is a nightlife destination in its own right and deserves to be kept in mind for a drop-in by anyone passing through Wicker Park at any hour. With three floors and 80,000 volumes of used, rare, and collectible books in 78 different subject areas, this is one of Chicago's largest used bookstores. Other perks include coffee, a poetry series Sun. at 7 P.M., and rotating art exhibits. Open Mon.–Sat. 11 A.M.–1 A.M., Sun. 11 A.M.–10 P.M.

N. Fagin Books
459 N. Milwaukee, 312/829-5252   C
This specialty store deals in used (particularly academic and rare) anthropology, archeology, botany, zoology, natural history, linguistics, and ethnic art books. Call ahead. You must be buzzed in.

New World Resource Center
1300 N. Western, 312/227-4011, *www.newworldresourcecenter.com* **W**
Founded in 1971 and run solely by volunteers, this non-profit, left-wing bookstore has a used book room with bargains galore. While some are the expected tomes on politics, economics, human rights, and various progressive causes, others reflect a broad range of subjects, and all are inexpensive. There's also a good collection of $2 paperbacks, mostly those classics you've been meaning to read one day. Open Tues.–Fri. 3 P.M.–9 P.M., Sat.–Sun. noon–7 P.M.

Powell's Book Stores
2850 N. Lincoln, 773/248-1444　　　　　　　　　　　　　　　**N**
Open Sun.–Fri. 11 A.M.–9 P.M., Sat. 10 A.M.–10 P.M.
1501 E. 57th, 773/955-7780　　　　　　　　　　　　　　　　**S**
Open daily 9 A.M.–11 P.M.
828 S. Wabash, 312/341-0748　　　　　　　　　　　　　　　**C**
Open Mon.–Fri. 10:30 A.M.–6 P.M., Sat. 10 A.M.–6 P.M., Sun. noon–5 P.M.
www.powellschicago.com
These large and much loved bookstores stock used and remaindered, serious, quality, and scholarly titles in over 100 different fields, with significant history, ancient history, medieval studies, classics, archaeology, philosophy, art, photography, and fiction collections. Each store is estimated to have at least a quarter of a million titles. **Powell's** and co-owner Brad Jonas are also involved in distributing reprints of Oxford University press titles, selling wholesale to other bookstores, running the CIROBE annual remainder show in Chicago, and other local book events.

Prairie Avenue Bookshop
418 S. Wabash, 312/922-8311, *www.pabook.com*　　　　　　　**C**
Called the "best architectural bookshop in the world" by the *London Financial Times*, the United States' largest architectural bookstore sells new and used books on architecture, interior design, and urban planning in a setting filled with architectural artifacts and furniture. Make sure to pop in next time you're downtown with some spare time on your hands. Open Mon.–Fri. 10 A.M.–6 P.M., Sat. 10 A.M.–4 P.M.

Selected Works
3510 N. Broadway, 773/975-0002　　　　　　　　　　　　　　**N**
This broad collection offers more academic subjects like classical studies, philosophy, anthropology, theology, history, psychology, poetry, and literature beside the more popular ones like sci fi, mystery, fiction, cookbooks, metaphysical, and second-hand sheet music. Open daily noon–9 P.M.

Shake Rattle & Read Book Box
4812 N. Broadway, 773/334-5311   **FN**
Let Ric Addy's special assemblage of books, vinyl, and a half-century of
pop culture grab your attention next time you're in Uptown in the middle of
the day. Books focus on pop culture, Hollywood, militaria, cookbooks,
mysteries, pulp fiction, and the latest paperback reads. The music section
has records (mostly rock and jazz), but also some CDs and cassettes. Then
there are comics, posters, and plenty of old magazines (check out the vintage
rock 'n' roll magazines). Open daily noon–6 P.M.

Children's Items

Clothes (infant–size 14), furniture (cribs, beds, bassinets, dressers, hi-
chairs), bedding and receiving blankets, toys (bikes, outdoor equipment,
plush stuffed animals), strollers, nursery decorations, and more make **First
Seconds Resale** (4266 N. Milwaukee, 773/777-2200) a great resource for
parents. Most items are sold on consignment, but cash is paid for toys and
furniture. **Once Upon A Child** (5316 N. Milwaukee, 773/594-1705,
www.ouac.com) has similar items, as do **The Second Child** (954 W.
Armitage, 773/883-0880, *www.2ndchild.com*) and **Children's Wearhouse**
(2640 W. Pratt, 773/761-3572), both of which carry maternity clothes as
well.

Clothing, Bridal

Cynthia's Consignments
2218 N. Clybourn, 773/248-7714
www.cynthiasconsignments.com/bridal.htm   **N**
With over 2,000 high-fashion wedding gowns—none over two years old—
Cynthia's has the largest and most impressive designer bridal consignment
in the city. In fact some of her stock is so current, the same dresses are still
selling at full-price on the racks of the area's elite bridal shops. Though
many of the dresses have been worn once, others are samples and exclusive
end-of-the season buyouts from those designer boutiques. Veils and bridal
accessories are also available. Everything is 50–80% off retail. Owner
Cynthia Hodgkins is a model and former Miss Illinois. Open Mon. 11 A.M.–7
P.M., Tues.–Sat. 11 A.M.–6 P.M., Sun. noon–5 P.M.

I–Do Designer Bridal Consignment
6742 W. Belmont, 773/205-1234   **FN**
Voted Chicago's #1 bridal resale shop by *Chicago* magazine two years in a

row, the store carries over 500 discontinued designs, floor samples, and vintage gowns from the 1930s to the present, as well as "once-worn" gowns (cleaned and bagged). In addition to a wide array of veils, tiaras, and petticoats, an excellent in-house seamstress is available for custom alterations. Open Tues.–Fri. noon–8 P.M., Sat.–Sun. noon–6 P.M.

Check out **Silver Moon** and **Wacky Cats** in the Vintage Clothing section (p. 395) for vintage wedding gear.

Clothing, Men's

Duomo Men's Designer Resale
2906 N. Broadway, 773/325-2325 N

In the spirit of Chicago's many designer resale and consignment shops for women, comes this one for men who want to dress fashionably without spending a fortune. Very particular in its selection, the store's stock includes end-of-season merchandise from the area's most exclusive boutiques along with cleaned and pressed consignment clothing no more than two seasons old. Expect Calvin Klein, Claude Montana, Hugo Boss, Armani, Versace, Gucci, Prada, Gautier, and peers on the labels. Open Mon.–Sat. 11 A.M.–7 P.M., Sun. noon–5 P.M.

Monitor Formal Wear
1422 W. Wilson, 773/561-0573, *www.monitorformalwear.com* N

While they promote their wares to entertainers, caterers, and waiters, **Monitor** probably has a piece of used or vintage formalwear just for you, too. Suits, tuxedos, dinner jackets, sports coats, vests, cummerbunds, shirts, shoes, scarves, canes, and jewelry are all available for an affordable special occasion transformation. Open Mon.–Fri. 10 A.M.–7 P.M., Sat. 10 A.M.–6 P.M.

Suitsmart
115 N. Wabash, 2nd Floor, 312/236-SUIT, *www.suitsmart.com* C

Known for their service as well as their selection, **Suitsmart** was the first in the area to handle gently-used men's clothing. (Their inventory also includes closeouts and overstocks.) Used and new items are all department store and designer brands, up-to-date in style, free of major flaws, and well-labeled with size information. Trade in your older suit for an updated style. Tailoring available. Open Mon.–Fri. 10 A.M.–6 P.M. (Thur. until 7 P.M.), Sat.–Sun. 11 A.M.–5 P.M.

Clothing, Vintage

Beatnix

3400 N. Halsted, 773/281-6933 **N**

Everything necessary for a 60s/70s look can be found here, and they may even be inching 80s-ward. Bell bottoms? Platform Shoes? Wigs? Something plaid, polyester, or otherwise wacky in texture, color, or cut? They've got it. Just maybe, you want a retro tux for say . . . catering or table waiting as they suggest? Plenty of leather and buckskin jackets, jewelry, purses, bags, belts, ties, and tiaras also await. Pop in late on the weekends for some last-minute clubbing get-up. Open Mon.–Thur. 11 A.M.–9 or 10 P.M., Fri.–Sat. 11 A.M.–11 P.M. or midnight, Sun. noon–9 P.M.

Hubba-Hubba

3309 N. Clark, 773/477-1414 **N**

If vintage spells romance for you, hurry over to Hubba-Hubba for items from the 1950s and earlier, as well as newer vintage-inspired articles. Start a search for that special occasion dress or tuxedo here or pick up a beaded sweater or gabardine jacket for everyday use. Dripping in lace, pearls, crystal, and rhinestones and perfumed with a floral scent, the second floor's jewelry, accessories, frames, housewares, and linens offer girly girl shopping at its best. Parking in rear. Open Mon.–Sat. 11 A.M.–7 P.M., Sun. noon–5 P.M.

Land of the Lost

614 W. Belmont, 773/529-4966 **N**

This small subterranean store is jam-packed with resale clothing that is among the best-priced in the city and guaranteed to add fashion flavor to aficionados of decades past. Leather jackets of various styles are a steal for around $20–$50 and the Levi's (in denim and corduroy) are all priced around $20. In addition, a nice mix of shirts from retro butterfly-collared to iron-on Ts are plentiful, and collectible lunchboxes, ashtrays, and miscellaneous items are scattered throughout the shop. Open daily noon–7 P.M.

Lost Eras Costumes & Props

1511 W. Howard, 773/764-7400, *www.losteras.com* **FN**

This third-generation family business has been costuming the public and theater and movie casts since 1969. Whether you need to create a historic or fantastic look, or merely have a theatrical fashion sense to tend to, *something* from their stock of 1,000,000 costumes, at least 10,000 of which are vintage, will call your name. Antiques, props, and miscellanous garage sale finds, too! Open Mon.–Sat. 10 A.M.–6 P.M., Sun. noon–5 P.M.

Night and Day
2252 W. Belmont, 773/327-4045   N
Previously Vintage Deluxe 2, this shop on the Belmont antique strip
specializes in men's and women's clothing from the 20s through 60s. They
have a good selection of extra-large clothing, which is often hard to find,
plus home furnishings and nifty knick-knacks. Open Wed.–Sun. 2 P.M.–7
P.M.

Shangrila
1952 W. Roscoe, 773/348-5090   N
Self-described as the "smallest and least expensive" of the local vintage
dealers, due to their high turnover, **Shangrila** mixes some contemporary
used clothing into their selection of goods from the 1930s to the 1970s.
Along with their casual and fancy attire, you'll find shoes, handbags, and
jewelry. Grab something from their collection of pulp novels and LPs to
help authenticate a new look. Open Mon.–Fri. noon–7 P.M., Sat noon –6 P.M.,
Sun. noon–5 P.M.

Silver Moon
3337 N. Halsted, 773/883-0222   N
They "don't do junk here" is what I'm told. Instead, they pack two rooms
with inviting vintage from the 1890s to the 1960s. One room is devoted to
clothing, with a notable selection of hats and men's suits, tails, and tuxes.
The other displays a collection of wedding gowns, jewelry, accessories,
shoes, and antiques and oddities from the 40s and earlier. Open Wed.–Sat.
noon–8 P.M., Sun. noon–5 P.M.

Strange Cargo
3448 N. Clark, 773/327-8090   N
Modern vintage of the 50s–70s comprises the strange cargo pedaled here.
Police jackets, Levi's 501s, overalls, bowling shirts, iron-ons, and old
models of athletic footwear—unused Converse, Nike, Keds, and more—top
the big sellers list. Also, women's casual and formal apparel, jewelry, and
hats. Open daily from 11 A.M.–6:45 P.M., closes Sun. at 5:30 P.M.

Wacky Cats
3012 N. Lincoln, 773/929-6701, *www.wackycats.com*   N
Wacky since 1988. Women's causal and formalwear, wedding gowns, men's
shirts and suits, hats, shoes, lingerie, and accessories dating from the 1920s
to the 1970s make up the **Wacky Cats** inventory. Open Mon.–Fri. noon–7
P.M., Sat. noon–6 P.M., Sun. noon–7 P.M.

Clothing, Women's

Any gal whose fashion sense is grander than her wallet needs a few favorite consignment shops to turn to...frequently. Their turnover system keeps stock fresh and seasonal—prices are typically marked down systematically over a period of weeks to keep things moving. And the better places take only clothes less than two years old that have been dry-cleaned (or at least washed), pressed, and supplied on a hanger. What's not sold in a reasonable amount of time is either returned to the consignor or donated to charity.

Buy Choice Resale
3860 N. Lincoln, 773/296-4525   **N**
Free of the downtown attitude, **Buy Choice** may actually deserve owner–sisters Cathy and Clay's self-election of their store as "Chicago's Friendliest Consignment Shop." Their selection includes everything from casual to formal department store and designer clothing (petite to plus sizes), along with shoes (to size 11), hats, jewelry, sunglasses, and purses. Open Tues.–Wed. noon–7 P.M., Thur.–Fri. noon–8 P.M., Sat.–Sun. noon–5 P.M.

Buy Popular Demand
2629 N. Halsted, 773/868-0404   **N**
Another friendly consignment shop, **Buy Popular Demand**'s only irksome quality is the overstuffed racks that make it hard to browse quickly. Get on their mailing list to be notified about their great seasonal sales. Open Mon.–Fri. 11 A.M.–7 P.M., Sun. 11 A.M.–5 P.M.

Cynthia's Consignments
2218 N. Clybourn, 773/248-7714, *www.cynthiasconsignments.com*   **N**
Cynthia's specializes in high-quality, top designer (Dolce & Gabana, Donna Karan, Prada, Versace, and cohorts) consignment clothing: cleaned, pressed, no more than two seasons old, and probably from a socialite more fashionable than thou—or me, at least. Other garments aren't even "gently used," rather stock overruns and year-end leftovers from exclusive city and North Shore boutiques. Evening gown rentals also available. See *Clothing, Bridal* on p. 392 for information on Cynthia's designer bridalwear bargains. Open Mon. 11 A.M.–7 P.M., Tues.–Sat. 11 A.M.–6 P.M., Sun. noon–5 P.M.

The Daisy Shop
67 E. Oak, 6th Floor, 312/943-8880, *www.daisyshop.com*   **C**
Called "a jewel of a resale shop" by local fashion editors and "sartorial resale splendor" by themselves, **The Daisy Shop** is the place to spend your money after simply browsing through the exclusive Oak Street boutiques.

(Because if you don't know their actual prices ahead of time, you won't realize what a discount you're getting for your hundreds-of-dollars something.) Armani, Chanel, Lagerfeld, Hermes, Escada, and Mizrahi are but a few of the 75 couturiers the shop discriminatingly accepts—its 2,000-item inventory gleaned from the best dressed women in Chicago, Boston, New York, and Palm Beach. Lest you have nothing to complement your haute purchases, the shop also carries fine jewelry, appraised signed costume jewelry, and authenticated accessories on consignment for completing any ensemble. Open Mon.–Sat. 11 A.M.–6 P.M., Sun. noon–5 P.M.

Designer Resale East
658 N. Dearborn, 312/587-3312   **C**
Don't be surprised to find certain price tags here inching perilously up into the hundreds of dollars. The designer and couture clothing, shoes, and accessories sold are likely closeouts or consigned by that sliver of society who can afford to buy things they never wear—you'll find the original tags still on some of this stuff. Yet, there are big bargains for what it is, as well as bargains for the rest of us, especially when pieces are marked down to move. Open Mon.–Fri. 11 A.M.–6 P.M., Sat.–Sun. 11 A.M.–5 P.M.

I Saw It First
2153 W. Irving Park, 773/866-0188   **N**
This brand new (July 2004) women's resale and consignment shop is making a strong start with an opening selection of fun, cute, vintage-inspired, and trendy clothing and accessories. Open Mon., Wed., Fri. 3 P.M.–7 P.M., Sat. 11 A.M.–6 P.M., Sun. 12:30 P.M.–5 P.M.

McShane's Exchange
815 W. Armitage, 773/525-0282   **N**
1141 W. Webster, 773/525-0211   **N**
Great prices and selection make designer clothing accessible to women of all budgets at these extremely popular consignment shops. As they like to say: We're "14 blocks above Bendel's [Henri Bendel's at 900 N. Michigan Avenue] and about 80% below." Open Mon.–Fri. 11 A.M.–7 P.M., Sat. 10 A.M.–6 P.M., Sun. noon–5 P.M.

My Closet
3350 N. Paulina, 773/388-9851   **N**
This newer Roscoe Village shop offers a mix of high-end resale and vintage clothes. You'll find plenty of funky vintage dresses for $10 or less, and rows of brand name dresses, skirts, tops, and jeans for bargain prices. Lots of Express dresses go for around $14, but expect to pay $20 or more for big

labels like Ralph Lauren or Donna Karan. A rack of vintage Levi's are mostly priced under $10. The store's walls are lined with shelves of barely or never-worn major label shoes that range from $15 to $25. In terms of quality and selection, this is definitely one of the nicest consignment stores this shopper has seen in a long time. Open Mon.–Fri. 11 A.M.–8 P.M., Sat 11 A.M.–6 P.M., Sun. noon–5 P.M.

My Sister's Closet
5413 W. Devon, 773/774-5050   **FN**
This 22-year-old Edgebrook business deals in resale clothing and "samples" for women and children. Accessories available include shoes, purses, scarves, and jewelry (fine, antique, and costume). Maternity wear, perfume, home decor, and antiques are also sold. Open Mon.–Fri. 10 A.M.–6 P.M., Sat. 10 A.M.–5 P.M., Sun. 11 A.M.–4 P.M.

Secret Closet
4617 N. Lincoln, 773/293-2903   **N**
Specializing in newer, nicer women's clothing, the stand-out feature of this Lincoln Square boutique are the daily colored tag sales. The percentage of each color changes often, but you can find clothes 20–80% off everyday. They also sell children's clothing, accessories, and some antique furniture. Open Mon.–Fri. 1 P.M.–7 P.M., Sat. 11 A.M.–7 P.M., Sun. 11 A.M.–5 P.M.

Selections
2152 N. Clybourn, 773/296-4014   **N**
Armani, Escada, DKNY, Ralph Lauren, Dana Buchman . . . these are the types of labels (and relative price tags) to expect from **Selections'** selection of better consignment clothing and accessories. There's also a small men's section. Open Mon.–Thur. 11 A.M.–7 P.M., Fri. 11 A.M.–6 P.M., Sat. 10 A.M.–6 P.M., Sun. noon–5 P.M.

Clothing, Women's and Men's

Disgraceland
3338 N. Clark, 773/281-5875   **N**
Disgraceland specializes in high-quality casual wear (mostly current, some vintage) from labels like the Limited, Gap, and Betsy Johnson. Expect lots of jeans, shoes, and boots, as well as jewelry, hats, scarves, and accessories. Open Mon.–Sat. 11 A.M.–7 P.M., Sun. noon–6 P.M.

Ragstock
812 W. Belmont, 2nd floor, 773/868-9263   N
Open Mon.–Fri. 10 A.M.–9 P.M., Sat. 10 A.M.–10 P.M., Sun. noon–8 P.M.
226 S. Wabash #2, 312/692-1778   C
Open Mon.–Fri. 10 A.M.–8 P.M., Sat. 10 A.M.–7 P.M., Sun. noon–6 P.M.
6431 N. Sheridan, 773/465-1539   FN
Open Mon.–Fri. 10 A.M.–8 P.M., Sat. 10 A.M.–7 P.M., Sun. noon–5 P.M.
www.ragstock.com
This mish-mash of 60s–80s retrowear, flannels, military surplus, kimonos, hoodies, cute skirts, and miscellanous inexpensive, new clothing caters to those inclined towards mix-and-match creative dressing.

Recycle
1474 N. Milwaukee, 773/645-1900   W
This vintage and designer consignment boutique for women and men does carry the contemporary labels those old guard and new-arrival Wicker Park kids are wearing, but their inventory is broad enough to appeal to a more diverse clientele. Open Mon.–Sat. 11 A.M.–7 P.M., Sun 11 A.M.–5 P.M.

Threads, Etc.
2327 N. Milwaukee, 773/276-6411   N
Their better casual and formal threads for men and women cram the huge first floor space (furniture, houseware, and more on the second floor). Brooks Brothers, Armani, Polo, Mark Shale, Ann Taylor, Ann Klein, Liz Claiborne, Gap, Levi's, Express, and Banana Republic typify the labels available here. Notable collections includes jeans, leather, formalwear, shoes, accessories, purses, belts, jewelry, and some vintage items. Open Mon.–Fri. 11 A.M.–7 P.M., Sun. 11 A.M.–5 P.M.

Computers

Chicago Cyber Exchange
455 W. North, 312/337-4882, *www.ccenow.com*   C
Though used computer games and software are the big-sellers here, they're just some of the ways that one can save on the high costs of being a technophile. Used hardware is also available, including complete computer systems, laptops, printers, scanners, digital cameras, and networking equipment. Staff members can build, fix, restore, maintain, and network systems too for a reasonable price. All software is checked for viruses and to ensure it's in proper working order. Store credit available for your old products. Open Mon.–Fri. 10 A.M.–7 P.M., Sat. 10 A.M.–1 P.M.

Furniture, Home

Used furniture dealers and resale shops with a significant furniture selection dot the city. Here are some good choices to start your hunt for just the right living room, dining room, bedroom, and kitchen furniture that are more reliable, established, and diverse in their offerings. You can also pick up carpeting, major appliances, antiques, and lighting at many of them, too. Head northwest for the biggest concentration of resale furniture shops: **AAA Furniture Harlem Thrift Store** (7186 W. Grand, 773/889-0639), **Best Thrift** (3115 W. Irving Park, 773/583-2880), **Junk 'n' Treasures** (4041 N. Milwuakee, 773/283-2002), **Millennium Liquidators Thrifty Resale** (2911 N. Central, 773/725-3130), and **RPN Sales** (4415 N. Milwaukee, 773/736-1925). Further north, there are **Chicago Recycle Shop** (5308 N. Clark, 773/878-8525) and **Economy Furniture on Clark** (6600 N. Clark, 773/338-6560), and to the west, **Value Bedding Liquidation Center** (1850 S. Kostner, 773/522-1045). On the South Side, visit **Bowman's Used Furniture** (720 E. 63rd, 773/493-2125), **Oldies But Goodies** (71 E. 43rd, 773/536-1545), and **McCoy Real New & Used Furniture & Appliance** (7257 S. Halsted, 773/994-9000).

Furniture, Hotel/Motel

Cooper Furniture Inc.
1929–33 S. Halsted, 312/226-2299   **C**
Don't stay at the Four Seasons, Ambassador East, Hyatt, Hilton, or Marriott as often as you would like? Maybe you need a trip to this 7-floor jungle to pick up some used pieces from these hoteliers for your own home. **Cooper Furniture** has been in the business for 65+ years, redistributing hotel items like bedding, carpeting, lobby furniture, chandeliers, mirrors, paintings and prints, telephones, electronics, and tablecloths to the public. Open Mon.–Fri. 8 A.M.–6 P.M., Sat. noon–5 P.M.

Less monstrous are **Fort Pitt Associates** (1400 W. 37th, 773/247-3523) and **Windy City Furniture** (2221 S. Michigan, 312/225-9777), which also deal in used hotel/motel furniture. Armoires, dressers, beds, sofas, chairs, tables, lamps, mirrors, and carpets: they resell nearly everything but the "Do Not Disturb" signs.

Furniture, Office

While these stores don't offer garage sale deals, their office furniture is still available well below the list price. On the Near North Side, choose between **Stein Office Furniture** (1030 W. North, 4ᵗʰ floor, 312/649-7100) and **Gently Used Office Furniture** (1300 W. North, 773/276-6200). Further north is the **Direct Office Furniture Warehouse** (5041 N. Western, 773/271-3000). Near south, there's **Redux Office Furniture** (244 W. 16ᵗʰ, 312/829-7711). All carry a wide variety of chairs, desks, file cabinets, and workstations/modular units. Sometimes there's even wallpaper, carpeting, hanging files, manila folders, storage disks, and the like to be found.

Music, CDs/Records/Cassettes

Beverly Records

11612 S. Western, 773/779-0066, *www.beverlyrecords.com*   FSW

Have you been searching for just the right music for that Western roundup or 50s sock hop you're throwing? Perhaps a ditty from the roaring 20s or even the soundtrack of *Camelot*? Look no further. Chances are **Beverly Records** (est. 1967) will have exactly what you've been searching for and more. Noted the #1 source in the Midwest for out of print titles, their full catalog includes 45s, LPs, and even those 8-tracks! DJs swarm this store for those hard-to-find 12" vinyl selections. Open Mon.–Fri. 10 A.M.–6 P.M. (Thur. until 7 P.M.), Sat. 9:30 A.M.–6 P.M., Sun. 11 A.M.–3 P.M.

Crazy Man Records

1655 W. Division, 773/489-9848   W

Eddie Fisher, the man behind **Crazy Man Records** and far from crazy, specializes in vinyl old and new (yes, they still produce LPs). Imports and collectibles are also for sale. DJs, collectors, and fans of the 33 rpm are regular customers. All genres but classical are sold, bought, and traded. Open Tues.–Sun. noon–9 P.M., that is, he usually tries to open by noon and stays open as late at 9 P.M. depending on how busy it is.

Dr. Wax

5210 S. Harper, 773/493-8696   S

1121 W. Berwyn, 773/784-3333   N

Records, tapes, and CDs. Alternative, jazz, reggae, rock, soul, and imports. The Berwyn store has more indy rock and a greater overall mix, the Hyde Park shop more R&B and urban offerings. Open Mon.–Sat. 11 A.M.–8 P.M., Sun. noon–6 P.M.

Dusty Groove America

1120 N. Ashland, 773/342-5800, *www.dustygroove.com*   W

With new and used vinyl and CDs representing jazz, hip hop, soul, neo-soul, funk, deep funk, Latin, Brazilian, reggae, world music, gospel, abstract sounds, and spoken word, this groovy place with slick digs is more cutting edge then dusty. Come on—they even have a "take-out" window to pick up orders you place online! Open daily 10 A.M.–8 P.M.

Evil Clown Compact Disc
3418 N. Halsted, 773/472-4761, *www.evilclowncd.com*   **N**
Buy, sell, or exchange new and used CDs (some cassettes and records) in urban, hip, and edgy genres like alternative, Britpop, dance, electronica, Gothic, imports, indie rock, industrial, jungle, Krautrock, new wave, old jazz, punk, and technopop.

George's Music Room
3915 W. Roosevelt, 773/762-8910   **W**
A must-know-about West Side classic, **George's Music Room** specializes in African-American music, particularly older styles and the hard-to-find elsewhere. Look for blues, jazz, R&B, soul, hip hop, and rap as records and CDs. Open Mon.–Thur 11 A.M.–8 P.M., Fri.–Sat. 11 A.M.–9 P.M., Sun. 11 A.M.–6 P.M.

Gramaphone Records
2663 N. Clark, 773/472-3683, *www.gramaphonerecords.com*   **N**
Calling themselves Chicago's premier dance and electronic music store, this 35-year-old Clark Street staple deals in records, tapes, and CDs. They also carry pop, rock, hip hop, trance, and underground. Open Mon.–Fri. 11 A.M.–9 P.M., Sat. 10:30 A.M.–8:30 P.M., Sun. noon–7 P.M.

Great Scott Records & Tapes
9523 S. Jeffery, 773/734-5317   **FSW**
Records, tapes, and CDs. **Great Scott** has an oldies specialty, with R & B, pop, gospel, rap, and hip hop sections. Open Mon.–Sat. 10 A.M.–8 P.M., Sun. 11 A.M.–6 P.M.

Hi-Fi Records
2570 N. Clark, 773/880-1002, *www.hifirecords.com*   **N**
Open Mon.–Sat. 11 A.M.–8 P.M., Sun. noon–7 P.M.
3728 N. Clark, 773/388-3885   **N**
Open daily at noon and open at least until 6 P.M. Usually open until 10:30 P.M. Thur.–Sat., but closing time depends on who's playing next door at the **Metro** (see p. 255).
Another great new-and-used independent "record" store with sundry genres and formats, including imports, underground, LPs, 12", CDs, and DVDs.

The store adjacent to the Metro (3728) carries more alternative rock, indie labels, dance, rap, hip hop, and electronic.

Hot Jams

5012 S. Pulaski, 773/581-5267   **SW**

This small store gives Southwest Siders the chance to buy discs you can't find elsewhere. Most styles, including acid, hip hop, house, jungle, rap, and techno, seem to find a place here. In addition to tapes and CDs, there are hundreds of vinyl records in rows and rows of bins, and you're likely to find some real bargains. Open daily 1 P.M.–9 P.M.

Jazz Record Mart

444 N. Wabash, 312/222-1467, *www.jazzrecordmart.com*   **C**

Not just the world's best, largest collection of jazz and blues, **Jazz Record Mart** is an entity unto itself and an important player in the jazz/blues world. Owner Bob Koester has also been running his Chicago's jazz and blues label, Delmark Records, since 1953, one of the oldest independent labels still owned and operated by its founder. His downtown depository of tens of thousands of new and used items (LPs, CDs, tapes, 45s, 78s, and memorabilia) extends well beyond the signature collections to gospel, R&B, world music, spoken word (say, Beat poets or Lenny Bruce), and even things like country, lounge, acid, or wacky futuristic sounds. Keep an ear open for their special events. Open Mon.–Sat. 10 A.M.–8 P.M., Sun. 10 A.M.–5 P.M.

Laurie's Planet of Sound

4639 N. Lincoln, 773/271-3569

http://lauriesplanetofsound.tripod.com   **N**

Already a Lincoln Square fixture, Laurie's sells a respectable selection of alternative videos and books, zines, posters, and other music paraphernalia side by side with their new and used records, CDs, and tapes. Open Mon.–Sat. 10 A.M.–10 P.M., Sun. 11 A.M.–7 P.M.

Out of the Past Records

4407 W. Madison, 773/626-3878   **W**

LPs, 45s, CDs, tapes, and 8-tracks. Dusties, jazz, R&B, and gospel. Open Mon.–Fri. 11:30 A.M.–7 P.M., Sat. 11:30 A.M.–8:30 P.M., Sun. 11:30 A.M.–6:30 P.M.

Raffe's Record Riot

4350 N. Cicero, 773/725-1327   **NW**

Tapes, CDs, and 100,000 records, as well as memorabilia and collectibles. Open Mon.–Sat. noon–6 P.M. (usually).

Reckless Records

3157 N. Broadway, 773/404-5080   **N**

1532 N. Milwaukee, 773/235-3727   **W**

www.reckless.com

This new-and-used store has been a consistent Lakeview staple since 1989, and now they're in Wicker Park, too. They carry "everything," which naturally includes the unusual, interesting, rare, and imported (records, tapes, CDs, videos, and laserdiscs). The main focus is on alternative rock, but the store does boast a healthy jazz section, as well as modest soul, blues, and country categories. Even better, some racks are devoted to rock sub-categories like psychedelia or 50s/60s. This may be a hindrance for some, but a credit to others seeking a specific title or genre. Frequent markdowns. Open Mon.–Sat. 10 A.M.–10 P.M., Sun. 10 A.M.–8 P.M.

Record Dugout Used Records

6055 W. 63rd, 773/586-1206   **SW**

Records (45s, LPs, and 78s) of the 50s, 60s, and 70s and . . . baseball cards. Open Mon.–Fri. noon–7 P.M., Sat.–Sun. noon–5 P.M.

Record Emporium

3346 N. Paulina, 773/248-1821, *www.recordemporium.com*   **N**

This last of the old-time record stores (but they do have CDs!) describes themselves as going out of business since 1979 and the model for the record store in the movie *High Fidelity*. They specialize in alternative rock, classic rock, blues, jazz, Americana, and being that kind of great indy store people like to hang out in and be loyal to. Open Mon.–Sat. 11 A.M.–7 P.M., Sun. noon–6 P.M.

2nd Hand Tunes

1377 E. 53rd, 773/684-3375, *www.2ndhandtunes.com*   **S**

Open daily 10 A.M.–8 P.M.

Sound Gallery

1821 W. North, 773/235-8472, *www.chicagosoundgallery.com*   **W**

Open daily noon–8 P.M.

Chicago's oldest (est. 1976) and largest used LP, CD, VHS, and DVD chain with two city and two suburban stores. They carry the rare, out-of-print, and obscure along with newer and more popular sounds. **Sound Gallery** also carries books, audio supplies, and record-inspired accessories.

Sporting Goods

The Northcenter neighborhood sports two used athletic equipment stores where goods are bought, sold, consigned, and exchanged: **Play It Again Sports** (2101 W. Irving Park, 773/463-9900, *www.playitagainsports.com*) and **Chicago Sports Exchange** (3839 N. Western, 773/583-7283). Play It Again is larger, brighter, pricier, and more neatly organized. They also carry new items as well as providing a good-sized driving range for customers to test out golf clubs. Closer in spirit to the typical resale shop is the crammed Sports Exchange, where they just might let you wrangle over a price or two.

Several small neighborhood shops afford good deals on used bicycles and bike parts. **Blackstone Bike Co-op** (see p. 380) and **Urban Bikes** (p. 380) were discussed previously, but **Recycle** (1465 S. Michigan, 312/987-1080) and **Upgrade Cycle Works** (1130 W. Chicago, 312/226-8650) should also be checked for low-priced used and new bicycles.

Stereos and Electronics

Stereo Exchange
4743 N. Western, 773/784-0004, *www.turntablerepair.com*   N
Primarily a repair shop where electronics are sent from around the country to be fixed, **The Stereo Exchange** also buys, sells, trades, and installs stereos, radios, amps, receivers, speakers, phonographs, turntables, TVs, VCRs, 8-track players, keyboards, synthesizers, car alarms, and other home and auto electronics. Posted hours of Mon. & Fri. noon–6 P.M., Wed. & Thur. noon–5 P.M., and Sat. 11 A.M.–2 P.M. may fluctuate, so call ahead.

Typewriters!

Independence Business Machines
1623 W. Montrose, 773/248-5548   N
Owner Steve Kazmierski has been in the typewriter repair business since 1964, and he can repair anything from an IBM Selectric to a 100-year-old Underwood. Complete refurbishment may cost as much as $175, but the machines will look new; various examples are for sale in the shop window. Semi-retired, Kazmierski says, "People don't want to let me retire completely." He's optimistic about the future, too; citing both sales to big business clients and young people, he adds, "I think typewriters are coming back." Open Mon.–Fri. 10 A.M.–2 P.M., Sat. 10 A.M.–1 P.M. (maybe not Saturdays in summer).

Non-Profit Resale Stores

When you don't mind picking and hunting, when you want the real bargains, or when you have a pet cause you like to support, take your business to one of the following shops.

The Ark Thrift Shop
1302 N. Milwaukee, 773/862-5011   **W**
3345 N. Lincoln, 773/248-1117   **N**
Medical, dental, barber/beautician, and job counseling services are among the many free offerings that **The Ark**—a Jewish social welfare agency—provides its constituents. They also run the only Kosher food pantry in the city, deliver Kosher meals to seniors and people with disabilities, and assist Russian Jews trying to establish themselves in the United States. The Ark is well-known for the high quality of their ever-changing stock, especially in the furniture and housewares departments.

Brown Elephant Resale
3651 N. Halsted, 773/549-5943   **N**
3939 N. Ashland, 773/244-2930   **N**
The **Brown Elephant** stores benefit the Howard Brown Health Center—a health and human services organization serving the gay and lesbian community and offering extensive programs for AIDS patients and those who are HIV+. The concept behind this pioneering resale shop, which does well over $1 million in annual sales, has since spread to other American cities. Goods are priced a little higher here, but you're also likely to find newer, cooler, more interesting stuff, too.

The Chicago Resale Store
118 S. Halsted, 312/491-2004   **C**
Racks and racks of men's, women's, and children's clothing, suits, shirts, pants, shoes, jackets, and prom dresses. If you have radiator heat in Chicago

---

Free Shopping in Chicago?

Sure, on "Trashing Day." According to North Sider Nina Sandlin, Chicago's most popular moving days, May 1st and Oct 1st, are the best days for "trashing." That's visiting the alleys and dumpsters in better neighborhoods—especially those with a high concentration of renters—to recover some of the goods those with plenty of *disposable* income discard when they move. Some of her regular finds include housewares, furniture, plants, expensive clothing, plastics, office supplies, and gift wrap!

you'll like to know that they sell humidifiers, dehumidifiers, space heaters, and air purifiers. TVs, baby toys, grills, refrigerators, bikes, tools, plates, glassware, and new and old games are all organized and cleaned. Items are nice and the prices are extremely good, and to entice you even more if the ticket doesn't say "full price" you can take half off! Run by the Chicago Christian Industrial League—all proceeds go directly to their programs for the homeless. Closed Sun.–Mon.

Hidden Treasures
46 E. Chicago, 312/943-7761 **C**
Supporting Northwestern Memorial Hospital's Patients First program, this shop carries lots of books, quality women's clothing, shoes, and accessories, and better home furnishings.

National Council of Jewish Women's Thrift Shop
1524 W. Howard, 773/764-2364 **FN**
Monies from this shop provide non-sectarian help, primarily to local women and children, through support for battered women, children's scholarships, and more. Some funds are used for international women's causes.

Roseland Christian Community Thrift Store
33 E. 111th, 773/468-0262 **FSE**
This store's income benefits the surrounding community in many ways— through a food pantry, a homeless shelter, summer programs for kids, job opportunities and economic development, emergency funds, and Christian ministry.

Salvation Army
1515 N. Milwaukee, 773/489-5194	**W**
2024 S. Western, 773/254-1127	**W**
2270 N. Clybourn, 773/477-1300	**N**
3055 W. 63rd, 773/476-8718	**SW**
3301 W. Montrose, 773/588-7343	**NW**
3837 W. Fullerton, 773/276-1955	**NW**
4220 W. Belmont, 773/205-7446	**NW**
5112 S. Ashland, 773/737-3335	**SW**
5713 W. Chicago, 773/287-9774	**W**

Not usually the pick of the litter, but worth checking out for the low prices and sheer quantity of stuff that gets donated.

Society of St. Vincent DePaul Resale Shops

2145 N. Halsted, 312/943-6776	N
5413 S. Kedzie, 773/434-0109	SW
9321 S. Western, 773/881-0600	FSW

The chain of St. Vincent DePaul resale stores serves the poor, low-income, and bargain-hunting members of the Chicago populace in a variety of ways. Each store employs nearly 75 people—including seniors and the mentally disabled—providing training, new job skills, and advancement opportunities. Individuals in need are given vouchers for clothing and household supplies, allowing them to shop with dignity in the stores. Revenue supports S.V.D.P. programs that help with utility, rent, clothing, and basic supplies for the homeless and those who need to get back on their feet. Non-useable goods are recycled in a responsible manner.

White Elephant Shop of Children's Memorial Hospital

2380 N. Lincoln, 773/883-6184   N

Buying an $8,000 Bob Mackie dress for $135 was among the recent ways a resale shopper helped the Children's Memorial Hospital's **White Elephant Shop** assist low-income families pay their children's medical bills. Good finds at good prices are the norm here—look for designer clothing for women, men, and children, artwork, TVs, telephones, appliances, furniture, and more. Other programs the shop supports include assistance to families of children with catastrophic illnesses, temporary relocation for people who have been displaced from public housing for asbestos and lead removal, and organ transplant research.

Other shops' causes can be determined from their names: **Council for Jewish Elderly Good Byes Resale Shop** (3503 W. Lawrence, 773/583-5118), **Mount Sinai Hospital Resale Shop** (814 W. Diversey, 773/935-1434), and **N.S.A.R. (Northwest Suburban Aid to the Retarded) Thrift Shoppe** (7710 W. Touhy, 773/631-6230). The proceeds from the **Luther North High School Thrift Shop** (6059 W. Addison, 773/725-4406) go into the general school operating budget to help defray tuition costs. **The Right Place** (5219 N. Clark, 773/561-7757) raises scholarship funds for the B. Zell Anshe Emet Day School, a private Jewish grammar school.

The Annex (6056 N. Broadway, 773/761-8318), **Firman Community Services Thrift Shop** (120 E. Garfield, 773/373-1433), **Marillac House Thrift Shop** (2859 W. Jackson, 773/638-0186), **St. Pius Parish Store** (1701 W. 18th Place, 312/226-6234), and **Our Lady of Sorrows Resale** (3149 W. Jackson, 773/722-0861) all support various local programs for the disadvantaged.

Other Resale Stores

Finally, the most complete list anywhere of Chicago's plethora of second-hand shops. Consult it when you need to find someplace close or when you feel like browsing in another part of town.

FAR NORTH

- **Almost New Resale**, 8254 W. Balmoral, 773/792-3260
- **American Thrift Store**, 3125 N. Central, 773/685-5566
- **Antique and Resale Shop**, 7214 N. Harlem, 773/631-1151
- **Chicago Recycle Shop**, 5308 N. Clark, 773/878-8525
- **Norwood Park Home Thrift Shop**, 6019 N. Nina, 773/763-3775
- **Resale House**, 7129 N. Clark, 773/743-5616
- **Village Discount Outlet**, 4898 N. Clark, (no phone)

NORTH

- **Best Thrift**, 3115 W. Irving Park, 773/583-2880
- **Land of the Lost**, 614 W. Belmont, 773/529-4966
Among their general stock of vintage and resale clothes and collectibles, **Land of the Lost** has special collections of casual clothes, games, signs, glassware, and clocks.
- **Something Old Something New**, 1056 W. Belmont, 773/271-1300
- **Unique Thrift Store**, 4445 N. Sheridan, 773/275-8623
- **Village Discount Outlet**, 2855 N. Halsted, (no phone)
- **Village Discount Outlet**, 2032 N. Milwaukee, (no phone)
- **Village Discount Outlet**, 2043 W. Roscoe, (no phone)

NORTHWEST

- **A Niche In Time**, 6052 N. Avondale, 773/631-3880
- **All Saints Resale Shop**, 2816 N. Laramie, 773/545-6818
- **Amara's Resale Shop**, 4712 W. Diversey, 773/283-1862
- **American Thrift Store**, 2874 N. Milwaukee, 773/292-0994
- **Everything Under the Sun**, 5122 W. Grand, 773/622-1181
- **Fullerton Ave. Thrift Store**, 346 W. Fullerton, 773/782-1798
- **The Thrift Store**, 3012 N. Central, 773/622-2400
- **Unique Thrift Store**, 3748 N. Elston, 773/279-0850
- **Unique Thrift Store**, 4441 W. Diversey, 773/227-2282
- **Village Discount Outlet**, 4635 N. Elston, (no phone)
- **Village Discount Outlet**, 3301 W. Lawrence, (no phone)

WEST

- **American Thrift Store**, 1718 W. Chicago, 312/243-4343
- **American Thrift Store**, 4425 W. 16th, 773/685-5566
- **Ann's Thrift Store**, 5 N. Cicero, 773/378-6023
- **Wonderland Multivintage**, 1339 N. Milwaukee Ave., 773/235-3110

Wonderland sells old toys, jewelry, records, glassware, plates, and other vintage items, but we suggest you stop by if you're in the market for vintage barware or games.

SOUTHWEST

- **Unique Thrift Store**, 2329 S. Kedzie, 773/762-7510
- **Unique Thrift Store**, 3000 S. Halsted, 312/842-0942
- **Unique Thrift Store**, 3542 S. Archer, 773/247-2599
- **Unique Thrift Store**, 5040 S. Kedzie, 773/434-4886
- **Victory Resale Center**, 1022 W. 63rd, 773/476-4812
- **Village Discount Outlet**, 6419 S. Kedzie, (no phone)
- **Village Discount Outlet**, 4020 W. 26th, (no phone)
- **Village Discount Outlet**, 2514 W. 47th, (no phone)

FAR SOUTHEAST

- **Caring Closet**, 1745 E. 71st, 773/947-9043
- **Jackson Resale Shop**, 6756 S. Stony Island, 773/667-9189
- **Oh's First and Second Shop**, 519 E. 79th, 773/783-3984
- **South End Thrift Shop**, 8533 S. Cottage Grove, 773/873-0717

FAR SOUTHWEST

- **Crystal Thrift Shop**, 8018 S. Halsted, 773/994-2228
- **Unique Thrift Store**, 9341 S. Ashland, 773/239-3127
- **Village Discount Outlet**, 7443 S. Racine, (no phone)

Markets and Bazaars

FLEA markets and bazaars: an ideal leisurely weekend activity for browsing for your cheap buys and watching others browse for theirs.

Ashland Swap-O-Rama
4100 S. Ashland, 708/344-7300   **SW**
The owners of this 110,000-square-foot, year-round flea market in the Back of the Yards neighborhood like to brag that you can find "everything that's

legal to sell" here and they may not be exaggerating too much. With 450 stores inside and another 200 outside, stadium-sized bathrooms, multi-ethnic concessions, and kiddie distractions it's easy for shoppers to stay all day. Tues. & Thur. 7 A.M.–3 P.M. (outdoors only), Sat.–Sun. 7 A.M.–4 P.M. (inside and out).

Boyajian's Bazaar
1305 E. 53rd, 773/324-2020   **S**
The international bazaar brought indoors! Beads, gifts, crafts, folk art, clothing, wall hangings, carvings, trinkets from Africa, the Middle East, Asia, and Latin America: Boyajian's brings you everything but the haggling. Typically open Mon.–Fri. 11 A.M.–6 P.M.

Buyer's Flea Market
4545 W. Division, 773/227-1889, *www.chicagofleamarket.com*   **W**
This year-round weekend flea market features hundreds of dealers indoors, with more outdoors as the weather allows (though it is covered), many selling at a bargain the day-to-day stuff you'd otherwise be picking up elsewhere. Ample parking on the premises, decent bathrooms, and a food court. The CTA's Division Street bus will drop you off in front of the place. Open Sat.–Sun. 8 A.M.–5 P.M.

(The New) Maxwell Street Market
Canal Street between Roosevelt Road and 17th Street   **C**
Over 100 years old, the **Maxwell Street Market** was at one time the largest open-air market in the world. Some thought this bargain hunters' nirvana should have received landmark designation. Others with more power thought it was a dump and had been trying to shut it down or relocate it for years—especially because of the expanding University of Illinois. These folks succeeded a few years back. As of September 1994, the market has been located a few blocks east of its original location (Halsted & Maxwell St.) on Canal Street. This new site has room for only half of the regular Maxwell Street vendors, but retains much of the commotion of the original Maxwell Street Market, including nearly 400 vendors, musicians, food booths (particularly Mexican stands and carts), and haggling efforts. Sun. 7 A.M.–3 P.M.

Supermall
52nd & Pulaski, 773/581-9200   **SW**
Atmosphere can be half the fun of a good shopping experience, and if ambiance is important to you, be sure and check out this shopping arena. **Supermall** is a huge indoor bazaar with dozens of individual merchants

leasing small booth space to sell their wares. You'll find lots of clothing, especially western wear, cowboy boots, team hats for Mexican soccer teams, leather jackets, beautiful holiday clothing for children, and even utilitarian items like bundles of socks and kitchen ware. Prices vary from one booth to the next, which in most cases works to the shopper's advantage. Open Mon.–Sat. 10 A.M.–8 P.M., Sat. 10 A.M.–7 P.M.

Similar malls in different neighborhoods are also popular with immigrants—both as shoppers and vendors—and make great places to experience some of Chicago's cultural diversity while bargain hunting: **The Clark Mall** (7212 N. Clark, 773/764-7091) and the **Logan Square Discount Mega Mall** (2500 N. Milwaukee, 773/489-2525). The **Logan Square Mall** has a particularly wide assortment of international food booths that serve up a bounty of American fast food favorites, Asian dishes, Mexican specialties, and traditional Puerto Rican fare. Both malls are open Mon.–Sat. 10 A.M.–8 P.M., Sun. 10 A.M.–7 P.M.

Public Auctions

Chicago Police Department's
Evidence and Recovered Property Auction
Westside Technical Institute, 2800 S. Western, 312/747-6224   SW
One Saturday a month, the **CPD's Evidence and Recovered Property Unit** auctions off a mountain of unclaimed merchandise from tools and bicycles to shoes and stereo equipment. The auction begins at 10 A.M. and ends when everything has been sold—usually about 3 P.M. or 4 P.M. Sale items can be viewed on the Friday afternoon before the auction from 1 P.M. to 3 P.M. and on the morning of the auction from 8 A.M. to 9:55 A.M. Call the above number to get a list of upcoming auction dates, because the Saturday varies from month to month. No entrance fee.

Susanin's Chicago Auctions
900 S. Clinton, 312/832-9800, *www.auctionsmart.com*   C
In a new 35,000-square-foot facility, this 10-year-old auction house holds weekly auctions of general property recovered from homes throughout the city. An assortment of affordable furniture, paintings, collectibles, rugs, jewelry, silver, and more are available for viewing throughout the week from 10 A.M. to 5 P.M. before the Saturday auction gets underway around noon (doors open at 10 A.M.). Items are also available for viewing on their Web site. In addition, those of you wondering the value of that hand-me-down

china can take advantage of free appraisals on Thursdays, no appointment necessary.

Direct Auction Galleries
7232 N. Western, 773/465-3300, *www.directauction.com*   **FN**
In business for almost 40 years, this auction house auctions off 600–700 items for anywhere from $20 to $20,000 every other Tues. from 3 P.M. until as late as 11 P.M. and beyond. They also sell cheap beverages and snacks— good to know if you'll be settling in for an evening of bidding. Viewings are the Monday before the auction, 3:30 P.M.–7:30 P.M., and the day of the auction, 2 P.M.–3 P.M. Those who go regularly swear by the great deals on a wide range of items from antique furniture, chandeliers, china, rugs, glassware, artwork, and more. Visit the Web site to view items, see the schedule, and get on the e-mail list, but also for FAQs on the consignment and auction processes.

9

KEEPING INFORMED

The Chicago Cultural Center, home of the Office of Tourism's Visitor Information Center, is a great place to get informed before your adventures in the city. *Photo by Bill Arroyo.*

The historic Water Tower is widely recognized for being one of only two downtown public buildings to survive the Great Chicago Fire of 1871.
Photo by Bill Arroyo.

KEEPING INFORMED

A NATIVE'S GUIDE TO CHICAGO will help you navigate through permanent, or at least, semi-permanent Chicago. To stay current, however, with the changing, developing, and fleeting Chicago requires additional and ongoing effort. The phone, radio, television, Internet, and print resources listed in this chapter should keep you moving with the day-to-day news and events that enliven our city.

Phone Numbers/Hotlines to Know

Tip: One-and-a-half phone numbers to remember: 311 and the main branch of the Chicago Public Library (312/747-4300). If it at all pertains to the city, whether it's graffiti and flooding or concerts in the park, call 311. For in-depth information on city institutions, history, etc., have the reference desk at the Harold Washington Library Center steer you in the right direction.

Basics

City Council Information   312/744-3081
www.cityofchicago.org
Emergency   911

Fire Department (non-emergency)	311
www.cityofchicago.org/fire	
Fire Department (outside of Chicago)	312/744-5000
Library—Main Branch (Harold Washington Lib. Center)	312/747-4300
www.chipublib.org	
Mayor's Office of Inquiry and Information	311
Mayor's Office of Inquiry (outside of Chicago)	312/744-5000
Police Department (non-emergency)	311
www.cityofchicago.org/police	
Police Department (outside of Chicago)	312/744-5000
Post Office	800/275-8777
www.usps.com	

Cultural Events

Chicago Architecture Foundation	312/922-3432
www.architecture.org	
Chicago Arts Programming Hotline	312/346-3278
Chicago Department of Cultural Affairs	312/744-6630
Chicago Live Concerts (Popular Music)	312/666-6667
Chicago Music Alliance (Opera/Classical)	312/987-9296
Grant Park Music Festival	312/742-4763
www.grantparkmusicfestival.com	
Jazz Hotline	312/427-3300
Mayor's Office of Special Events	
www.cityofchicago.org/specialevents	

The place to call for information on parades, summer festivals, art shows, concerts, etc.

• **General**	312/744-3315
• **24-Hour Hotline**	312/744-3370
• **Film**	312/744-6415
• **TTY**	312/744-2964

Lodging

Hot Rooms (Discount Rooms Downtown)	773/468-7666
www.hotrooms.com	
Illinois Hotel & Lodging Association	877/456-3446
www.stayillinois.com	

Sports and Recreation

Chicago Park District   312/742-7529
Chicago Park District/TTY   312/747-2001
www.chicagoparkdistrict.com

Tickets

Hot Tix
www.hottix.org
Ticket Master   312/559-1212
www.ticketmaster.com

Tourist Information

Chicago Convention & Tourism Bureau   877/244-2246
Chicago Convention & Tourism Bureau/TTY   866/710-0294
www.choosechicago.com
Illinois Bureau of Tourism   800/226-6632
www.enjoyillinois.com
Illinois Bureau of Tourism/TTY   800/785-6055

Transportation

American United Cab   773/248-7600
Amtrak Fare & Scheduling Information   800/872-7245
www.amtrak.com
Chicago Transit Authority (CTA)   888/968-7282
www.transitchicago.com
Chicago Transit Authority (CTA)/TTY   888/282-8891
Flash Cab   773/561-4444
Greyhound Bus   800/231-2222
www.greyhound.com
Illinois Department of Transportation   312/368-4636
www.dot.state.il.us
Illinois Tollway   773/242-3620
www.illinoistollway.com
METRA (suburban commuter trains)   312/322-6774
www.metrarail.com

Midway Airport	773/838-0600
www.ohare.com/midway/home.asp	
O'Hare International Airport	773/686-2200
www.ohare.com/ohare/home.asp	
Pace Bus (suburban buses)	847/364-7223
www.pacebus.com	
Regional Transit Authority (RTA)	312/836-7000
Skyway Information	312/747-8383
Yellow Cab	312/829-4222

Radio Programming

News/Talk

WBBM–AM (780 AM) News *www.wbbm780.com*
On air tip: Chicagoans know to tune in to WBBM for traffic and weather on the eights, every ten minutes, round the clock. Many also rely on the *Noon Business Hour*.

WBEZ–FM (91.5 FM) Chicago Public Radio .... *www.wbez.org*
On air tip: For interview, news, essays, panels, and documentaries with a local orientation, join Steve Edwards, host of the award-winning weekday morning news magazine, *Eight Forty-Eight* (named for the stations' Navy Pier address), 9:35 A.M.–11 A.M. Sunday mornings 10 A.M.–11 A.M., *Hello Beautiful!* collects and replays segments of Chicago arts coverage that aired on other shows during the week. This is also the place on the dial to hear NPR shows and BBC news.

WCKG–FM (105.9 FM) Talk.. *www.wckg.com*
On air tip: Catch Steve Dahl on the airwaves, weekdays 2 P.M.–7 P.M. Dahl has been a local radio legend since shortly after his arrival in 1979 to be a rock DJ for WLUP. He invited fans to blow up their disco records in between games at a Comiskey Park doubleheader. "Disco Demolition" made broadcasting history when the explosion and resulting debris incited thousands of fans to rush the field and others to start fires and otherwise riot, causing the White Sox to forfeit the game.
Noteworthy Trivia: CKG's newest talk DJ, Frankie "Hollywood" Rodriguez, made a name for himself in the early and mid-1980s as a popular club and radio DJ playing and creating the very disco-like house music developing in Chicago at that time.

WGN–AM (720 AM) Chicago's news and talk .... *www.wgnradio.com*
Need to know: WGN stands for **W**orld's **G**reatest **N**ewspaper (*Chicago Tribune*) and operates from the base of the Tribune Tower on Michigan Avenue, where one studio looks out onto the Equitable Fountain Plaza and passersby can hear the broadcast from an outdoor speaker. While every station has its loyal listeners, WGN's loyal listeners tend to listen for years, or decades, and most true-blue Chicagoans tune in at least occasionally to one of its shows. For many, WGN is synonymous with the Cubs, and even a few minutes of the distinctive sound of their Wrigley Field broadcast in the background is enough for folks from around the region to know it's summertime and that all is right with the world. WGN hosts and Cubs announcers, past and present, are local celebrities, period.
On air tip: Though most WGN programming is very local and Chicago-focused, don't miss veteran journalist Rick Kogan's *The Sunday Papers*, 6:30 A.M.–9 A.M., for a weekly Chicago lovefest. To be locally literate, you might also want to know what these hosts' shows are all about: Kathy & Judy (mid-day girlfriends), Steve and Johnnie (husband-and-wife team are city's #1 overnight show), and Milt Rosenberg (U of C prof leads intellectual discussions with top local, national, and international thinkers and players of all stripes).

WLS–AM (890 AM) News & Talk .... *http://wlsam.com*
Noteworthy Trivia: This 80-year-old station was originally owned by Sears Roebuck and Co., the **W**orld's **L**argest **S**tore. One of WLS's first shows was the *National Barn Dance* program, what would become the most popular and longest running country-and-western shows in history after *The Grand Old Opry*.
On air tip: Chicago PM, weekdays 6 P.M.–7 P.M., pairs up top reporter Bill Cameron with top talk show host Jay Marvin to dissect and discuss the stories of the day and their effect on Chicago and Chicagoans. Night owls can get their Chicago fix from Carol O'Keefe's public affairs program, *Connected to Chicago*, Mon. midnight – 1 A.M.

WVON–AM (1450 AM) News/talk .... *www.wvon.com*
Need to Know: WVON began over 35 years ago as "Voice of the Negro," when one could hear interviews with the Rev. Martin Luther King, Jr. and other leading lights of the day alongside the best in African-American music. On what's now known as the "Voice of the Nation," listeners can tune in to such personalities as Professor Willie Dixon, a staff historian with the DuSable Museum, for talk shows particularly relevant to Chicago's black community. This part-time station broadcasts daily 10 P.M.– 1 P.M.

College

The college-sponsored radio stations and the stations that air independently from local college campuses are a heartening substitute for commercial radio. Try them for new, local, experimental, and hybrid music; quirky and passionate programming; and alternative news and views.

WCRX–FM (88.1 FM) Columbia College.............................*www.crx.net*
Need to know: Columbia College is the home of Chicago's most popular radio education program.
On air tip: In addition to billing themselves as "Chicago's Underground" for the variety of new, local music they showcase, WCRX has an extensive public affairs lineup, including *Ask the Alderman*. On the third Tuesday of each month at 7 P.M., Chicago aldermen answer questions live from their studio.

WHPK–FM (88.5 FM)
University of Chicago.....................................*http://whpk.uchicago.edu/info*
On air tip: A music schedule that includes rap, rock, folk, jazz, blues, electronic, and classical is already impressive, but there's more: reggae, calypso, Middle Eastern, Korean, unintelligent dance music, soul, doowop, funk, synthpop, ambient, industrial...

WLUW–FM (88.7 FM) Loyola University..........................*www.wluw.org*
On air tip: A staggering schedule includes shows devoted to future music, live bluegrass, New Orleans music, punk/hardcore, and music by and for the gay community. Other programs focus specifically on covering Chicago's Ethiopian and Bulgarian populations and the broader Rogers Park, Edgewater, and Uptown neighborhoods. Another category covers news from progressive and social-justice standpoints, including those from a Catholic activist perspective.

WIIT–FM (88.9 FM) Illinois Institute of Technology ... *http://radio.iit.edu*
On air tip: Tune in for house, gospel, alternative, Indian, fusion, rock, electronic, tropical, dance, lounge, jazz, and world music.

WNUR–FM (89.3 FM) Northwestern University.................*www.wnur.org*
On air tip: This is Northwestern and their station is "Chicago's Sound Experiment," so in addition to the expected diversified musical offerings, many have fancy names, like rhythmic noise, dark ambient, digital hardcore, breakbeat, tech house, and avant-classical. WNUR is also home to

Chicago's longest running reggae show and First World Report, a public affairs program devoted to Chicago issues from an African-American viewpoint. Not surprisingly, this is one of the leading college radio stations in the country and one of the best-funded, too.

WRRG–FM (88.9 FM) Triton College .... *www.wrrg.org*
On air tip: Primarily spinning progressive and indie rock, the Triton DJs will also delve into jazz, metal, hip hop, and electronic.

WZRD–FM (88.3 FM)
Northeastern Illinois Univ. .... *http://orion.neiu.edu/~wradio/indexf.htm*
On air tip: Many find "The Wizard" on the dial to hear the daily Pacifica News reports at 4:30 P.M. and 10 P.M.

Music

WBBM–FM (96.3 FM) New Pop, Dance, Urban *www.b96.com*

WDRV–FM (97.1 FM) Timeless Rock .... *www.wdrv.com*

WFMT–FM (98.7 FM) Classical .... *www.networkchicago.com/wfmt*
Need to know: WFMT is one of only a few commercial radio stations in the country still dedicated to classical music and the fine arts, 24/7/365.
Web tip: Events tab has links to local fine arts events, city fests, family activities, and Chicago recommendations from local PBS TV shows.

WGCI–AM (1390 AM) Gospel *http://207.230.156.205/main.html*
On air tip: Hear the preaching of Chicago's own Rev. Jesse Jackson, Sun. 7 A.M.–8 A.M.

WGCI–FM (107.5 FM) Hip-Hop and R&B .... *www.wgci.com*

WJMK–FM (104.3 FM) Oldies, mostly 60s and 70s .... *www.wjmk.com*
On air tip: Don't miss Rock and Roll Hall of Fame inductee, DJ Dick Biondi.

WKQX–FM (101.1 FM) Alternative Rock *www.q101.com*
On air tip: Home to Chicago's very own shock jock, Mancow.

WKSC–FM (103.5 FM) Contemporary Hits................. *www.kiss1035.com*

WLIT–FM (93.9 FM) Light Rock .... *www.litefm.com*

WLUP–FM (97.9 FM) Rock, mostly Classic .... *www.wlup.com*

WNND–FM (100.3 FM)
Not-So-Oldies: Hits of the 80s and 90s .... *www.wnnd.com*

WNUA–FM (95.5 FM) Smooth Jazz .... *www.wnua.com*
On air tip: Grammy-award-winning jazz pianist Ramsey Lewis hosts the morning show, weekdays 5 A.M.–9 A.M.

WRLL–FM (1690 AM) Real Oldies................... *www.realoldies1690.com*
On air tip: If you ever wondered what happened to WLS's Larry Lujack and Tommy Edwards, and more important, their infamous "Animal Stories," Uncle Lar' and L'il Tommy now run the weekday morning show, with daily Animal Stories segments, at WRLL.

WTMX–FM (101.9 FM) Rock Mix, mostly new ....*www.wtmx.com*
Web tip: Morning hosts Eric and Kathy's "Entertainment Chicago" listing covers upcoming fests, concerts, sporting events, appearances, and miscellaneous fun stuff.

WUSN–FM (99.5 FM) Country *www.us99.com*
Need to know: US–99 is wildly popular beyond what most culture-watchers would expect and perhaps the top major market country station in the U.S. They can take a lot of credit for introducing new country acts like Shania Twain, Alan Jackson, and the Dixie Chicks to an urban audience and the growing cross-over success of country music stars.

WVAZ–FM (102.7 FM) R&B Hits and Old School *www.v103.com*

WXRT–AM (93.1 FM) Rock .... *www.wxrt.com*
Need to know: The oldest (30+ years) and most influential "progressive rock" station in the country, few stations have the success and longevity of WXRT, which has always been at the forefront of musical trends, from punk to grunge. Among rock stations, none have outlasted it. Unlike nearly all commercial music stations, WXRT allows their jocks to pick what songs they play. Their music library consists of thousands of CDs and vinyl, spanning the entire course of rock-and-roll history.
On air tip: Tune in Sunday mornings 9 A.M.–11 A.M. for *Breakfast with The Beatles*. Host Terri Hemmert, XRT's most recognized DJ and Chicago's first female morning drive personality (1981), has been with the station

almost since its inception and is considered to be one of the world's foremost Beatles experts. The *Saturday Morning Flashback* show (8 A.M.– noon), one of the city's most-listened to programs, spotlights the news, music, movies, TV shows, political events, and sports news of a different bygone year each week.

WZSR–FM (105.5 FM) Adult Contemporary.................*www.star105.com*

WZZN–FM (94.7 FM)
Harder, louder, faster side of new Rock *www.947thezone.com*

Sports

WCSN –AM (820 AM)
Sporting News Radio....................................*http://radio.sportingnews.com*

WMVP–AM (1000 AM) ESPN Radio..........................*www.am1000.com*
Web tip: Click on a team's logo, college teams included, to see their schedule and read the latest news.

WSCR–AM (670 AM) Sports Talk.........................*www.670thescore.com*
Need to know: One of the first all-sports stations in the country, "The Score" quickly became the most-listened to station among men 25–54 in the city, even though they were originally a daytime-only station. Then there's Mike North. He went from selling hot dogs at a stand just blocks away from the studios to a multi-million-dollar radio personality at the station.

Ethnic

WCEV–AM (1450 AM) Multi-ethnic, including Polish, Irish, Croatian, and Lithuanian
Noteworthy Trivia: Chicagoland's Ethnic Voice is run by Lucyna Migala, whose family has been involved in Polish broadcasting in Chicago for three generations.

Wietrzne Radio (1080 AM)................................. *www.wietrzneradio.com*
Web tip: Mówi po polsku? If so, you'll be able to navigate their site and benefit from the community calendar and information relevant to Chicago's Polish community.

WIND–AM (560 AM) Spanish....................................*www.univision.com*

On air tip: Catch host Javier Salas weekdays 5 A.M.–10 A.M. on *Un Nuevo Día*, a call-in and discussion show that covers many Chicago topics, particularly those of interest to Chicago Latinos.

WKTA–AM (1330 AM)
Polish, Korean, Russian, Austrian/German .... *www.pclradio.com*

WLEY–FM (107.9 FM) Spanish................................ *www.laley1079.com*
On air tip: The only Spanish station in Chicago known for supporting local musical talent.

WNVR–AM (1030 AM) Polish..................................... *www.pclradio.com*

WOJO–FM (105.1 FM) Spanish .... *www.univision.com*

WPNA–FM (1490 AM) Polish *www.wpna1490am.com*

WVIX–FM (93.5 & 103.1 FM) Spanish .... *www.univision.com*

Chicago Radio on the Internet

Broadcasting in Chicago: 1921–1989 (and thereafter)
www.richsamuels.com/index1.html
This must-visit site for anyone interested in various aspects of Chicago radio history, with special emphasis on the NBC Studios in the Merchandise Mart, includes articles, photos, audio files, and memories for all.

DJ Headlines
www.djheadlines.com
Step inside the world of Chicago radio with DJ Headlines' current events, insider news, links to every station, studio photos, and a directory of "Where Are They Now," where you can find out what's up with your favorite on air personalities.

Radio Hall of Fame
www.radiohof.org
Until the Radio Hall of Fame re-opens within the new Museum of Broadcast Communications Building, find them here on the Net.

Internet Sites

Comprehensive Chicago Pages

AOL CityGuide: Chicago
www.digitalcity.com/chicago
If it's hot, the best, or coming soon, AOL's Chicago city guide will let you know about it, as well as providing news, personals, chat room, and storehouses of local sports, entertainment, dining, shopping, and tourism knowledge.

Chicago Convention & Tourism Bureau
www.choosechicago.com
Some of the most current information on the Internet about what's going on in Chicago—from theater and gallery offerings to specialty tours, events, and festivals. There's the expected general whatnot on visiting the city, Navy Pier, and McCormick Place, but like all repositories of Chicago

---

E-Chicago

A useful way of knowing what's new and what's going on in the city without doing much work is to put yourself on the following free, weekly e-mail lists. While they may be a little too trendy, youthful, or corporate for some, the content is not always predictable—sometimes the writers really do their homework. Each e-newsletter will arrive Thursday or Friday, just in time for weekend planning, and is full of catchy headlines tempting you to click through and be in the know. If nothing else, the ever rotating lineup of coverage and re-mixing and matching of the establishments in their deep databases will remind you of the things you've been meaning to get around to.

- **Citysearch**
  Click on "My CitySearch" in top right corner of page
  (*http://chicago.citysearch.com*) above category tabs to sign up.
- **AOL CityGuide**
  Sign up at: *www.digitalcity.com/chicago/weekendeguide*.
- **Metromix**
  You must register at *www.chicagotribune.com* (click on "Registration") and check the box for the weekly Metromix mailing.

information these days, they're beginning to get more creative with their reporting and their reach into the neighborhoods is expanding.

Chicago Metromix
www.metromix.com
The *Chicago Tribune*'s online guide for the savvy urbanite includes massive searchable databases for nightclubs, film, art & culture, recreation, shopping, family, and more, plus new feature articles posted daily in various departments.

City of Chicago Page
www.cityofchicago.org
The City of Chicago's official site contains a wealth of information both for tourists (interactive downtown map, electronic tour guide, information for student travelers, safety tips, current events, etc.) and residents (directory of city services and departments, public school and public library information, date/time of next city council meeting, special events, and more). This is a good starting point for a search on anything related to Chicago.

Citysearch: Chicago
http://chicago.citysearch.com
Another all-purpose, full-service, up-to-the-minute Web site devoted to fun times in Chicago. Special sections cover restaurants, bars & nightlife, movies, spas & beauty, hotels, and tickets & events. On a given day, features might highlight exotic cocktails at swanky lounges, dog-friendly outings, budget attractions, classic Italian beef joints, and new restaurants opening in a trendy neighborhood.

Chicago Area Statistics and General Facts

Chicago Area Government Information Locator
www.chicagoinfo.gov
Chicagoland information gateway for federal, state, and local government services for individuals, businesses, and nonprofits.

Chicago Demographics Subject Locator
www.cagis.uic.edu/demographics/subject_locator.html
An alphabetical list of dozens of demographic category that will lead you to fascinating sub-categories and statistics on various aspects of Chicago's 74 official communities: What types of transportation do residents of Uptown take to work? What languages do those in Logan Square speak at home? What percentage of people in West Englewood have served in the Military?

Chicago Fact Book
www.ci.chi.il.us/PlanAndDevelop/ChgoFacts
Facts, stats, and Chicago fun from the city's Department of Planning and Development: geography, climate, demographics, education, business, conventions, housing, health care, industry, international trade, labor force, retail sector, and more.

Chicago Public Library Chicago Information
www.chipublib.org/004chicago/004chicago.html
The Chicago Public Library's "Learn Chicago" page leads to all things Chicago: details such as the city motto, charter, corporate seal, flower, and flag; bios and pictures of past mayors; a master timeline of Windy City history; a directory of city organizations; bibliographies and reading lists on local topics; and their special collections, like the Chicago Blues archives.

Chicago Public Library's Frequently Requested Phone Number List
www.chipublib.org/004chicago/chicfreq.html
A list of the phone numbers, and Internet links where relevant, most often requested from the Chicago Public Library: AIDS information and testing, Alcoholics Anonymous, contacting your alderman, the arson hotline, Better Business Bureau, CTA route information, grammar hotlines at local universities, homework hotline, legal services for low income families, museum contacts, passport information, tenants rights, travel information for adjacent states, voter information, and many more.

Chicago Vocabulary
http://members.aol.com/mistamoose/vocab.html
A glossary of Chicago vernacular, shorthand, acronyms, and in-the-know phrases, such as the fact that we use "alderman" for both male and female council members, what we prefer to call our sports stadiums regardless of corporate naming rights, slogans from long-running local TV commercials, and nicknames for local personalities. A good start, but take advantage of their suggestion request to help them expand.

Television

Web tip: If you've never been to a local station's Web site, it's time to check one out. They all have breaking news and video, other current news stories and updates, an instant view of local weather conditions, and easy ways to submit story ideas for your favorite segments. There are also contests, promotions, community events calendars, and public service announcements like product recalls, school closings, fraud advisories, etc.

Network TV

WBBM/CBS (Channel 2).. *www.cbs2chicago.com*
Local weekday news: 5 A.M., 11 A.M., 4:30 P.M., 5 P.M., and 10 P.M.
Saturdays: 8 A.M., 5 P.M., and 10 P.M.
Sundays: 6 A.M., 10 A.M., 5 P.M., and 10 P.M.
Look for recurring segments "Table for 2" and "Inside Chicago" on the local news. "Table for 2" has everyday Chicagoans recommending and discussing their favorite places to eat. Inside Chicago takes reporter Vince Gerasole anywhere around town imaginable from the Hilton's laundry room to women's favorite shoe stores.

WMAQ/NBC (Channel 5)... *www.nbc5.com*
Local weekday news: 5 A.M.–7 A.M., 11 A.M.–11:30 A.M., 4:30 P.M., 5 P.M., and 10 P.M.
Saturdays: 6 A.M., 5 P.M., and 10 P.M.
Sundays: 6 A.M., 8 A.M., 5 P.M., and 10 P.M.
As on NBC's *Today* show, viewers are invited to the northwest corner of the 401 N. Michigan building next to the NBC Tower on Columbus Drive to watch the local morning newscasts live from the street-side "Studio5."

WLS/ABC (Channel 7)... *www.abc7chicago.com*
Local weekday news: 5 A.M., 5:30 A.M., 6 A.M., 11 A.M., 4 P.M., 5 P.M., 6 P.M., and 10 P.M.
Saturdays: 6 A.M., 5 P.M., and 10 P.M.
Sundays: 6 A.M., 7 A.M., 8 A.M., 5 P.M., and 10 P.M.
ABC–Channel 7 has led the market in local news coverage since 1986. Chicago segments to watch out for are Steve Dolinsky's "The Hungry Hound" food and restaurant reports Wednesdays and Fridays on the 11 A.M. news and Harry Porterfield's "Someone You Should Know" Tuesdays and Thursdays on the 5 P.M. program. Porterfield has been introducing Chicagoans to the notable people and organizations next door since 1977.
Shows to know:
  • **Chicagoing!** (Sun. 11:30 A.M.)
  In the longest-running show of its kind (15 years and counting), veteran news reporter Bill Campbell engages in serious and lighthearted conversations and profiles on the past, present, and future of Chicago.

  • **190 North** (Sun. 10:35 P.M., re-aired Sun. 11 A.M.)

Local news pro Janet Davies explores what's new, fun, and unusual in Chicago. Episodes of the past year have taken the audience to up-and-coming and overlooked neighborhoods; Tiki lounges; motorcycle rallies; DJ, bartending, and French pastry schools; and the Pedway system.

WGN (Channel 9) .... *www.wgntv.com*
Local weekday news: 5 A.M.– 9 A.M., noon, and 9 P.M.
Saturdays: midnight and 9 P.M.
Sundays: 9 P.M.
WGN has a reputation as one of the country's most popular local television stations and home of the Chicago Cubs' games, but other than the news and the Cubbies, WB shows dominate Channel 9's programming. For fun local stuff catch their 5-minute "Lunchbreak" segment on the noon show and "Unsung Heroes" and "Chicago's Very Own Stories" bits on the weekend news.

WTTW/PBS (Channel 11) .... *www.networkchicago.com/wttw*
Shows to know:
   • **Check, Please!** (Fri. 8 P.M., re-aired Sat. 2 P.M., Sun. 11 P.M.)
Every week, host Alpana Singh invites three new guests who are not professional restaurant critics—though there's the occasional local celebrity—to try each other's restaurant recommendations, then discuss them on this wildly popular show.
   • **Chicago Tonight** (Mon.–Fri. 7 P.M., re-aired Mon.–Fri. midnight, 1:30 A.M., 4:30 A.M.)
Channel 11 has recently merged most of their specialty Chicago programming with the long-running *Chicago Tonight* public affairs show, which has a new one-hour format hosted by Bob Sirott. The first half-hour is still the more serious current events interviews and panel discussions with co-host Phil Ponce. The latter portion of the show devotes 5–10 minute chunks of time to subjects previously covered by such shows as *Artbeat Chicago* (arts and culture), *Chicago Stories* (the people, places, and events of Chicago's past), and *Wild Chicago*. Not to be missed for all Chicago junkies and any time you need to re-connect with your city.

WYCC (Channel 20) .... *www.ccc.edu/wycc*
WYCC is the television station of Chicago's City Colleges.
Shows to know:
   • **Ben Around Town** (Fri. 7 P.M., re-aired Sun. 7:30 P.M.)
Host Ben Hollis's latest venture in publicly airing his passion for Chicago, specifically its zanier side. Previous efforts of the same, in

Wild Chicago and *Ben Loves Chicago*, brought him Emmys.

WCIU (Channel 26)... *www.wciu.com*
Need to know: WCIU–TV (Chicago's 1ˢᵗ UHF) became Chicago's first UHF station in 1964, and is one of the last locally owned and operated independent major-market stations in the country.
Noteworthy trivia: Always aiming to reach the "underserved" in Chicago, WCIU is the birthplace of *Soul Train*, the first African-American youth dance program on TV.
Show to know:
  • **Svengoolie** (Sat. 9 P.M.)
    In the annals of local TV hosts, Rich Koz ranks up there with the favorites and the memorables. Chicago's King of the Horror Flicks for almost three decades, Koz is Svengoolie, emcee of the evening's featured scary movie. Svengoolie, with his musical sidekick Doug Graves and talking skull Tombstone, provides comedy, commentary, musical interludes, commercial parodies, sounds effects, and dialogue revisions throughout the show to enhance movies that would otherwise be frightful. Yes, he used to be the *Son of Svengoolie*, but original Svengoolie Jerry G. Bishop granted him full Svengoolie-hood in the early 90s.

FOX/WFLD (Channel 32)... *www.foxchicago.com*
Local weekday news: 5 A.M.–7 A.M., 7 A.M.– 9 A.M., and 9 P.M.
Saturdays: 9 P.M.
Sundays: 9 P.M.
Need to know: Bob Sirott, a former Top 40 DJ with WLS and now with *Chicago Tonight*, reinvented morning news shows with the development of the Emmy-winning *Fox Thing in the Morning*, which he then hosted for several years, mingling the news with his sharp wit, amplified banter, Chicago memories, fondness for records, and gimmicks like interviewing celebrities in bed. The current *Fox News in the Morning* has replaced it.

Cable TV

Chicago Access Network Television/CAN TV.................. *www.cantv.org*
CAN TV is a non-commercial, 90% local group of public access television stations, recognized nationally for its model programming and services (such as training and facilities) in the realm of community media.

- **CAN TV 19**

Programming covers various music genres, ethnic news, neighborhood issues and commentary, labor, seniors, sports, and nonprofits.

- **CAN TV 21**

Schedule includes the Education bulletin board with a fax-on-demand feature for obtaining applications and forms at home; "Chicago Learns TV" Chicago Public Schools programming; weeknight call-in shows devoted to health, education, economic development, and local politics; and the new Illinois Channel, a state version of C-SPAN where we'll be able to see the state government in action.

- **CAN TV 27**

Channel 27 is "FYI Chicago," where nonprofits can run video brochures of their organizations. The Illinois Labor History Society, the Chicago Reporter, and the Community Media Workshop also have regular sports.

- **CAN TV 42**

CAN–CALL TV 42 is an interactive community bulletin board for the posting of events, jobs, educational activities, and nonprofit resources. Viewers can dial a local number and punch in a 3-digit code to read about the item that interests them on TV.

Chicago Cable–TV 25
Show to know:
- **Nude Hippo: Your Chicago Show** (Thur. 7 P.M.–8 P.M.)
www.nudehippo.com
Tony Lossano and company's magazine-style show covers the people, places, and events of Chicago in a fun-loving, independent, and winging-it style during its two back-to-back half-hour shows.

Chicago Municipal Television Channel (Channel 23) and the **Chicago Arts Channel** (Channel 49) are low-powered cable stations delivering 24-hour municipal news and information. While some of the programming is heavily overlaid with cheerleading for the current administration, this is still interesting stuff. For most of us, it provides a rare look into the schools, parks, community centers, libraries, and social services beyond our own neighborhoods, *and* our only experience at all behind the scenes in many city departments, utilities, industrial facilities, train yards. *CHAnge* takes a look at positive developments in the Chicago Housing Authority, also an eye-opener for many, and *Connections* shows viewers all the places you can go with the Chicago Transit Authority.

CLTV (Channel depends on cable service) .... *www.cltv.com*
The aptly named Chicagoland TV declares that they are "around Chicago, around the clock," and it's true. Without the usual stunts or sensation, but with eyes, ears, and a heart for its character, CLTV consistently provides outstanding coverage of Chicago as a city and as a region in all its complexity.
Show to know:
* **Metromix: The TV Show** (Thur. 8:30 P.M., re-aired Fri. 11:30 A.M., 7:30 P.M., and 11:30 P.M., Sat. 6:30 A.M. and 11:30 A.M., and Sun. 11:30 A.M.)
Hosted by local broadcasting personality LeeAnn Trotter, this televised version of the Tribune company Web site (www.metromix.com) focuses on the best local entertainment options, particularly nightlife and weekend activities.

Publications

At the Newsstand

Chicago Magazine... *www.chicagomag.com*
Chicago Magazine's slick and polished coverage of Chicago-area personalities, politics, dining, culture, society, trends, real estate, fashion, and lifestyle issues actually appeals to a broader, more generalized audience than its pages of high-end advertising would suggest.

Chicago Reporter... *www.chicagoreporter.com*
This monthly, award-winning paper has been delivering investigative journalism of race and poverty issues in Chicago since 1972.

Chicago Sun-Times .... *www.suntimes.com*
A daily circulation of about 450,000 papers makes the *Chicago Sun-Times* one of the 10 largest daily newspapers in the U.S.

Chicago Tribune... *www.chicagotribune.com*
Founded in 1847 and run for over a century by the local Medill–McCormick family dynasty, the *Chicago Tribune* is one of the nation's foremost newspapers with its 23 Pulitzer Prizes, a daily circulation close to 700,000, and a Sunday circulation topping 1,000,000.

Crain's Chicago Business .... *www.crainschicagobusiness.com*
One of the country's chief regional business publications, *Crain's* provides
a diverse lineup of breaking news, features, and opinions on the Chicagoland
business scene to almost a quarter of a million people weekly.

Daily Herald .... *www.dailyherald.com*
Four generations of the Paddock family built a chain of weekly newspapers
into the *Daily Herald* over the last 120 years. Based in the Northern
Suburbs, this daily is now the third largest newspaper in the state.

Daily Southtown .... *www.dailysouthtown.com*
A daily, regional paper based in the South Suburbs and primarily serving
those communities and their adjoining city neighborhoods.

Free and Topical

These ubiquitous papers, often found in banks, bars, libraries, restaurants,
and stores are invaluable resources for keeping in touch with neighborhood
and city happenings, especially those in your areas of interest. Keep an eye
out, too, for established and emerging neighborhood papers.

African-American

N'DIGO
401 N. Wabash; Chicago, IL 60611; 312/822-0202
www.ndigo.com
The largest weekly publication aimed at black Chicagoans, *N'Digo* covers
events, entertainment, fashion, people, health, jobs, and finance, mostly for
a middle-class and progressive audience.

Chicago for Residents

Chicago Learning Guide
1823 W. Iowa; Chicago, IL 60622; 773/782-0901
www.chicagolearningguide.com
A quarterly directory of professional, personal, and recreational classes
available in and around Chicago, the *Learning Guide* includes articles and
photography on learning activities, plus indexed listings of hundreds of class
providers, private instructors, classes, and learning events.

Chicago Reader
11 E. Illinois; Chicago, IL 60611; 312/828-0350
www.chireader.com
At least the size of the Sunday paper, the *Reader* may be the largest free alternative weekly in the United States. This is a weekly must-have for many Chicagoans who rely on its comprehensive coverage of art, movies, music, and theatre goings-on; an overwhelming classified section that will hook you up with anything you need in Chicago—job, car, apartment, date, friends, activities, enlightenment—anything; and its in-depth cover stories. Pick one up practically anywhere free newspapers are stacked.

Newcity
770 N. Halsted, Suite 306; Chicago, IL 60622; 312/243-8786
www.newcitychicago.com
A weekly Chicago news and arts paper with extensive event listings—a good bet if the *Reader* overwhelms you.

The Onion
3023 N. Clark, #908; Chicago, IL 60657; 773/404-9910
www.theonion.com
Billed as "America's Finest News Source," this weekly parody paper, originally from Madison, Wisconsin, now has serious local reviews, ads, and information on what's happening around town in the back section after all the funny stuff.

UR
655 W. Irving Park, Suite 209; Chicago, IL 60613; 773/529-5100
www.urchicago.com
In a previous incarnation, the "University Reporter" for college kids, UR has grown up into covering Chicago culture, sounds, and attitude (lots of attitude) for those 20-something spirits of all ages. The journalism's on the light side, but in revealing the city life and night life around them, the staff usually takes a refreshing and imaginative approach. P.S. There's also a raunch-factor to some of the columns unsuitable for most people's parents.

Chicago for Tourists

Chicago Official Visitors Guide
McCormick Place on the Lake
2301 S. Lake Shore Drive; Chicago, IL 60616, 312/567-8500
www.choosechicago.com
The quarterly visitors' guide published by the Chicago Convention and

Tourism Bureau covers seasonal events and attractions, nightlife, dining, shopping, and sightseeing, and includes a fold out map of the most-visited neighborhoods by tourists.

Key Magazine
904 W. Blackhawk; Chicago, IL 60622; 312/943-0838
http://keymagazine.com/chicago
This weekly visitors' information guide has been around since 1920. Find it in hotels, convention facilities, information centers, and airports.

WHERE Magazine
1165 N. Clark; Chicago, IL 60610; 312/642-1896
www.wheremagazine.com
WHERE has been publishing those glossy, monthly magazines that cue visitors on the best current events, shopping, dining, attractions, cultural options, and entertainment to be found in those central enclaves of a city tourists are most likely to visit for 65 years and is now the largest global publisher of such. Pick one up wherever you and fellow tourists congregate.

Children and Parents

Chicago Parent
141 S. Oak Park Avenue; Oak Park, IL 60302; 708/386-5555
www.chicagoparent.com
Considered one of the best local parenting publications in the country, this hefty, all-purpose monthly newsmagazine not only provides information on Chicagoland events and resources, but covers general topics from a Chicago perspective and relies on Chicago writers and experts to do so.

Gay and Lesbian

Chicago Free Press
3714 N. Broadway, Chicago, IL 60613; 773/325-0005
www.chicagofreepress.com
"A common voice for a diverse community," this newsweekly caters to Chicago's gay and lesbian community. Formed a few years ago when staff members walked out of the *Windy City Times*, the *Free Press* now makes Chicago a two-GLBT-paper town. "Freetime," their nightlife and entertainment section, has club listings and party pics. "FreeStyle" covers books, music, film, theater, and food.

Gay Chicago Magazine
3115 N. Broadway; Chicago, IL 60657; 773/327-7271
www.gaychicagomagazine.com
A 20-year-old weekly newsmagazine for gay men filled with local and national news, theater and restaurant reviews, columnists, events and nightlife calendar, and extensive classifieds.

Windy City Media Group
1115 W. Belmont, #2-D; Chicago, IL 60657; 773/871-7610
www.windycitymediagroup.com
"The Voice of Chicago's Gay, Lesbian, Bi, and Trans Community Since 1985" publishes a number of periodicals including:
- *Windy City Times*
A newsweekly covering local and national news, books, theater, and events.
- *Nightspots*
A weekly publication devoted to gay nightlife and local events
- *Identity*
A monthly publication for the black gay and lesbian community.

Jewish

Chicago Jewish Star
Star Media Group, Inc.
P.O. Box 268; Skokie, IL 60076-0014; 847/674-STAR
www.skokienet.org/cjstar1
Chicago's oldest, largest-circulation, independent Jewish newspaper, the twice-monthly *Chicago Jewish Star* offers fresh and award-winning coverage of local, national, and international news; commentary; and a useful calendar of events.

Music

Chicago Jazz Magazine
P.O. Box 737; Park Ridge, IL 60068; 847/322-3534
www.chicagojazzmagazine.com
This all-purpose monthly for true-blue and jazz-curious fans dispenses educational columns on the nuts, bolts, and fringes of the genre; book and CD reviews; interviews with local musicians; obits; photos; and club schedules for recurring and touring acts.

Illinois Entertainer
2250 E. Devon; Des Plaines, IL 60018; 708/298-9333
www.illinoisentertainer.com
A heavy duty monthly newsmagazine for those in greater Chicagoland (up to Milwaukee and down to downstate) who are in, aspiring to be in, or appreciate all forms of rock bands. With serious features, columns, and reviews on local and touring groups, music culture, and equipment; directories of local bands, clubs, labels, and studios; and classifieds that make it easy to find lessons, used equipment, and bandmates.

New Age

The Monthly Aspectarian
TMA Communications, Inc.
6407 W. Elm St.; Morton Grove, IL 60053; 847/966-1110
www.lightworks.com/MonthlyAspectarian
The premier New Age publication for the Chicago/Northwest Indiana/Milwaukee/Madison region, this 100-page monthly has been bringing readers articles, resources, and events related to heightened consciousness, holistic health, and physical, mental, and spiritual growth since 1979. Look for it in vegetarian restaurants, health food stores, and metaphysical shops.

Socially Conscious for the Countercultural

Conscious Choice
920 N. Franklin; Suite 202; Chicago, IL 60610; 312/440-4373
www.consciouschoice.com
This ample monthly newsmagazine promotes holistic and sustainable living, political awareness, socially-responsible business and lifestyles, ecology, and wellness through in-depth features, columns, calendars of events, and resource listings that focus on the local and regional but sometimes extend to national and international levels.

Socially Conscious for the Upscale

Chicago Social
200 W. Hubbard; Chicago, IL 60610; 312/274-2500
www.Modernluxury.com
An oversized, glossy, "luxury" monthly for an upscale crowd, covering local social events, big ticket charity functions, fashion, art, food, and wine.

Sports

Chicago Athlete Magazine
7842 N. Lincoln Ave.; Skokie, IL 60077; 847/675-0200
www.chicagoaa.com
Aimed at active and competitive athletes, particularly runners, cyclists, and triathletes, *Chicago Athlete* is a monthly mag providing comprehensive coverage of news, race results, events, clubs, stores, and new products, along with feature articles.

The Chicago Sports Review
216 W. Jackson Blvd., Ste. 925; Chicago, IL 60606; 312/658-1200
www.chicagosportsreview.com
If you can identify with the sense that there is no such thing as too much sports, get yourself to their Web site and sign up for the daily e-mail newsletter. The publication itself is monthly and available in many popular sports bars. CSR keeps you current with professional, college, high school, amateur, and fantasy sports.

Windy City Sports
1450 W. Randolph; Chicago, IL 60607; 312/421-1551
www.windycitysportsmag.com
A monthly magazine for the Chicago athlete, particularly those who like to compete, train, and swoon over gear. With in-depth articles, local resources, and schedules of events.

Theater

PerformInk
3223 N. Sheffield; Chicago, IL 60657; 773/296-4600
www.performink.com
A biweekly publication devoted to the Chicago theater scene, focusing particularly on items of interest to actors and others in the business.

Women

Today's Chicago Woman
Leigh Communications, Inc.
233 E. Ontario Street, Suite 1300; Chicago, IL 60611; 312/951-7600
www.todayschicagowoman.com
This large and enduring monthly newspaper primarily for and about profes-

sional women covers the lighter topics of health, beauty (lots of cosmetic surgery), fashion, shopping, luxury items, food, wine, and events, along with politics, business, finance, networking, and the stories of influential local women.

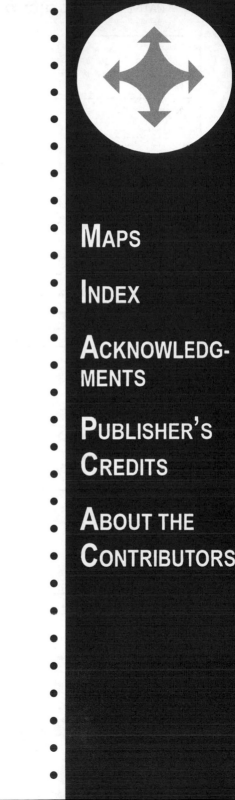

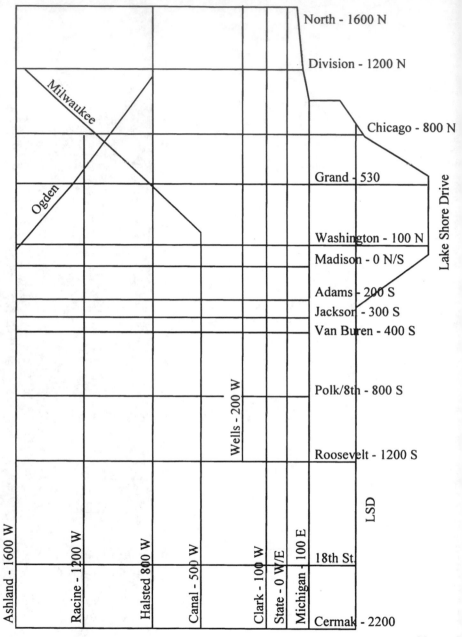

North - 1600 N

Division - 1200 N

Chicago - 800 N

Grand - 530

Washington - 100 N

Madison - 0 N/S

Adams - 200 S

Jackson - 300 S

Van Buren - 400 S

Polk/8th - 800 S

Roosevelt - 1200 S

18th St.

Cermak - 2200

Milwaukee

Ogden

Lake Shore Drive

LSD

Wells - 200 W

Ashland - 1600 W

Racine - 1200 W

Halsted 800 W

Canal - 500 W

Clark - 100 W

State - 0 W/E

Michigan - 100 E

Central

N
W ← → E
S

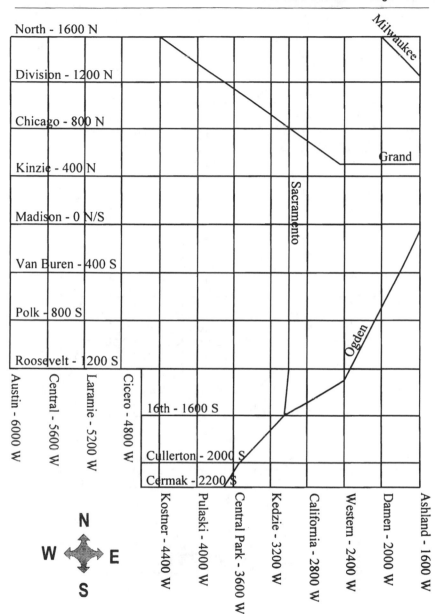

North - 1600 N

Division - 1200 N

Chicago - 800 N

Kinzie - 400 N

Madison - 0 N/S

Van Buren - 400 S

Polk - 800 S

Roosevelt - 1200 S

16th - 1600 S

Cullerton - 2000 S

Cermak - 2200 S

Milwaukee

Grand

Sacramento

Ogden

Austin - 6000 W

Central - 5600 W

Laramie - 5200 W

Cicero - 4800 W

Kostner - 4400 W

Pulaski - 4000 W

Central Park - 3600 W

Kedzie - 3200 W

California - 2800 W

Western - 2400 W

Damen - 2000 W

Ashland - 1600 W

N
W E
S

West

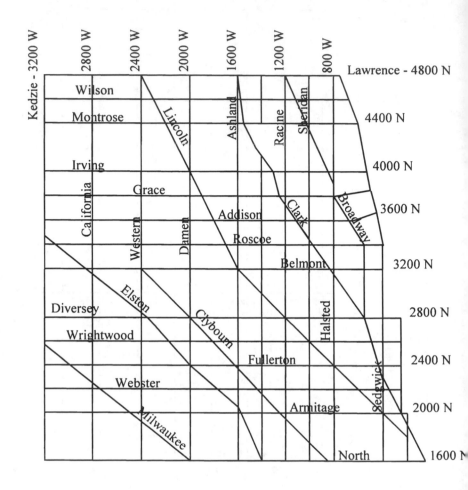

North

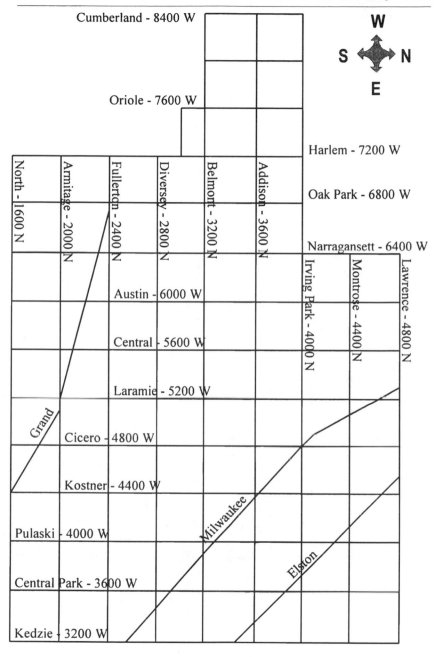

Northwest

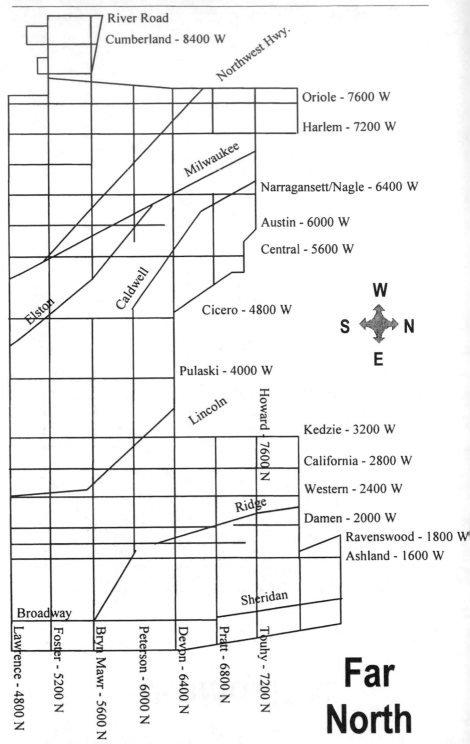

River Road
Cumberland - 8400 W
Northwest Hwy.
Oriole - 7600 W
Harlem - 7200 W
Milwaukee
Narragansett/Nagle - 6400 W
Austin - 6000 W
Central - 5600 W
Caldwell
Elston
Cicero - 4800 W
Pulaski - 4000 W
Lincoln
Howard - 7600 N
Kedzie - 3200 W
California - 2800 W
Western - 2400 W
Ridge
Damen - 2000 W
Ravenswood - 1800 W
Ashland - 1600 W
Sheridan
Broadway
Lawrence - 4800 N
Foster - 5200 N
Bryn Mawr - 5600 N
Peterson - 6000 N
Devon - 6400 N
Pratt - 6800 N
Touhy - 7200 N

W
S ← → N
E

Far North

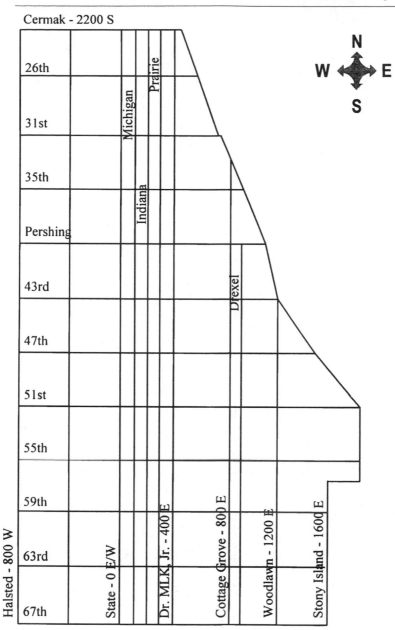

South

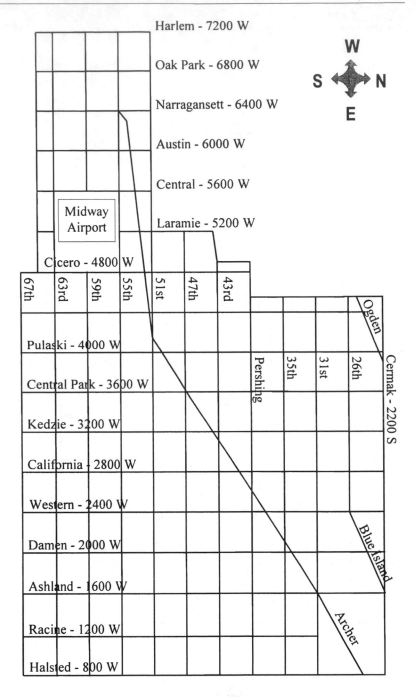

Harlem - 7200 W

Oak Park - 6800 W

Narragansett - 6400 W

Austin - 6000 W

Central - 5600 W

Laramie - 5200 W

Midway
Airport

Cicero - 4800 W

67th · 63rd · 59th · 55th · 51st · 47th · 43rd

Pulaski - 4000 W

Central Park - 3600 W

Kedzie - 3200 W

California - 2800 W

Western - 2400 W

Damen - 2000 W

Ashland - 1600 W

Racine - 1200 W

Halsted - 800 W

Pershing · 35th · 31st · 26th

Cermak - 2200 S

Ogden

Blue Island

Archer

W / S / N / E

Southwest

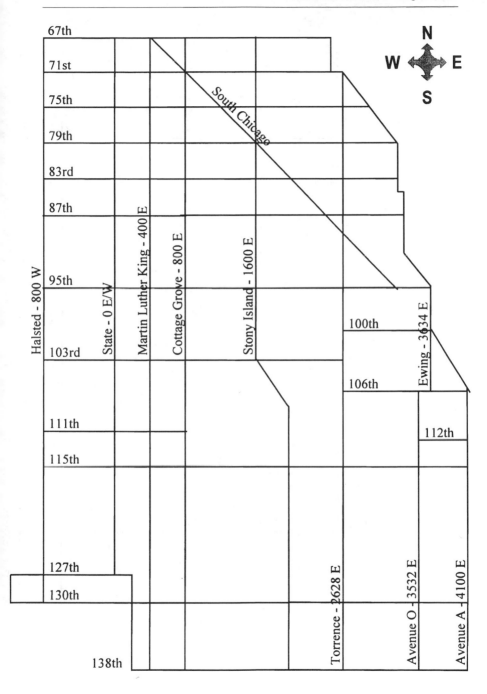

Far Southeast

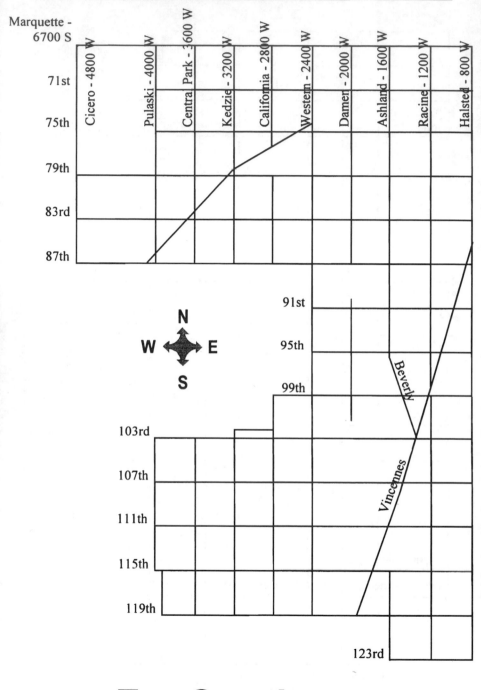

Far Southwest

Index

Wholesale Mattress Factory Outlet, 371
Wicker Park, 108, 139
Wicker Park Chess Club, 105
Wicker Park's Summerfest, 297
Wiener Circle, The, 173, 322
Wiggly Field, 108
Wikstrom's Gourmet Foods, 308
Wild Goose, 202
Wild Hare, 252
Wildwood Park, 133, 138
Williams Park, 115, 141
Willows Hotel, 347
Wilson Community Center, 140
Wilson Park (Frank J.), 133, 138
Wilson Park (John P.), 140
Wilson Skate Park, 121
Windward Sports, 122
Windy City Darters, 107
Windy City Furniture, 400
Windy City Sailing, 120
Windy City Urban Inn, 348
wine, 388
Wine Discount Center, 369
Wing & Groove Theatre, 275
Wing Wah Lau, 160
Wise Fools Pub, 254
Wishbone, 228
WNEP Theatre, 273
Wolf Lake/William Powers Conservation
    Area, 70–71, 319
Wolfe Playground, 98, 141
Women and Children First, 308
Womens Park & Gardens, 49
Wonderland Multivintage, 410
Wooded Island and Lagoon, 71, 337
Wooded Isle Suites, 348
Woodhull Playground, 141
World Bocce Association, 99
world music, 255
World's Finest Chocolate Outlet Store, 237
Wright, Frank Lloyd, 25, 27, 30, 60
Wrightwood Park, 129, 138
Wrightwood Playground, 118
Wrigley Building, 19
Wrigley Field, 335
Wrigleyville News, 382
Wrigleyville's Addison-Clark Street Fair, 297

Xavier's, 279
Xpedx Paper Store, 371–372

Yardifacts, 368
Yesterday, 387
Yoga, 135
Yojimbo's Garage, 379–380
Young Park, 140

Zaiqa, 183
Zanzibar Motel, 355
Zebra Lounge, 251
Zella's, 315
Zentra, 256, 315
Zephyr Ice Cream Restaurant, 182
Zeppo Theater, 275
Zoolights, 51
zoos, 13–14
Zorba's House, 197

Acknowledgments

INSTEAD of getting simpler, each successive edition of *A Native's Guide To Chicago* becomes more involved and draws more people into its creation. For this fourth edition, that meant the invaluable help of over a dozen contributing writers who took on the project of updating the last edition and keeping up with the ever-growing number of establishments worthy of inclusion. It also meant painstaking fact-checking and proofreading not only by freelancers, but by friends and family as well. Graphic designer Timothy Kocher once again updated the cover, and Bill Arroyo is to thank for the new photos. "We couldn't have done it without you" is hardly sufficient to recognize everyone's individual contributions. A million thanks! Finally, our tremendous appreciation to all those at the other ends of letters, phone calls, emails, and surprise visits, who supplied either suggestions or information to help make this the best version of *A Native's Guide to Chicago* yet! You've each provided an important piece of the final product and we're truly grateful for your participation. —Lake Claremont Press

Publisher's Credits

COVER design by Timothy Kocher. Editing, layout, and interior design by Sharon Woodhouse. Photographs by Bill Arroyo and Rames Shrestha. Maps by Bill Arroyo and Sharon Woodhouse. Fact checking by Elizabeth Daniel, Amy Formanski, Karen Formanski, Steven Kaszynski, Mary McNulty, Ken Woodhouse, Sandie Woodhouse, Sharon Woodhouse, and Sheryl Woodhouse-Keese. Proofreading by Elizabeth Daniel, Karen Formanski, Steven Kaszynski, and Sharon Woodhouse. Indexing by Elizabeth Daniel, Karen Formanski, Steven Kaszynski, and Brian Keese. Contributing writers: Susan Blumberg, Ella Bramwell, Christina Bultinck, Nicole Bultinck, Sheila Elliot, Amy Formanski, Karen Formanski, Keir Graff, John Greenfield, Mary Houlihan, Mary McNulty, James Porter, Heather Shouse, Matt Wolka, Ken Woodhouse, and Sharon Woodhouse. With special entries by Bill Lucas, Andrew Plonka, and Ken Polson.

Typography

THE text of *A Native's Guide To Chicago* was set in Times New Roman, with heads and subheads in Arial Narrow.

Notice

Contributors

SUSAN BLUMBERG is a native Chicagoan and recent South Side convert. She works in publishing at the University of Chicago and is also a freelance writer.

ELLA BRAMWELL is a well-seasoned native of the South Side of Chicago. Ella holds a Masters degree in Marketing and Marketing Communications and serves as a part-time faculty member at Columbia College in the Arts, Entertainment, and Marketing Department. The owner and president of Untamed Marketing, Inc., she has executed marketing programs within the music and entertainment industries for over ten years and currently specializes in youth and ethnic marketing programs. She's been married for nearly 20 years and is the mother of two boys.

While CHRISTINA BULTINCK'S parents dreamed of raising their kids in the "country," Christina dreamt of living in the city, which she now does, though her geographic partiality is equally divided. She enjoys snagging a deal at eclectic stores, grabbing a meal at ethnic restaurants, and blabbing her spiel at area bars.

NICOLE BULTINCK had a great time researching and reviewing natural spaces, recreation, restaurants/bars, lodging, and outlet stores in portions of Wicker Park, West Town, the Near West Side, the Loop, Printer's Row, and Mount Greenwood. Nicole recently completed a Bachelor of Business Administration degree and has started working on her MBA.

SHEILA ELLIOTT is a journalist with many years of experience reporting on Chicago's Southwest Side and its suburban communities. Raised in Chicago, she now calls Oak Park home.

AMY FORMANSKI, a lifelong Chicagoan, answers an astounding variety of questions daily at a local library. She freelances as a factchecker and proofreader for LCP when needed. You might see her around the North Side on her mission to keep all neighborhood indie coffeehouses and resale clothing stores in business. She is currently pursuing her MLIS degree from Dominican University

KAREN FORMANSKI has been Assistant Publisher at LCP since September, 2000. Despite having an incurable travel bug, she has always embraced

Chicago as her hometown. In her spare time she enjoys exploring the city's neighborhoods, volunteering and taking lessons at the Old Town School of Folk Music, and experimenting with vegan cuisine.

KEIR GRAFF may not be a Chicago native, but he's been more than happy to adopt the city as his new hometown. He reviews books for *Booklist*, and has contributed features, essays, and criticism to publications such as Playboy.com, the *Chicago Tribune*, the *Chicago Reader*, the *Daily Herald*, *Billiards Digest*, *NewCity*, and *CS*. He's also a playwright and a screenwriter—he just signed a contract to adapt his play, *Driving a Bargain*, for Luminair Films.

JOHN GREENFIELD has spent his entire adult life in Chicago. A bicycle messenger for most of the nineties, he now works as Bicycle Parking Coordinator for the Chicagoland Bicycle Federation. Greenfield also writes occasionally for the *Chicago Reader* and leads the rock band Illinois First!, playing songs about the history and geography of the Land of Lincoln.

MARY HOULIHAN writes about theater, music, and the arts for the *Chicago Sun-Times*.

A virtual native of Chicago, **MARY McNULTY** fell in love with the city the first time she drove down Lake Shore Drive and saw the Buckingham Fountain in full spurt. Since that momentous day, Mary has learned to dress in layers, collected stories on the Archer Avenue bus, and become a die-hard White Sox fan. Her work has appeared in the *Chicago Tribune*, the *Daily Herald*, *West Suburban Living*, and *American Profile*.

JAMES PORTER is a Chicago native who, in addition to writing about music, entertainment and local color for *Newcity*, *Illinois Entertainer*, *No Depression*, *Living Blues*, *Blender*, and other magazines, was a major contributor to the book *Bubblegum Music Is The Naked Truth* (Feral House, 2001).

HEATHER SHOUSE is a local writer who contributed to the food, music, and shopping sections. While not a Chicago native, the Columbia College journalism graduate considers the Second City her second home. Her writing on music, food, arts, and entertainment has appeared in the *Chicago Tribune*, *Chicago Reader*, *CS*, and various national publications. In addition, she is the Chicago editor of *Flyer* magazine, a monthly culture guide distributed in major cities nationwide.

MATTHEW WOLKA works as a church musician and spends most of the day cruising Chicago neighborhoods for 8-tracks. While attending Northwestern University, he fell in love with the city and, with the exception of a four year stint in the Navy and a whimsical three month adventure in Poland, hasn't lived anywhere else since.

KEN WOODHOUSE is a third-generation, lifelong Chicagoan and a 2003 graduate of the University of Illinois at Urbana-Champaign. He is an avid, amateur musician and stays active in the local music scene as the General Manager for Lakeside Pride Musical Ensembles and as a Unison choir member with Windy City Performing Arts. He is currently serving as an AmeriCorps volunteer with Teaming for Technology at the United Way.

SHARON WOODHOUSE is the publisher of Lake Claremont Press and a faithful Chicagoan who falls smitten with cities everywhere, particularly New York City. But don't tell anyone. She has written about Chicago for Metromix.com, *American Bookseller*, *Publishers Weekly*, and several other local, national, and online publications.

Lake Claremont Press

Where the Second City is second to none . . .

- Preserving the past
- Exploring the present
- Ensuring a future sense of place for our corner of the globe

In a highly-mobile, rootless world where places can easily lose their individual character, **Lake Claremont Press books foster and reveal Chicago's special identity by sharing what's distinctive about our city's history, culture, geography, built environment, spirit, people, and lore**.

In an age of giant media mergers at one end of the spectrum, Lake Claremont Press represents the alternative at the other end: **a small, independent, niche publisher specializing in a subject that we know better than anyone**. As such, we stand shoulder-to-shoulder with the publishing houses of that *other* big city.

Founded by Sharon Woodhouse in 1994, Lake Claremont Press has published 30 titles, including local bestseller *Chicago Haunts: Ghostlore of the Windy City* and award-winners *Hollywood on Lake Michigan: 100 Years of Chicago and the Movies*, *The Chicago River: A Natural and Unnatural History*, and *Near West Side Stories: Struggles for Community in Chicago's Maxwell Street Neighborhood*. Our staff of three full-time and one part-time employee releases four to seven new titles annually with the help of a crew of talented freelance production professionals.

LCP authors and their books have been featured in hundreds of local and national newspapers, magazines, and Internet publications, and on dozens of local and national radio programs, television shows, and cable channels, including the *Chicago Sun-Times*, *Chicago Tribune*, *Chicago Magazine*, *Crain's Chicago Business*, the *Wall Street Journal*, the BBC, CNN, National Public Radio, A&E, The History Channel, The Travel Channel, The National Geographic Channel, WGN, *Chicago Tonight*, and the *Chicago Stories* series. Our staff and authors are actively involved in promoting and sharing our love and knowledge of Chicago with our community and the world beyond.

We welcome new and established authors to submit book proposals and finished manuscripts on all things Chicago. We publish nonfiction trade paperbacks only at this time; we do not publish memoirs, coffee table books, photography, fiction, or poetry.

Other Lake Claremont Press Books

Award Winners

The Chicago River: A Natural and Unnatural History
by Libby Hill
Hill presents an intimate biography of a humble, even sluggish, stream in the right place at the right time—the story of the making and perpetual re-making of a river by everything from geological forces to the interventions of an emerging and mighty city. **Winner of a 2001 American Regional History Publishing award and a 2000 Midwest Independent Publishers Association award. Nominated for best new book in public works history.**
1-893121-02-X, Aug. 2000, softcover, 302 pp., 78 maps and photos, $16.95

The Streets & San Man's Guide to Chicago Eats
by Dennis Foley
Tongue-in-Cheek Style and Food-in-Mouth Expertise certified by the City of Chicago's *Department of Lunch*. Streets & San electrician Dennis Foley shares his and his co-workers' favorite lunch joints in all reaches of the city. Enjoy Chicago's best mom-and-pop eateries at fast-food prices and never eat in chain restaurants again! Warning: requires a sense of humor, a sense of adventure, and a large appetite. **Winner of two 2004 Midwest Independent Publishers Association Awards!**
1-893121-27-5, June 2004, softcover, 117 pp., 83 reviews, 25 coupons, $12.95

Finding Your Chicago Ancestors:
A Beginner's Guide to Family History in the City and Cook County
by Grace DuMelle
Trace your Chicago lineage with this step-by-step guide by Grace DuMelle, owner of the Heartland Historical Research Service and a family historian with the Newberry Library. This book is designed to be simple enough for beginners and useful for anyone doing research on their family's Chicago connections. **Winner of a 1st place 2005 Midwest Independent Publishers Association Award, a 2006 Illinois Woman's Press Association Communications Contest award, and a 2006 National Federation of Press Women Award.**
1-893121-25-9, March 2005, softcover, 329 pp., heavily illustrated, $16.95

Near West Side Stories:
Struggles for Community in Chicago's Maxwell Street Neighborhood
by Carolyn Eastwood
An ongoing story of unequal power in Chicago. Four extraordinary "ordinary" people representing ethnic groups that have had a distinct territorial presence on Chicago's Near West Side—one Jewish, one Italian, one African-American, and one Mexican—reminisce fondly on life in the old neighborhood and tell of their heroic

struggles to save it and the 120-year-old Maxwell Street Market that was at its core from the contrary plans of some of the biggest power players in a city of clout. **Winner of a 2002 Midwest Independent Publishers Association Award.**
1-893121-09-7, June 2002, softcover, 368 pp., 113 photos, $17.95

Regional History

A Chicago Tavern: A Goat, a Curse, and the American Dream
by Rick Kogan
In the summer of 1934, a baby goat fell off a truck, limped into a saloon owned by Greek immigrant William Sianis, and a Chicago icon was born. The Billy Goat Inn became a haven for newspaper reporters, policemen, politicians, and anyone else drawn to the hospitality and showmanship of hardworking "Billy Goat" Sianis and his often antic, uniquely comforting establishment. But did Billy jinx the Cubs? When he and one of his goats were barred from entering Wrigley Field during the 1945 World Series, the Cubs' loss to Detroit fueled a legend as enduring as their fans' "Wait 'til next year" mantra. Rick Kogan's affectionate salute invites you to pull up a barstool next to some of the Billy Goat's cherished patrons: regulars, visitors, and luminaries like Mike Royko, and young stars John Belushi, Bill Murray, and Don Novello, who immortalized the tavern in the *Saturday Night Life* "Cheezborger, Cheezborger" skits. In these echoes and images, Kogan reminds us why the American tavern is still the friendliest place in town and offers his toast to a Chicago original.
1-893121-49-6, Sept. 2006, softcover, 118 pp., 47 photos, $10

The Politics of Place: A History of Zoning in Chicago
by Joseph Schwieterman and Dana Caspall
How the face of Chicago—renowned for its distinctive skyline, Loop business district, and diverse neighborhoods—came to be is a story of enterprise, ingenuity, opportunity . . . and zoning. Here's that story: bold visions compromised by political realities, battles between residents and developers, and occasional misfires from City Council and City Hall.
1-893121-26-7, February 2006, oblong, softcover, 291 pp., 150 photos, $19.95

Wrigley Field's Last World Series:
The Wartime Chicago Cubs and the Pennant of 1945
by Chuck Billington
Relive the Chicago Cubs' historic 1945 season, the last time the team won a pennant. Charles Billington paints an evolving portrait of the season and its players, and chronicles the effect of World War II on the wider national scene during this unique period in baseball history. Featuring the photography of George Brace. Hailed in Chicago and sports publications as: "required reading for baseball history buffs," "impeccable research mixed with obvious passion and an intimate, highly readable style," "an eloquent social commentary of the times," "a page-turner," "a great read," and "a gripping 'I was there' account of the season."
1-893121-45-3, May 2005, softcover, 321 pp., 25 historic photos, $16.95

The Golden Age of Chicago Children's Television
by Ted Okuda and Jack Mulqueen

At one time every station in Chicago a maximum of five, until 1964—produced or aired some programming for children. From the late 1940s through the early 1970s, local television stations created a golden age of children's television unique in American broadcasting. Though the shows often operated under strict budgetary constraints, these programs were rich in imagination, inventiveness, and devoted fans. Discover the back stories and details of this special era from the people who created, lived, and enjoyed it—producers, on-air personalities, and fans.

1-893121-17-8, June 2004, softcover, 251 pp., 78 photos, $17.95

Chicago's Midway Airport: The First Seventy-Five Years
by Christopher Lynch

Training ground of heroes and daredevils. Transportation hub to the nation. Heart of a neighborhood. Outpost of glamour. Crossroads of the world. Birthplace of the major airlines. Contemporary success story. Learn why Midway Airport may be Chicago's most overlooked treasure and the country's most historic airport with this collection of oral histories, historic narrative, and fascinating photos.

1-893121-18-6, Jan. 2003, oblong, softcover, 201 pp., 205 photos, $19.95

Great Chicago Fires: Historic Blazes That Shaped a City
by David Cowan

As Chicago changed from agrarian outpost to industrial giant, it would be visited time and again by some of the worst infernos in American history—fires that sparked not only banner headlines but, more importantly, critical upgrades in fire safety laws across the globe. Cowan tells the story of the other "great" Chicago fires, noting the causes, consequences, and historical context of each. In transporting readers beyond the fireline and into the ruins, he brings readers up close to the heroism, awe, and devastation generated by the fires that shaped Chicago.

1-893121-07-0, Aug. 2001, oblong, softcover, 167 pp., 80 historic photos, $19.95

Regional Travel & Guidebooks By Locals

A Cook's Guide to Chicago: Where to Find Everything
You Need and Lots of Things You Didn't Know You Did, 2nd Edition
by Marilyn Pocius

With the locally best-selling first edition of *A Cook's Guide to Chicago*, chef Marilyn Pocius took food lovers and serious h me cooks on a tasty romp into Chicago's secret culinary corners and forever changed the way they shop, cook, and eat. Get in on the knowing as she continues her explorations of local foodways. Discover how specialty food and equipment shops like gourmet stores, health food emporiums, butchers, fish mongers, produce stands, spice shops, ethnic grocers, and restaurant supplies dealers can make your life delicious. With new Kosher, Balkan, and multi-ethnic store sections, and the 2,000+ ingredient index that makes it easy to find everything you didn't know you needed!

1-893121-47-X, Feb. 2006, softcover, 344 pp., with "Top 10s" & recipes, $15.95

A Field Guide to Gay & Lesbian Chicago
by Kathie Bergquist & Robert McDonald
Kathie and Robert are here to set the record straight, er, queer, with this first and only book to give gay and lesbian travelers the inside (and hilarious) scoop on gay-friendly accomodations, shopping, recreation, music, theater, dining, and nightlife in the Windy City. Topics also include transportation, safety, Chicago's gay history, the "gayborhoods," hooking up, and their own personal adventures.
1-893121-03-8, June 2006, softcover, 329 pp., 65 photos, 3 maps, $15.95

Ghostlore and Haunted History

Chicago Haunts: Ghostlore of the Windy City
by Ursula Bielski
Bielski captures over 160 years of Chicago's haunted history with her distinctive blend of lively storytelling, in-depth historical research, exclusive interviews, and insights from parapsychology. Called "a masterpiece of the genre," "a must-read," and "an absolutely first-rate-book" by reviewers, *Cl cago Haunts* continues to earn the praise of critics and readers alike.
0-9642426-7-2, Oct. 1998, softcover, 277 pp., 29 photos, $15

More Chicago Haunts: Scenes from Myth and Memory
by Ursula Bielski
Chicago. A town with a past. A people haunted by its history in more ways than one. A "windy city" with tales to tell . . . Bielski is back with more history, more legends, and more hauntings, including the personal scary stories of *Chicago Haunts* readers.
1-893121-04-6, Oct. 2000, softcover, 312 pp., 50 photos, $15

Creepy Chicago: A Ghosthunter's Tales of the City's Scariest Sites
by Ursula Bielski, illustrated by Amy Noble
Chicago's famous phantoms, haunted history, and unsolved mysteries for readers ages 8–12. *Chicago Haunts* for kids!
1-893121-15-1, Aug. 2003, softcover, 19 illustrated stories, glossary, 136 pp., $8

Muldoon: A True Chicago Ghost Story: Tales of a Forgotten Rectory
by Rocco A. Facchini and Daniel J. Facchini
Poverty, crime, politics, scandal, revenge, and a ghost: Fresh out of the seminary in 1957, Father Rocco Facchini was appointed to his ᶠrst assignment at the parish of St. Charles Borromeo on Chicago's Near West Side. Adjusting to rectory life with an unorthodox, dispirited pastor and adapting to the needs of the rough, impoverished neighborhood were challenges in themselves. Little did he know that the rectory and church were also being haunted by a bishop's ghost! These are the untold stories of the last days of St. Charles parish by the last person able to tell them. The *Chicago Sun-Times* reported it as "The hot new read among Chicago priests"; countless others have declared it "reads like a novel. I couldn't put it down!" Discover for yourself the mysteries of Muldoon.
1-893121-24-0, Sept. 2003, softcover, 268 pp., 44 photos, $15

Also from LCP

*Chicago TV Horror Movie Shows:
From Shock Theatre to Svengoolie*

*On the Job: Behind the Stars
of the Chicago Police Department*

Today's Chicago Blues

*Wrigley Field's Last World Series:
The Wartime Chicago Cubs and the
Pennant of 1945*

*A Chicago Tavern: A Goat, A Curse,
and the American Dream*

*The Golden Age of Chicago
Children's Television*

*Chicago's Midway Airport: The
First Seventy-Five Years*

*Great Chicago Fires:
Historic Blazes That Shaped a City*

*The Firefighter's Best Friend:
Lives and Legends of
Chicago Firehouse Dogs*

Graveyards of Chicago

*Chicago Haunts:
Ghostlore of the Windy City*

More Chicago Haunts

Creepy Chicago (for kids 8–12)

*Muldoon: A True Chicago Ghost
Story: Tales of a Forgotten Rectory*

Award Winners

A Cook's Guide to Chicago

*The Politics of Place: A History of
Zoning in Chicago*

*Finding Your Chicago Ancestors: A
Beginner's Guide to Family History
in the City and Cook County*

*The Streets & San Man's Guide to
Chicago Eats*

*The Chicago River: A Natural and
Unnatural History*

*Near West Side Stories: Struggles
for Community in Chicago's
Maxwell Street Neighborhood*

*Hollywood on Lake Michigan:
100 Years of Chicago & the Movies*

*A Field Guide to
Gay & Lesbian Chicago*

Coming Soon

*From Lumber Hookers to the
Hooligan Fleet: A Treasury of
Chicago Maritime History*

*Rule 53: Capturing Hippies, Spies,
Politicians, and Murderers in an
American Courtroom*

*For Members Only: A History
and Guide to Chicago's
Oldest Private Clubs*

Order Form

A Native's Guide to Chicago, 4th Ed.	_____ @ $15.95 =	_____
A Cook's Guide to Chicago, 2nd Ed.	_____ @ $15.95 =	_____
The Streets & San Man's Guide to Chicago Eats	_____ @ $12.95 =	_____
Finding Your Chicago Ancestors	_____ @ $16.95 =	_____
The Golden Age of Chicago Children's Television	_____ @ $17.95 =	_____
The Chicago River	_____ @ $16.95 =	_____
The Politics of Place: A History of Zoning in Chgo	_____ @ $19.95 =	_____
Chicago's Midway Airport	_____ @ $19.95 =	_____
Chicago Haunts	_____ @ $15.00 =	_____
_____	_____ @ $_____ =	_____
_____	_____ @ $_____ =	_____

Subtotal: _____
Less Discount: _____
New Subtotal: _____
9% Sales Tax for Illinois Residents: _____
Shipping: _____
TOTAL: _____

Name_____

Address_____

City_____**State**_____**Zip**_____

Email_____

☐ *Add me to the LCP monthly customer e-mail newsletter list.*

Please enclose check, money order, or credit card information.

Visa/MC/AmEx/Discover#_____**Exp.**_____

Signature_____

Discounts when you order multiple copies!
2 books—10% off total, 3–4 books—20% off,
5–9 books—25% off, 10+ books—40% off

—Low shipping fees—
$3.50 for the first book and $.50 for each additional book,
with a maximum charge of $10.

Order by mail, phone, fax, or e-mail.
All of our books have a no-hassle, 100% money back guarantee.

LAKE CLAREMONT PRESS
P.O. Box 25291 • Chicago, IL 60625
312/226-8400 • 312/226-8420 (fax)
lcp@lakeclaremont.com • www.lakeclaremont.co